THE CHILD AS MUSICIAN

THE CHILD AS MUSICIAN

A handbook of musical development

Edited by

GARY E. McPHERSON

Marilyn Pflederer Zimmerman Endowed Chair in Music Education,
University of Illinois at Urbana-Champaign, USA

OXFORD

UNIVERSITY PRESS

Great Clarendon Street, Oxford OX2 6DP

Oxford University Press is a department of the University of Oxford.
It furthers the University's objective of excellence in research, scholarship,
and education by publishing worldwide in

Oxford New York

Auckland Cape Town Dar es Salaam Hong Kong Karachi
Kuala Lumpur Madrid Melbourne Mexico City Nairobi
New Delhi Shanghai Taipei Toronto

With offices in

Argentina Austria Brazil Chile Czech Republic France Greece
Guatemala Hungary Italy Japan Poland Portugal Singapore
South Korea Switzerland Thailand Turkey Ukraine Vietnam

Oxford is a registered trade mark of Oxford University Press
in the UK and in certain other countries

Published in the United States
by Oxford University Press Inc., New York

© Oxford University Press 2006

British Library Cataloguing in Publication Data

Data available

Library of Congress Cataloging in Publication Data

Data available

Typeset by Newgen Imaging Systems (P) Ltd., Chennai, India
Printed in Great Britain
on acid-free paper by
Biddles Ltd., King's Lynn

ISBN 0–19–853031–5 (Hbk.)   978–0–19–853031–2 (Hbk.)
ISBN 0–19–853032–3 (Pbk.)   978–0–19–853032–9 (Pbk.)

10 9 8 7 6 5 4 3 2 1

PREFACE

The contributions in this book celebrate the richness and diversity of the many different ways in which children can engage in and interact with music. It presents theory—both cutting edge and classic—in an accessible way for readers by surveying research concerned with the development and acquisition of musical skills. The intended focus is on musical development from conception to late adolescence, although the bulk of the coverage concentrates on the period when children are able to begin formal music instruction (from around age 3) until the final year of formal schooling (around age 18).

There are a number of elements that distinguish this volume from others in the literature. First, chapter authors have focused their attention and interpretation on citations that apply to and have relevance for the age groups studied. This means that the majority of references deal with actual studies of the types of children being depicted in the chapter, rather than attempts to extrapolate information from studies with adults. Second, I wanted to ensure that authors synthesized the available literature from the UK, North America, and Europe (as well as other regions such as Australia). The volume therefore attempts to bring together the main research traditions, in a way that would maximize its appeal worldwide.

Third, the book is broad in its scope, but is not intended to be comprehensive. Even before contacting the authors, I realized that no survey of the magnitude provided here could ever hope to cover every dimension of musical development in a single volume. I especially became aware of deficiencies in various parts of the literature, and of the need to focus the author's efforts on the main threads that help to explain how children develop musically. I am particularly aware that many more studies deserve to be undertaken that address children's musical development, especially in informal and non-Western contexts. I have tried to address these important aspects by including special chapters devoted to these topics, but I acknowledge also that there is still much to learn from how children in various non-Western cultures interact with music, and how this might be different from musical engagement in Western cultures. Finally, the intention of the book is to provide an overview of the biological, environmental, social, cultural, and historical factors that have shaped the acquisition of musical skills, understandings, and attitudes. To achieve this aim the chapters draw on research from a variety of disciplines, including music, psychology, education, sociology, philosophy, and medicine.

There is obviously no single or unanimous voice that can be used to explain musical development but rather a rainbow of ideas and opinions. Consequently, in the early stages when I was considering the content, I was keen to ensure that the volume would include authors who study musical development from a range of angles and research traditions. During the editorial process, I therefore allowed authors to retain their own personal voice to explain from whatever perspective they may work the aspect of musical development that they had been assigned. The result is that readers are able to enjoy a range of approaches to the 24 chapters that reflect the different paradigms the 30 authors work from and the wealth of experience they have brought to the project.

In the general field of educational psychology there are a number of publications that survey the issues surrounding child and adolescent development. Some of the more innovative present research and theories, and their educational implications, in a style that stresses the fundamental interplay among the biological, environmental, social, and cultural influences at each stage of a child's development. Until now, no similar overview has existed for child and adolescent development in the field of music. *The child as musician* attempts to address this imbalance, while complementing the now extensive range of music psychology publications available in the Oxford University Press catalogue.

As can be seen from the title, this volume acts as a 'handbook' on musical development. But the use of the term 'development' is used with caution because there are many conceptions of how musical development might take place, just as there are for other disciplines and areas of human potential. This is an important point to remember because, as Jeanne Bamberger reminds us in her chapter, progress in research is not so much characterized by a striving to reach consensus as it is a refinement of the debate. What I hope this volume will help achieve, therefore, is to highlight the diversity in current literature dealing with how we think about and conceptualize children's musical development. This is the prime goal of this book, as individually the authors search for better and more effective ways to explain in their own words and according to their own perspectives the remarkable ways in which children can become engaged with music.

The book is intended for a range of different groups of readers. The development of national curricula and national standards in various countries during the 1980s and 1990s demonstrated that music educators internationally are becoming increasingly interested in developmental issues concerned with children's engagement with music, and are keen to explore the practical applications of the various strands of research that impact on their day-to-day work. For this reason, the main group of readers will be music educators, especially those with a specific interest or expertise in music psychology and research. Another major target group consists of music psychologists and educational researchers who I hope will also welcome the publication of an authoritative account of the development and acquisition of musical skills and understandings, and use this as the theoretical basis for subsequent work in the area.

The 24 chapters in this volume are organized according to five loosely constructed sections—*Development, Engagement, Differences, Skills* and *Contexts*—even though I realize that some of the contributions could have easily been included in another section of the book. The first section (*Development*) deals with fundamental issues of development; two chapters on the critical months and years from conception to the end of infancy, and three chapters dealing with how the musical brain develops, ways of understanding musical development, and the nature of musicality. Section two (*Engagement*) scrutinizes claims about the non-musical benefits of exposure to music by critically examining whether music makes you smarter. This is followed by four thorough literature reviews dealing with musical preference and taste, literacy, aesthetic response, and the perception of emotion in music.

Section three (*Differences*) focuses on those issues that explain and identify individual differences. One of the most obvious, yet also one of the most multifaceted, concerns how motivation for experiencing and studying music changes throughout childhood. Information on this topic is followed by a chapter that provides a framework for defining giftedness and talent in music, plus two chapters on children with disabilities—one focusing on musical development and the other on music in therapy. Each of the chapters in this section is written from a very different perspective. Together they provide a powerful explanation of the importance and value of music in the lives of all children.

Five chapters cover *skills* that can develop as a result of exposure to music. Informal activities associated with musical play and the use of computers and technology complement chapters dealing with the acquisition of vocal and instrumental skills, as well as the individual and social worlds of children's musical creativity.

The final section of the book discusses five musical *Contexts*. The first of these surveys four different formal settings from the past: the English Medieval Song Schools, Instrumental Instruction in 18th century Britain, School Music Teaching in late 19th century Europe, and Recapitulation and Musical Childhoods in the 20th century. The intention is to provide readers with information that will assist them make comparisons between how children learned and developed their musical capacities in the past, and current opportunities. Importantly, an additional two chapters focus on children's musical involvement in non-Western cultures. The first of these discusses global practices with the second focusing on cultural traditions. The authors of these two chapters remind us that any conception of music must encompass the ways in which children mature musically as a result of enculturation, training, and education. Likewise, we are also reminded that music provides children with a sense of cultural identity.

The book concludes with two chapters focusing on important new research dealing with youth musical engagement and the transition from child to adult. Each of these chapters helps frame the developmental issues that have been covered earlier in the book, while at the same time reminding readers that the decisions young people make about the value and importance of music in their lives are often shaped by their emerging sense of self.

As a young university student about 30 years ago, I have a vivid memory of asking one of my lecturers, 'How do you keep up with research on children's musical development?' Her reply was something like, 'Gary, I don't have any problems because there is only a small stream of research being published.' This statement could not be made today—in fact the explosion of ideas and literature generated in the last 10 to 15 years has revolutionized the ways in which we can study, define, and debate the many issues surrounding children's engagement with music. With this as our basis, the current volume attempts to provide a timely summary of where we are up to with our thinking, while at the same time identifying many of the challenges that lie ahead in our quest to better understand children's musical development. My sincere hope is that readers will find the information illuminating and interesting and that it will encourage them to think more deeply about the many different ways in which music can affect children's lives and the quality of life in communities throughout the world. I also hope that the information provided here will help those who have to defend music education to articulate even more precisely why all children deserve to have access to music throughout their childhood.

Gary E. McPherson
2006

ACKNOWLEDGEMENTS

The first draft of each chapter was independently reviewed by the editor and three additional reviewers, who included a selection of other authors from the book and anonymous external reviewers. Regarding the latter, I am grateful to: Eckart Altenmüller, Klaus-Ernst Behne, Martin Brody, Jean Callaghan, Lori Custodero, John Flohr, Alf Gabrielsson, Françoys Gagné, John Geake, Miraca Gross, Chris Hasty, Eve Harwood, Jere Humphreys, Wilfried Gruhn, Patrik Juslin, William Lee, Andreas Lehmann, Esther Mang, Michael Mark, Jacqueline Robarts, Carlos Xavier Rodriguez, Leon Thurman, Slava Senyshyn, John Sloboda, Teresa Volk, Jackie Wiggins, and Ellen Winner.

I take this opportunity to thank the various representatives of Oxford University Press. I am especially grateful to the OUP Commissioning Editor Martin Baum and his assistant Carol Maxwell for answering all of my questions and steering me in the right direction whenever I had a problem. Their enthusiasm for producing this book is appreciated. I would also like to thank my son Glen, who helped with the design of the cover.

Most of all, I extend my heartfelt thanks to each of the authors for agreeing to be involved. I am extremely grateful to them for putting up with the endless correspondence and the many suggestions from the reviewers. They deserve praise for their commitment to the project and the quality of their work.

Now that all of the authors can see their chapters in the context of the whole book, I hope that they will agree that our journey together has been worthwhile. I hope also, that our readers enjoy the fruits of our labour.

Gary E. McPherson
February, 2006

CONTENTS

CONTRIBUTORS

James Austin is Associate Professor and Chair of Music Education at the University of Colorado – Boulder. He received a Bachelor's degree in music education from the University of North Dakota and earned graduate degrees (MA, PhD) from the University of Iowa. Previously, he taught instrumental music (grades 4–12) in Minnesota public schools, served as a graduate assistant at the University of Iowa, and was on the music education faculty at Ball State University. His research and publication areas include student motivation and self-concept development, teacher education, classroom-level assessment, and arts policy implications of educational reform. James Austin regularly presents papers at national and international conferences and currently serves on editorial boards for the *Bulletin of the Council for Research in Music Education, Psychology of Music,* and *Research and Issues in Music Education.* From 2000 to 2005, he served as Program Chair and Chair for the Music Education SIG of the American Educational Research Association, and is currently serving as Chair of the MENC Measurement and Evaluation SRIG. In 2004, he was awarded the Richard Bern Trego Faculty Fellowship by the College of Music at CU-Boulder.

Jeanne Bamberger is Professor of Music and Urban Education, emerita at the Massachusetts Institute of Technology and Visiting Professor in the Graduate School of Education at the University of California, Berkeley, where she continues to teach music theory and music cognition. Her research is interdisciplinary: integrating music theory and practice, modes of representation, and recent approaches to cognitive development, she focuses on close analysis of children and adults in moments of spontaneous learning. Jeanne Bamberger, was a student of Artur Schnabel and Roger Sessions, performed extensively in the US and Europe as piano soloist and in chamber music ensembles. She attended Columbia University and the University of California at Berkeley receiving degrees in philosophy and music theory. Her most recent books include *The mind behind the musical ear* (1995),and *Developing musical intuitions: A project based introduction to making and understanding music* (2000). Other recent publications include: 'The development of intuitive musical understanding: A natural experiment,' *Psychology of Music* (2003), and 'Music as embodied mathematics: A study of a mutually informing affinity' (with A. diSessa), *International Journal of Computers for Mathematical Learning* (2004).

Margaret S. Barrett is Associate Professor of Music Education in the Faculty of Education at the University of Tasmania. Her research interests include the study of: children's musical thinking as composers and notators; creativity in music and the arts; children's communities of musical practice; the meaning and value of the arts in children's and young musicians' lives; the developmental psychology of music; and aesthetic education. Margaret Barrett has published in key journals in music and early childhood education and contributed book chapters to a number of edited collections in music education. She was National President of the *Australian Society for Music Education* (1999–2001) and is the editor of the journal *Research Studies in Music Education.*

Leslie Bunt is Professor in Music Therapy at the University of the West of England, Director of the postgraduate diploma course in music therapy at the University of Bristol and Director of The MusicSpace Trust, a registered charity with a network of community-based centres for music therapy. He read music at the University of Bristol and after a period of music teaching trained in music therapy with Juliette Alvin in 1976 at the Guildhall School of Music and Drama, London. His doctoral study at City University, London evaluated the effects of music therapy with children with special needs, the first such study in the UK. Leslie Bunt has worked extensively as a music therapist with children and adults of all ages and has been involved in postgraduate training of music therapists for over twenty years. His first book *Music therapy: An art beyond words* (Routledge 1994) has been translated into six languages. He is Vice-President of the *British Society of Music Therapy* and a Fellow of the *Royal Society of Arts.* He is a conductor of choral and operatic groups in his home city of Bristol.

Karen Burland is a lecturer in the School of Music at the University of Leeds where she teaches courses in the psychology of music, aesthetics, and criticism and popular music. She studied music at the University of Sheffield, where she remained to complete an MA in the Psychology of Music and subsequently her PhD. Her published work addresses collaborative composition, environmental influences on the acquisition of musical skill, the professional development of musicians, and the nature of musical identities. Karen performs regularly with a number of jazz groups and orchestras in Sheffield.

Pamela Burnard is a Senior Lecturer in the Faculty of Education at the University of Cambridge, England where she lectures on undergraduate, graduate and postgraduate courses in Music and Arts Education, Children and Creativity, coordinates the MPhil in Educational Research Course and supervises MEd, MPhil and PhD students. She is co-editor of the *International Journal of Music Education: Practice,* an associate editor of *Psychology of Music,* and on the editorial boards of the *British Journal of Music Education, Music Education Research* amongst other editorial boards.She is also a member of the Board of Directors of the *International Society for Music Education.* Her research interests include musical creativity, creative thinking, creative learning, musical composition and improvisation, teacher creativity and thinking and pupil voice. Pamela Burnard also convenes with Anna Craft and Teresa Grainger the British Educational Research Association Special Interest Group, Creativity in Education.

Patricia Shehan Campbell is Donald E. Peterson Professor of Music at the University of Washington, where she teaches courses at the interface of education and ethnomusicology. She is the author of *Teaching music globally* (2004) (and co-editor of the Oxford University Press series, *Global music: Experiencing music, expressing culture*), *Songs in their heads: Music and its meanings in children's lives* (1998), *Lessons from the world* (1991/2001), *Music in cultural context* (1996), and co-author of *Music in childhood* (2005, 3rd edition), numerous publications on content and method of world music cultures. She has lectured on the pedagogy of world music and children's musical involvement throughout the United States, in much of Europe and Asia, in Australia, New Zealand, and South Africa. She is a member of various editorial boards, and was recently named to the board of Smithsonian Folkways.

Gordon Cox is Senior Lecturer in Education at the University of Reading. After studying at the Royal Academy of Music, London, he taught for some years in schools and colleges in England and Canada. He was a graduate student in the Department of Folklore at the Memorial University of Newfoundland, and received his PhD in music education from the University of Reading. His research focuses upon music education history. Gordon Cox is co-editor of the *British Journal of Music Education,* and is author of *Folk music in a Newfoundland outport* (1980), *A history of music education in England 1872–1928* (1993), *Living music in schools 1923–1999* (2002), and *Sir Arthur Somervell on music education* (2003).

Jane W. Davidson is Chair of Music at both the University of Sheffield and the University of Western Australia. She has a background in music psychology, musicology, vocal performance, and contemporary dance. A former editor of *Psychology of Music,* she is currently Vice-President of the *European Society for the Cognitive Sciences of Music.* She has taught at undergraduate and post-graduate levels for many years, contributing to courses on: psychological approaches to performance, development of musical ability, psychology for musicians, music therapy, music in the community, gender studies in music, opera and music theatre studies, vocal pedagogy and movement classes. She has written more than one hundred scholarly contributions on performance, expression, therapy and the determinants of artistic abilities. Her edited volume the *Music Practitioner* explores the uses of research for the practising musician. She has held visiting posts at the Hong Kong Institute of Education, the University of New South Wales, the University of Western Sydney, the Guildhall School of Music and Drama, and the Luzerne Konservatorium. Jane Davidson also works as a professional stage director in opera and music theatre, having collaborated with Andrew Lawrence-King, *Opera North,* and *Drama per Musica.*

Susan Hallam is Professor of Education at the Institute of Education, University of London and currently Head of the Institute's School of Lifelong Education and International Development. She pursued careers as both a professional musician and a music educator before becoming an academic in 1991. Her research interests include disaffection from school, ability grouping and homework and issues relating to learning in music, practising, performing, musical ability, musical understanding and the effects of music on behaviour and studying. She is the author of ten books including *Instrumental teaching: A practical guide to better teaching and learning* (1998), *The power of music* (2001) and *Music psychology in education* (2005) and over one hundred other scholarly contributions. She is currently editor of *Psychology of Music,* and is past editor of the *Psychology of Education Review* and *Learning Matters.* She is Chair of the Education Section of the *British Psychological Society,* Treasurer of the *British Educational Research Association,* an auditor for the *Quality Assurance Agency* and an Academician of the *Learned Societies for the Social Sciences.*

David J. Hargreaves is Professor of Education at Roehampton University, and Visiting Professor at the Universities of Gothenburg and Macau. He is a Fellow of the British

Psychological Society, and has been Editor of *Psychology of Music* and Chair of the Research Commission of the *International Society for Music Education*. His books, which have been translated into 14 languages, include *The developmental psychology of music* (1986), and *Musical communication* (with Dorothy Miell and Raymond MacDonald, 2005), as well as numerous journal articles and book chapters in psychology, music and education. Current projects include pupils' experiences of school music; teacher and pupil identities in secondary school music; musical creativity and improvisation. He has appeared on BBC TV and radio as a jazz pianist and composer, and is organist at his local village church. He was recently awarded an honorary doctorate by the Faculty of Fine and Applied Arts in the University of Gothenburg, Sweden for his 'most important contribution towards the creation of a research department of music education' in that University.

Maud Hickey is an Associate Professor of Music Education at Northwestern University in Evanston, Illinois. Her research interests include creative thinking in music, music composition, music technology, and the intersections of these areas. She is current chair of the editorial committee for the *Music Educators Journal* (until 2006), and is serving on the editorial board for the *Journal of Technology in Music Learning*. Maud Hickey is a Vice President and board member for the *International Society for Improvisation in Music*, and has served as a member of the board for the *College Music Society*. Her work has been published in the *Journal of Research in Music Education*, the *Journal of the Centre for Research and Education in the Art*, and the *Journal of Technology in Music Learning*, among others. She is the editor (and a chapter author) for the book *Why and how to teach music composition: A new horizon for music education* (2003).

Donald A. Hodges is Covington Distinguished Professor of Music Education and Director of the Music Research Institute at the University of North Carolina at Greensboro. He received his undergraduate degree from the University of Kansas, and M.M. and Ph.D. from the University of Texas. Previous academic appointments include the Philadelphia public schools, the University of South Carolina, Southern Methodist University, and the University of Texas at San Antonio. He is contributing editor of the *Handbook of music psychology* and the accompanying *Multimedia companion I* (CD-ROMs, Vols. 1 & 2). He has authored more than 100 book chapters, papers, and multimedia programs in music education and music psychology and has made presentations to numerous state, national, and international conferences. Recent research efforts have included a series of brain imaging studies of pianists, conductors, and singers using PET, MRI, and fMRI. Additional research, papers, and presentations have been on Williams Syndrome musicians, tonality judgments in popular music, the nature of human musicality, the evolutionary basis for musicality, and biomusic.

Judith A. Jellison is the Mary D. Bold Regents Professor of Music, University Distinguished Teaching Professor, and Head of the Division of Music and Human Learning at the University of Texas at Austin. A devoted advocate for children's quality music experiences, her career began as a choral and instrumental public school music teacher in classrooms with widely diverse populations of children and as a music therapist in hospital settings. These early experiences shaped her philosophy of inclusive education, guiding her later work in higher education, first as founder and Director of Music Therapy at the University of Minnesota and now as Head of Music and Human Learning at UT. An active contributor to professional organizations, she is the recipient of the Senior Researcher Award from *MENC-The National Association for Music Education*, and the Publication Award from the *American Music Therapy Association*.

Kathryn Marsh is Chair of Music Education at the Sydney Conservatorium of Music, University of Sydney, where she teaches subjects relating to primary and early childhood music education, multicultural music education and music education research methods. Her research interests include children's musical play, children's creativity, and multicultural and Aboriginal music education. She has written a variety of scholarly and professional publications and has been actively involved in curriculum development and teacher training for many years. Kathryn Marsh is a member of the editorial board of the *International Journal of Music Education* and has been the recipient of major national research grants which have involved large scale international cross-cultural collaborative research into children's musical play in Australia, Europe, the UK, USA and Korea.

Gary E. McPherson is the Marilyn Pflederer Zimmerman Endowed Chair in Music Education at the University of Illinois at Urbana-Champaign, and President of the *International Society for Music Education* (2004–2006). He studied music education at the Sydney Conservatorium of Music before completing a Master of Music Education at Indiana University and a PhD at the University of Sydney. He worked at the University of New South Wales in Sydney, Australia, for many years, where he helped to develop undergraduate and postgraduate courses in music education and undertook longitudinal research with children learning music in schools. During this time, he also served as National President of the *Australian Society for Music Education* (1995–1997). Between 2002 and 2005, he was Professor of Creative Arts at the Hong Kong Institute of Education where he served as Head of Department and Acting Dean. His published research addresses visual, aural and creative aspects of music performance, motivation, and teaching and learning processes in music. Together with Richard Parncutt, he edited *The Science and Psychology of Music Performance* (Oxford University Press, 2002). Gary McPherson has served on the editorial boards of most research journals in music education, and was editor of *Research Studies in Music Education* from its inception in 1993 until December 2004. As a musician, he has been awarded a Licentiate and Fellowship in trumpet performance from Trinity College, London, and performed with several of Australia's leading ensembles.

Janet Mills is a Research Fellow at the Royal College of Music, London, where she teaches, and runs several music education research projects. She studied music and mathematics at the University of York, trained as a teacher at the University of Leeds, and holds a doctorate from the University of Oxford. Following posts as head of music in secondary schools, she was a teacher educator at Westminster College, Oxford and the University of Exeter, and then HM Inspector of Schools and Ofsted's Specialist Adviser for Music for ten years. She has worked as a teacher, researcher, adviser or inspector in over 800 primary, special and secondary schools, and also in the community. She is author of *Music in the primary school* (Cambridge University Press) and *Music in the school* (Oxford University Press), and many articles on music education and education in research journals, books and magazines. She is an officer or former officer of several music education associations, and a member of the editorial board of the *British Journal of Music Education*. Her principal instrument is violin. In 2004 she won a National Teaching Fellowship.

Adrian C. North is a Senior Lecturer in Psychology at the University of Leicester in the United Kingdom. He obtained his first degree in psychology from the University of Manchester in 1993 before completing a PhD in music psychology at the University of Leicester in 1996. His research concerns music in adolescence, music and consumer behaviour, and experimental aesthetics.

Susan A. O'Neill is a Research Associate in the Faculty of Education at Simon Fraser University in British Columbia, Canada. She received her Baccalaureate in Music from the University of Ottawa, and completed her graduate degrees in England (MA in Performance Studies, MA in Education, PhD in Psychology). She was Senior Lecturer in Psychology at Keele University until 2004, and Associate Director of the Unit for the Study of Musical Skill and Development. She was awarded a Visiting Research Fellowship from the University of Michigan for 2001–2003 where she was a Research Affiliate with the Gender and Achievement Research Program. Her research interests include motivation, identity, ethnicity and gender issues associated with young people's engagement in music. As a consultant she has developed professional training programs for music practitioners and teachers, and has contributed to policy planning for youth music programs. She was Director of the Young People and Music Participation Project funded by the Economic and Social Research Council and has published widely in the fields of music psychology and music education. Her other contributions to edited books include *The Social Psychology of Music* (1997), *Music and Emotion: Theory and Research* (2001), *The Science and Psychology of Music Performance* (2002), and *Musical Identities* (2002), all published by Oxford University Press.

Richard Parncutt is Austria's first Professor of Systematic Musicology, a position created at the University of Graz in 1998. He studied physics and music at the University of Melbourne, and his doctoral degree in physics, psychology, and music was granted by the University of New England, Australia. He has researched and lectured at TU München, KTH Stockholm, TU Berlin, Dalhousie University (Halifax), McGill University, Université de Montréal, and Keele University (England). He is author of *Harmony: A psychoacoustical approach* (Springer-Verlag, 1989), co-editor with Gary McPherson of *The Science and psychology of music performance* (Oxford University Press, 2002), and author of numerous peer-reviewed research articles on the perception of harmony, tonality, and rhythm. He is, or has been, a member of the editorial advisory boards of all leading international journals in music psychology and systematic musicology. In 2004 he conceived of and organized the first Conference on Interdisciplinary Musicology in Graz. He has performed internationally as a pianist and piano accompanist in various genres.

James Renwick is a lecturer in music education at the Sydney Conservatorium of Music, where he teaches research methods and instrumental pedagogy. He is also completing doctoral research at the University of New South Wales, collaborating with Gary McPherson and John McCormick on a study funded by the Australian Research Council that investigates associations between students' motivational beliefs, their practising behaviour and performance achievement. James' previous research has focused on detailed observational analyses of children's practising strategies. A musicology graduate of the University of Sydney, James Renwick also works as a clarinet and saxophone teacher and examiner.

E. Glenn Schellenberg is Professor of Psychology at the University of Toronto at Mississauga. He holds degrees in psychology and linguistics from the University of Toronto (BSc), and in psychology, cognitive studies, and statistics from Cornell University (PhD). His research focuses on reciprocal influences between music and cognition—how psychological predispositions influence musical structures and how exposure to music affects cognitive abilities. He is also interested in emotional responses to music, including the musical dimensions that influence such responses as well as listeners' preferences for certain pieces and genres. His teaching responsibilities include courses in developmental psychology and cognitive development. Throughout his childhood and adolescence he trained as a pianist. He subsequently performed in many rock bands and composed music for film and television, including the theme song for a children's television program.

Emery Schubert is an Australian Research Council Research Fellow at the School of Music and Music Education, University of New South Wales in Sydney, Australia. His research includes the time series analysis of emotion in music, and investigating emotion and expression in performances of Baroque, Romantic and other styles of music. His tertiary teaching includes music perception and music technology, and he also continues links with the school band movement. He received the UNSW Vice-Chancellors postdoctoral fellowship and completed postdoctorates in the School of Physics with the Music Acoustics Group (also at UNSW), and MARCS at the University of Western Sydney. In 2002 he was a recipient of the ESCOM 10th Anniversary Award with Dr. Dorottya Fabian for the discovery of the 'kerning illusion'. He has served as Publications Editor for the journal *Research Studies in Music Education* and is currently a Co-Editor of *Acoustics Australia*.

Mark Tarrant is Lecturer in Psychology at Keele University, UK. His major research interests are in social development and experimental social psychology. His research on social development focuses broadly on how developmental outcomes (e.g., self-concept, experiences of developmental tasks) during adolescence are negotiated in group contexts. His work in experimental social psychology focuses principally on three topics within the area of intergroup relations: The role of emotion in intergroup discrimination; meta-stereotyping; and group-based responses to deviance. He was awarded his PhD (entitled *Music and social development in adolescence*) from the University of Leicester in 2000. His research has been published in a variety of music psychology and social-developmental psychology journals.

Sandra E. Trehub is Professor Emeritus in the Department of Psychology at the University of Toronto at Mississauga. She completed an undergraduate degree in economics and philosophy and a PhD in experimental psychology from McGill University. Her research focuses primarily on the musical abilities of infants and young children as well as the changes in ability that result from formal and informal exposure to music. She also studies the musical performances that mothers provide in the course of caring for their infants. In addition, she has begun documenting the music perception and production skills of congenitally deaf children who hear 'electrically' rather than acoustically by means of cochlear implants. For the most part, Sandra Trehub's research is conducted under controlled laboratory conditions. At times, however, she ventures to remote villages (e.g., in Gabon, India, Papua New Guinea, Turkey) to observe mothers' use of music in child-care.

Robert Walker is Post-Graduate Coordinator in the School of Music and Music Education, University of New South Wales, Sydney, Australia. He moved to Australia from Canada in 1998, where he served as a full professor at the University of British Columbia with one of the country's largest doctoral programmes in music education, and full professor at Simon Fraser University, where he forged links between education and the School of Contemporary Arts. While in Canada, he was editor of the *Canadian Music Educator* and the *Canadian Journal of Research in Music Education*. He has served as Chief Examiner for Music and Coordinator of Arts programmes for the International Baccalaureate Organisation and Chair of the Research Commission of the *International Society for Music Education*. Educated in England, he took his BMus (Hons – Convocation 1st Prize winner) and PhD in the Music Department at Kings College, University of London. He was an organist and singer, a member of Lichfield and Ely Cathedral choirs, Director of Music at the Kings School, Ely, and head of music at two large grammar schools before moving to university teaching. Robert Walker is the author of nine books and over 100 research papers.

Peter R. Webster is the John Beattie Professor of Music Education and Technology at the School of Music, Northwestern University in Evanston, Illinois. He is now serving as the Associate Dean of Academic Affairs and Research as well as Director of Doctoral Studies. He holds degrees in music education from the University of Southern Maine (BS) and the Eastman School of Music at the University of Rochester (MM, PhD). His teaching responsibilities at Northwestern include courses in research, music technology, and creative thinking in music. His published work includes articles and book chapters on technology, perception, preference, and creative thinking in music that have appeared in journals and handbooks in and outside of music. Peter Webster is co-author with David Williams of *Experiencing music technology*, 3rd edition (Wadsworth/Schirmer, 2006), the standard textbook and DVD used in introductory college courses in music technology. He is also the author of *Measures of creative thinking in music*, an exploratory tool for assessing music thinking using quasi-improvisational tasks.

Graham F. Welch holds the Institute of Education, University of London Established Chair of Music Education and is Head of the Institute's School of Arts and Humanities. He is Chair of the *Society for Education, Music and Psychology Research* (SEMPRE) and recent past Co-Chair of the Research Commission of the *International Society for Music Education* (ISME). He also holds Visiting Professorships at the Universities of Sydney, Limerick (Eire) and Roehampton (UK), as well as the Sibelius Academy in Finland, and has acted as a consultant to the National Center for Voice and Speech (NCVS) in the USA and the Voice Research Centre in Stockholm (Sweden) on aspects of children's singing and vocal development. Research and publications number over one hundred and seventy five and embrace a variety of aspects of musical development and music education, teacher education, psychology of music, singing and voice science, special education and disability.

Aaron Williamon is the Research Fellow in the Psychology of Music at the Royal College of Music, London, where he heads the Centre for the Study of Music Performance. He also holds a research fellowship in the Faculty of Medicine at Imperial College, London. He was awarded a BA in music and BSc in psychology from the Honors College of the University of South Carolina before subsequently completing his PhD at Royal Holloway, University of London. His research focuses on music cognition, expert performance and (in particular) applied psychological and health-related initiatives that enable musicians to perform at their peak. His recent book, *Musical excellence*, is published by Oxford University Press. It draws together the findings of initiatives from across the arts and sciences, with the aim of offering musicians new perspectives and practical guidance for enhancing performance and managing performance-related stress. In addition, he is interested in how audiences perceive and evaluate performances and, in 1998, was awarded the Hickman Prize by the *Society for Education, Music, and Psychology Research* (SEMPRE) for his work on this topic. He has performed as a trumpeter in chamber and symphony orchestras, brass bands, and brass quintets in both Europe and North America.

Susan Young lectures in early childhood studies and music education in the School of Education and Lifelong Learning, the University of Exeter, UK. She is also Senior Research Fellow at the Centre for International Research in Music Education, Roehampton University, London, where for many years she was a member of the academic staff. Susan Young studied at the Royal College of Music, London, the Institut Jaques-Dalcroze, Switzerland and the Institute of Education, London before embarking on a varied teaching career that included primary, secondary education and a specialist music school. She has increasingly focused on music in early childhood and is frequently asked to give presentations on this topic at national and international occasions. She has written and presented widely on the topic of music education, particularly in the early years and published in a range of journals, both in the UK and internationally. Recent books include *Music with the under fours* and the co-authored *Music in the early years.*

CHAPTER 1

PRENATAL DEVELOPMENT

RICHARD PARNCUTT

Introduction

Infants have a wide range of skills that can be described as musical (see Chapter 2). What is the origin of those skills? This chapter considers the possibility that they are—at least in part—learned before birth, as the fetus becomes familiar with the internal sound patterns of its mother's body and associates these patterns with her physical and emotional state. The chapter begins by presenting background information about the fetal sound environment and musically relevant fetal abilities and behaviours that may be related to musical abilities as they emerge after birth. It goes on to consider the question of how to evaluate and reconcile conflicting research findings on prenatal musicality, and concludes with specific, tentative recommendations for expectant mothers or parents interested in the musical development of their fetus. The chapter aims to give readers background material in the controversial area of prenatal musical psychology, so that they can make informed decisions about the validity of published claims for themselves.

The fetal sound environment

The most important sounds to which the human fetus is regularly exposed are its mother's voice, her heartbeat, her movements (including footsteps), her breathing, and her digestion (stomach growling or borborygmi—the rumbling sounds caused by gas moving through the intestines) (Lecanuet, 1996). Less important, but often still audible, are sounds produced by the fetus itself (heartbeat, movement) and sounds from outside the mother's body. In the following, I will use the word 'audible' in the sense of 'audible for a human adult with normal hearing', and will return later to the question of whether the fetus can hear these sounds.

The internal sounds of the mother's body may reach the fetal ears by different paths. For example, maternal heartbeat sounds may be transmitted directly from the heart, the umbilical artery, the uterine artery, or uteroplacental blood flow. For this and other reasons, the loudness or audibility of each kind of sound may be different in different parts of the amniotic cavity, so fetal perception depends on the fetus's physical orientation.

All the sounds to which the fetus is exposed, regardless of whether they originate inside or outside the mother's body, are *muffled*. The high frequencies are attenuated by the amniotic fluid and body of the mother, which act as a *low-pass filter* (Armitage *et al.*, 1980; Richards *et al.*, 1992). Sounds below about 300 Hz may not be attenuated at all, while higher frequencies are increasingly attenuated; frequencies beyond about 2 kHz are generally inaudible (Abrams *et al.*, 1998).

Audible sounds from outside the mother's body include the voices of other people, sounds in the environment, and music. The intensity of these sounds is attenuated considerably (typical estimate: 30 dB) by comparison with internal sounds, as they pass through the mother's body. This makes them more susceptible to drowning out (complete masking) by internal sounds (Querleu *et al.*, 1988; Peters *et al.*, 1993). This presumably explains why newborns can recognize their mother's but not their father's voice, even if they were regularly exposed to both before birth, and even though the father's voice is less affected by low-pass filtering (DeCasper & Prescott, 1984).

The speech of an expectant mother would be largely intelligible to her fetus, if it could understand speech. Uterine muffling does not affect the ups and downs in pitch (prosody or intonation), the timing of phonemes (rhythm), variations in loudness (accentuation), or variations in pitch register (including the difference between male and female voices) (Smith *et al.*, 2003). As all but a few lower partials are rendered inaudible, the timbre of the mother's speech, which includes the identity of individual vowels and consonants, is strongly affected. It is nevertheless still possible for both adult listeners and the fetus itself to distinguish between different phonemes (vowels and consonants) in uterine recordings of the mother's voice (Querleu *et al.*, 1988, Decasper *et al.*, 1994). The relative salience of pitch (as opposed to timbre) in prenatally audible speech may explain in part why infants are more interested in maternal singing than maternal speech (cf. Trehub & Nakata, 2001–02). A further possibility is that learning is facilitated when expression is exaggerated in any modality (Masataka, 1998).

Musically relevant fetal abilities and behaviours

Postnatal musicality involves not only hearing but also movement, balance (essential for dance), and emotion. All of these depend on neurocognition, and all have roots in the prenatal period (Hepper, 1992).

The brain
Before birth, different brain regions develop at different rates, and sensory organs initially develop independently of the brain regions to which they will later be connected. Connections between peripheral sense organs and the central nervous system start to mature in about the 25th week,[1] after which sensory learning can begin in earnest (Oerter & Montada, 1995; Chapter 3, this volume). From this point, brain development is influenced by external sensory stimulation (Panicker *et al.*, 2002).

---

[1] The age of the fetus is referred to throughout this chapter in the conventional way as gestational age, or age since last menstruation. This is 2 weeks greater than conceptual age. For example, normal birth at 40 weeks gestation age corresponds to 38 weeks since conception. The term *embryo* applies during the first 8–12 weeks of gestation, while gross body structures and internal organs are developing; the term *fetus* applies from the third month (Oerter & Montada, 1995).

Hearing

The most important organ for hearing is the cochlea of the inner ear.[2] Here, vibrations are converted to neural impulses, and different frequencies are separated. A range of studies, both behavioural (Hepper & Shahidullah, 1994) and physiological (Rubel & Ryals, 1983; Pujol et al., 1991), have demonstrated that the fetal auditory system begins to process sounds between about 16 and 20 weeks, before it is anatomically mature.[3] The range of frequencies to which the cochlea responds is initially small and lies somewhere between 200 and 1000 Hz (Rubel & Ryals, 1983; Hepper & Shahidullah, 1994). As the frequency response of the cochlea gradually broadens, so too does its ability to separate simultaneous frequencies (frequency discrimination), to separate rapid sequences of sounds as in ordinary speech (temporal discrimination), and to perceive very quiet sounds (auditory threshold). At birth, all these abilities approach adult levels (cf. Ptok & Ptok, 1996). Numerous empirical studies are consistent with this general picture (for reviews see Busnel & Granier-Deferre, 1983; Lecanuet, 1996).

An important, survival-promoting function of postnatal hearing is the *localization* of sound sources (Blauert, 1997). Different cues indicate the direction from which a sound arrives in the left–right dimension (interaural time and intensity differences), the up–down dimension (spectral envelope variations due to reflections from the irregular shape of the pinna), and the front–back dimension (acoustic shadow cast by the pinna). The distance of the sound source is estimated on the basis of known relationships between loudness and distance for specific sound sources in specific situations. All these cues depend on frequency. Although babies can localize in the left–right dimension at birth (Morrongiello et al., 1994; Furst et al., 2004), they could hardly have had prenatal practice at this task. First, the fetal head does not cast an acoustic shadow at the relatively low frequencies that are available in the uterus. Second, interaural time differences, which are important for sound localization by adults at low frequencies (Wightman & Kistler, 1992), are an order of magnitude smaller for the fetus than for an adult due to the smaller size of the fetal head and the faster speed of sound in fluid. Thus, anecdotal reports of the fetus turning its head towards a sound (e.g., Bitnour, 2000) are implausible.

Balance and orientation

A discussion of the prenatal development of musicality would be incomplete without a consideration of the prenatal development of balance and orientation. First, music is associated with dance in all known musical cultures (Blacking, 1979). Second, the cochlea (organ

---

[2] Vibration can also be perceived through the skin or by bone conduction to the inner ear (Gerhardt et al., 1996); but experimental attempts to demonstrate this in animal fetuses (e.g., Parkes et al., 1991) have been unsuccessful. The mucus that fills the fetal middle ear throughout the prenatal period does not prevent it from functioning (Keith, 1975), but it may cause some attenuation (Abrams et al., 1995).

[3] Anatomical maturity involves several developmental stages. At about 10 weeks, hair cells begin to appear on the basilar membrane; at about 20 weeks, the efferent innervation of the outer hair cells begins; and at about 24–28 weeks, the cochlear receptors and auditory synapses mature (Pujol et al., 1991). The organ and tunnel of Corti are present in all turns of the cochlea at about 26 weeks (Altmann, 1950). The auditory pathway (from cochlear nerve to inferior colliculus) undergoes myelination between weeks 26 and 28, which improves the speed and synchronization of auditory impulses (Morre et al., 1995).

of hearing) and vestibule (organ of balance) are anatomically and physiologically united (Todd & Cody, 2000) and develop prenatally in parallel (Lai & Chan, 2002).

The vestibular system enables adults to perceive and monitor orientation (up versus down) and acceleration. The vestibular sense or *proprioception* begins to function before the fetus first shows a *righting reflex* at 25 weeks (Hooker, 1952) and may play a part in bringing the fetus into a head-down (cephalic) position before birth (Hepper, 1992).

Like all other senses, the vestibular sense needs stimulation to develop normally. Animal experiments (e.g., Ronca & Alberts, 2000) have demonstrated that prenatal proprioceptive abilities are not only present, but also trained before birth, consistent with the existence of fetal cognitive representations of orientation and acceleration.

Movement and heart rate responses to sounds

Fetal hearing can be investigated by checking whether fetal heart rate and movements consistently change after repeated exposure to a sound. Fetal movements are especially interesting for musical development because of the connection between music and dance.

Heart rate accelerations or decelerations in response to sound begin at about 20 weeks (Lecanuet, 1996) and occur in most human fetuses from about 26 weeks (Abrams, 1995). Spontaneous fetal movements begin at 6–9 weeks, but are not felt by the mother until about 20 weeks (Hooker, 1952; Oerter & Montada, 1995). Motor responses to loud, broad-band noises begin at about 24 weeks (Lecanuet, 1996); responses to pure tones begin a few weeks later. Motor responses to sound become consistent at 28–32 weeks (Birnholz & Benacerraf, 1983; Kisilevsky *et al.*, 1992). Motor and heart rate responses to music are more frequent at 38 than at 32 weeks (Wilkin, 1995/96). Responses have greater amplitude (e.g., greater heartbeat acceleration or deceleration) and are more likely when the fetus is awake, and depend on levels of alertness within sleep/wake states.

A problem with such behavioural measures is that the fetus may perceive something and not react to it (Hepper, 1992). However, no consistent auditory brainstem responses (auditory evoked potentials) have been observed before 25–30 weeks (Lecanuet, 1996).

Emotional communication

The relevance of emotional communication between mother and fetus for musical development lies in its potential to help explain an important—and still somewhat mysterious—property of music: the emotional implications of sound and movement patterns (cf. Juslin & Persson, 2002). The sophisticated emotional communicative abilities and sensitivities of infants suggest that they had prenatal practice; and the importance of emotional communication for infant survival suggests that there is evolutionary pressure for prenatal development of emotional communication.

Young infants communicate emotion through crying, babbling, facial expressions, and bodily gestures (Trevarthen, 1985; Zeifman, 2001). These messages inform the mother or other carer about the infant's physical and emotional state (which are largely inseparable) and hence about its current needs. The nature and origins of these processes can be explained by speculating on their contribution to infant survival in prehistoric human and prehuman societies (evolutionary psychology). The primary evolutionary purpose of infant–adult communication is presumably to motivate carers to help infants survive into childhood, when language gradually takes over the function of communicating needs.

Psychologists study the behavioural, physiological, and experiential aspects of emotion, and the relationships among them (Strongman, 2003). As experiential aspects of fetal emotion are absent or inaccessible, fetal emotion can only be investigated by tracking changes in physiological and behavioural states (Van den Bergh, 1992).

Physiological emotional communication

This may be said to occur when emotionally implicated biochemicals pass from the mother to the fetus (or from the fetus to the mother) via the placenta and umbilical cord, and reach the fetal brain. Specific biochemicals are associated with specific behaviours and emotions; for example, hormones are associated with anger, fear, sex, love, stress, or exertion, and endorphines are for example associated with pain, stress, hunger, digestion. As all biochemicals have multiple functions, and as all such mappings depend strongly on operational definitions of terms such as 'anger', they should be approached with caution.

As the fetus is anatomically connected to the mother, but physiologically to some extent independent of her, it shares some, but not all, of its mother's physiological states. For example, the maternal and fetal heartbeat correlate from about 32 weeks (DiPietro *et al.*, 2004); the coupling mechanism is presumably biochemical. The placenta is a filter that primarily passes nutrients and oxygen in one direction and wastes and carbon dioxide in the other. It partly filters out bacteria, viruses, toxins, drugs, and chemicals including alcohol, nicotine, and cocaine. For example, fetal steroids are highly lipophilic and so easily cross the placenta (Welberg & Seckl, 2001).

Recent years have seen considerable progress in the area of biochemistry of stress. Stress is associated with activation of the hypothalamic–pituitary–adrenal (HPA) axis and the sympathetic nervous (or sympatho-adrenomedullar) system (SA) (Van den Bergh, 1992). Stressors produce responses in a variety of endocrine systems and involve hormones such as cortisol, adrenaline (epinephrine), noradrenaline (norepinephrine), prolactin, thyroxine, insulin, and testosterone (Mason, 1975) as well as corticotrophin-releasing hormone (CRH) and adrenocorticotrophic hormone (ACTH) (Mulder *et al.*, 2002). Levels of neuropeptides such as CRH in the amygdala, hypothalamus, and pituitary gland are associated with emotionality, anxiety, and stress (cf. Brown & Gray, 1988; Davis, 1992). Corticosteroids, a class of steroid hormones, are involved in stress and immune responses and associated with fear and anxiety (Korte, 2001). Stress and fear affect levels of glucocorticoids, of which cortisol is the most important (Welberg & Seckl, 2001). Hormone release in response to stressors depends not only on the stressor itself, but also on a range of genetic, personality, and environmental factors.

Such research can shed light on the question of prenatal emotional communication. Changes in maternal physical and emotional state (such as stress or relaxation) affect fetal behaviours such as heart rate, heart rate variability, body movements, and breathing movements (Van den Bergh, 1992 cites numerous studies). These effects are presumably biochemically mediated. These effects are presumably biochemically mediated. For example, maternal anger can be communicated to the fetus via high cortisol and adrenaline and low dopamine and serotonin levels (Field *et al.*, 2002).

In both humans and other mammals, maternal emotion and stress affect the offspring's *physiology* (neurochemistry, endocrine function) and *psychology* (emotion, cognition) (Maret, 1997; Weinstock, 1997; Buitelaar *et al.*, 2003). Against a background of steadily increasing blood concentrations of CRH, ACTH, and cortisol throughout the pregnancy, information about maternal stress can reach the fetus as a temporary reduction in blood flow, transfer of maternal hormones across the placenta, or release of placental CRH; CRH enters fetal circulation via the umbilical vein, whereas cortisol enters via the umbilical arteries (Mulder *et al.*, 2002). Prenatal exposure to glucocorticoids such as cortisol affects fetal development (Coe *et al.*, 2003), produces hypertension and other medical and behavioural problems in later life (Seckl, 2001), affects the development of internal organs including the ear (Canlon *et al.*, 2003), and plays a part in the aetiology of schizophrenia (Koenig *et al.*, 2002). The intrauterine hormonal environment affects development of the fetal hippocampus and amygdala, and hence programming of the HPA axis (Matthews, 2002). The neuroendocrine system acts as a link between prenatal biochemical, neurodevelopmental variables such as plasma levels of ACTH and cortisol, and elements of the maternal psychosocial environment such as stress, social support, and personality (Wadhwa *et al.*, 1996). Maternal prenatal stress and associated placental levels of adrenocorticotrophin, endorphins, and CRH can lead to premature (preterm) delivery, adverse neurodevelopment, and chronic degenerative diseases and psychopathologies in adulthood (Wadhwa *et al.*, 2002; Huizink *et al.*, 2004).

Elevated prenatal cortisol levels caused by excessive maternal stress can cause temperamental, behavioural, emotional, motor, and cognitive problems in infants (De Weerth *et al.*, 2003). Infants of 'emotionally disturbed women' are 'typically described as restless, irritable, poor sleepers, and prone to gastrointestinal difficulties'; and 'mothers under severe emotional stress tend to have hyperactive fetuses' (Van den Bergh, 1992, pp. 159 and 160, citing various studies). Children of women treated with the glucocorticoid receptor agonist dexamethasone (DEX), which readily passes the placenta (Welberg & Seckl, 2001), are shyer, more avoidant, and more emotional (Trautman *et al.*, 1995). The effect of prenatal stress on cognitive development and temperament of infants is stronger when it occurs later in the pregnancy (Buitelaar *et al.*, 2003).

Biochemical-emotional communication between mother and fetus is not always associated with stress. Oestrogen and testosterone levels can influence the probability of hyperactivity and social and emotional problems (Williams *et al.*, 2003). Oxytocin is not only used to induce labour (Loghis *et al.*, 1999)—it is also associated with singing (Grape *et al.*, 2003), social contact, and sexuality (Keverne & Curley, 2004), and has therefore been implicated in aspects of mother–infant bonding such as breastfeeding and lullabies. Melatonin helps the circadian rhythms of fetus and mother to synchronize (Reppert & Weaver, 1988).

The word 'communication' implies that information travels in both directions. An example of two-way biochemical communication between mother and fetus is the process leading to the onset of labour. An increase in fetal plasma androgen concentration leads to increases in maternal plasma oestrogen, oxytocin, and amnion fibronectin concentrations (Mecenas *et al.*, 1996). Fetal cortisol levels trigger subsequent maternal endocrine changes leading to labour (Wu *et al.*, 2001). These levels are sensitive not only to onset of labour, but also to mode of delivery—whether normal/spontaneous, instrumental, or Caesarean (Mears *et al.*, 2004).

The claims I have made in this section should be treated with caution. All emotionally implicated biochemicals have other, non-emotional functions, and the link between bio-chemicals and emotion tends to be quite indirect (Korte, 2001). Changes in biochemical levels may be due to circadian variations rather than emotion (Walsh *et al.*, 1984). Emotion-ally implicated biochemicals may be associated only with arousal and not with emotional valence. Ongoing research in this area will doubtless generate important new insights and surprises in the coming years.

Behavioural emotional communication

Behavioural emotional communication between mother and fetus may be said to occur when the fetus picks up emotionally informative patterns of sound and movement from within the mother's body. As already pointed out, the most clearly audible sound sources are the voice, breathing, heartbeat, digestion, and walking. In each case, the sound or movement pattern depends strongly on the mother's physical and emotional state (e.g., heart rate: Ekman *et al.*, 1983; respiratory changes: Averill, 1969; uterine contractions, Moawad, 1973). Mastropieri and Turkewitz (1999) explain:

> For example, changes in voice intonation associated with an emotional state such as anger may be accompanied by increased respiration, causing a different pattern of diaphragmatic movements, as well as increased muscular tension and an increase in heart rate. Additionally, those physiological changes involved in the production of speech and which contribute to vocal intonation may also be detectable to the fetus, particularly because autonomic changes immediately precede and influence changes in voice intonation (Scherer, 1986). Temporal relationships between distinctive prosodic acoustic stimulation and distinctive responses associated with maternal physiological changes would provide an opportunity for associative learning (via classical conditioning) in utero. This form of learning would serve as a basis for the perception of and a differential response to different vocal expressions of emotion after birth. (p. 205)

What might motivate the fetus to become sensitive to patterns of sound and movement and their emotional connotations? Again, evolutionary psychology can provide tentative answers.

- Fetal survival is threatened by premature delivery, regardless of whether the mother survives the birth. The fetus is therefore under evolutionary pressure to prepare appropriately for premature delivery.
- After birth, the baby is under evolutionary pressure to be sensitive and adapt to the changing physical and emotional states of its mother (or other caretaker), so that the demands it makes on the mother can generally be met. To begin to acquire this ability before birth, it must monitor its mother's physical and emotional state by attending to biochemical correlates of emotion and emotionally informative sound and movement patterns.

Prenatally available sources of information about the mother's state can be associated with each other by *classical conditioning* (Parncutt, 1993, 1997). The existence of fetal classical conditioning was demonstrated by Spelt (1948) and discussed by Hepper (1992). As changes in maternal sound and movement patterns in response to an external event are faster than associated biochemical changes, they are also predictive of those biochemical changes. Once the different responses have been linked by association, the faster sound and movement responses can act as an early warning system.

This theory is consistent with recent empirical findings. Fetal physiology is plastic in the sense that it responds to environmental factors, preparing the fetus to respond optimally to environmental conditions outside of the uterus (Welberg & Seckl. 2001). The fetuses of anxious women tend to be more active (Van den Bergh *et al.*, 1989). Prenatal stress increases the likelihood of premature delivery, low birth weight, and small head circumference (Dunkel-Schetter *et al.*, 1998). All these phenomena either increase the chance of surviving premature birth or may be a result of preparing for premature birth due to maternal accident, illness, or emotional turmoil. The fetus can evidently go into a state akin to shock, shutting down all developmental processes to maximize chances of survival in a potentially hostile external environment. Mothers who survive fetal death are also usually in shock (Rogers *et al.*, 1999).

Fetal sensitivity to the emotional state of the mother plays a part in postnatal bonding. Infant behaviour is influenced by facial and vocal expression (Campos *et al.*, 2003) and infants as young as 3 months can detect depression in their mothers (Weinberg & Tronick, 1998). A baby that responds to the emotional state of the mother can better co-ordinate with her, again enhancing its chances of survival. This may explain why infants are sensitive to emotional implications of pitch contours in both speech (Mastropieri & Turkewitz, 1999) and music (Trehub & Nakata, 2001–02). Such sensitivities could be prenatally learned (Parncutt, 1993, 1997), genetically predetermined (Trehub, 2003), or both.

Auditory learning and memory

Without auditory learning and memory, there could be no prenatal psychological or musical development. It is therefore interesting in this context to investigate the prenatal emergence of learning and memory. Learning may be defined as storage of information, and in the absence of language, its existence can be investigated by observing behaviour. Prenatal memory is not memory in the everyday sense of remembering a phone number or what happened yesterday, which presupposes adult, linguistically mediated consciousness; it may therefore be more accurate to speak of 'transnatal retention of auditory experience' (Arabin, 2002, p. 428).

The only studies convincingly demonstrating fetal memory have involved many stimulus repetitions (details follow). For that reason, I assume that fetal memories are *procedural* (or *implicit*)—and no more than that. In adults, for example, procedural memory underlies technical skills on a musical instrument, or the ability to drive a car—things that we do mainly automatically, without thinking. In the fetus, procedural memory enables associations to be formed between stimuli that frequently occur in close temporal proximity (classical conditioning). Fetal memories clearly cannot be *declarative* (*explicit*) or *semantic* (*conceptual*) in the everyday adult sense, as the fetus has no language. I know of no direct, convincing evidence of fetal *episodic* (*autobiographical*) memory, or fetal memory for individual events; and the arguments in this chapter do not require that assumption.

Experiments on prenatal auditory learning can be divided into two categories: those where both exposure and behavioural demonstration of learning are prenatal, and those in which exposure is prenatal and behavioural demonstration is postnatal.

Prenatal–prenatal memory

The fetus can habituate (get used and stop responding) to a repeated stimulus (Peiper, 1925), even if it is as complex as music (Cassidy & Standley, 1995; Wilkin, 1995/96). Experiments on habituation do not *necessarily* demonstrate learning, because the subject may also stop responding for reasons of perceptual or motor fatigue; but as prenatal learning occurs in many animals, it is not surprising that it occurs in humans (Hepper, 1992).

Prenatal–postnatal memory

Newborns' sensitivity to heartbeat sounds may be due to prenatal conditioning by the sound of the mother's cardiovascular system (Salk, 1962; Dettermann, 1978). Hepper (1991) demonstrated that babies who had heard a specific piece of music regularly before birth (the theme from the TV soap opera *Neighbours*) but not after birth (before the experimental session) responded with heightened alertness, lower heart rate and fewer movements; but 3 weeks after birth, the infants seemed to have forgotten the music (or were no longer interested in it). Conflicting data were obtained by British music psychologist Alexandra Lamont, who found that memories for prenatally heard music can last as long as a year (Jones, 2001). In a comparable postnatal–postnatal study, 7-month infants presented with the same music daily for 2 weeks remembered it for a further 2 weeks (Saffran *et al.*, 2000). Further research is needed on the postnatal duration of prenatally established auditory memories under different conditions. Presumably, postnatal memory for prenatal sounds lasts longer when those sounds are heard very often, such as the mother's voice and sounds associated with her movements and digestion, and lasts longest when those sounds occur almost constantly, such as the mother's heartbeat and breathing sounds.

Survival value of prenatal hearing

Why can the fetus hear? If prenatal hearing and musical development are related, an answer to this question may contribute to an understanding of musical development and perhaps of music itself. Mammals that hear before birth include humans, sheep, goats, and guinea pigs; those that do not include ferrets, gerbils, rats, and cats (cf. Hepper, 1992; Sohmer & Freeman, 1995). This raises the question of the survival value of prenatal hearing. Consider the following three possibilities.

Preparation for perception

Prenatal perception (including prenatal hearing) may 'serve as a "running-in" period for the sensory systems' (Hepper, 1992, p. 145). The physiological development of the sensory systems depends on sensory input, and the sensory systems need practice with a restricted range of stimuli in order to be able to cope with the greater diversity of stimuli to which they will be exposed after birth. Prenatal sensory learning may provide a foundation for future sensory learning ability.

Preparation for language

A child typically learns to *understand* language long before s/he can *produce* language at the same level (Karmiloff & Karmiloff-Smith, 2001). This suggests that prenatal (passive) language exposure speeds up postnatal (active) language acquisition and increases the baby's chance of survival (Seebach *et al.*, 1994).

Preparation for bonding

Prenatal hearing indirectly promotes postnatal bonding (or attachment) between baby and mother (Hepper, 1992, 1996), which in turn promotes infant survival. Thanks to prenatal hearing, newborns can distinguish their mother's voice from the voice of other new mothers (DeCasper & Fifer, 1980), and may recognize (Kolata, 1984) or even prefer (DeCasper & Spence, 1986) a story they heard repeatedly before birth, or people speaking their mother's language to another language (Moon *et al.*, 1993). Such studies are evidence for a sophisticated prenatal ability to memorize complex sound patterns. They suggest that the ability to process gestural aspects of language (prosody, intonation, contour), which inform the listener about the intentions and emotions of the speaker, begins before birth (Childs, 1998; Karmiloff & Karmiloff-Smith, 2001).

Evaluating research on prenatal musicality

Research relevant to prenatal musicality is a minefield of poorly defined terms, inappropriately motivated research, poor communication between research groups with different backgrounds and underlying assumptions, and tenuous connections between research results and practical applications (including applications in music education). Popular sources (such as Tsiaras, 2003) are not always reliable. The value and applicability of literature can depend strongly on researchers' motives. Searching the internet can be a problem, because much of the easily accessible literature is politically motivated (e.g., the pro-life, anti-abortion movement).

Consider the following example. Several sources (Karmiloff & Karmiloff-Smith, undated; Whitwell, undated; Wilkin, 1995/96) report that the fetus moves in time to music ('dances'). I could find no plausible empirical evidence for this claim, which seems to be a misinterpretation or exaggeration of the fetus's tendency to change its pattern of movements depending on the kind of stimulation it receives—regardless of whether adults hear that stimulation as music. Any repeated movement can be regarded as rhythmic, but synchronization to music is another matter. Children do not learn to synchronize their movements to a beat, at least temporarily, until their second postnatal year (Moog, 1963). Moreover, there is no evolutionary reason why the fetus should possess this ability.

The following discussion aims to help readers develop a feel for the contradictions in the literature and their origins, and in this way to obtain plausible answers to their questions.

Scientific-conservative versus romantic-progressive research

Gooch (1972, cited in Boyce-Tillman, 2004) classified human cultures into two types, according to the way in which they construct knowledge. 'Type A' systems focus on products, objectivity, impersonal logic, detachment, and discrete categories of knowledge based on proof and scientific evidence. 'Type B' systems favour being, subjectivity, emotion, magic, involvement, association, belief, spirituality, and non-causal knowledge, and are suppressed in modern Western culture. The literature on prenatal psychology may be similarly divided into two categories, which I call *scientific-conservative* and *romantic-progressive.*

Scientific-conservative literature relies on carefully controlled experiments, and is represented by respected medical journals such as the *Journal of Obstetrics and Gynecology* and the numerous journals associated with the American Psychological Association. While these traditions exemplify high academic standards and successful quality control mechanisms, they are not perfect. Scientific-conservative medical research still downplays apparently successful paramedical approaches that are difficult to investigate empirically or reconcile with a Western, materialist approach. And this tradition has not entirely eliminated its patriarchal and sexist traditions and tendencies (e.g., Bickel *et al.*, 1996; Woodward, 1999; Yedidia & Bickel, 2001). The association between fetal psychology and women's bodies and issues may explain why, until a few decades ago, the scientific and medical mainstream showed remarkably little interest in fetal psychology. Scientific-conservative and patriarchal (or stereotypically masculine) thinking is also strong within the field of cognitive psychology, which traditionally treats the brain as a computer separate from the human body and the physical/social environment, and regards quantitative research methods (statistical analysis of numerical data) as superior to qualitative methods (content analysis of linguistic data).

Romantic-progressive researchers tend to the other extreme—united in their opposition to groups as diverse as conservative scientists, the political right wing, and feminists (Verny, 1999). They address scientifically problematic topics such as the interaction between emotional and physical health, paramedical healing, and spirituality. Their flagship journal is the *Journal of Prenatal and Perinatal Psychology and Health.*

Romantic-progressive claims are often undeniably valid and important. Regarding 'prenatal and birth themes and symbols in dance, movement, art, dreams, language, myth, ritual, play, and psychotherapy', Menzam (2002, abstract) wrote: 'Although we cannot prove that specific movement patterns re-enact prenatal and birth events, we can conclude that prenatal and birth themes appear to present everywhere in our lives'. Nor is there always a clear distinction between romantic-progressive and scientific-conservative research. For example, the scientific-conservative Hepper (1992) adopted a progressive stance when he pointed out the danger of underestimating fetal abilities: 'a fetus may sense a stimulus, but exhibit no response' (p. 133).

Some romantic-progressive researchers wildly exaggerate fetal abilities. For example, Cheek (1986) found evidence for out-of-body prenatal memories in memories accessed through hypnotic regression. The call for papers of the 16th International Congress of the International Society for Prenatal and Perinatal Psychology and Medicine (ISPPM Heidelberg 2005) begins as follows: 'Research in the field of prenatal psychology has extended our life-history back to conception and beyond—right back to our parents' thoughts and plans for a child of their own.' The theme of the 12th International ISPPM (London, 1998) was *Conscious Birth: The Experience of a Lifetime,* and the website explained:

> The dawning awareness that the human baby is normally conscious at birth lays the
> foundation for a paradigm shift with immense consequences. The Congress will review the

now irrefutable tide of evidence for prenatal and perinatal consciousness, examine its impact on the dynamics of the human condition, survey the history of the emergence of the new paradigm and the reaction it has met and explore the implications for a range of fields.

Chamberlain (1993) drew on anecdotal evidence from psychotherapy to support claims of 'fetal intelligence' and 'thinking before birth'. Sallenbach (1993) even wondered when the 'intelligent' prenate has 'the capacity to formulate hypotheses' (p. 77). These authors failed to distinguish between intelligence and the more elementary abilities to learn and react. Intelligence is normally understood to involve both the possession of knowledge and the ability to use it efficiently and adaptively in real and unexpected situations (Sternberg, 1985). It is misleading to apply this term to the fetus.

Every field of research has its radicals and conservatives, but seldom is the gap between them as large as in prenatal psychology. We can only guess the reason. Perhaps it stems from the strong emotions that babies evoke in adults—combined with the mystery and fascination of a largely inaccessible experimental subject (the fetus). Adults are strongly motivated to meet babies' needs by caring for and playing with them, which has clear survival value (Bjorklund *et al.*, 2002). To what extent should researchers in pre- and perinatal psychology be objective about these feelings? Parenting behaviours are incompatible with the airs of self-importance traditionally cultivated by university professors to maintain the respect of their students and of the general public, who may not be in a position to evaluate their research and intellectual competence by less superficial means. This is an important issue for music educators, whose parental instincts can motivate them to devote their lives to the good cause of child musicality, but at the same time cloud their judgement when confronted with scientific questions related to their research. It is a classic example of the tension between objectivity and subjectivity, or between facts and values, in scientific research (Lassman & Speirs, 1994).

This chapter aims to steer a middle course between 'Type A' scientific-conservative and 'Type B' romantic-progressive extremes. I acknowledge not only the explanatory power of 'Type A' systems but also the descriptive relevance of 'Type B' systems for musical experience and meaning. Like a scientific-conservative, I avoid claims that contradict the best empirical literature. Like a romantic-progressive, I consider promising theories and scenarios for which little or no empirical evidence yet exists. I support my claims with available empirical literature, abstract logic, evolutionary arguments, and everyday experience. I acknowledge, and attempt to combine, the different (tacit) philosophies and criteria of 'truth' that characterize the sciences and the humanities: empiricism, rationalism, intersubjectivity, pragmatism. This radically (and perhaps dangerously) interdisciplinary approach is my attempt to creatively resolve the profound fragmentation of the field of prenatal psychology and, in that way, to contribute to its coming of age.

Definition of talent, music, and consciousness

Terminology in prenatal development can be misleading and inconsistent. Scientific conservatives may overuse scientific jargon, while romantic progressives may project adult or postnatal concepts onto the fetus.

Talent

Musical performance skills (Chapter 5 and 12) are clearly unavailable and irrelevant to the fetus. Fetuses may nevertheless vary in their musical *potential* (giftedness, talent, propensity, musicality, aptitude). If musical potential is genetically determined, it exists before birth and presumably influences the prenatal perceptual-cognitive abilities of hearing, processing, memorizing, recalling, recognizing pitch-time patterns, and associating these with emotion.

Like any other ability, musical ability emerges from an interaction between genes and environment (Plomin & Bergeman, 1991). Presumably, this process begins as soon as the fetus begins to hear. Behaviourally, babies vary in many ways, for example in their irritability (e.g. the frequency of occurrence, duration, and intensity of their crying), which can be regarded as an aspect of personality (Kohnstamm *et al.*, 1989). The extent to which a baby's irritability might be genetically determined is unclear, because it is strongly influenced by the prenatal environment (see 'Emotional communication'). The same presumably applies to a baby's musical ability.

The relative significance of the prenatal stage for long-term musical development is unknown—but unlikely to be comparable with the childhood stage, in which a range of factors influence long-term musical success, including the presence of musical instruments, parents who love music, meaningful (family) musical activities, understanding teachers, parental tolerance of informal practice, and so on. Empirical studies (e.g., Howe *et al.*, 1998) have demonstrated that musical skill depends almost entirely on the amount and quality of practice; but this depends in turn on the motivation to practice long and hard, which may have a considerable genetic–biological component.

Music

What does a fetus perceive, when it perceives *music*? Clearly, not what an adult perceives. First, the fetus has no language or reflective awareness with which to process the music. Second, music perception always depends strongly on previous musical experience (as ethnomusicological research makes clear). Thus, it is important to define what is meant by music. If music is an integral feature of human culture, then it can hardly be relevant to the fetus, which—romantic-progressive objections to the contrary—has not yet been initiated into that culture. For that initiation runs parallel to the acquisition of language (Noble & Davidson, 1996) and does not begin until about one year after birth.

To understand fetal responses to music, it is instructive to consider music perception by non-human animals, which—like the fetus—do not contribute actively or directly to human culture and therefore, presumably, do not experience music (or anything else) in the way human children or adults do. Cows, for example, may produce more milk when exposed to slow music and less when exposed to fast music, because a slow beat reduces stress and a faster beat increases it (North & MacKenzie, 2001). Similarly, the human fetus may prefer musical tempos close to the resting heart rate of the mother (Whitwell, undated). Such work can shed light on inborn responses to specific musical parameters (here, beat and tempo), but not on music in the sense of human musical culture.

Consciousness

Progressive-romantic researchers who are also psychotherapists, psychoanalysts, or hypnotists such as Cheek (1986) often suggest that the fetus has a kind of consciousness (or awareness). Whereas a term such as 'sentient prenate' (Chamberlain, 1994) may be appropriate, as the word sentient refers merely to perception, the parallel claim that 'unborn children are sensitive and aware' (abstract) is unfounded and misleading, and the claim that 'consciousness may not be dependent on the central nervous system, or even on the body' (Wade, 1998, abstract), does not distinguish the fetus from other living or non-living things. A scientific-conservative approach regards the anecdotal experience of therapists and clients in psychoanalysis, psychotherapy, and hypnosis as unreliable, because the various factors that may influence it cannot be separated and controlled.

The confusion about consciousness in the literature on prenatal psychology is unsurprising considering the continuing confusion in the general philosophical, psychological, and neuroscientific literature on consciousness (e.g. Baier, 1999). This confusion appears to stem from variations in both the (operational) definition of consciousness and underlying philosophical assumptions. Often, neither of these is clearly explained. Some possible definitions or components of consciousness are listed below; the most interesting and mysterious of these may be termed *reflective consciousness*, or simply *reflection*.

Regarding philosophical beliefs, scientific-conservatives often seem to be philosophical materialists who believe that only the physical world exists, whereas other researchers may be mind–body dualists. Popper and Eccles (1977) acknowledged the existence of 'three worlds': the physical world, including the brain and all its anatomical and physiological contents (World 1); the world of private experiences—sensations and emotions (2); and the world of information, knowledge, and culture (3). According to their approach, mind–body dualism is about Worlds 1 and 2. But reflection involves (linguistic) description of one's private world of experience, and is therefore an interaction between Worlds 2 and 3. This is consistent with the thesis that reflection and language emerged in parallel, both phylogenetically (in human evolution) and ontogenetically (in child development) (Noble & Davidson, 1996).

By definition, reflection can only be directly observed from within, that is, by introspection. We guess and assume that other people can reflect, but have no direct evidence. The term consciousness is often used in a more general sense that includes observable behaviours such as wakefulness, attention, and preference, as well as unobservable cognitive phenomena such as working memory and cognitive representations. I will consider each of these in turn with regard to the fetus.

The concept of *fetal wakefulness* is unproblematic. It is also directly relevant to prenatal musicality, as fetuses—like newborns—are more likely to react to and process sound when they are awake, and are much more often asleep than awake. An infant's eye, body and respiratory movements allow five behavioural states to be identified—two sleep states (non-REM, REM) and three states of wakefulness (Prechtl, 1974). At 36 weeks gestational age, four of these five neonate states can be identified from fetal heart rate and its variability: quiet sleep, active or REM sleep, quiet wakefulness, and active wakefulness; and the amount of time the fetus spends per day in each state gradually changes as it develops (Nijhuis *et al.*,

1982). It is also possible to determine sleep/wake states from prenatal body movements using ultrasound (Arabin & Riedewald 1992). Sleep-state differentiation begins somewhere between 14 weeks (Oerter & Montada, 1995) and 28 weeks (Awoust & Levi, 1983; Selton *et al.*, 2000). The circadian rhythms of the fetus are synchronized to those of the mother: the fetus tends to be most awake and active when the mother sleeps (Reppert & Weaver, 1988). Incidentally, the fact that the fetus 'dreams' (as babies do in REM sleep: Roffwarg *et al.*, 1966) is no evidence of reflection, since REM sleep also occurs in other animals.

As already noted, the fetus is capable of learning. According to Baddeley's (1986) concept of working memory, stimuli must be processed in working memory before they can be memorized, implying that the fetus also has working memory. If working memory is 'an essential contributor to the neural basis of consciousness' (Osaka, 2003), the fetus may be conscious in this sense. But a scientific approach should preferably distinguish concepts such consciousness, attention, perception, and working memory (Baars, 1997).

The concept of fetal *attention* is less straightforward. The word 'listening' (as opposed to merely hearing) implies attention, which may be psychologically defined as a state of heightened wakefulness or vigilance in response to a stimulus, coupled with selective perception of that stimulus. The fetus cannot turn towards an external sound source, because it has no means of determining its direction (see *sound localization* above). A change in fetal behavioural state in response to a stimulus does not necessary imply attention, either. However, many studies have shown that the fetus *habituates* to a repeated stimulus (Lecanuet, 1996). If habituation is defined as a discontinuation of attention, then it is also evidence for the existence of attention. Attention is not the same as consciousness, but is involved in the selection and maintenance of conscious contents (Baars, 1997).

Musical *preferences* begin early. Babies can show preferences for different sounds by sucking in different ways on a pacifier (DeCasper & Fifer, 1980). Newborns prefer the sound of their mother's voice when the high frequencies had been filtered out so that it more closely resembled the muffled sound of the mother's voice *in utero* (Querleu *et al.*, 1984; Fifer & Moon, 1988). Presumably, the fetus could also show preferences if an experimental paradigm could be designed to demonstrate it (perhaps some kind of brain scan, cf. Weiskopf, 2003) or if fetal behavioural reactions (movements, heart rate) characteristic of preference could be identified. All this is unsurprising, as it is normal for non-human animals to show preferences, such as for different foods. The existence of preferences is therefore no evidence for reflection.

Psychologists distinguish between *sensation*, the initial message from the senses, and *perception*, the extraction of information and meaning from sensations (Hepper, 1992), but also use the blanket term perception to cover both. In a cognitive approach, perception involves the construction of *cognitive representations* of environmental objects, usually by comparing sensory inputs in different sense modalities. The concept of prenatal bonding (e.g. Sallenbach, 1993) implies that the fetus forms a cognitive representation of the mother: it combines auditory, movement, biochemical, and other signals that it picks up from the mother so as to construct her as a unified object. Oberhoff (2005) has suggested that this cognitive representation has two essential qualities that might enable a later connection to music: it is *big* and *moving*, just as music is often considered to have virtual spatial properties that are associated with bodily motion and independent of the physical spatial locations of musical instruments (Eitan & Granot, 2004). Again, this is no evidence for fetal reflection, as it is normal for non-human animals to form cognitive representations of environmental objects.

Reflection distinguishes humans from non-humans. Associated with reflection are uniquely human behaviours such as *realizing* that one is attending to or doing something, doing things deliberately (*intentionality*), knowing that one knows something (*metacognition*), and knowing that others have separate reflective consciousness (*theory of mind*) (Noble & Davidson, 1996; Szendre, 1996; Garfield *et al.*, 2001). We cannot conclusively disprove that fetal reflection exists, because if the fetus had a private world of reflection adults would have no access to it. The only known way to access the reflection of another being or group is through language. However, current knowledge about the role of language in the ontogenesis of reflection makes the existence of fetal reflection seem very unlikely. Phylogenetically, the gradual prehistoric emergence of human speech and language presumably ran parallel to the gradual emergence of reflection and associated characteristically human behaviours (Corballis, 2004). Ontogenetically, babies acquire language, reflection, and a concept of self gradually as they interact imitatively and socially with caretakers; the process begins actively around the age of 1 and continues for at least 10 years (Slobodchikov & Tsukerman, 1992; Papoušek & Papoušek, 1995; Flavell *et al.*, 1999; Asendorpf, 2002; Decety & Chaminade, 2003).

 It seems to be human nature to attribute mental processes, including one's inner life and reflective consciousness of sensations and emotions, to other beings or objects such as pets (Archer, 1997). This process, sometimes called *animistic projection*, plays a part in theories of the origin of art (Wulf, 1947) and religion (Roheim, 1932), and in the psychological concept of theory of mind. As animistic projection involves the assumption or attribution of human characteristics, it may be regarded as a form of *anthropomorphism* (also called *anthropomorphization* or *personification*), which is an important issue in fields as diverse as veterinary science, ethology (animal behaviour), animal welfare, evolutionary biology, anthropology, primatology, psychology, history, philosophy, and literary criticism (Mitchell *et al.*, 1997). In the sciences, human qualities may be projected on to animals such as dolphins (Hafemann, 1987), while in areas addressed by the humanities (religion, myths, fairy tales, children's literature), reflection and intentionality may be projected on to living and non-living objects, non-human animals, and gods. The more specific Freudian concept of *projection*—a defence mechanism by which feelings or impulses are attributed to another person (Baumeister *et al.*, 1998)—also plays a part in religion (Beit-Hallahmi & Argyle, 1975). The psychological function of animistic projection may be to overcome the loneliness that accompanies the discovery of self, which in turn accompanies the onset of reflection (cf. Davis & Franzoi, 1986).

 Animistic projection on to (and hence anthropomorphism of) the fetus begins when a mother starts to feel her fetus move at about 20 weeks, and gets the impression that it is kicking on purpose, or trying to communicate (Gloger-Tippelt, 1988). Later, adults project reflection on to a baby or child during infant–adult vocal play (otherwise known as *motherese*: Papoušek & Papoušek, 1995; also Chapter 2, this volume); that is, they speak and behave as if the baby or child can reflect.

Children appear to learn both reflection and animistic projection by imitating the behaviour of their carers. Animistic projection is also taught directly when adults project reflection on to animals or other objects during adult–child interactions. Such behaviours help the baby or child to gradually discover that adults (as well as other animals and objects) have different minds, and to conclude that they have their own (Garfield *et al.*, 2001). The child also projects its own reflective consciousness on to objects and animals, when such assignment is plausible and meaningful (Szendre, 1996).

The concepts of animistic projection and anthropomorphism can explain why so many romantic-progressive researchers accept and promote the idea of prenatal reflection. It can also explain the prevalence of the belief that the womb is a safe and happy place, in which the fetus experiences well-being and perfection (Montagu, 1962; Whitwell, undated; I committed the same logical error in Parncutt, 1993, 1997). But even if the fetus could reflect, it could only be 'happy' if it could compare its present state with a previous, less ideal, 'sadder' state. Sounds associated with prenatal 'experience' are not, therefore, necessarily associated with positive emotions. To imagine things from the perspective of the fetus, it is necessary to leave all aspects of the adult world behind, including associations between happiness and abundance, and between sadness and work or responsibility.

Summarizing this section, fetal 'consciousness' is limited to *wakefulness, attention, perception*, and *preference*. These capabilities are shared by non-human animals (as well as non-human fetuses), suggesting the prenatal human development is not essentially different (and therefore no more wonderful) than prenatal development in other animals. Neither the fetus nor the baby is capable of *reflection*. As the expression 'prenatal experience' (as used for example by Hepper, 1992 and Lecanuet, 1996) implies reflection (consider, in everyday language, the 'experience' of a holiday on a Greek island), it is misleading and should be avoided.

Prenatal music education

Can and should music education begin before birth? The following two arguments suggest that it should:

- *Fetal abilities.* During the third trimester, the fetus is mature enough to survive birth. It can hear, process, and remember musical patterns of sound, and associate them with emotions. Moreover, sound is the most complex (and therefore interesting) prenatally available stimulus: as soon as the baby is born, the amount of competing information that it can potentially extract from the other senses (primarily vision) increases dramatically, while the simultaneous increase in available acoustic information is relatively small. This point can explain the contrast between newborn's striking perceptual musical abilities and the relatively slow rate at which infants learn specific musical structures such as tonality (Krumhansl & Keil, 1982, cited in Trehub, 2003).

- *Parental motivation.* The parents' desire for a child increases steadily during pregnancy and reaches a peak just before the birth (Gloger-Tippelt, 1988). During the last 10 weeks, expectant mothers actively imagine the appearance and behaviour of their baby and what it will be like to care for it. During that time, the parents (and especially the mother) are highly motivated to participate in activities that will promote the health and well-being of their child.

Is this not a perfect window of opportunity to get the child started on musical development? Should parents take advantage of this period to give their child a head start on musical education? The answer would be 'yes' if it could be demonstrated that prenatally stimulated babies or children had superior musical abilities. And a number of studies seem to have shown that prenatal sensory-motor stimulation—beyond the wealth of sounds and other stimulation normally available in the mother's body—can contribute not only to musical development but also to general sensory-motor, language, emotional, social, and even physical development (Manrique et al., 1993; Panthuraamphorn, 1993; Chen et al., 1994).

Unfortunately, all such studies are methodologically problematic. No researcher has yet succeeded in clearly separating effects of prenatal stimulation from postnatal effects on musical development. For example, Lafuente et al. (1997) attempted to 'advance the intellectual and physical development of the fetus by means of musical stimuli' (abstract). Fetuses between 28 and 40 weeks were regularly exposed to violin sounds, and their postnatal development was monitored. The authors claimed that the babies in the experimental group were 'superior in gross and fine motor activities, linguistic development, some aspects of body-sensory co-ordination and certain cognitive behaviours'. If that were true, it would be a sensation. Why might violin sounds have such specific effects, while the sound of the mother's voice and the multitude of other sounds to which the fetus is exposed do not? The fetus has no way of distinguishing between speech and music. More plausibly, Tafuri and Villa (2002) suggested that prenatally musically educated babies produce musical vocalizations (babbling) earlier, more frequently and with musically higher quality than controls. But again it was not possible to control or eliminate postnatal effects on musical development. We thus have no convincing evidence that prenatal fetal acoustic, tactile, or movement stimulation influences intelligence, creativity, or later development. Hepper (1992) wrote: 'My own studies indicate that there may be some benefits resulting from prenatal stimulation, but this appears to be not the result of stimulation *per se*, but rather the results of increasing the interest of the mother in her pregnancy, which has 'knock-on' effects for development after birth' (p. 149).

If prenatal exposure to music indeed gives the fetus a headstart in the development of musical abilities, which is certainly possible, what kind of music should the mother listen to? Should the mother *like* the music, encouraging the fetus to associate it with positive emotions that might later motivate it to become actively involved in music? Or should the mother choose music whose emotion she feels strongly, regardless of whether those feelings are positive or negative, given that memories associated with strong emotions are more salient and last longer (Kulas et al., 2003; Phelps, 2004)? Again, confounds make this question hard to verify empirically; and it is not (yet) possible to investigate fetal preferences.

A further problem is the holistic, amodal nature of fetal and infant perception (Sallenbach, 1993). Neither the fetus nor the infant distinguishes between music and speech; infant–adult vocal play is a combination of speech and music, suggesting that children do not begin to separate the two until their second year. Similarly, the idea of talking to the fetus to encourage prenatal bonding (e.g. Sallenbach, 1993) can only work in one direction: the mother may get the impression of bonding (Bitnour, 2000), but the fetus has no 'idea' that speech is normally directed toward people, and has no possible way of 'knowing' whether speech is directed toward it or someone else.

In summary, empirical studies have not yet demonstrated the success of prenatal music education. The best musicians tend to be those who work the hardest, and the ones who work the hardest are the ones who are most motivated to work and most persistent when the going gets tough (O'Neill & McPherson, 2002). There is no known way of promoting the prenatal development of these attributes.

Contraindications

The problem is not only that benefits of prenatal music education cannot be verified. Attempts to educate the fetus by regularly playing music or other sounds through a loud-speaker strapped to the mother's abdomen could be also dangerous—or at least negatively affect development—in the following ways.

- *Hearing damage.* The fetus is not evolutionarily prepared to hear sound more loudly than the mother does, as it may do when a loudspeaker is strapped to its mother's abdomen. In this situation, the mother may not be in a position to adjust the loudness to an appropriate level. Children of mothers who were working in noisy environments such as factories while pregnant, which is now illegal in some countries (Brezinka *et al.*, 1997), may be more likely to develop high-frequency hearing loss; evidence has been presented both for this claim (Lalande *et al.*, 1986; Pierson, 1996) and against it (Ohel *et al.*, 1987; Arulkumaran *et al.*, 1991).

- *Stress.* Prenatal noise can have other long-term effects. For example, aeroplane noise can lead to a reduction in newborn body weight and height at age 3 years (Kawada, 2004). Noise-induced stress may impair the development of the fetal immune system (Sobrian *et al.*, 1997). Again, these findings are controversial; some investigators (e.g., Hartikainen-Sorri *et al.*, 1991) found no effects of noise.

- *Sleep.* An abdominal loudspeaker could disturb the wake/sleep cycle of the fetus (Nijhuis *et al.*,1982) and disrupt the timing of brain development (Fifer, reported in Bitnour, 2000). The same applies to fetal massage or games. The fetus is much more often asleep than awake, and sleep is important for physiological development. Interrupted sleep may be regarded as a kind of prenatal stress. No one would place a blaring loudspeaker next to a sleeping baby (DiPietro, reported in Bitnour, 2000). It is presumably important at least to ensure that the fetus is awake (moving) before applying such techniques.

- *Bonding.* Prenatal music education via an abdominal loudspeaker could inhibit prenatal bonding. From the viewpoint of the fetus, bonding with the mother involves perceiving her in all sense modalities. A loudspeaker could disrupt and confuse the development of a cognitive representation of the mother.

- *Uncertainty.* Researchers do not yet know enough about the developing fetal brain and auditory system to be sure about the possible positive or negative effects of deliberate prenatal auditory stimulation. Its consequences (like, for example, the consequences of eating genetically modified foods) are hard to predict. Until things become clearer, it may be better to avoid such procedures altogether.

Ethics

Is it *ethical* to try to educate the fetus? Clearly, it cannot hurt if the fetus gets a headstart on musical skill acquisition that will later help it to compete with musical peers. But:

- *Parentification.* Parents who feel inadequate about themselves may try to compensate by encouraging their children to make up for their own failures—such as their (perceived) lack of musical talent. This is an example of *co-dependence*, which involves shame-proneness, low self-esteem, and *parentification* (Wells *et al.*, 1999). Children are 'parentified' when they are expected to take on the role of caretaker to their siblings or even to their own parents (Chase, 1999). Parents should avoid projecting their wishes on to their child, who has (or will develop) its own wishes, and instead focus on creating a loving environment in which the child can develop in its own, individual way.

- *Pressure.* If too much emphasis is placed on achievement and 'hothousing' in early childhood, the child may achieve less rather than more, miss out on valuable childhood experiences, and develop psychological problems (Hyson *et al.*, 1991). Placing unreasonable expectations on the fetus may set up a negative and lasting dynamic between parents and children. Modern children are under enough pressure (Elkind, 1981) without it starting before birth (DiPietro, reported in Bitnour, 2000).

- *Priorities.* We cannot foresee the contribution a fetus will later make to society. Music is one of countless positive alternatives, but surely not the most important. The world is threatened by poverty, war, and environmental change. Because tomorrow's adults will have to solve these problems, they are a challenge to education in general. Peer and teacher–student interactions are important for social development (Kim & Stevens, 1987). Parents can contribute by nurturing their children's natural altruism (Hurlbut, 2002), promoting situations that encourage them to think clearly, independently, and critically, and nurturing their natural abilities and tendencies. 'Our ultimate objective, of course, is to help create not a musical genius but a person well integrated in his [sic.] physical, emotional, intellectual and spiritual self' (Whitwell, undated).

Recommendations

In conclusion, the following recommendations can be made to expectant mothers wishing to support their unborn child's musical development. Because the empirical evidence is incomplete, the recommendations are necessarily tentative and intuitive.

- *General health.* Promote general fetal development by eating and exercising wisely. A chronic lack of important nutrients can restrict fetal growth and permanently affect cardiovascular, endocrine, and metabolic systems (Bertram & Hanson, 2002).

- *Stress.* Restrict stress to reasonable limits. Recent research (cited above) has clearly and repeatedly demonstrated that *excessive* maternal stress is bad for the fetus. Conversely, *mild* stress is normal and may even promote development (DiPietro, 2004).

- *Auditory health.* Minimize the chance of hearing problems by avoiding infections. The most common cause of prenatal hearing loss is viral infection by cytomegalovirus or rubella. In Western countries, rubella has become rare due to vaccination (Lagasse *et al.*, 2000). As it is unclear whether prenatal noise affects postnatal hearing, avoid long-term exposure to high sound levels in discos or factories. The fetus may be affected primarily by the stress you feel when exposed to loud sounds; the noise itself may be secondary.

- *Music.* Listen to and play a lot of music—provided you enjoy the music yourself. The more music the fetus hears, the more it will learn about it, at least in the sense of storing pitch-time patterns in memory. Maternal enjoyment may also promote the development of positive emotional associations to music, and is certainly more important than arbitrary aesthetic judgements of musicologists; 'classical' music is not necessarily better (cf. Cook, 1998). However, do not force yourself to play or listen to music, as stress is problematic (see above) and negative connotations may cancel out the positive effect of neutral exposure. Avoid very loud music (see above), but remember that moderately quiet music will be inaudible to the fetus. Some researchers claim that music with a clear beat is preferable and that you should listen to the same music regularly, but the evidence for this is weak.

- *Singing.* If you enjoy singing, sing. The quality of your singing (e.g., in the sense of staying in tune or in key) doesn't matter: your fetus is very accommodating! Nor does it matter whether you sing, speak, or something in between. If it helps you to imagine that your fetus is listening, and this makes music making (and listening) more enjoyable, OK—but be aware that the fetus is unable to reflect on what it hears. Regardless of its prenatal effect, singing to your fetus can give you a headstart on bonding with your baby (Fridman, 2000) and get you into the habit of singing lullabies after the birth, which is musically, cognitively, emotionally, and socially beneficial (cf. Chapter 2, this volume).

- *Living.* Paradoxically, the best way to promote a child's musical ability before its birth may be to do nothing specifically musical at all. Just eat, sleep, walk, talk, and experience emotional ups and downs as usual. All these activities produce sound patterns that stimulate the prenatal development of hearing, auditory pattern recognition, and the emotional connotations of sound patterns that underlie music.

Acknowledgements

I am grateful to Ellen Dissanayake, Michaela Gosch, Gunter Kreutz, Donald Hodges, Thomas Hutsteiner, Annekatrin Kessler, Carol Krumhansl, Peter Liebmann-Holzmann, Gary McPherson, Bernd Oberhoff, William Noble, Kazue Semba, Glenn Schellenberg, Günter

Schulter, Caroline Traube, and Sandra Trehub for helpful suggestions and discussions. This research was supported in part by NSERC Grant #228175-00 and VRQ Grant 2201-202 to Daniel J. Levitin and was carried out in part during sabbatical leave from the University of Graz.

References

Abrams, R. M. (1995). Some aspects of the fetal sound environment. In I. Deliège and J. Sloboda (eds), *Perception and cognition of music* (pp. 83–101). Hove, Sussex, England: Psychology Press.

Abrams, R. M., Gerhardt, K. J., & Peters, A. J. M. (1995). Transmission of sound and vibration to the fetus. In J. P. Lecanuet *et al.* (eds), *Fetal development: A psychobiological perspective* (pp. 315–330). London: Lawrence Erlbaum Associates.

Abrams, R. M., Griffiths, S. K., Huang, X., Sain, J., Langford, G., & Gerhardt, K. K. (1998). Fetal music perception: The role of sound transmission. *Music perception*, 15, 307–317.

Altmann, E. (1950). Normal development of the ear and its 2 mechanics. *Archives in Otolaryngology*, 52, 725–730.

Arabin, B. (2002). Opinion: Music during pregnancy. *Ultrasound in Obstetrics and Gynecology*, 20, 425–430.

Arabin, B. & Riedewald, S. (1992). An attempt to quantify characteristics of behavioural states. *American Journal of Perinatology*, 9, 115–119.

Archer, J. (1997). Why do people love their pets? *Evolution and Human Behaviour*, 18(4), 237–259.

Armitage, S. E., Baldwin, B. A., & Vince, M. A. (1980). The fetal sound environment of sheep. *Science*, 208, 1173–1174.

Arulkumaran, S., Skurr, B., Tong, H., Kek, L. P., Yeoh, K. H., & Ratnam, S. S. (1991). No evidence of hearing loss due to fetal acoustic stimulation test. *Obstetrics & Gynecology*, 78, 283–285.

Asendorpf, J. B. (2002). Self-awareness, other-awareness, and secondary representation. In W. Prinz & A. N. Meltzoff (eds), *The imitative mind: Development, evolution, and brain bases* (pp.63–73). New York, NY: Cambridge University Press.

Averill, J. R. (1969). Autonomic response patterns in sadness and mirth. *Psychophysiology*, 5, 399–414.

Awoust, J. & Levi, S. (1983). Neurological maturation of the human fetus. *Ultrasound in Medicine and Biology, Suppl.* 2, 583–587.

Baars, B. J. (1997). Some essential differences between consciousness and attention, perception, and working memory. *Consciousness and Cognition*, 6, 363–371.

Baddeley, A. (1986). *Working memory.* Oxford: Clarendon.

Baier, W. R. (ed.) (1999). *Bewusstsein.* Graz: Leykam.

Baumeister, R. F., Dale, K., & Sommer, K. L. (1998). Freudian defense mechanisms and empirical findings in modern social psychology: Reaction formation, projection, displacement, undoing, isolation, sublimation, and denial. *Journal of Personality*, 66, 1081–1124.

Beit-Hallahmi, B. & Argyle, M. (1975). God as a father-projection: The theory and the evidence. *British Journal of Medical Psychology*, 48, 71–75.

Bertram, C. E. & Hanson, M. A. (2002). Prenatal programming of postnatal endocrine responses by glucocorticoids. *Reproduction*, 124, 459–467.

Bickel, J., Croft, K. & Marshall, R. (1996). *Enhancing the environment for women in academic medicine.* Washington, DC: Association of American Medical Colleges.

Birnholz, J. & Benacerraf, B. (1983). The development of human fetal hearing. *Science*, 222, 516–518.

Bitnour, M. B. (2000). What's it like in the womb? *WebMD Feature Archive*, http://my.webmd.com/content/article/11/3608_285.htm

Bjorklund, D. F., Yunger, J. L., & Pellegrini, A. D. (2002). The evolution of parenting and evolutionary approaches to childrearing. In M. Bornstein, M. (ed.), *Handbook of parenting*, Vol. 2: *Biology and ecology of parenting* (2nd edn, pp. 3–30). Mahwah, NJ: Lawrence Erlbaum Associates.

Blacking, J. (ed.) (1979). *The performing arts: Music and dance.* The Hague: Mouton.

Blauert, J. (1997). *Spatial hearing: The psychophysics of human sound localization.* Cambridge, MA: MIT Press.

Boyce-Tillman, J. (2004). Towards an ecology of music education. *Philosophy of Music Education Review*, 12, 102–125.

Brezinka, C., Lechner, T., & Stephan, K. (1997). Der Fetus und der Lärm (The fetus and noise). *Gynäkologisch-geburtshilfliche Rundschau*, 37(3), 119–129.

Brown, M. R. & Gray, T. S. (1988). Peptide injections into the amygala of conscious rats: Effects on blood pressure, heart rate and plasma catecholamines. *Regulatory Peptides*, 21, 95–106.

Buitelaar, J. K., Huizink, A. C., Mulder, E. J., Robles de Medina, P. G., & Visser, G. H. A. (2003). Prenatal stress and cognitive development and temperament in infants. *Neurobiology of Aging*, 24 (Suppl. 1), S53–S60.

Busnel, M. C., & Granier-Deferre, C. (1983). And what of fetal audition? In Oliveito, A. & Zappella, M. (eds), *The behavior of human infants* (pp. 93–126). New York: Plenum.

Campos, J. J., Thein, S., & Owen, D. (2003). A Darwinian lebacy to understanding human infancy. *Annals of the New York Academy of Sciences*, 1000, 110–134.

Canlon, B., Erichsen, S., Nemlander, E., Chen, M., Hossain, A., Celsi, G., & Ceccatelli, S. (2003). Alterations in the intrauterine environment by glucocorticoids modifies the developmental programme of the auditory system. *European Journal of Neuroscience*, 17, 2035–2041.

Cassidy, J. W. & Standley, J. M. (1995). The effect of music listening on physiological responses of premature infants in the NICU. *Journal of Music Therapy*, 32, 208–227.

Chamberlain, D. B. (1993). Prenatal intelligence. In Blum (ed.), *Prenatal perception, learning, and bonding.* Hong Kong: Leonardo.

Chamberlain, D. B. (1994). The sentient prenate: What every parent should know. *Journal of Prenatal and Perinatal Psychology and Health*, 9(1), 9–31.

Chase, N. D. (1999). *Burdened children. theory, research, and treatment of parentification.* Thousand Oaks, CA: Sage.

Cheek, D. B. (1986). Prenatal and perinatal imprints: Apparent prenatal consciousness as revealed by hypnosis. *Pre- & Peri-Natal Psychology Journal*, 2(2), 97–110.

Chen, D. G., Huang, Y. F., Zhang, J. Y., & Qi, G. P. (1994). Influence of prenatal music- and touch-enrichment on the IQ, development and behaviour of infants. *Chinese Journal of Psychology*, 8, 148–151.

Childs, M. R. (1998). Prenatal language learning. *Journal of Prenatal and Perinatal Psychology and Health*, 13, 99–122.

Coe, C. L., Kramer, M., Cvéh, B., Gould, E., Reeves, A. J., Kirschbaum, C., & Fuchs, E. (2003). Prenatal stress diminishes neurogenesis in the dentate gyrus of juvenile rhesus monkeys. *Biological Psychiatry*, 54, 1025–1034.

Cook, N. (1998). *Music: A very short introduction.* Oxford University Press.

Corballis, M. C. (2004). The origins of modernity: Was autonomous speech the critical factor? *Psychological Review*, 111, 543–552.

Davis, M. (1992). The role of the amygdala in fear and anxiety. *Annual Review of Neuroscience*, 15, 353–375.

Davis, M. H. & Franzoi, S. L. (1986). Adolescent loneliness, self–disclosure, and private self–consciousness: a longitudinal investigation. *Journal of Personality and Social Psychology*, 51(3), 595–608.

De Weerth, C., van Hees, Y., & Buitelaar, J. K. (2003). Prenatal maternal cortisol levels and infant behavior during the first 5 months. *Early Human Development*, 74, 139–151.

DeCasper, A. J. & Fifer, W. (1980). Of human bonding: Newborns prefer their mothers' voices. *Science*, 208, 1174–1176.

DeCasper, A. J. & Prescott, P. A. (1984). Human newborns' perception of male voices: preference, discrimination, and reinforcing value. *Developmental Psychobiology*, 17(5), 481–491.

DeCasper, A. J. & Spence, M. J. (1986). Prenatal maternal speech influences newborns' perception of speech sound. *Infant Behaviour and Development*, 9, 133–150.

DeCasper, A. J., Lecanuet, J. P. Maugais, R., Granier-Deferre, C., & Busnel, M. C. (1994). Fetal reactions to recurrent maternal speech. *Infant Behaviour and Development*, 17, 159–164.

Decety, J. & Chaminade, T. (2003). When the self represents the other: A new cognitive neuroscience view on psychological identification. *Consciousness and Cognition*, 12, 577–596.

Dettermann, D. K. (1978). The effect of heartbeat on neonatal crying. *Infant Behavior ad Development*, 1, 36–48.

DiPietro, J. A. (2004). The role of prenatal maternal stress in child development. *Current Directions in Psychological Science*, 13, 71–74.

DiPietro, J. A., Irizarry, R. A., Costigan, K. A., & Gurewitsch, E. D. (2004). The psychophysiology of the maternal-fetal relationship. *Psychophysiology*, 41, 510–520.

Dunkel-Schetter, C. (1998). Maternal stress and preterm delivery. *Prenatal and Neonatal Medicine*, 3, 39–42.

Eitan, Z. & Granot, R. Y. (2004). Musical parameters and spatio-kinetic imagery. In S. D. Lipscomb, R. Ashley, R. O. Gjerdingen, & P. Webster (eds), *Proceedings of the 8th International Conference on Music Perception & Cognition* (pp. 57–63). Adelaide, Australia: Causal Productions.

Ekman, P., Levenson, R. W., & Friesen, W. V. (1983). Autonomic nervous system activity distinguishes between different emotions. *Science*, 221, 1208–1210.

Elkind, D. (1981). *The hurried child*. Reading, MA: Addison-Wesley.

Field, T. M., Diego, M., Hernandez-Reif, M. A., Salman, F., Schanberg, S., Kuhn, C., Yando, R., & Bendell, D. (2002). Prenatal anger effects on the fetus and neonate. *Journal of Obstetrics and Gynaecology*, 22, 260–266.

Fifer, W. P. & Moon, C. (1988). Auditory experience in the fetus. In W. P. Smotherman & S. R. Robinson (eds), *Behaviour of the fetus* (pp. 175–188). Telford, England: Caldwell.

Flavell, J. H., Green, F. L., Flavell, E. R., & Lin, N. T. (1999). Development of children's knowledge about unconsciousness. *Child Development*, 70 (2), 396–412.

Fridman, R. (2000). The maternal womb: The first musical school for the baby. *Journal of Prenatal and Perinatal Psychology and Health*, 15, 23–30.

Furst, M., Bresloff, I., Levine, R. A., Merlob, P. L., & Attias, J. J. (2004). Interaural time coincidence detectors are present at birth: Evidence from binaural interaction. *Hearing Research*, 187(1–2), 63–72.

Garfield, J. L., Peterson, C. C., & Perry, T. (2001). Social cognition, language acquisition and the development of the theory of mind. *Mind and Language*, 16, 494–541.

Gerhardt, K. J., Huang, X., Arrington, K. E., Meixner, K., Abrams, R. M., & Antonelli, P. J. (1996). Fetal sheep in utero hear through bone conduction. *American Journal of Otolaryngology*, 17, 374–379.

Gloger-Tippelt, G. (1988). Die Entwicklung des Konzeptes "eigenes Kind" im Verlauf des Übergangs zur Elternschaft. In E. Brähler & A. Meyer (eds), *Partnerschaft, Sexualität und Fruchtbarkeit. Beiträge aus Forschung und Praxis*, Berlin: Springer.

Gooch, S. (1972). *Total man: Towards an evolutionary theory of personality*. London: Allen Lane, Penguin.

Grape, C., Sandgren, M., Hansson, L, O., Ericson, M., & Theorell, T. (2003). Does singing promote well-being? An empirical study of professional and amateur singers during a singing lesson. *Integrative Physiological and Behavioral Science*, 38, 65–74

Hafemann, M. (1987). Delphine—Totem-Tiere des New Age? (Dolphins: totem animals of the New Age?) *Psychologie heute*, 14 (8), 28–33.

Hartikainen-Sorri, A. L., Kirkinen, P., Sorri, M., Anttonen, H., Tuimala, R. (1991). No effect of experimental noise exposure on human pregnancy. *Obstetrics and Gynecology*, 77, 611–615.

Hepper, P. G. (1991). An examination of fetal learning before and after birth. *Irish Journal of Psychology*, 12, 95–107.

Hepper, P. G. (1992). Fetal psychology: An embryonic science. In J. G. Nijhuis (ed.), *Fetal behaviour* (pp. 129–156). Oxford: Oxford University Press.

Hepper, P. G. (1996). Fetal memory: Does it exist? What does it do? *Acta Paediatrica Supplement*, 416, 16–20.

Hepper, P.G. & Shahidullah, B.S. (1994). Development of fetal hearing. *Archives of Disease in Childhood*, 71, F81–F87.

Hooker, D. (1952). *The prenatal origin of behaviour*. Lawrence, KS: University of Kansas Press.

Howe, M. J. A., Davidson, J. W., & Sloboda, J. A. (1998). Innate talents: Reality or myth? *Behavioural and Brain Sciences*, 21, 399–407.

Huizink, A., Mulder, E., & Buitelaar, J. (2004). Prenatal stress and risk for psychopathology: Specific effects or induction of general susceptibility? *Psychological Bulletin*, 130, 115–142.

Hurlbut, W. B. (2002). Empathy, evolution, and altruism. In S. G. Post, L. G. Underwood, J. P. Schloss, & W. B. Hurlbut (eds), *Altruism & altruistic love: Science, philosophy, & religion in dialogue* (pp. 309–327). London: Oxford University Press.

Hyson, M.C., Hirsh-Pasek, K., Rescorla, L., Cone, J., & Martell-Boinske, L. (1991). Ingredients of parental 'pressure' in early childhood. *Journal of Applied Developmental Psychology*, 12, 347–365.

Jones, N. (2001). Babies' musical memories formed in womb. *New Scientist*, 11 July.

Juslin, P. N. & Persson, R. S. (2002). Emotional communication. In R. Parncutt & G. E. McPherson (eds), *Science and psychology of music performance* (pp. 219–236). New York: Oxford University Press.

Karmiloff, K. & Karmiloff-Smith, A. (2001). *Pathways to language: From fetus to adolescent*. London: Harvard University Press.

Karmiloff, K. & Karmiloff-Smith, A. (undated). Hören: *Das Leben Ihres ungeborenen Babys* (The life of your unborn baby). Germany: Pampers. See also www.pampers.com

Kawada, T. (2004). The effect of noise on the health of children. *Journal of Nippon Medical School*, 71, 5–10.

Keith, R. W. (1975). Middle ear function in neonates. *Archives of Otolaryngology*, 101, 376–379.

Keverne, E. B. & Curley, J. P. (2004). Vasopressin, oxytocin and social behaviour. *Current Opinion in Neurobiology*, 14, 777–783.

Kim, Y. O. & Stevens, J. H. (1987). The socialization of prosocial behavior in children. *Childhood Education*, 63, 200–206.

Kisilevsky, B. S., Muir, D. W., & Low, J. A. (1992). Maturation of human fetal responses to vibroacoustic stimulation. *Child Development*, 63(6), 1497–1508.

Koenig, J. I., Kirkpatrick, B., Lee, P. (2002). Glucocorticoid hormones and early brain development in schizophrenia. *Neuropsychopharmacology*, 27(2), 309–318.

Kohnstamm, G. A., Bates, J. E., & Rothbart, M. K. (eds) (1989). *Temperament in childhood*. Chichester, England: Wiley.

Kolata, G. (1984). Studying learning in the womb. *Science*, 225, 302–303.

Korte, S. M. (2001). Corticosteroids in relation to fear, anxiety and psychopathology. *Neuroscience and Behavioral Reviews*, 25, 117–142.

Krumhansl, C. L. & Keil, F. C. (1982). Acquisition of the hierarchy of tonal functions in music. *Memory and Cognition*, 10, 243–251.

Kulas, J. F., Conger, J. C. & Smolin, J. M. (2003). The effects of emotion on memory: An investigation of attentional bias. *Journal of Anxiety Disorders*, 17(1), 103–113.

Lafuente, M. J., Grifol, R., Segerra, J., Soriano, J., Gorba, M. A., & Montesinos, A. (1997). Effects of the Firstart method of prenatal stimulation on psychomotor development. The first six months. *Pre- and Perinatal Psychology Journal*, 11, 151–162.

Lagasse, N., Dhooge, I., & Govaert, P. (2000). Congenital CMV-infection and hearing loss. *Acta Otorhinolaryngologica Belgica*, 54(4), 431–436.

Lai, C.H. & Chan Y.S. (2002). Development of the vestibular system. *Neuroembryology*, 1, 61–71.

Lalande, N. M., Hetu, R., & Lambert, J. (1986). Is occupational noise exposure during pregnancy a risk factor of damage to the auditory system of the fetus? *American Journal of Industrial Medicine*, 10, 427–35.

Lassman, P. & Speirs, R. (1994). *Weber: Political writings*. Cambridge: Cambridge University Press.

Lecanuet, J.-P. (1996). Prenatal auditory experience. In I. Deliège and J. Sloboda (eds), *Musical beginnings* (pp. 3–34). Oxford: Oxford University Press.

Loghis, E., Salamalekis, N., Vitoratos, N., Panayotopoulos, D., & Kassanos, C. (1999). Umbilical cord blood gas analysis in augmented labour. *Journal of Obstetrics and Gynaecology*, 19, 38–40.

Manrique, B., Contasi, M., Alvarado, M. A., Zypman, M., Palma, N., Ierrobino, M. T., Ramirez, I., & Carini, D. (1993). Nurturing parents to stimulate their children from prenatal stage to three years of age. In T. Blum (ed.), *Prenatal perception, learning and bonding* (pp. 153–186). Berlin, Germany: Leonardo.

Maret, S. (1997). *The prenatal person: Frank Lake's maternal-fetal distress syndrome*. New York: University Press of America.

Masataka, N. (1998). Perception of motherese in Japanese sign language by 6-month-old hearing infants. *Developmental Psychology*, 34, 241–246.

Mason, J. W. (1975). A historical view of the stress field. *Journal of Human Stress*, 1, 6–12.

Mastropieri, D. & Turkewitz, G. (1999). Prenatal experience and neonatal responsiveness to vocal expressions of emotion. *Developmental Psychobiology*, 35, 204–214.

Matthews, S. G. (2002). Early programming of the hypothalamo-pituitary-adrenal axis. *Trends in Endocrinology and Metabolism*, 13, 373–380.

Mears, K., McAuliffe, F., Grimes, H., & Morrison, J. J. (2004). Fetal cortisol in relation to labour, intrapartum events and mode of delivery. *Journal of Obstetrics and Gynaecology*, 24(2), 129–132.

Mecenas, C. A., Giussani, D. A., Owiny, J. R., Jenkins, S. L., Wu, W. X., Honnebier, B. O., Lockwood, C. J., Kong, L., Guller, S., & Nathanielsz, P. W. (1996). Production of premature delivery in pregnant rhesus monkeys by androstenedione infusion. *Nature Medicine*, 2(4), 443–448.

Menzam, C. (2002). Dancing our birth: Prenatal and birth themes and symbols in dance, movement, art, dreams, language, myth, ritual, play, and psychotherapy. *Dissertation Abstracts International, Section B (Sciences & Engineering)*, 63(1-B), 567.

Mitchell, R., Miles, L., & Thompson, N. (eds), (1997). *Anthropomorphism, anecdotes, and animals*. New York: SUNY Press.

Moawad, A. H. (1973). The sympathetic nervous system and the uterus. In J. B. Josimivich (ed.), *Problems of human reproduction*, Vol. 1: *Uterine contractions—side effects of steroidal contraceptives* (pp. 65–82). New York: Wiley.

Montagu, A. (1962). *Prenatal influences*. Springfield, IL: Charles Thomas.

Moog, H. (1963). *Beginn und erste Entwicklung des Musikerlebens im Kindesalter. Eine empirisch-psychologische Untersuchung*. Köln: Wasmund.

Moon, C., Cooper, R. P., & Fifer, W. P. (1993). Two-days-old infants prefer their native language. *Infant Behaviour and Development*, 16, 495–500.

Morre, J. K., Perazzo, L. M., & Braun, A. (1995). Time-course of axonal myelination in the human brain-stem auditory pathway. *Hearing Research*, 87, 21–31.

Morrongiello, B. A., Fenwick, K, D,, Hillier, L., & Chance, G. (1994). Sound localization in newborn human infants. *Developmental Psychobiology*, 27(8), 519–538.

Mulder, E. J. H., Robles de Medina, P. G., Huizink, A. C., Van den Bergh, B. R. H., Buitelaar, J. K., & Visser, G. H. A. (2002). Prenatal maternal stress: Effects on pregnancy and the (unborn) child. *Early Human Development*, 70, 3–14.

Nijhuis, J. G., Prechtl, H. F. R., Martin Jr, C. B., & Bots, R. S. G. M. (1982). Are there behavioural states in the human fetus? *Early Human Development*, 6, 177–195.

Noble, W. & Davidson, I. (1996). *Human evolution, language and mind: A psychological and archaeological inquiry*. Cambridge: Cambridge University Press.

North, A. & MacKenzie, L. (2001). 'Moosic Study' reveals way of increasing milk yields. Leicester, England: Press and Publications Office, University of Leicester. http://www.le.ac.uk/press/press/moosicstudy.html

Oberhoff, B. (2005). Das Fötale in der Musik. Musik als 'Das Große Bewegende' und 'Die Göttliche Stimme'. In B. Oberhoff (ed.), *Die seelischen Wurzeln der Musik. Psychoanalytische Erkundungen* (pp. 41–63). Gießen: Psychosozial-Verlag.

Oerter, R. & Montada, L. (1995). *Entwicklungspsychologie* (Developmental psychology) (3rd edn). Weinheim, Germany: PsychologieVerlagsUnion.

Ohel, G., Horowitz, E., Linder, N., & Sohmer, H. (1987). Neonatal auditory acuity following in utero vibratory acoustic stimulation. *American Journal of Obstetrics & Gynecology*, 157, 440–441.

O'Neill, S. A. & McPherson, G. E. (2002). Motivation. In R. Parncutt & G. E. McPherson (eds), *Science and Psychology of Music Performance* (pp. 31–46). New York: Oxford University Press.

Osaka, N. (2003). Working memory-based consciousness: An individual difference approach. In N. Osaka (ed.), *Neural basis of consciousness* (pp. 27–44). Amsterdam, Netherlands: John Benjamins Publishing Company.

Panicker, H., Wadhwa, S., & Roy, T. S. (2002). Effect of prenatal sound stimulation on medio-rostral neo-striatum/hyperstriatum ventrale region of chick forebrain: A morphometric and immunohistochemical study. *Journal of Chemical Neuroanatomy*, 24, 127–135.

Panthuraamphorn, C. (1993). Prenatal infant stimulation program. In T. Blum (ed.), *Prenatal perception, learning and bonding* (pp. 187–220). Berlin, Germany: Leonardo.

Papoušek, H. & Papoušek, M. (1995). Intuitive parenting. In M. H. Bornstein (ed.), *Handbook of parenting, Volume 2: Biology and ecology of parenting* (pp. 117–135). Mahwah, NJ: Lawrence Erlbaum Associates.

Parkes, M. J., Moore, P. J., Moore, D. R., Fisk, N. M., & Hanson, M. A. (1991). Behavioral changes in fetal sheep caused by vibroacoustic stimulation: The effects of cochlear ablation. *American Journal of Obstetrics and Gynecology*, **164**, 1336–1343.

Parncutt, R. (1993). Prenatal experience and the origins of music. In T. Blum (ed.), *Prenatal perception, learning, and bonding* (pp. 253–277). Berlin: Leonardo.

Parncutt, R. (1997). Pränatale Erfahrung und die Ursprünge der Musik. In L. Janus & S. Haibach (eds), *Seelisches Erleben vor und während der Geburt* (pp. 225–240). Neu-Isenburg, Germany: LinguaMed.

Peiper, A. (1925). Sinnesempfindungen des Kinds vor seiner Geburt. *Monatsschrift für Kinderheilkunde*, **29**, 237–241.

Peters, A. J. M., Abrams, R. M., Gerhardt, K. J., & Griffiths, S. K. (1993). Transmission of airborne sound from 50–20,000 Hz into the abdomen of sheep. *Journal of Low Frequency Noise and Vibration*, **12**, 16–24.

Phelps, E. A. (2004). Human emotion and memory: Interactions of the amygdala and hippocampal complex. *Current Opinion in Neurobiology*, **14**(2), 198–202.

Pierson, L. L. (1996). Hazards of noise exposure on fetal hearing. *Seminars in Perinatology*, **20**, 21–29.

Plomin, R. & Bergeman, C. S. (1991). The nature of nurture: Genetic influence on 'environmental' measures. *Behavioral and Brain Sciences*, **14**, 373–427. (with open peer commentary)

Popper, K. R. & Eccles, J. C. (1977). *The self and its brain*. Berlin: Springer.

Prechtl, H. F. R. (1974). The behavioural states of the newborn infant (a review). *Brain Research*, **76**, 185–212.

Ptok, M. & Ptok, A. (1996). Die Entwicklung des Hörens. *Sprache Stimme Gehör*, **20**, 1–5.

Pujol, R., Lavigne-Rebillard, M., & Uziel, A. (1991). Development of the human cochlea. *Acta Otolaryngologica (Stockholm)*, **482**, 7–12.

Querleu, C., Lefebvre, C., Titran, M., Renard, X., Morillion, M., & Crepin, G. (1984). Réactivité du nouveau-né de moins de deux heures de vie à la voix maternelle. *Journal de gynecologie, obstetrique et biologie de la reproduction*, **13**, 125–134.

Reppert, S. M. & Weaver, D. R. (1988). Maternal transduction of light-dark information for the fetus. In W. P. Smotherman & S. R. Robinson (eds), *Behaviour of the fetus* (pp. 119–139). Telford, England: Caldwell.

Richards, D. S, Frentzen, B., Gerhardt, K. J., McCann, M. E., & Abrams, R. M. (1992). Sound levels in the human uterus. *Obstetrics & Gynecology*, **80**, 186–90.

Roffwarg, H. A., Muzio, J. N., & Dement, W. C. (1966). Ontogenetic development of the human sleep-dream cycle. *Science*, **152**, 604–619.

Rogers, F. B., Rozycki, G. S., Osler, T. M., Shackford, S. R., Jalbert, J., Kirton, O., Scalea, T., Morris, J., Ross, S., Cipolle, M., Fildes, J., Cogbill, T., Bergstein, J., Clark, D., Frankel, H., Bell, R., Gens, D., Cullinane, D., Kauder, D., & Bynoe, R.P. (1999). A multi-institutional study of factors associated with fetal death in injured pregnant patients. *Archives of Surgery*, **134**, 1274–1277.

Roheim, G. (1932). Animism and religion. *Psychoanalytic Quarterly*, **1**, 59–112.

Ronca, A. E. & Alberts, J. R. (2000). Effects of prenatal spaceflight on vestibular responses in neonatal rats. *Journal of Applied Physiology*, 89(6), 2318–2324.

Rubel, E. W. & Ryals, B. M. (1983). Development of the place principle: Acoustic trauma. *Science*, 219, 512–514.

Saffran, J. R., Loman, M. M., & Robertson, R. R. W. (2000). Infant memory for musical experiences. *Cognition*, 77, B15–B23.

Salk, L. (1962). Mother's heartbeat as an imprinting stimulus. *Transactions of the New York Academy of Science*, 24, 121–124.

Sallenbach, W. B. (1993). The intelligent prenate: Paradigms in prenatal learning and bonding. In T. Blum (ed.), *Prenatal perception, learning and bonding* (pp. 61–106). Berlin, Germany: Leonardo.

Scherer, K. R. (1986). Vocal expression: Review. *Psychology Bulletin*, 9, 143–165.

Seckl, J. R. (2001). Glucocorticoid programming of the fetus; adult phenotypes and molecular mechanisms. *Molecular and Cellular Endocrinology*, 185, 61.71.

Seebach, B. S., Intrator, N., Lieberman, P., & Cooper, L. N. (1994). A model of prenatal acquisition of speech parameters. *Proceedings of the National Academy of Science of the USA*, 91, 7473–7476.

Selton, D., Andre, M., & Hascoet J. M. (2000). Normal EEG in very premature infants: Reference criteria. *Clinical Neurophysiology*, 111(12), 2116–2124.

Slobodchikov, V. I. & Tsukerman, G. A. (1992). The genesis of reflective consciousness at early school age. *Journal of Russian and East European Psychology*, 30(1), 6–27.

Smith, S. L., Gerhardt, K. J., Griffiths, S. K., Huang, X., & Abrams, R. M. (2003). Intelligibility of sentences recorded from the uterus of a pregnant ewe and from the fetal inner ear. *Audiology & Neuro-otology*, 8, 347–353.

Sobrian, S. K., Vaughn, V. T., Ashe, W. K., Markovic, B., Djuric, V., Jankovic, B. D. (1997). Gestational exposure to loud noise alters the development and postnatal responsiveness of humoral and cellular components of the immune system in offspring. *Environmental Research*, 73, 227–241.

Sohmer, H. & Freeman, S. (1995). Functional development of auditory sensitivity in the fetus and neonate. *Journal of basic and clinical physiology and pharmacology*, 6(2), 95–108.

Spelt, D. K. (1948). The conditioning of the human fetus *in utero*. *Journal of Experimental Psychology*, 38, 338–346.

Sternberg, R. J. (1985). *Beyond IQ: A triarchic theory of human intelligence*. Cambridge: Cambridge University Press.

Strongman, K. T. (2003). *The psychology of emotion: From everyday life to theory* (5th edn). Chichester, West Sussex: Wiley.

Szendre, E. N. (1996). Children's assignment of intentionality to people, animals, plants, and objects: Challenges to theory of mind and animism. *Dissertation Abstracts International, Section B Sciences and Engineering*, 57(3-B), 2184.

Tafuri, J. & Villa, D. (2002). Musical elements in the vocalisations of infants aged 2–8 months. *British Journal of Music Education*, 19, 73–88.

Todd, N. P. McA. & Cody, F. (2000). Vestibular responses to loud dance music: A physiological basis for the 'rock and roll threshold'? *Journal of the Acoustical Society of America*, 107, 496–500.

Trautman P. D., Meyer-Bahlburg, H. F., Postelnek, J., & New, M. I. (1995). Effects of early prenatal dexamethasone on the cognitive and behavioral development of young children: Results of a pilot study. *Psychoneuroendocrinology*, 20, 439–449.

Trehub, S. E. (2003). The developmental origins of musicality. *Nature Neuscience*, 6, 669–673.

Trehub, S. E. & Nakata, T. (2001–02). Emotion and music in infancy. *Musicae Scientiae* (special issue), 37–61.

Trevarthen, C. (1985). Facial expressions of emotion in mother-infant interaction. *Human Neurobiology*, 4, 21–32.

Tsiaras, A. (2003). *Wunder des Lebens: Wie ein Kind entsteht* (transl. of *From conception to birth: A life unfolds*, 2002). Munich, Germany: Knaur.

Van den Bergh, B. R. H. (1992). Maternal emotions during pregnancy and fetal and neonatal behaviour. In J. G. Nijhuis (ed.), *Fetal behaviour* (pp. 157–208). Oxford: Oxford University Press.

Van den Bergh, B. R. H., Mulder, E. J. H., Visser, G. H. A., Poelmann-Weesjes, G., Bekedam, D. J., & Prechtl, H. F. R. (1989). The effect of (induced) maternal emotions on fetal behavior: A controlled study. *Early Human Development*, 19, 9–19.

Verny, T. R. (1999). Finding our voice. *Journal of Prenatal and Perinatal Psychology and Health*, 13, 191–200.

Wade, J. (1998). Two voices from the womb: Evidence from a physically transcendent and a cellular source of fetal consciousness. *Journal of Prenatal and Perinatal Psychology and Health*, 13, 123.148.

Wadhwa, P. D., Dunkel-Schetter, C., Chicz DeMet, A., Porto, M., & Sandman, C. A. (1996). Prenatal psychosocial factors and the neuroendocrine axis in human pregnancy. *Psychosomatic Medicine*, 58, 432–446.

Wadhwa, P. D., Glynn, L., Hobel, C. J., Garite, T., Porto, M. Chicz DeMet, A., Wiglesworth, A. K., & Sandman, C. A. (2002). Behavioural perinatology: Biobehavioural processes in human fetal development. *Regulatory Peptides*, 108(2–3), 149–157.

Walsh, S. W., Ducsay, C. A., & Novy, M. J. (1984). Circadian hormonal interactions among the mother, fetus, and amniotic fluid. *American Journal of Obstetrics and Gynecology*, 150, 745–53.

Weinberg, M. K. & Tronick, E. Z. (1998). Emotional characteristics of infants associated with maternal depression and anxiety. *Pediatrics*, 102(5) supplement, 1298–1304.

Weinstock, M. (1997). Does prenatal stress impair coping and regulation of hypothalamic-pituitary-adrenal axis? *Neuroscience and Biobehavioral Reviews*, 21, 1–10.

Weiskopf, N., Veit, R., Erb, M., Mathiak, K., Grodd, W., Goebel, R., & Birbaumer, N. (2003). Physiological self-regulation of regional brain activity using real-time functional magnetic resonance imaging (fMRI): Methodology and exemplary data. *NeuroImage*, 19, 577–586.

Welberg, L. A. M. & Seckl, J. R. (2001). Prenatal stress, glucocorticoids and the programming of the brain. *Journal of Neuroendocrinology*, 13, 113–128.

Wells, M., Glickauf Hughes, C., & Jones, R. (1999). Codependency: A grass roots construct's relationship to shame-proneness, low self-esteem, and childhood parentification. *American Journal of Family Therapy*, 27, 63–71.

Whitwell, G. E. (undated). *The importance of prenatal sound and music.* http://www.birthpsychology.com/lifebefore/sound1.html. Read on 31.5.2004.

Wightman, F. L. & Kistler, D. J. (1992). The dominant role of low-frequency interaural time differences in sound localization. *Journal of the Acoustical Society of America*, 91(3), 1648–1661.

Wilkin, P. E. (1995/96). A comparison of fetal and newborn responses to music and sound stimuli with and without daily exposure to a specific piece of music. *Bulletin of the Council of Research in Music Education*, 127, 163–169.

Williams, J. H. G., Greenhalgh, K. D., & Manning, J. T. (2003). Second to fourth finger ratio and possible precursors of developmental psychopathology in preschool children. *Early Human Development*, 72, 57–65.

Woodward, C. A. (1999). Medical students' attitudes toward women: Are medical schools microcosms of society? *Canadian Medical Association Journal*, **160**, 347–348.

Wu, W. X., Ma, X. H., Unno, N., & Nathanielsz, P. W. (2001). In vivo evidence for stimulation of placental, myometrial, and endometrial prostaglandin G/H synthase 2 by fetal cortisol replacement after fetal adrenalectomy. *Endocrinology*, **142**(9), 3857–3864.

Wulf, M. (1947). L'mahuta shel haomanut (About the nature of art). *Ofakim*, **4**(3), 2–9.

Yedidia, M. J. & Bickel, J. (2001). Why aren't there more women leaders in academic medicine? The views of clinical department chairs. *Academic Medicine*, **76**, 453–465.

Zeifman, D. M. (2001). An ethological analysis of human infant crying: answering Tinbergen's four questions. *Developmental Psychobiology*, **39**, 265–85.

CHAPTER 2

INFANTS AS MUSICAL CONNOISSEURS

SANDRA E. TREHUB

The term *connoisseur* is generally reserved for experts in matters of taste, especially with reference to the expressive or culinary arts. In the case of music, a connoisseur would be a discerning listener in a narrow or literal sense—having keen perceptual skills—and in a broader, more important sense—distinguishing musical compositions and performances of high quality from those of lesser quality. The latter skill necessitates extensive knowledge of the musical conventions of a particular culture, such knowledge being beyond the reach of inexperienced listeners. How, then, might infants qualify as musical connoisseurs? In my view, their precocious music listening skills, excellent memory for music, highly musical environment, and intense interest in expressive musical performances compensate for their obvious ignorance of musical conventions. In the pages that follow, I outline the scientific evidence in these domains and explore the implications of that evidence.

Assessing the fine-tuning of infant ears

How do researchers establish which aspects of music are perceptible, memorable, and even pleasurable for very young and inexperienced listeners? Early in life, infants cannot report what they hear, nor can they follow instructions. Unlike dogs, whose raised earflaps indicate attentive listening, infants provide no obvious clues to what they hear. To circumvent such response limitations, researchers try to develop procedures to yield information about infant skills while minimizing the potential biases of adult observers. In the most commonly used procedure, 6–10-month-old infants watch a live puppet show directly in front of them while a repeating musical pattern (e.g., a sequence of five to 10 notes) plays in the background from a loudspeaker off to one side (Trehub *et al.*, 1987). Infants become engrossed in the puppet show, seemingly oblivious to the background music, but their responses to subtle changes in the music indicate otherwise. The occurrence of a melodic or rhythmic change typically leads infants to turn toward the loudspeaker, as if checking the reason for the change. Turns immediately following a change (i.e., correct responses) are rewarded by the presentation of age-appropriate visual displays for a few seconds. Because turns at other times (i.e., incorrect responses) bring no such rewards, infants can maximize the available 'entertainment' by continuing to watch the puppet show except when opportunities arise for new visual treats (e.g., some change in the music). Most 6–10-month-old infants learn the rules of this game within a few minutes, at which time they proceed to the test phase, which features trials with musical changes (i.e., change trials) and trials without changes (i.e., no-change trials). Systematic turning on change trials but not on no-change trials provides evidence that infants can detect the change under consideration.

The other commonly used procedure assesses infant listening preferences (e.g., Trainor, 1996). First, infants' attention is attracted to a visual display that appears on their left or right side. Looking at the display results in the presentation of one musical pattern (e.g., one rendition of a song), which stops playing when infants look away. Their attention is then attracted to a similar visual display on the opposite side, which results in the presentation of a contrasting musical pattern (e.g., another rendition of the same song) until infants look away. The procedure continues, with infant listening times to each musical pattern accumulated over successive trials. Longer cumulative listening time to one pattern reveals, at the very least, that infants can differentiate the two patterns. Differential listening times to the contrasting musical samples also provide insight into infants' musical preferences. For example, if infants listen longer to one of two performances differing only in tempo, pitch level, or voice quality, that would imply not only that they notice the difference but that they prefer one version to the other. Advantages of the preference procedure include its ease of use and applicability over a relatively wide age range. One disadvantage is the difficulty of interpreting equivalent listening times to contrasting musical pieces. In some cases, infants may fail to notice the differences. In other cases, their evaluation of the musical samples, whether favourable or unfavourable, may be similar.

Precocious music listening skills: pitch patterns

The use of these techniques has revealed a great deal about infants' listening skills. For example, we have learned that infants can detect pitch differences of a semitone or less, even when such subtle differences are embedded in a melody (e.g., Trehub *et al.*, 1999). In other words, infants are sensitive to the smallest meaningful pitch distinctions in the music of all cultures. Although smaller (i.e., microtonal) variations are present in Indian and Arab-Persian music, such variations are considered relevant to intonation rather than pitch structure (Burns, 1999). In any case, music listening is not about pitch resolution but about pitch relations, especially the relations that underlie the perceptual equivalence of transposed melodies. For example, knowing a tune means recognizing it regardless of its key or starting note. Some years ago, it became apparent that after limited exposure to a melody (e.g., a few repetitions), infants treat transpositions of that melody—all pitches changed but pitch relations preserved—as equivalent to the original (Trehub *et al.*, 1987). By contrast, infants perceive a melody as novel when a single note changes the melodic contour, or the pattern of directional changes in pitch (Trehub *et al.*, 1985).

Infants' ability to perceive relational aspects of pitch does not mean that they ignore absolute pitch cues. In some situations, infants seem to focus on absolute rather than relative pitch cues (Saffran & Griepentrog, 2001; Saffran, 2003). In others, they focus on relative pitch cues (Trehub, 2003; Plantinga & Trainor, 2005). The nature of the input and task demands influence infants' inclination to focus on absolute or relational cues in the input (Saffran *et al.*, 2005), which may also be the case for adults. In general, adults focus on relative pitch cues in music, which enables them to recognize or reproduce familiar tunes at different pitch levels. In some situations, however, they show surprisingly good memory for the pitch level of familiar recordings. For example, they recognize the pitch level of music that accompanies their favourite television programmes, as reflected in their ability to distinguish the original music from renditions that are identical in every respect except for a pitch-shift of one or two semitones (Schellenberg & Trehub, 2003). Presumably, the combined performance cues of the original make it sound more authentic than the pitch-shifted versions.

For infants, the most salient feature of a melody is its pitch contour (i.e., successive directional changes in pitch direction), which is also the most salient feature of maternal speech (Fernald, 1991). Even when two melodies are separated by several seconds, infants notice overall contour differences (Chang & Trehub, 1977a). Under certain conditions, they also detect subtle interval changes, most notably when the melodies are consonant (i.e., containing intervals that sound pleasant) rather than dissonant (i.e., containing intervals that sound unpleasant). For example, they respond to a single semitone change in the context of melodies based on the major triad (e.g., C-E-G-E-C to C-E-G#-E-C) but not those based on the augmented triad (e.g., C-E-G#-E-C to C-E-G-E-C) (Trainor & Trehub, 1993). They also respond to a semitone change in the context of a repeating perfect fifth sequence (e.g., C-G-C-G-C-G) but not in the context of a repeating tritone (e.g., C-F#-C-F#-C-F#) (Schellenberg & Trehub, 1996).

Aside from infants' response to specific consonant and dissonant intervals, they also perceive more general qualities that distinguish consonance from dissonance. As a result, they perceive the similarity among harmonic intervals, or simultaneous tone combinations, on the basis of their consonance or dissonance rather than the size of the pitch distance that separates them (Schellenberg & Trainor, 1996). Moreover, when provided with listening choices in a highly controlled laboratory context, infants prefer consonant to dissonant music. For example, 2-month-olds listen longer to consonant intervals than to dissonant intervals (Trainor et al., 2002), as do 6-month-olds (Trainor & Heinmiller, 1998). Detailed coding of the behaviour of 4-month-olds indicates that aside from listening longer to consonant than to dissonant instrumental music, they are more likely to squirm, fuss, and turn away when they hear dissonant music (Zentner & Kagan, 1996).

There are indications that non-human listeners have very different sound preferences. For example, when tamarin monkeys are tested in a two-arm maze, one arm of which results in the presentation of consonant intervals and the other, dissonant intervals, they distribute their time equally in both areas (McDermott & Hauser, 2004). This contrasts with their unambiguous preference, in the same test context, for positive over negative calls by members of their own species. Their indifference to consonance is most apparent, however, in their choice of silence over consonant music (McDermott, 2005). In short, the qualities that underlie human musical preferences across cultures have little attraction for tamarin monkeys.

Some adult–infant similarities in pitch pattern processing seem to reflect skills that are present from birth or shortly thereafter. Undoubtedly, the ultimate level of skill is affected by the quality and extent of musical exposure. In general, musical exposure and training lead to improvement in the detection of contour and interval information (Fujioka et al.,

2004). At times, however, naïve music listeners outperform adult listeners who have had long-term exposure to music (Trainor & Trehub, 1992; Trehub *et al.*, 1999). For example, Western infants and adults both detect a semitone change in one note of a tonal melody when the changed note is outside the key of the original melody, but infants detect other changes that are difficult for adults to notice, such as those remaining within the key and implied harmony of the original (Trainor & Trehub, 1992). Moreover, unlike Western adults, who are more sensitive to tuning changes in melodies based on familiar scales (e.g., major) rather than unfamiliar scales (e.g., Javanese pelog), young Western infants are equally sensitive to changes in both scale types (Lynch *et al.*, 1990; Trehub *et al.*, 1999). Presumably, young infants perceive music in a culture-general rather than a culture-specific manner. By contrast, adults' implicit knowledge of the tonal and harmonic conventions of their culture interferes with their detection of subtle pitch differences in foreign contexts, just as knowledge of their native language interferes with the perception of some foreign speech sounds (Werker & Tees, 1984). By 12 months of age, infants show some signs of culture-specific processing of pitch patterns, as indicated by their greater sensitivity to tuning changes in melodies based on the major scale than on the Javanese pelog scale (Lynch & Eilers, 1992).

Precocious music listening skills: rhythmic patterns

As adults listen to music, they group the unfolding auditory events into meaningful chunks, they detect relations among those chunks, and they generate expectations about what sounds are likely to follow and when they will occur. There are indications that infants do likewise. For example, 6- and 8-month-old infants group the component tones of auditory patterns on the basis of similarities in their pitch, loudness, and timbre, as do 5-year-old children and adults (Fitzgibbons *et al.*, 1974; Thorpe *et al.*, 1988; Thorpe & Trehub, 1989). Moreover, 8-month-olds generally perceive a long-duration note as a boundary between groups or phrases (Trainor & Adams, 2000). Infants show their sensitivity to musical phrasing by their preference for musical pieces with pauses added *between* phrases, which maintain the integrity of phrases, over pauses added *within* phrases, which disrupt the phrasing (Krumhansl & Jusczyk, 1990; Jusczyk & Krumhansl, 1993).

Just as infants respond primarily to relative pitch cues, they also respond primarily to relative duration cues. Accordingly, they treat sound patterns as equivalent when they have comparable rhythmic groups (e.g., 3-1 or 2-2) despite changes in tempo (Chang & Trehub, 1977b; Trehub & Thorpe, 1989; Lewkowicz, 2003). Nonetheless, they are also capable of detecting changes in tempo (Pickens & Bahrick, 1995).

Metrical aspects of rhythm enable adults and children to synchronize their behaviour when singing, dancing, or clapping with others. The universality of synchronized rhythmic behaviour implies that listeners readily discern the metrical structure of music. In fact, adults tend to perceive strong–weak patterns even when there are no durational cues or accents (Brochard *et al.*, 2003). There are indications that infants are also sensitive to metrical cues. For example, 10-month-olds distinguish musical performances that differ only in the performer's intended metre (Palmer *et al.*, 2001). Moreover, after limited exposure to different rhythms that induce the same metre, 7-month-olds listen preferentially to novel rhythms that induce a novel metre than to novel rhythms that induce the metre heard previously (Hannon & Johnson, 2005).

The presence of metrical variations across cultures makes it possible to explore the consequences of musical exposure on metre perception. Simple duration ratios (1:1 and 2:1) and isochrony (i.e., a uniform underlying pulse) abound in Western music, but complex duration ratios and complex metres occur, along with simple metres, in Eastern Europe, South Asia, Africa, and the Middle East (London, 1995). For example, many dance tunes from Bulgaria and Macedonia consist of short and long durations that alternate in a 2:3 ratio. After 2 minutes of exposure to unfamiliar Balkan or Macedonian tunes, North American adults differentiate variations that disrupt the metrical structure of the original from those that preserve it, but they do so only in the case of simple metres (Hannon & Trehub, 2005a). By contrast, 6-month-old infants differentiate metre-disrupting from metre-preserving variations in complex as well as simple metrical contexts, much like Bulgarian and Macedonian adults do (Hannon & Trehub, 2005a). These findings challenge the widespread belief of inherent or innate biases for simple metres. Instead, young infants seem to be relatively flexible in their perception of metre, unlike adults, who tend to assimilate the music they hear into familiar metrical frameworks.

Surprisingly, adult-like biases for culture-specific metres emerge after relatively limited exposure to music. By 12 months of age, Western infants are no longer able to differentiate metre-preserving from metre-disrupting variations in the context of complex metres, but they continue to make the differentiation in the context of simple metres (Hannon & Trehub, 2005b). Nevertheless, a mere 2 weeks of daily exposure to melodies with complex metre can eliminate the simple-metre bias in 12-month-olds but not in adults (Hannon & Trehub, 2005b). Following such exposure, 12-month-olds perform as well on complex metres as they do on simple metres, but adults remain unable to distinguish metre-disrupting from metre-preserving variations in the context of complex metres. Long-term exposure to the music of a particular culture may lead to highly entrenched representations of metrical structure that are resistant to change. It seems that 'old habits die hard,' even in the case of music listening. Entrenched representations may also account for adults' difficulty perceiving subtleties in unfamiliar musical scales (Lynch & Eilers, 1992; Trehub et al., 1999) and in foreign speech (Werker & Tees, 1984). The available evidence is consistent with greater flexibility in younger than in older brains. For example, children show similar patterns of brain activation when they are engaged in melodic and rhythmic processing, in contrast to adults, who show right hemisphere dominance for melodic processing and left hemisphere dominance for rhythmic processing (Zatorre et al., 2002; Overy et al., 2004).

Music perception obviously involves interpretation as well as hearing, but it may involve much more. The tendency to move our bodies in time to music may influence how we perceive and remember it. In the early months of life, infants do not move spontaneously to music, as we do, but their parents often rock or bounce them while singing. How do such movements affect infants' perception of the music? In a recent study, 7-month-old infants heard 2 minutes of a drum rhythm that was ambiguous because it lacked intensity or duration accents (Phillips-Silver & Trainor, 2005). During the presentation of the pattern, some infants were bounced on every second beat, and others were bounced on every third beat.

In a subsequent preferential listening test that featured one version with intensity accents on every second beat (duple) and another version with accents on every third beat (triple), infants listened longer to the version that matched the previous bouncing pattern. The matching of rhythm across sound and movement patterns was evident only for infants who had experienced the bouncing motion. Other infants who simply watched an adult bouncing up and down on every second or third beat did not show differential responsiveness to the versions with intensity accents. In short, concurrent movement influences how infants perceive music, which may also be the case for adults.

Long-term memory for music

For obvious reasons, infants lack the extended listening experience that enables adults to recognize familiar tunes after hearing the initial few notes (Dalla Bella *et al.*, 2003). Nevertheless, they seem to remember complex musical passages after relatively limited exposure. Following 2 weeks of brief daily exposure to portions of a Mozart sonata, infants are able to distinguish it from an unfamiliar Mozart sonata (Saffran *et al.*, 2000). Similarly, a week of exposure to a synthesized rendition of an English folk melody enables 6-month-old infants to distinguish it from a contrasting folk melody (Trainor *et al.*, 2004). However, 6-month-olds seem unable to remember the pitch level of the folk melody heard at home, as reflected in their failure to respond differentially when the melody is presented at the original pitch level or at a pitch level shifted upward or downward by six or seven semitones (Plantinga & Trainor, 2005). Infants may be able to remember more musical features from music that is relevant to their experience or interests. For example, after 2 weeks of daily exposure to recordings of an unfamiliar, expressively sung lullaby, 7-month-old infants respond differentially to versions sung at the original pitch level or at a pitch level four semitones higher or lower (Volkova *et al.*, in press). This finding implies that aspects of the original performance, including its pitch level, are part of infants' long-term representation of musical pieces that are meaningful to them. In short, the use of expressive vocal music reveals abilities that are not evident in the context of synthesized instrumental music. What remains unclear is the relative contribution of the voice, the expressiveness of the rendition, and the structure of the musical materials.

Infants' rich musical environment

If infants have such precocious listening skills, it is reasonable to ask whether they have opportunities for using those skills in everyday life. They do, indeed. For one thing, caregivers around the world—mothers, fathers, grandparents, and siblings—speak to infants well before they can understand anything about the verbal content. This infant-directed speech differs from conventional, or adult-directed, speech in its high pitch register, sustained vowels, rhythmic quality, repetitiveness, and expanded pitch contours (Fernald, 1991; Papoušek *et al.*, 1991; Cooper, 1997). The result is quasi-musical speech or sing-song that falls somewhere between speech and music. Infant-directed speech provides pre-verbal listeners with engaging sound effects while giving mothers an opportunity to share their feelings (see Chapter 10). Obviously, this mode of emotion sharing is inaccessible to deaf caregivers who communicate manually. Interestingly, deaf mothers add expressiveness to their infant-directed sign language by increasing the rhythmicity, repetitiveness, and fluidity of their communicative gestures (Erting *et al.*, 1990; Masataka, 1992), which results in graceful, dance-like movement.

Regardless of their culture of origin, most infants experience music-like input from the incomprehensible but pleasant-sounding speech of their hearing mother or from the visually pleasing manual gestures of their deaf mother. Most infants also experience 'real' music in the form of sung performances by their mother or primary caregiver (Trehub & Trainor, 1998; Custodero *et al.*, 2003). Except for unusual circumstances involving extreme stress or illness, mothers across cultures sing to their infants in the course of routine care (Brakeley, 1950; Tucker, 1984; Trehub & Schellenberg, 1995), although *what* they sing and *how* they sing may differ (Trehub & Trainor, 1998). Every culture has a dedicated genre of music for infants, which includes lullabies in all cases and play songs in some cases. North American mothers generally sing play songs to their infants (Trehub *et al.*, 1997a), often with accompanying movements, but mothers in more traditional cultures typically sing lullabies (Trehub & Schellenberg, 1995; Trehub & Trainor, 1998). One source of difference in song choice is the widespread (but non-North American) practice of mothers remaining in close physical contact with infants, even during sleep (Super & Harkness, 1986; Morelli *et al.*, 1992). Another source of difference involves divergent conceptions of infancy. Contemporary North American mothers are inclined to 'stimulate' their infants by means of lively songs, speech, and physical play with a view to optimizing their development. They expect infants to respond by smiling, laughing, or providing other overt signs of enjoyment. By contrast, mothers in traditional cultures strive for infant contentment, which accounts for their provision of soothing rather than arousing interactions, along with constant contact (Toda *et al.*, 1990). For them, a calm or sleeping infant is ample reward for their efforts.

The distinctiveness of infant-directed singing goes beyond the repertoire, or *what* the mother sings, to *how* she sings. In general, North American mothers sing to their infants at a higher pitch level and slower tempo than they usually use for the same songs (Trehub *et al.*, 1993b, 1997; Trainor, 1996; Trainor *et al.*, 1997). These features of the maternal singing style are related to emotional expressiveness, with elevated vocal pitch associated with joyful feelings (Murray & Arnott, 1993; Bachorowski & Owren, 1995), and slow tempo associated with affection and tenderness (Fonagy & Magdics, 1963; Davitz, 1964).

Singing in the course of caregiving often extends beyond infancy, which provides opportunities for observing the fine-tuning of maternal performances. When mothers sing the same song to their infant and preschool child, their renditions are about a semitone higher for their infant than for their preschooler, and the lyrics are pronounced more precisely for the preschooler (Bergeson & Trehub, 1999), both adjustments being appropriate to the needs of these listeners. In general, adult listeners readily distinguish performances for infants from other informal performances of the same song by the same singer, even when they are unfamiliar with the language and culture of the singer (Trehub *et al.*, 1993a, 1997b). The transparency of these performances arises largely from their warm vocal tone. The mere presence of an infant has emotional consequences for the mother, which, in turn, affects the expressiveness of her spoken or sung communications. Such expressiveness is not exclusive to mothers or to experienced caregivers. Preschool siblings also sing more expressively than usual in the presence of their infant siblings (Trehub *et al.*, 1994).

The singing of fathers is more difficult to study because of their lesser availability and greater self-consciousness. Many fathers are averse to observations of their vocal interactions with infants, in contrast to their public displays of active physical play, including tossing infants in the air. When fathers do sing, they adjust their sung performances for infants in much the same way as mothers do, elevating their usual pitch level and slowing their tempo (Trehub *et al.*, 1997b). As in their physical play, which differs from that of mothers, fathers tend to provide arousing performances of songs for their baby boys and soothing performances for their baby girls (Trehub *et al.*, 1997a).

One intriguing aspect of maternal singing is its stereotypy, which may facilitate infants' recognition of specific songs and singing voices. When mothers sing the same song to their infant on different days, their renditions are nearly identical in pitch level and tempo (Bergeson & Trehub, 2002) so long as the infant is in a comparable state on both occasions. Not surprisingly, changes in infant state are usually accompanied by appropriate adjustments in singing style, with soothing renditions offered for fretful or sleepy infants and lively renditions for alert, playful infants.

Infants may experience musical forms other than the live expressive performances of parents and siblings. Increasingly, caregivers are exposing infants to musical toys, commercial audio and video recordings, and television programmes that target infant audiences. Moreover, infants are likely to overhear some of the recorded music for which parents or siblings are the intended audience.

In general, infants receive musical or quasi-musical input for much of their waking time. In contrast to the recorded music that dominates adults' experience, live, improvised performances dominate the experience of most infants. In a sense, mothers function as infants' first musical mentors. Their singing may not meet professional standards of tuning or timing, but it seems unsurpassed in its suitability for the intended listener.

Infants' responsiveness to maternal speech and song

Infants respond to infant-directed speech with greater attentiveness and more positive affect than they accord to adult-directed speech (Fernald, 1991; Werker *et al.*, 1994; Cooper, 1997). Nevertheless, it is unclear which aspects of maternal speech attract and maintain infants' attention. Maternal speech has a larger pitch range and greater dynamic range (whisper to loud) than ordinary adult speech, which may contribute to infant preferences. There are indications, however, that the emotional expressiveness of maternal speech is the principal factor underlying its attractiveness for infant listeners (Singh *et al.*, 2002). Emotional expressiveness may also account for infants' preference for infant-directed over adult-directed sign language (Masataka, 1996), even for hearing infants with no prior exposure to sign language (Masataka, 1998).

From the earliest days of life, infants prefer infant-directed singing to other styles of informal singing (Trainor, 1996; Masataka, 1999). The elevated pitch level of infant-directed singing may contribute to infant preferences. For example, they prefer the higher-pitched of two performances of the same song by the same singer (Trainor & Zacharias, 1998; O'Neill *et al.*, 2001), but their preference for higher-pitched singing may not apply to all circumstances. For lullabies sung at slow tempi, infants prefer the lower-pitched of two versions (Volkova *et al.*, in press). Perhaps infants simply prefer the more expressive of two performances, which would account for their high-pitch preference in the case of play songs and their low-pitch preference in the case of lullabies.

When 6-month-old infants are given a choice between recorded audiovisual performances of their own mothers' speech and singing, they show more sustained interest in the singing (Nakata & Trehub, 2004). They seem to be mesmerized by the sung performances, which prompt them to stop moving and stare at their mother's on-screen image for extended periods. The maternal speech performances, while engaging, are not nearly as captivating as the singing. Maternal singing is thought to regulate infant arousal, which is consistent with measurements of a stress-related hormone (cortisol) in infants' saliva. For healthy, non-fussy infants who have slightly elevated arousal levels, maternal singing results in subtle decreases in arousal; for those with lower arousal levels, maternal singing results in subtle increases (Shenfield *et al.*, 2003). Perhaps maternal singing optimizes infant arousal or mood. The presumed arousal-modulating benefits of music are leading to its increased use in neonatal intensive care (Lorch *et al.*, 1994; Cassidy & Standley, 1995).

Individual differences

As noted, infants prefer consonant to dissonant music (Zentner & Kagan, 1996; Trainor & Heinmiller, 1998), and they are attracted to expressive singing (Trainor, 1996; Masataka, 1999). Just as infants prefer speech that expresses positive emotions (Singh *et al.*, 2002), they prefer music that expresses happiness rather than sadness (Nawrot, 2003).

In the case of adults, there are individual differences in attitudes and reactions to traditional art music, contemporary art music, popular music, heavy metal, or hip hop. These differences arise from a variety of factors, including age, education, personality (Kemp, 1997; Rentfrow & Gosling, 2003), prior exposure (Peretz *et al.*, 1998), and mood (Knobloch & Zillmann, 2002). In the case of infants, temperament (calm vs. excitable) may also affect musical preferences. In one study, 6- and 9-month-old infants received audiovisual versions of soothing and lively performances of the same nursery songs (e.g., 'Twinkle, Twinkle, Little Star'), and their listening preferences were assessed (Trehub *et al.*, 2002). Although no overall preferences were evident for either age group, some infants listened considerably longer to the soothing than to the playful version, while others exhibited the reverse preference. Infants who listened to both types of music for relatively long periods preferred the soothing renditions, and those who listened for much shorter periods preferred the playful renditions. Interestingly, mothers of 'long-listeners' described their infants as calm and easy-going, in contrast to mothers of 'short-listeners' who described their infants as highly active. It is possible, then, that infants' preferred song tempo is related to their personal style or tempo, as is the case for adults. Clearly, more research in this realm is warranted.

Reflections on young and older listeners

The aforementioned evidence is consistent with claims of infant musical precocity (Trehub, 2000). Well before their first birthday, infants discern subtle melodic and rhythmic distinctions in music, whether that music originates from their musical culture-to-be or from another musical culture (Lynch *et al.*, 1990; Trehub & Hannon, 2005a). They link the sounds that they hear to the movements that they feel, which affects their perception of musical rhythm (Phillips-Silver & Trainor, 2005). In some situations, infants' music perception and learning skills outstrip those of adults (Trehub *et al.*, 1999; Hannon & Trehub, 2005a,b), especially when novel or unusual music is involved. Infants' relative inexperience with music may generate a kind of open-mindedness that enables them to notice subtle musical distinctions that are missed by experienced or expert listeners. The duration of this window of open-mindedness or perceptual flexibility remains unclear. What is clear is that the process of musical enculturation begins much earlier than was thought previously (Cuddy & Badertscher, 1987; Krumhansl, 1990), as evidenced by the culture-specific metrical biases (Hannon & Trehub, 2005b) and pitch processing biases (Lynch & Eilers, 1992) of 12-month-olds. One important difference in the musical biases of 12-month-olds and adults is their apparent ease of reversibility in the case of infants (Hannon & Trehub, 2005b). Undoubtedly, adults could learn the subtleties of complex Balkan metres with sufficient exposure, but such learning is impeded by their implicit understanding of Western metrical structure. Perhaps dancing or moving to novel music would facilitate adults' acquisition of its metrical structure, as it does for infants (Phillips-Silver & Trainor, 2005). An important challenge for future research is to identify the different ways in which familiarity with the music of one's culture assists and impedes the acquisition of skills and structures relevant to other musical cultures.

Beyond the precocious perceptual skills that characterize the early months of life is infants' incredible interest in music. Although mothers are seemingly unaware of infants' musical abilities and inclinations, they intuitively provide them with a daily diet of live, expressive performances of music—simple songs that are playful or soothing. Infants react with rapt attention, which undoubtedly encourages maternal encores. Regardless of their ignorance of musical conventions or standards, infants still qualify as connoisseurs in the sense used here. Perhaps they could even be considered musical prodigies, who become the protégés of their adoring caregivers. For their part, caregivers indulge infants with intimate musical performances, which enhance their overall well-being and nurture their interest in music.

Unfortunately, little is known about the course of perceptual development or the 'natural' musical environment in the years between infancy and school entry. Research in that period has focused largely on music production skills (e.g., Gérard & Drake, 1990; Mitroudot, 2001) and, increasingly, on the non-musical benefits of musical training (Rauscher & Zupan, 2000; Anvari *et al.*, 2002; Chapter 6, this volume). It is likely that preschoolers' music perception skills exceed those of 12-month-olds in a number of respects, but some aspects of musical enculturation proceed slowly. For example, children's understanding of implied harmony (Trainor & Trehub, 1994) and the tonal hierarchy (Krumhansl & Keil, 1982) remains limited until about 7 years of age, and continued refinement of this knowledge is apparent for several years (Lamont & Cross, 1994; Costa-Giomi, 2003). Nevertheless, preschoolers outdo older children in their unbridled enthusiasm for music, which is apparent in the spontaneity and inventiveness of their chants and songs in playgrounds throughout the world (Opie & Opie, 1969; Kartomi, 1980). Preschoolers' relative freedom from the constraints of societal standards or conventions may make a substantial contribution to their inventiveness (Gardner *et al.*, 1990).

A word on formal and informal education for infants and toddlers

For some music educators (e.g., Feierabend, 1996; Gordon, 1996), the keen perceptual skills of very young listeners and their enthusiasm for music justify systematic exposure to *good* music and *appropriate* musical activities as early as possible. In their view, musical aptitude should be nurtured, first, by guided listening, next, by guided movement to music and, subsequently, by guided music-making. Many parents are tempted by appeals for early musical training, not necessarily for the anticipated musical consequences but for the cognitive consequences that are heralded, often uncritically, in the popular media. Despite the absence of scientific support for long-range musical or non-musical benefits of *very early* training, music programmes for infants and toddlers are increasing in number and popularity. In some cases, the programmes provide positive experiences for parents, including opportunities for connecting with other parents, revitalizing the joy of music-making, and increasing parents' repertoire of children's songs and games. In other cases, well-meaning but misguided instructors provide authoritative prescriptions for 'proper' music, a course of action that threatens parents' intuitive musical interactions as well as their self-esteem. Such instructors have important lessons to learn from the sensitive musical mentoring that most parents provide for their infants and toddlers.

Music educators' promotion of very early musical exposure or training implies a critical or sensitive period during which musical training has unique benefits. To date, the only music-related skill that is known to depend on early musical training (before 6 years of age) is *absolute pitch* (Takeuchi & Hulse, 1993; Trainor, 2005). Although musicians with absolute pitch typically began music lessons before 6 years of age, most musicians with comparable early training do not have absolute pitch, which implies that genetic predispositions are also implicated (Baharloo *et al.*, 1998). Absolute pitch is commonly regarded as a sign of musical giftedness, but its value is overrated (see Chapter 12). The essence of music resides in relative aspects of pitch and timing, and there are indications that musicians with absolute pitch are poorer at relative pitch processing than are musicians without absolute pitch (Miyazaki, 1995).

Finally, there is no evidence that formal musical exposure or training beginning in infancy or the preschool period is necessary for the highest levels of musical achievement in adolescence or adulthood. Instead, there are indications that a supportive early home environment, one that encourages spontaneous expressiveness, is important for optimizing musical achievement (Manturzewska, 1990; Moore *et al.*, 2003). Casual observers as well as experienced music educators are well aware of preschoolers' technical limitations in singing and other forms of music-making. From what we know about infants' and toddlers' perceptual and motor abilities, it is highly unlikely that preschoolers' production 'problems' have perceptual origins. Instead, limitations in motor control (e.g., producing the intended note) and self-monitoring (e.g., noticing pitch or timing deviations from a model) must be implicated. In general, such limitations are outgrown in the normal course of development, but progress is likely to be accelerated by training. In the case of very young children, music educators and parents should consider whether the expected benefits of training—more rapid achievement of some musical milestones—involve any hidden costs. Perhaps the greatest challenge for early music educators is to sustain the joy of music and the musical creativity that are so clearly evident in the months or years that precede formal instruction.

Acknowledgements

The preparation of this chapter was assisted by funding from the Natural Sciences and Engineering Research Council and the Social Sciences and Humanities Research Council of Canada.

References

Anvari, S. H., Trainor, L. J., Woodside, J., & Levy, B. A. (2002). Relations among musical skills, phonological processing, and early reading ability in preschool children. *Journal of Experimental Child Psychology*, 83, 111–130.

Bachorowski, J. A. & Owren, M. J. (1995). Vocal expression of emotion: Acoustical properties of speech are associated with emotional intensity and context. *Psychological Science*, 6, 219–224.

Baharloo, S., Johnston, P. A., Service, S. K., Gitschier, J., & Freimer, N. B. (1998). Absolute pitch: An approach for identification of genetic and nongenetic components. *American Journal of Human Genetics*, 62, 224–231.

Bergeson, T. R. & Trehub, S. E. (1999). Mothers' singing to infants and preschool children. *Infant Behavior & Development*, 22, 51–64.

Bergeson, T. R. & Trehub, S. E. (2002). Absolute pitch and tempo in mothers' songs to infants. *Psychological Science*, 13, 72–75.

Brakeley, T. C. (1950). Lullaby. In M. Leach & J. Fried (eds), *Standard dictionary of folklore, mythology, and legend* (pp. 653–654). New York: Funk & Wagnalls.

Brochard, R., Abecasis, D., Potter, D., Ragot, R. & Drake, C. (2003). The 'ticktock' of our internal clock: Direct brain evidence of subjective accents in isochronous sequences. *Psychological Science*, 14, 362–366.

Burns, E. M. (1999). Intervals, scales, and tuning. In D. Deutsch (ed.), *The psychology of music* (pp. 215–264). San Diego: Academic Press.

Cassidy, J. W. & Standley, J. M. (1995). The effect of music listening on physiological responses of premature infants in the NICU. *Journal of Music Therapy*, 32, 208–227.

Chang, H. W. & Trehub, S. E. (1977a). Auditory processing of relational information by young infants. *Journal of Experimental Child Psychology*, 24, 324–331.

Chang, H. W. & Trehub, S. E. (1977b). Infants' perception of temporal grouping in auditory patterns. *Child Development*, 48, 1666–1670.

Cooper, R. P. (1997). An ecological approach to infants' perception of intonation contours as meaningful aspects of speech. In C. Dent-Read & P. Zukow-Goldring (eds), *Evolving explanations of development: Ecological approaches to organism-environment systems* (pp. 55–85). Washington, DC: American Psychological Association.

Costa-Giomi, E. (2003). Young children's harmonic perception. *Annals of the New York Academy of Sciences*, **999**, 477–484.

Cuddy, L. L. & Badertscher, B. (1987). Recovery of the tonal hierarchy: Some comparisons across age and levels of musical experience. *Perception & Psychophysics*, **41**, 609–620.

Custodero, L. A., Britto, P. R., & Brooks-Gunn, J. (2003). Musical lives: A collective portrait of American parents and their young children. *Journal of Applied Developmental Psychology*, **24**, 553–572.

Dalla Bella, S., Peretz, I., & Aronoff, N. (2003). Time course of melody recognition: A gating paradigm study. *Perception & Psychophysics*, **65**, 1019–1028.

Davitz, J. R. (ed.) (1964). *The communication of emotional meaning*. New York, NY: McGraw-Hill.

Erting, C. J., Prezioso, C., & O'Grandy Hynes, M. (1990). The interactional context of deaf mother-infant communication. In V. Volterra & C. J. Erting (eds), *From gesture to language in hearing and deaf children* (pp. 97–106). Berlin: Springer.

Feierabend, J. M. (1996). Music and movement for infants and toddlers: Naturally wonder-full. *Early Childhood Connections*, **2**, 19–26.

Fernald, A. (1991). Prosody in speech to children: Prelinguistic and linguistic functions. *Annals of Child Development*, **8**, 43–80.

Fitzgibbons, P. J., Pollatsek, A., & Thomas, I. B. (1974). Detection of temporal gaps within and between perceptual tonal groups. *Perception & Psychophysics*, **16**, 522–528.

Fonagy, I. & Magdics, K. (1963). Emotional patterns in intonation and music. *Zeitschrift für Phonetik*, **16**, 293–326.

Fujioka, T., Trainor, L. J., Ross, B, Kakigi, R., & Pantev, C. (2004). Musical training enhances automatic encoding of melodic contour and interval structure. *Journal of Cognitive Neuroscience*, **16**, 1010–1021.

Gardner, H., Phelps, E., & Wolf, D. P. (1990). The roots of adult creativity in children's symbolic products. In C. N. Alexander & E. J. Langer (eds), *Higher stages of human development: Perspectives on adult growth* (pp. 79–96). London: Oxford University Press.

Gérard, C. & Drake, C. (1990). The inability of young children to reproduce intensity differences in musical rhythms. *Perception & Psychophysics*, **48**, 91–101.

Gordon, E. E. (1996). Music aptitude and music achievement. *Early Childhood Connections*, **2**, 11–13.

Hannon, E. E. & Johnson, S. P. (2005). Infants use meter to categorize rhythms and melodies: Implications for musical structure learning. *Cognitive Psychology*, **50**, 354–377.

Hannon, E. E. & Trehub, S.E. (2005a). Metrical categories in infancy and adulthood. *Psychological Science*, **16**, 48–55.

Hannon, E. E. & Trehub, S. E. (2005b). Tuning in to musical rhythms: Infants learn more readily than adults. *Proceedings of the National Academy of Sciences*, **102**, 12639–12643.

Jusczyk, P. W. & Krumhansl, C. L. (1993). Pitch and rhythmic patterns affecting infants' sensitivity to musical phrase structure. *Journal of Experimental Psychology: Human Perception and Performance*, **19**, 627–640.

Kartomi, M. J. (1980). Childlikeness in play songs—A case study among the Pitjantjara at Yalata, South Australia. *Miscellanea Musicologica*, **11**, 172–214.

Kemp, A. E. (1997). Individual differences in musical behaviour. In D. J. Hargreaves (ed.), *The social psychology of music* (pp. 25–45). London: Oxford University Press.

Knobloch, S. & Zillmann, D. (2002). Mood management via the digital jukebox. *Journal of Communication*, 52, 351–366.

Krumhansl, C. L. (1990). *Cognitive foundations of musical pitch*. New York: Oxford University Press.

Krumhansl, C. L. & Jusczyk, P. W. (1990). Infants' perception of phrase structure in music. *Psychological Science*, 1, 70–73.

Krumhansl, C. L. & Keil, F. C. (1982). Acquisition of the hierarchy of tonal functions in music. *Memory & Cognition*, 10, 243–251.

Lamont, A. & Cross, I. (1994). Children's cognitive representations of musical pitch. *Music Perception*, 12, 27–55.

Lewkowicz, D. J. (2003). Learning and discrimination of audiovisual events in human infants: The hierarchical relation between intersensory temporal synchrony and rhythmic pattern cues. *Developmental Psychology*, 39, 795–804.

London, J. (1995). Some examples of complex meters and their implications for models of metric perception. *Music Perception*, 13, 59–77.

Lorch, C. A., Lorch, V., Diefendorf, A. O., & Earl, P. W. (1994). Effect of stimulative and sedative music on systolic blood pressure, heart rate, and respiratory rate in premature infants. *Journal of Music Therapy*, 31, 105–118.

Lynch, M. P. & Eilers, R. E. (1992). A study of perceptual development for musical tuning. *Perception & Psychophysics*, 52, 599–608.

Lynch, M. P., Eilers, R. E., Oller, D. K., & Urbano, R. C. (1990). Innateness, experience, and music perception. *Psychological Science*, 1, 272–276.

Manturzewska, M. (1990). A biographical study of the life-span development of professional musicians. *Psychology of Music*, 18, 112–139.

Masataka, N. (1992). Motherese in a signed language. *Infant Behavior & Development*, 15, 453–460.

Masataka, N. (1996). Perception of motherese in a signed language by 6-month-old deaf infants. *Developmental Psychology*, 32, 874–879.

Masataka, N. (1998). Perception of motherese in Japanese sign language by 6-month-old hearing infants. *Developmental Psychology*, 34, 241–246.

Masataka, N. (1999). Preference for infant-directed singing in 2-day-old hearing infants of deaf parents. *Developmental Psychology*, 35, 1001–1005.

McDermott, J. (2005). *Probing the evolutionary origins of music perception*. Presented at The Neurosciences and music–II: From perception to performance, Leipzig, Germany.

McDermott, J. & Hauser, M. (2004). Are consonant intervals music to their ears? Spontaneous acoustic preferences in a nonhuman primate. *Cognition*, 94, B11–B21.

Mitroudot, L. (2001). Infant's melodic schemas—analysis of song productions by 4 and 5-year old subjects. *Musicae Scientiae*, 5, 83–104.

Miyazaki, K. (1995). Perception of relative pitch with different references: Some absolute-pitch listeners can't tell musical interval names. *Perception & Psychophysics*, 57, 962–970.

Moore, D. G., Burland, K., & Davidson, J. W. (2003). The social context of musical success: A developmental account. *British Journal of Psychology*, 94, 529–549.

Morelli, G. A., Rogoff, B, Oppenheim, D., & Goldsmith, D. (1992). Cultural variation in infants' sleeping arrangements; Questions of independence. *Developmental Psychology*, 28, 604–613.

Murray, I. R. & Arnott, J. L. (1993). Toward the simulation of emotion in synthetic speech: A review of the literature on human vocal emotion. *Journal of the Acoustical Society of America*, 93, 1097–1108.

Nakata, T. & Trehub, S. E. (2004). Infants' responsiveness to maternal speech and singing. *Infant Behavior & Development*, 27, 455–464.

Nawrot, E. S. (2003). The perception of emotional expression in music: Evidence from infants, children and adults. *Psychology of Music*, 31, 75–92.

O'Neill, C., Trainor, L. J., & Trehub, S. E. (2001). Infants' responsiveness to fathers' singing. *Music Perception*, 18, 409–425.

Opie, I. & Opie, P. (1969). *Children's games in the street and playground*. Oxford: Clarendon Press.

Overy, K., Norton, A.C., Cronin, K. T., Gaab, N. *et al.* (2004). Imaging melody and rhythm processing in young children. *NeuroReport*, 15, 1723–1726.

Palmer, C., Jungers, M. K., & Jusczyk, P. W. (2001). Episodic memory for musical prosody. *Journal of Memory & Language*, 45, 526–545.

Papoušek, M., Papoušek, H., & Symmes, D. (1991). The meanings of melodies in motherese in tone and stress languages. *Infant Behavior & Development*, 14, 415–440.

Peretz, I., Gaudreau, D., & Bonnel, A. (1998). Exposure effects on music preference and recognition. *Memory & Cognition*, 26, 884–902.

Phillips-Silver, J. & Trainor, L. J. (2005). Feeling the beat: Movement influences infant rhythm perception. *Science*, 308, 1430.

Pickens, J. & Bahrick, L. E. (1995). Infants' discrimination of bimodal events on the basis of rhythm and tempo. *British Journal of Developmental Psychology*, 13, 223–236.

Plantinga, J. & Trainor, L. J. (2005). Memory for melody: Infants use a relative pitch code. *Cognition*, 98, 1–11.

Rauscher, F. H. & Zupan, M. A. (2000). Classroom keyboard instruction improves kindergarten children's spatial-temporal performance: A field experiment. *Early Childhood Research Quarterly*, 15, 215–228.

Rentfrow, P. J. & Gosling, S. D. (2003). The do re mi's of everyday life: The structure and personality correlates of music preferences. *Journal of Personality & Social Psychology*, 84, 1236–1256.

Saffran, J. R. (2003). Absolute pitch in infancy and adulthood: The role of tonal structure. *Developmental Science*, 6, 35–43.

Saffran, J. R. & Griepentrog, G. J. (2001). Absolute pitch in infant auditory learning: Evidence for developmental reorganization. *Developmental Psychology*, 37, 74–85.

Saffran, J. R., Loman, M. M., & Robertson, R. R W. (2000). Infant memory for musical experiences. *Cognition*, 77, B15–B23.

Saffran, J. R., Reeck, K., Niebuhr, A., & Wilson, D. (2005). Changing the tune: The structure of the input affects infants' use of absolute and relative pitch. *Developmental Science*, 8, 1–7.

Schellenberg, E. G. & Trainor, L. J. (1996). Sensory consonance and the perceptual similarity of complex-tone harmonic intervals: Tests of adult and infant listeners. *Journal of the Acoustical Society of America*, 100, 3321–3328.

Schellenberg, E. G. & Trehub, S. E. (1996). Natural musical intervals: Evidence from infant listeners. *Psychological Science*, 7, 272–277.

Schellenberg, E. G. & Trehub, S. E. (2003). Good pitch memory is widespread. *Psychological Science*, 14, 262–266.

Shenfield, T., Trehub, S. E., & Nakata, T. (2003). Maternal singing modulates infant arousal. *Psychology of Music*, 31, 365–375.

Singh, L., Morgan, J. L., & Best, C. T. (2002). Infants' listening preferences: Baby talk or happy talk? *Infancy*, 3, 365–394.

Super, C. M. & Harkness, S. (1986). The developmental niche: A conceptualization at the interface of child and culture. *International Journal of Behavioral Development*, 9, 545–569.

Takeuchi, A. H. & Hulse, S. H. (1993). Absolute pitch. *Psychological Bulletin*, 113, 345–361.

Thorpe, L. A. & Trehub, S. E. (1989). Duration illusion and auditory grouping in infancy. *Developmental Psychology*, 25, 122–127.

Thorpe, L. A., Trehub, S. E., Morrongiello, B. A., & Bull, D. (1988). Perceptual grouping by infants and preschool children. *Developmental Psychology*, 24, 484–491.

Toda, S., Fogel, A., & Kawai, M. (1990). Maternal speech to three-month-old infants in the United States and Japan. *Journal of Child Language*, 17, 279–294.

Trainor, L. J. (1996). Infant preferences for infant-directed versus noninfant-directed playsongs and lullabies. *Infant Behavior & Development*, 19, 83–92.

Trainor, L. J. (2005). Are there critical periods for musical development? *Developmental Psychobiology*, 46, 262–278.

Trainor, L. J. & Adams, B. (2000). Infants' and adults' use of duration and intensity cues in the segmentation of tone patterns. *Perception & Psychophysics*, 62, 333–340.

Trainor, L. J. & Heinmiller, B. M. (1998). The development of evaluative responses to music: Infants prefer to listen to consonance over dissonance. *Infant Behavior & Development*, 21, 77–88.

Trainor, L. J. & Trehub, S. E. (1992). A comparison of infants' and adults' sensitivity to Western musical structure. *Journal of Experimental Psychology: Human Perception and Performance*, 18, 394–402.

Trainor, L. J. & Trehub, S. E. (1993). What mediates infants' and adults' superior processing of the major over the augmented triad? *Music Perception*, 11, 185–196.

Trainor, L. J. & Trehub, S. E. (1994). Key membership and implied harmony in Western tonal music: Developmental perspectives. *Perception & Psychophysics*, 56, 125–132.

Trainor, L. J. & Zacharias, C. A. (1998). Infants prefer higher-pitched singing. *Infant Behavior & Development*, 21, 799–805.

Trainor, L. J., Clark, E. D., Huntley, A., & Adams, B. (1997). The acoustic basis of preferences for infant-directed singing. *Infant Behavior & Development*, 20, 383–396.

Trainor, L. J., Tsang, C. D., & Cheung, V. H. W. (2002). Preference for sensory consonance in 2- and 4-month-old infants. *Music Perception*, 20, 187–194.

Trainor, L. J., Wu., L., & Tsang, C. D. (2004). Long-term memory for music: Infants remember tempo and timbre. *Developmental Science*, 7, 289–296.

Trehub, S. E. (2000). Human processing predispositions and musical universals. In N. L. Wallin, B. Merker & S. Brown (eds), *The origins of music* (pp. 427–448). Cambridge, MA: MIT Press.

Trehub, S. E. (2003). Absolute and relative pitch processing in tone learning tasks. *Developmental Science*, 6, 46–47.

Trehub, S. E., & Hannon, E. E. (in press). Infant music perception: Domain-general or domain-specific mechanisms? *Cognition*.

Trehub, S. E. & Schellenberg, E. G. (1995). Music: Its relevance to infants. *Annals of Child Development*, 11, 1–24.

Trehub, S. E. & Thorpe, L. A. (1989). Infants' perception of rhythm: Categorization of auditory sequences by temporal structure. *Canadian Journal of Psychology*, 43, 217–229.

Trehub, S. E. & Trainor, L. J. (1998). Singing to infants: Lullabies and play songs. *Advances in Infancy Research*, 12, 43–77.

Trehub, S. E., Thorpe, L. A., & Morrongiello, B. A. (1985). Infants' perception of melodies: Changes in a single tone. *Infant Behavior & Development*, 8, 213–223.

Trehub, S. E., Thorpe, L. A., & Morrongiello, B. A. (1987). Organizational processes in infants' perception of auditory patterns. *Child Development*, **58**, 741–749.

Trehub, S. E., Unyk, A. M., & Trainor, L. J. (1993a). Adults identify infant-directed music across cultures. *Infant Behavior & Development*, **16**, 193–211.

Trehub, S. E., Unyk, A. M., & Trainor, L. J. (1993b). Maternal singing in cross-cultural perspective. *Infant Behavior & Development*, **16**, 285–295.

Trehub, S. E., Unyk, A. M., & Henderson, J. L. (1994). Children's songs to infant siblings: Parallels with speech. *Journal of Child Language*, **21**, 735–744.

Trehub, S. E., Hill, D. S., & Kamenetsky, S. B. (1997a). Parents' sung performances for infants. *Canadian Journal of Experimental Psychology*, **51**, 385–396.

Trehub, S. E., Unyk, A. M., Kamenetsky, S. B., Hill, D. S., Trainor, L. J., Henderson, J. L., & Saraza, M. (1997b). Mothers' and fathers' singing to infants. *Developmental Psychology*, **33**, 500–507.

Trehub, S. E., Schellenberg, E. G., & Kamenetsky, S. B. (1999). Infants' and adults' perception of scale structure. *Journal of Experimental Psychology: Human Perception and Performance*, **25**, 965–975.

Trehub, S. E., Nakata, T., & Bergeson, T. (2002). *Infants' responsiveness to soothing and playful singing.* Presented at the International Conference on Infant Studies, Toronto.

Tucker, N. (1984). Lullabies. *History Today*, **34**, 40–46.

Volkova, A., Trehub, S. E., & Schellenberg, E. G. (in press). Infants' memory performances. *Developmental Science*.

Werker, J. F., & Tees, R. C. (1984). Cross-language speech perception: Evidence for perceptual reorganization during the first year of life. *Infant Behavior & Development*, **7**, 49–63.

Werker, J. F., Pegg, J. E., & McLeod, P. J. (1994). A cross-language investigation of infant preference for infant-directed communication. *Infant Behavior & Development*, **17**, 323–333.

Zatorre, R. J., Belin, P., & Penhune, V. B. (2002). Structure and function of auditory cortex: Music and speech. *Trends in Cognitive Sciences*, **6**, 37–46.

Zentner, M. R. & Kagan, J. (1996). Perception of music by infants. *Nature*, **383**, 29.

CHAPTER 3

THE MUSICAL BRAIN

DONALD A. HODGES

How does it happen that all children possess a musical brain? This question forms the focus of this chapter, which describes the development of the musical brain from before birth through the teenage years. As early as the last months of pregnancy, the fetus responds to musical sounds and children naturally engage in musical experiences that shape inherited neural systems toward the eventual adult musical brain. Children who begin formal music instruction at an early age develop different brains from those who do not receive such training. As adults, these musicians will have stronger and faster brain responses to musical tasks than naïve listeners. It is becoming increasingly apparent that all human beings are biologically equipped to be musical and that this genetic predisposition for musicality has important consequences for us not only artistically, but emotionally and socially, as well. The first section of this chapter describes general brain growth and development, while the second reviews research literature dealing specifically with the development of the musical brain.

General brain development

Figures used to describe the adult brain are almost beyond comprehension. For example, the brain has billions of neurons (brain cells) that may have as many as a quadrillion (1000 trillion) connections with each other (Gopnik *et al.*, 2001). In the motor cortex, a single neuron may take part in as many as 60 000 synapses (connections) and there are over 200 million fibres in the corpus callosum (a bundle of fibres connecting the two halves of the brain; it plays a major role in transferring and integrating information between the two hemispheres; see Figure 3.1) (Ashwell *et al.*, 2000). Just these few figures are enough to convince one of the enormous complexity of the human brain. But how does it get that way?

Growing a brain is a dynamic, interactive process that is driven by genetics and shaped by experiences in living. Some aspects of brain development show a smooth continuous growth, while others alternate between plateaus with no growth and spurts of rapid growth. There are also instances of significant overgrowth followed by retrenchment.

At birth, the brain is 30% of adult weight, by age 2 it reaches 70%, and by 6 it is 90% (Berk, 2004). From birth to adulthood the brain quadruples in volume (weight), with most of the increase coming from growth of dendrites (fibres bringing information into the cell body), increased synapses (synaptogenesis), fibre bundles, and myelin (a fatty sheath covering

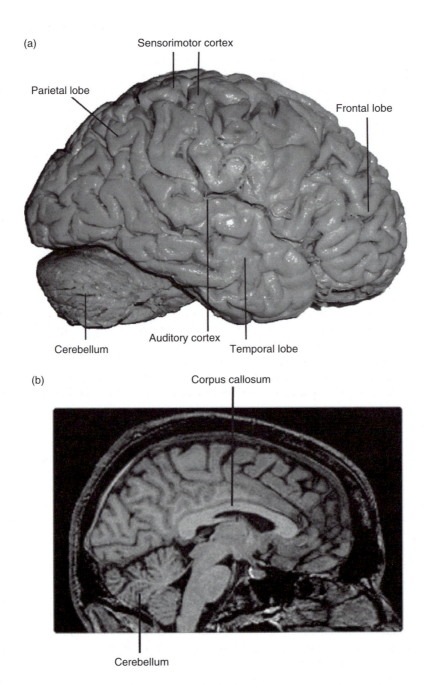

(a)

Sensorimotor cortex

Parietal lobe

Frontal lobe

Cerebellum

Auditory cortex

Temporal lobe

(b)

Corpus callosum

Cerebellum

Figure 3.1 Major areas of the brain. (a) The exterior of the right hemisphere. (b) The interior of the brain.

axons) (Johnson, 1998). Most of the brain cells are in place by the end of the sixth month of fetal development (Johnson, 2001); in fact, beginning around day 42 after conception and for the next 120 days, brain cells proliferate at the rate of 580 000 per minute (Bruer, 1999). Even though additional brain cells are not produced in most brain areas after this time, another contribution to brain growth is that glial cells (which support and nourish neurons) continue to increase rapidly even after birth.

This overall growth moves in localized spurts, with some parts of the brain growing and changing rapidly at the same time that other parts are more static. These growth spurts are connected with changes in cognitive functioning. For example, rapid growth in the auditory and visual areas in the first year corresponds to dramatic gains in auditory and visual perception. Peak growth rates in the frontal circuits of the corpus callosum between the ages of 3 and 6 result in greater ability to sustain focused attention and to plan new actions (Thompson et al., 2000). Another part of the corpus callosum shows rapid, peak growth rates (up to 80%) between the ages of 11 and 15, having to do with spatial association and language development. Ages 6–15 see growth in temperoparietal systems also implicated in language and spatial relationships.

By studying large samples of children from ages 2 months to early adulthood, researchers have found overall continuous growth, but many examples of discrete growth spurts in specific regions at specific times (Thatcher et al., 1987). In general, the right hemisphere shows more steady, sustained growth, with spurts between birth and 2 and between 8 and 10. Left hemisphere growth is characterized by more abrupt spurts, particularly between 3 and 6. Left hemisphere pairings from front to back reach 90% of adult values by age 5, but the right hemisphere does not reach this level until age 9. Interestingly, growth patterns seem to broadly correspond to Piaget's stages of development.

After age 15, growth is bilateral, primarily in frontal lobe connections, with few changes found elsewhere (Sowell et al., 1999). The cerebral cortex and hippocampus are the slowest parts of the brain to develop (Johnson, 2001). As the brain grows, it folds in upon itself as a means of including more tissue into a constrained space. This cortical folding (gryrification) begins as early as the 11–16th week of gestation, reaches adult levels soon after birth, continues until the 38th week when it reaches 118% of adult values, then regresses and stabilizes by age 20 (Zilles et al., 1997).

As a demonstration of cortical folding, try this simple experiment: cup the hands facing each other with fingertips touching. Notice the distance from the first knuckle on each finger to the first knuckle on the finger opposite. Roll the fingers inward so that the first knuckles on all fingers are touching. This can be repeated so that the second knuckle on each finger is touching the second knuckle on the finger opposite. Rolling the fingers inward to make the total hand area smaller roughly approximates how the brain folded in upon itself as it developed over the millennia from a brain of approximately 500 mL to one of over 1300 mL (Cowan, 1979).

The next subsections of this review provide information on additional concepts that help to refine an understanding of brain development, including myelination, plasticity, pruning, and critical periods. A final subsection in this general discussion covers the development of the auditory cortex.

Myelination

Myelination is a process of coating the neuronal axons with a fatty sheath that improves message transfer with respect to accuracy and speed. Axons are fibres that transmit information away from a cell body. Myelination begins in the fourth month after gestation and continues for the next 30 years (Sowell *et al.*, 1999). It occurs in different brain regions at different times and, in general, proceeds from bottom to top and from back to front. The brainstem and cerebellum come first and the frontal lobes last. The reticular formation (which maintains alertness and consciousness) becomes coated throughout childhood into adolescence (Berk, 2004), accounting for improved concentration. The corpus callosum does not begin to myelinate until the end of the first year. As indicated previously, there are spurts of rapid growth in different parts of the corpus callosum at different ages that continue to age 15 (Thompson *et al.*, 2000). Myelination is related to cognitive functioning (Webb *et al.*, 2001) and because the process is not a smooth, continuous one, development of cognitive functioning is also not a smooth, continuous process.

Plasticity

Plasticity refers to the notion that brain structures are not rigidly defined, rather that they are malleable. Brain structures can change over time as a result of learning experiences. This has specific relevance for brain injury, in that when a portion of the brain is destroyed other parts may take over that function (Chugani *et al.*, 1996). This is more likely to be the case the earlier the damage occurs and the more limited it is. Plasticity, however, is not just a response to brain injury, but a central feature of the brain development and learning that persists throughout life as experiences change the brain (Stiles, 2000). Plasticity can be influenced by both negative (e.g., injury) and positive (e.g., learning) experiences (Nelson & Bloom, 1997).

Mounting evidence suggests that musicians' brains are models of neuroplasticity (Pantev *et al.*, 2001a, 2003; Schlaug, 2001; Münte *et al.*, 2002; Ross *et al.*, 2003). Studies of the effects of musical experiences on brain plasticity are reviewed subsequently under the heading 'Experiential factors in musicality'.

Pruning

A surprising feature of brain growth is that in the early years, there is a massive overproduction and redundancy of synapses (Berk, 2004), with peaks of synaptic density coming at different times for different regions (Johnson, 2001). Overproduction is as high as 50% (Stiles, 2000). This, along with fuel expenditure during the coating of axons, leads to a doubling of glucose metabolism in the frontal cortex from ages 2 to 4 (Thompson *et al.*, 2000), which reaches 190% to 226% of adult values between 3 and 8 (Chugani *et al.*, 1993).

Genes and experience work together in a process called neural pruning, whereby the brain is sculpted into its eventual configuration. There is a severe, spatially localized loss of brain tissue of up to 50% between the ages of 7–11 and 9–13 (Thompson *et al.*, 2000) and from 20 to 80% of cortical neurons and synapses may be lost in specific regions (Stiles, 2000). Pruning can be 'experience-expectant' or 'experience-dependent'. In experience-expectant systems (e.g., language or music), development is based on expectations that experience will provide the necessary influences to select the appropriate subset of synaptic connections (Webb *et al.*, 2001). Experience-dependent systems (e.g., vocabulary or specific musical skills) are unique to each individual as a result of specific learning experiences. Competition, particularly in terms of input, leads to both cell death and synaptic reduction (Stiles, 2000). Synaptic connections that are infrequently or never activated are eliminated, while those that are frequently used are retained and strengthened (Gopnik *et al.*, 2001). As the brain learns, it imposes restrictions on itself, such that what is learned influences what can be learned (Quartz, 2003).

Neural pruning illustrates the interplay between nature and nurture. Genetic instructions richly endow a youngster's brain with numerous possibilities. Actual experiences sculpt the brain toward its eventual adult makeup. For example, a child who is reared in a bilingual home easily learns two languages. Whether these two are Japanese and Italian or English and Spanish depends entirely on what she has the opportunity to learn and which sounds she makes that are constantly reinforced.

Imagine, for a moment, a child growing up in an English-only home. During interactions with adults, the infant is presented with 'parentese' speech with exaggerated visual and aural models. She gazes at the lips and tongue of the speaker and tries to copy those facial gestures. Similarly, she listens intently and tries to mimic the sounds she hears. Numerous faulty attempts may go unacknowledged, but when there is a vocalization that approximates a real word (e.g., ma-ma, da-da), there is a veritable explosion of reinforcement. The infant is encouraged to try, try again. Gradually, what the novice speaker learns to do becomes easier and easier and this, in turn, imposes a structure on awareness. Slowly, the infant loses the ability either to hear or to produce certain sounds as she gains facility in hearing and producing the English language. For example, adult English-only speakers are mostly incapable of hearing or producing the Vietnamese name 'Ng' as native speakers can.

This scenario with language is much the same as with music. Thousands of Japanese children have grown up to be bimusical as they learned both the traditional music of their culture and Western classical music through Suzuki instruction. Children are born with the capacity to learn any musical genre (an experience-expectant system); the specific musical style or styles (experience-dependent systems) depend on the culture in which one is raised. To an adolescent who has been exposed only to Western music, the microtunings and polyrhythms inherent in non-Western music may be difficult, if not impossible, to apprehend or produce (Patel *et al.*, 2004).

Critical periods

As different regions of the brain go through growth spurts, there are critical periods during which time appropriate stimulation is vital for normal development (Berk, 2004). If appropriate stimuli are not provided during critical periods, proper connections will not be made and deficits will occur. Physical, social, and emotional growth can be severely stunted when children are raised in abnormal environments. For example, social and economic problems in Romania in the 1980s caused a large number of infants to be placed in orphanages where they received inadequate care and attention. The result was mild neurocognitive impairment, impulsivity, and attention and social deficits (Chugani *et al.*, 2001).

In children, critical periods are more clearly marked for basic, species-specific traits, such as were previously identified as experience-expectant systems. The story of Genie details how a child who led a severely deprived life until the age of 13 was thereafter extremely limited in her use of language, even after years of concentrated efforts on the part of therapists (Curtiss, 1977; Rymer, 1993). However, for experience-dependent systems, the window of opportunity for learning may never be permanently shut and Bruer (1999) cautions against an over-reliance on critical periods as rigid determinants of human learning.

In contrast to critical periods, optimal periods are growth phases during which time learning may come more easily and more quickly. If appropriate experiences do not occur during optimal periods, learning may still occur at a later time, though it may be more difficult. (See Flohr & Hodges, 2002, for a discussion of this concept in a musical context.)

Once again, consider first a linguistic, then a musical example. Everyday experiences teach us that while adults can learn a new language, it is more easily done at a young age. A monolingual adult is less likely to learn to speak a second language without an accent. A classic example is an adult Japanese speaker learning to speak English, who is unable to distinguish 'l' from 'r' as in pray/play or rake/lake. Such a person is unable to hear or produce the requisite sounds.

An examination of professional musicians supports the common perception that an early start is essential to eventual success as a concert artist (D. Moore *et al.*, 2003). Conversely, *It's never too late* (Holt, 1978) documents the author's experiences in learning to play the cello as an adult. It can be done, but as with language, it is more easily accomplished in earlier years. In *Tone deaf and all thumbs? An invitation to music-making for late bloomers and non-prodigies*, Wilson (1986) presents a neurological explanation of music learning, with implications for adult beginners.

Development of the auditory cortex

The auditory cortex follows the general developmental scheme as outlined previously. Neurons are in place and functional such that during the last 3 months of pregnancy the fetus responds to sounds (Lecanuet, 1996; R. Moore *et al.*, 2001). Cortical evoked potentials (measuring electrical activity) in response to sound have been recorded in the fetus during labour (Staley *et al.*, 1990). Musical sounds presented during the last 3 months before birth can have an effect on subsequent infant behaviour (Olds, 1985), an indication that the fetal brain is at least able to register and remember musical sounds.

After birth, there is a rapid burst of synaptic development in the auditory cortex between months 3 and 4, reaching 150% of adult values between 4 and 12 months (Johnson, 1998). Correspondingly, localized glucose expenditure peaks somewhat later, between ages 3 and 8, with a slower decline from 9 to 15, and eventually reaching adult values (Chugani *et al.*, 1993). Auditory deprivation leads to less myelination and fewer projections to and from the auditory cortices. Congenitally-deaf adults have the same total volume of auditory cortex as hearing controls, although they have higher gray–white matter ratios (Emmorey *et al.*, 2003). (The outer layer of the cortex is comprised of gray matter, which is involved in more complex functions of the brain. It is organized in six layers. White matter forms an inner core of fibres that connect functional areas of the cortex.)

Neural activity in the auditory cortex that is functional and mature is restricted largely to the top, outer layer (layer I) of gray matter before 4 months of age; infants' ability to process auditory information is thus most likely due to brainstem analysis (J. Moore, 2002; see Figure 3.2). By age 2, axons are beginning to reach deeper layers (layers IV, V, and VI), and interconnections increase significantly over the next few years. This development from 6 months to age 5 reflects transmission of information from inner ear and brainstem to the auditory cortex and results in increasing perceptual skills (e.g., for language and music). From age 5 to 11 or 12, mature axons appear in layers II and III connecting the two hemispheres and areas within hemispheres (e.g., auditory association areas). These corticocortical connections are reflected in increasingly mature auditory perceptual skills. For example, the ability to discriminate auditory stimuli has been studied in 2-, 3-, 4-, and 6-month-old infants. Although 2-month-old infants can discriminate between standard and altered patterns, a clear developmental path was seen in that adult-like responses were found in 31% of infants at 3 months, 58% at 4 months, and in most infants by 6 months (Trainor et al., 2003a).

Differences in left and right hemispheric auditory processing are issues of interest with musical implications that will be discussed subsequently. In 65% of adults, the left auditory association area is larger than the corresponding area on the right (Johnson, 1998). This same leftward asymmetry is seen in congenitally deaf adults and suggests that left–right

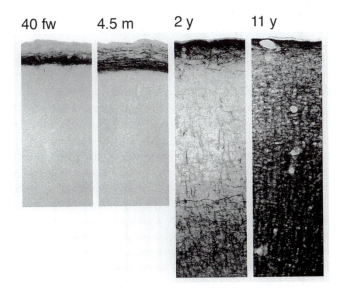

Figure 3.2 Neurofilament-immunostained sections of cortical tissue. At 40th fetal week (fw) and at 4.5 months' postnatal age, mature axons are present only in marginal layer. By 2 years of age, mature neurofilament-expressing axons are entering deeper cortical layers. By 11 years, mature axons are present with adult-like density in all cortical layers. Reprinted from Moore, J. (2002) Maturation of human auditory cortex: Implications for speech perception. *The Annals of Otology, Rhinology & Laryngology*, 111, 7–10. Used with permission.

differences are not a result of auditory experience but may, in fact, be present from birth (Emmorey *et al.*, 2003). Development to this state is not smooth. At 29 weeks, the left side is already larger than the right; however, in many cases the right develops sooner than the left. Changes in absolute threshold to pure tones can be seen over time, representing development of the auditory cortex. At 2 weeks, absolute threshold is as much as 50 dB poorer than adults; at 3 months the gap is 15–30 dB, and from 6 to 12 months it is 10–15 dB (Aslin *et al.*, 1998). These differences are also reflected in frequency and intensity discriminations, with 6-month-olds requiring twice the levels of frequency and intensity as adults to detect changes.

A fundamentally important aspect of auditory processing—segregation of sound streams—has been studied using EEG measurements of newborn infants (2–5 days old) and of young adults (18–23 years old) as they listen to a series of tones (Winkler *et al.*, 2003). Results confirm that newborns are already capable of segregating the sound streams just as adults are. This means they come into the world able to focus attention selectively on such tasks as separating the sound of their mothers' voices from background noise. Following a review of hearing in terms of both language and music perception, Aslin *et al.* (1998) provide evidence for a general auditory mechanism adapted for both modes, though this interpretation is not without controversy.

Musical brain development

There is abundant observational evidence indicating that the fetus responds to musical sounds during the last 3 months of pregnancy and that these prenatal music listening experiences may have an effect on subsequent behaviour (Lecanuet, 1996). Infants selectively respond to music at very early ages (Panneton, 1985; Fassbender, 1996; Papoušek, H., 1996), express preferences for consonance over dissonance (Trainor *et al.*, 2002), and possess many musical processing skills (e.g., detection of changes in melody, in terms of pitches, rhythms, tempo, and contour) (Trehub, 2001, 2003, 2004; also see Chapter 2). In turn, infant preverbal speech and singing show musical qualities (e.g., modulation of timbre, melodic contour, timing, etc.) at early ages (Fridman, 1973; Papoušek, M., 1996). Development of musicality continues throughout childhood (Hargreaves, 1996; Sloboda & Davidson, 1996). Few studies supporting these notions utilize direct measurements of brain responses, though the brain's involvement is clearly presupposed. The prevailing notion is that when infants display listening and musical processing skills it is due more to inborn capabilities and less to learning (Imberty, 2000; Trehub, 2000). Although learning takes place from the beginning, infants do not need extensive experience to process musical sounds in adult-like ways.

Neural wiring makes the pathway from the inner ear to the auditory cortex stronger to the opposite hemisphere than to the same side, with approximately 70% of the fibres crossing over (Handel, 1989). Strong left ear advantages are evident for music timbre discrimination in 4-day-old neonates; because of the cross-over connections, this indicates preference for right hemispheric processing (Bertoncini *et al.*, 1989). These findings were confirmed in 2-, 3-, and 4-month-old infants (Best *et al.*, 1982). Eight-and-a-half-month-old infants demonstrated more sophisticated responses, with definite preferences for melodic processing, left ear (right hemisphere) for contour-altered changes and right ear (left hemisphere) for contour-preserved changes (Balaban *et al.*, 1998). These hemispheric differences persist as 5–7 year olds had a slight increase in right hemispheric activation in the auditory cortex for melodic processing as compared with rhythmic processing (Overy *et al.*, 2004). The fact that these left–right differences are smaller than those found in adults (Samson *et al.*, 2001; Zatorre, 2001) suggests a developmental trajectory.

Timbre discrimination is an important component of both speech and music perception. Infants as young as 2 days old can recognize the sound of their mothers' voices (DeCasper & Fifer, 1980) and make limited musical timbre judgements at 1 week (O'Connell, 2003), indicating that they come into the world prepared to make important timbral discriminations. Eight-month-old infants are able to discriminate spectral slope differences that are most frequently found in speech and music (Tsang & Trainor, 2002). Timing is important, too, as newborns from 2 to 6 days old show electrical brain responses to durational changes in complex, harmonic tones that are similar to older children and adults (Cheour *et al.*, 2002).

Electrical brain responses (electroencephalogram or EEG) to music have been monitored in 3-, 6-, 9-, and 12-month-old infants (Schmidt *et al.*, 2002). Three orchestral pieces representing happiness, sadness, and fear were presented to determine whether there were differences in responses across age or affect. Although overall EEG power increased from 3 to 12 month olds, the distribution varied across age. Development of the frontal lobe (implicated in decision-making, planning, and critical thinking) was indicated by the fact that younger infants (3 and 6 months) showed no differences between frontal and parietal activity, while older infants (9 and 12 months) had more activation at frontal than parietal sites. Furthermore, affective music caused a significant increase in brain activity in 3 month olds, had little effect on 6 and 9 month olds, and caused a decrease in 12 month olds. Seven-month-old infants display sophisticated music listening skills, in that they can remember music that they hear (Saffran *et al.*, 2001).

Four-year-old children listened to classical music for 1 hour a day for 6 months (Malyrenko *et al.*, 1996). At the end of that time, significant positive changes in electrical brain activity were found in comparison with controls. Likewise, brain responses of 4-year-old Suzuki-trained students were significantly greater than those who were not taking music lessons (Trainor *et al.*, 2003b).

Flohr and colleagues have examined EEG in 4–6-year-old children during musical tasks. In one study, EEG data were gathered from children as they: (1) were in eyes open, quiet rest; (2) tapped rhythms to classical music; and (3) tapped rhythms to an Irish folk song (Flohr & Miller, 1993). Alpha levels (brain waves from 8.5 to 12.0 Hz) decreased at all sites, possibly indicating greater cognitive involvement. In another study, one group of children from the ages of 4 to 6 received special music instruction while students in a control group did not (Flohr *et al.*, 1996). These children were monitored during: (1) eyes open, quiet rest; (2) listening to classical music; and (3) puzzle assembly. The musically trained children exhibited EEG activations indicating increased cognitive processing and greater relaxation.

Seven- to 9-year-old children who start music instruction between the ages of 3 and 5 perform better on both melodic and prosodic language perception tasks than children who do not receive musical training; these differences in performance run parallel with significant differences in electrophysiological brain responses (Magne *et al.*, 2003). Although the results as reported are preliminary and should be considered with caution, findings are comparable with performances of adult trained and untrained musicians. This indicates that musical training enables these children to detect pitch variations in both music and language better than those who have not had training. Whether this translates into improved linguistic competency is still being studied.

Genetic factors in musicality

To what extent do genes shape the musical brain? The issue of nature versus nurture is always a difficult one because musicality consists of physical, physiological, cognitive, and dispositional traits in a complex series of interactions. That some aspects are genetic, others dependent on environment, and many on genetic–environmental interactions is assumed; however, precise contributions are as yet unknown (Oerter, 2003).

Although the Human Genome Project (http://www.ornl.gov/sci/techresources/Human_ Genome/home.shtml) may have raised expectations that musical genes would be identified, evidence of genetic instructions creating differences in musical brains remains circumstantial. The role of genetic instructions has been studied in those with absolute pitch (AP) because populations can be divided into those with and without AP. Evidence for the importance of genes comes from an unequal distribution among populations (there is a higher incidence among Asians), differences in brain morphology (a more exaggerated leftward asymmetry of the auditory association cortex), and higher prevalence among siblings and identical twins, with a corresponding deficit for melodic processing among those with congenital amusia (Zatorre, 2003). Brain activations indicate that AP possessors do not access working memory, as do those with relative pitch; rather they activate distinctive areas involved in associative learning. Finally, there is the known importance of early music learning experiences. Without early training, development of AP is highly unlikely.

Baharloo *et al.* (1998) studied more than 600 musicians and found that AP tended to cluster in families, providing support for nature. However, the greater preponderance of those with AP started their musical training before the age of 4, supporting the notion that both genes and experience play a part in musicality. Early childhood musical training, particularly with the use of 'fixed do', enhances the probability of AP in genetically susceptible individuals, but is not an absolute requirement. Factoring out different ethnicities (e.g., Chinese, Korean, Japanese) and early onset of music instruction, researchers believe that persons of Asian descent still have a higher incidence of musical AP (i.e., not AP for tonal languages) than those of other backgrounds; why this is so is not known (Gregersen *et al.*, 2001). In a study of identical and fraternal twins, Drayna *et al.* (2001) estimated heritability of AP at 0.71–0.80 based upon performances on a distorted tunes test; however, they, too, acknowledge the important role of learning.

In contrast to studying those with special abilities like AP, one can also study the absence of such traits. Peretz (2001) has coined the term 'congenital amusia' to refer to the fact that some persons may be born with deficits in musical processing. Amusia refers to the loss of musical skills due to brain damage. Congential amusia, then, infers that this brain damage is present at birth. (It is also possible, however, that the deficits are not inborn, but rather a result of a lack of appropriate stimulation during critical periods.) Just as aphasia, which deals with loss of language skills due to selective destruction of neural tissue, consists of many particularized deficits (e.g., Broca's aphasia, loss of ability to speak coherently; Wernicke's aphasia, loss of speech comprehension, etc.), amusia includes both receptive and expressive limitations and can involve deficits in pitch, rhythm, timbre processing, and so on (Hodges, 1996; Brust, 2001).

A number of cognitive impairments, based on known genetic defects, provide insights into the heritability of musicality. Musical savants may display extraordinary perform-ance skills, yet be severely limited in other cognitive domains (Miller, 1989). In Williams syndrome, individuals are mentally asymmetric, often showing proclivities in music and lan-guage with strong deficits in other cognitive domains (Levitin & Bellugi, 1998); linguistic and musical skills may be based on more generic acoustical memory skills. Prodigies, of course, do not have a cognitive impairment, but their situations may be similar in that their amazing skills appear so early and provide evidence of heritability. It is not yet pos-sible to explain the exceptional degree of musicality in musical savants, Williams syndrome musicians, or musical prodigies. However, these behaviours are not merely a result of learning experiences; clearly neural structures are intact that allow for these specialized skills. Furthermore, these neural structures appear to be strongly influenced by genetic instructions.

Experiential factors in musicality

Although genetic influences are important, there are also indications that musical training changes the brain and that the earlier musical instruction begins, the greater the changes. These changes can be seen in structure (i.e., morphological or anatomical changes) and in function (i.e., brain activations in terms of cerebral blood flow, electrophysiological responses, etc.). Nearly all this research has been conducted on adults; however, when sig-nificant differences are found between trained and untrained musicians, these data purport to give evidence of the effects of music learning experiences. This is especially true when other variables have been factored out and where differences are greater when the inception of musical studies was at an early age.

When children begin music lessons at a relatively early age, they are often likely to study piano, a skill that makes relatively equivalent demands of both hands. The results of these demands are seen in the brains of adult pianists who started studying before the age of 7, in that they have more symmetrical left and right motor cortices (Amunts et al., 1997). They also demonstrate increased motor cortex activations, controlling the fingers, in response to learning piano exercises, both actual and imagined (Pascual-Leone et al., 1995) or when listening to learned pieces in the absence of actual movement (Haueisen & Knösche, 2001). In fact, increases in motor activations appeared as quickly as 20 minutes in beginners who received piano instruction (Bangert & Altenmüller, 2003). In contrast, professional pianists showed less activation in primary and secondary motor cortex than controls, suggesting greater efficiency (Jäncke et al., 2000). That is, once the task is learned, and perhaps habituated (e.g., scales), fewer neural resources are required. Finally, learning to read music activates an area of the brain (superior parietal cortex on both sides) that is not activated in non-learners (Stewart et al., 2003).

In contrast to pianists, string players require fine movements in the fingers of the left hand and relatively gross movements of the right hand. Consequently, they have a larger and more responsive right primary somatosensory cortex (which controls the fingers of the left hand) than controls (Elbert *et al.*, 1995). Once again, these effects are larger for those who start music lessons at an early age.

The concept of use-dependent adaptation is that areas of the brain that are constantly stimulated and that are required for successful task performance change in response. Thus, children who begin musical studies at an early age will later show an enlarged corpus callosum (Schlaug *et al.*, 1995a ; Lee *et al.*, 2003), reflecting the need for hand co-ordination and for information sharing between the two hemispheres. They will also have a larger cerebellum (Hutchinson *et al.*, 2003), reflecting the need to synthesize motor, sensory, and cognitive information and to co-ordinate responses. As trained musicians they will show increased gray matter (Sluming *et al.*, 2002; Gaser & Schlaug, 2003), reflecting motor learning and the ability to translate musical notation into motor output.

Studying music at an early age also causes increases in the left auditory association cortex (Schlaug *et al.*, 1995b; Zatorre *et al.*, 1998), reflecting increased auditory processing demands. An alternative possibility is that left–right ratios are a result of neural pruning in the right auditory association cortex among musicians (Keenan *et al.*, 2001). Use-dependency is also seen in the fact that auditory cortex in both hemispheres responding to piano tones is 25% larger among experienced musicians and, again, the effect is greater for those who begin musical studies at an early age (Pantev *et al.*, 1998). Also, violinists and trumpeters are more responsive to the tones of their own instrument (Pantev *et al.*, 2001b). Numerous studies have shown differences in electrical brain responses between trained and untrained musicians (e.g., Faita & Besson, 1994; Lopez *et al.*, 2003; Nager *et al.*, 2003; Tervaniemi & Huotilainen, 2003). In general, musicians show faster and stronger electrical responses than controls, reflecting a greater ability to process musical information and to complete musical tasks successfully.

Concluding statement

The development of the musical brain follows general brain development. Certain musical processing abilities appear very early in life, others come at later stages. Musical abilities as reflected in the musical brain appear to be influenced by both genetic instructions and learning experiences. The musical brain is highly plastic, though significant changes are likely to be smaller and weaker at later ages.

Information presented in this chapter may leave the reader with the impression that a great deal is known about the development of the musical brain and a considerable amount is indeed known. However, there is still so much yet to be learned. In fact, so little is known that so-called brain-based music education is, for the most part, premature. Bruer's (2002) comments about brain-based education being no more than folk theory are apropos.

Consider but one example. Previously, it was stated that research supports the common notion that early inception of music instruction is critical for later success. On that basis, one might begin to advocate for increased amounts of practice time for young beginners. However, closer investigation reveals that professional musicians actually practised less as children than those who later became amateur musicians (D. Moore *et al.*, 2003). What, then, made the difference? Social factors, such as parental support, teacher's personality, and peer interactions, were central to their success. This clearly illustrates the need to place neuromusical findings within a larger context. The musical brain does not grow in isolation. It grows inside a whole person, who lives in a particular home environment, possesses internal proclivities, experiences external motivations, and so on. Those concerned with the musical development of children are encouraged to stay abreast of neuromusical literature, but also to consider the context and to make applications with caution. With patience and persistence, neuromusical researchers will undoubtedly provide a much better picture of how children develop a musical brain.

References

Amunts, K., Schlaug, G., Jancke, L., Steinmetz, H., Schleicher, A., Dabringhaus, A., & Zilles, K. (1997). Motor cortex and hand motor skills: Structural compliance in the human brain. *Human Brain Mapping*, 5, 206–215.

Ashwell, K., Tancred, E., & Paxinos, G. (2000). The brain's anatomy. In E. Gordon (ed.), *Integrative neuroscience* (pp. 87–108). Amsterdam: Harwood Academic Publishers.

Aslin, R., Jusczyk, P., & Pisoni, D. (1998). Speech and auditory processing during infancy: Constraints on and precursors to language. In E. Kuhn & S. Siegler (eds), *Handbook of child psychology*, Vol. 2, (5th edn). (pp. 147–198). New York: Wiley & Sons.

Baharloo, S., Johnston, P., Service, S., Gitschier, J., & Freimer, N. (1998). Absolute pitch: An approach for identification of genetic and nongenetic components. *American Journal of Human Genetics*, 62, 224–231.

Balaban, M., Anderson, L., & Wisniewski, A. (1998). Lateral asymmetries in infant melody perception. *Developmental Psychology*, 34(1), 39–48.

Bangert, M. & Altenmüller, E. (2003). Mapping perception to action in piano practice: A longitudinal DC-EEG study. BMC Neuroscience, 4:26, Available from http://www.biomedcentral.com/1471-2202/4/26. [Accessed 3 May 2004].

Berk, L. (2004). *Development through the lifespan*, 3rd edn. New York: Allyn & Bacon.

Bertoncini, J., Morais, J., Bijeljac-Babic, R., McAdams, S., Peretz, I., & Mehler, J. (1989). Dichotic perception and laterality in neonates. *Brain and Language*, 37, 591–605.

Best, C., Hoffman, H., & Glanville, B. (1982). Development of infant ear asymmetries in speech and music. *Perception and Psychophysics*, 31, 75–85.

Bruer, J. (1999). *The myth of the first three years*. New York: The Free Press.

Bruer, J. (2002). Avoiding the pediatrician's error: How neuroscientists can help educators (and themselves). *Nature Neuroscience Supplement*, 5, 1031–1033.

Brust, J. (2001). Music and the neurologist: A historical perspective. In R. Zatorre & I. Peretz (eds), *The biological foundations of music. Annals of the New York Academy of Sciences*, Vol. 930, pp. 143–152.

Cheour, M., Kushnerenko, E., Ceponiene, R., Fellman, V., & Näätänen, R. (2002). Electric brain responses obtained from newborn infants to changes in duration in complex harmonic tones. *Developmental Neuropsychology*, 22(2), 471–479.

Chugani, H., Phelps, M., & Mazziotta, J. (1993). Positron emission tomography study of human brain functional development. In M. Johnson (ed.), *Brain development and cognition* (pp. 125–143). Cambridge, MA: Blackwell Publishers.

Chugani, H., Müller, R.-A., & Chugani, D. (1996). Functional brain reorganization in children. *Brain & Development*, 18, 347–356.

Chugani, H., Behen, M., Muzik, O., Juhász, C., Nagy, F., & Chugani, D. (2001). Local brain functional activity following early deprivation: A study of postinstitutionalized Romanian orphans. *NeuroImage*, **14**, 1290–1301.

Cowan, W. (1979). The development of the brain. *Scientific American*, **241**(3), 113–33.

Curtiss, S. (1977). *Genie: a psycho linguistic study of a modern-day 'wild child'*. New York: Academic Press.

DeCasper, A. & Fifer, W. (1980). Of human bonding: Newborns prefer their mothers' voices. *Science*, **208**(4448), 1174–1176.

Drayna, D., Manichaikul, A., de Lange, M., Snieder, H., & Spector, T. (2001). Genetic correlates of musical pitch recognition in humans. *Science*, **291**, 1969–1971.

Elbert, T., Pantev, C., Wienbruch, C., Rockstrub, B., & Taub, E. (1995). Increased cortical representation of the fingers of the left hand in string players. *Science*, **270**(5234), 305–307.

Emmorey, K., Allen, J., Bruss, J., Schenker, N., & Damasio, H. (2003). A morphometric analysis of auditory brain regions in congenitally deaf adults. *PNAS Neuroscience*, **100**(17), 10049–10054.

Faita, F. & M. Besson. (1994). Electrophysiological index of musical expectancy: Is there a repetition effect on the event-related potentials associated with musical incongruities? In I. Deliege (ed.), *Proceedings of the 3rd international conference for music perception and cognition* (pp. 433–435). Liege, Belgium.

Fassbender, C. (1996). Infants' auditory sensitivity towards acoustic parameters of speech and music. In I. Deliège & J. A. Sloboda (eds), *Musical beginnings: Origins and development of musical competence* (pp. 56–87). New York: Oxford University Press.

Flohr, J. & Hodges, D. (2002). Music and neuroscience. In R. Colwell & C. Richardson (eds), *The new handbook of research on music teaching and learning* (pp. 991–1008). New York: Oxford University Press.

Flohr, J. & Miller, D. (1993). Quantitative EEG differences between baseline and psychomotor responses to music. *Music Education Research Reports*. Austin, TX: Texas Music Educators Association, 1–7.

Flohr, J., Miller, D., & Persellin, D. (1996). Children's electrophysiological responses to music. Paper presented at the 22nd International Society for Music Education World Conference (Amsterdam, Netherlands) and at the International Society for Music Education Early Childhood Commission Seminar (Winchester, England). ERIC Document PSO25654.

Fridman, R. (1973). The first cry of the newborn: Basis for the child's future musical development. *Journal of Research in Music Education*, **21**(3), 264–69.

Gaser, C. & Schlaug, G. (2003). Brain structures differ between musicians and non-musicians. *The Journal of Neuroscience*, **23**(27), 9240–9245.

Gopnik, A., Meltznoff, A., & Kuhl, P. (2001). *The scientist in the crib*. New York: Perennial.

Gregersen, P., Kowalsky, E., Kohn, N., & Marvin, E. (2001). Early childhood music education and predisposition to absolute pitch: Teasing apart genes and environment. *American Journal of Medical Genetics*, **98**(3), 280–282.

Handel, S. (1989). *Listening: An introduction to the perception of auditory events*. Cambridge, MA: MIT Press.

Hargreaves, D. (1996). The development of artistic and musical competence. In I. Deliège & J. A. Sloboda (eds), *Musical beginnings: Origins and development of musical competence* (pp. 145–170). New York: Oxford University Press.

Haueisen, J. & Knösche, T. (2001). Involuntary motor activity in pianists evoked by music perception. *Journal of Cognitive Neuroscience*, **13**, 786–792.

Hodges, D. (1996). Neuromusical research: A review of the literature. In D. Hodges (ed.), *Handbook of music psychology* (2nd edn), (pp. 197–284). San Antonio, TX: IMR Press.

Holt, J. (1978). *Never too late: My musical life story*. New York: Delacorte.

Hutchinson, S., Lee, L., Gaab, N., & Schlaug, G. (2003). Cerebellar volume of musicians. *Cerebral Cortex*, 13, 943–949.

Imberty, M. (2000). The question of innate competencies in musical communication. In N. Wallin, B. Merker & S. Brown (eds), *The origins of music* (pp. 449–462). Cambridge, MA: The MIT Press.

Jäncke, L., Shah, N., & Peters, M. (2000). Cortical activations in primary and secondary motor areas for complex bimanual movements in professional pianists. *Cognitive Brain Research*, 10, 177–183.

Johnson, M. (1998). The neural basis of cognitive development. In E. Kuhn & S. Siegler (eds), *Handbook of child psychology*, Vol. 2, (5th edn), (pp. 1–49). New York: Wiley & Sons.

Johnson, M. (2001). Infants' initial 'knowledge' of the world: A cognitive neuroscience perspective. In F. Lacerda, C. von Hofsten, & M. Heimann (eds), *Emerging cognitive abilities in early infancy*, (pp. 53–72). Mahwah, NJ: Lawrence Erlbaum Associates.

Keenan, J., Thangaraj, V., Halpern, A., & Schlaug, G. (2001). Absolute Pitch and Planum Temporale. *NeuroImage*, 14, 1402–1408.

Lecanuet, J. (1996). Prenatal auditory experience. In I. Deliège & J. A. Sloboda (eds), *Musical beginnings: Origins and development of musical competence* (pp. 3–34). New York: Oxford University Press.

Lee, D., Chen, Y., & Schlaug, G. (2003). Corpus callosum: Musician and gender effects. *NeuroReport*, 14, 205–209.

Levitin, D. & Bellugi, U. (1998). Musical abilities in individuals with Williams Syndrome. *Music Perception*, 15(4), 357–389.

Lopez, L., Jürgens, R., Diekmann, V., Becker, W., Ried, S., Grözinger, B., & Erné, E. (2003). Musicians versus nonmusicians: A neurophysiogical approach. In G. Avanzini, C. Faienza, D. Minciacchi, L. Lopez, L., & M. Majno (eds), *The neurosciences and music. Annals of the New York Academy of Sciences*, 999, 124–130.

Magne, C., Schön, D., & Besson, M. (2003). Prosodic and melodic processing in adults and children: Behavioral and electrophysiologic approaches. In G. Avanzini, C. Faienza, D. Minciacchi, L. Lopez, & M. Majno (eds), *The neurosciences and music. Annals of the New York Academy of Sciences*, 999, 461–476.

Malyrenko, T., Kuraev, G., Malyrenko, Y., Khvatova, M., Romanova, N., & Gurina, V. (1996). The development of brain electrical activity in 4-year-old children by long-term sensory stimulation with music. *Human Physiology*, 22(1), 76–81.

Miller, L. (1989). *Musical savants: Exceptional skill and mental retardation.* Hillsdale, NJ: Lawrence Erlbaum Associates.

Moore, D., Burland, K., & Davidson, J. (2003). The social context of musical success: A developmental account. *British Journal of Psychology*, 94, 529–549.

Moore, J. (2002). Maturation of human auditory cortex: Implications for speech perception. *The Annals of Otology, Rhinology & Laryngology*, 111, 7–10.

Moore, R., Vadeyar, S., Fulford, J., Tyler, D., Gribben, C., Baker, P., James, D., & Gowland, P. (2001). Antenatal determination of fetal brain activity in response to an acoustic stimulus using functional magnetic resonance imaging. *Human Brain Mapping*, 12, 94–99.

Münte. T., Eckart Altenmüller, E., & Jäncke, L. (2002). The musician's brain as a model of neuroplasticity. *Nature Neuroscience*, 3, 473–378.

Nager, W., Kohlmetz, C., Altenmüller, E., Rodriguez-Fornells, A. & Münte, T. (2003). The fate of sounds in conductors' brains: an ERP study. *Cognitive Brain Research*, 17, 83–93.

Nelson, C. & Bloom, F. (1997). Child development and neuroscience. *Child Development*, 68(5), 970–987.

O'Connell, D. (2003). *The effects of prenatal music experiences on one-week-old infants' timbre discrimination of selected auditory stimuli.* (Doctor of Philosophy, University of North Carolina at Greensboro). *Dissertation Abstracts International*, 64/06-A, 2018. (University Microfilms No. 3093879).

Oerter, R. (2003). Biological and psychological correlates of exceptional performance in development. In G. Avanzini, C. Faienza, D. Minciacchi, L. Lopez, & M. Majno (eds), *The neurosciences and music. Annals of the New York Academy of Sciences*, **999**, 451–460.

Olds, C. (1985). Fetal response to music. *Midwives Chronicle*, **98**(1170), 202–203.

Overy, K., Norton, A., Cronin, K., Gaab, N., Alsop, D., Winner, E., & Schlaug, G. (2004). Imaging melody and rhythm processing in young children. *NeuroReport*, **15**, 1723–1726.

Panneton, R. (1985). Prenatal auditory experience with melodies: Effects on postnatal auditory preferences. (Doctor of Philosophy, The University of North Carolina at Greensboro). *Dissertation Abstracts International* 47/09-B, 3984. University Microfilms No. 8701333).

Pantev, C., Oostenveld, R., Engelien, A., Ross, B., Roberts, L. E., & Hoek, M. (1998). Increased auditory cortical representation. *Nature*, **392**, 811–813.

Pantev, C., Roberts, L., Schulz, M., Engelien, A. & Ross, B. (2001b). Timbre-specific enhancement of auditory cortical representations in musicians. *NeuroReport*, **1**, 169–174.

Pantev, C., Engelien, A., Candia, A., & Elbert, T. (2001a). Representational cortex in musicians: Plastic alterations in response to musical practice. In R. Zatorre & I. Peretz (eds), *The biological foundations of music. Annals of the New York Academy of Sciences*, **930**, 300–314.

Pantev, C., Ross, B., Fujioka, T., Trainor, L., Schulte, M., & Schulz, M. (2003). Music and learning-induced cortical plasticity. In G. Avanzini, C. Faienza, D. Minciacchi, L. Lopez, & M. Majno (eds), *The neurosciences and music. Annals of the New York Academy of Sciences*, **999**, 438–450.

Papoušek, H. (1996). Musicality in infant research: Biological and cultural origins of early musicality. In I. Deliège & J. A. Sloboda (eds), *Musical beginnings: Origins and development of musical competence* (pp. 37–55). New York: Oxford University Press.

Papoušek, M. (1996). Intuitive parenting: A hidden source of musical stimulation in infancy. In I. Deliège & J. A. Sloboda (eds), *Musical beginnings: Origins and development of musical competence* (pp. 88–112). New York: Oxford University Press.

Pascual-Leone, A., Dand, N., Cohen, L., Braskil-Neto, J., Cammarota, A., & Hallett, M. (1995). Modulation of muscle responses evoked by transcranial magnetic stimulation during the acquisition of new fine motor skills. *Journal of Neurophysiology*, **74**(3), 1037–45.

Patel, A., Iversen, J., & Ohgushi, K. (2004). Cultural differences in rhythm perception: What is the influence of native language? In S. Lipscomb, R. Ashley, R. Gjerdingen, & P. Webster (eds), *Proceedings of the 8th International Conference on Music Perception and Cognition*. Evanston, IL: Northwestern University. CD-ROM.

Peretz, I. (2001). Brain specialization for music: New evidence from congenital amusia. In R. Zatorre & I. Peretz (eds), *The biological foundations of music. Annals of the New York Academy of Sciences*, **930**, 153–165.

Quartz, S. (2003). Learning and brain development: A neural constructivist perspective. In P. Quinlan (ed.), *Connectionist models of development* (pp. 279–309). New York: Psychology Press.

Ross, D., Olson, I., & Gore, J. (2003). Cortical plasticity in an early blind musician: An fMRI study. *Magnetic Resonance Imaging*, **21**, 821–828.

Rymer, R. (1993). *Genie: an abused child's flight from silence*. New York: HarperCollins Publishers.

Saffran, J., Loman, M., & Robertson, R. (2001). Infant long-term memory for music. In R. Zatorre & I. Peretz (eds), *The biological foundations of music. Annals of the New York Academy of Sciences*, **930**, 397–400.

Samson, S., Ehrle, N., & Baulac, M. (2001). Cerebral substrates for musical temporal processes. In R. Zatorre & I. Peretz (eds), *The biological foundations of music. Annals of the York Academy of Sciences*, **930**, 166–178.

Schlaug, G. (2001). The brain of musicians. A model for functional and structural adaptation. In R. Zatorre & I. Peretz (eds), *The biological foundations of music. Annals of the New York Academy of Sciences*, **930**, 281–299.

Schlaug, G., Jäncke, L., Huang, Y., Staiger, J. F., & Steinmetz, H. (1995a). Increased corpus callosum size in musicians, *Neuropsychologia*, **33**, 1047–1055.

Schlaug, G., Jäncke, L., Huang, Y., & Steinmetz, H. (1995b). In vivo evidence of structural brain asymmetry in musicians. *Science*, **267**(5198), 699–701.

Schmidt, L., Trainor, L., & Santesso, D. (2002). Development of frontal electroencephalogram (EEG) and heart rate (ECG) responses to affective musical stimuli during the first 12 months of post-natal life. *Brain and Cognition*, **52**, 27–32.

Sloboda, J. & Davidson, J. (1996). The young performing musician. In I. Deliège & J. Sloboda (eds), *Musical beginnings: Origins and development of musical competence* (pp. 171–190). New York: Oxford University Press.

Sluming, V., Barrick, T., Howard, M., Cezayirli, E., Mayes, A., & Roberts, N. (2002). Voxel-based morphometry reveals increased gray matter density in Broca's Area in male symphony orchestra musicians. *Neuroimage*, **17**, 1613–1622.

Sowell, E., Thompson, P., Holmes, C., Jernigan, T., & Toga, A. (1999). In vivo evidence for post-adolescent brain maturation in frontal and striatal regions. *Nature Neuroscience*, **2**(10), 859–861.

Staley, K., Iragui, V., & Spitz, M. (1990). The human fetal auditory evoked potential. *Electroencephalography and Clinical Neurophysiology*, **77**(1), 1–5.

Stewart, L., Henson, R., Kampe, K., Walsh, V., Turner, R., & Frith, U. (2003). Brain changes after learning to read and play music. *NeuroImage*, **20**, 71–83.

Stiles, J. (2000). Neural plasticity and cognitive development. *Developmental Neuropscyhology*, **18**(2), 237–272.

Tervaniemi, M. & Huotilainen, M. (2003). The promises of change-related brain potentials in cognitive neuroscience of music. In G. Avanzini, C. Faienza, D. Minciacchi, L. Lopez, & M. Majno (eds), *The neurosciences and music. Annals of the New York Academy of Sciences*, **999**, 29–39.

Thatcher, R., Walker, R., & Giudice, S. (1987). Human cerebral hemispheres develop at different rates and ages. *Science*, **236**(4805), 1110–1113.

Thompson, P., Giedd, J., Woods, R., MacDonald, D., Evans, A., & Toga, A. (2000). Growth patterns in the developing brain detected by using continuum mechanical tensor maps. *Nature*, **404**(9), 190–193.

Trainor, L., Tsang, C., & Cheung, V. (2002). Preference for consonance in two-month-old infants. *Music Perception*, **20**(2), 185–192.

Trainor, L., McFadden, M., Hodgson, L., Darragh, L., Barlow, J., Matsos, L., & Sonnadara, R. (2003a). Changes in auditory cortex and the development of mismatch negativity between 2 and 6 months of age. *International Journal of Psychophysiology*, **51**, 5–15.

Trainor, L., Shahin, A., & Roberts, L. (2003b). Effects of musical training on the auditory cortex in children. In G. Avanzini, C. Faienza, D. Minciacchi, L. Lopez, & M. Majno (eds), *The neurosciences and music. Annals of the New York Academy of Sciences*, **999**, 506–513.

Trehub, S. (2000). Human Processing Predispositions and Musical Universals. In N. Wallin, B. Merker, & S. Brown (eds), *The origins of music* (pp. 428–448). Cambridge, MA: MIT Press.

Trehub, S. (2001). Musical predispositions in infancy. In R. Zatorre & I. Peretz (eds), *The biological foundations of music. Annals of the New York Academy of Sciences*, **930**, 1–16.

Trehub, S. (2003). The developmental origins of musicality. *Nature Neuroscience*, **6**(7), 669–673.

Trehub, S. (2004). Foundations: Music perception in infancy. In J. Flohr (ed.), *The musical lives of young children* (pp. 24–29). Upper Saddle River, NJ: Prentice-Hall.

Tsang, C. & Trainor, L. (2002). Spectral slope discrimination in infancy: Sensitivity to socially important timbres. *Infant Behavior & Development*, 25, 183–194.

Webb, S., Monk, C., & Nelson, C. (2001). Mechanisms of postnatal neurobiological development: Implications for human development. *Developmental Neuropsychology*, 19(2), 147–171.

Wilson, F. (1986). *Tone deaf and all thumbs? An invitation to music-making for late bloomers and non-prodigies.* New York: Viking Press.

Winkler, I., Kushnerenko, E., Horváth, J., Ceponiene, R., Fellman, V., Huotilainen, M., Näätänen, R., & Sussman, E. (2003). Newborn infants can organize the auditory world. *Proceedings of the National Academy of Sciences*, 100(20), 11812–11815.

Zatorre, R. (2001). Neural specializations for tonal processing. In R. Zatorre & I. Peretz (eds), *The biological foundations of music. Annals of the New York Academy Sciences*, 930, 193–210.

Zatorre, R. (2003). Absolute pitch: A model for understanding the influence of genes and development on neural and cognitive function. *Nature Neuroscience*, 6, 692–695.

Zatorre, R., Perry, D., Beckett, C., Westbury, C., & Evans, A. (1998). Functional anatomy of musical processing in listeners with absolute pitch and relative pitch. *Proceedings of the National Academy of Sciences*, 95, 3172–3177.

Zilles, K., Schleicher, A., Langemann, C., Amunts, K., Morosan, P., Palomero-Gallagher, N., Schormann, T., Mohlberg, H., Bürgel, U., Steinmetz, H., Schlaug, G., & Roland, P. (1997). Quantitative analysis of sulci in the human cerebral cortex: Development, regional heterogeneity, gender difference, asymmetry, intersubject variability and cortical architecture. *Human Brain Mapping*, 5, 218–221.

CHAPTER 4

WHAT DEVELOPS IN MUSICAL DEVELOPMENT?

JEANNE BAMBERGER

And we must bear in mind that musical cognition implies the simultaneous cognition of a permanent and of a changeable element, and that this applies without limitation or qualification to every branch of music. We shall be sure to miss the truth unless we place the supreme and ultimate, not in the thing determined, but in the activity that determines.

Aristoxenus, cited in Strunk (1950, p. 31)

But in our zeal to explain music, it has been tempting to forget the hypothetical and constructed nature of such categories and to imagine that it is these ideas themselves that have the power to produce our experience.

Hasty (2000, p. 100)

Introduction

Revisiting my earlier studies of musical development now from a greater distance, I find that many aspects need to be re-thought. For example, in the case studies of children from which most of my results have been drawn, the influence of cognitive developmental theory tempted me to focus more on the regularities I could find in their behaviour, while underplaying the anomalies and enigmas that are often more telling with respect to development. Further, I find that I stopped too soon—specifically, before the emergence of aspects that would help to illuminate later phases in the course of musical development. What, for instance, might we mean by *musical complexity* and what are the apparent *simplicities* from which it grows?

In this chapter I expand the field of interest to provide a broader and also more detailed framework for thinking about musical development. For example, in the quote that heads this chapter, the fourth century, BC music theorist, Aristoxenus, confronts head on a paradoxical presence in musical cognition—the simultaneous presence of a permanent and a changeable element. In what follows, there is a primary focus on the tension between the permanence of the score and the changeable perceived meanings of entities it encodes in asking what we take to be 'progress' in musical development. In turn, I will ask: How is 'progress' related to notions of musical complexity—in the unfolding of a developing composition, and in developing a 'hearing' and a performance of it as well?

Hasty (2001) raises a related enigma: What is the role of our analytic categories and what are their implications in coming to understand the development of musical *experience*?

What assumptions are implicit in a particular analysis and how do these influence our understanding of how musical experience develops in expected and unexpected ways?

Enigmas and organizing constraints

In confronting the enigmas inherent in notions of musical development, I will propose a first and basic assumption: developing a 'hearing' of a composition as it unfolds in time is a *performance* and performances (both silent and out-loud) involve a process of active sense-making occurring in real-time.[1]

But to say this only raises more enigmas: First, a hearing as it is happening is, perhaps paradoxically, a silent affair; by its very nature it is private, an internal experience. And as one cannot hear the hearings that another makes, how can we study how specific hearings develop and change?

Second, and it is to this that much of what follows is addressed: If, in our performances, we are actively organizing incoming musical phenomena as they are occurring through time, what are the present, momentary *constraints* we bring to bear in guiding these generative organizing processes? How do these constraints evolve, develop, and change, and how can we find out? Putting it another way: in our creative responses back and forth with material out there, what are the productive interactions and even tensions among organizing constraints that shape our potential for making coherence in particular ways?[2]

Cognitive developmental traditions

Despite the wide and varied studies of cognitive development over the last several decades, certain criteria for 'progress' are generally shared among them. Briefly, cognitive developmental progress is characterized as transformations that occur over time in how individuals organize their perceptions and the strategies they bring to bear in constructing their understandings of the world around them:

- Initially, young children participate primarily in present contexts where properties, events, and relations are perceived to change their function and meaning in response to their unique embedding in these immediately experienced situations.

- Subsequently, the older child is able to subsume the flux of the passing moment through the mental construction of outside fixed reference systems in relation to which properties are abstracted from a present context, invariantly named, placed, classified, and their relations consistently measured in spite of a change in situation.

It is not surprising that in the spirit of these traditional trajectories, musical developmental studies have typically focused on 'progress' as meaning the capacities of children to abstract, name, measure, and hold musical elements constant (e.g., pitch, duration, interval) across

---

[1] The basic sense of a 'hearing' that I use throughout the chapter derives from common practice among musicians. For example, one member of a quartet might say to another, 'But how are you *hearing* that phrase— beginning on the downbeat or on the upbeat of the previous measure?'

[2] In using the term, constraints, I am influenced, in part, by Stravinsky (1947) who couples the term not with a sense of restriction or containment but rather with a role in creating freedom. He says, in *The poetics of music*: 'The more constraints one imposes, the more one frees one's self of the chains that shackle the spirit' (p. 64).

changing contexts (Seashore, 1938/67; Zimmerman, 1971; Gordon, 1979; Krumhansel, 1990; see overview, Shuter-Dyson, 1982). In response, much early music instruction tends to give primary attention to musical 'literacy.' It is at least tacitly assumed that through learning to recognize and produce a notated pitch and to name it as the same when or wherever it occurs, the child will learn to overcome earlier responsiveness to the continuous fluctuation in the properties of objects according to the change of situation.

It is important to remember, in this regard, that because of their power and efficacy in providing stable 'things to think with' and shared means of communication, professionals and educators in all disciplines give privileged status to symbolic notations and theoretic categories associated with their domain. However, the utility of these symbolic expressions depends importantly on the cogent and practical selections made over time with respect to the kinds and levels of phenomena to which symbolic expressions in a discipline are to refer.

As a result of this evolving selectivity, symbol systems associated with all disciplines are necessarily partial and they are so in two senses: they are incomplete and they are also 'partial-to' certain features while minimizing the importance of others. At the same time, by giving privileged status to these symbol systems, their referents, and their modes of description (sometimes thought to be explanations), users run the risk of coming to believe that the features and relations to which the symbols refer are the only 'things,' the only objects that exist in the domain. At the most extreme, this implicit ontological commitment has the potential of becoming a kind of ontological imperialism.

Reflections on development

In the light of these comments, how are we to approach the questions and enigmas raised with respect to the study of musical development? As an admittedly tentative first approximation, I propose that:

> Musical development is enhanced by continuously evolving interactions among multiple organizing constraints along with the disequilibrium and sensitivity to growing complexity that these entanglements entrain.

Thus, I argue that rather than being a unidirectional process, musical development is a spiralling, endlessly recursive process in which multiple organizing constraints are concurrently present, creating an essential, generative tension as they play a transformational dance with one another. Paradoxically, the constraints most closely related to the unidirectional trajectory of developmental theory are just those that are the most explicitly co-present and generative in musical development:

- *Situational meaning-making:* situational organizing constraints guide perceptual meaning-making that focuses on the present and unique function of events within the context in which they occur. When pitch/time properties associated with an event (a motive or a harmony) are embedded in a new situation, the invariant properties change their identity and function in response to where and when they occur.

- *Abstract meaning-making:* abstract organizing constraints guide meaning-making in isolating and extracting the pitch/time properties of events from the situation in which they occur. Holding them constant in spite of change in situation, events are perceived in relation to a generalizable outside, fixed reference structure (a scale, a metric). Extracting properties from their context is necessary to giving them invariant names and reciprocally, the mental construction of fixed reference structures is necessary to understanding the referents of conventional symbols.

Following traditional development theory, the simultaneous presence and generative tension between organizing constraints is more often taken to be a 'from-to' progression favouring abstraction. As a result, we tend to see behaviour associated with this co-presence as anomalous, chalking it up to a student's confusion or to being developmentally behind, instead of recognizing the moment as evidence of significant learning going on.

An essential tension: both the same and different

Enigmas and traditional views of musical development, become more explicitly problematic when juxtaposed to descriptions of performance practice by professional musicians. Here is David Soyer, the former cellist in the Guarnari String Quartet, talking about his development of a 'hearing' and performance of a passage in the Beethoven Quartet Op. 59, No. 2 (see Figure 4.1):

> The passage begins in the key of G-sharp minor; the G natural in bar 216 is clearly a simplified way of writing F double-sharp, which, as the leading note, has an upwards attraction towards the tonic G sharp (m. 218). For this reason I'd avoid using the open G-string and would play the passage on the C string. When G natural comes again [bar 224], its harmonic function is altered; it's now the fifth degree of C major and thus not sharpened. The subsequent G sharp [bar 225] is no longer the tonic but acts as the leading note in a minor and should be sharpened. This is the explanation from the harmonic standpoint, but your hearing once sensitized to such things, will often be able to put you there quite of itself without your needing to think it out.

> cited in Blum (1986, p. 33)

Soyer stresses particularly the importance of developing 'a sensitivity' to the changing function of the same notated pitch in response to a change in its contextual (harmonic) embedding. In doing so, his description raises the paradoxical issues of musical development to a new level of both complexity and relevance: How does a 'hearing' evolve? How does one become 'sensitized' to 'such things' so that the 'same' becomes both the same and different? How does a performer benefit from the invariance of pitch class notation and still use it as a means for projecting change in functional musical meaning? The questions suggest a further paradox: It would be impossible even to notice the remarkable shifts in meaning that the same notated pitch may undergo, if one were unable to recognize that, indeed, it is the same pitch.

Simples and complexity

Going on to further questions of what we might mean by 'simple' and 'complex', I argue that we initially enter into the complexity of multiple organizing constraints such as seen in Soyer's remarks, through the door of commonplaces, the 'structural simples' embodied by tunes we all learn as children (Bamberger, 1991/1995). These form the scaffolding upon

Figure 4.1 Beethoven, Op. 59 No. 2: first movement (Coda).

which our earliest musical sense-making develops. Of these commonplaces, *Twinkle Twinkle Little Star* is probably the most emblematic—a kind of *ur*-tune. Calling them 'archetypes,' Rosner and Meyer (1982) point out that: '[Archetypes] establish fundamental frameworks in terms of which culturally competent audiences ... perceive, comprehend, and respond to works of art ... they may be and usually are internalized as habits of perception and cognition operating within a set of cultural constraints.' (p. 318).

Composers, listeners, and performers do not *discard* these common cultural organizing constraints, rather complexity is *functionally dependent* on them. For example, in developing a hearing of an unfamiliar and complex work, we initially seek out just these familiar pitch-time relations, only later reconstructing them as features unique to the particular work. Indeed, in developing an appropriate hearing of a complex work, the performer is continuously learning as the piece, itself, develops and learns.

To provide evidence for these conjectures concerning music development and the emergence of musical complexity, I begin with two, closely analysed examples of children working with commonplace tunes, while confronting in real time, the tensions between situational and abstract organizing constraints. The third example shifts to a fully worked out composition—three conflicting hearings of a Beethoven Sonata movement. The differences among the hearings embody tensions among organizing constraints that are seen already in nascent form in the children's work. In doing so, the three hearings illustrate three phases in the course of musical learning and development.

Part II: Tune building

In the first of two examples I return to my previous reports (Bamberger, 1986, 1991/1995, 2005) of research on children building commonplace tunes with the Montessori bells. However, I intend the examples now to illustrate most sparely and unambiguously a fleeting moment in which we see learning and development happening as a child confronts and creatively resolves an emergent tension between organizing constraints.

In working with participants in these task situations I make a beginning assumption: no matter how obscure or confused a child's actions, decisions, or descriptions may seem, there is reason in what he or she has done; it is my job to probe for and to find the sense made. This is particularly important when a participant's observed behaviour seems most anomalous with respect to some deeply embedded musical assumptions. Barbara McClintock, the Noble prize winning biologist, puts it this way in describing her observations of cells: 'Anything ... even if it doesn't make much sense, it'll be there. ... So if the material tells you, "It may be this," allow that. Don't turn it aside and call it an exception, an aberration, a contaminant. ... That's what's happened all the way along the line with so many good clues.' (Quoted in Keller, 1983, p. 179).

To find out and to appreciate what 'the material is [telling] you,' the adult and the child have an advantage over McClintock's cells—they can speak to one another. Thus, teacher/researcher and participant can work together bringing issues to the surface that otherwise might remain hidden, the result being that adult and child could unknowingly pass one another by.

In each example, while the child continues to deal with the same musical material, his behaviour shows him initially invoking situational organizing constraints and subsequently invoking (if only tentatively) abstract, invariant property constraints. Thus, it is not whether or not the child can successfully complete the given task because almost all can, but rather the process through which he or she does so.

Jeff: parallel play

The first example is borrowed from the stories of Jeff in *The mind behind the musical ear* (Bamberger, 1991/1995). The task: given five Montessori bells, build the tune, *Hot Cross Buns*. Nine-year-old Jeff built a bell-path for *Hot Cross Buns* that was typical of young children and even some musically novice adults (Figure 4.2).

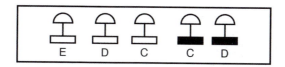

Figure 4.2 *Hot Cross Buns:* bell path.

Characteristic of novice tune-builders, Jeff's focus was on the emerging present situation: he built the tune cumulatively with each bell added as it was needed in order of occurrence in the tune. With the important exception of repeated figures, as well as immediately repeated single pitches, there is a bell standing for and playing each event as it comes along in the tune.

In his performance of *Hot* on the bells, the tune as sounding events, of course continues ever onward in time. But Jeff's action path 'turned back' in space as he played the repeating first figure and later its return. His actions are evidence that through immediate repetition, he implicitly recognized the integrity of motivic groupings, marking them and making them in action, as bounded entities. The structural entities were also spatially marked by the gap Jeff made between bells separating the middle figure from the beginning and ending figures (Figure 4.3).

To probe and test my understanding of Jeff's focus on groupings and the situational functions of the bells as events within groups, I made an on-the-spot experiment: pointing to the first brown bell in the second group, I asked Jeff if he could find a match for it among the white bells. The matching C-bells were, of course, positioned adjacent to one another but across a spatial and structural divide. I wanted to see if I could provoke Jeff from his current hearing/seeing the bells as situated, functional tune events to seeing/hearing the bells as function-less, position-less, simply property-holding objects. Could Jeff conceive of bells detached from the concrete situation in which they were embedded?

In response to my request, Jeff played the now isolated brown bell, tested and rejected the white E and D bells. Trying the white C-bell, Jeff looked up with an expression of some surprise, and nodded his head in recognition that they sounded the same (Figure 4.4).

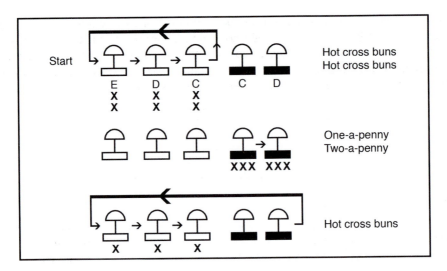

Figure 4.3 Action path: bounded entities.[3]

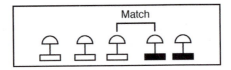

Figure 4.4 A match.

At this point, Jeff was faced with two strategies for giving meaning to the two bells—strategies that I believed were incommensurable:

- *the two bells were different:* situationally, they stood for and played tune events that were unique in their starkly different functions (an ending and a beginning) along the action and bell paths.
- *the two bells were the same:* extracted from their embedded context along the action and bell paths, they were simply objects that 'sounded the same'—they shared the same invisible property, pitch.

To again probe my understanding, I made another on-the-spot experiment, this time to probe further into what seemed an implicit tension between the two disparate meanings. I

---

3   The graphics I have used reveal, in their inadequacy, the difficulties encountered in making a static representation of actions moving through time: There are, of course, only five bells and not 15 as in the picture; the bells, themselves do not 'happen' again; nor in travelling the action path are you able, as in the picture, to see the past, present, and future all at the same time. But how else can one represent 'after' or even 'next' in a flat, two dimensional, fixed printing surface?

asked: 'Well, since those brown and white bells you just played sound the same, I bet you could play HOT without the brown bell since you have a white one that matches it already.'

Jeff paused, then quietly produced a solution that ingeniously dissipated the tension I had presumed and implicitly reconciled the potentially conflicting meanings (Figure 4.5): taking one bell in each hand, *he simply switched their positions!*

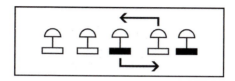

Figure 4.5 Switch.

Jeff's solution to my inquiry suggested multiple organizing constraints in imminent transaction: the comparison task had been successful in helping Jeff extract properties from their functional roles but his ingenious solution allowed him to maintain his strongly held situational stance, as well:

• The two bells were the same thus they could be exchanged; they could stand in for one another.

• The two bells were different thus both bells needed to be present. Each was a stepping stone along the action and tune paths, and each was necessary to performing its unique, situational function in the unfolding of the tune.

I could, of course, have easily seen Jeff's performance in response to my probe as simply an example of confusion or a kind of tease. However, making the assumption that there was reason in Jeff's response, on reflection I recognized it as a potentially generative moment. It was a kind of 'parallel play.' Jeff's invention was also a source for mutual reflection and for further experimenting—the kind of moment that is generative of musical development. (For Jeff's further development, see Bamberger, 1991/1995.)

Conan: double classification

This second example illustrates essential tensions playing out in a quite different context— the work of a gifted violinist who has already achieved significant musical recognition. Ten-year-old Conan was a member of the Young Performers Program, a special programme for musically gifted children in a community music school in Cambridge, Massachusetts. Conan had recently played an impressive performance of a Mozart violin concerto with the school orchestra, and of course read music fluently.

Over a period of 6 months previous to enlisting Conan along with five other young violinists as participants in bell tasks, I attended the children's private violin lessons, chamber music rehearsals, coaching sessions, and sat in on theory classes, orchestra rehearsals, and public performances.

Most memorable in these observations was the persistence with which teachers and coaches encouraged children to shift their focus among what I have called 'fields of attention.' The strategy was in an effort to encourage the children to experiment with playing a passage in differing ways. This, in turn, contributed to the young performers' development of a network of multiple ways of actively understanding, thinking about, and performing a passage, a motive, or even a single note (Bamberger, 1986). In short, the teachers and coaches were nurturing the kinds of transactions that I have suggested are fundamental to musical learning and development. It is not surprising, then, that in Conan's work we see a three-way transaction occurring among possible organizing constraints.

Conan was asked to build *Twinkle Twinkle Little Star* with the Montessori bells. He was given nine bells—the C-Major set plus two Gs and two Cs. It was expected that, given his experience with reading music notation and performing, Conan would begin by simply building the C-Major scale. Indeed, slightly older children in the programme (11–12 year olds) did exactly that. But surprisingly, Conan began just as Jeff and other musically novice children did—cumulatively searching for and introducing bells in order of occurrence as he needed them in building up the tune (Figure 4.6).

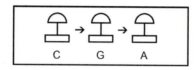

Figure 4.6 In order of occurrence.

However, at the end of the first phrase Conan deviated from this strategy: turning back (left) along his tune-ordered bell path, *he struck the G-bell again* thus giving the same bell dual function in the tune: initially an 'on-the-way, middle event,' the same bell served also as a 'phrase ending.' In contrast, most musical novices of any age continue their initial organizing strategy by simply adding another G-bell, giving it unique function as the ending of the phrase and of the currently cumulating bell-path (Figure 4.7).[4]

Conan's 'turn-back' move, which already suggested his potential for invoking mixed organizing constraints, provoked a moment of direct confrontation between organizers. By turning back (left) to strike the G-bell again, there was no longer a single, ordered series unified by a common direction and chronology in space and time. Conan's bell-path (the sequence of bells in table-space), and the tune-path (the sequence of events unfolding in time) were no longer in direct correspondence.

Moreover, Conan's next move makes clear that his move left also had the implication of 'going down' as if on the piano keyboard.[5] Following this downward momentum of a well-practised scale (A to G), Conan continued this downward move from G onward to the left, obviously expecting to find the F-bell there—the next lower in the scale after G and the bell he needed for the next event in the tune. Instead, he struck the C-bell that was, of course, still there as first-in-tune (Figure 4.8).

Conan's view of the line-up of unmarked bells was transforming and multiple organizing constraints were clearly in confrontation: On hearing the C-bell, Conan hesitated, backed

---

[4] Conan's 'turning back' differs from Jeff's in its function—Jeff's 'turn-back' involved literal repetition of a whole structural element–thus no change in function; Conan's 'turn back' gave new meaning to a single pitch.

[5] Conan, like the other children in the programme, had also played the piano.

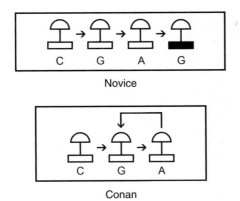

Figure 4.7 The single G-bell is given dual function.

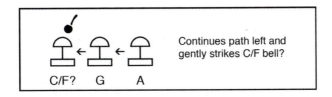

Figure 4.8 Confronting organizing constraints.

off, and swinging his mallet *between* the C and G bells, said, 'Yah, it has to go there'. Opting for the fixed reference scale organizer, the 'it' was clearly the F-bell (Figure 4.9).

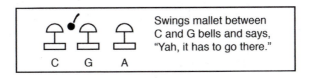

Figure 4.9 Opting for the fixed reference organizer.

In his initial construction, the line-up of bells was a row of uniquely situated, order-of-occurrence tune-events (C-G-A); now, with his critical move 'down,' he saw the same line-up as an ordered pitch series arranged high-to-low, right-to-left.

Pursuing his new view, Conan found an actual F-bell among the remaining, unused bells on the table. Breaking open the tune-ordered bell-path, he moved the C-bell to the left (for 'down'), and inserted the found F-bell in the space he made for it (Figure 4.10).

With this and his next moves, Conan ingeniously resolved the tension between organizing constraints by inventing a scheme that, like Jeff's, invoked both kinds of organizing

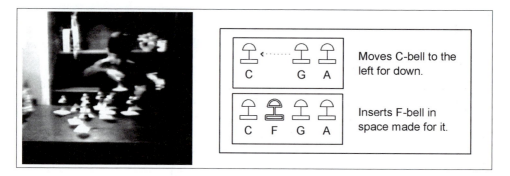

Figure 4.10 Inserts F-bell in the space between C and G.

constraints simultaneously. Using his initial organizer, he continued to add bells to his bell path in order of occurrence (F → E → D). And with his subsequent organizer, the fixed reference scale co-present, he positioned each new bell to the left of the previous one as next lower (D ← E ← F) (Figure 4.11).

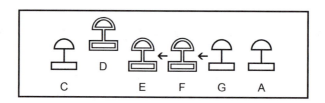

Figure 4.11 Double classification.

Conan had invented a *double classification strategy* that resolved the emergent conflict between situational and abstract organizers. And as a fortuitous function of the 'gap-fill' structure[6] of the melody, the history of Conan's construction mirrored the history of the unfolding tune—an emblematic case of analysis-in-action.

Once the first part of the tune was built with the bell-path now the embodiment of the familiar scale, Conan quickly completed the rest of the tune by simply moving about on it. Indeed, if visitors had come into the room at this point, they might have assumed that Conan had begun his tune construction by first building the C-Major scale.

Demonstrating his experience with musical problem-solving and engaging the complexity of multiple representations, Conan had moved through transactions among three organizing constraints:

- a cumulative bell-path—finding and placing bells to the right as they occurred temporally in the tune;

[6] 'Gap-fill melodies consist of two elements: a disjunct interval—the gap—and conjunct intervals which fill the gap.' (Meyer, 1973, p. 145).

- going 'backward' and 'down' (left in space) to give double function to a single (G) bell; and

- joining order of occurrence in the tune with the fixed reference scale to make a *double classification* organizing scheme.

The other five young violinists at the same moment in the tune construction, the end of the first phrase, confronted much the same conflict among situational and abstract organizing constraints. Probably it was more than chance that the conflict occurred at a structural boundary as it had with Jeff. All of the children also found ingenious ways to resolve the tensions they confronted but each did so in a different and unique way (Bamberger 1986, 2005).

The work of Jeff and Conan could be seen as a spontaneous performance that held generative potential, but only if noticed as such and encouraged. Instances such as these are emblematic occasions for mutual reflection between teacher and student, for drawing out the multiple perspectives and even the tacit analysis implicit in the children's spontaneous actions. For the gifted violinists, such conversations might productively develop into questions such as those that emerged from Soyer's comments: How can they, as performers, benefit from the invariance of pitch notation and still use it as a means for projecting change in functional musical meaning?

Part III: Evolving complexity—three hearings of a Beethoven sonata movement

As the previous examples have shown and as experience tells us, individuals with no formal music instruction spontaneously invoke powerful organizing constraints guiding their apprehension of the familiar music of our culture. In the example that follows, I introduce descriptions of hearings made by three students who are at differing stages in their musical experience. In doing so, I return to some of the questions that motivated this essay: What characterizes the organizing constraints at different phases in musical development? What do we take to be 'progress' and how is 'progress' related to experience and training? In turn, how are these factors related to notions of musical complexity—in the unfolding of a developing composition, and in developing a 'hearing' and a performance of it, as well?

Accounts of the students' diverse hearings of the Beethoven Sonata movement are not verbatim transcripts as the previous examples were, but rather an amalgam of many that I have heard over the years: Clem is typical of those who have had no formal music instruction. Peter's hearing is most like those who have recently completed a general music class in high school but who do not play an instrument. Anya represents the most experienced student, one who has taken a high school music theory class, and as a pianist, has actually performed the Beethoven Sonata movement.

I want to emphasize, as I have with the previous examples, that despite their differences, each description reflects a focus on real, possible, and legitimate features of the music—those that contribute to the coherence that each student has made. At the same time, the scenario is intended to demonstrate the distinctive aspects that characterize hearings at different phases during a process in which learning and development are interactively joined.

After listening to a performance of the movement played twice (with repeats), the students were asked simply to 'tell me what you heard in the piece.' The score was available for the students but only as a reference for those who could use it to check out disagreements. (Bar numbers are inserted for the convenience of the reader) (Figure 4.12).

Clem

I heard three parts in the piece. In the first part I heard the same tune most of the time (bars 1–16). Then, after what seems to be an argument going on, another tune starts that sounds different, sadder. The argument seems to get resolved, here, but not happily. This new sad tune makes up the second part (bars 20–25). Then the first part comes back again much like it was at the beginning (bars 33–44). After that, something else happens, but I'm not sure what. Then the sad, second tune comes back followed by the first part again. So, as I said, there are really three parts—the second one is different and the first and third are alike. Or you could say that there are just two parts, if what you are counting are *kinds* of things.

Peter

My hearing is quite different from Clem's. I heard three parts, as well, but they aren't the same three parts. For instance, as the piece is a minuet or scherzo its in 3/4 time, and as I expected, it turns out to have the typical minuet form (he draws):

$$\| : A : \| : B + A' : \|$$

The A section has two phrases, both the same length, the whole A section is in the major mode.

The B section is a development (bars 9–33). It begins with a change in key and there are several more key changes. What Clem called the new tune isn't a new section at all. It comes in the middle of this development section, and its in the minor mode. Maybe that's why he heard it as sadder.

The third part, 'A',' ends with a short coda and then B + A' is repeated exactly. Its interesting that Clem was able to hear the return to A' and the repeat of his 'sad tune,' so I don't understand why he didn't hear that the whole B and A' sections are just repeated, exactly.

Anya

Well, I'd say that Peter stopped where my hearing begins. I also heard those three large parts, but its how Beethoven creates them that I'm paying most attention to—at least when I'm playing. For instance, the little motive right at the beginning. (*Anya plays opening motive*) (Figure 4.13.)

Beethoven plays with that opening motive through the whole movement, transforming it to change its role as the piece goes along. For instance, there is one place that I find particularly amazing—the transformations Beethoven makes as he gets into what Clem called the 'sad tune.'

Figure 4.12 Beethoven Sonata, Op 2, No. 2 (Scherzo).

Figure 4.13 Opening motive.

Remember, at the beginning of the development, we heard those two balanced phrases where Beethoven switches registers—the opening tune switches from the right hand to the left hand (plays bars 9–16). Well, in going on, Beethoven really disrupts the evenness of those phrases as he moves very quickly through a four-step series of transformations while heading for Clem's sad tune.

Right at the end of the second phrase, he takes just its last two notes—an accented note and a weak-beat ending (bar 16); he then moves this two-note little fragment down a little and uses it to form a stand-alone, two-note hanging fragment still ending on a weak beat (bar 17). Then, third, in a kind of slight-of-hand, he extends the two-beat beginning accented figure into a three-beat end-accented figure (bar 19) that feels like a resolution—an arrival at momentary stability (plays bars 16–19) (Figure 4.14).

Figure 4.14 A series of transformations.

But instead of letting you stop there, Beethoven, in a fourth step, takes the rhythm of that three-beat, now end-accented fragment, and playing it as three repeated notes, turns it into the head of the new 'sad tune.' So, in a way, it isn't a new tune at all; its simply the last in this series of transformations (plays bars 18–23) (Figure 4.15).

Its really hard to play that passage, by the way: after what seems like a stop, a resolution, you have to quickly go on, shift into a very different mood and a different tune, slow down, and at the same time make it feel like a continuing development.

Figure 4.15 The head of the new sad tune.

Clem: When you hear the sad tune that was where I had the feeling that the argument was resolved, right?

Anya: Yes, and it's partly because for the first time there's a melody with a clear accompaniment, and a clear phrase boundary (plays bars 20–23) (Figure 4.16).

Figure 4.16 Clear phrase boundary.

Peter: But still, that so-called sad tune is not a new section; it's just a part of the development or B section.

Anya: Of course, but you're focusing on the piece as an example of a type, collapsing its unique details into this prototype so you can say, 'Oh yeah, it's one of those.' It reminds me of something I read in a book by Polya called *How to Solve It*: 'This principle is so perfectly general that no particular application of it is possible.'

Peter: Well, I think it's important to hear the piece as an example of a type, too. After all, you couldn't even talk about *unique details* if you didn't have the general scheme in your head already.

Anya: O.K. but what about the return of A? It's not just that the first part comes back again, but rather the *way* Beethoven gets there. He makes the transition to the return by taking that same, end-accented, repeated three note motive that forms the head of the new tune, tosses it around and shortens it until it disappears into silence. And out of this tense silence the opening motive reappears just like it was in the beginning. But, you know, when I play the opening motive here, it always sounds different to me. I guess it's because so much has happened to it along the way (plays bars 27–36) (Figure 4.17).

Peter: I think you're making too much of this transformation business, just look at the score!

Figure 4.17 The return of A.

Anya: I suppose I hear the return as both the same and as different; but the same notes in a new context, a new situation, sound different to me. And I think I play it differently, too. As for the coda, all of a sudden it seems like we're in duple meter instead of triple (plays bars 41–44). As a result, you get the feeling that the whole thing speeds up to a running finish (Figure 4.18).

Figure 4.18 The coda.

Peter: Besides, can you really *hear* all that or are you just making a lot of it up? And another thing: are you going to tell me that Beethoven knew he was doing all that transformation while he was writing the piece?

Anya: There's no way we'll ever know; and what difference would it make anyhow? It's how *we* hear the finished product that's the point.

Clem: But do you really need to go into all that detail to play the piece?

Anya: Actually, in truth, when I'm learning a piece and when I'm playing it, it's all in experimenting with how it sounds as I listen back, and how the piece feels in my hands. I never actually said any of those things out loud before, or even to myself, for that matter. It was really interesting trying to put it into words.

Revisiting the Scherzo

The three hearings of the Beethoven movement were meant to be, first of all, a view-in-action of my argument that a hearing is itself, a *performance*: what each student believes he or she simply found in the music is, instead, an active process of making sense guided by the organizing constraints that each has available and/or has brought to bear. Keeping in mind that these were amalgams of typical students' reports, what, then, are the salient differences in the aspects that students with differing musical backgrounds attend to? How are these different foci influenced by learning and experience? What does this tell us about emergent organizing constraints and their relation to musical development?

The three students' different hearings of similarity or difference produced the most telling arguments. Clem, as is typical of musically novice students, focused on 'tunes'; as evidence, the same tune in a different register at the beginning of the B section was not a difference that made a difference for Clem. Anya, typifying an experienced performer, does single out the change in register as a salient feature, taking the contrast to mark the beginning of a new section. Peter, more typical of a musically 'schooled' good student, also heard the passage as different from the opening, but selected change of key as the significant feature.

Most important, the students' differing hearings of similarity or difference as influenced by their preferred objects of attention, in turn influenced their hearings of *structural boundaries*. These influences were clear in this first example, and continued throughout their descriptions of the larger design.

For instance, Clem, in contrast to Peter, failed to hear the literal repeat of the beginning of the B section after the Coda. Hearing literal repeats is a common problem among novice students. In a classroom situation, for example, it is tempting to say that Clem and others who fail to hear literal repeats, are simply getting it wrong or have 'poor ears.' Students, themselves, when asked to account for their 'mis-perception,' will often attribute it simply to 'bad memory.' But if it were simply a question of 'bad memory,' how can we account for why a novice student like Clem has no trouble remembering the 'sad tune' when it is played again and also the return to A when it occurs again? As it turns out these are critical issues for musical development.

Bartlett (1932), in his seminal book, *Remembering*, has taught us that *what* we remember, and thus what we are able to recognize as the same when it occurs again, depends upon *how* we have made sense of the phenomena in the first place, and particularly *when* it occurred—in what context. Memory, then, rather than being a kind of simple recording device, which is sometimes defective, might better be construed as a process of active re-construction. Bartlett says: 'Every incoming change contributes its part to the total 'schema' of the moment *in the order in which it occurs*. . .so in order to maintain the 'schema' as it is, it must continue to be done in the same order.' (p. 201).

Bartlett emphasizes the importance of an event occurring in the same chronological order if we are to recognize it as the same when it occurs again. The differences in the way the three passages in question occur when they are literally repeated provides good evidence for Bartlett's claim. Clem recognizes the reappearance of the two events that occur in exactly the same order: the sad tune (bar 20) and the A section (bar 33). However, Clem does not recognize the literal repeat of the passage with which the B section occurs. Following Bartlett's theory, this is not surprising as the passage does not occur in the same order or in the same situation as in its initial occurrence: the repeat of B begins after material that is new and different from its initial appearance after A and it occurs without any interruption or preparation. In contrast, the repeat of both the sad tune and A appear not only in the same chronological order, but after the preparation by an unstable, fragmented transition passage out of which they emerge as an arrival at welcomed stability. Chronological order is, then, another example of a constraint that guides the construction of meaning.

IV: Comparative cultures

Let me propose, now, that it is useful to look at the participants' responses in the task situations as anthropologists might look at the behaviour of individuals belonging to different cultures. For instance, in considering the issue of boundary making, or 'segmentability,' the ethnomusicologist, Agawu (1999) says: 'The issue of music's physical segmentability is less interesting ... than what might be called its cultural segmentability. To segment culturally is to draw on a rich culturally specific body of formal and informal discourses in order to determine a work's significant sense units. Such units are not neutrally derived; nor are they value-free.' (pp. 142–143).

Following Agawu, we might think about the disagreements among the students with respect to their hearings of structural boundaries or 'segmentability' in the Scherzo as arising from the students' membership in different 'developmental cultures.' This would be a way of viewing their perceptual disagreements in terms, for instance, of ontology (what each is taking to exist), along with their belief systems, values, and preferences. For instance, Peter favoured invariant structural 'types or schemes,' over Anya valuing transformations and the changing meanings they entrain.

Or we might even consider our professional culture and the beliefs it holds with respect to our experience of music moving through time. For example, once having learned to respond to the sign :‖ as if by a conditioned reflex, we easily wipe out the fact that while this is an instruction for the performer to 'turn back' in the score, within the culture of the novice listener, music like time, can never 'turn back.'

Indeed, 'going back' in pitch-space while 'going on' in time harks back to Conan's confrontation (can we say 'culture conflict?') between his initial order of occurrence, situational construction and his abrupt shift to an abstract, scale-oriented focus. Conan's confrontation revealed his ability to engage multiple organizers that Peter, within his schooled culture and his belief in the playing out of the 'typical minuet form,' seemed reluctant to do. Perhaps these cultural confrontations should serve as a reminder that, within our culture of knowledgeable musicians, we may sometimes be impoverishing our more educated hearings.

But continuing the anthropological stance, we should be attentive to the values of schooled culture and the organizing constraints they entrain, as well—learning to classify, and to name invariant properties, relations, and forms. These are organizing constraints that Peter had learned to value and to use in his performances as listener. These learned constraints make it possible for him to recognize the same properties occurring again even out of context, and to generalize his knowledge of form given a new instance of a type. And this learning was also what made it possible for Soyer to notice and respond in his playing to the remarkable shifts in meaning that the same notated pitch could undergo; it would have been unremarkable if he had not been able to recognize that, indeed, it was the same pitch.

Learning and knowledge *about* music, can take different forms, be put to different uses, result in different hearings, and can be seen as evidence of developmental progress or not depending on the theories to which you ascribe and the cultures to which you belong.

V: Finale

At the outset of this essay I confessed the need to re-think some of my earlier views about musical development. I mentioned that I had underplayed observed anomalies and enigmas that are often more telling with respect to development, and I had stopped too soon—specifically, before asking, for instance, what might we mean by *musical complexity?*

While I have addressed these matters through emphasizing the tensions among organizing constraints and argued that such tensions are essential to learning and development, there is another particularly contentious issue that has been lurking behind much of the discussion thus far: Is 'development' to be differentiated from 'learning,' or are development and learning dependent on one another, continuously evolving together? Vygotsky (1978) is clearly on the latter side of this debate. He states:

> The conception of maturation as a passive process cannot adequately describe complex [developmental] phenomena. Any psychological process, whether the development of thought or voluntary behaviour, is a process undergoing changes right before one's eyes. The development in question can be limited to only a few seconds, or even fractions of seconds. . .one can, under laboratory conditions, provoke development (as is the case in normal perception). It can also (as in the case of complex mental processes) last many days and even weeks. (p. 19)

In analysing the work of the participants (real or derived), it should be clear that, influenced by Vygotsky, I view learning and development as instrumentally interactive—a single system. I have ascribed to the notion that . . . *one can, under laboratory conditions, provoke development.* Most specifically, during the tune building tasks that Jeff and Conan carried out (probably due particularly to the novelty of the bell materials) we were able to see tensions among organizing constraints leading to moments of musical development occurring right before our eyes.

What then, are the educational implications if learning and development are seen as inextricably intertwined? I propose that we should notice and appreciate organizing constraints such as those of Jeff and Clem that are naturally acquired through familiarity with the commonplaces of our culture and not be tempted to *turn them aside and call them an exception, an aberration, a contaminant.* On this view, if students are helped from the beginning to reflect on and value their hearings, including the puzzles and conflicts that might emerge, they are more likely to build on rather than forego their musical intuitions. In doing so, they are more likely to gain Anya's capacity to embrace conflicts, to make multiple hearings, and perhaps after passing through a stage such as Peter's schooled culture, learn to choose selectively among possibilities depending on when, where, and what for.

So, as educators and as researchers, rather than arguing about what counts as progress in the course of musical development and what determines a hearing that counts as better than another, it seems more productive to follow the view of Clifford Geertz (1973), the cultural anthropologist, who proposes that '. . . progress is marked less by a perfection of consensus than as a refinement of debate. What gets better is the precision with which we vex one another' (p. 29).

Looking onward and outward from this reflective turn, progress is potentially inherent, then, in our experience of each new hearing and each new performance if we engage them as unique encounters and if each of their inevitable puzzlements is seriously embraced.

> *Artur Schnabel*: I am quite content to be one-sided. . . . I love those works which never cease to present new problems and therefore are an ever-fresh experience.
>
> cited in Saerchinger (1957, p. 309)

> *Roger Sessions*: I would prefer by far to write music which has something fresh to reveal at each new hearing than music which is completely self-evident the first time, and though it may remain pleasing makes no essential contribution thereafter.
>
> cited in Prausnitz (2002, p. vii)

References

Agawu, K. (1999). The challenge of semiotics. In N. Cook & M. Everist (eds), *Rethinking Music* (pp. 138–160). Oxford University Press: Oxford.

Aristoxenus (*c*.300 BC). *The Harmonic elements*. In O. Strunk (ed., 1950), *Source readings in music history: Antiquity and the middle ages* (pp. 27–31). New York: W.W. Norton & Co.

Bamberger, J. (1986). Cognitive issues in the development of musically gifted children. In R. J. Sternberg & J. E. Davidson (eds), *Conceptions of giftedness* (pp. 388–413). Cambridge: Cambridge University Press.

Bamberger, J. (1991/1995). *The mind behind the musical ear*. Cambridge, MA: Harvard University Press.

Bamberger, J. (2005). How the conventions of music symbol systems shape musical perception. In D. Miehl, J. Macdonald, & D. Hargreaves (eds), *Musical communication* (pp. 143-170). Oxford: Oxford University Press.

Barlett, F. C. (1932). *Remembering: A study in experimental and social psychology*. Cambridge: Cambridge University Press.

Blum, D. (1986). *The art of quartet playing: The Guarneri quartet in conversation with David Blum*. New York: Alfred A. Knopf.

Geertz, C. (1973). *The interpretation of cultures*. New York: Basic Books.

Gordon, E. E. (1979). *Primary measures of music audiation*. Chicago, IL: G.I.A.

Hasty, C. (2000) Music's evanescence and the question of time after structuralism. In M. P. Soulsby & J. T. Fraser (eds), *Time: Perspectives at the millenium* (pp. 97–109). Westport CT: Bergin & Garvey.

Keller, E. F. (1983). *A feeling for the organism: The life and work of Barbara McClintock*. New York: W. H. Freeman & Co.

Krumhansl, C. L. (1990). *The cognitive foundations of musical pitch*. Oxford: Oxford University Press.

Prausnitz, F. (2002) *Roger Sessions: How a 'difficult' composer got that way*. New York: Oxford University Press.

Rosner, B. S. & Meyer, L. B. (1982). Melodic processes and perception of music. In D. Deutch (ed.), *The Psychology of music* (pp. 317–340). New York: Academic Press.

Saerchinger, C. (1957). *Artur Schnabel*. New York: Dodd, Mead & Co.

Seashore, C. E. (1938/1967). *Psychology of music*. New York: Dover Publications, Inc.

Shuter-Dyson, R. (1982). Musical ability. In D. Deutch (ed.), *The Psychology of music*, (pp. 391–412). New York: Academic Press.

Stravinsky, I. (1947). *Poetics of Music*. Cambridge, MA: Harvard University Press.

Strunk, O. (1950). *Source readings in music history.* New York: W. W. Norton.

Vygotsky, L. (1978). *Mind in society: the development of higher psychological processes* (M. Cole, *et al.* (eds). Cambridge, MA: Harvard University Press.

Zimmerman, M. (1971). *Musical characteristics of children: From research to the music classroom.* Reston, VA: Music Educators National Conference.

CHAPTER 5

MUSICALITY

SUSAN HALLAM

What do we mean by musicality?

There is no consensus among academics regarding the meaning of the term 'musicality'. An objective source, the *Oxford Dictionary*, refers to it as the state of being 'musical', which, in turn, is defined as being fond of, or skilled in, music. The adjective 'musical' is often attached to a range of other terms, for example, ability (defined as capacity or power), aptitude (natural propensity or talent), talent (a special aptitude or faculty), and potential (coming into being or action, latent). In the literature these terms are often used interchangeably, although there has been a tendency for the term 'musicality' to be adopted in considerations of whether being musical is a species-specific characteristic of human beings. This involves speculation about the evolutionary basis of musical behaviour (see, for instance, Hodges, 1996) and consideration of evidence that examines whether the neural structures that facilitate the perception and appreciation of music and the development of musical skills are universal. Other terms tend to be adopted when individual differences in musical skills are considered.

Musical ability, often, although not exclusively, is used to refer to the current level of musical skills that an individual exhibits whether acquired through genetic inheritance or learning, while aptitude, talent, and potential tend to refer to musical skills perceived to be based on inherited factors. There are no universally agreed definitions of these terms. Their meanings are constructed by each author who adopts them and reflect the cultural, political, economic, and social factors pertaining in that place, at that time (Blacking, 1971). For instance, in the Western world, historically, studies of musical ability have focused on the development of tests to assess potential for engaging in music. These determined musical opportunities for children in the same way that tests of intelligence determined general educational opportunities. In this chapter the terminology adopted will reflect that of the research to which it refers.

The development of testing of musicality

The development of the testing of musicality, at the time more usually referred to as 'musical ability', paralleled the development of the testing of intelligence. In the early and mid-twentieth century, there was an assumption that individuals were endowed with different levels of 'intelligence' that were genetically based, relatively immutable and unchanging. Early tests, to identify those children who truly 'were unable to profit from the instruction given in ordinary schools' and would benefit from remedial education (Binet & Simon, 1916/1973, p. 9) were age normed. Stern (1912/1965) developed these procedures further to enable a single measure of intelligence to be arrived at for any individual regardless of their age—the Intelligence Quotient (IQ) (mental age divided by chronological age). This marked the beginning of what has come to be known as the psychometric approach to the study of intelligence. Within this tradition, procedures for test construction and statistical analysis were developed and refined. These were then used as the basis for factor analysis, which was used to explore the underlying nature of intelligence. The number of factors identified varied depending on the particular tests, samples and analyses adopted. In some studies, a single general intelligence emerged, in others a single main factor with other 'special' abilities, and in others as many as 120 separate factors were identified (Gardner *et al.*, 1996). During this early period, as now, there was intense debate about the nature of intelligence.

The first test of musical ability was developed in 1883 by Carl Stumpf, who suggested a number of simple tests that music teachers might undertake to select pupils. These proved successful in discriminating between experienced musicians and self-confessed unmusical students and heralded the tradition of musical ability testing (Shuter-Dyson & Gabriel, 1981) (see Table 5.1 for details of the major tests of musical aptitude from 1919 of 1982). Seashore *et al.* (1960) believed that musical ability was a set of loosely related basic sensory discrimination skills, which had a genetic basis and would not change over time except for variation due to lapses of concentration. He did not believe that subtest scores should be combined to give a single measure of musical ability, but rather that a profile should be obtained that could be divided into a number of clearly defined characteristics that were unrelated to each other. These were pitch, loudness, rhythm, time, timbre, and tonal memory. This conception contrasted with that of Wing, who believed in a general ability to perceive and appreciate music rather than a profile. The Wing Standardized Tests of Musical Intelligence (1981) include seven elements, three involving ear acuity (chord analysis, pitch, and melodic memory), and four that assessed appreciation of music (rhythm, harmony, intensity, and phrasing). Revesz (1953) produced a more extensive battery of tests and

Table 5.1 The major tests of musical aptitude 1919–1982 (derived from Hodges & Haack, 1996).

Measures of musical ability	Dates of original measures and revisions
Seashore measures of musical talents	1919, 1925, 1939, 1956, 1960
Kwalwasser–Dykema music tests	1930, 1954
Wing Standardized Tests of Musical Intelligence	1939, 1948, 1957, 1960, 1961, 1981
Gretsch–Tilson musical aptitude test	1941
Test of Musicality (Gaston)	1942, 1950, 1956, 1957
Kwalwasser music talent test	1953
Musical aptitude profile (Gordon)	1965
Measures of musical abilities (Bentley)	1966
Primary measures of audiation (Gordon)	1979
Intermediate measures of audiation (Gordon)	1982

adopted the term 'musicality' to denote the ability to enjoy music 'aesthetically', which was assessed by establishing the depth to which a person could listen to and comprehend the artistic structure of a composition. Later authors sought to produce material that would be more relevant to actual musical activities. Drake (1957) devised a test of musical memory where a melody had to be recognized from a selection that varied because of change of key, time or notes. In the United Kingdom, Bentley (1966) devised the Measures of Musical Abilities, which tested pitch discrimination, tonal memory, chord analysis, and rhythmic memory. These were combined into a single score.

More recent developments have acknowledged that any measure of musicality can only be considered within prevailing musical cultural norms. Karma (1985) suggests that musical aptitude is the ability to structure acoustic material, sense of tonality, rhythm, and harmony each seen as cultural-specific reflections of a general structuring ability. Gordon (1979) used the term 'audiation' to describe the ability to give meaning to what is heard. He identified five stages of audiation. The first two, perceiving and giving meaning to the sound through tonal and rhythmic patterns, for him, constituted musical aptitude. In stages 3–5, the listener asks what they have just heard, where they have heard it and what they will hear next. These stages assess achievement. Gordon has developed a series of tests which cover age ranges from pre-school to adulthood: Audie, a test for 3–4-year-old children (Gordon, 1989b), the Primary Measures of Musical Audiation for children aged 4–8 years (PMMA, Gordon, 1979); the Intermediate Measures of Musical Audiation for children from 5 to 11 (IMMA, Gordon, 1982); the Music Aptitude Profile for Children and Adults (11 years and older) (Gordon, 1965); and the Advanced Measures of Musical Audiation, which is used for entrance into higher education music courses (AMMA, Gordon, 1989a).

The most recent development in musical ability testing reflects the technological advances of the latter half of the twentieth century. Individualized computer-based systems assess the recognition of change in synthesizer-produced melodies of four to nine notes in length, which become increasingly more difficult. The tests allow for individual speed of responding increasing validity and reliability (Vispoel & Coffman, 1992; Vispoel, 1993) through minimizing the reliance on the general cognitive processing skills needed to perform well on earlier tests (Doxey & Wright, 1990).

The rationale underlying all of these tests is that 'musicality' has its basis in aural perception. The individual is a passive respondent to, rather than an active maker of, music. While alternative, more active, measures of selecting pupils for learning to play an instrument have been adopted by teachers, these have tended not to be formalized. Perhaps the most common of these has been selection based on the child's ability to sing. However, the relationship between developmental tonal aptitude and use of the singing voice may be very small (Rutkowski, 1996). Singing in tune seems to be more related to motor response schema and can be improved by training where knowledge of results is given (Welch *et al.*, 1989). Other active measures include tests of musical performance (Watkins & Farnum, 1954). However, these have tended to be conceptualized as tests of achievement rather than aptitude or potential.

Historically, the measurement of musicality has been focused on a narrow range of aural perceptual skills perceived as 'internal' to the individual paralleling the types of testing used to measure intelligence. In recent years, changes in society, brought about by technological advances, have led to a global need for a more highly educated work force with a wider range of skills, cognitive and social. This, alongside increased concern in at least some societies with issues of equity, has meant that narrow definitions of intelligence that focus solely on logical reasoning and assume a stable and inherited single entity are no longer appropriate.

Modern conceptions of the nature of intelligence

Modern theories of intelligence share the view that it is complex and multifaceted. They all take much greater account of the environment and the way that the individual adapts to it, and acknowledge the importance of the context of learning. However, they vary in the extent to which they develop and emphasize different aspects. The pioneers of this work were Gardner (1983/1993) and Sternberg (1985, 1988, 1996). Each proposes multiple intelligences, although the basis for these is very different.

The only theory that identifies music as an identifiable intelligence is Gardner's theory of multiple intelligences (1983/1993). The latest version of his work (1999) proposes nine separate intelligences: linguistic, logico-mathematical, spatial, musical, bodily-kinaesthetic, interpersonal, intrapersonal, naturalist, and spiritual/existential. The last of these is suggested tentatively as Gardner proposes a number of criteria that he believes should be satisfied before the existence of a particular intelligence can be justified. These are potential isolation by brain damage, the existence of prodigies and other exceptional individuals, an identifiable core operation or set of operations, a distinctive developmental history, along with a definable set of expert end-state performances, an evolutionary history and evolutionary plausibility, support from experimental psychological tasks, support from psychometric findings, and susceptibility to encoding in a symbol system. Gardner believes that intelligences are educable—the result of a constant interaction among biological and environmental factors—potentials that will or will not be activated depending on the values of a particular culture, the opportunities available in that culture and the personal decisions made by individuals and their families (Gardner, 1999). The theory suggests that we each have a unique blend of intelligences that leads to variation in our performance on a range of skills. Gardner also stresses that there is a distinction between an individual's preferences for materials, intelligences and their capacities in these spheres (Gardner, 1999, p. 81), a point that will be returned to later in discussing the relevance of this work to understanding expert musical end-states.

Gardner's theory has particularly resonated with educators and been influential in supporting the need for a broad curriculum in schools to facilitate the development of all of the 'intelligences'. It has also fostered an interest in inter- and intrapersonal intelligences and their importance in our functioning in everyday life, leading to the theorizing of 'emotional' intelligence (see for example, Goleman, 1996).

In contrast to Gardner, Sternberg's (1985) triarchic theory conceptualizes intelligence in terms of a series of subtheories. The first, the componential subtheory is concerned with the internal functioning of individuals when they think intelligently, for instance, by analysing, judging, evaluating, comparing, and contrasting. This subtheory is closely related to the psychometric approach to studying intelligence. The second subtheory, the experiential subtheory is concerned with the way that experience affects an individual's intelligence and conversely how intelligence affects the kinds of experiences an individual has. The final subtheory, the contextual subtheory considers intelligence in relation to the culture and environment of the external world, that is how a person's interactions in the world affect his or her intelligence and how that intelligence affects the world in which she or he lives.

Both of these theories have had enormous impact on the way that intelligence is conceptualized. For instance, Ceci (1990) acknowledges that his bio-ecological theory owes much to the work of Sternberg. He, like Sternberg, outlines the importance of information processing, experience, and context, but he places much greater emphasis on the latter, including motivational forces, the social and physical environment or task, the subject domain in which the task is embedded and its impact on complex problem solving. He emphasizes the key role that knowledge plays in understanding individual differences echoing findings from the study of expertise (see Chi *et al.*, 1988). Basic low-level mental processing is seen to enable the acquisition of knowledge, while that processing itself is affected by that knowledge. In other words ability is merely a reflection of what the individual has learnt in the past—knowledge and ability are viewed as fundamentally inseparable. Ceci also argues against the notion of a single underlying intelligence and claims that there are multiple cognitive potentials that have a biological basis. Cognitive potentials, context, and knowledge are interwoven in such a way that it is not possible to analyse environmental contributions separately from the biological contributions to intellectual functioning. They are in a constant state of symbiosis (Ceci *et al.*, 1990).

Two major theories, those of Anderson (1992) and Demetriou (1993; Demetriou & Valanides, 1998) attempt to address the relationships between intelligence and cognitive development. Anderson, in contrast to other theorists adopts a narrow focus on information processing. He details what he calls a minimum cognitive architecture and provides a framework for explaining how cognitive abilities increase, how individual differences remain stable with development, how abilities covary, and why there are specific cognitive abilities and universal abilities. In contrast, Demetriou, also adopting a development approach, conceives the mind as a hierarchical, multisystem and multidimensional universe involving two knowledge levels, one oriented toward the environment, one oriented toward itself. Each level involves several systems, each representing and processing different aspects of the world. At the intersection of these levels there is a processing system that constrains the type and amount of information that can be processed and the efficiency with which it is processed. Because of its multilevel and multisystem nature, the mind develops along multiple paths. Development at different levels or in different systems of mind takes place through different developmental mechanisms. Learning varies across hierarchical levels or systems. So far, seven environmentally oriented systems have been identified, the categorical, the quantitative, the causal, the spatial, the prepositional, the social, and the pictographic. Demetriou does not identify a specific 'musical' system.

All of the theories outlined above acknowledge the importance of learning and see intelligence as educable. However, Perkins (1995), in a theory, which like Gardner's has been embraced by educators, has particularly stressed the importance of learning how to learn. He identifies three broad trends in the kinds of psychological resources people offer to explain differences in intelligence: a neural viewpoint (intelligence with IQ), an experiential viewpoint (knowledge and experience), and a reflective viewpoint (the importance of good mental management). Perkins suggests that learning leading to deep understanding, high levels of retention and the ability to apply knowledge in a wide range of situations arises from thoughtful, active engagement with the content being learned. Learning is argued to require reorganization, which is divided into five broad categories: strategies (strategies that redirect thinking), metacognition (monitoring and directing thinking), dispositions (a tendency in thinking), distributed cognition (use of cultural artefacts, e.g. books, computers, diagrams), and transfer (carrying learning from one context to another) (Goodrich *et al.*, 1998). These all have relevance to the consideration of the development of musical skills.

Before moving on to consider the challenges that have been made to traditional conceptions of musicality, it is worth noting that Western concerns with the nature and measurement of intelligence are not shared universally. In some Eastern cultures, children's attainment is seen to depend on effort not innate ability (Stevenson & Lee, 1990). In those cultures, there has been little concern with issues relating to intelligence and its measurement. This reinforces postmodern discourse, which acknowledges that human thinking is rooted in specific historical and cultural situations, that knowledge is open, ambiguous, and based on different perspectives, and that it is validated through cultural practices (Kvale, 1992).

Recent conceptions of the nature of musicality

In parallel with the challenges to traditional views of the nature of intelligence, the concept of musicality has been severely criticized in recent years. Focusing on the importance of effort, some have proposed that it is time spent practising that underpins the development of expert performance, not inherited ability. Ericsson *et al.* (1993) suggested a monotonic relationship between 'deliberate practice' and an individual's acquired performance, a relationship supported by Sloboda *et al.* (1996) who, comparing five groups of young musicians of different capabilities, found greater levels of practice at all ages from the 'best' group, increasing over time to lead to large cumulative differences. Interviews with the parents of these children revealed that singing by the child at an early age was the only sign that distinguished those children who later succeeded in being accepted by a high status music school. These results reinforce the practice explanation (Howe *et al.*, 1995). However, not all the evidence is supportive. Sloboda and Howe (1991) found that students identified as having greater ability by their teachers had undertaken less practice in their main instrument, their practice time having been spread more equally across three instruments. Wagner (1975) found that increased practice did not lead to any greater improvement in performance over an 8-week period and Zurcher (1972) found no relationship between total practice time and performance achievement. Reported correlations between achievement and time spent practising also vary considerably and are only moderate (Sloboda *et al.*, 1996). It may be that it is the overall length of time over which learning has taken place rather than the specific amount of practice that is important (Hallam, 1998a, 2004). In addition, skills can be developed through playful practice and playing in groups, not only through deliberate practice. Social factors such as parental support, teacher's personality, and peer interactions have also been shown to be more important than amount of practice time in achieving a high level of musical performance (Moore *et al.*, 2003).

There has also been a tendency in much of this research to neglect the issue of drop-outs— those who may have undertaken extensive practice, been unsuccessful and dropped out. While Sloboda *et al.* (1996) demonstrated that those who had dropped out had undertaken less practice and achieved less than those who continued, in much of the research on drop-outs no single explanatory factor has emerged. Rather a number of factors, including socio-economic status, self-concept in music, reading achievement, scholastic ability, measured musical ability, math achievement, and motivation are all valid predictors of continuing to play a musical instrument (Young, 1971; Mawbey, 1973; McCarthy, 1980; Klinedinst, 1991, Hallam, 1998a). Frakes (1984) found significant differences between musical achievement, academic achievement and attitudes towards musical participation between drop-outs, non-participants, and participants in musical activity. Drop-outs perceived themselves as less musically able, received less family encouragement, tended to feel musically inadequate, and turned to sport and other leisure activities instead of music. Frakes concluded that positive self-perceptions of musical skills were linked to the desire to continue music education voluntarily. Supporting this, Hurley (1995) found that students who dropped out viewed continuing to play as demanding too great a time cost for the relatively small rewards it offered.

When the quality of performance has been considered rather than the level of expertise attained, the amount of practice undertaken is not a good predictor (Hallam, 1998a; Williamon & Valentine, 2000). Hallam (2004) demonstrated that other factors, in particular, teachers' ratings of musical ability, self-esteem, and involvement in extracurricular music activities were better predictors of examination marks than time spent practising. Longer-term outcomes in relation to becoming a professional musician or being involved in music in an amateur capacity were best predicted by self-esteem, self-efficacy, and enjoyment of performing. Professional aspirations were also supported by membership of high-quality performing groups and effective practising strategies. Amateur aspirations were predicted by parental support (Hallam, 2004). Quality of performance seems to depend on complex interactions between the way the musician implements the various skills needed to produce high-quality musical performance and the performing context.

A further issue is that measures of time spent practising do not take account of the effectiveness of the practice undertaken. There are certainly differences in the practising strategies adopted by students and their metacognitive skills, although, as the theories of intelligence discussed earlier indicate their development seems to be inextricably intertwined with the acquisition of knowledge (Hallam, 2001a,b).

Taken together the research suggests that there are complex relationships between prior knowledge, motivation, effort, and perceived efficacy. Motivation, through intermediate processes involving self-esteem and reward may be related to prior knowledge, skills, and expertise. When a child begins to learn an instrument, prior musical knowledge will affect ease of learning and the time needed to achieve mastery of a task. While undertaking additional practice may compensate for lack of prior knowledge, this has a time cost and also requires perseverance. If a task proves challenging the effort required to complete it may be perceived as too great and the individual may give up playing. Such difficulties may be attributed to a lack of musical ability leading to a loss of self-esteem, loss of motivation, less practice, and a downward spiral leading to the termination of lessons (Chandler *et al.*, 1987; Asmus, 1994).

On the basis of a range of evidence, Sloboda (1996) has argued for the deconstruction of musical ability indicating that the 'talent' account of individual differences in musical expressivity should not so much be 'disproved as dissolved into a whole set of complex interacting factors and causes, each of which has its own logic and determining conditions' (p. 123). He and colleagues have argued that the 'talent' conception of musical ability that postulates innately determined differences between individuals in their capacity for musical accomplishment is 'folk psychology' (Sloboda *et al.*, 1994). Findings from a survey that indicated that more than 75% of a sample of educational professionals believed that playing an instrument, singing, and composing required a special gift or natural talent supports this argument (Davis, 1994).

Others have also recognized the contribution of a wide range of skills to musical attainment. In 1979, Gilbert devised tests of motor skills, performance on which was highly correlated with musical attainment (Gilbert, 1981). The importance of creativity in music has been acknowledged and ways of assessing it devised (Vaughan, 1977; Webster, 1988), the evidence suggesting that generally, musical creativity factors seemed to be discrete from those assessed by musical ability tests (Swanner, 1985). In relation to instrumental playing, McPherson (1995, 1996) identified five distinct skills: sight reading; performing rehearsed music; playing from memory; playing by ear, and improvising, while Hallam (1998b) suggested that 'musical skills' included aural, cognitive, technical, musicianship, performance, and learning skills. There has also been an increasing acknowledgement that individual musicians have differing strengths and weaknesses within their profile of musical skills.

The social construction of musical ability

Although there have been challenges to the very existence of musical ability in recent years, and some consideration of the need to broaden its conception to explain different musical end-states (Hallam, 1998b), the concept itself has not received the same level of theoretical development as intelligence. However, a number of researchers have explored its conceptualization by different groups in society. Haroutounian (2000) analysed the level of importance attached to particular criteria in identifying musically able children. General behaviours of 'sustained interest' and 'self-discipline' received higher mean responses than music-specific characteristics indicative of music aptitude. A performance assessment scale showed note and rhythmic accuracy rated highest in importance followed by steady rhythmic performance, dynamic contrasts, and technical fluency. Originality received the lowest rating. However, interviews with experts across the musical fields of research, performance, psychology, and education, teachers involved in gifted education programmes and others regularly involved in the identification of gifted children revealed categories of perceptual awareness and discrimination; meta-perception; creative interpretation; behaviour/performance; and motivation. The most decisive factor perceived to determine musical potential in children rested on criteria related to the child's creative expressive involvement in musical activities. This contrasted with the questionnaire survey that found that creativity was found to be an inadequate measure reinforcing the complexity and difficulty of defining and identifying musical potential.

In a series of studies Hallam and colleagues (Hallam & Prince, 2003; Hallam & Shaw, 2003; Hallam & Woods, 2003) explored the conceptions of musical ability held by a cross section of the population including adults and children, musicians and non-musicians, using both qualitative and quantitative research methods. Six categories emerged from the initial qualitative study: aural skills, receptive responses to music; generative activities, the integration of a range of skills, personal qualities, and the extent to which musical abil- · ity was perceived as being learned or inherited. Overall, 28% of the sample mentioned aural skills as indicative of musical ability, 32% included listening and understanding, 24% having an appreciation of music, and 15% being responsive to music. By far the largest response in any category was that musical ability was being able to play a musical instrument or sing (cited by 71% of the sample). This response was highest in children who did not take part in extracurricular music (86%), and adults not involved in education (83%). The integration of a range of skills was cited by 9% of respondents. Personal qualities including motivation, personal expression, immersion in music, total commitment, and metacognition (being able to learn to learn) were cited most by musicians. The findings did not indicate a general conception of musical ability as genetically determined.

Overall, the musicians gave more complex responses, including many more elements in their statements. The category most frequently cited by musicians was shared with other groups in that it focused on being able to sing or play an instrument (56%). This was followed by listening and understanding (47%), emotional expression (41%), having a musical ear (39%), motivation (31%), communication and interpretation (30%), having a sense of rhythm (29%), being able to compose (29%), personal commitment and expression (28%), technical skills (27%), appreciation of music (24%), responsiveness to music (23%), and progression and development (20%).

A follow-up study (Hallam & Shaw, 2003), based on responses to rating scales derived from the qualitative research indicated that musical ability was most strongly conceptualized in relation to rhythmic ability, organization of sound, communication, motivation, personal characteristics, integration of a range of complex skills and performing in a group. Having a musical ear came lower in the list than might have been expected given its prominent position with regard to musical ability historically (see Figure 5.1). The conception of rhythm as being most important may reflect its central role in much popular music. No statistically significant differences were found between respondents from different groups in relation to the total scores for musical ear; rhythmic ability; listening and understanding; response to music; being able to play a musical instrument or sing; being able to read music; metacognition or relating to the origins of musical ability. Significant differences were found in relation to all the other categories. Musicians expressed the strongest agreement that musical ability was related to communication, being able to play in a group, emotional sensitivity and the organization of sound indicating that these skills are crucial at the highest levels of expertise.

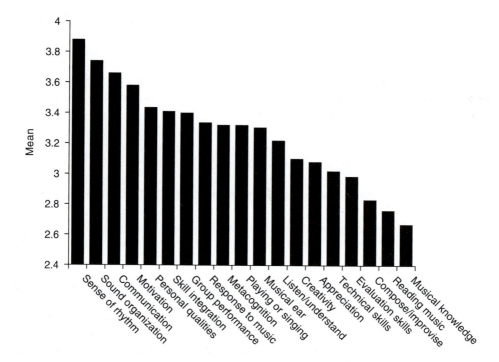

Figure 5.1 Mean ratings of elements of musical ability.

The final study in the series focused on the conceptions of instrumental teachers (Hallam & Woods, 2003) with findings similar to those described above. Most of the teachers (89%) conceptualized the term musical ability to encompass a variety of skills and qualities and believed that musical ability depended on learning and natural aptitude (88%); 81% believed that some pupils had a natural 'talent' for music. Specifically mentioned in relation to this were speed of learning and communication skills. Even where teachers supported the notion of 'natural talent' they accepted that this would not develop without considerable effort. In a similar study, Brandstrom (1999) studied Swedish music teachers' everyday conceptions of musicality. Two major categories evolved: an absolute view suggesting that musicality was biologically inherited and a more relativistic one that assumed equal musical possibilities for everyone. All considered musical attainment to be the result of a mixture of inherited factors and environmental opportunities.

Overall, the conceptions of musical ability generated by this research are complex and multifaceted and reflect the wide range of expert end-states that occur in the music profession. They also bear comparison with the broadening conceptions of intelligence discussed earlier. Key questions that emerge from this line of research concern whether we need to reconstruct our conception of 'musicality', or whether Gardner's theory of multiple intelligences can explain musical learning in relation to its various expert end-states.

Relationships between conceptions of multiple intelligences and musicality

The research exploring people's conceptions of musical ability suggests that for many it is defined by an end-state—being able to play, sing, improvise, or compose. Analysis of the emergent conceptual categories against Gardner's multiple intelligences suggests that most end-states and activities can be accounted for by the operation of other intelligences apart from music. Gardner, himself, acknowledges that for 'what is involved in particular musical tasks, like conducting, performing, or composing music a single construct of "musical intelligence" is far too gross' (Gardner, 1999, p. 103). The end-states of musical intelligence draw on combinations of several intelligences as do all complex activities.

All of the intelligences are implicated in musical activity, although naturalist intelligence, which is concerned with our understanding of the natural world, may only be applied in relation to the making and maintenance of instruments. Spatial intelligence is claimed by Gardner to be relevant in the compositional process and also in the structural analysis of music. Verbal intelligence appears to be linked to labelling skills in relation to notation, identifying the names and styles of music and understanding the historical and cultural frameworks within which music was written and will be performed. There has also been a close relationship between mathematics and music since the time of Pythagoras. In medieval times, and in some non-Western cultures, the study of music has shared many features with the study of mathematics, including an interest in proportions, ratios and recurring patterns. Twelve-tone music, computer-generated and computer-mediated composition has sustained these links. The performance of music, in particular in relation to rhythm also has close links with mathematics. Bodily-kinaesthetic intelligence is involved in the learning and performance of technical skills and intrapersonal skills play an important part in the emotional aspects of performance, in enabling the performer or composer to be self-aware, providing a rich source of emotional material on which to draw in the development of ideas for composition or interpretation. Interpersonal intelligence is important for communicating with an audience and also where musicians need to work together in preparing for performance. Table 5.2 indicates how each intelligence might be implicated at the professional level.

What the theory of multiple intelligences (Gardner, 1999) fails to address is the issue of motivation and commitment to music and the relationship between these, the various intelligences and their end-states. To learn to play an instrument, sing, or compose requires practice and dedication. Those involved in teaching music are very aware of this. For commitment to be sustained, this motivation needs to be generated from within the individual, not derived from external pressures (Hallam, 1998a). Gardner argues that an individual may be motivated in a domain unrelated to his or her abilities in that domain. Individuals may have high levels of measured musical ability and no interest in music or vice versa. However, those who are interested in music and spend more time engaged with it will increase their 'ability'. In addition, lack of progress in learning music and interpretation of this as perceived lack of ability often leads to a reduction in motivation and pupils giving up playing. These findings have important implications for the ways in which pupils are selected to participate in musical activities.

Table 5.2 Gardner's multiple intelligences applied to music.

	Ways that the intelligences might be utilized in music
Logical-mathematical	Analysis, performance, and sight reading of rhythms, analysis of the structure of music, composition
Spatial	Reading of notation, identifying and understanding the structure of music
Bodily-kinaesthetic	Technical skills, movement involved in the communication of interpretation
Intrapersonal	Understanding emotions, drawing on internal emotional resources for developing interpretation, self-knowledge of strengths and weaknesses, metacognition, control of anxiety
Interpersonal	Communication with an audience, teaching, working with other musicians
Linguistic	Reading music, critical analysis of music and performance, understanding the historical and cultural contexts of music
Naturalist	Probably not influential in music performance although the understanding of natural materials is important in the making of instruments and their maintenance
Spiritualist/existential	This may contribute towards the 'emotional' and 'aesthetic' aspects of performance

Gardner also has little to say about the processes involved in the acquisition of musical skills and the way that the various intelligences operate together. His original theory proposed no 'executive' processing system that would co-ordinate, monitor, and evaluate the functioning of the other intelligences, although in response to criticism Gardner has argued that the intrapersonal intelligence takes on this role. The theories of Ceci (1990) and Perkins (1995), with their greater focus on learning, Anderson (1992) and Demetriou (1993), which take account of development changes within and across domains, and research focusing on the development of expertise (Ericsson *et al.*, 1993) may be more helpful in this respect. The challenge is to develop an integrated theory that can take account of the many factors that contribute towards a range of expert musical end-states. Whether this should be framed in relation to music as a single 'intelligence' or should draw on a range of 'intelligences' is a matter for debate.

Is musicality inherited or learned?

Underlying much of the controversy about musicality are questions relating to its origins. There are two debates relating to the heritability of musicality. The first focuses on whether humans as a species have a capacity for music; the second is concerned with individual differences. The two are often confused. In relation to the first debate there is an increasing body of evidence that all humans have the potential to make music and that musicality is as universal as linguistic ability (Messenger, 1958; Blacking, 1971; Wallin *et al.*, 2000). Recent neurological research supports this view suggesting that there are two key elements to musical processing, one concerned with the encoding of pitch along musical scales, and one ascribing regular beat to incoming events. The universal capacity for appreciation of music fits well with the notion of specialized musical structures in the brain that are present and functional early in human development (Peretz, 2003).

The second debate focuses on whether there are genetically determined individual differences in musical ability. This parallels similar debates relating to intelligence. Early studies focused on comparisons of measured musical ability between identical and fraternal twins and other family relationships. The evidence from this research is mixed (Shuter-Dyson & Gabriel, 1981; Shuter-Dyson, 1999; Hodges, 1996; Gardner, 1999). While little recent research has focused specifically on musical ability, it is now accepted that there is a strong environmental influence on measured intelligence. Indeed, this is the only possible explanation for the evidence that IQ scores have risen dramatically in recent years (Flynn, 1987). Advances in research on genetics, to date, have increased our knowledge little in relation to the heritability of intelligence or musical skills. Few human behaviours or traits have been traced to specific gene pairs and it is likely that those who exhibit musical skills are drawing on a range of different gene combinations, which exert an influence on our physical makeup in addition to our cognitive and emotional development. Further, interactive rather than additive models of the relationship between the environment and genetic inheritance are now being proposed (Ceci, 1990) supported by evidence from studies of expertise that demonstrate that the acquisition of knowledge, in itself, affects the efficiency and effectiveness of the processes by which more knowledge is acquired.

This is supported by evidence that the cerebral cortex has an amazing ability to self-organize in response to outside stimuli including music (Rauschecker, 2003). Cortical activation during music processing reflects personal musical experiences accumulated over time. Listening to music, learning to play an instrument, formal instruction, and professional training result in multiple representations of music that seem to be, in part, interchangeable and rapidly adaptive (Altenmuller, 2003). Schlaug (2003) argues that while self-selection for musicianship by individuals with innate functional and structural brain differences cannot be completely ruled out, there is ever increasing evidence that musical training itself leads to changes in brain function and structure. This suggests that whatever genetic inheritance an individual may have is greatly enhanced by a musically enriched environment.

The most difficult phenomenon to explain without resorting to some notion of inherited differences in musicality is the evidence of idiot savants and child prodigies. The former are children whose general cognitive functioning is below normal levels but who nevertheless are able to undertaken some activities, for instance, drawing, calculating calendar dates, playing music, with apparent ease and outstanding skill. The evidence from these children suggests that some cognitive functions operate independently (Sloboda *et al.*, 1985; Young & Nettlebeck, 1995). Miller (1989) asserts that one of the outstanding characteristics of many musical savants was absolute pitch, which enabled some of the savants to make confident and rapid judgement of pitch and complex chords. On some tasks they were able to perform at a similar level to competent adult musicians. They were also sensitive to rules reflecting harmonic relationships and the structure of musical compositions. It is difficult to explain these skills without resorting to genetic explanations, although many of these children have limited sight and language disorders, which may have led to increased development of auditory processing skills and the use of music as a means of communication. They also spend a great deal of time practising their skills, in part because they receive considerable positive reinforcement for their musical expertise. Williams syndrome individuals present another intriguing problem. With IQs typically in the range 65–70, their cognitive asymmetry is caused by a genetic defect (microdeletion on chromosome 7), which normally leaves them very poor at mathematics and spatial reasoning, but more adept than might be expected in relation to language and musical skills, the development of the latter depending on them having appropriate opportunities for acquisition.

There are remarkable similarities between many of the characteristics of the savants and child prodigies. Recently, Ruthsatz and Detterman (2003) reported a case of a musical prodigy who had no formal tuition on an instrument, did no formal practice and had gained his skills by listening to other performers and improvising his own musical pieces. His family had no particular musical background, although his mother played the piano. He could sing in two languages and had taught himself to play numerous instruments. His musical behaviours seemed self-motivated—he engaged in them spontaneously and with pleasure, in particular entertaining people. He spent a great deal of time in playful imitation of other musicians but the improvement in his performance was a by-product of this practice not the product of it. He had extremely high scores on tests of musical ability and intelligence, the latter revealing an extraordinary memory as measured within his cognitive profile. Any theoretical explanations of musical ability need to take account of these factors.

Conclusions

Current methodologies and technologies do not enable us to state beyond doubt whether observed differences in musical ability in children are the sole result of genetic inheritance, learning or an interaction between the two. There is abundant evidence that humans as a species are 'musical', that we share similar brain structures that respond to music, and that exposure to music and engagement with it improve measured musicality. Evidence so far from the study of genetics suggests that there are unlikely to be single genes responsible for any complex behaviours including those relating to music and that differences in musical attainment are likely to depend on complex interactions between a range of skills and experiences that are likely to have an equally complex genetic basis. It may be that we will never be able to establish, beyond doubt, to what extent individual musical ability is learned or inherited. Pragmatically, we should provide all children with opportunities from the earliest age to develop their musical skills. If resources are limited and selection has to be made, interest in music and motivation to engage with it may prove to be better determinants of success than traditional tests of musicality. If motivational criteria are used for selection, the musical skills developed are likely to be well utilized in the long term, in some aspect of musical activity even if it is not what was originally intended. For instance, a child offered an opportunity to play the violin may not become a professional violinist but may become a composer, a music critic, maintain a lasting interest in listening to music or take part in amateur music making in a folk group. What will be sustained over time is the child's interest in music and the use of the particular musical skills that s/he acquired in the musical environment to which s/he was exposed. In a society where it is not possible, or desirable, for everyone to become professionally engaged in music, this is surely the most valuable educational outcome.

References

Altenmuller, E. O. (2003). How many music centres are in the brain? In I. Peretz & R. Zatorre (eds), *The Cognitive neuroscience of music* (pp 346–356). Oxford: Oxford University Press.

Anderson, M. (1992). *Intelligence and development: A cognitive theory.* Oxford: Blackwell.

Asmus, E. P. (1994). Motivation in music teaching and learning. *The Quarterly Journal of Music Teaching and Learning*, 5(4), 5–32.

Bentley, A. (1966). *Measures of musical abilities.* Windsor: NFER-NELSON.

Binet, A. & Simon, T. (1916/1973). *The development of intelligence in children.* (The Binet-Simon Scale) (Elizabeth S. Kite, Trans.) New York: The Arnos Press. (Original work published 1916.)

Blacking, J. A. R. (1971). Towards a theory of musical competence. In E. DeJager (ed.), *Man: Anthropological essays in honour of O.F. Raum.* Cape Town: Struik.

Brandstrom, S. (1999). Music teachers' everyday conceptions of musicality. *Bulletin of the Council for Research in Music Education*, **141**, 21–25.

Ceci, S. J. (1990). *On intelligence ... more or less: a bio-ecological treatise on intellectual development.* Englewood Cliffs, NJ: Prentice Hall.

Ceci, S. J., Ramey, S. L., & Ramey, C. T. (1990). Framing intellectual assessment in terms of a person-process-context model. *Educational Psychologist*, 25(3/4), 269–291.

Chandler, T. A., Chiarella, D., & Auria, C. (1987). Performance expectancy, success, satisfaction and attributions as variables in band challenges. *Journal of Research in Music Education*, 35(4), 249–258.

Chi, M. T. H., Glaser, R., & Farr, M. J. (1988). *The nature of expertise.* Hillsdale, NJ: Lawrence Erlbaum Publishers.

Davis, M. (1994). Folk music psychology. *The Psychologist*, 7(12), 537.

Demetriou, A. (1993). *Cognitive development: Models, methods, and applications.* Thesalonika: Art of Text.

Demetriou, A., & Valanides, A. (1998). A three-level theory of the developing mind: Basic principles and implications for instruction and assessment. In R. J. Sternberg & W. M. Williams (eds), *Intelligence, instruction and assessment: Theory into practice* (pp. 149–199). Mahwah, NJ: Lawrence Erlbaum Associates.

Doxey, C. & Wright, C. (1990). An exploratory study of children's music ability. *Early Childhood Research Quarterly*, 5, 425–440.

Drake, R. M. (1957). *Manual for the Drake musical aptitude tests* (2nd edn). Chicago, IL: Science Research Associates.

Ericsson, K. A., Krampe, R. T., & Tesch-Romer, C. (1993). The role of deliberate practice in the acquisition of expert performance. *Psychological Review*, **100**(3), 363–406.

Flynn, J. R. (1987). Massive IQ gains in fourteen nations: What IQ tests really measure. *Psychological Bulletin*, 101, 171–191.

Frakes, L. (1984). *Differences in music and achievement, academic achievement and attitude among participants, dropouts and non-participants in secondary school music.* PhD Thesis, University of Iowa.

Gardner, H. (1983/1993). *Frames of mind.* London: Fontana Press.

Gardner, H. (1999). *Intelligence reframed: Multiple intelligences for the 21st century.* New York: Basic Books.

Gardner, H., Kornhaber, M. L., & Wake, W. K. (1996). *Intelligence: Multiple perspectives.* New York: Harcourt Brace College Publishers.

Gilbert, J. P. (1979). Assessment of motoric music skill development in young children: Test construction and evaluation procedures. *Psychology of Music*, 7(2), 3–12.

Gilbert, J. P. (1981). Motoric music skill development in young children: A longitudinal investigation. *Psychology of Music*, 9(1), 21–25.

Goleman, D. (1996). *Emotional intelligence: Why it can matter more than IQ.* London: Bloomsbury.

Goodrich Andrade, H. L. & Perkins, D. N. (1998). Learnable intelligence and intelligent learning. In: R. J. Sternberg & W. M. Williams (eds), *Intelligence, Instruction and Assessment: Theory into practice.* Mahwah, NJ: Lawrence Erlbaum Associates.

Gordon, E. E. (1965). *Musical aptitude profile manual.* Boston, MA: Houghton Mifflin.

Gordon, E. E. (1979). *Primary measures of music audiation.* Chicago, IL: GIA.

Gordon, E. E. (1982). *Intermediate measures of music audiation.* Chicago, IL: GIA.

Gordon, E. E. (1989a). *Advanced measures of music audiation.* Chicago, IL: GIA.

Gordon, E. E. (1989b). *Audie: A game for understanding and analysing your child's musical potential.* Chicago, IL: GIA.

Hallam, S. (1998a). The predictors of achievement and drop out in instrumental music tuition. *Psychology of Music,* 26(2), 116–132.

Hallam, S. (1998b). *Instrumental teaching: A practical guide to better teaching and learning.* Oxford: Heinemann.

Hallam, S. (2001a). The development of metacognition in musicians: Implications for education. *The British Journal of Music Education,* 18(1), 27–39.

Hallam, S. (2001b). The development of expertise in young musicians: strategy use, knowledge acquisition and individual diversity. *Music Education Research,* 3(1), 7–23.

Hallam, S. (2004). How important is practising as a predictor of learning outcomes in instrumental music? In S. D. Lipscomb, R. Ashley, R. O. Gjerdingen, & P. Webster (eds), *Proceedings of the 8th International Conference on Music Perception and Cognition, Evanston, IL, 2004.* CD-ROM.

Hallam, S. & Prince, V. (2003). Conceptions of musical ability. *Research Studies in Music Education,* 20, 2–22.

Hallam, S. & Shaw, J. (2003). Constructions of musical ability. *Bulletin of the Council for Research in Music Education,* 153/4, 102–107.

Hallam, S. & Woods, C. (2003). *Instrumental music teachers' perceptions of musical ability.* Paper presented at the Third International Research in Music Education Conference, 8–12th April, University of Exeter.

Haroutounian, J. (2000). Perspectives of musical talent: a study of identification criteria and procedures. *High Ability Studies,* 11(2), 137–160.

Hodges, D. A. (1996). Human musicality. In D. A. Hodges (ed.), *Handbook of music psychology* (pp. 29–68). San Antonia: IMR Press.

Hodges, D. A. & Haack, P. A. (1996). The influence of music on human behaviour. In D. A. Hodges (ed.), *Handbook of music psychology* (pp. 469–555). San Antonia: IMR Press.

Howe, M., Davidson, J., Moore, D., & Sloboda, J. A. (1995). Are there early childhood signs of musical ability? *Psychology of Music,* 23, 162–176.

Hurley, C. G. (1995). Student motivations for beginning and continuing/discontinuing string music tuition. *The Quarterly Journal of Music Teaching and Learning,* 6, 44–55.

Karma, K. (1985). Components of auditive structuring: Towards a theory of musical aptitude. *Bulletin of the Council for Research in Music Education,* 82, 18–31.

Klinedinst, R. E. (1991). Predicting performance achievement and retention of fifth-grade instrumental students. *Journal of Research in Music Education,* 39(3), 225–238.

Kvale, S. (1992). Postmodern psychology: a contradiction in terms? In S. Kvale (ed.), *Psychology and Postmodernism* (pp. 31–57). London Sage Publications

Mawbey, W. E. (1973). Wastage from instrumental classes in schools. *Psychology of Music,* 1, 33–43.

McCarthy, J. F. (1980). Individualised instruction, student achievement and drop out in an urban elementary school program. *Journal of Research in Music Education*, **28**, 59–69.

McPherson, G. E. (1995). Redefining the teaching of musical performance. *The Quarterly Journal of Music Teaching and Learning*, VI(2), 56–64.

McPherson, G. E. (1996). Five aspects of musical performance and their correlates. *Bulletin of the Council for Research in Music Education*, **127**, 115–121.

Messenger, J. (1958). Esthetic talent. *Basic College Quarterly*, **4**, 20–24.

Miller, L. K. (1989). *Musical savants: Exceptional skill in the mentally retarded*. Hillsdale, NJ: Lawrence Erlbaum Associates.

Moore, D., Burland, K., & Davidson, J. (2003). The social context of music success: A developmental account. *British Journal of Psychology*, **94**, 529–549.

Peretz, I. (2003). Brain specialization for music: new evidence from congenital amusia, In I. Peretz & R. Zatorre (eds), *The cognitive neuroscience of music* (pp. 192–203). Oxford: Oxford University Press.

Perkins, D. (1995). *Outsmarting IQ: The emerging science of learning intelligence*. New York: The Free Press.

Rauschecker, J. P. (2003). Functional organization and plasticity of auditory cortex. In I. Peretz & R. Zatorre (eds), *The cognitive neuroscience of music* (pp. 357–365). Oxford: Oxford University Press.

Revesz, G. (1953). *Introduction to the psychology of music*. London: Longmans.

Ruthsatz, J. & Detterman, D. K. (2003). An extraordinary memory: The case of a musical prodigy. *Intelligence*, **31**, 509–518.

Rutkowski, J. (1996). The effectiveness of individual/small group singing activities on kindergartners' use of singing voice and developmental music aptitude. *Journal of Research in Music Education*, **44**, 353–368.

Schlaug, G. (2003). The brain of musicians. In I. Peretz & R. Zatorre (eds), *The cognitive neuroscience of music* (pp. 366–381). Oxford: Oxford University Press.

Seashore, C. E., Lewis, L., & Saetveit, J. G. (1960). *Seashore measures of musical talents*. New York: The Psychological Corporation.

Shuter-Dyson, R. & Gabriel, C. (1981). *The psychology of musical ability*. London: Methuen.

Shuter-Dyson, R. (1999). Musical ability. In D. Deutsch (ed.), *The psychology of music* (pp. 627–651). New York: Harcourt Brace and Company.

Sloboda, J. A. (1996). The acquisition of musical performance expertise: deconstructing the talent account of individual differences in musical expressivity. In K. A. Anders (ed.), *The road to excellence: The acquisition of expert performance in the arts and sciences, sports and games* (pp. 107–126). Mahwah, NJ: Lawrence Erlbaum Associates.

Sloboda, J. A. & Howe, M. J. A. (1991). Biographical precursors of musical excellence: An interview study. *Psychology of Music*, **19**(1), 3–21.

Sloboda, J., Hermelin, B., & O'Connor, N. (1985). An exceptional musical memory. *Musical Perception*, **3**, 155–170.

Sloboda, J. A., Davidson, J., & Howe, M. J. A. (1994). Is everyone musical? *The Psychologist*, **7**(8), 349–354.

Sloboda, J. A., Davidson, J. W., Howe, M. J. A., & Moore, D. G. (1996). The role of practice in the development of performing musicians. *British Journal of Psychology*, **87**, 287–309.

Stern, W. (1912/1965). The psychological methods for testing intelligence. In R. J. Herrnstein & E. G. Boring (eds), *A source book in the history of psychology*. Cambridge, MA: Harvard University Press. (Original work published 1912.)

Sternberg, R. J. (1985). *Beyond IQ: A triarchic theory of human intelligence*. Cambridge: Cambridge University Press.

Sternberg, R. J. (1988). *The triarchic mind: A new theory of human intelligence.* New York: Viking-Penguin.

Sternberg, R. J. (1996). *Successful intelligence.* New York: Simon & Schuster.

Swanner, D. L. (1985). *Relationships between musical creativity and selected factors, including personality, motivation, musical aptitude, and cognitive intelligence as measured in third grade children.* Unpublished dissertation, Case Western Reserve University, Cleveland, OH.

Stevenson, H. & Lee, S. (1990). Contexts of achievement: A study of American, Chinese and Japanese children. *Monographs of the Society for Research in Child Development,* Vol. 221 (55), Nos 1–2. Chicago, IL: University of Chicago

Vaughan, M. M. (1977). Measuring creativity: Its cultivation and measurement. *Bulletin of the Council for Research in Music Education,* 50, 72–77.

Vispoel, W. P. (1993). The development and evaluation of a computerized adaptive test of tonal memory. *Journal of Research in Music Education,* 41, 111–136.

Vispoel, W. P. & Coffman, D. D. (1992). Computerized-adaptive and self-adapted tests of music listening skills: Psychometric features and motivational benefits, *Applied measurement in Education,* 7, 25–51.

Wagner, M. J. (1975). The effect of a practice report on practice time and musical performance. In C. K. Masden, R. D. Greer, & C. H. Madsen, Jr (eds), *Research in music behaviour* (pp. 125–130). New York: Teachers' College Press.

Wallin, N., Merker, B., & Brown, S. (2000). *The origins of music.* Cambridge, MA: The MIT Press.

Watkins, J. G. & Farnum, S. E. (1954). *The Watkins-Farnum performance scale.* Winnona, MN: Hal Leonard Music.

Webster, P. R. (1988). New perspectives on music aptitude and achievement. *Psychomusicology,* 7(2), 177–194.

Welch, G. F., Howard, D. M., & Rush, C. (1989). Real-time visual feedback in the development of vocal pitch accuracy in singing. *Psychology of Music,* 17(2), 146–157.

Williamon, A. & Valentine, E. (2000). Quantity and quality of musical practice as predictors of performance quality. *British Journal of Psychology,* 91(3), 353–376.

Wing, H. D. (1981). *Standardised tests of musical intelligence.* Windsor, England: National Foundation for Educational Research.

Young, L. & Nettelbeck, T. (1995). The abilities of a musical savant and his family. *Journal of Autism and Developmental Disorders,* 25(3), 231–247.

Young, W. T. (1971). The role of musical aptitude, intelligence and academic achievement in predicting the musical attainment of elementary instrumental music students. *Journal of Research in Music Education,* 19(4), 384–398.

Zurcher, W. (1972). The effect of model-supportive practice on beginning brass instrumentalists. In C. K. Madsen, R. D. Greer, & C. H. Madsen (eds), *Research in music behavior: Modifying music behavior in the classroom* (pp. 125–130). New York: Teachers College Press.

CHAPTER 6

EXPOSURE TO MUSIC: THE TRUTH ABOUT THE CONSEQUENCES

E. GLENN SCHELLENBERG

In this chapter, I examine claims about non-musical consequences of exposure to music. Over the past 10 years, the possibility that *music makes you smarter* has sparked the imagination of researchers, the popular press, and the general public. But is there any truth to this idea? If so, what is the evidence? My goal here is to answer these questions as well as possible by reviewing the relevant scholarly literature.

At the outset, we might ask why people care about non-musical side-effects of exposure to music. Do we have similar concerns about other subjects taught in school and university, such as mathematics, English, or chemistry? Would we value physics *less* if we knew that it did *not* lead to improvements in drama? Although the question is tongue-in-cheek, it highlights the fact that all academic disciplines are not considered equal. In my view, the most likely explanation for the disparity is that music is both an art form *and* an academic discipline. Somehow, its status as an art form reduces its status as a discipline. Studying fine arts is considered to be icing on the cake in a typical scholarly meal, whereas mathematics and science are the meat and potatoes. As such, music is more likely than other subjects to be eliminated from the school curriculum when budgets are reduced. Indeed, in the neo-conservative, belt-tightening climate of the late twentieth century, music education programmes were often slashed or threatened. Consequently, the idea that music might have collateral benefits was welcomed with open arms as a way of saving or reviving programmes. It suggested that music could be *more* than just an art form. In fact, music could be a conduit for improvements in other domains.

These historical and contextual factors helped to exaggerate the timeless and universal appeal of quick fixes to complex problems. Competition for admission to the best schools and universities is stiff, and a few extra IQ points could make an important difference. It is also well known that IQ is predictive of academic performance, job performance, income, health, longevity, and dealing successfully with the demands of everyday life (e.g., Brody, 1997; Ceci & Williams, 1997; Gottfredson, 1997; Sternberg *et al.*, 2001; Deary *et al.*, 2004; Gottfredson & Deary, 2004). Thus, it is no wonder that the public and the media paid attention to the proposal that simply exposing oneself to music leads to a boost in IQ. It is difficult to imagine a simpler fix (music) to such a complex problem (intelligence).

In Western society, exposure to music typically takes one of two forms: listening and performing. Music listening is everywhere, both by design and by accident. People buy CDs, they watch and hear music videos on TV, they listen to music on the radio, they download

MP3 files from the internet, and they attend concerts. They also *overhear* music in shopping malls, at the dentist, from the neighbour's home or car, and so on. By contrast, performing music is relatively rare in Western society. Many children take lessons for a year or two. Only a relatively small minority study music year in and year out, practising regularly on a daily basis. Moreover, the stark contrast between simply listening to music on the one hand, and actively pursuing a musical education or performing music regularly on the other hand, makes it highly unlikely that the two activities would have similar effects on non-musical aspects of human behaviour. As I have argued previously (Schellenberg, 2001, 2003), it is important to treat these two forms of exposure to music separately. Accordingly, the first section of this chapter examines consequences of music listening. The second section examines consequences of music lessons and performing.

Music listening

Current interest in side-effects of exposure to music stems largely from the publication of an article in *Nature* in 1993 (Rauscher *et al.*, 1993). The researchers tested the spatial abilities of undergraduates after 10 minutes of exposure to classical music, relaxation instructions, or silence. The tests were three subtests from the Stanford-Binet Intelligence Scale (Thorndike *et al.*, 1986), a widely used test of IQ. Performance on the spatial tests proved to be better after listening to music than in the other two conditions. Because the musical piece was a recording composed by Mozart, the effect became known as the *Mozart effect*. It is important to note that the effect was short-lived, as one would expect from simply listening to music for a mere 10 minutes. In fact, although each participant completed all three spatial tests after the exposure phase, the advantage for the Mozart group was evident only on the first test.

Why did the findings create such a fuss? One likely reason is that the authors reported their results as IQ scores, which the media translated as revealing a very simple fix to a complex problem, namely that listening to Mozart increases intelligence. Another reason is that the authors did not consider well-established findings from psychology or neuroscience to explain the link between music listening and test performance. Instead, they suggested that passive listening to 'complex' music (e.g., the Mozart piece they used as a stimulus) enhances abstract reasoning in general, including spatial reasoning. In other words, they proposed a direct causal link between listening to Mozart and spatial abilities, which the media extended to intelligence in general.

Researchers subsequently tried to replicate and extend the effect using a variety of outcome measures and different pieces of music. They were successful in some instances but not in others (for reviews, see Chabris, 1999; Hetland, 2000b). For example, performance on the original tests of spatial abilities was found to improve after listening to music composed by Mozart (Rauscher *et al.*, 1995; Rideout & Laubach, 1996; Rideout & Taylor, 1997; Rideout *et al.*, 1998) or by Yanni, a New Age composer (Rideout *et al.*, 1998), but not after listening to minimalist music composed by Philip Glass (Rauscher *et al.*, 1995). Other researchers found no effect of listening to Mozart on a test of working memory (Steele *et al.*, 1997), on an alternative test of spatial abilities (Carstens *et al.*, 1995), or on tests of abstract reasoning (Stough *et al.*, 1994; Newman *et al.*, 1995).

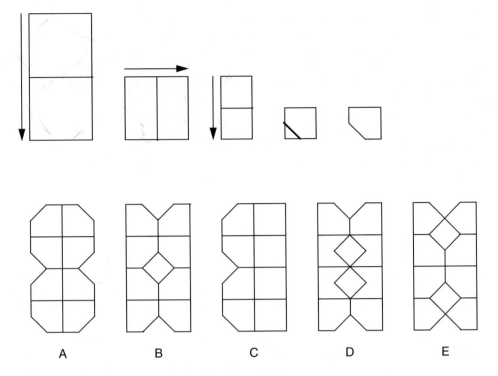

Figure 6.1 An example of a test item similar to those on the paper-folding-and-cutting test of spatial abilities. The upper portion illustrates folding and cutting manipulations to a rectangular piece of paper. The respondent chooses the option in the lower portion that corresponds to the paper after it is unfolded. The correct answer is B.

In order to explain the discrepant results, Rauscher and her colleagues (Rauscher *et al.*, 1995; Rauscher & Shaw, 1998) narrowed the scope of the proposed causal link between music listening and abstract reasoning. Their revised hypothesis limited the effect to tests of *spatial-temporal* abilities, those requiring 'mental imagery and temporal ordering' (Rauscher, 1999, p. 827). Only one of the three subtests from their original article met this new criterion: *paper-folding-and-cutting* (PF&C). The PF&C test illustrates folding and cutting manipulations performed on a rectangular piece of paper (see Figure 6.1). Participants choose which of five alternatives corresponds to the piece of paper when it is unfolded. Their final score is the total number of correct responses. Re-analysis of the original results from 1993 showed that the Mozart effect was reliable only for this particular test (Rauscher & Shaw, 1998). None the less, some researchers have failed to replicate the effect even when they used this particular outcome measure (Steele *et al.*, 1999a–c). These null findings suggest that the effect is fleeting or highly sensitive to minor procedural differences.

With a somewhat different approach, my colleagues and I (Nantais & Schellenberg, 1999; Thompson *et al.*, 2001; Husain *et al.*, 2002; Schellenberg & Hallam, 2005; Schellenberg *et al.*, in press) conducted a series of studies that sought to (1) replicate the original effect, and (2) make systematic alterations to the method in order to highlight the underlying mechanisms driving the effect. The first study (Nantais & Schellenberg, 1999) consisted of two experiments. In the first, participants were college undergraduates tested on two occasions with alternate versions of the PF&C task that were equivalent in difficulty. The students completed the tests in a sound-attenuating booth after listening to music or sitting in silence for 10 minutes. The music was the same Mozart piece used by Rauscher *et al.* (1993) or another piece composed by Schubert from the same CD (i.e., with the same performers, recording quality, and so on). Both groups of students had higher scores on the PF&C test after listening to music than after sitting in silence (see Figure 6.2, upper panel).

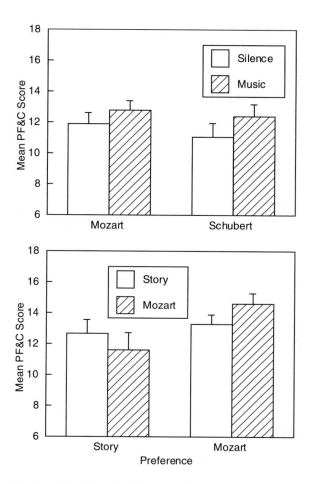

Figure 6.2 Results from Nantais and Schellenberg (1999) experiments 1 (upper) and 2 (lower). The upper panel illustrates that performance on the paper-folding-and-cutting (PF&C) test was better after listening to music composed by Mozart (left) or Schubert (right) than after sitting in silence. In the lower panel, Mozart was contrasted with a narrated story. Performance on the PF&C task was better after listening to the story for participants who preferred the story (left), but after listening to Mozart for those who preferred Mozart (right). Error bars are standard errors.

In other words, we replicated the Mozart effect and found a Schubert effect that was similar in magnitude.

The results from this first experiment left it unclear, however, whether the effect was due to music listening *per se*, or because the music conditions were simply more interesting than sitting in silence. In the second experiment (same procedure and equipment), we contrasted listening to Mozart with listening to a narrated story. Both conditions had auditory stimuli, with the story selected to be about as interesting as listening to Mozart. The logic was that if the effect was actually due to *music* listening, it should also be evident when the control condition consisted of an auditory but non-musical stimulus. This time, however, the advantage for Mozart disappeared. The participants were also asked which stimulus they preferred (the music or the story). Further analysis of the data revealed that performance varied reliably as a function of preference (see Figure 6.2, lower panel). Those who preferred Mozart did better on the PF&C test after listening to Mozart. Those who preferred the story did better after listening to the story. The results indicated that the so-called Mozart effect is not specific to Mozart in particular or to music in general. Moreover, it seems highly likely that the positive effects of music in experiment 1 were a consequence of the fact that participants preferred listening to music over sitting in silence.

In a second study (Thompson *et al.*, 2001), we explored the idea of listeners' preferences in greater detail. We hypothesized that preferences in the initial study were related to differences in emotional states, particularly listeners' arousal levels and moods. Music is known to have reliable effects on listeners' emotional states (Thayer & Levenson, 1983; Krumhansl, 1997; Gabrielsson, 2001; Peretz, 2001; Schmidt & Trainor, 2001; Sloboda & Juslin, 2001), and people listen to music precisely for its emotional impact (Sloboda, 1992). Arousal (i.e., how alert or fatigued one feels) and mood (i.e., how positive or negative one feels) correspond to the two dimensions of emotions described by a well-known theory of emotions (Russell, 1980). Effects of arousal and mood on test performance are well established (Isen *et al.*, 1992; Khan & Isen, 1993; Cahill & McGaugh, 1998; Dutton & Carroll, 2001; Cassady & Johnson, 2002; Eich & Forgas, 2003; Grawitch *et al.*, 2003). According to the *arousal and mood hypothesis*, the 'special link' between music composed by Mozart and spatial (or spatial-temporal) abilities is actually just one example of a stimulus that affects arousal and mood, which, in turn, affect performance on a wide variety of tests. The main advantage of this perspective is that it explains the seemingly mysterious Mozart effect in a straightforward manner with well-established psychological findings.

As in Nantais and Schellenberg (1999), undergraduates came to the lab on two occasions. They completed the PF&C test after listening to music on one occasion, and after sitting in silence on the other. For half of the participants, the music was the same Mozart sonata used previously. The sonata is an up-tempo, happy sounding piece in a major key. For the other half, the music was Albinoni's Adagio—a slow-tempo, sad sounding piece in a minor key that is often played at funerals. On both visits, arousal and mood were measured at the beginning and the end of the testing session. Compared with the baseline (i.e., silence) condition, we expected that the Mozart piece would increase arousal levels and improve listeners' mood, whereas the Albinoni piece should decrease arousal and worsen mood.

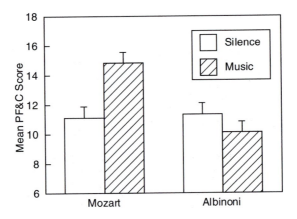

Figure 6.3 Results from Thompson *et al.* (2001) illustrating that performance on the paper-folding-and-cutting (PF&C) task was better after listening to Mozart compared with sitting in silence (left), but not after listening to Albinoni (right). Error bars are standard errors.

Accordingly, we also predicted that we would find a music advantage on the PF&C test for the Mozart group but not for the Albinoni group. The data were completely consistent with these predictions (see Figure 6.3). Moreover, when we used statistical means to hold constant participants' changes in arousal and mood, the Mozart advantage on the PF&C task disappeared.

In a third study (Husain *et al.*, 2002), we examined which features of the Mozart sonata led to changes in arousal and mood, which, in turn, led to enhanced performance on the PF&C task. We created four versions of the same Mozart piece that varied in tempo (fast or slow) and mode (major or minor). Undergraduates heard one of the versions and then completed the PF&C task. Arousal and mood were measured at the beginning and end of the testing session. As expected, performance on the PF&C task was better among listeners who heard the fast rather than slow versions, and for those who heard the major rather than the minor versions (see Figure 6.4). Another interesting finding was that the tempo and mode manipulations had different effects on arousal and mood. The tempo manipulation influenced arousal but not mood, whereas the mode manipulation influenced mood but not arousal. As in Thompson *et al.* (2001), changes in arousal and mood accounted for most of the variance in PF&C scores (i.e., whether participants performed well or poorly), with higher scores associated with higher levels of arousal and more positive moods.

In the fourth study in this series (Schellenberg *et al.*, in press), we attempted to find the few missing pieces of evidence that were needed to support the arousal and mood account of the Mozart effect. Our goals were to show that the Mozart effect generalized to (1) tests that do not measure spatial-temporal abilities, and (2) any type of music that is enjoyable for the particular group of listeners. To this end, we conducted two experiments. In the first, undergraduates listened to the Mozart piece on one

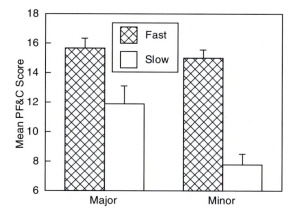

Figure 6.4 Results from Husain *et al.* (2002) illustrating performance on the paper-folding-and-cutting (PF&C) task after listening to one of four versions of a Mozart sonata. Performance was better after the fast compared with the slow versions, and after the major compared with the minor versions. Error bars are standard errors.

visit to the laboratory and the Albinoni piece on another visit. Instead of administering the PF&C test, we administered two subtests from the Wechsler Adult Intelligence Scale—Third Edition (Wechsler, 1997), one on each visit. Neither subtest measured spatial-temporal abilities. One (Symbol Search) was a speeded test of pattern recognition. The other (Letter–Number Sequencing) was a measure of working memory. Testing order of the music (Mozart then Albinoni or vice versa) was counterbalanced with testing order of the particular subtest (Symbol Search then Letter–Number Sequencing or vice versa). Arousal and mood were measured at the beginning and the end of both testing sessions.

At the first test session, the different music-listening experiences had a small effect on mood (i.e., moods were more positive after listening to Mozart than to Albinoni) but no effect on arousal. Perhaps the testing environment (sitting in a sound-attenuating booth wearing headphones) was too unusual for this particular group of listeners for the music to have much of an arousing effect. At the second session, however, we found reliable differences in arousal *and* in mood as a consequence of music listening, with increases in arousal and positive mood after listening to Mozart, but decreases in arousal and positive mood after listening to Albinoni. Because music listening affected arousal *and* mood at the second session but only mood at the first session, we expected that music listening would have a stronger impact on performance on the IQ subtests at the second test session compared with the first. Indeed, at the first session, music listening did not affect performance on the IQ subtests. At the second session, however, we found a reliable difference for one of our two outcome measures (see Figure 6.5). Performance on the Symbol Search subtest was better after listening to Mozart than after listening to Albinoni. In short, when there was a reliable difference in arousal and in mood as a consequence of music listening, there was

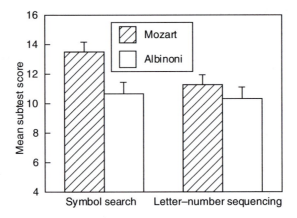

Figure 6.5 Results from experiment 1, Schellenberg *et al.* (in press), illustrating that performance on the symbol search subtest was better after listening to Mozart than to Albinoni (second test session). The Mozart advantage on the letter–number sequencing subtest was not significant. Error bars are standard errors.

also a reliable difference on one of the IQ subtests. When there was no difference in arousal, there was no evidence of a Mozart effect.

In a second experiment (Schellenberg *et al.*, in press), we sought to generalize the findings even further by examining the creative abilities of Japanese 5-year-old children. Each child was provided with paper and 18 crayons and asked to make a drawing after a lunch break that included exposure to music. The outcome measures were time spent drawing (relative to a baseline measure), as well as judgements of creativity that adults made for the drawings. Exposure to music consisted of listening to the Mozart or the Albinoni piece (used earlier) during lunch, listening to familiar children's songs during lunch, or singing children's songs for 20 minutes after lunch. For young children, we doubted that listening to classical music (i.e., Mozart or Albinoni) would optimize arousal and mood. Rather, hearing or singing familiar songs would be more likely to do so. In line with this view, the results revealed that (1) the children spent a longer time drawing after exposure to familiar music compared with classical music (Figure 6.6, upper), and (2) creative ratings were higher for the drawings the children made after exposure to familiar music (Figure 6.6, lower). In a separate investigation, we (Schellenberg & Hallam, 2005) showed that cognitive benefits are more likely after 10- and 11-year-olds listen to popular music than to Mozart.

To summarize, the results from this series of studies make it clear that specific characteristics of music affect arousal and mood, which, in turn, affect performance on cognitive tasks. In one sense, then, the Mozart effect describes a reliable phenomenon. The term is misleading, however, because the effect does not depend on listening to Mozart, or even on listening to music. Moreover, the claim of a specific causal link between listening to music composed by Mozart and spatial-temporal abilities is without merit.

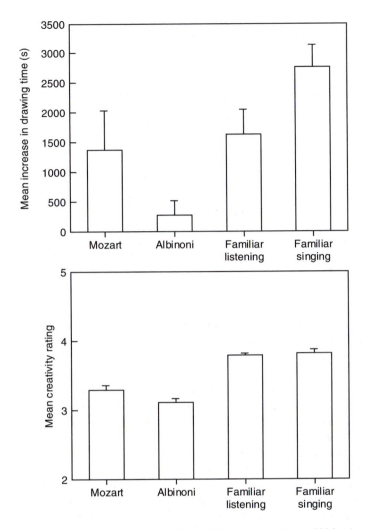

Figure 6.6 Results from experiment 2, Schellenberg *et al.* (in press), illustrating that 5-year-olds' drawing times (upper panel) were longer (compared with baseline) after exposure to familiar music (listening or singing) than to classical music (Mozart or Albinoni). In addition, adults' ratings of creativity (lower panel) were higher for drawings from the children who drew after exposure to familiar music than for those who drew after listening to classical music. Error bars are standard errors.

Music lessons

I now examine whether music *lessons* affect cognitive abilities. Before I begin, it is important to highlight a few critical issues. Our personal experiences can change us—how we think or feel, what we believe to be true, how we look at things (works of art, legal contracts), and so on. It should come as no surprise, then, that taking music lessons not only improves our music-performance abilities, but also our music-listening skills (Dowling & Harwood, 1986; Smith, 1997). These perceptual and cognitive improvements include better recognition of melodies (e.g., Dowling, 1978; Bartlett & Dowling, 1980; Orsmond & Miller, 1999) and a greater likelihood of hearing music in line with predictions from music theory (e.g., understanding that *doh* is more stable than *ti* in a musical context; Krumhansl, 1990). Musical training also leads to differential brain-activation patterns in response to musical stimuli (e.g., Fujioka *et al.*, 2004). Although musical skills are obviously useful for musicians, the benefits are more or less logical outcomes of taking music lessons and playing music. In other words, if we want to say something interesting and provocative about positive benefits of music lessons, we need to show that taking music lessons improves abilities in one or more *non-musical* domains.

A second point involves the *specificity* of observed links between music lessons and cognitive abilities. Music lovers might like to be able to claim that taking music lessons makes you smarter in one way or another. If the claim is to have any real meaning, it is important to show that music is special or unique in this regard. Reading, chess, ballet, and swimming lessons could all confer similar benefits. The claim would then be misleading because it would be far more specific than required. It would be more accurate to say that out-of-school activities *in general* have cognitive benefits.

A third point is that taking music lessons is associated with other demographic variables that are known to be predictive of cognitive advantages. For example, children who take music lessons tend to come from families with higher incomes than average families, and their parents tend to have more education than the average parent (Sergeant & Thatcher, 1974; Curtis, 2004; Schellenberg, in press). To make matters even more complicated, family income and education are both associated positively with measures of cognitive abilities, including IQ scores (e.g., Ceci & Williams, 1997). These associations make it difficult to make definitive conclusions about observed associations between music lessons and cognitive functioning, because family income and parents' education could be the real source of the effect. In short, when one is comparing children with different amounts of musical training, one is— *at the same time*—comparing children from different family backgrounds. Before we can attribute any observed associations to music lessons, contributions from these extraneous factors need to be ruled out in some way. One possibility is to recruit children from families who are equivalent or similar in terms of their background. Another possibility is to partial out the effects of variables such as family income and parents' education by statistical means. These statistical methods adjust the results so that it is *as if* one were testing children from similar family backgrounds.

But even after accounting for potential confounding variables, the presence of positive associations between music lessons and cognitive abilities does not allow researchers to conclude that music lessons are actually *causing* increases in intelligence. In fact, the direction of causation could be in the opposite direction: children with better cognitive abilities might be more inclined than other children to take music lessons. All *correlational studies* and *quasi-experiments* suffer from this limitation. Whereas correlational studies examine whether two or more variables (e.g., duration of musical training and intellectual abilities) increase or decrease in tandem, quasi-experiments compare children that are categorized into groups based on their pre-existing characteristics (e.g., no music lessons vs. some training). Either way, because the children are not assigned at random to music lessons, no inferences about causation can be made.

The only way to infer causation is to conduct a true experiment with random assignment of children to music lessons. The random assignment assures that it is extremely unlikely that extraneous variables (e.g., family income, parents' education, involvement in non-musical activities) would differ between conditions. Even then, the extent of the inferences is limited by the particular comparison conditions. For example, one could recruit a sample of children and assign half of them randomly to music lessons, with the other half receiving no lessons. After a year or two of lessons, the music group might have higher scores on one or more tests of intellectual abilities. One could then infer appropriately that music lessons were indeed the source of the difference between groups. Unfortunately, it would remain unclear whether the *music* part of the lessons played a central role. As noted, a possible alternative is that other types of extracurricular activities could have similar effects. In other words, because the comparison group received no additional lessons of any kind, one cannot rule out the possibility that non-musical aspects of the lessons (e.g., additional contact with an adult instructor) were the source of the effect, and that similar effects would be evident for other out-of-school activities.

In light of these rather far-reaching problems, let us turn to the available research. What do we know about non-musical side-effects of music lessons? As a first pass, we might ask whether musical abilities tend to be correlated with other abilities, or, alternatively, whether they are in a league of their own. Gardner's (1993) theory of *multiple intelligences* implies that musical abilities (which he calls musical *intelligence*) are distinct and independent from other abilities (or other intelligences). Accordingly, if the human mind is truly *modular* (Fodor, 1983), with autonomous and independent mechanisms handling specific types of input (i.e., linguistic, musical, spatial, and so on), improvements in musical abilities are unlikely to be accompanied by improvements in non-musical domains.

When researchers have examined whether musical *aptitude* (natural musical ability) is associated with other cognitive skills, participants are typically selected without regard to musical training and administered two or more tests. At least one of the tests measures musical abilities and at least one other test measures a non-musical ability. Because the goal is to measure aptitude rather than explicit knowledge of music, musical abilities are often measured by asking participants to identify whether two musical patterns have the same melody or rhythm. Performance on these types of task tends to be correlated positively with general intelligence (Lynn *et al.*, 1989), as well as with more specific components of intelligence such as verbal abilities (Barwick *et al.*, 1989; Lamb & Gregory, 1993; Douglas & Willatts, 1994; Anvari *et al.*, 2002), symbolic reasoning (Gromko & Poorman, 1998a), spatial abilities (Hassler *et al.*, 1985), and reasoning by analogy (Nelson & Barresi, 1989). Because musical aptitude is associated with a variety of other abilities including general intelligence, the simplest explanation of these findings is that more intelligent children perform better on a variety of tests. Another possibility is that improving musical aptitude through musical training could be accompanied by *general* cognitive improvements.

Some researchers believe, however, that taking music lessons is associated with benefits in *specific* non-musical abilities. For example, Rauscher (1999, 2002) proposes that taking music lessons leads to long-term improvements in spatial-temporal abilities, in exactly the same way that listening to music leads to short-term benefits. Another school of thought holds that non-musical benefits of music lessons are primarily linguistic (Chan *et al.*, 1998; Ho *et al.*, 2003), possibly as a consequence of improvements in auditory temporal processing (Jakobson *et al.*, 2003). Yet another view suggests that musical and mathematical abilities are linked closely. This view is a common piece of folk wisdom, and supporters of the spatial-temporal hypothesis also believe that spatial-temporal abilities are linked with mathematical abilities (Rauscher, 1999, 2002; Shaw, 2000). These different theoretical viewpoints lead researchers to use specific types of tests in their investigations (e.g., tests of spatial-temporal *or* linguistic abilities, but not both). But evidence of an association with music lessons in one domain (e.g., spatial-temporal abilities) does not rule out the possibility that a similar association could be evident in another domain (e.g., linguistic abilities).

When considered as a whole, the available correlational and quasi-experimental studies provide evidence that is consistent with the *general* hypothesis (i.e., music lessons affect intellectual abilities generally). They are also consistent with the possibility that children with high IQs—who do well on many outcome measures—are more likely than other children to take music lessons. For example, a relatively recent review (Hetland, 2000a) concluded that taking music lessons is predictive of improved spatial-temporal abilities. Another review (Butzlaff, 2000) reported that taking music lessons is associated positively with reading ability. Yet another review (Vaughn, 2000) found that taking music lessons is predictive of enhanced mathematical skills. Other positive associations have been identified between taking music lessons and a variety of outcome measures, including tests of visual-motor integration (Orsmond & Miller, 1999), selective attention (Hurwitz *et al.*, 1975), and memory for verbal stimuli (Chan *et al.*, 1998; Kilgour *et al.*, 2000; Ho *et al.*, 2003; Jakobson *et al.*, 2003). In sum, the available data from correlational and quasi-experimental studies point to small but reliable associations between music lessons and intellectual abilities in general, without informing us about the direction of the association.

Are smarter children more likely than other children to take music lessons? Or do music lessons improve intellectual abilities? Or could both of these hypotheses be true? Let us turn now to the experimental studies that have examined whether music lessons affect cognitive abilities. In one such study (Rauscher & Zupan, 2000), kindergarten children were assigned to one of two conditions. In one condition, the children served as a control group (no music lessons). In the other condition, children received 20-minute keyboard lessons twice a week for 8 months. The children were administered a set of three spatial tasks (two spatial-temporal, one spatial memory) before the lessons began (pre-test) and after they were completed (post-test). Compared with the no-music group, the keyboard group had significantly higher increases from pre- to post-test on all three spatial measures. These effects disappeared a year later for children who stopped taking lessons, but they continued to increase for children who continued taking music lessons (Rauscher, 2002). In fact, children who took lessons continuously from kindergarten through third grade proved to have better spatial skills than children who started lessons in second grade. These results suggest that musical training, particularly training that begins early in life, is associated with benefits in spatial abilities (see also Gromko & Poorman, 1998b). Unfortunately, it is unclear whether similar benefits would be found for verbal or mathematical abilities, or for general intelligence. It is also unclear whether other types of training (in drama, gymnastics, etc.) would have similar benefits.

In another experimental study (Costa-Giomi, 1999), 9-year-old children received 3 years of weekly individual piano lessons, or no lessons. Children were administered a short test of cognitive abilities that provided an overall score as well as separate subscores for verbal, quantitative, and spatial abilities. The test was administered at the beginning of the study and each year thereafter. The groups did not differ at the beginning or at the end of the study, but the results revealed small but temporary advantages for the music group on the overall score after the second year, and on the spatial subtest after the first and second years. Studying children who begin music lessons at an earlier age might yield results that are stronger, more interpretable, and less temporary.

Rather provocative findings came from a study that provided four first-grade classes with a 7-month programme in the arts that included specialized training in music and visual arts (Gardiner et al., 1996). The music lessons were taught in the Kodály method, which emphasizes clapping, hand signs, dancing, and singing. The four special-arts classes were compared with four others who received the standard curriculum. Although the children in the special-arts classes were behind the other classes before the study began, after the programme was finished they matched the other classes in reading ability and surpassed them in mathematics. These results are particularly exciting because the outcome measures included real-world outcomes (i.e., measures of academic achievement) rather than abstract measures of intelligence or its subcomponents. None the less, it is impossible to attribute the positive outcomes to the music lessons rather than the visual component of the special-arts programme. Moreover, even if the results were a consequence of the music curriculum, it would remain unclear whether they were due to music rather than to one or more features of the particular teaching method.

In a recent field experiment (Schellenberg, 2004), I tried to rectify some of the problems that precluded clear interpretations of the earlier findings (Gardiner et al., 1996; Gromko & Poorman, 1998b; Costa-Giomi, 1999; Rauscher & Zupan, 2000). Families of 6-year-old children were recruited by placing an ad in a local newspaper, offering 'free arts lessons'. Parents were then interviewed on the telephone and at their homes to ensure that: (1) they were interested in participating regardless of the condition to which their child was assigned; (2) they had a keyboard in their home with at least four octaves of full-size keys; (3) their child was registered in public school; and (4) their child had never taken music lessons previously. A group of 144 families was selected based on these criteria. Unlike previous studies, the children were assigned individually and at random to one of four groups: keyboard lessons, voice (Kodály) lessons, drama lessons, or no lessons. The lessons were weekly lessons taught in groups of six for 36 weeks. (The no-lessons group received keyboard lessons the following year.) All of the lessons were taught at the Royal Conservatory of Music, which is the oldest and most prestigious institution of its type in Canada. The instructors were certified female professionals who taught music or drama professionally on a regular basis. The drama lessons provided a control condition (in addition to the no-lessons group) that, like music, was an arts activity that had a primary auditory component and incorporated memorization, practice, and rehearsal.

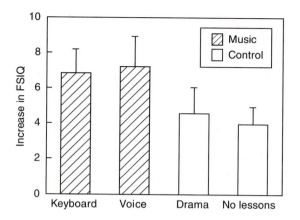

Figure 6.7 Results from Schellenberg (2004), illustrating that children who took music lessons (keyboard or voice) had larger increases in FSIQ than children who took drama lessons or no lessons. Error bars are standard errors.

Each child was tested once before the lessons began (before entering first grade) and again after the lessons were over (in the summer between first and second grades). Twelve of the 108 children in the keyboard, voice, and drama groups stopped going to the lessons mid-way through the year and were not available for the second testing session. The outcome measures included the entire Wechsler Intelligence Scale for Children—Third Edition (WISC-III; Wechsler, 1991), which has 12 subtests that measure a wide variety of skills. The subtests are combined to give a full-scale IQ score (FSIQ), as well as four index scores (Verbal Comprehension, Perceptual Organization, Processing Speed, and Freedom from Distractibility), that correspond to the *principal components* (i.e., independent dimensions) of the test. The children were also administered the Kaufman Test of Educational Achievement (K-TEA; Kaufman & Kaufman, 1985), which is a standardized test of academic ability that includes five subtests of specific mathematical and reading abilities. A parent completed the Behavioural Assessment System for Children—parent report form (BASC; Reynolds & Kamphaus, 1992), which provides measures of adaptive and maladaptive social behaviour. The K-TEA was included to test whether any potential differences in WISC-III scores would translate to applied differences in scholastic ability. The BASC was included to test whether potential side-effects of music lessons would extend beyond cognitive abilities to social behaviour.

Across the four groups, the children had reliable increases in FSIQ from the pre-test to the post-test session that averaged 5.7 points. This finding is likely to be a consequence of attending school, which is known to raise IQ (Ceci & Williams, 1997). When these increases were analysed as a function of the various conditions, the two music groups (keyboard and voice) had similar increases in FSIQ, as did the two control groups (drama and no-lessons). When the music groups were compared with the control groups, however, a reliable difference was found (see Figure 6.7). The control groups had increases in FSIQ that averaged 4.3 points, whereas the music groups had an average increase of 7.0 points. Because the experiment included random assignment of children to the four groups, the

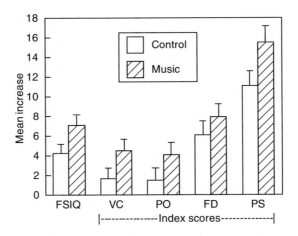

Figure 6.8 Results from Schellenberg (2004), illustrating that the advantage for the music groups (keyboard or voice lessons) over the control groups (drama or no lessons) was consistent across the four index scores of the WISC-III (VC: Verbal Comprehension, PO: Perceptual Organization, FD: Freedom from Distractibility, PS: Processing Speed) as well as full-scale IQ (FSIQ).

results allow one to infer causation, namely that taking music lessons led to greater increases in FSIQ than taking drama lessons or no lessons at all.

The findings refute suggestions of links between music education and specific aspects of cognition. Compared with the control groups, the music groups had greater increases on all four index scores of the WISC-III (see Figure 6.8), and on 10 of its 12 subtests—all but Arithmetic and Information. The Arithmetic subtest requires children to do basic mental addition, subtraction, multiplication, and division in response to real-world questions, whereas Information is a test of verbal abilities that measures participants' knowledge of common events, objects, places, and people. Because the *control* groups actually had larger improvements (not significantly) on these two subtests, the findings provide rather compelling evidence that musical training does *not* lead to special improvements in mathematical or verbal abilities. Moreover, other subtests that measured spatial-temporal abilities (Object Assembly), verbal abilities (Vocabulary), or processing speed (Symbol Search, Coding) did not stand out in terms of the improvements that could be attributed to music lessons. In fact, improvements on these tests was no different in magnitude than the improvement noted on subtests of working memory (Digit Span), understanding similarities between concepts (Similarities), and so on.

Having shown that taking music lessons causes small but significant increases in FSIQ, one might ask whether these benefits have any applied relevance that extends to performance in traditional school subjects. When the music and control groups were compared on the five subtests of the K-TEA, they did not differ significantly in any case. None the less, the music group had larger improvements on each of the five subtests. If the null hypothesis of 'no difference between groups' were actually true in each case, it should be like flipping a coin five times in a row. The odds of *heads* coming up (or the music group having a larger increase) each time is 1 in 32, which is less than 0.05 and therefore statistically significant by the rules of science.

A separate analysis asked whether side-effects of music lessons would be limited to intellectual abilities (e.g., IQ, academic performance) or whether they might also improve social skills. Results from the BASC revealed that levels of maladaptive behaviour were very low across groups and did not change over the year of the study. This null finding was to be expected because the items measuring maladaptive behaviour are designed to identify at-risk children who require clinical intervention. On the measure of *adaptive* social skills, however, the drama group showed a significant improvement over the course of the study. This improvement was not evident for any of the other groups, and the difference between the drama and other groups was highly significant. Although this finding was not predicted in advance, it seems sensible in hindsight. The interactive and essentially social nature of drama lessons appears to improve adaptive social skills, such as cooperating with peers, and behaving politely and appropriately in interactions with adults and other children.

These findings represent the first clear pieces of evidence that taking music lessons *causes* positive intellectual benefits. It is important to keep in mind that the benefits were relatively small (slightly less than 3 points). Moreover, when the findings are considered as a whole, they suggest that extracurricular activities *in general* may be beneficial for child development, with different activities (e.g., music or drama) conferring benefits in different areas (e.g., intellectual or social skills, respectively). The results also raise an important question: Would the benefits of music lessons continue to grow with additional lessons? Unfortunately, this question is almost impossible to answer using a true experiment. In the Schellenberg (2004) study, one of every nine children in the music and drama groups dropped out of the study before it was completed. Although this rate of attrition was considered to be acceptable, higher rates would make the experiment invalid because children who drop out are likely to differ systematically from children who persevere (e.g., in terms of motivation, ability to concentrate, and so on). This problem becomes especially troublesome when rates of attrition differ for the different groups.

As an alternative, we can address the issue with a correlational design, by looking at children with different amounts of music lessons to determine whether intellectual abilities tend to increase with amount of training. Strictly speaking, this approach means that causation cannot be determined. In principle, positive results could mean that (1) music lessons cause intellectual benefits, (2) intellectually gifted children are more likely than other children to take music lessons, or (3) some other variable is causing increases in the likelihood of taking music lessons and scoring well on measures of intellectual abilities. Obvious candidates for these other variables include parents' education, family income, and involvement in non-musical out-of-school activities. Fortunately, these variables can be measured relatively accurately—and held constant in the statistical analyses—simply by asking parents to provide the relevant information. In short, the correlational approach allows us to test whether the most likely extraneous variables are the true source of any observed effects. If these can be ruled out, the results from the earlier experimental study provide evidence about the direction of causation.

In the first of two correlational studies (Schellenberg, in press), 147 children were recruited from the local area. The families ranged from lower-middle to upper-middle

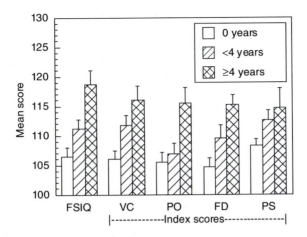

Figure 6.9 Results from Schellenberg (in press), illustrating full-scale IQ (FSIQ) and WISC-III index scores (VC: Verbal Comprehension, PO: Perceptual Organization, FD: Freedom from Distractibility, PS: Processing Speed) for children 6–12 years of age as a function of years of music lessons. Error bars are standard errors.

class in terms of social status (i.e., family income and parents' education), and they were very mixed with respect to ethnic background. The children came to the laboratory with a parent on a single occasion. Each child was administered the complete WISC-III and the K-TEA. A parent completed the BASC as well as a detailed questionnaire asking for background information about the child's history of music lessons, the child's involvement in non-musical out-of-school activities, the parents' highest level of education, and total family income. In addition, parents were asked to provide a photocopy of the child's most recent report card. (Report cards are standardized across publicly funded schools in the province of Ontario and thus comparable.) For each child, we used the grades on the report card to calculate an average grade in school.

The main predictor variable was the total number of months of private and group music lessons taken outside of school. As predicted, this variable was correlated positively with FSIQ ($r = 0.35$; see Figure 6.9). The association was smaller but still reliable after holding constant individual differences in family income, parents' education, involvement in non-musical activities, and age. (Age was included because for any individual child, age always increases with total months of music lessons.) In general, parents' education was a better predictor than music lessons of performance on the WISC-III measures, but musical training was a better predictor than family income. Involvement in non-musical activities was not associated with WISC-III scores. The association between music lessons and the various WISC-III outcome measures was strongest for FSIQ, but it was statistically significant for each index score and for all but one of the 12 individual subtests. The exception was Object Assembly, the only WISC-III subtest that measures spatial-temporal abilities. Once again, the results provide evidence against all of the theories that link music lessons with specific subsets of intellectual functioning. Instead, they point to a small but very *general* association. Moreover, there was no evidence that non-musical out-of-school activities have similar intellectual benefits.

When music lessons were used to predict school average and performance on the standardized test of academic abilities (K-TEA), a similar pattern emerged. Both of these outcome measures had a reliable positive association with music lessons, and the associations remained reliable (albeit smaller) after accounting for individual differences in parental education, family income, non-musical activities, and age. As in the experimental study (Schellenberg, 2004), music lessons had no association with adaptive or maladaptive social functioning. In sum, the results from this correlational study were completely consistent with those from the experiment, and they provided the first evidence that, on average, the intellectual benefits caused by music lessons increase as duration of musical training increases. Obviously, other differences among children in motivation, peer groups, social status, number of siblings, and so on, are likely to play a part in determining both how long a child takes music lessons and how much intellectual benefit is accrued.

A second correlational study of 150 undergraduates (Schellenberg, in press) tested whether taking music lessons in childhood and adolescence confers intellectual benefits that last until early adulthood. The students came individually to the laboratory and were administered the entire Wechsler Adult Intelligence Scale—Third Edition (WAIS-III; Wechsler, 1997), which is similar to the WISC-III but designed for testing adults rather than children. The students also provided detailed information about their musical background, which included years of private music lessons (group lessons outside of school were rare) as well as years of playing music on a regular basis. The latter measure was included to account for the likelihood that effects of musical training would differ, for example, between one student who took music lessons for 3 years but never played a note afterward, and another student who also took music lessons for 3 years but continued to play regularly for an additional 4 years. Accordingly, the main predictor variable was years of playing music regularly (i.e., years of private lessons plus additional years of regular playing). The students also provided information about their high-school average, their parents' highest level of education, and their family income.

Years of playing music regularly had a reliable positive association with FSIQ ($r = 0.21$; see Figure 6.10). The effect was smaller than it was in childhood, probably because more time had elapsed since the musical training ended. The association remained reliable after accounting for parents' education and family income. Examination of the WAIS-III index and subtest scores revealed significant associations for some outcome measures but not for others. None the less, the results were not consistent with any proposals of links between music lessons and specific subsets of intellectual abilities. Moreover, playing music had the strongest predictive power for FSIQ, which is an aggregate measure that is formed from *all* of the subtests. Playing music also had a small but reliable positive association with high-school average that could not be attributed to family income or parents' education. These results suggest that associations between music lessons and intellectual abilities are small but very general and long-lasting, continuing some years after the lessons have ended.

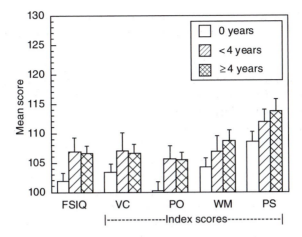

Figure 6.10 Results from Schellenberg (in press), illustrating full-scale IQ (FSIQ) and WAIS-III index scores (VC: Verbal Comprehension, PO: Perceptual Organization, WM: Working Memory, PS: Processing Speed) for undergraduates as a function of years of playing music regularly. Error bars are standard errors.

Conclusions

On the one hand, studies of music listening show that the Mozart effect is relatively reliable. On the other hand, the results also make it clear that the effect is not specific to music composed by Mozart in particular, or even to music in general. Moreover, the effects go well beyond tests of spatial-temporal abilities to other components of intelligence, such as creativity or recognizing patterns rapidly. Is it fair, then, to say that listening to music confers intellectual benefits? Yes, but it is misleading to suggest that music is somehow special in this regard. Specific characteristics of music (e.g., tempo or mode) can induce changes in listeners' arousal levels and their moods, but so can drinking a cup of coffee, or receiving a gift of $5. As noted above, it is well established that changes in arousal affect performance on tests of cognitive abilities, as do changes in mood. In other words, there are many simple but temporary and small fixes to the problem of intelligence.

Studies of formal training in music tell a different but related story. The available findings reveal small but reliable and consistent associations between taking music lessons and intellectual abilities. The association appears to be causal and cannot be attributed to extraneous variables that are associated with taking music lessons or cognitive abilities. The available evidence also indicates that associations between music lessons and cognitive abilities are general—extending broadly across the various subcomponents of intelligence and cognition—rather than limited to a specific subset of abilities. Other out-of-school activities (e.g., drama lessons) do not appear to have similar intellectual benefits, although they may have benefits for other aspects of child development (e.g., social skills).

If the effects of music listening are due to changes in arousal and mood, can we explain the effects of learning to play music with similar underlying mechanisms? Despite some speculation that this is indeed possible (Rauscher, 1999, 2002), the answer *must* be 'no' for at least two reasons: (1) taking music lessons and practising regularly over a period of time could not conceivably have the same emotional impact day in and day out, and (2) in studies of effects of music training, the outcome variables are *never* measured directly after listening to music.

How, then, can we explain the effect? There are at least four distinct possibilities. One is that the effect is simply an extension of the well-known fact that schooling raises IQ (Ceci & Williams, 1997). From this perspective, other out-of-school activities that are scholastic in nature (e.g., reading, maths, or chess lessons) could have similar effects. Music lessons could still be unique because, unlike reading, maths, or chess lessons, they represent a scholarly out-of-school activity that many children *enjoy*. Another possibility is that the intellectual benefits of music lessons stem from one or more of the wide array of abilities that are trained and improved when learning to play music. These include fine-motor skills, learning to read music, learning to perceive and express emotions in music, memorization of extended passages, acquired knowledge of musical structures (e.g., scales, chords, intervals, cadences and other harmonic progressions), and so on. Most of these factors (memorizing, reading, fine-motor skills, perceiving/expressing emotion) are *not* specific to music. Thus, it is possible that a non-musical activity that incorporated some or all of these factors could confer similar benefits. A third possibility is that something specific about music is driving the effect. A musical tune is an *abstraction*, which means that it can be recognized whether it is played fast or slow, or high or low. In other words, a tune is defined by the pitch and temporal relations that establish its identity. Learning explicitly about the abstract nature of music could lead to an improved ability to reason abstractly in general, which would, in turn, explain the observed increases on measures of intellectual ability. Yet another possibility is that learning to play music is similar to learning a second language. Bilingualism is known to confer some non-linguistic cognitive advantages (Bialystok, 2001).

Although the source of the effect of music *listening* on intellectual abilities has been identified (at least to my satisfaction), the source of the effect of music *lessons* remains more elusive. I have offered some ideas to explain the effect but researchers will undoubtedly continue to examine this question in more detail in the future. None the less, I think that it is safe to conclude at this point that a reasonable amount of out-of-school activities is good for child development. Music lessons represent one option that appears to confer small but general intellectual benefits. When considered in conjunction with the cost and effort required to master a musical instrument, it is clear that music lessons are *not* a simple fix to a complex problem, or an easy way to raise intelligence. Deciding which activity is most appropriate for a particular child depends on many factors, primarily the child's interests and abilities, what the family can afford, and what can fit into the busy schedules of modern lives.

Acknowledgements

Preparation of this chapter was supported by the Natural Sciences and Engineering Research Council of Canada and the Social Sciences and Humanities Research Council of Canada. Correspondence should be sent to Glenn Schellenberg, Department of

Psychology, University of Toronto at Mississauga, Mississauga, ON, Canada L5L 1C6 (e-mail: g.schellenberg@utoronto.ca).

References

Anvari, S. H., Trainor, B. J., Woodside, J., & Levy, B.A. (2002). Relations among musical skills, phonological processing and early reading abilities in pre-school children. *Journal of Experimental Child Psychology*, **83**, 111–130.

Bartlett, J. C. & Dowling, W. J. (1980). Recognition of transposed melodies: A key-distance effect in developmental perspective. *Journal of Experimental Psychology: Human Perception and Performance*, **6**, 501–515.

Barwick, J., Valentine, E., West, R., & Wilding, J. (1989). Relations between reading and musical abilities. *British Journal of Educational Psychology*, **59**, 253–257.

Bialystok, E. (2001). *Bilingualism in development: Language, literacy, and cognition.* New York: Cambridge University Press.

Brody, N. (1997). Intelligence, schooling, and society. *American Psychologist*, **52**, 1046–1050.

Butzlaff, R. (2000). Can music be used to teach reading? *Journal of Aesthetic Education*, **34**(3/4), 167–178.

Cahill, L. & McGaugh, J. L. (1998). Mechanisms of emotional arousal and lasting declarative memory. *Trends in Neurosciences*, **21**, 294–299.

Carstens, C. B., Huskins, E., & Hounshell, G. W. (1995). Listening to Mozart may not enhance performance on the revised Minnesota Paper Form Board Test. *Psychological Reports*, **77**, 111–114.

Cassady, J. C. & Johnson, R. E. (2002). Cognitive test anxiety and academic performance. *Contemporary Educational Psychology*, **27**, 270–295.

Ceci, S. J. & Williams, W. M. (1997). Schooling, intelligence and income. *American Psychologist*, **52**, 1051–1058.

Chabris, C. F. (1999). Prelude or requiem for the 'Mozart Effect'? *Nature*, **400**, 826–827.

Chan, A. S., Ho., Y.-C., & Cheung, M.-C. (1998). Music training improves verbal memory. *Nature*, **396**, 128.

Costa-Giomi, E. (1999). The effects of three years of piano instruction on children's cognitive development. *Journal of Research in Music Education*, **47**, 198–212.

Curtis, P. (2004, October 22). Music lessons 'dominated by middle-class girls'. *The Guardian*.

Deary, I. J., Whiteman, M. C., Starr, J. M., Whalley, L. J., & Fox, H. C. (2004). The impact of childhood intelligence on later life: Following up the Scottish Mental Surveys of 1932 and 1947. *Journal of Personality and Social Psychology*, **86**, 130–147.

Douglas, S. & Willatts, P. (1994). The relationship between musical ability and literacy skills. *Journal of Research and Reading*, **17**, 99–107.

Dowling, W. J. (1978). Scale and contour: Two components of a theory of memory for melodies. *Psychological Review*, **85**, 341–354.

Dowling, W. J. & Harwood, D. L. (1986). *Music cognition.* Orlando, FL: Academic Press.

Dutton, A. & Carroll, M. (2001). Eyewitness testimony: Effects of source of arousal on memory, source-monitoring, and metamemory judgments. *Australian Journal of Psychology*, **53**, 83–91.

Eich, E. & Forgas, J. P. (2003). Mood, cognition, and memory. In A. F. Healy & R. W. Proctor (eds), *Handbook of psychology: Experimental psychology: Vol. 4.* (pp. 61–83). New York: Wiley.

Fodor, J. A. (1983). *The modularity of mind.* Cambridge, MA: Bradford.

Fujioka, T., Trainor, L. J., Ross, B., Kakigi, R., & Pantev, C. (2004). Musical training enhances automatic encoding of melodic contour and interval structure. *Journal of Cognitive Neuroscience*, 16, 1010–1021.

Gabrielsson, A. (2001). Emotions in strong experiences with music. In P. N. Juslin & J. A. Sloboda (eds), *Music and emotion: Theory and research* (pp. 431–449). New York: Oxford University Press.

Gardiner, M. F., Fox, A., Knowles, F., & Jeffrey, D. (1996). Learning improved by arts training. *Nature*, 381, 284.

Gardner, H. (1993). *Frames of mind: The theory of multiple intelligences* (2nd edn). New York: Basic Books.

Gottfredson, L.S. (1997). Why g matters: The complexity of everyday life. *Intelligence*, 24, 79–132.

Gottfredson, L. S. & Deary, I. J. (2004). Intelligence predicts health and longevity, but why? *Current Directions in Psychological Science*, 13, 1– 4.

Grawitch, M. J., Munz, D. C., Elliott, E. K., & Mathis, A. (2003). Promoting creativity in temporary problem-solving groups: The effects of positive mood and autonomy in problem definition on idea-generating performance. *Group Dynamics*, 7, 200–213.

Gromko, J. E. & Poorman, A. S. (1998a). Developmental trends and relationships in children's aural perception and symbol use. *Journal of Research in Music Education*, 46, 16–23.

Gromko, J. E. & Poorman, A. S. (1998b). The effect of music training on preschoolers' spatial-temporal task performance. *Journal of Research in Music Education*, 46, 173–181.

Hassler, M., Birbaumer, N., & Feil, A. (1985). Musical talent and visual spatial-ability: A longitudinal study. *Psychology of Music*, 13, 99–113.

Hetland, L. (2000a). Learning to make music enhances spatial reasoning. *Journal of Aesthetic Education*, 34(3/4), 179–238.

Hetland, L. (2000b). Listening to music enhances spatial-temporal reasoning: Evidence for the 'Mozart effect'. *Journal of Aesthetic Education*, 34(3/4), 105–148.

Ho, Y.-C., Cheung, M.-C., & Chan, A. S. (2003). Music training improves verbal but not visual memory: Cross sectional and longitudinal explorations in children. *Neuropsychology*, 17, 439–450.

Hurwitz, I., Wolff, P. H., Bortnick, B. D., & Kokas, K. (1975). Nonmusical effects of the Kodály music curriculum in primary grade children. *Journal of Learning Disabilities*, 8, 167–174.

Husain, G., Thompson, W. F., & Schellenberg, E. G. (2002). Effects of musical tempo and mode on arousal, mood, and spatial abilities. *Music Perception*, 20, 151–171.

Isen, A. M., Niedenthal, P., & Cantor, N. (1992). An influence of positive affect on social categorization. *Motivation and Emotion*, 16, 65–78.

Jakobson, L. S., Cuddy, L. L., & Kilgour, A. R. (2003). Time tagging: A key to musicians' superior memory. *Music Perception*, 20, 307–313.

Kaufman, A. S. & Kaufman, N. L. (1985). *Kaufman Test of Educational Achievement*. Circle Pines, MN: American Guidance Service.

Khan, B. E. & Isen, A. M. (1993). The influence of positive affect on variety-seeking among safe, enjoyable products. *Journal of Consumer Research*, 20, 257–270.

Kilgour, A. R., Jakobson, L. S., & Cuddy, L. L. (2000). Music training and rate of presentation as mediators of text and song recall. *Memory & Cognition*, 28, 700–710.

Krumhansl, C. L. (1990). *Cognitive foundations of musical pitch*. New York: Oxford University Press.

Krumhansl, C. L. (1997). An exploratory study of musical emotions and psychophysiology. *Canadian Journal of Experimental Psychology*, 51, 336–352.

Lamb, S. J. & Gregory, A. H. (1993). The relationship between music and reading in beginning readers. *Educational Psychology*, 13, 19–27.

Lynn, R., Wilson, R. G., & Gault, A. (1989). Simple musical tests as measures of Spearman's g. *Personality and Individual Differences*, 10, 25–28.

Nantais, K. M. & Schellenberg, E. G. (1999). The Mozart effect: An artifact of preference. *Psychological Science*, 10, 370–373.

Nelson, D. J. & Barresi, A. L. (1989). Children's age-related intellectual strategies for dealing with musical and spatial analogical tasks. *Journal of Research in Music Education*, 37, 93–103.

Newman, J., Rosenbach, J. H., Burns, K. L., & Latimer, B. C. (1995). An experimental test of the 'Mozart Effect': Does listening to his music improve spatial ability? *Perceptual and Motor Skills*, 81, 1379–1387.

Orsmond, G. I. & Miller, L. K. (1999). Cognitive, musical and environmental correlates of early music instruction. *Psychology of Music*, 27, 18–37.

Peretz, I. (2001). Listen to the brain: A biological perspective on musical emotions. In P. N. Juslin & J. A. Sloboda (eds), *Music and emotion: Theory and research* (pp. 105–134). New York: Oxford University Press.

Rauscher, F. H. (1999). Prelude or requiem for the 'Mozart effect'? *Nature*, 400, 827–828.

Rauscher, F. H. (2002). Mozart and the mind: Factual and fictional effects of musical enrichment. In J. Aronson (ed.), *Improving academic achievement: Impact of psychological factors on education* (pp. 267–278). San Diego: Academic Press.

Rauscher, F. H. & Shaw, G. L. (1998). Key components of the Mozart effect. *Perceptual and Motor Skills*, 86, 835–841.

Rauscher, F. H. & Zupan, M. A. (2000). Classroom keyboard instructions improve kindergarten children's spatial-temporal performance: A field experiment. *Early Childhood Research Quarterly*, 15, 215–228.

Rauscher, F. H., Shaw, G. L., & Ky, K. N. (1993). Music and spatial task performance. *Nature*, 365, 611.

Rauscher, F. H., Shaw, G. L., & Ky, K. N. (1995). Listening to Mozart enhances spatial-temporal reasoning: Towards a neurophysiological basis. *Neuroscience Letters*, 185, 44–47.

Reynolds, C. R. & Kamphaus, R. W. (1992). *Behavior assessment system for children*. Circle Pines, MN: American Guidance Service.

Rideout, B. E. & Laubach, C. M. (1996). EEG correlates of enhanced spatial performance following exposure to music. *Perceptual and Motor Skills*, 82, 427–432.

Rideout, B. E. & Taylor, J. (1997). Enhanced spatial performance following 10 minutes exposure to music: A replication. *Perceptual and Motor Skills*, 85, 112–114.

Rideout, B. E., Dougherty, S., & Wernert, L. (1998). Effect of music on spatial performance: A test of generality. *Perceptual and Motor Skills*, 86, 512–514.

Russell, J. A. (1980). A circumplex model of affect. *Journal of Personality and Social Psychology*, 39, 1161–1178.

Schellenberg, E. G. (2001). Music and non-musical abilities. *Annals of the New York Academy of Sciences*, 930, 355–371.

Schellenberg, E. G. (2003). Does exposure to music have beneficial side effects? In I. Peretz & R. J. Zatorre (eds), *The cognitive neuroscience of music* (pp. 430–448). Oxford: Oxford University Press.

Schellenberg, E. G. (2004). Music lessons enhance IQ. *Psychological Science*, 15, 511–514.

Schellenberg, E. G. (in press). Long-term positive associations between music lessons and IQ. *Journal of Educational Psychology*.

Schellenberg, E. G. & Hallam, S. (2005). Music listening and cognitive abilities in 10- and 11-year-olds: The Blur effect. *Annals of the New York Academy of Science*, 1060, 202–209.

Schellenberg, E. G., Nakata, T., Hunter, P. G., & Tamoto, S. (in press). Exposure to music and cognitive performance: Tests of children and adults. *Psychology of Music*.

Schmidt, L. A. & Trainor, L. J. (2001). Frontal brain electrical activity (EEG) distinguishes valence and intensity of musical emotions. *Cognition and Emotion*, 15, 487–500.

Sergeant, D. & Thatcher, G. (1974). Intelligence, social status, and musical abilities. *Psychology of Music*, 2, 32–57.

Shaw, G.L. (2000). *Keeping Mozart in mind*. San Diego: Academic Press.

Sloboda, J. A. (1992). Empirical studies of emotional response to music. In M. R. Jones & S. Holleran (eds), *Cognitive bases of musical communication* (pp. 33–46). Washington, DC: American Psychological Association.

Sloboda, J. A. & Juslin, P. N. (2001). Psychological perspectives on music and emotion. In P. N. Juslin & J. A. Sloboda (eds), *Music and emotion: Theory and research* (pp. 71–104). New York: Oxford University Press.

Smith, J. D. (1997). The place of musical novices in music science. *Music Perception*, 14, 227–262.

Steele, K. M., Ball, T. M., & Runk, R. (1997). Listening to Mozart does not enhance backwards digit span performance. *Perceptual and Motor Skills*, 84, 1179–1184.

Steele, K. M., Brown, K. M., & Stoecker, J. A. (1999a). Failure to confirm the Rauscher and Shaw description of recovery of the Mozart effect. *Perceptual and Motor Skills*, 88, 843–848.

Steele, K. M., Bass, K. E., & Crook, M. D. (1999b). The mystery of the Mozart effect: Failure to replicate. *Psychological Science*, 10, 366–369.

Steele, K. M., Dalla Bella, S., Peretz, I., Dunlop, T., Dawe, L. A., Humphrey, G. K., Shannon, R. A., Kirby Jr., K. L., & Olmstead, C. G. (1999c). Prelude or requiem for the 'Mozart effect'? *Nature*, 400, 827.

Sternberg, R. J., Grigorenko, E. L., & Bundy, D. A. (2001). The predictive value of IQ. *Merrill-Palmer Quarterly*, 47, 1–41.

Stough, C., Kerkin, B., Bates, T., & Mangan, G. (1994). Music and spatial IQ. *Personality and Individual Differences*, 17, 695.

Thayer, J. F. & Levenson, R. (1983). Effects of music on psychophysiological responses to a stressful film. *Psychomusicology*, 3, 44–54.

Thompson, W. F., Schellenberg, E. G., & Husain, G. (2001). Arousal, mood and the Mozart effect. *Psychological Science*, 12, 248–251.

Thorndike, R. L., Hagen, E. P., & Sattler, J. M. (1986). *The Stanford-Binet Intelligence Scale* (4th edn). Chicago: Riverside.

Vaughn, K. (2000). Music and mathematics: Modest support for the oft-claimed relationship. *Journal of Aesthetic Education*, 34(3/4), 149–166.

Wechsler, D. (1991). *Wechsler intelligence scale for children* (3rd edn). San Antonio, TX: Psychological Corporation.

Wechsler, D. (1997). *Wechsler adult intelligence scale* (3rd edn). San Antonio, TX: Psychological Corporation.

CHAPTER 7

MUSICAL PREFERENCE AND TASTE IN CHILDHOOD AND ADOLESCENCE

DAVID J. HARGREAVES, ADRIAN C. NORTH, AND MARK TARRANT

Introduction

Music is all around us in twenty-first century life—in shops, restaurants, workplaces, dental surgeries, and on recorded phone messages, as well as in the concert hall and the media. Two recent studies have estimated that approximately 40–50% of most people's everyday lives involve music in some way, whether in passive listening, or in more active participation (Sloboda *et al.*, 2001; North *et al.*, 2004). Because we hear music in so many different circumstances and contexts, and because it fulfils so many different functions in our lives, it is hardly surprising that our musical tastes and preferences are in a constant state of flux.

In this chapter we look for regularities in the complex and ever-changing pattern of individual preferences, with a particular focus on age changes from early childhood through to adolescence. These questions are of vital concern to musicians, teachers, and audiences: and in this chapter, we approach them from our own perspective as psychologists. If any such developmental patterns can be identified, it is our job as psychologists to try to explain rather than merely to describe them. We will review the nebulous and scattered literature on the development of taste and preference, and try to explain the main findings in terms of three main theoretical approaches: experimental aesthetics, developmental approaches, and social identity theory (SIT).

To be clear at the outset, we use the term *preference* to refer to a person's liking for one piece of music as compared with another at a given point in time, and *taste* to refer to the overall patterning of an individual's preferences over longer time periods (for a further discussion of these issues of definition, and the relationship with other terms such as *attitudes, emotional responses, opinions*, and *behavioural intentions*, see Hargreaves, 1986). We propose that any explanation of taste and preference must take into account the characteristics of the three main components of any listening situation, namely the *person* (e.g., age, gender, cultural group, musical training), the *music* (e.g., structure, style, complexity, familiarity), and the *listening situation* (e.g., work, leisure, entertainment situations, presence/absence of others), and we start the chapter with a brief description of a 'reciprocal feedback' model of musical response that will enable us to specify how these different factors may interact in giving rise to a preference response, which may then feed into longer-term patterns of taste.

The rest of the chapter is organized around the main theoretical approaches mentioned above. First, we review research in the field of *experimental aesthetics*, which has traditionally focused on the characteristics of the musical stimulus itself, and on how these affect different types of response in the listener. The two main types of explanation within experimental aesthetics are those that explain preferences in terms of the levels of arousal that different stimulus configurations arouse in the listener, and the opposing 'preference for prototypes' model. We compare and contrast these two approaches, and summarize their relative contributions to the explanation of developmental issues.

Other developmental research has focused on explaining age-related changes in musical behaviour. We review those studies that have looked specifically at age changes in musical preference and taste, mostly in childhood and adolescence (though there are also smaller research literatures on prenatal preferences, and those in old age). Some of this research assumes that age-related changes in preference derive from changes in cognitive maturation, though authors differ in the extent to which they explicitly espouse the idea of developmental stages (see discussion by Hargreaves, 1996). One of the main objections to the existence of stages is that any regular individual developments are swamped by the massive influence of social and cultural factors arising from the media, from popular culture, and many other external sources, such that current socio-cultural research on the development of preferences is more likely to investigate specific social groups, musical styles, or situations.

This leads on to the third major theoretical approach, that of SIT (Tajfel & Turner, 1979). This proposes that we all categorize ourselves as members of certain social groups (ingroups), that we correspondingly define other social groups as outgroups, and that we use the distinction between the two as a basis for self-evaluation. This approach is used in explaining childhood and adolescent identity issues, and the importance of music to adolescents has stimulated some of our own studies on the social functions of musical preference and taste in adolescence. In this part of the chapter we review some empirical research on social comparison and musical taste in adolescence, and also consider areas in which a social identity perspective can be fruitfully employed in the future.

A reciprocal feedback model of musical response

Responses to music are determined by the variables involved in the three interacting components of any given listening situation, namely the *listener*, the *music*, and the *listening situation*. Figure 7.1 summarizes our conception of how these interactions take place and how each, individually and in interaction, gives rise to a *response* in the listener. We describe it as a 'reciprocal feedback' model because each of the three components can exert a simultaneous influence upon each of the other two, and because these mutual influences are bidirectional in each case.

The model shown in Figure 7.1, which is elaborated and described in more detail by Hargreaves *et al.* (2005), describes the determinants of an immediate response to a specific musical stimulus at a given point in time. The *music* itself can be characterized, and be seen

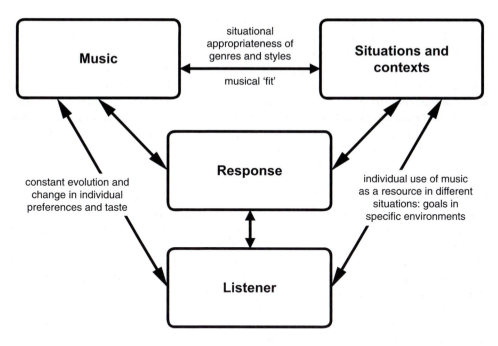

Figure 7.1 Reciprocal feedback model of musical response.

to vary, in several different ways. As we shall see in the next section, research in experimental aesthetics describes the different 'collative variables' of a given stimulus, such as its complexity, familiarity, or orderliness, and other researchers emphasize its *prototypicality*—the extent to which a piece is typical of the genre or style that it represents. Listeners' immediate reactions in terms of style or genre can sometimes have a more powerful influence on preference than the piece itself (North & Hargreaves, 1997).

Listeners vary with respect to 'individual difference' factors such as age, gender, personality, and specific musical training, knowledge, and experience, and these will all determine preference responses, and Rentfrow and Gosling (2003) have carried out some intriguing new research on the personality correlates of preferences. Figure 7.1 shows how we can conceptualize the reciprocal feedback relationship between the music and the listener: individuals' immediate responses to new stimuli are shaped by their longer-term taste patterns, but significant new responses can correspondingly change those longer-term patterns, as the system is in a constant state of change and evolution.

Situations and contexts, which complete the triangle, might include features of the listener's immediate situation (e.g., the presence or absence of others, or simultaneous engagement in other ongoing activities): the immediate social or institutional context (e.g., concert hall, shop, restaurant, workplace, school classroom, consumer or leisure environment), and also broader factors relating to regional or national influences (e.g., music associated with sports clubs, political movements, or national figures). The reciprocal feedback relationship between situations and contexts and the listener refers in Figure 7.1 to the interaction between the effects of music on a listener in a specific situation, and the ways in which individuals in contemporary society use music as a resource, for example in managing emotional states or moods. We have demonstrated elsewhere that people have specific arousal-state and other goals in specific environments, and that they consciously use music to achieve these goals (see North & Hargreaves, 2000a).

The final link in the reciprocal causal chain is that between the music and the situation and/or context within which it is heard. Our work on music and consumer behaviour shows very clearly that different genres and styles are generally perceived as being more or less appropriate to different environments, for example: a shop selling fashion wear to young people will typically play loud contemporary pop music, an antique shop may discreetly play Vivaldi or Mozart, and the retail industry invests a good deal of time and money into creating appropriate 'in-store ambience' by optimizing the musical 'fit' with specific products and environments. Music can also influence responses to specific situations, however: we were able to demonstrate empirically that variations in the music played in a cafeteria was systematically related to diners' reactions to and behaviour within it (North & Hargreaves, 1996).

This is a general model of responses to music, and not all responses to music include preference responses, of course: we shall draw on the distinction between the affective and cognitive components of musical response later in the chapter. The model nevertheless provides a perspective from which we can explain preference responses, and these in turn shape people's longer-term tastes, and ultimately their musical identities (see Hargreaves *et al.*, 2002).

Experimental aesthetics

Over the past 10–20 years, research on experimental aesthetics has focused on one issue, namely the relative importance of two theories concerning arousal-mediating and cognitive variables respectively (see e.g., Boselie, 1991; Hekkert & Snelders, 1995; Konečni, 1996). The arousal-based approach is best associated with Berlyne (1971). He argued that when someone hears music, he or she collates several of its informational properties such as complexity and familiarity. The theory claims that liking for the music is determined principally by the effect of these collative stimulus properties on activity in the autonomic nervous system. Music that possesses intermediate degrees of what has been termed *arousal potential* is supposedly liked most, giving rise to what has been termed an 'inverted-U' relationship between preference and collative properties (see Figure 7.2). Indeed, numerous studies carried out in the 1970s supplied broad support for Berlyne's theory (see review in Hargreaves, 1986).

The next major development in the field occurred in the 1980s when other researchers (e.g., Martindale & Moore, 1988) began to challenge this approach. They argued instead that preference is determined by the extent to which a particular stimulus is typical of its class. Explanations of this have tended to invoke neural network models of human cognition: this approach claims that preference is positively related to prototypicality because typical stimuli give rise to stronger activation of the salient cognitive categories, and allow the perceiver to make greater sense of the world.

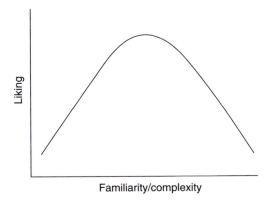

Figure 7.2 The inverted U relationship between liking for music and its arousal-evoking qualities.

Consequently by the mid-1980s there were essentially two competing camps. One comprised adherents to Berlyne's theory who argued that the collative properties of art works were most important because preference was determined by arousal of the autonomic nervous system. Although not behaviourists themselves the researchers had clearly been influenced by elements of the approach, favouring precise manipulations of artificial stimuli followed by measurement of the observable physical effects of these. The other camp comprised a younger group of cognitive psychologists who argued that the prototypicality of a given art work of the more general category to which it belonged was most important; and that this was because preference was determined by the activation of cognitive categories in the mind of the perceiver. Although these researchers continued the tradition of careful manipulation of (usually artificial) artistic stimuli, they had far fewer concerns about discussing the effect of these on mental states and abstract cognitive constructs.

The degree of conflict was increased by the nature of much of the research on what might be termed the *preference for prototypes* model. Understandably, a considerable portion of this considered the relative extent to which prototypicality and stimulus arousal potential were able to explain liking for aesthetic objects. The consistent conclusion of this research was that variations in preference are more closely associated with stimulus prototypicality. For example, Martindale and Moore (1989) report that complexity accounted for 4% of the variance in participants' preference for classical music themes, whereas 51% was accounted for by typicality measures (see similar findings by Whitfield & Slatter, 1979; Whitfield, 1983; Moore & Martindale, 1983; Hekkert & van Wieringen, 1990; Martindale *et al.*, 1990). Martindale *et al.* (1988) argued that results such as these 'suggest that collative variables are probably a good deal less important in determining preference than Berlyne thought them to be. Furthermore, they probably determine preference via mechanisms different than those proposed by Berlyne' (p. 94).

Taken at face value, this implies that Berlyne's theory should be discarded. However, as two of us have argued elsewhere (North & Hargreaves, 2000b), this is not necessarily the case. Although there are other arguments we could cite, perhaps the most compelling is that variations in the arousal potential of a piece of music (i.e., an arousal-mediating variable) also affect the typicality of a piece of music of the class from which it is drawn. For example, some of Stockhausen's music would score very highly on measures of arousal potential, and supporters of Berlyne's theory would argue that this explains its unpopularity relative to say Beethoven, although this may raise some deeper issues for musicologists. Nevertheless, the same erratic nature that gives this music its arousal potential also makes it untypical of the category 'classical music'. In short, arousal-mediating variables contribute to the prototypicality of a stimulus. In other words, both approaches can consider the same aspects of music as being important. The discrepancy still remains, however, concerning the causal mechanisms proposed by the two theories, with one focusing on the autonomic nervous system and the other focusing on unobservable cognitive mechanisms. However, even this apparent distinction presupposes that the nervous system arousal and cognitive functioning are wholly unrelated. This of course is certainly not the case, and there is no evidence of which we are aware to suggest that just because a piece of music produces nervous system arousal it cannot also affect the listener's cognitive processing. Consequently, the battle between the two theories may to some extent constitute a 'red herring' for those concerned with more practical issues.

Nevertheless, this degree of theoretical confusion perhaps explains why so little research has considered specifically developmental issues. Consequently it is worthwhile speculating on how the two theories may be applied in future research aiming towards understanding young people's developing musical preferences. Although it is possible to formulate numerous hypotheses we instead focus on two that seem particularly likely to bear fruit.

First of all let us consider research that might be carried out more overtly within the approach of Berlyne's theory. One concept that remains almost entirely unresearched concerns increasing acculturation over the lifespan to a broad range of musical styles. As we noted earlier, technological advances mean that music is perhaps more prevalent in our everyday lives now than at any previous point in time. It is important to remember that not all this exposure to music is voluntary, as we also hear music in the context of other media (e.g., television advertising) and in numerous places outside the home (e.g., restaurants). This means that over the course of the lifespan there is a continuous growth in the number of hours we have been exposed to a variety of musical styles. For example, a pop-music-loving 5 year old will have heard less classical music than a pop-music-loving 15 year old, who in turn will have heard less classical music than a pop-music-loving 35 year old.

This increasing exposure over the lifespan has interesting implications in terms of Berlyne's theory. The more we hear a particular piece of music or musical style so the easier it is to understand it. In short, the music becomes less erratic and varied to our own individual ear, and this of course means that it would be perceived as less complex. In short, with increasing age, a piece of music or musical style moves from right to left along the inverted-U relationship between liking and arousal potential. The process is demonstrated in Figure 7.3. Graph A shows the position of three pop songs at one particular point in time, and Graph B shows how the position of these songs on the inverted-U should change following repeated exposures. This suggests one interesting model for how musical preferences could evolve through the lifespan. Increasing age could well be associated with a preference

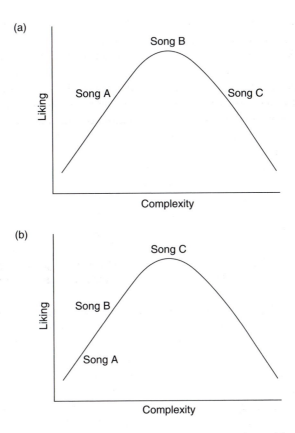

Figure 7.3 (a,b) The effect of increasing similarity over time on the subjective complexity of three songs.

for increasingly complex music. Whereas Song B might be moderately arousing to young ears (see Graph A) it could be could be too simplistic to older ears (Graph B): Song C might seem uninterpretable to children (Graph A), but could be moderately arousing to older people (Graph B). Such a process could only occur for music common to our culture, but does suggest one means by which liking for individual pieces or even entire styles (with their characteristic levels of complexity) might evolve as people age.

Similarly, the preference for prototypes theory may also be able to shed light on the development of musical taste across the lifespan. Holbrook (1995) found that preferences for several types of musical and other stimuli tended to peak for those 'encountered during a *critical period* of development associated with late adolescence or early adulthood' (p. 57), and consistent with this are data concerning specifically pop music reported by North and Hargreaves (1995). Two hundred and seventy-five participants aged 9–78 years were asked to nominate their most eminent pop musicians. The 'top 10' list for each age group implied one very interesting pattern. Although there was a tendency for all age groups to nominate the 'greats' of pop music such as The Beatles, the remaining nominations seemed to be

Table 7.1 The 'top 10' most eminent pop musicians in 1995 according to different age groups.

9–10 year olds	14–15 year olds	18–24 year olds	25–49 year olds	50+ year olds
1. 2 Unlimited	1. Madonna/ Wet Wet Wet/ The Beatles	1. The Beatles	1. The Beatles	1. The Beatles
2. Wet Wet Wet		2. U2	2. David Bowie	2. Simon and Garfunkel
3. The Beatles/Elvis Presley		3. Madness	3. Simon and Garfunkel	3. Perry Como/Shirley Bassey/Cliff Richard/Harry Belafonte/Andy Williams
	4. Elvis Presley	4. Elvis Presley	4. Elvis Presley	
5. Pet Shop Boys	5. Bryan Adams	5. Eurythmics	5. Eurythmics/ The Rolling Stones	
6. Madonna/ Michael Jackson	6. Whitney Houston	6. Madonna		
	7. Haddaway	7. Jimi Hendrix	7. The Police	
8. Ace of Base	8. U2/Take That	8. The Police	8. Jimi Hendrix	8. The Shadows
9. Jazzy Jeff and the Fresh Prince		9. George Michael	9. The Beach Boys	9. The Bachelors
10. Take That/ Janet Jackson	10. Pet Shop Boys	10. The Rolling Stones	10. U2	10. Petula Clarke

awarded to artists who were themselves at the peak of their fame during the participants' adolescence/early adulthood (see Table 7.1).

In direct contrast to the idea proposed earlier, this suggests that our notion of what constitutes 'music' does not evolve over time, and instead becomes fixed forevermore during the adolescence/early adulthood 'critical period'. If this central category of 'music' does not change then any new piece of music should be evaluated according to the extent to which it corresponds with that which we heard when in adolescence/early adulthood. In short, today's music will always be evaluated by yesterday's criteria. Such an argument might explain why many aspects of our musical preferences remain consistent throughout life.

Developmental approaches

Age changes in the perception, production, and performance of music are of great interest to musicians and educators as well as to psychologists, and a good deal of research has looked at this. Swanwick and Runfola (2002) have recently reviewed this field in Colwell and Richardson's *New Handbook of Research on Music Teaching and Learning*, drawing extensively on an earlier review by Hargreaves and Zimmerman (1992) in the original *Handbook*. They cite in particular Gordon's music learning theory (e.g., Gordon, 1976), Serafine's (1988) account of 'music as cognition', the numerous contributions of Howard

Gardner and other researchers associated with Harvard Project Zero, notably Davidson and Scripp, and Bamberger; Swanwick and Tillman's (1986) developmental spiral, and Hargreaves and Galton's (1992) descriptive model of parallel age-related developments across the different art forms.

Swanwick and Runfola's (2002) title, 'Developmental characteristics of learners', implies that age-related changes in musical behaviour are primarily determined by the character-istics of the learner, and a good deal of the research they review implicitly adopts the view that these changes have their origins in cognitive maturation, which is often linked with the proposal of Piagetian-style developmental stages. Many contemporary developmental psychologists in the UK and elsewhere reject stage-type theories for a number of different reasons, however (e.g., Goswami, 2001), and the postulation of age-related stages or phases in musical development is problematic.

These considerations of age developments in competencies, skills, or abilities may be less likely to apply to musical preferences and tastes, as likes and dislikes are presumably less dependent on the maturation of competencies and skills than performing or composing abilities, for example. This is not necessarily true, however: one of the more prominent explanations of age-related changes in preferences is that the putative cognitive structures underlying musical behaviour at different ages do exert a direct influence upon individual likes and dislikes. The notion of general 'cognitive aesthetic development' was used by one of us, for example, in summarizing the findings of several empirical investigations of developmental changes in children's aesthetic judgements about visual art works (see Hargreaves & Galton, 1992).

Bearing this in mind, it is useful to evaluate the literature on the development of musical preference and taste by keeping a clear distinction in mind between the capabilities that appear to be involved in making a particular preference decision, and the actual content of that decision. Concerning the first of these, a small body of research has built up on the devel-opment of what has become known as 'musical style sensitivity', i.e., the ability to distinguish between exemplars of different musical styles. The terminology is confusing in this field. Six different types of response to musical style—stylistic sensitivity, discrimination, knowledge, liking, tolerance and competence—have been proposed in the research literature, and we have tried to spell out the differences between these (Hargreaves & North, 1999).

Gardner (1973), in a pioneering study in this area, found that 11–19-year-old groups were better able than 6–11 year olds to discriminate between excerpts drawn from different styles of classical music, for example, but that the 11 year olds scored highest overall; the tendency to respond to music using style labels as such only became apparent among the 14 year olds in this study, and this was supported by Hargreaves' (1982) finding that the spontaneous use of musical style labels increased regularly with age. Castell (1982) repeated Gardner's study including pop and jazz music alongside classical pieces, and by using a more user friendly task; she found that all the members of her sample were much more accurate on the task with pop than with classical styles, and that her 8–9 year olds scored higher with pop music styles than 10–11 year olds.

Following these early studies, several other researchers have carried out cross-sectional studies that have used different age groups, musical styles, and task procedures (e.g., Addessi et al., 1995; Hargreaves & North, 1999). Marshall's (2001) doctoral thesis, which incorporates six separate empirical studies, showed that systematic variations in different aspects of the experimental procedure and testing situation could influence participants' level of success on the tasks. These included the participants' level of motivation (investigated by introducing competition and rewards), variations in the personal characteristics of the test administrator, and the school timetabling context within which the tasks were administered. He also showed that the level of contrast between the musical excerpts selected as representative of different styles and genres could exert a critical influence on participants' ability to make stylistic discriminations.

Given Marshall's findings, and the generally disparate results from the other studies in this field, our interim conclusion is that although some age-related changes in stylistic discrimination and knowledge do seem to exist, their manifestation is strongly dependent on the range of genres under investigation, the degree of contrast between the style exemplars that are selected, and on the experimental procedures employed. The best way to explain this, following the conclusions of our own study (Hargreaves & North, 1999), is to distinguish between the cognitive and affective components of responses to musical styles—i.e., in people's abilities to understand and discuss them on the one hand, and their subjective responses to them, including likes and dislikes, on the other. There may be more consistent age-related changes in the former—in stylistic knowledge, for example, which will increase through acculturation and learning, than in the latter—but both aspects are influenced directly by the social and cultural connotations of the particular pieces under investigation.

This takes us on to the more extensive body of research on the *content* of the musical preferences of different age groups, which was comprehensively reviewed by both Finnäs (1989) and LeBlanc (1991). Finnäs was interested in the extent to which musical preferences can be modified, from an educational point of view, and he divided his review into those studies dealing with: (1) specific characteristics of the music; (2) effects of familiarity and repetition; (3) the contrast between 'intramusical' and 'intrapersonal' strategies of influencing preference; and (4) social influences. LeBlanc's (1991) comprehensive review was specifically devoted to the effects of 'maturation/ageing' on music listening preference, however, and we have drawn extensively upon it in compiling Table 7.2. This table summarizes the participants and musical stimuli employed in most of the studies reviewed by LeBlanc, and also includes the few that have been conducted in the intervening years.

LeBlanc (1991) used the concept of 'open-earedness', a term that was first used in the psychological research literature by Hargreaves (1982) and by Castell (1982), in explaining the overall pattern of these results. We originally used the term as a shorthand way of conveying our impression that that younger children were more readily able to listen to and maybe also enjoy unconventional or unusual (e.g., 'avant garde', aleatory, or electronic) musical forms, as they may 'show less evidence of acculturation to normative standards of 'good taste' than older children' (Hargreaves, 1982, p. 51). LeBlanc then proposed four generalizations on the basis of his review: that 'younger children are more open-eared … open-earedness declines as the child enters adolescence … there is a partial rebound of open-earedness as the listener matures from adolescence to young adulthood … open-earedness declines as the listener matures to old age' (pp. 36–38).

A closer look at Table 7.2 shows that with one or two exceptions, LeBlanc's generalizations receive general support. The 'dip' in open-earedness in later childhood seems to occur at

Table 7.2 Summary of empirical studies of age differences in stylistic preference.

	Participants	Music	Results
Rubin-Rabson (1940)	70 adults 20–70 y	24 art music orchestral works 1750–1925: 'classic', 'transitional', 'modern' periods	'classic' and 'modern' preference decreased with age
Fisher (1951)	251 grades 6, 9, 10, and college students	art music of differing levels of formality	grade 6 preferred Gould (least formal) to Haydn (most), college students vice versa
Keston & Pinto (1955)	202 college students at 3 age levels	'serious classical', 'popular classical', 'dinner', 'popular'	$r = 0.38$ between age and preference for 'good' music
Rogers (1957)	635 grades 4, 7, 9, 12	'seriously classical', 'popular classical', 'dinner', 'popular'	preference for classical decreased with age, diversity of preferences decreased between grades 4 and 12
Baumann (1960)	1410 12–20 y	range of styles within 'art music', 'popular', 'traditional'	popular preference decreased with age, classical preference increased with age
Taylor (1969)	800 8–11 y	paired excerpts of art music by composers from 6 historical periods	preference for twentieth century composers decreased with age, for later baroque composers increased with age
Meadows (1970)	982 grade 7 college students	30 excerpts from 10 'popular' and 'art music' styles	art music preference increased with age
Greer et al. (1974)	134 grades K–6	'top 20 rock' and 'non-rock' styles, operant listening task	older Ps preferred 'rock', becoming significant at grade 2
Bragg & Crozier (1974)	12 at each of 8–9, 14–15, 20+ y	random electronic stimuli at 6 complexity levels: studies I, II, III with different preference tasks	I older Ps preferred more complex on verbal rating scale task: II no age effect on paired comparison task: III no age effect on untimed task younger Ps listened for longer than older
Eisenstein (1979)	64 grades 2–6	Webern tone rows	
Geringer (1982)	40 × grades 5/6, college music and non-music majors	popular and art music, operant listening task	college music majors preferred art music, other two groups preferred popular
May (1985)	577 grades 1–3	24 pieces representing 9 generic styles including art music, popular music, non-Western music	overall preference decreased with age, decline for 'rock' and 'country' styles less than for other styles

Table 7.2 (Continued)

	Participants	Music	Results
Hargreaves and Castell (1987)	96, 16 in each of grades K, 2, 4, 6, 9, college	familiar/unfamiliar real melodies, near/far approximations to music	preference for approximations decreased with age; preference for real melodies suggest inverted U preference function with age
Haack (1988)	108 25–54 y	pop song titles 1945–1982: selection of 'top 10 of all time'	preference for music popular in mid-20s
LeBlanc et al. (1988)	926 grades 3, 5, 7, 9, 10, 11, 12, college	24 trad jazz pieces at different tempo levels	preferences summed over tempo levels: U-shaped curve with age
Le Blanc et al. (1993)	2262 6–91 y	'art music', trad jazz, rock	preference decreased in adolescence, increased in adulthood, decreased in old age
Hargreaves et al. (1995)	278 grades 7, 11	ratings of 12 style category labels	overall liking decreased with age, especially for 'serious' styles
North & Hargreaves (1995)	275 9–78 y	nominations of 30 most eminent pop artists 1955–94	general preference for artists from late adolescence/early adulthood: Beatles/Elvis nominated by all
Hargreaves & North (1999)	275 9–78 y	ratings of liking for self-nominated styles	liking for rock/pop styles decreased with age, for classical increased with age: 'crossover' in middle age?
Gembris & Schellenberg (2003)	591 grades K-6	popular, classical, avant garde, ethnic	overall preference decreased with age: grade 1 most positive, grade 6 most negative, overall preference for pop

around the age of 10 or 11 years, and this typically shows itself in very strongly expressed preferences for a narrow range of pop styles, and strong general dislike for all other styles. After this, there seems to be a general decline in liking for popular music styles across the rest of the lifespan, and a corresponding general increase in 'classical' styles—although this does not necessarily seem to apply to more contemporary art music (e.g., Taylor, 1969). There may be some kind of interaction with the familiarity or complexity of the music (cf. Hargreaves & Castell, 1987), and several of the studies suggest that age and musical training are associated with preference for more 'serious' music, but there is insufficient evidence to propose any causal links between these findings.

The studies by Haack (1988) and North and Hargreaves (1995), both using eminence judgements, clearly demonstrate a general preference for artists/musicians who were popular during the listeners' late adolescence/early adulthood: the latter study also reveals the intriguing finding that some popular artists, Elvis Presley and the Beatles in particular, are consistently rated as eminent by all age groups over the last 30 years or so. Given that the studies in Table 7.2 vary widely with respect to their theoretical rationales, their participant groups and age ranges, the actual genres and styles under investigation, and the assessment techniques employed, it is perhaps surprising that LeBlanc's generalizations do seem to hold true—this is still the case for the most recent study, by Gembris and Schellenberg (2003).

These generalizations about age differences in 'open-earedness' with respect to 'popular' and 'classical' or 'serious' styles may be valid because they work at a high level of generality: they refer to broad genres rather than to specific styles within those genres, and thus side-step the problems of cohort or historical effects. By obtaining the eminence rankings of participants aged between 9 and 78 years for specific popular musicians over the last half of the last century, for example, North and Hargreaves (1995) produced clear evidence for such effects: but it was nevertheless possible to make generalizations about preferences that were not bound to specific historical periods. Investigating preferences for specific current popular styles would present huge practical problems because those styles themselves are changing and evolving more rapidly than ever in today's postmodern and increasingly globalized society.

Social identity theory

SIT (Tajfel & Turner, 1979) is based on the idea that individuals seek to evaluate their social group memberships—however these are defined—positively; that is, they strive for positive social identity. A wealth of research has supported this simple idea in both real and artificial (i.e., experimentally created) social groups. This research has demonstrated that the need for positive social identity underpins a broad range of group-based phenomena, including personal motivation to adopt group norms (e.g., Noel et al., 1995), beliefs about group variability (e.g., Doosje et al., 1995) and also willingness to engage in group-protecting behaviours (i.e., intergroup discrimination: Branscombe & Wann, 1994).

We recently completed a series of studies that investigated how SIT can be used to predict adolescents' musical behaviour. These studies have been reviewed elsewhere (Tarrant et al., 2002) and so we do not need to elaborate them again in detail here. The most important point to convey, however, is that expressions of musical preference in adolescence seem to be guided by *group norms* that can be drawn upon in contexts in which social identity needs are salient.

In one study (Tarrant *et al.*, 2001a), we demonstrated that adolescents associated their own peer group with music that was valued positively by the group (e.g., popular music, dance music) to a greater extent than they associated an outgroup with that same music. At the same time, they associated the outgroup with music that was valued negatively (e.g., classical music, country music) to a greater extent than they associated the ingroup with that music. A separate study (Tarrant *et al.*, 2001b) established that musical behaviour is *more* important to social identity processes than certain other behaviours, such as those related to other media activities and sport: Adolescents relied primarily on statements about music in order to distinguish the ingroup from an outgroup.

An understanding of the normative processes underlying adolescents' musical preferences enables the generation of hypotheses concerning what should happen when group norms are violated (i.e., when individuals fail to behave in line with a group norm). Research into the so-called 'black sheep effect' (Marques *et al.*, 1988) seems particularly informative here. This research has elaborated the ways in which groups deal with members who violate group norms. It has been demonstrated that the presence of an antinormative (deviant) member can represent a threat to the distinctiveness of the group; when such a threat is perceived, a common response is to derogate the deviant (thereby removing the threat: Castano *et al.*, 2002). The presence of antinormative members does not automatically raise concerns about group distinctiveness, however: when the deviant behaviour can be attributed to factors outside of the deviant's personal control (e.g., to an unfavourable social situation), deviants seem to be treated equally as favourably as members who do not violate a norm (De Cremer & Vanbeselaere, 1999).

Tarrant *et al.* (2004) investigated this idea in an experimental context in which a musical norm was implicitly violated. Adolescents in this study were asked to imagine that members of an ingroup and an outgroup had either been listening to a radio station that played pop/dance music (positively valued behaviours) or had been listening to a radio station that played country/classical music (negatively valued behaviours). Participants were asked to explain the behaviour of the group members. Results showed that, relative to the outgroup, negative behaviours of the ingroup were attributed to factors external to the group (cf. Islam & Hewstone, 1993). That is, participants tended to say that the ingroup members would be comparatively *unlikely* to perform the behaviour again and that they would be *unlikely* to perform similar behaviours in the future (i.e., they implied that the behaviour was an isolated incident). In short, participants seemed to be more forgiving of the antinormative behaviour when it was performed by a member of the ingroup (see Hornsey *et al.*, 2002).

Most recently, research into the black sheep effect has focused on the consequences of norm violation in a *developmental* context, and it is in this regard that we see the social identity perspective making a particularly valuable contribution to music research in the future. This research has addressed the issue of *when* group-based responses to norm violation are likely to emerge. While children as young as 4 or 5 years of age have been shown to exhibit consistent preferences for their own social groups (Bennett *et al.*, 1998; Nesdale *et al.*, 2003), the ability to determine when a group norm has been violated does not seem to emerge until later in childhood, when social cognition is more sophisticated (Abrams *et al.*, 2003).

In terms of understanding the development of musical preference, the finding that sensitivity to norm violation emerges in late childhood may help explain the corresponding reduction in open-earedness at that time. As described earlier, younger children seem willing to embrace multiple styles of music (i.e., they are open-eared). At this age specific styles of music do not seem to have been assigned normative value within a group context (or at least children have not yet developed the ability to recognize when a preference norm has been violated). As such, a child who expresses preference for one particular style of music would not be expected to be treated any differently to a child who expresses a preference for a different style.

However, when sensitivity to norm violation emerges in later childhood, we would expect children who violate a preference norm (e.g., those who continue to demonstrate open-earedness) to attract the scrutiny of others. If the behaviour of such children cannot be attributed to external factors (e.g., as in Tarrant et al., 2004), we would expect them to be labelled as 'black sheep', and derogated accordingly. In short, the development of normative awareness would be expected to exert pressure on older, but not younger, children to adhere to normative standards of musical preference.

We suggest that research now seeks to clarify precisely the ways in which sensitivity to norm violation helps to structure children's developing musical preferences. Elaboration of this process will also likely prove informative to an understanding of more general self-processes in childhood and adolescence. On this basis, it seems possible that the expression of preference for 'appropriate' music might be one means by which young people can strategically ensure acceptance by their group, and ultimately avoid the negative consequences for self that are associated with peer rejection (Boivin & Bégin, 1989; Parker & Asher, 1993).

So far, research that has applied a social identity perspective to musical behaviour has focused largely on how expressions of musical preference facilitate group distinctiveness, and ultimately intergroup discrimination. In the last part of this section we turn briefly to research that has considered how music can be used to help facilitate improvements in social relations.

Drawing on Gaertner et al.'s (1993) 'common ingroup identity' model, Bakagiannis and Tarrant (2006) showed how statements about musical preference can influence adolescents' cognitive representations and subsequent treatment of different groups. Participants in this study were first assigned to social groups created for the purpose of the experiment (cf. Tajfel et al., 1971) and were then led to believe that the two groups either had very similar or very different musical preferences (the nature of the musical preferences was not specified). A third group was not told anything about the groups' musical preferences. After this, participants rated each group along a series of trait adjectives. In line with the common ingroup identity model, the introduction of a common social identity appeared to lead to a reduction in levels of discrimination. Specifically, compared with participants who were not told anything about the two groups' musical preferences, those who believed the groups had very similar preferences were less likely to perceive that the groups were different along the trait adjectives.

This study represents an encouraging first step towards highlighting ways in which music can help improve relations between social groups. Of course, a limitation of the above study is that it used artificial groups and these allowed for the relatively easy manipulation of musical preference beliefs. A goal for future research therefore should be to extend this analysis to real social contexts using groups whose musical preferences are more firmly established. On the basis of the research discussed in this section and elsewhere (Tarrant *et al.*, 2002), we believe that the continued adoption of the social identity perspective is likely to prove instrumental in this regard.

Conclusions

The purpose of this chapter has been to review the fundamental mechanisms governing the development of preference and taste from the psychological point of view, as well as to review the research literature on the course of development of those preferences. Our main contention forms the essence of the musical response model presented in Figure 7.1: that any adequate explanation of these developments must take into account the interactions between the person, the music, and their social and cultural context, and the model represents a first attempt to do so.

Although the model operates at a very broad and imprecise level, it nevertheless provides a framework within which we can conceptualize the interplay between different theoretical approaches. Experimental aesthetics deals mainly with 'the music' in the model, albeit at a very general level, and would benefit enormously from further contributions from music theory. Developmental approaches focus on one important 'listener variable', age, which of course interacts with many other aspects of individual differences. SIT deals specifically with the ways in which one important aspect of 'situations and contexts', the presence of significant others, directly affects the listener's immediate responses, and thereby incorporates much more long-term and deep-seated aspects of personal identity.

Given the immense importance of musical taste and preference in the everyday lives and social identities of young people, and the commercial significance of the music business, we suggest that the issues raised in this chapter have profound implications for education and social policy (see e.g., Lamont *et al.*, 2003; North & Hargreaves, 2003). The power of music is increasingly apparent in all of our lives, and the development of psychological theory and research in this area has the potential to tell us much more about how this influence works, and about how it might be used to promote social and educational well-being.

References

Abrams, D., Rutland, A., & Cameron, L. (2003). The development of subjective group dynamics: Children's judgments of normative and deviant in-group and out-group individuals. *Child Development*, **74**, 1840–1856.

Addessi, A. R., Baroni, M., Luzzi, C., & Tafuri, J. (1995). The development of musical stylistic competence in children. *Council for Research in Music Education Bulletin*, **127**, 8–15.

Bakagiannis, S. & Tarrant, M. (2006). Can music bring people together? Effects of shared musical preference on intergroup bias in adolescence. *Scandinavian Journal of Psychology*, **47**, 129–136.

Baumann, V. H. (1960). Teen-age music preferences. *Journal of Research in Music Education*, **8**, 75–84.

Bennett, M., Lyons, E., Sani, F., & Barrett, M (1998). Children's subjective identification with the group and ingroup favoritism. *Developmental Psychology*, 34, 902–909.

Berlyne, D. E. (1971). *Aesthetics and psychobiology*. New York: Appleton-Century-Crofts.

Boivin, M. & Bégin, G. (1989). Peer status and self-perception among early elementary school children: The case of the rejected children. *Child Development*, 60, 591–596.

Boselie, F. (1991). Against prototypicality as a central concept in aesthetics. *Empirical Studies of the Arts*, 9, 65–73.

Branscombe, N. R. & Wann, D. L. (1994). Collective self-esteem consequences of outgroup derogation when a valued social identity is on trial. *European Journal of Social Psychology*, 24, 641–657.

Bragg, B. W. E. & Crozier, J. B. (1974). The development with age of verbal and exploratory responses to sound sequences varying in uncertainty level. In D. E. Berlyne (ed.), *Studies in the new experimental aesthetics: Steps towards an objective psychology of aesthetic appreciation*. Washington, DC: Hemisphere.

Castano, E., Paladino, M. P., Coull, A., & Yzerbyt, V. Y. (2002). Protecting the ingroup stereotype: Ingroup identification and the management of deviant ingroup members. *British Journal of Social Psychology*, 41, 365–385.

Castell, K. C. (1982). Children's sensitivity to stylistic differences in 'classical' and 'popular' music. *Psychology of Music, Special Issue*, 22–25.

De Cremer, D. & Vanbeselaere, N. (1999). I am deviant, because . . .: The impact of situational factors upon the black sheep effect. *Psychologica Belgica*, 39, 71–79.

Doosje, B., Ellemers, N., and Spears, R. (1995). Perceived intragroup variability as a function of group status and identification. *Journal of Experimental Social Psychology*, 31, 410–436.

Eisenstein, S. R. (1979). Grade/age levels and the reinforcement value of the collative properties of music. *Journal of Research in Music Education*, 27, 76–86.

Finnäs, L. (1989). How can musical preferences be modified? A research review. *Bulletin of the Council for Research in Music Education*, 102, 1–58.

Fisher, R. L. (1951). Preferences of different age and socioeconomic groups in unstructured musical situations. *Journal of Social Psychology*, 33, 147–152.

Gaertner, S. L., Dovidio, J. F., Anastasio, P. A., Bachman, B. A., & Rust, M. C. (1993). The common ingroup identity model: Recategorization and the reduction of intergroup bias. In W. Stroebe & M. Hewstone (eds), *The European Review of Social Psychology* (pp. 1–26). Vol. 4. Chichester: Wiley.

Gardner, H. (1973). Children's sensitivity to musical styles. *Merrill-Palmer Quarterly*, 19, 67–77.

Gembris, H. & Schellenberg, G. (2003). *Musical preferences of elementary school children* (p. 324). Abstracts of the 5th ESCOM conference, University of Hanover, Germany.

Geringer, J. M. (1982). Verbal and operant music listening responses in relationship to age and training. *Psychology of Music, Special Issue*, 47–50.

Gordon, E. E. (1976). *Learning sequence and patterns in music*. Buffalo: Tometic Associates Ltd.

Goswami, U. (2001). Cognitive development: No stages please—we're British. *British Journal of Psychology*, 92, 257–277.

Greer, R. D., Dorow, L. G., & Randall, A. (1974). Music listening preferences of elementary school children. *Journal of Research in Music Education*, 22, 284–291.

Haack, P. A. (1988). *An exploratory study of popular music preferences along the age continuum*. Paper presented at the meeting of the Music Educators National Conference, Indianapolis, Indiana, USA.

Hargreaves, D. J. (1982). The development of aesthetic reactions to music. *Psychology of Music, Special Issue*, 51–54.

Hargreaves, D. J. (1986). *The developmental psychology of music.* Cambridge: Cambridge University Press.

Hargreaves, D. J. (1996). The development of artistic and musical competence. In I. deLiège & J.A. Sloboda (eds), *Musical beginnings: The origins and development of musical competence* (pp. 145–170). Oxford: Oxford University Press.

Hargreaves, D. J. & Castell, K. C. (1987). Development of liking for familiar and unfamiliar melodies. *Council for Research in Music Education Bulletin,* 91, 665–669.

Hargreaves, D. J. & Galton, M. (1992). Aesthetic learning: psychological theory and educational practice. In B. Reimer & R. A. Smith (eds), *1992 N.S.S.E. yearbook on the arts in education* (pp. 124–150). Chicago: N.S.S.E.

Hargreaves, D. J. & North, A. C. (1999). Developing concepts of musical style. *Musicae Scientiae,* 2, 193–213.

Hargreaves, D. J. & Zimmerman, M. (1992). Developmental theories of music learning. In R. Colwell (ed.), *Handbook for research in music teaching and learning* (pp. 377–391). New York: Schirmer/Macmillan.

Hargreaves, D. J., Comber, C. J. F., & Colley, A. M. (1995). Effects of age, gender, and training on the musical preferences of British secondary school students. *Journal of Research in Music Education,* 43, 242–250.

Hargreaves, D. J., MacDonald, R. A. R., & Miell, D.E. (2002). What are musical identities, and why are they important? In R. A. R. MacDonald, D. J. Hargreaves, & D. E. Miell (eds), *Musical identities* (pp. 1–20). Oxford: Oxford University Press.

Hargreaves, D. J., Miell, D. E., & MacDonald, R. A. R. (2005). How do people communicate using music? In D. E. Miell, R. A. R. MacDonald, & D. J. Hargreaves (eds), *Musical Communication* (pp. 1–25). Oxford: Oxford University Press.

Hekkert, P. & Snelders, H. M. J. J. (1995). Prototypicality as an explanatory concept in aesthetics: a reply to Boselie. *Empirical Studies of the Arts,* 13, 149–160.

Hekkert, P. & van Wieringen, P. C. W. (1990). Complexity and prototypicality as determinants of the appraisal of cubist paintings. *British Journal of Psychology,* 81, 483–495.

Holbrook, M. B. (1995) An empirical approach to representing patterns of consumer tastes, nostalgia, and hierarchy in the market for cultural products. *Empirical Studies of the Arts,* 13, 55–71.

Hornsey, M. J., Oppes, T., & Svensson, A. (2002). 'It's OK if we say it but you can't': Responses to intergroup and intragroup criticism. *European Journal of Social Psychology,* 32, 293–307.

Islam, R. & Hewstone, M. (1993). Intergroup attributions and affective consequences in majority and minority groups. *Journal of Personality and Social Psychology,* 64, 936–950.

Keston, M.J. & Pinto, I.M. (1955). Possible factors influencing music preference. *Journal of Genetic Psychology,* 86, 101–113.

Konečni, V. J. (1996). Daniel E. Berlyne (1924–1976): two decades later. *Empirical Studies of the Arts,* 14, 129–142.

Lamont, A. M., Hargreaves, D. J., Marshall, N., & Tarrant, M. (2003). Young people's music in and out of school. *British Journal of Music Education,* 20(3), 1–13.

LeBlanc, A. (1991). Effect of maturation/aging on music listening preference: A review of the literature. Paper presented at the Ninth National Symposium on Research in Music Behavior, Canon Beach, Oregon, USA.

LeBlanc, A., Colman, J., McCrary, J., Sherrill, C., & Malin, S. (1988). Tempo preferences of different age music listeners. *Journal of Research in Music Education,* 36, 156–168.

LeBlanc, A., Sims, W. L., Siivola, C., & Obert, M. (1993). Music style preferences of different-age listeners. Paper presented at the Tenth National Symposium on Research in Music Behavior, University of Alabama, Tuscaloosa, Alabama, USA.

Marques, J. M., Yzerbyt, V. Y., & Leyens, J.-P. (1988). The black sheep effect: Judgmental extremity towards ingroup members as a function of ingroup identification. *European Journal of Social Psychology*, 18, 1–16.

Marshall, N. A. (2001). *Developing concepts of musical style*. Unpublished PhD thesis, University of Durham.

Martindale, C. & Moore, K, (1988). Priming, prototypicality, and preference. *Journal of Experimental Psychology: Human Perception and Performance*, 14, 661–670.

Martindale, C. & Moore, K. (1989). Relationship of musical preference to collative, ecological, and psychophysical variables. *Music Perception*, 6, 431–455.

Martindale, C., Moore, K., & West, A. (1988). Relationship of preference judgements to typicality, novelty, and mere exposure. *Empirical Studies of the Arts*, 6, 79–96.

Martindale, C., Moore, K., & Borkum, J. (1990). Aesthetic preference: Anomalous findings for Berlyne's psychobiological theory. *American Journal of Psychology*, 103, 53–80.

May, W. V. (1985). Musical style preference and aural discrimination skills of primary grade school children. *Journal of Research in Music Education*, 32, 7–22.

Meadows, E. S. (1970). The relationship of music preference to certain cultural determiners. *Dissertation Abstracts International*, 31, 6100A.

Moore, K. & Martindale, C. (1983). Preference for shapes varying in color, color typicality, size, and complexity. Paper presented at the International Conference on Psychology and the Arts, Cardiff.

Nesdale, D., Maas, A., Griffiths, J., & Durkin, K. (2003). Effects of ingroup and outgroup ethnicity on children's attitudes towards members of the ingroup and outgroup. *British Journal of Developmental Psychology*, 21, 177–192.

Noel, J. G., Wann, D. L., & Branscombe, N. R. (1995). Peripheral ingroup membership status and public negativity towards outgroups. *Journal of Personality and Social Psychology*, 68, 127–137.

North, A. C. & Hargreaves, D. J. (1995). Eminence in pop music. *Popular Music and Society*, 19, 41–66.

North, A. C. & Hargreaves, D. J. (1996). The effects of music on responses to a dining area. *Journal of Environmental Psychology*, 16, 55–64.

North, A. C. & Hargreaves, D. J. (1997). Liking for musical styles. *Musicae Scientiae*, 1, 107–126.

North, A. C. & Hargreaves, D. J. (2000a). Musical preferences during and after relaxing and exercising. *American Journal of Psychology*, 113, 43–67.

North, A. C. & Hargreaves, D. J. (2000b). Collative variables versus prototypicality. *Empirical Studies of the Arts*, 18, 13–17.

North, A. C. & Hargreaves, D. J. (2003). Is music important? Two common misconceptions. *The Psychologist*, 16(8), 406–410.

North, A. C., Hargreaves, D. J., & Hargreaves, J. J. (2004). Uses of music in everyday life. *Music Perception*, 22, 41–77.

Parker, J. G. & Asher, S. R. (1993). Friendship and friendship quality in middle childhood: Links with peer group acceptance and feelings of loneliness and social dissatisfaction. *Developmental Psychology*, 29, 611–621.

Rentfrow, P. J. & Gosling, S. D. (2003). The do re mi's of everyday life: Examining the structure and personality correlates of music preferences. *Journal of Personality and Social Psychology*, 84(6), 1236–1256.

Rogers, V.R. (1957). Children's musical preferences. *Elementary School Journal*, 57, 433–435.

Rubin-Rabson, G. (1940). The influence of age, intelligence, and training on reactions to classic and modern music. *Journal of General Psychology*, 22, 413–429.

Runfola, M. & Swanwick, K. (2002). Developmental characteristics of learners. In R. Colwell & C. P. Richardson (eds), *New handbook of research on music teaching and learning* (pp. 373–397). Oxford: Oxford University Press.

Serafine, M. L. (1988). *Music as cognition: The development of thought in sound.* New York: Columbia University Press.

Sloboda, J. A., O'Neill, S. A., & Ivaldi, A. (2001). Functions of music in everyday life: an exploratory study using the Experience Sampling Method. *Musicae Scientiae*, 5, 9–32.

Swanwick, K. & Tillman, J. (1986). The sequence of musical development. *British Journal of Music Education*, 3, 305–39.

Tajfel, H. & Turner, J. C. (1979). An integrative theory of intergroup conflict. In W. G. Austin & S. Worschel (eds), *The social psychology of intergroup relations* (pp. 33–47). Monterey, CA: Brooks/Cole.

Tajfel, H., Flament, C., Billig, M. G., & Bundy, R. P. (1971). Social categorization and intergroup behaviour. *European Journal of Social Psychology*, 1, 149–178.

Tarrant, M., Hargreaves, D. J., & North, A. C. (2001a). Social categorization, self-esteem, and the estimated musical preferences of male adolescents. *Journal of Social Psychology*, 141, 565–581.

Tarrant, M., North, A. C., Edridge, M. D., Kirk, L. E., Smith, E. A., & Turner, R. E. (2001b). Social identity in adolescence. *Journal of Adolescence*, 24, 597–609.

Tarrant, M., North, A. C., & Hargreaves, D. J. (2002). Youth identity and music. In R. A. R. MacDonald, D. J. Hargreaves, & D. Miell (eds), *Musical identities* (pp. 134–150). Oxford: Oxford University Press.

Tarrant, M., North, A. C., & Hargreaves, D. J. (2004). Adolescents' intergroup attributions: A comparison of two social identities. *Journal of Youth and Adolescence*, 33, 177–185.

Taylor, S. (1969). Development of children aged seven to eleven. *Journal of Research in Music Education*, 17, 100–107.

Whitfield, T. W. A. (1983). Predicting preference for familiar, everyday objects. An experimental confrontation between two theories of aesthetic behaviour. *Journal of Environmental Psychology*, 3, 221–237.

Whitfield, T. W. A. & Slatter, P. E. (1979). The effects of categorization and prototypicality on aesthetic choice in a furniture selection task. *British Journal of Psychology*, 70, 65–75.

CHAPTER 8

MUSICAL LITERACY

JANET MILLS AND GARY E. MCPHERSON

What do we mean when we say that a child is 'musically literate?' How can musical literacy be defined and what types of competencies might it infer? Because this term is widely used, it makes sense to address it in this book. As will become evident during the discussion to follow, however, our view, consistent with approaches to language literacy, is that *literacy* in situations related to Western classical music occurs as a result of children having developed their capacity to make music, reflect on the music in which they are engaged, express their views on music which they play, hear or create, speak about and listen to music in order to form judgements, and read, write, comprehend and interpret staff notation. Each of these aspects of literacy has been dealt with elsewhere in this volume, so most of our comments in this chapter will detail the fundamental aspects of learning how to use staff notation, even though we recognize that this is only one dimension of the literacy acquisition process, and that staff notation is only one type of music notation.

Literacy or literacies?

An obvious way to define and thereby understand what 'musical literacy' means is to draw parallels with the ways that children become 'literate' as they learn to read and write their spoken mother tongue. A common assumption is that literacy involves the simple ability to read and write, through processes involved in decoding letters, and groups of letters, into sounds and vice versa. However, literacy in language development is far more complex.

Although researchers still debate the best methods and techniques for teaching children to read language, and teachers find that each child needs an individual mix of methods and techniques, they agree that language reading is best achieved through speech, after the basic structure and vocabulary of the language has first been established (Cooper, 2003). There is also an increasing recognition of the importance of communication in real-world situations and the need to develop children's capacities to speak, listen, read, write, and think (Cooper, 2003). Thus, literacy in reading and writing can involve developing a large set of structures 'ranging from individual skills, abilities, and knowledge to social practices and functional competencies to ideological values and political goals' (Soares, 1992, pp. 8–10, cited in Hansen *et al.*, 2004). This is why some language researchers prefer the term *literacies* in recognition that there is no single unitary literacy (Soares, 1992), but rather a complex of abilities (Harris & Hodges, 1995). One of the fundamental assumptions in this literature is that children should be exposed to a wide variety of literacy experiences and considerable direct or explicit instruction, beginning with experiences in listening and speaking, which in due course lead on to, and continue to develop alongside, reading and writing (Cooper, 2003).

Much of this parallels theoretical conceptions of musical development where an expanded view of musical literacy is the norm (McPherson & Gabrielsson, 2002). This is one reason why some music educators (including the authors of this chapter) try to avoid using the term 'musical literacy', because it is so easily misunderstood. There are usually other ways of saying whatever it is that you want to say when describing a child as musically literate—or as not musically literate.

Ask anyone who uses the term 'musical literacy' to say what they mean by it, and they will often speak—in effect—of the ability to function fluently as a musician. But delve deeper to find out what is meant by 'function', 'fluently', or 'musician', and it becomes clear that views of 'musical literacy' often focus exclusively on the ability to decode written staff notation and turn it 'accurately' into sound. And this is where problems start to emerge, for while many musicians around the world can decode written staff notation fluently:

1. There are many modes of music making in which notation plays no part.

2. No child needs to be able to decode staff notation accurately *before* starting to learn to make the sorts of music where staff notation is used customarily.

3. Learning to read music before, or separately from, learning to make music can lead to misunderstandings.

4. Too early an exposure to staff notation can lead people to overlook the features of music that are not its focus. Staff notation of a melody provides Western classical musicians with information about which note (from the Western classical scale) to play, when it should start, and (provided that the tempo remains constant) when the next note should start. It says little about timbre, articulation, how long a note should be sustained within the space of time allotted to it, dynamics, tempo change, and so forth. And this is just what it does not say about melody. Bring harmony or any of the other dimensions of music into the equation, and the partial nature of the information provided by staff notation becomes even more apparent.

5. Undue emphasis on staff notation can lead to atrophy of musicians' creative abilities, and their ability to memorize.

6. Some people who do not read music at all nevertheless become fluent even within the realm of the music where composers and performers customarily use staff notation. Examples include adults who sing complex Western classical choral works entirely from memory, or who can sit down at a piano to 'improvise' or play pieces in the style of named Western classical composers that they recall from aural and physical memory.

Contexts involving musical literacy

Traditionally, many Western classical performing musicians have developed their literacy skills through childhood instrumental lessons that addressed instrumental skills, music reading skills, and related skills as part of the same package. However, as highlighted in other chapters (see Chapters 21 and 22), and also in other writing (e.g., Mills, 2005) children who grow up in a culture where music is valued and plentiful, and where there are role models of people who describe themselves, and are described by others as 'musicians', often grow up to be musicians themselves, in effect at their mother or somebody else's knee, just as they learn to speak, to walk, to wash themselves, or to make friends, and so forth. We are not suggesting here that becoming a musician is (literally) innate, or that one becomes a musician simply by being in the right place for the right length of time. Growing up to be a musician involves engaging, in some way, with musicians, just as growing up to speak a foreign language involves engagement with other people who can speak it. There is tuition, of a kind, involved, but it is not necessarily the sort that must take children out of their culture in order to give them trumpet lessons in a distant studio, or piano lessons in their school.

Farrell (2001) writes of the *gharanas* (literally 'households') of India that are based on familial lineage and have musical styles that are distinct, but adapt with the times. Wiggins (1996) writes of the challenge, when learning Ghanaian drum music in Ghana, of keeping up with teenage boys who have grown up with it around them, and who cannot understand why he finds it so challenging to play. Green and Bray (1997) write of Cheryl who is aged 13. Cheryl, who lives in England, plays in her father's folk band but has had no formal music training. Despite this, she is the most accomplished member of the band. Cheryl is a fluent musician, arguably 'literate' in the music she is playing, who has learnt through engagement with other, older, musicians—and who has developed skills that surpass theirs. Her fluency as a musician—her musical literacies—have been shaped by factors including:

- developing an ability to play by ear;
- development of her musical memory;
- the absence of any curb on her creative and expressive abilities;
- the familiar music of her father's folk band;
- the physical characteristics and timbral possibilities of the instruments available to her; and
- other people, especially her participation and involvement with older musicians.

Cheryl's school music education truly acknowledged neither the unique abilities she brought to lessons nor the musicianship she had developed outside school. In many countries it is possible to visit classrooms where a well-meaning teacher tries to teach young children what is seen as the basics of staff notation, although they have no immediate musical need for it given that they learn songs aurally, remember their compositions or record them using invented symbols or electronically, and so forth. One also sometimes sees early instrumental lessons in which equally well-meaning instrumental teachers inadvertently give children the impression that a musician cannot play a note that has not first been decoded from the printed page, or where children are being distracted from listening to, enjoying, and refining the sounds that they are making through being required to simultaneously decode staff notation.

So, given all these caveats, how do children learn to read staff notation? While there are respects in which music is not a language, there may nevertheless be lessons here from the ways in which children learn to read their own verbal language, be it English or a language that uses another alphabet or symbol system.

Parallels between language and music literacy development

The most important principle we have observed from studies on written verbal language development is that children should become competent with spoken verbal language before they grapple with written verbal language (Kirby, 1988; Adam, 1994). In most countries children speak for as long as 5 years before being obliged to start learning to read on entry to school, and only after they have gained a great deal of prior experience with their native language and reached the mental age necessary to maximize their success as readers (Mills, 1991a; Adam, 1994; McPherson & Gabrielsson, 2002). By this age, the home experiences of most children of having been read to by their mothers and seen their parents and others reading will have prepared them for the nature of how words and thoughts can be represented in symbols (Adams, 1994). They are thus ready to begin to read for themselves.

It does not follow from the above that children should engage formally with music aurally for as long as 5 years before being introduced to some form of staff notation, as they will come to their first formal lessons having heard a great deal of music during their infancy and early childhood. Even so, it may be unwise to introduce children to music reading in their early music lessons, especially if they are learning an instrument and still working out the basics of sound production. Rather, children should be encouraged to experience and enjoy music first, so that the acquisition of formal musical skills can occur *inductively* as a natural outcome of this process (Hargreaves, 1986). An activity that can prepare young beginners for learning to read staff notation is to encourage them to invent their own notations to represent pieces they already know. This provides them with the metamusical awareness that will enhance their progress towards understanding why staff notation looks and works the way it does (Upitis, 1990, 1992; McPherson & Gabrielsson, 2002).

Most 5- or 6-year-old children's knowledge about how music can be represented in any form of notation will be below their level of understanding of how verbal language can be represented in print. Thus, children younger than 6 probably learn an instrument best when teaching emphasizes learning to play pieces that they already know by sound, and rote learning of unfamiliar pieces, in order to establish ear-to-hand co-ordination skills that lay a foundation for introducing notation later and also keep their imaginative skills alive (McPherson & Gabrielsson, 2002).

We know from studies with young learners that the functional literacy of knowing where to put your fingers after having seen a visual cue on a score, represents a very limited form of comprehending staff notation (McPherson, 1993, 2005; Schleuter, 1997). The knowledge of letter names and note patterns needs therefore to be practised in various contexts, leading from familiar patterns to more challenging previously unknown patterns.

Another important principle is that even after children have learnt to read and write verbal language, they still speak it. As they become fluent users of staff notation, and when they have achieved fluency, they still need opportunities to work free of staff notation, in order to develop and sustain the full range and depth of their musical literacy.

As mentioned above, children are exposed to a great deal of written verbal language in their environment for several years before they learn to read it. They see when adults use it, and when they do not, such as when a mother helps her infant by pointing to the words as she reads the story. This is related to the practice within the Anglican choral tradition whereby a new chorister may be paired with an older chorister who is expected to point to the music as he or she sings, with younger choristers joining in sections that they can recall, long before they have learned to read music autonomously (Mills & Barrett, in press).

Finally, in their early stages as readers of spoken verbal language, children learn to read words that they already know. Long before they can read fluently, they may pick out words such as their name on birthday cakes or cards (Mills, 2005). When their formal reading begins, they first learn to read simple words that are already in their spoken vocabulary. The opportunity to cross-check material that they are reading with material that they know, and to relate it within an aural system that they already understand, could be useful also in music. This is why the general rule recommended by McPherson and Gabrielsson (2002) is for children to learn to read pieces they already know by ear, before pieces they do not know which require more sophisticated levels of processing. This principle underpinned some of the early published band methods (Brittin & Sheldon, 2004).

The mechanics of reading music notation

When reading aloud we are saying the words from one section while reading the words from the section that immediately follows. Likewise when performing and interpreting music from notation our eyes may run ahead of what is actually being played (Sloboda, 2005). Studies show that expert sight-readers are able to recognize 'chunks' or patterns of up to seven notes after the music has been removed (Dodson, 1983; Schleuter & Schleuter, 1988; Sloboda, 1988, 2005). Most importantly, the evidence also suggests that reading skills are developed through experience and familiarity with the symbols being read, such that it is easier to look ahead and anticipate the flow of the music when the notation contains predictable or straightforward patterns (Sloboda, 2005). Problems involving visual processing therefore do not always explain poor reading ability. As with reading text, poor readers of musical notation are probably the tail end of a continuous distribution, rather than a peculiar group whose reading processes are different from more efficient readers. By this we mean that they probably display deficits on skills that more able readers can do better, rather than employ processes that are entirely different (Meadows, 1993).

In the very beginning stages of learning to read staff notation, a young child will need to learn that music is read by moving your eyes from left to right, top to bottom on the page. As a child learns to distinguish common familiar patterns in the pieces being studied he or she becomes more capable of integrating a more varied array of patterns into his or her repertoire, and begins to differentiate and predict patterns from the overall shape or start of the particular pattern. It is advantageous in all stages of development for the child to have the sound of the music in his or her mind, because this will enable the young musician to draw on these aural recollections in order to 'read ahead'.

Many children exposed to a traditional approach to music instruction begin learning notation from the very first lessons. Without being taught to link the sound of musical patterns with notated patterns these children will probably learn to rely on sight vocabulary, going directly from the visual image to the fingering required to execute this on their instrument. This is what Schleuter (1997) refers to as 'button pushers' to whom notation indicates only what fingers to push down. In such cases the player goes from eye to hand, without necessarily connecting this with his or her ear, or from visual perceptions to the reproduction of the written notation on the instrument (King, 1983). Being aware of the sound of the music and also of being able to link this auditory perception with the visual perception, however, is especially important if the child is to be able to develop the repertoire of musical patterns required to perform more difficult passages. Establishing each of the links between eye, ear, and hand is also necessary if the child is to develop the capacity to deal with unfamiliar patterns when performing a new piece of music (King, 1983).

It is probably true also that there are various stages leading up to the skilled ability to read notation and that the nature of reading staff notation, as with most other musical skills, changes substantially during the first 5 or 6 years of the formal learning process. For example, McPherson's (1993, 1994a, 2005) studies with beginning to advanced level children learning musical instruments shows wide differences between sight-reading ability occurred even within the first 12 months, and that the main predictor of the children's ability to process notation was the strategies they used to aid their performance (see Chapter 17 for further reading).

In summary, the mechanics of reading notation involve the co-ordination of a number of differing skills. Highly developed readers of notation display an ability to link the sound with the notation (McPherson, 1993, 1994b, 2005; Schleuter, 1997). Young instrumentalists, however, may have more trouble with reading rhythm than pitch, because 'pitch production with many instruments is possible without internalization of pitch, while rhythm production is difficult without auditory coding' (Dodson, 1983, p. 4). As an example, McPherson (1993, 1994a) examined a group of wind instrumentalists, all of whom had been studying their instrument for more than 2 years. He found that students of all ability levels made approximately three times as many rhythm errors as compared with pitch errors. These results can be interpreted as follows. Sight-singing involves processes whereby the child will need to comprehend both pitch and rhythm in order to successfully 'sing' the passage being performed. In this sense, the task of sight-singing demands an ability to inwardly 'hear', or what Gordon (2003) refers to as 'audiate' (i.e., comprehend), both pitch and rhythm. However, when sight-reading on an instrument, the player does not need to audiate pitch at the same level as is needed to bring meaning to the rhythm. When most children see the pitches 'F-G-E-F', for example, they would know that this is fingered in a certain way on their instrument. They therefore do not necessarily need to be able to hear the passage in their mind, in order to be able to perform it on their instrument. But with rhythm, they will need to know how the pattern sounds. There are therefore subtle differences between sight-singing and sight-reading in the way that musicians process pitch and rhythm. The ability to self-correct errors is important for efficient sight-reading and sight-singing (Mills, 1983).

Hierarchical levels

There are few studies that help us conceptualize how young children develop their ability to read unfamiliar melodies from staff notation. One, by Cantwell and Millard (1994), involves an attempt to identify the different hierarchical levels at which reading traditional staff notation can be analysed. These researchers speculated that processing staff notation has similarities with processing text and used Kirby's (1988) work on processing text to construct an eight-level hierarchy of operational levels that they believe are required when children process staff notation. Cantwell and Millard's (1994) theoretical synthesis of Kirby's work can be abbreviated as follows:

1. *Features:* the markings on the page that form the basis of notation. These involve awareness of the features of the lines and curves of the musical symbols and notes, and knowledge that they are both systematic and meaningful.

2. *Letters/musical notes and signs:* consistent interpretation of features allows the child to attend to and recognize basic symbol units such as individual notes, clef signs, time signature, dynamic markings, sharps, flats, and so forth.

3. *Syllables/intervals:* structural analysis of melodic patterns involves recognizing the systematic relationships between adjoining notes (e.g., intervals).

4. *Words/groups:* the transition from individual notes to groups of notes occurs via structural analysis of the component intervals, or by visual scanning of the whole musical idea (e.g., chord, scale run). This represents the first level of musical meaning; however, at this level, the meanings attached to individual clusters are decontextualized and isolated.

5. *Word groups/motifs or note grouplets:* combinations of clusters form a *motif* or *motif grouplet*, a level of musical meaning equivalent to understanding individual phrases and clauses in text. These may vary in length according to their musical function.

6. *Ideas/musical phrase or figure:* in music, an individual idea is expressed by combining motifs into a musical phrase.

7. *Main idea/musical idea:* the combination of musical phrases yields a musical idea, equivalent in text processing terms to the construction of a main idea from a paragraph.

8. *Themes/musical subject:* understanding of the musical subject involves imposing a sense of musicality on to the score such that the component musical phrase and subject are taken beyond technical proficiency to include variations of sound, mood, dynamics, and so forth in ways that allow for individualized interpretation of the score (Cantwell & Millard, 1994, pp. 47–49).

The above hierarchy suggests that children first become aware of the features of staff notation as they start to develop a sense of what reading notation is all about, and begin to learn how music is notated on the score. Next, consistent interpretation of the features of staff notation allows the child to attend to basic symbol units of the medium. In staff notation, this includes being able to recognize individual notes, clef signs, time and key signatures, dynamic markings, sharps, flats, and so forth. During this stage the size of the notation is important as children learn to process the notation and focus their eyes on the line of the staff notation. If the symbols are too close together, then they may have difficulty perceiving differences, or may even skip over important details such as a flat or sharp.

From here, further development will be hampered unless the child has already learnt to link the auditory sound with the visual notation. They will need to develop their capacity to recognize motifs and patterns, such as sequences, and cope with pulse, meter, and rhythm as well as key, tonality, and pitch. These relationships form the basis for learning to comprehend or 'audiate' what is seen in notation, and of being aware of the syntax of the music being performed. At the most sophisticated level, the child will learn how to use what he or she has seen in the notation to enhance the expression of their performance.

A number of implications arise from the above hierarchy, two of which are highlighted by Cantwell and Millard (1994). The first involves the need for teachers to explicitly cue their students to focus their processing operations at a higher level on the hierarchy than they are currently working. For example, young learners could be cued to translate the individual notes and patterns that they are learning to read into a meaningful entity of a melody or phrase such as by singing the melody while following the notation before they commence to play it on an instrument. Focusing children's attention on the flow of a melody and the expressive detail in a score, or even encouraging them to play the passage with a different kind of expression can help them develop a more sophisticated awareness of the broader purpose of notation. As they develop further, students can then be encouraged to focus their attention on the upper two levels (*musical ideas* and *themes*), so that they understand how notation can help them develop a personalized conception of the musical score.

A second implication of the study concerns ways in which 'deep' rather than 'surface' levels of processing can be encouraged during teaching, based on the premise that the development of deeper processing skills when reading notation is just as important as the development of technical skill on an instrument.

Practice leads to automaticity, allowing children to quickly and accurately discern key features in the staff notation, and then use these to co-ordinate motor movements that allow them to either sing or play the melody represented in notation. Such automaticity allows musicians to direct their attention to higher levels such as the expressive detail or the overall flow of the melody and how it might be interpreted. Practice, in the form of drill and practice exercises, can help a child to react quickly to the symbols they see in notation. But drill and practice activities can also be boring and frustrating for learners, and not necessarily the most efficient form of learning. Guided meaningful reading of a range of musical repertoires in which the student's attention is directed to relevant technical and expressive characteristics that are embedded in the music itself helps to instil confidence and knowledge that can be applied in other contexts. Allied with these experiences are kinaesthetic relationships such as being able to recognize the 'key terrain' of the piece. On the piano, for example, each key has a kinaesthetically distinct feel (E major being quite different from C major, for example). A child will have a better chance of learning how to read staff notation, if he or she is able to recognize the 'key terrain' of the passage of the piece being learned.

As an extension of these points, McPherson and Gabrielsson (2002) propose that children need to acquire some knowledge of how to attend to individual details and decode the basic elements of pitch and rhythm. They will need to learn, for example, that a quarter note (or crotchet) is one beat in length in many contexts and that music is represented by notes on a five line staff that can be more easily remembered using mnemonic aids (e.g., 'F-A-C-E' for the spaces on a treble clef; this is levels 1 and 2 on the above hierarchy). However, learning can be extremely tedious and frustrating if the process concentrates too much on these types of fine detail such that a child's attention is constantly focused on learning the names of individual notes and rhythmic patterns divorced from the sound of the music itself. This is especially evident in situations where knowledge of this kind is not immediately put into practice so that it can be integrated into the child's growing awareness of how the actual music really sounds.

Following on from this it would be incorrect to assume that children need to memorize a wide range of 'facts' before they will be successful in learning how to read and comprehend notation. The process of reading music can be extremely slow and tortuous for children when the learning process introduces elements of music that are not immediately applied in the musical examples performed or studied by the children themselves. Thus, the old style of instrumental 'method' books, which displayed all the rhythmic patterns (from whole notes leading down to quarter, sixteenth, and thirty second note values), and a full range of pitches within as well as above and below the musical stave, have long been dismissed by music educators as a very ineffective way of introducing children to notation. Most contemporary method books for teaching children to play an instrument now include only the information needed at the time of learning to play a specific melody, so that the child does not have to learn information that is not immediately put into practice.

Children will not always acquire efficient reading skills by exclusively starting on letter name/note duration and then working up. Right from the start, they need to operate at a higher level of abstraction to extract the sense of the passage they are attempting to read. Equally important are the small-scale predictions built up through a knowledge of form, style, and larger units such as chords, measures, beats, and phrases, which must be understood before music reading becomes meaningful (Sloboda, 2005). In this sense, unless the beginner knows the music through repeated hearings and has been able to form a mental blueprint internally, then it will be more difficult and frustrating to try and read it note by note.

Finally, and as mentioned previously, it is important to remind ourselves that children will vary widely in their progress toward fluent reading. As shown in McPherson's (1993, 2005) longitudinal studies with young beginners (see Chapter 17), wide differences in reading abilities appear in the first weeks of learning, with some children struggling to read while others pick up notation skills relatively easy. Unfortunately, children who have problems often do not receive the type of supportive instruction that will improve their abilities with the result that they often cease instruction. Educators would not allow such wide differences to occur in everyday instruction of children learning to read their spoken language, and nor should we allow them to occur in music. Learning to read staff notation involves a complex of skills, and no two students will follow exactly the same line of development.

In summary then, a key principle of effective learning is that any new concept or piece of information about staff notation should be linked wherever possible to structurally mean-ingful entities such as phrases and melodies (i.e., the upper levels of the above hierarchy) rather than individual notes, so that the child's focus of attention is on the main reason for learning—access to music making. In the very early stages of learning, unless the sound of the melody the child is trying to read or perform is in his or her mind, then the act of reading the notation is more likely to be frustrating and tedious.

An example of the music reading process

With the above as our guide, we now turn to a practical example of the very earliest stages of learning to read musical notation. If reading staff notation is in any way similar to reading words, then at its most basic level there are probably two distinct ways in which a child can decode notation. First, the child could break down the individual notes and sound them out before they are blended together to form a meaningful whole. In this method the child would see for example, a meaningful whole (Figure 8.1) and try to decode this by breaking it down into individual notes (Figure 8.2).

Figure 8.1 A meaningful whole.

Figure 8.2 Individual notes.

A major problem with this approach is that the emphasis is on moving from symbol to action (fingerings) to sound, rather than symbol to sound to action (McPherson & Gabrielsson, 2002; see also Mainwaring, 1933, 1941, 1951). This is how many young beginners who are taught to read music from the very first lessons often practise at home—by stumbling over individual notes as they continue playing, sometimes so slowly and hesitantly that they no longer are able to perceive the music they are attempting to perform (McPherson, 1993; McPherson & Renwick, 2001; McPherson & Gabrielsson, 2002). In such situations children may have insufficient cognitive resources left to devote to manipulating their instrument and listening to what they are playing because so much of their attention is focused on reading notation (McPherson & Gabrielsson, 2002). This is particularly important to note, given that vision tends to dominate and inhibit the processing of signals from other modalities (Posner *et al.*, 1976; Smyth, 1984). As Bamberger (1996, 1999) explains, beginners find these types of learning experiences extremely frustrating, especially when they are taught to look at the smallest objects such as single notes and to classify these without any knowledge of their context or functional meaning. Asking beginners to focus on notation too early, according to Bamberger (1996), means asking them to 'put aside their most intimate ways of knowing—figures, felt paths, context and function' (p. 44). Too early an emphasis on notation can therefore lead to a decreased aural sensitivity for the natural unified patterns that children spontaneously observe when listening to music.

A second more direct method would be for the child to link the patterns of a group of notes directly to the overall sound that is represented in the notation. This is more like the processes that seem to be used by children who are given the opportunity to play by ear, for example:

> Amy [age 32 months] is not one to 'plink-plonk' on the piano, but loves to watch her father play. He shows her how to play E-D-C: she copies him and says 'That's *Three Blind Mice*'. She works out how to continue *Three Blind Mice*, playing E-D-C E-D-C G-F-E G-F-E. She then stops abruptly, and goes off to play with some toys.
>
> Mills (2005, p. 164)

In a related approach to music reading, the child would be encouraged to learn to comprehend groups of notes such as in Figure 8.3 ('comprehending patterns'), and to associate these with the aural image already formed of a well known piece of music, such as the repeated pattern at the beginning of *Three Blind Mice*. Obviously, this is a more direct and musical approach as young readers work more holistically to connect what they see with the sound of each pattern or phrase. This *direct* or holistic approach is how many children exposed to rote teaching techniques would learn to process notation. For example, in the Suzuki method children learn a large repertoire of pieces by rote before learning to perform the same repertoire when notation is introduced. In this approach they already have a mental image of what the music sounds like and how it can be reproduced on their instrument, and therefore only need to learn how to link the symbol of what they see with this mental image. In contrast to the first method above, the emphasis is more musical as the young musician learns to work from symbol to sound to action (McPherson & Gabrielsson, 2002).

Figure 8.3 Comprehending patterns.

There may be times when all children will use both methods for analysing notation, depending on the level of difficulty of the music being performed. For example, young musicians who are skilled readers will tend to work at the holistic level, performing with ease the musical patterns that they have come to know and internalize. However, when they encounter a difficult or unusual rhythmic or pitch pattern they may stumble before breaking the pattern down into simpler units and then gradually piecing it together in order to perform it as a whole. However, it is important to note that research in reading words (Kirby, 1988) suggests that poor readers find it difficult to rely exclusively on a 'phonological approach', whereby they break a word down into individual letters before sounding it out and eventually blending it together. Reading staff notation can cause a similar type of problem, because when individual notes are broken down into isolated units, and divorced from the meter or key in which they operate, their meaning can be destroyed. This is why Gordon (2003) and others stress the importance of learning to read notation in context, and why staff notation will only have relevance when the child learns to feel the beat or tonality of the patterns he or she is trying to reproduce from notation. It is also the reason why teachers will often use rhythmic and tonal syllables as an aid to reading development and why young children learning an instrument will often be taught to tap out the beat using large motor movements as an aid to learning to feel the rhythm of a pattern they are about to learn to perform. However, tapping out rhythms, rather than a pulse, can be problematic, as we will see below.

Common problems

Learning to decipher staff notation can be very confusing for a child. Music uses a number of ordinary sounding words that mean something different from their usage in everyday life: high and low being just one pair of examples. The relationship between hearing and comprehending high and low pitch in music and physically learning how to play it on an instrument can be very mystifying. On the piano high and low notes go from right to left, on the guitar the highest string is at the bottom, and on the cello the sound goes up as you slide your hand down a string.

The common practice of teaching children to read rhythms by tapping or clapping is also very problematic. Rhythms have durations as well as onsets, but a 'long' tap or clap is the same length as a 'short' tap or clap: only the silence after the tap or clap changes in length. The first author (Mills, 1991b,c) worked with children ages 8–10, to learn more about the information they pick up from rhythms that are clapped or played to them. She based her experiment on a simple rhythmic pattern used in earlier research by Bamberger (1988) (see Figure 8.4). The response of one child was typical of many of the children who

Figure 8.4 Experimental rhythmic pattern.

took part in the Bamberger research (see Figure 8.5). Lucy had recently started learning the violin:

> After listening to the clapped rhythm, she drew her hand and showed, through labelling the fingers from 'beat 1' to 'beat 5' that she had spotted that the rhythm repeated, and also that the repeating cell consisted of five claps. She also showed that 'beats 3–5' were a group of some sort (Figure 8.5a). [The researcher] asked Lucy if she could think of another way of drawing the rhythm. She drew five teddy bears that she numbered 1–5, labelling clasps 3–5 'fast'. Lucy's response seemed reasonable . . . there is a sense in which 'beats 3–5' sound like a group. However, the US research had judged responses like Lucy's to be immature, and to suggest that she had not heard the rhythm properly.
>
> Mills (2005, pp. 101–103)

In a subsequent session a couple of weeks later, the researcher returned with a very simple electronic keyboard, so that she could investigate how Lucy might respond to rhythms that were sustained. Instead of clapping rhythms, Lucy was taught to play them on a single note using the electronic keyboard that would sustain the sound until the key was lifted. After learning the rhythm shown in Figure 8.5(b), Lucy was asked to draw something that would remind her of the rhythm that she had just learned.

> Lucy drew ten pigs, which she numbered from one to ten. She labelled pigs 2, 3, 7 and 8 as 'fast'. Next ....without prompting.., she clapped the rhythm and labelled pigs 4 and 9 'fast' too. It was as though the rhythm that she was hearing had changed into one that could be written more accurately using the notation shown below the pigs. Thereafter, Lucy gave up drawing until she had first clapped a rhythm that she had learnt to play on the keyboard.
>
> Mills (2005, p. 103)

Her responses to three further rhythms are shown in Figure 8.5(c–e).

Finally, the researcher returned to the original rhythm (Figure 8.5f). Lucy's response was the same as when she had not used the sustaining instrument, except that she produced squares instead of teddies, and wrote out the repetition of the first 'bar'. Her notation could be interpreted as:

- inaccurate, duration-based notation of the rhythms;
- notation based on something other than duration;
- accurate, duration-based, notations of rhythms reconstructed from the previously clapped rhythms.

Given that in the rhythm shown in Figure 8.5(b) Lucy changed her accurate notation after clapping, the third of these interpretations is the most sensible:

> A long clap is no longer than a short clap: only the silence between vary in length. So Lucy is entitled to reconstruct the clapped rhythms like this if she wishes.

Why did Lucy clap?

> The answer is that her violin teacher has trained her to clap rhythms before playing them. When Lucy plays a rhythm, her teacher cannot tell whether any mistakes result from inaccurate rhythmic perception or technical difficulties such as plucking a string, or

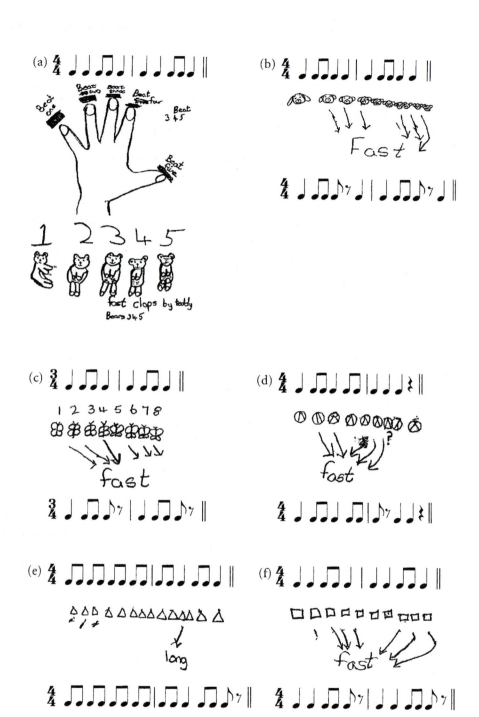

Figure 8.5 (a–f) Drawings illustrating the notation and perception of rhythm by Lucy (aged 8).

changing bow, at the moment intended. Asking Lucy to sing the rhythm on a single note does not work either, because Lucy learns in a group, and the teacher cannot tell whether an individual is, for example, sustaining a crotchet for the duration of a minim. Asking Lucy to clap makes things easier for the teacher, who can see if Lucy is not clapping in the right place, even when she is clapping in a group. The problem is that Lucy's teacher had not noticed that clapping changes Lucy's rhythmic perception. There is nothing intuitive about an assumption that a clap represents a note which lasts until the next clap is heard. When the teacher claps a rhythm she may, as [adult musicians often] do, 'hear' a tone that sustains until the onset of the next clap. But Lucy seems not to do this. She may learn to.

Mills (2005, pp. 103–104)

However, it is unlikely that clapping rhythms before she has played them will prove helpful. Problems such as Lucy's are embedded deeply within systems of music education. For example, syllabuses sometimes suggest activities such as clapping the rhythm of a known song, or clapping short rhythmic patterns. What, exactly, is the rhythm of a song? How can a clap be anything other than short?

Coda

This chapter has considered how children develop into 'literate' musicians. As has become evident in the discussion and other chapters in this volume, any conception of what it is to be 'musically literate' is fraught with problems related to defining what is meant by music and the various situations in which children might be engaged musically. Consequently, one of the main purposes of this chapter has been to disentangle some issues related to literacy as it applies to music, and to do so in ways that will help readers understand one of the most easily misunderstood areas of a child's musical development.

In the final analysis, it is important to acknowledge how many children learn to read staff notation and achieve a level of proficiency that enables them to function musically. Equally, however, many children are failed by the ways in which they are taught to read music, and give up playing completely. Reading staff notation is not a prerequisite for successful engagement with and appreciation of music, and exclusive concentration on reading has held back the progress of countless learners, while putting many others off completely (Priest, 1989; Schenck, 1989; Mills, 1991b,c, 2005; McPherson, 1993, 2005).

References

Adams, M. J. (1994). *Beginning to read: Thinking and learning about print*. Cambridge, MA: MIT Press.

Bamberger, J. (1988). Les structurations cognitives de l'apprehension et de la notation de rhythmes simples. In H. Sinclair (ed.), *La production de notations chez le jeune enfant* (pp. 99–121). Paris: Presses Universitaires de France.

Bamberger, J. (1996). Turning music theory on its ear. *International Journal of Computers for Mathematical Learning*, 1, 33–55.

Bamberger, J. (1999). Learning from the children we teach. *Bulletin of the Council for Research in Music Education*, 142, 48–74.

Britton, R. & Sheldon, D. C. (2004). An analysis of band method books: Implications of culture, composer and type of music. *Bulletin of the Council for Research in Music Education*, **161/162**, 47–56.

Cantwell, R. H. & Millard, Y. (1994). The relationship between approach to learning and learning strategies in learning music. *British Journal of Educational Psychology*, 64, 45–63.

Cooper, D. (2003). *Literacy: Helping children construct meaning* (5th edn), New York: Houghton Mifflin.

Dodson, T. A. (1983). Developing music reading skills: Research implications. *Update*, 1(4), 3–6

Farrell, G. (2001). India. In D. J. Hargreaves & A. C. North (eds), *Musical development and learning: The international perspective* (pp. 56–72). London: Continuum.

Gordon, E. E. (2003). *Learning sequences in music: Skill, content and patterns*. Chicago, IL: GIA Publications.

Green, S. & Bray, D. (1997). *Differentiation: a guide for music teachers*. Northampton: NIAS.

Hanson, D., Bernstorf, E., & Stuber, G. M. (2004). *The music and literacy connection*. Washington, DC: MENC, the National Association for Music Education.

Hargreaves, D. J. (1986). *The developmental psychology of music*. Cambridge: Cambridge University Press.

Harris, T. L. & Hodges, R. E. (eds) (1995). *The literacy dictionary: The vocabulary of reading and writing*. Newark, DE: International Reading Association.

King, D. W. (1983). *Field-dependence/field-independence and achievement in music reading*. Doctoral dissertation, University of Wisconsin, Madison, 1983.

Kirby, J. R. (1988). Style, strategy, and skill in reading. In R. R. Schmeck (ed.). *Learning strategies and learning styles* (pp. 229–273). New York: Plennum Press.

Mainwaring, J. (1933). Kinaesthetic factors in the recall of musical experience. *British Journal of Psychology*, XXIII(3), 284–307.

Mainwaring, J. (1941). The meaning of musicianship: A problem in the teaching of music. *British Journal of Educational Psychology*, XI(3), 205–214.

Mainwaring, J. (1951). Psychological factors in the teaching of music. *British Journal of Educational Psychology*, XXI, 105–121.

Meadows, S. (1993). *The child as thinker: The development and acquisition of cognition in childhood*. London: Routledge.

McPherson, G. E. (1993). *Factors and abilities influencing the development of visual, aural and creative performance skills in music and their educational implications*. Doctor of Philosophy, University of Sydney, Australia. *Dissertation Abstracts International*, 54/04–A, 1277. (University Microfilms No. 9317278).

McPherson, G. E. (1994a). Factors and abilities influencing sight-reading skill in music, *Journal of Research in Music Education*, 42(3), 217–231.

McPherson, G. E. (1994b). Improvisation: Past, present and future. In H. Lees (ed.), *Musical connections: Tradition and change. Proceedings of the 21st World Conference of the International Society for Music Education, held in Tampa, Florida, USA* (pp. 154–162). Auckland, New Zealand: University of Auckland Press.

McPherson, G. E. (2005). From child to musician: Skill development during the beginning stages of learning an instrument. *Psychology of Music*, 33, 5–35.

McPherson, G. E. & Gabrielsson, A. (2002). From sound to sign. In R. Parncutt & G. E. McPherson (eds), *The science and psychology of musical performance: Creative strategies for music teaching and learning* (pp. 99–115). Oxford: Oxford University Press.

McPherson, G. E. & Renwick, J. M. (2001). A longitudinal study of self-regulation in children's musical practice. *Music Education Research*, 3(2), 169–186.

Mills, J. (1983). *Identifying potential orchestral musicians.* Unpublished DPhil, Oxford University.

Mills, J. (1991a). *Music in the primary school.* Cambridge: Cambridge University Press.

Mills, J. (1991b). Clapping as an approximation to rhythm. *Canadian Music Educator*, 33, 131–138.

Mills, J. (1991c). Out for the count: confused by crotchets—part 2. *Music Teacher*, 70(6), 12–15.

Mills, J. (2005). *Music in the school.* Oxford: Oxford University Press.

Mills, J. & Barrett, M. (in press). Raising boys' achievement? Music as everyday life. *Proceedings of the International Society for Music Education World Conference*, July 16–21, 2006, Kuala Lumpur, Malaysia.

Posner, M. I., Nissen, M. J., & Klein, R. M. (1976). Visual dominance: An information-processing account of its origins and significance. *Psychological review*, 83(2), 157–171.

Priest, P. (1989). Playing by ear: Its nature and application to instrumental learning. *British Journal of Music Education*, 6(2), 173–191.

Schenck, R. (1989). Above all, learning an instrument must be fun! *British Journal of Music Education*, 6, 3–35.

Schleuter, S. (1997). *A sound approach to teaching instrumentalists.* (2nd edn), New York: Schirmer Books.

Schleuter, S. & Schleuter, L. (1988). Teaching and learning music performance: What, when, and how. In C. Fowler (ed.). *The Crane symposium: Toward and understanding of the teaching and learning of music performance* (pp. 63–87). Potsdam College of the State University of New York.

Sloboda, J. A. (1988). *Generative processes in music: The psychology of performance, improvisation, and composition.* Oxford: Clarendon Press.

Sloboda, J. A. (2005). *Exploring the musical mind: Cognition, emotion, ability, function.* Oxford: Oxford University Press.

Smythe, M. M. (1984). Perception and action. In M. M. Smythe & A. M. Wing (eds), *The psychology of human movement* (pp. 119–152). London: Academic Press.

Soares, M. B. (1992). Literacy assessment and its implication for statistical measurement. Paper prepared for UNESCO, Division of Statistics, Paris.

Upitis, R. (1990). Children's invented notations of familiar and unfamiliar melodies. *Psychomusicology*, 9, 89–106.

Upitis, R. (1992). *Can I play you my song? The compositions and invented notations of children.* Portsmouth, NJ: Heinemann Educational Books.

Wiggins, T. (1996). The world of music in education. *British Journal of Music Education*, 13, 21–29.

CHAPTER 9

AESTHETIC RESPONSE

MARGARET S. BARRETT

Introduction

'Aesthetic response' is one of a constellation of related terms and concepts (e.g., aesthetic experience, aesthetic judgement, aesthetic choice, affective response, musical appreciation, musical preference, musical taste) that have been employed in music education research, theory, and practice when attempting to describe and/or define the nature of music knowing, experience, and judgement. As such the concept of aesthetic response is deeply problematic, an 'essentially contested concept' (Gallie, 1964; Barrett, 2002). To separate the terms, the 'aesthetic' stems from a philosophical tradition established in the eighteenth century, which drew on the legacy of the Ancient Greeks in an attempt to determine the nature, meaning and value of the arts and sensory experience to human existence. The latter term 'response' implies the end-point of some form of interaction; one that could be the result of precipitate stimulation, behaviourist training, or, considered reflection. While originally located in the realm of philosophy, when wedded to 'response', and placed in the context of music education, 'aesthetic response' has also been the object of study within psychology and sociology.

This chapter examines the ways in which 'aesthetic response' has been described and used within the philosophy, psychology, and sociology of music education, and examines relevant research that has sought to identify the nature and developmental trajectory in children's musical engagement within and across these fields. In so doing, it explores a view of aesthetic response as 'performative' and constitutive of identity, and considers the implications of this view for theories of children's musical development.

The topic of 'aesthetics', whether couched in philosophical, psychological, or sociological terms has generated an extensive body of literature. It is beyond the scope of this chapter to deal with the diverse and complex theories that have arisen within the literature, or to add further to the numerous attempts to arrive at a definitive account of aesthetic response. Rather, the chapter is intended to alert the reader to the depth and complexity of theoretical work in relation to this concept, and to provoke further discussion. Necessarily, many perspectives are omitted, some dealt with in a cursory manner when deserving of a more thorough examination, while others are examined in more depth as a particular argument is pursued. For this reason, readers are encouraged to move beyond my omissions and 'prejudices'[1] and to explore the field in greater depth[2].

Philosophical views of aesthetic response

Philosophical views of aesthetic response arise from philosophical endeavour that has aimed to provide 'sustained, systematic and critical examination of belief' (Elliott, 2002, p. 85), and make 'the implicit explicit, with the ultimate aim of enriching both understanding and perception' (Bowman, 1998, p. 5). While the study of the nature of music, its effects, and human response, has been the topic of philosophical debate since the writings of Plato, Socrates, and Aristotle, the formalization of this debate under the term 'aesthetic', stems from the eighteenth century and the work of Alexander Gottlieb Baumgarten (1735[3]). Baumgarten created the term 'aesthetica' to describe a type of understanding that occurs through sensory experience of the world, that is, through perception rather than conception. He thereby created a complementary form of knowing and knowledge, a 'second-order' form of cognition. This idea of the aesthetic was taken up by Kant in his work *The critique of judgment* (1952/1790), and expanded upon in distinctive ways. For Kant, aesthetic experience consisted of the apprehension of beauty in an object, an apprehension that rests in our capacity to perceive formal qualities and make direct, personal judgements that are 'disinterested', that is, unmediated by consideration of external issues such as moral or ethical concerns. Unfortunately, Kant considered music's 'formal properties' as being too located in the realm of the sensuous as opposed to the contemplative, thus relegating music to a lowly form of aesthetic experience within the spectrum of the arts.

Throughout the eighteenth and nineteenth centuries a view of the aesthetic arose that sought to identify engagement with the arts as rational, cognitive, and separate from the powerful and seductive effects of the emotions and the sensuous. Philosophers strove to identify 'universal' and 'eternal' qualities that could be drawn on when making judgements about the nature and quality of arts works and experiences, and a unique kind of attention or 'aesthetic attitude' that was employed in such experiences[4]. This focus on universal and eternal qualities necessitated the discarding of all reference to context or qualities external to the work itself: the arts work became 'autonomous', an object or event to be judged solely through analysis of its 'internal' features, its 'form'. This is perhaps most powerfully illustrated in Eduard Hanslick's 'aesthetics of music' (1986) first published in 1854, where the capacity to appreciate the formal properties of musical works over sensuous or emotive properties, was emphasized. Hanslick's antipathy to the consideration of 'context'

---

[1] I use the term 'prejudice' in Gadamer's non-pejorative sense that 'all understanding necessarily involves some prejudice' (1982, p. 239).

[2] Analysis of primary sources and interpretations of these (e.g., Bowman, 1998) will provide a greater insight and understanding of the complexities of these debates in relation to music.

[3] *Meditationes Philosophicae de Nonnullus ad Poema Pertinentitous.*

[4] 'Aesthetic attitude' or *disinterest* theories may be traced from Kant, through the work of Schopenhauer (1818/1966), to Bullough's (1912) identification of 'psychical distance'.

or extra-musical features in making musical judgements is evidenced in his discussion of programme music, specifically Beethoven's overture to *Egmont*:

> The content of Beethoven's overture is not the character Egmont, nor his actions, experiences, attitudes, but these are the content of the portrait 'Egmont', of the drama *Egmont*. The contents of the overture are sequences of tones which the composer has created entirely spontaneously, according to logical musical principles. For aesthetical contemplation, they are wholly autonomous and independent of the mental image of Egmont, with which only the poetical imagination of the composer has brought them into connection, no matter whether, in some inexplicable way, the image was suitable for initiating the invention of that sequence of tones or whether he invented that sequence of tones and then found the image of Egmont consistent with it.
>
> Hanslick (1986, pp. 74–75)

For Hanslick, musical content consisted of the 'sequences of tones' rather than any extra-musical material, where music '. . . speaks not merely by means of tones, it speaks only tones' (1986, p. 78). In Hanslick's theory, musical content and form were 'fused in an obscure, inseparable unity' (1986, p. 80) that distinguished music from all other literary and visual arts. Feelings were a secondary effect in music as '. . . the more powerfully an effect from a work of art overwhelms us physically (and hence is pathological), the more negligible is its aesthetical component' (1986, p. 57). Hanslick (1986) instead promoted a 'deliberate pure contemplation' of music, that yielded an 'unemotional yet heartfelt pleasure', a 'mental satisfaction which the listener finds in continuously following and anticipating the composer's designs, here to be confirmed in his expectations, there to be agreeably lead astray' (p. 64).

This emphasis on the cognition of autonomous form as the determining factor in making meaning and judgements in music continues in various guises through the accounts of musical meaning offered by theorists such as Suzanne Langer (1942/1979) and Leonard B. Meyer (1956). Langer's theory of music does not exclude emotion and the sensuous, as she views music as a type of analogue of emotional experience, where the movement of musical tension mirrors that of emotional experience. However, in her view we do not experience the emotions *as* emotions, rather, we experience music as a 'presentational symbol' of emotions: as Bowman (2004) describes this approach, '. . . music shares common structural form with the realm of feeling (music sounds like feelings feel)' (p. 32).

Meyer also admits emotion into the ways in which we understand and make meaning in music. In his early work, Meyer (1956) provides an (somewhat behavioural) explanation of musical meaning where music and emotion (or affect) are described in terms of stimulus and response, with musical meaning and 'affect' arising from our close attention to the unfolding of musical patterns that both confirm and contradict our 'listener' expectations. For example, musical 'affect' may be achieved through the development of repetitive musical forms that lead the listener to expect certain musical resolutions that are subsequently interrupted or delayed, before being resolved in conventional or novel ways. Meyer's (2001) continued emphasis on 'expectancy' and arousal and resolution as the 'essential basis for aesthetic-emotional experience' (p. 353) is evident in later work. While emotion and 'affect' are admitted, they are only achieved through cognitive attention to pattern and structure within the musical work in a manner reminiscent of Hanslick's description of the 'unemotional yet heartfelt pleasure' gained from the 'deliberate pure contemplation of music'. For Meyer (2001), uncertainty is of aesthetic importance as 'When the tensions of instability are resolved to the cognitive security of stable patterning, functional relationships have at once articulated and unified musical structure' (p. 359).

Langer's and Meyer's theories are in varying degrees sensitive to stylistic and cultural differences, thereby beginning the move away from an emphasis on universal qualities in the ways in which we understand, make meaning, and respond to music. However, the terms by which Meyer's 'expectations' are unfolded within styles rests in a Western art music definition of 'style' that identifies 'intra-stylistic' features through the 'universal lens' of Western art music. This circular process inevitably judges all music from a common (Western art music) framework regardless of the acknowledgement of style-specific features within that framework, and tends to draw us back to a cognitive focus on autonomous form, albeit one that admits of a form of emotional engagement (for further discussion of the development of *emotional* response see Chapter 10).

Philosophical views: implications for children's musical development

The legacy of these (modernist) accounts of aesthetics and aesthetic response has been an exclusive focus on audience-listening as the key mode by which aesthetic response is elicited/demonstrated, where the listener's increasing ability to identify the interplay of formal features is taken as an indicator of aesthetic understanding and development. Adherence to these accounts of the aesthetic suggests that the development of aesthetic response in children rests in a growing capacity to identify and 'engage' in audience-listening mode with the formal features of musical works in particular musical styles. Specifically, a child's capacity to identify and respond to musical tension achieved through the manipulation of musical elements (Langer), or, to identify the ways in which musical patterns are established, developed, and resolved (Meyer), is indicative of aesthetic understanding and response.

Such an approach does not acknowledge that music has many roles and functions in our lives beyond that of being an 'object' of 'pure contemplation', roles that I shall explore in greater depth later in this chapter. Furthermore, postmodernist perspectives on aesthetics have challenged the verities that were the foundation of modernist aesthetic theory, those of autonomous form, universal and eternal qualities, and disinterestedness, suggesting that our attention in and to music encompasses more than a disinterested focus on formal properties. Acknowledgement of the particular and local, of plurality, the 'other', and of 'bias' or 'prejudice' in a non-pejorative sense move the aesthetic project away from a focus on definitive statements. As Bowman (1998) reminds us:

> The comforting belief that all music is evaluable by the same, strictly 'aesthetic' criteria has lost its persuasiveness, as has the noble vision of music as an inherently and inevitably 'humanizing' affair. The essentially musical core which 'masterworks' were once thought to represent abundantly is increasingly characterized as ideological and political subterfuge. What the term 'music' designates has become increasingly problematic, and its potential values have become radically multiple. (p. 394)

The admission of postmodernist theory to the discussion of aesthetics has generated considerable debate, and philosophical accounts of aesthetic response in music are contested heavily. However, within the discipline of the psychology of music, the study of aesthetic response has been subject to less debate. In the following section I shall explore the ways in which aesthetic response has been described and interrogated from this perspective.

Psychological views of aesthetic response

Psychological views of aesthetic response have arisen largely from the study of music perception and cognition in the field of psycho-acoustics, specifically, within the subfield of empirical or experimental aesthetics. Empirical aesthetics (Fechner, 1876/1978) was developed as a complementary area of study to that of philosophical aesthetics, and was intended to establish a means to scientific study of those concepts raised in philosophical aesthetics. This work was taken up by Berlyne (1970, 1971, 1974) who established the field of experimental aesthetics in an attempt to develop an 'objective' approach to the study of aesthetic appreciation in music that was *separate* from the 'speculative' nature of philosophical aesthetics.

Despite this distinction in the intentions of empirical and experimental aesthetics, both approaches have a philosophical foundation in modernist accounts of the aesthetic. This is perhaps a consequence of early parallel development wherein empirical and experimental aesthetics developed from *modernist* accounts of philosophical aesthetics, and have not been subject to recent *postmodernist* developments in the field. Within empirical and experimental aesthetics, the research enterprise works from 'universal' features of music (e.g., the perception of acoustic stimuli and/or pattern and form) to identify characteristic patterns of development in the aesthetic/affective perception and cognition of music. Consequently, psychological accounts of aesthetic response are subject to the criticisms levelled at modernist philosophical accounts of the aesthetic in their focus on autonomous form, universal and eternal qualities, and 'disinterested' response.

Studies of aesthetic response in the psychology of music have included the analysis of listener response to hearings of non-musical acoustic stimuli (Berlyne, 1971), of elements of musical systems, such as tuning (Lynch & Eilers, 1991), and of partial and/or complete performances of musical works (Madsen *et al.*, 1993). These studies have included the investigation of responses to auditory/musical experiences that require little prior knowledge or experience of music, and/or extensive knowledge and experience (Madsen & Geringer, 1990; Madsen *et al.*, 1993). The former of these approaches arises in part from nativist views of aesthetic thinking and response that argue that innate cognitive structures govern thinking, learning, and development, and seek to identify the nature of these, and the constraints of their operation. In contrast to the nativist position, contextualist views argue that culture and context play an instrumental role in thinking, learning, and development, and insist that the constructive influences of these factors be admitted to any study of aesthetic thinking and response. Research techniques employed in these studies have elicited both non-verbal and verbal response to listening experience. In the former, devices such as the 'Continuous Response Digital Interface' (CRDI) have been used as a means to accessing music response unmediated by language and the specialized vocabulary required for the discussion of music experience (Madsen & Geringer, 1990; Madsen *et al.*, 1993). The CRDI involves manipulation of a dial during listening experience, a process that produces a 'map' of emotional response to music experience that indicates the peaks and troughs of such response (in part an application of Langer's suggestion that music is a 'presentational symbol' of emotions). The view of 'aesthetic response' that emerges from this approach is one that highlights music's role in arousing feelings and emotions, rather than one that focuses on the identification of elements of musical structure and form. Essentially, the CRDI maps 'reflection-in-action', providing a means to monitor arousal states.

Non-verbal approaches have been employed also in developmental psychology research with infants and young children as a means to circumventing infants' actual and young children's perceived inability to verbalize a response to musical experience. Researchers examining infants' responses to music have adapted 'head-turn preference procedures' (HTPP) employed in developmental linguistics to test infants' abilities to discriminate between varying aural stimuli (Karmiloff & Karmiloff-Smith, 2001). This procedure has been used to identify infants' musical preferences for consonance over dissonance (Zentner & Kagan, 1996; Trainor *et al.*, 2002); musically phrased segmentation of melodies over non-musically phrased segmentation (Krumhansl & Juscyk, 1990); and tone repetition in melody (Schellenberg & Trehub, 1999). HTPP strategies have also been employed to identify infants' ability to detect changes in melodic contour (Trehub *et al.*, 1997), and in semi-tonal variations in interval size (Schellenberg & Trehub, 1996). These HTPP studies indicate that infants have established preferences and abilities from an early age, suggesting that music preferences and responses arise from innate structures. An alternative interpretation of these findings takes into account the considerable exposure to music that many infants experience *in utero* and during the first months of life, modifying a purely nativist account of this aspect of musical development to one that admits of the formative nature of culture and environment.

In a bid to address criticisms concerning the ecological validity of some methodological approaches to the psychological study of aesthetics (e.g., asking participants to respond to isolated tones or artificial stimuli that have little or no resemblance to music events) researchers working with child participants have sought increasingly to use complete musical works of varying length and complexity as a means to eliciting and studying aesthetic response. Strategies employed in these studies have included: eliciting verbal response during the aural event using 'think-aloud' protocols (Richardson, 1995); eliciting verbal response after the aural event using interview, verbal checklist, or written reflective responses (Hevner, 1936; Farnsworth, 1954; Flowers, 1984, 1988; Nelson, 1985; Preston, 1994; Rodriguez & Webster, 1997; Rodriguez, 1998; Swanwick & Franca, 1999; Barrett, 2000/2001); eliciting non-verbal 'aesthetic response' during the aural event using devices such as the CRDI (Byrnes, 1997); eliciting non-verbal response after the aural event using movement analogues (Gromko & Poorman, 1998; Fung & Gromko, 2001), adult-generated listening maps (Gromko & Russell, 2002), and graphic tasks (Hair, 1993/1994). In reviewing this body of research, questions may be raised in regard to the timing of the elicitation of the response (during or after the event): specifically, the distinction between responding in listening as a 'reflection-in-action' strategy as opposed to responding after listening as a 'reflection-on-action' strategy. While some would dispute whether listening is 'action', or indeed, capable of bearing the distinction between reflection 'in' rather than 'on' action, what is accessed 'in' rather than 'after' the event may be qualitatively different in ways that are important to understanding aesthetic thinking and response. Similarly, distinction needs to be made between arousal, affect, and enduring response. Further research is needed to explore these questions in relation to aesthetic response.

The employment of verbal strategies to elicit children's aesthetic response has not been without criticism as researchers have suggested that young children's ability to verbalize their ideas and responses is significantly less than their perceptual abilities (Hair, 1981, 1987). Nevertheless a number of studies have proposed developmental trends in children's verbal responses to listening experience. These include the observation that:

1. young children are more concerned with describing isolated properties of sound than with the affective aspects of music (Rodriguez & Webster, 1997);
2. musically untrained children's and adults' verbal responses are primarily concerned with 'extra-musical' references with some references to timbre, tempo, and dynamics (Flowers, 1990); and
3. children move progressively through stages dominated respectively by
    - a focus on the materials of music (isolated properties)
    - a focus on expressive properties, and
    - a focus on issues of form and structure (Swanwick & Franca, 1999).

The hierarchic separation of children's perception of isolated properties, expressive properties, and issues of form and structure that is outlined in these findings reflects the concerns of modernist aesthetics with the separation of affective issues from those of structure and form, a Cartesian separation of emotion from cognition. It could be speculated that these results reflect the underlying aesthetic theory of such research, in that a theoretical separation of affective and structural properties, of form and content, shapes the ways in which these issues are identified in participant responses, and subsequently interpreted: that is, a dualistic framework inevitably produces dualistic results.

In other approaches to the study of aesthetic response researchers have sought to examine modes of music engagement other than audience-listening as a means to accessing musical thinking and aesthetic decision-making, focusing on children's *musical* discourse as composers (Barrett, 1996, 1998). Findings from this research dispute the hierarchic separation of expressive properties and issues of form and structure in children's musical thinking, a finding that is supported by other research (Marsh, 1995). From this research, a view of the aesthetic as a situated interpretive 'dialogue' between the child, the music event, and the social and cultural contexts in which she experiences music and music-making is proposed (Barrett, 2002). The aesthetic 'transaction' is viewed as a form of contextually embedded action in which meanings and judgements of value are 'demonstrated' through a range of musical processes (Barrett, 2002, 2003a).

Psychological views: implications for children's musical development

Specific aesthetic theories are rarely outlined in many of the studies cited above. However, the emphasis on initiating and mapping response to formal/structural features in isolation from content and contextual features, suggests that the underlying aesthetic theory is formalist and modernist, that is, one that focuses on intra-musical features, and response to these 'aesthetic' qualities. These studies tend to work from musical materials developed within the Western classical or 'art' music tradition, further reinforcing a philosophical view of the aesthetic as autonomous, universal, eternal, creating a sense of internal congruence that results in broad similarities in the ways in which aesthetic experience and response is described (Lychner, 1998).

In these psychological approaches to the study of aesthetic response the development of aesthetic response in children appears to rest in a growing capacity to identify and 'engage' with the formal features of musical works. While researchers have moved beyond a solitary focus on audience-listening as the prime mode of engagement for aesthetic response, to one that acknowledges other forms of engagement, and admitted an expanded notion of 'music' to include music beyond that of the Western music canon, there is still considerable debate on the nature and developmental trajectory of aesthetic response. Indeed, the admission of issues of context and culture has served to add further complexity to the study of aesthetic response. Another element of complexity is evident in the emergence of interdisciplinary approaches to the study of music, music development, and aesthetic response.

While the field of cognitive neuroscience of music is not directly linked to that of experimental aesthetics or the psychological study of aesthetic response, the topics of study in this field have some overlap with the concerns of experimental aesthetics. For example, the study of the processing of emotions provoked by music experience relates to the sensuous aspects of aesthetic experience, and the mode of music engagement that is most often associated with aesthetic experience in music, that of audience listening. Studies that have mapped physiological response (heart and/or respiration rate, skin conductivity, blood flow) to music, suggest that 'music elicits a cascade of subconscious activity' (Trainor & Schmidt, 2003, p. 320). Trainor and Schmidt (2003) propose that 'music may be so intimately connected with emotional systems because caregivers use music to communicate emotionally with their infants before they are able to use language' (p. 310). This implicit linking of the cognitive and emotive through identifying communication as a function of early music engagement is also evident in the work of Dissanayake (2001). She argues that aesthetic imagination arises from the 'pretend play' of mother–infant interactions, interactions in which infants are active agents in their communicative interactions with mothers or caretakers in what are 'essentially *aesthetic* contexts' (2000, p. 219). Dissanayake (2000) observes that 'In these encounters, sensitivities to rhythmic and dynamic change are manipulated in order to co-ordinate the mother–infant pair emotionally and express its accord' (p. 219). This emphasis on interactive social engagement suggests a more holistic notion of aesthetic response that moves beyond a focus on intra-musical features (such as formal features of musical works) to a focus on the *uses* of music in social settings, in short, to sociological views of aesthetic response.

Sociological views of aesthetic response

As sociological studies are concerned with issues such as social organization, action and interaction between individuals and groups, and social processes involved in the production of culture and knowledge, sociological approaches to aesthetics have looked beyond intra-musical features to acknowledge the influence and impact of other processes in eliciting and shaping aesthetic response. Writing broadly of sociology, DeNora (2001) characterizes this move as one where 'sociologists across a wide range of specialist areas have devoted themselves to the question of how material-cultural and aesthetic media may be understood to provide models and candidate structures for the production and achievement of emotion and feeling within specific social settings' (p. 164). For music, this has resulted in a concern with 'how it is consumed and what it "does" in social life' (p. 164), and a focus on the practice of music in a range of social and cultural settings, rather than on 'autonomous music objects'. These concerns resonate with those of ethnomusicology, where the interests of musicologists and anthropologists intersect in the study of musical structures and materials (musicology), and their cultural function (anthropology) (Gregory, 1997). Discussion of some ethnomusicological approaches to the study of children's aesthetic engagement and response shall be addressed in this section.

DeNora (2000, 2001) suggests that when music is used to manipulate emotional, cognit-ive, and feeling states that it functions as a kind of 'aesthetic technology', an instrument of self and social ordering, of emotional and identity work. This enacted and enactive view of the aesthetic, where the focus is on 'use' not autonomous object provides a revitalized view of the aesthetic, one that emphasizes 'aesthetic agency' (DeNora, 2000). In this view, 'Music is a resource to which agents turn so as to regulate themselves as aesthetic agents, as feel-ing, thinking and active beings in their day-to-day lives' (DeNora, 2003, p. 95). This focus has also been taken up in philosophy by the pragmatist philosopher Richard Shusterman (2000) and is evidenced in his proposal of the discipline of 'somaesthetics' (I shall explore this further in the following section). The emergent view of the aesthetic from these diverse fields is one that is concerned with emotion, specifically, with the 'social distribution of emotion' (DeNora, 2001, p. 167), 'our need for beauty and intensified feeling' (Shusterman, 2000, p. 7), and our 'use' of aesthetic experiences in the structuring of our lives.

Within music, sociological views of aesthetic response have tended to focus on the issue of musical 'taste' or 'preference', under the broad rubric of 'musical appreciation' (Russell, 1997). The examination of the musical preferences of adolescents has been of particular interest to music educators and researchers working from a cross-disciplinary perspective in the social psychology of music (Zilman & Gan, 1997; North et al., 2000; Boal-Palheiros & Hargreaves, 2001). This interest reflects concerns that adolescents' enormous interest in and consumption of music in their lives beyond schools does not translate necessarily into a commensurate interest in engagement in school music (see further, Ross, 1995; Gammon, 1996). Much of the sociological research in aesthetic response has been concerned with exploring adolescents' preferences for specific genres of music and the links between such preferences and music-dependent behaviours (Frith & McRobbie, 1990; Shepherd & Giles-Davies, 1991; see also, Willis's 1978 study of bikeboys' use of music as a means to shaping their behaviour).

A number of studies have explored the relationship between gender and musical taste (Frith & McRobbie, 1990; Bryson, 1997) in an attempt to identify gender-based patterns of musical preference. For example, young girls' preference for romantic popular music and dance music (McRobbie, 2000) appears to differentiate their tastes from those of young boys. However, other research suggests that the differentiation on gender lines lies in the ways in which the respective groupings describe and discuss music rather than in the identification of specific musical works and styles (Richards, 1998). While much of this research has focused again on audience-listening as the main mode of aesthetic engagement, the nature of such listening has expanded beyond traditional 'concert-hall' notions of 'deliberate pure contemplation of music' to encompass types of 'performative listening', for example, listening in and through dance participation (McRobbie, 2000), and 'pairing music with a variety of other materials, practices, and postures' (DeNora, 2003, p. 94). In related work, feminist analyses of music and music experience interrogate the nature of audience-listening and criticism and the gendered assumptions that underlie modes of music engagement and forms of music analysis (McClary, 1991).

In other sociological investigations of aesthetic response researchers have investigated the musical preferences of younger children including the labels they use to describe such preferences (Suthers, 1999), their habits of listening at home and at school (Boal-Palheiros & Hargreaves, 2004), and the ways in which children 'use' music in their daily lives (Campbell, 1998, 2002). Campbell's (2002) study rests in the intersection between sociology, ethnomusicology, and anthropology as she argues that children 'use' music for a variety of purposes in their various musical cultures (p. 61). She identifies nine distinct functions of music in children's lives, those of: Emotional expression; Aesthetic enjoyment; Entertainment; Communication; Physical response; Enforcement of conformity to social norms; Validation of religious ritual; Continuity and stability of culture; and Integration of society (pp. 61–64). Campbell (2002) does not order these various functions in a developmental progression, rather, she emphasizes the diversity of uses of music in the lives of children of all ages. Crucially, the identification of these functions incorporates a variety of modes of music engagement. In other ethnomusicological work, children's songs and musical play have been identified as rich sources of information concerning the characteristic musical structures of adult culture (Nettl, 1990), and potentially a source for understanding the development of aesthetic preferences and practices in these cultures.

An acknowledged antecedent for Campbell's work lies in Blacking's seminal study of the music of the Venda people, and his analysis of children's song in this culture. Blacking's (1973/2000) emphasis was primarily ethnomusicological rather than anthropological as evidenced in his insistence on the analysis of music structure as a means to understanding the nature of music:

> We may never be able to understand exactly how another person feels about a piece of music, but we can perhaps understand the structural factors that generate the feelings. Attention to music's function in society is necessary only in so far as it may help us to explain the structures . . . I am concerned primarily with what music is, and not what it is used for. (p. 26)

While this emphasis may be viewed as a perpetuation of a modernist concern with accessing musical meaning through the analysis of music's constitutive elements, Blacking (1973/2000) asserted that musical structures were not separate from socio-cultural and biological structures:

> Functional analyses of musical structure cannot be detached from structural analyses of its social function: the function of tones in relation to each other cannot be explained adequately as part of a closed system without reference to the structures of the socio-cultural system of which the musical system is a part, and the biological system to which all music makers belong (p. 30).

In relation to the focus of this chapter, aesthetic response, Blacking's description of the embedded nature of the biological, the musical, and the socio-cultural reminds us that individual and collective experience of music in social and cultural settings is central to the development of aesthetic response, and is manifest in a range of musical modes of engagement.

Sociological views: implications for children's musical development

The sociological focus on the 'uses' of music in individual lives challenges traditional accounts of children's musical development in aesthetic response. Specifically, the 'uses' of music as a means to configure identity, relationships, and social and cultural institutions, suggests that aesthetic response is 'performative' and plays a key role in children's identity work. When these issues are taken into consideration, the study of children's aesthetic response necessitates a move from a singular focus on the musical work and children's response to this, to the study of children's musical action and agency, their active engagement in music in all modes of musical engagement (e.g., composing, improvising, listening, moving, performing, singing), and an admission of multiple ways in which aesthetic response may be 'performed'.

Aesthetic response and the child as musician

In the above discussion of philosophical, psychological, and sociological views of the aesthetic, it is evident that the bulk of research into aesthetic response has emerged in the field of psychology and its various subdisciplines. In terms of studying musical development, the child as musician has been viewed largely through the lens of developmental psychology, a lens that has been shaped by formalist views of the aesthetic that arose in modernist accounts of philosophical aesthetics. As such the development of the child as musician is described as a process whereby an autonomous individual engages with the phenomenon of Western music as it is presented in institutional Western music education practices. These latter tend to work from an 'atomised' rather than holistic account of music and music experience, where the study of music occurs through the isolated study of its constitutive elements rather than through holistic encounters with music practice. Lucy Green's (2002) analysis of the learning practices of popular musicians points the distinction between these formal and informal music learning practices. In what may be seen as a self-replicating process, research has focused on the study of individual response to the constitutive elements of music, presented variously in isolation, or complete musical contexts.

It is only recently that the child as musician has been viewed through other lenses, for example, that of sociology. Consequently, sociological accounts of children's aesthetic response are less common. Further, such accounts tend to be shaped around the study of social and cultural issues in aesthetic response such as gender, or social class, rather than developmental issues. Indeed, within the sociological study of childhood, many of the assumptions that are inherent in developmental psychological studies of childhood are challenged. This is evident in the emerging field of socio-cultural developmental psychology (Rogoff, 2003) where accounts of the nature and trajectory of development in a range of human functions are demonstrably different across social and cultural settings.

What is common in many accounts of the aesthetic and aesthetic response in both developmental psychology and sociology is a failure to acknowledge and interrogate the philosophical beliefs and values that underpin the research enterprise. I have attempted in the above discussions of psychological and sociological views to identify some of these underlying philosophical theories. It is significant that much of the research draws on formalist aesthetic theories that have been subject to considerable debate in recent years. Key criticisms of these theories include the adherence to universals, the separation of mind and body in human thought and action, and the elision of social and cultural variation. In what follows I shall explore an alternative account of aesthetic response that draws on recent aesthetic philosophy, and discuss the implications of such an account for our views of the development of the 'child as musician'.

Performing aesthetic identity

In a broad interdisciplinary approach to the study of the origins of 'art' and its meaning and function in human existence Dissanayake (1988/2002, 1992/1999, 2000) draws on diverse fields, including those of aesthetics, anthropology, evolutionary theory, biology and socio-biology, psychology, cognitive science, and neuroscience to propose a bioevolutionary theory of art. Dissanayake (2000) argues that the arts are intrinsic to human existence, that love and the arts are 'inherently related', and, that the origins of art lie in human intimacy. Her argument draws on evidence of 'psychobiological mechanisms', or 'rhythms and modes' that she proposes form the basis of mother–infant interactions and communication. While socio-cultural views of developmental psychology (Rogoff, 2003) may query Dissanayake's 'universal' characterization of mother–infant interactions, suggesting that these provide a 'Western' romanticized account of such early relationships, the theory provides a useful lens through which we may explore an alternative account of aesthetic response.

In earlier work Dissanayake comments that '. . . insofar as we respond *aesthetically* we are aware (at some level; it may well be inarticulate) of the code—of *how* not only *that* something is said. This awareness, which is cognitive, makes our fuller response possible, as we discriminate, relate, recognize, and otherwise follow the code's manipulations' (Dissanayake, 1988/2002, p. 165). Here, Dissanayake (1988/2002) identifies two kinds of appreciation, that of '. . . "ecstatic" response to sensual, psychophysiological properties in the artwork, and . . . "aesthetic" response to the manipulations of the code or pattern of expectations embodied in it' (p. 164). For Dissanayake, aesthetic response is a result of education whereas 'ecstatic' response arises from sensation. At one level this separation of the aesthetic from the ecstatic reflects the preoccupation of modernist aesthetic theory with separating body from mind, sensuous experience from cognition, a preoccupation that is countered by recent moves to 'embody' the mind (Damasio, 1994/2000, 2000, 2003; Lakoff & Johnson, 1999; Bresler, 2004). At another level, within Dissanayake's (2000) frame of a 'naturalistic aesthetic', the body and mind are brought together in a psychobiological explanation of aesthetic valuing and response that points towards the 'embodied mind'.

Dissanayake (2000) argues that the origins of the aesthetic lie in the human need for *mutuality*. She suggests that mutuality is characterized by the features of: belonging to; finding and making meaning; competence through handling and making; and, elaboration. Dissanayake's identification of these features draws on Trevarthen's (1998) concept of *innate intersubjectivity*. He argues that infants are predisposed to elicit, respond to, and regulate the mother's emotional as well as physical support and care, and identifies 'mutual action' and 'infant agency' as key components of this process. Mutuality and agency are also evident in Malloch's accounts of 'communicative musicality'. He describes 'communicative musicality' as the 'co-operative and co-dependent communicative interactions between mother and infant' (Malloch, 1999, p. 31) where human communication between mother and infant in the first year of life takes the form of an interactive dialogue shaped by the musical elements of pulse, quality, and narrative.

All of these accounts of the origins of the aesthetic emphasize the role of the infant as active agent rather than passive subject in the aesthetic transaction, and acknowledge that aesthetic response occurs as music-maker as well as music-listener. Others support this view of the child as active 'aesthetic' agent arguing that young children '. . . are culture-makers by nature . . . they are born into history and community' (Abbs, 2003, p. 55) and are engaged in a 'reciprocal relationship' between culture and self. Studies in the sociology of childhood assert that children '. . . are active contributors to, rather than simply spectators of the complex processes of cultural continuity and change' (James et al., 1998, p. 83). This is illustrated in studies of young children's meaning-making as song-makers (Barrett, 2000, 2003b) where young children are portrayed as active producers rather than simply re-producers of their musical culture, in short, that they work as 'meme engineers' (Barrett, 2003b) in the ways in which they construct musical meaning in and through their lives. Importantly, this early 'aesthetic work' plays a role in the ways in which young children come to understand themselves and others.

Richard Shusterman's (2002, 2004) concept of 'somaesthetics' constitutes one approach to a view of the aesthetic that embraces the sensual and the cognitive, the body and the mind. He defines somaesthetics as '. . . a discipline devoted to the critical ameliorative study of the experience and use of the body as a locus of sensory-aesthetic appreciation (*aesthesis*) and creative self-fashioning' (2004, p. 51), and suggests that this study addresses the central aims of philosophy, those of 'knowledge, self-knowledge, right action, justice, and the quest for the good life' (2004, p. 51). Shusterman outlines three forms of somaesthetics, analytic, pragmatic, and practical. While all three hold potential for developing our understanding of the development of aesthetic response in music, it is the latter, the practical, or experiential, that is my focus. For Shusterman, experiential somaesthetics' role is to inform us more fully about our feelings and emotions through attention to the embodiment of these. Knowledge of other courses of action and ways of being helps us 'retrain, reorganise and re-educate' (2004, pp. 56–58). Such awareness can lead us to better knowledge, understanding, and ultimately action in the ways in which we conduct our lives, issues that are closely linked to the development and maintenance of identity. Potentially, admission of somaesthetics may assist our understanding of the ways in which individuals draw on and enact music practices. It is worth noting that the music education system developed by Emile Jaques Dalcroze (1921/1980) holds as an underlying principle that musical understanding arises from developing awareness of kinaesthetic response to music and the subsequent conscious use of bodily movement as a means to explore music's structural and expressive properties. While Dalcroze's chief concern was the development of musical understanding in thought and action rather than self-knowledge and identity work, his philosophy and methods foreshadowed in many ways those of practical somaesthetics.

Three key elements emerge from the literature examined above: first, that the aesthetic is embodied, connecting the body and the mind in children's musical thought and action; second, that the 'child as musician' is engaged from infancy as 'aesthetic agent'; and, third, that children's 'aesthetic work' provides a means for them to 'perform' identity as they come to understand themselves and their worlds. In proposing a performative view of aesthetic identity, I seek to bring these three key elements together to promote a view of the child as aesthetic agent, engaged through mind and body in crucial identity work in and through music. That music is central to identity work is indisputable. Drawing on Judith Butler's performative account of identity, Bowman (2002) sets forth as a 'pivotal claim' for music's ethical and educational significance the view that:

> . . . we are what we do, and do repeatedly. Music's ritualistic actions and the dispositions that undergird them are fundamental to the formation of character, both collective and individual. More strongly still, music plays a fundamental role in the social production and regulation of identity. If music is an important part of the machinery by which people's individual and collective identities are constructed, reconstructed, maintained, and regulated, music education becomes something dramatically more momentous and problematic than an act of overseeing the development of musical skills, musicianship, or 'aesthetic sensibilities'. The view on which this claim is based is performative, one that sees identities not as natural facts, but cultural performances. (pp. 75–76)

I have quoted Bowman's claim in full as it holds significance for any discussion of children's musical development, and of the 'aesthetic'. If we endorse Bowman's central claim, that music is foundational in the construction, reconstruction, maintenance, and regulation of identity, the development of the 'child as musician' becomes a process of 'self-creation' that is concerned not just with the 'sonorous event' but also with the rich interplay of individual, social, cultural, and environmental factors that are part of that event, and the changes and transformations effected in the individual through engagement with all these factors.

In this view the development of aesthetic understanding as evidenced in aesthetic response is a process of growth, not of acquisition, '...more a process of "becoming" than a process of becoming aware or of "Becoming knowledgeable"' (Bowman, 2004, p. 44).

Significantly, developing aesthetic understanding and response is not the sole preserve of the listening subject: the possibility of aesthetic response is present in all modes of music engagement as children construct and 'perform' their emergent aesthetic identities.

References

Abbs, P. (2003). *Against the flow: Education, the arts and postmodern culture.* London: RoutledgeFalmer.

Barrett, M. S. (1996). Children's aesthetic decision-making: An analysis of children's musical discourse as composers. *International Journal of Music Education,* **28**, 37–62.

Barrett, M. S. (1998). Children composing: A view of aesthetic decision-making. In B. Sundin, G. E. McPherson, & G. Folkestad (eds), *Children composing* (pp. 57–81) Malmo: Lund University Press.

Barrett, M. S. (2000/2001). Perception, description and reflection: Young children's aesthetic decision-making as critics of their own and adult compositions. *Bulletin of the Council for Research in Music Education.* 147, 22–29

Barrett, M. S. (2002). Towards a 'situated' view of the aesthetic in music education. *Journal of Aesthetic Education,* **36**(3), 67–77.

Barrett, M. S. (2003a). Freedoms and constraints: Constructing musical worlds through the dialogue of composition. In M. Hickey (ed.), *Composition in the schools: A new horizon for music education* (pp. 3–27). Reston, VA: MENC.

Barrett, M. S. (2003b). Meme engineers: Children as producers of musical culture. *International Journal of Early Years Education,* **11**(3) 195–212.

Berlyne, D. E. (1970). Novelty, complexity, and hedonic value. *Perception and psychophysics,* **8**, 279–286.

Berlyne, D. E. (1971). *Aesthetics and psychobiology.* New York: Appleton Century Crofts Publishers.

Berlyne, D. E. (1974). *Studies in the new experimental aesthetics: Steps towards an objective psychology of aesthetic appreciation.* Toronto: John Wiley.

Blacking, J. (1973/2000). *How musical is man?* Seattle: University of Washington Press.

Boal-Palheiros, G. & Hargreaves, D. J. (2001). Listening to music at home and at school. *British Journal of Music Education,* **18**(2), 103–118.

Boal-Palheiros, G. & Hargreaves, D. J. (2004). Children's modes of listening to music at home and at school. In J. Tafuri (ed.), *Proceedings of the 20th seminar of the ISME Research Commission* (pp. 31–38). Bologna: Conservatorio di Musica.

Bowman, W. (1998). *Philosophical perspectives on music.* New York: Oxford University Press.

Bowman, W. (2002). Educating musically. In R. Colwell & C. Richardson (eds), *The new handbook of research on music teaching and learning* (pp. 63–84). New York: Oxford University Press.

Bowman, W. (2004). Cognition and the body: Perspectives from music education. In L. Bresler (ed.), *Knowing bodies, moving minds: Toward embodied music teaching and learning* (pp. 29–50). Dordrecht: Kluwer Academic Publishers.

Bresler, L. (2004). *Knowing bodies, moving minds: Toward embodied music teaching and learning.* Dordrecht: Kluwer Academic Publishers.

Bryson, B. (1997). 'Anything but heavy metal': Symbolic exclusion and musical dislikes. *American Sociological review,* **61**, 884–899.

Bullough, E. (1912). 'Psychical distance' as a factor in art and as an aesthetic principle. *British journal of Psychology,* **5**, 87–98.

Byrnes, S. R. (1997). Different-age and mentally handicapped listeners' response to Western art music selections. *Journal of Research in Music Education,* **45**(4), 568–579.

Campbell, P. S. (1998). *Songs in their heads: music and its meaning in children's lives.* New York: Oxford University Press.

Campbell, P. S. (2002). The musical cultures of children. In L. Bresler & C. Marme Thompson (eds), *The arts in children's lives: Context, culture, and curriculum* (pp. 57–69). Dordrecht: Kluwer Academic Publishers.

Dalcroze, E. J. (1921/1980). *Rhythm, music and education.* London: The Dalcroze Society.

Damasio, A. (1994/2000). *Descartes' error: Emotion, reason and the human brain.* New York: Quill (Harper Collins).

Damasio, A. (2000). *The feeling of what happens: Body, emotion and the making of consciousness.* London: Vintage.

Damasio, A. (2003). *Looking for Spinoza: Joy, sorrow, and the feeling brain.* New York: Harcourt.

DeNora, T. (2000). *Music in everyday life.* Cambridge: Cambridge University Press.

DeNora, T. (2001). Aesthetic agency and musical practice: New directions in the sociology of music and emotion. In P. N. Juslin & J. A. Sloboda (eds), *Music and emotion: Theory and research* (pp. 161–180). Oxford: Oxford University Press.

DeNora, T. (2003). *After Adorno: Rethinking music sociology.* Cambridge: Cambridge University Press.

Dissanayake, E. (1988/2002). *What is art for?* Seattle: University of Washington Press.

Dissanayake, E. (1992/1999). *Homo aestheticus: Where art comes from and why.* Seattle: University of Washington Press.

Dissanayake, E. (2000). *Art and intimacy: How the arts began.* Seattle: University of Washington Press.

Dissanayake, E. (2001). Becoming *homo aestheticus*: sources of aesthetic imagination in mother-infant interactions. *SubStance*, **94/95**, 85–103.

Elliott, D. J. (2002). Philosophical perspectives on research. In R. Colwell & C. Richardson (eds), *The new handbook of research on music teaching and learning* (pp. 85–102). New York: Oxford University Press.

Farnsworth, P. R. (1954). A study of the Hevner adjective list. *Journal of Aesthetics and Art Criticism*, **13**, 97–103.

Fechner, G. (1878/1978). *Die forschule der aesthetik (The introduction to aesthetics).* Hildesheim: Geor Holms.

Flowers, P. (1984). Attention to elements of music and effect of instruction in vocabulary on written descriptions of music by children and undergraduates. *Psychology of Music*, **12**, 17–24.

Flowers, P. (1988). The effects of teaching and learning experiences, tempo, and mode on undergraduates' and children's symphonic music preferences. *Journal of Research in Music Education*, **36**, 19–34.

Flowers, P. (1990). Listening: The key to describing music. *Music Educators Journal*, **77**, 21–23.

Frith, S. & McRobbie, A. (1990). Rock and sexuality. In S. Frith & A. Goodwin (eds), *Pop, Rock and the written word* (pp. 371–389). London: Routledge.

Fung, V. & Gromko, J. (2001). Effects of active versus passive listening on the quality of children's invented notations and preferences for two Korean pieces. *Psychology of Music*, **29**(2), 128–138.

Gadamer, H.-G. (1982). *Truth and method.* New York: Crossroads Press.

Gallie, W. B. (1964). *Philosophy and the historical understanding*, (2nd edn). New York: Schocken Books.

Gammon, V. (1996). What's wrong with school music? A response to Malcolm Ross. *British Journal of Music Education*, **3**, 101–122.

Gregory, A. H. (1997). The roles of music in society: the ethnomusicological perspective. In D. J. Hargreaves & A. C. North (eds), *The social psychology of music* (pp. 123–140). Oxford: Oxford University Press.

Green, L. (2002). *How popular musicians learn: A way ahead for music education.* Aldershott: Ashgate Publishing.

Gromko, J. & Poorman, A. S. (1998). Does perceptual-motor performance enhance perception of patterned art music? *Musicae Scientiae: The Journal of the European Society for Cognitive Sciences of Music*, 2(2), 157–170.

Gromko, J. & Russell, C. (2002). Relationships among young children's aural perception, listening condition, and accurate reading of graphic listening maps. *Journal of Research in Music Education*, 50(4), 333–342.

Hair, H. (1981). Verbal identification of musical concepts. *Journal of Research in Music Education*, 29, 11–21.

Hair, H. (1987). Descriptive vocabulary and visual choices: Children's responses to conceptual changes in music. *Bulletin of the Council for Research in Music Education*, 91, 59–64.

Hair, H. I. (1993/1994). Children's descriptions and representations of music. *Bulletin of the Council for Research in Music Education*, 119, 41–48.

Hanslick, E. (1986). *On the musically beautiful: A contribution towards the revision of the aesthetic of music.* (trans. G. Payzant from the 8th edn, 1891). Indianapolis, Indiana: Hackett Publishing Company.

Hevner, K. (1936). Experimental studies of the elements of expression in music. *American Journal of Psychology. XLV*, 111, 245–268.

James, A., Jenks, C., & Prout, A. (1998). *Theorizing childhood.* New York: Teachers College Press.

Kant, I. (1952). *The critique of judgement.* (trans. J. C. Meredith) Oxford: Clarendon Press.

Karmiloff, K. & Karmiloff-Smith, A. (2001). *Pathways to language: From fetus to adolescent.* Cambridge, MA.: Harvard University Press.

Krumhansl, C. L. & Juscyk, P. W. (1990). Infants' perception of phrase structure in music. *Psychological Science*, 1, 70 – 73.

Lakoff, G. & Johnson, M. (1999). *Philosophy in the flesh: The embodied mind and its challenge to western thought.* New York: Basic Books.

Langer, S. (1942/1979). *Philosophy in a new key: a study in the symbolism of reason, rite, and art.* (3rd edn). Cambridge, MA.: Harvard University Press.

Lychner, J. A. (1998). An empirical study concerning terminology relating to aesthetic response to music. *Journal of Research in Music Education*, 46(2) 303–319.

Lynch, M. P. & Eilers, R. E. (1991). Children's perception of native and nonnative music scales. *Music Perception*, 9, 121–132.

Madsen, C. K., Brittin, R. V., & Capparella-Sheldon, D. A. (1993). An empirical investigation of the aesthetic response to music. *Journal of Research in Music Education*, 41, 57–69.

Madsen, C. K., Byrnes, S. R., Capparella-Sheldon, D. A., & Brittin, R. V. (1993). Aesthetic responses to music: Musicians versus non-musicians. *Journal of Music Therapy*, 30(3), 174–191.

Madsen, C. K. & Geringer, J. M. (1990). Differential patterns of music listening: Focus of attention of musician s versus non-musicians. *Bulletin of the Council for Research in Music Education*, 105, 45–47.

Malloch, S. (1999). Mothers and infants and communicative musicality. *Musicae Scientiae, Special Issue*, 29–57.

Marsh, K. (1995). Children's singing games: Composition in the playground? *Research Studies in Music Education*, 4, 2–11.

McClary, S. (1991). *Feminine endings: Music, gender and sexuality.* Minneapolis: University of Minnesota Press.

McRobbie, A. (2000). *Feminism and youth culture*, (2nd edn). Basingstoke, UK: MacMillan.

Meyer, L. B. (1956). *Emotion and meaning in music.* Chicago, IL: University of Chicago Press.

Meyer, L. B. (2001). Music and emotion: Distinctions and uncertainties. In P. N. Juslin & J. A. Sloboda (eds), *Music and emotion: Theory and research* (pp. 341–360). Oxford: Oxford University Press.

Nelson, D. J. (1985). Trends in the aesthetic responses of children to the musical experience. *Journal of Research in Music Education*, 33(3) 193–203.

Nettl, B. (1990). *Folk and traditional music of the western continent* (3rd edn), Englewood Cliffs, NJ: Prentice-Hall.

North, A. C., Hargreaves, D. J., & O'Neill, S. (2000). The importance of music to adolescents. *British Journal of Educational Psychology*, 70, 255–272.

Preston, H. (ed.), (1994). Listening, appraising, and composing: Case studies in music. *British Journal of Music Education*, 11(2), 15–55.

Richards, C. (1998). *Teen spirits: Music and identity in media education*. London: UCL Press.

Richardson, C. P. (1995). The musical listening processes of the child: An international perspective. In H. Lee, & M. Barrett (eds), *Honing the craft: Improving the quality of music education* (pp. 212–219). Hobart: Artemis Publishing Consultants.

Rodriguez, C. X. (1998). Children's perception, production and description of musical expression . *Journal of Research in Music Education*, 46, 48–61

Rodriguez, C. X. & Webster, P. R. (1997). Development of children's verbal interpretative responses to music listening. *Bulletin of the Council for Research in Music Education*, 134, 9–30.

Rogoff, B. (2003). *The cultural nature of human development*. New York: Oxford University Press.

Ross, M. (1995). What's wrong with school music? *British Journal of Music Education*, 12(3), 185–201.

Russell, P. A. (1997). Musical tastes and society. In D. J. Hargreaves & A. C. North (eds), *The social psychology of music* (pp. 141–158). Oxford: Oxford University Press.

Schellenberg, E. G. & Trehub, S. E. (1996). Natural intervals in music: a perspective from infant listeners. *Psychological Science*, 7, 272–277.

Schellenberg, E. G. & Trehub, S. E. (1999). Culture-general and culture specific factors in the discrimination of melodies. *Journal of Experimental Child Psychology*, 74, 107–127.

Schopenhauer, A. (1818/1966). *The world as will and representation* (vols. 1 & 11). E. F. J. Payne (trans.) New York: Dover publications.

Shepherd, J. & Giles-Davies, J. (1991). Music, text and subjectivity. In J. Shepherd (ed.), *Music as social text* (pp. 174–187). Cambridge: Polity Press.

Shusterman, R. (2000). *Performing live: Aesthetic alternatives for the ends of art*. Ithaca, NY: Cornell University Press.

Shusterman, R. (2004). Somaesthetics and education: Exploring the terrain. In L. Bresler (ed.), *Knowing bodies, moving minds: Toward embodied music teaching and learning* (pp. 51–60). Dordrecht: Kluwer Academic Publishers.

Suthers, L. (1999). 'I sang games': An investigation of the labels used by young children to describe music experiences. In M. S. Barrett, G. E. McPherson, & R. Smith (eds), *Children and music: Developmental perspectives* (pp. 306–310). Launceston, Tasmania: Uniprint.

Swanwick, K. & Franca, C. C. (1999). Composing, performing and audience-listening as indicators of musical understanding. *British Journal of Music Education*, 16, 5–19.

Thompson, W. F. & Schellenberg, E. G. (2002). Cognitive constraints on music listening. In R. Colwell & C. Richardson (eds), *The new handbook of research on music teaching and learning* (pp. 461–485). New York: Oxford University Press.

Trainor, L. F., Tsang, C. D., & Cheung, V. H. W. (2002). Preference for musical consonance in 2-month-old infants. *Music Perception*, 20, 185–192.

Trainor, L. F. & Schmidt, L. A. (2003). Processing emotions induced by music. In I. Peretz & R. Zatorre (eds), *The cognitive neuroscience of music* (pp. 310–324). New York: Oxford University Press.

Trehub, S. E., Schellenberg, E. G., & Hill, D. S. (1997). The origins of music perception and cognition. A developmental perspective. In I. Delige & J. Sloboda (eds), *Perception and cognition of music* (pp. 103–128). Hove, UK: Psychology Press.

Trevarthen, C. (1998). The concept and foundation of human intersubjectivity. In S. Braten (ed.), *Inter-subjective communication and emotion in early ontogeny* (pp. 15–46). Cambridge: Cambridge University Press.

Willis, P. (1978). *Profane culture.* London: Routledge.

Zenter, M. R. & Kagan, J. (1996). Perception of music by infants. *Nature, 383,* 29.

Zilman, D. & Gan, S.-L. (1997). Musical taste in adolescence. In D. J. Hargreaves & A. C. North (eds), *The social psychology of music* (pp.161–187). Oxford: Oxford University Press.

CHAPTER 10

THE PERCEPTION OF EMOTION IN MUSIC

EMERY SCHUBERT AND GARY E. MCPHERSON

At what age can children perceive emotion in music? How might this evolve as they mature? These two questions form the focus of this review of literature concerning the perception of emotion in music from birth to adolescence. Drawing on available evidence, we propose a theoretical framework that can be used to understand how children develop their abilities to perceive emotion in music. We begin by providing a definition for emotion and the mechanisms for connecting emotion and music before surveying the general development of emotional perception throughout childhood. Importantly, the main part of our chapter draws on literature that helps explain how children perceive emotion in music rather than the emotion a child experiences in response to music. The theoretical position we propose is that throughout childhood different forces work in parallel in a spiral like manner and that decoding emotional information from music is a dynamic combination of one-to-one (veridical) connections and general (schematic) associations. This view is expanded in our examination of the methodological issues where we discuss limitations concerning how this topic has been studied to date, and our conclusions that provide a speculative model for understanding the development of the perception of emotion in music from infancy to adolescence.

What is an emotion?

Defining precisely what is meant by emotion is difficult even for the most specialized scholar (Solomon, 1993) but can be simplified if we begin by separating its *function* from its *structure*.

There are numerous ways of thinking about the *function* of emotion. Most show that emotional states occur spontaneously rather than as a result of conscious effort, that they can produce physiological changes (such as an increase in heart rate when feeling angry), and that the emotion producer does not have to focus on the emotion-inducing event or situation, because the emotion itself serves as an identifying marker with its own set of predetermined patterns (such as crying or laughing or being worried). Emotions therefore, are an elongation of a state and a communicative marker to others and the self that identifies and extends the state of the individual (Izard *et al.*, 1984; Mandler, 1984, 1990; Oatley & Jenkins, 1996; Rolls, 2002).

Emotions can also be defined *structurally* as a collection of entities (such as happiness, sadness, anger, fear) (Izard *et al.*, 2000) or, alternatively as dimensional constructs, lying along scales of negative to positive emotion (i.e., the valence dimension), activity and sleepiness (i.e., the arousal dimension), and so forth (Russell, 1997, but see also Schimmack 2002; Schimmack *et al.*, 2002 regarding some complications of this simplified view of emotional structure).

Emotions are often connected with other actions, associations, behaviours, and environmental stimuli. For example, Lang (1979) demonstrated how emotions can be triggered through a network of interacting nodes representing the emotion inducing stimulus (such as seeing a snake), the representations of physiological states (increased heart rate) and the associated thought patterns that occur as a result (such as running away). Bower (1981) further developed this way of understanding emotion by suggesting that emotion nodes (one representing happiness, another sadness, another anger, and so on) are able to activate memory structures (e.g., the memory of a snake, or even a piece of music), and vice versa.

Such network models have been used to explain musical expectation. Bharucha (1987, 1994) described two mechanisms through which musical information is primed during the listening process: when listening to a melody, what do we expect the next note to be? One process is the *veridical* (one to one) expectation: so a node, which in this case represents a single note of a melody, then activates a node representing the next node of that melody. We expect to hear the next note of the melody because its node is being 'prepared' by the currently activated node. Here, a melody (or piece of music) is well known, and rehearing it produces the expectation of the note that follows. For example, if you heard the notes C4 C4 G4 G4 A4 A4, the veridical memory of *Twinkle Twinkle Little Star* would facilitate an expectation of a G4—the next note of that tune.

Another mechanism is referred to as *schematic* expectancy. Here, the listener has acquired (without any necessary conscious attention) the rules of music in a particular style, and can therefore predict the next note of a melody of that style when the melody is unfamiliar. A typical example is the leading tone toward the end of a musical phrase. There are so many examples in which we hear this note rise to the tonic in Western music (e.g., B4 to C5 in the key of C major) that when a new piece is heard coming to the end of the phrase with a leading tone, we have a deeply ingrained, schematic expectation that the next note will be the tonic. Bharucha (1987) argues that these schematic expectancies emerge through exposure.

Definition of two processes for connecting emotion with music

Meyer's (1956) landmark monograph, *Emotion and meaning in music*, describes two broad ways in which emotions and music can be connected by listeners: *referentialism*—where the meaning in music comes from direct associations made with the situations, mood, and so forth and the music: Something outside the music is connected and associated with the music. *Absolutism* suggests that the meaning in music comes from within the structure of the music itself, without any need to make reference to something outside the music. This shares remarkable similarities with Bharucha's notion of veridical and schematic expectation. The veridical connection is that which occurs between a specific event and a specific piece of

Figure 10.1 Example of a tune associated with a cartoon villain.

music (that special song on a first date), as an example of Meyer's referentialism. And when many exemplars of a particular mood are connected with similar musical structures (e.g., music in the minor key representing a general sadness or negative emotions) we can say that there is a general, or schematic representation of emotion and music, as might be the case for absolutism. In this way, absolutism (and therefore schemata) may be understood here as a subconscious abstraction of musical and extramusical rules, so the listener *thinks* that the connection with emotions is part of the musical structure, but it has actually been built up from numerous exemplars of different veridical connections. As will become evident later in our discussion, these two mechanisms—veridical and schematic—can be used to provide a framework for answering the two aims of this chapter, which are to understand how children perceive emotion in music, and how their perceptions evolve as they mature.

Consider the following scenarios.

In the first, we see a young boy sitting in front of a TV watching a cartoon in which a villain is creeping around a corner. The associated soundtrack outlines a minor triad, such as the one shown in Figure 10.1.

Each step taken by the villain is mimicked by each note in the soundtrack, which provides the context for the child to pair the villain's movements with the character of the melody in the soundtrack. The emotion evoked by the situation may be suspenseful fear, and if the connection is strong, then later hearings can evoke the image, situation, or the emotional feelings made in the initial, veridical connections, even in the absence of the villain. The music itself is sufficient to evoke the emotion. This form of association occurs as children and adults are acculturated into the norms of emotional meaning in music through conscious or unconscious exposure (Zajonc, 2000) during the early years of their life, and well beyond.

In the second scenario, the boy mentioned above has seen so many cartoons where similar pairings occur that the emotional connotation conveyed by the music is thoroughly absorbed. The child has, without deliberate attention or explicit knowledge, learnt the rule that the minor chord harmony (of the kind outlined in Figure 10.1) presents a schematic, general connection to the negative emotion that was once only associated with a particular villain. We refer to this kind of association as *schematic*.[1]

The apparently *intrinsic* ability of music to convey emotional information can also occur in other ways. One of the earliest and more important examples is an infant who is startled by an unexpected *subito forte* chord while being exposed to an orchestral work. Some

---

[1] While we make the connection between schematic connections and absolutisim, it is worth noting that Meyer actually refers to emotional meaning that is intrinsic to musical structure as *absolute expressionism*. While this may be viewed as a subset of absolutism, the term absolutism is frequently used to mean what Meyer refers to as absolute expressionism (e.g., Trainor & Trehub, 1992b). For a further discussion of this nomenclature, see Hargreaves (1986, p. 8).

researchers believe that this type of reflexive response to an acoustic signal is a hard-wired connection that is phylogenetically present (Gaston, 1951; Masterson & Crawford, 1982). This requires an extension to our current definition of schematic expectation (the emergence of the general from numerous veridical connections): schematic associations can be made with emotion that is subconsciously or *intrinsically* connected with musical structure. The intrinsic schematic connection is present at birth and enables general, possibly universal, rules of music and emotion to be known.

Previous research on the perception of emotion in music has described what children can do at different ages so the framework we provide here is intended to help explain patterns in the data. Establishing the corresponding developmental paths for *veridical* and *schematic* activation is important for understanding how children develop their capacity to perceive emotion in music. While both veridical and schematic associations can operate in parallel, a more interesting question concerns the extent to which one may dominate over the other at various stages of a child's development. Before turning to this question, however, it is important to understand how emotional perception develops throughout childhood.

Perception of emotion in general: birth to late childhood

In their first 10 weeks of life, babies are able to show interest, distress, disgust, and content-ment and in the subsequent weeks and months of their development, leading up to about 7 months, they extend these to include happiness, sadness, anger, joy, surprise, and fear (Izard *et al.*, 1995). Researchers believe that these primary (basic) emotions are biologically programmed because they emerge in normal infants from all cultural backgrounds at about the same age (Malatesta, 1989; Camras, 1992). By 7 months infants are also able to identify and distinguish facial emotional expressions (Walker-Andrews & Dickson, 1997) and by 10 months to use social cues to decide how to act in ambiguous situations (Striano & Rochat, 2000).

Secondary (complex) emotions such as embarrassment, shame, guilt, envy, and pride, begin to appear in the second year as young infants start to experience situations when they feel self-conscious and begin to gain an understanding of rules and standards for evaluating their own and other people's conduct (Shaffer, 1999). These types of emotions depend on infants having developed some understanding of themselves. Because they are more sophisticated than primary emotions, these secondary emotions are also more culturally specific, in that they tend to vary more than primary emotions, depending on the social setting and the types of human interactions that govern what is appropriate in any given culture (Bee, 1997).

By 3 years of age infants are able to display nearly the entire range of adult emotions (Lewis, 2000) and their capacity to do this is part of a more generalized ability that allows them to make decisions through social referencing (Feinman, 1982). Infants of this age are able to make assertions about situations in their environment based on emotional informa-tion they gain from others, particular their mothers. For example, a child's examination of a parent's emotional response to a stranger or a toy (such as a fearful expression) determines the way the child responds in the new situation, and can impinge on their response at a later time (for example, a fearful response to the stranger or toy at a later interaction). Social referencing of this type suggests a high level of interpretation about events, and emotional information from the caretaker is used as a key or a kind of glue for associating information about new people and objects.

Between 3 and 6 years of age, children's understanding of the external causes and consequences of their emotions continues to improve and in the years that follow, they become increasingly better at integrating the perceptions and cues they learn (from observing other people) into a more complete understanding of their own and others' emotional reactions (Shaffer, 1999). By the age of 4 years children are able to verbally explain the emotional states of others, but tend to do them as consequences of external events ('He is sad because the other boy took his ball away'), rather than internal states. From the age of 4 children's ability to attribute emotion to both external and internal causes continues to improve (Levine, 1995) with a gradual shift toward them being able to decode accurately complex emotional situations (Lagattuta et al., 1997). For example, at about 4 years of age, children tend to simply use the content of spoken messages to decipher emotional information, even if the 'paralinguistic' (i.e., emotions and other messages transmitted via inflections and prosody) contradict the message (e.g., saying 'What a beautiful day' with an angry voice). Morton and Trehub (2001) demonstrated that in these situations 4 year olds are probably processing both language content and paralinguistic emotional cues (even though they are responding only to the content) because their reaction times in these conditions are longer than when content and paralinguistic cues are concordant. That is, the reaction time increase provides evidence of the difficulty of the task. By the time the child has reached the Piagetian concrete operational stage at about the age of 6 or 7, they have not only acquired the ability to understand the consequences of emotions, but are able to appropriately interpret and resolve many such complex emotional situations.

However, there are still some limitations in children's emotion-perception skills that take time to develop to the level of the typical adult. For example, as children approach the age of 6 years, they become aware of the thoughts and feelings different people have, but often confuse them. In contrast, children over 7 years of age are normally able to understand when more than one emotion is present simultaneously, and subsequently are able to hide socially undesirable emotions. During the period from 7 to 12 years of age children are able to empathize and take the perspective of different people in a self-reflective manner. For example, if a child is teasing another in a joking way, but the other child takes the joke seriously and becomes upset, the first child is able to identify what has happened, and to provide an understanding explanation such as 'I was only joking, I'm sorry that I upset you'. Selman (1977) refers to this as 'self-reflective perspective taking'. Improvements in children's perception of complex emotional situations and dilemmas therefore result as a consequence of increasing levels of sophistication and socialization (Selman, 1977; Gurucharri & Selman, 1982).

Infancy to 2 years

Musical interactions between a mother and her infant emerge out of an evolutionary necessity for bonding, and as such are a critical and biologically programmed part of infant (and parent) functionality (Dissanayake, 2000). During the months before birth, the developing fetus hears a range of nuances expressed in his or her mother's voice, such as the changes in vocal quality when she is happy or sad, excited or relaxed. Immediately after birth, newborn babies show an awareness of various emotional signals they perceive from their caregivers through their own vocalizations and hand movements (Malloch, 1999/2000; Nadel & Butterworth, 1999). The slow high-pitched utterances involved in infant-directed speech help them attend to and grasp messages in their parents' tone of voice long before they are capable of understanding what is actually being said (Fernald, 1992, 1993; Trehub & Nakata, 2001), and the pitch variations associated with infant-directed speech facilitate the communication of emotional messages (Slaney & McRoberts, 2003). In the weeks and months that follow birth, the infant's innate communicative capacities, supported by his or her parent's intuitive behaviour, provide the catalyst for an intimate dialogue between parent and infant. This typically involves a type of turn taking in which parent and child respond to each other in a way that is responsive to the infant's communicative needs. Malloch (1999/2000) describes this process as *communicative musicality*, because the parent–child interaction has a music-like rhythmic and melodic quality. Communication occurs not as a result of the infant understanding the words said to it by the mother, but through the intentions of these words and the affect they evoke, as expressed through the 'music-like' qualities of their joint vocalizations and the 'dance-like' gestures of their facial expressions and bodily movements.

A central question in research on infant-directed speech has been to determine the extent to which an infant gains cues about its caregiver's emotional state through vocal communication, including the musical elements used while singing. Evidence shows that infants have a distinct preference for infant-directed 'motherese' compared with normal adult speech inflection patterns because emotional information through this type of prosody is the only verbal channel available to the pre-linguistic, speech-listening infant in the absence of knowledge about the meaning of words (Werker & McLeod, 1989; Cooper *et al.*, 1997; Kitamura & Burnham, 1998; Trehub & Nakata, 2001). So it stands to reason that musical signals that share characteristics of speech also share its meaning (Trehub & Schellenberg, 1995), or as Fernald (1992) puts it:

> The communicative force of the mother's vocalizations derive not from their arbitrary meanings in a linguistic code, but more from their immediate musical power to arouse and alert, to calm and to delight. Through this distinctive form of vocal communication the infant begins to experience emotional communion with others, months before communion through symbols is possible. (p. 148).

Other studies suggest that infants are biologically predisposed not only to extracting emotional meaning from vocal signals, but also from lullabies, because of the soothing nature of the melodic, dynamic, rhythmic, and tempo features of the music that characterizes this genre (Trehub *et al.*, 1993; Trehub & Schellenberg, 1995; Trehub & Trainor, 1998).

If infants are predisposed to extracting emotional information from auditory signals, the question remains whether the baby is processing the various elements of the signal (contour variations, tempo, etc.) and quickly developing a repertoire of emotional associations based on an analysis of these signals, or whether emotional perception is hard-wired and automated as though the auditory signal is processed as an emotional whole (or 'gestalt'), without the need for prior processing of the auditory parameters. The prevailing view is that: 'emotion perception occurs as soon as the child learns to attend to the relevant stimulus cues and to decode the specified emotion. Emotion cognition is thought to develop later, as the child gains more sophisticated cognitive skills, has more experience in social interactions, and begins to acquire culture-specific display rules.' (Boone & Cunningham, 1998, p. 1008).

This view is in accord with the emotion-perception latency argument that some musical features *can* be reliably detected by infants under 12 months of age (Trehub & Schellenberg, 1995; Trehub, 2001; also Chapter 2, this volume). For example, even though infants' hearing is relatively underdeveloped, in that they are not capable of detecting subtle changes in loudness and duration until 5–8 years of age (Trehub & Schellenberg, 1995), to other parameters they are fairly sensitive. This includes contour, where they can detect alternations in pitch as small as a semitone from 7 months of age (Trehub *et al.*, 1986; Trainor & Trehub, 1992a). The infant auditory system is therefore highly sophisticated, even though not fully developed, at a very early age.

While keeping this in mind, it may also be the case that infants process musical and prosodic information as an emotional gestalt (Levi, 1978), and that this occurs before they are able to perceive separate musical parameters. So, a more radical interpretation would be that emotional understanding is innate, and that this form of understanding is more important for an infant than being able to abstract musical and acoustic features from an auditory signal (see Gentile, 1998). Evidence that the human affect processing system develops before the cognitive processing system supports this view (Zajonc, 1984).

In summary, we argue that infants are born with basic kinds of mechanisms that enable them to interpret the emotional meaning of sounds in the environment and, in particular, from their caregiver. This suggests the presence of a strong schematic, hard-wired mechanism that may well provide the young infant with an evolutionary advantage. While the situation with music is made more complex because of the problem of musical feature detection versus emotion abstraction primacy, we conclude from studies on infants' perception of emotion in music, and from the infant-directed-speech literature, that it is likely that some acoustic signals will also signal emotional meaning to the infant. That is, the mechanism for emotional detection by the infant is primarily, though not exclusively, schematic.

Three to 7 years

From the age of 3 children are already able to identify the emotions of sadness and happiness in music and by 4 can perceive the basic emotional labels of happiness, sadness, anger, and fear (Cunningham & Sterling, 1988; Boone & Cunningham, 2001). The age of 4 marks the beginning of a period of increasing sophistication, as children develop their capacity to encode verbally emotional meaning across a range of non-verbal media including the face and voice (Boone & Cunningham, 2001).

In a novel study by Adachi and Trehub (1998), performances (as distinct from perception) by children were recorded on video for later analysis. They found that children as young as 4 manipulate tempo, dynamics, and pitch of familiar songs when they are asked to present them in a happy or sad way. However, while older children used appropriate musical devices, the 4 year olds tended to use more idiosyncratic and varied devices such as physical gestures to facilitate the emotional communication. This parallels the perception of emotion in more culturally appropriate responses (both production and perception) commencing around this age, which reach their full potential at about the age of 7 or 8 years (see Chapter 2).

Gardner (1973; Gardner & Perkins, 1989) asserts that infants have developed enough knowledge and maturation to be able to start manipulating symbols by reading and writing from the age of 3 years. For example, he proposes that children around the age of 3 can describe music in terms of simplified musical features such as loud, fast, and so on—what he refers to as part of a pre-conventional stage of creative development—but by the age of 7 are more likely to use descriptive adjectives (Gardner & Perkins, 1989; Gardner et al., 1990).

One of the most fascinating changes in children's perception of emotion in music in Western culture from the ages of 3 to 7 is the gradual development of the major-happy, minor-sad connection. Recent literature suggests that infants are able to perceive happiness in music (Gentile, 1998; Nawrot, 2003). However, up to the age of 4 the young child does not appear to use the mode relationship to do so (Kastner & Crowder, 1990). In fact, responses are significantly less accurate in decoding happy and sad emotions from music in comparison with adult responses. The reason appears to be because 4-year-old decisions tend to rely too heavily on other musical parameters such as tempo, rather than mode (major/minor) (Crowder et al., 1991; Dalla Bella et al., 2001). With a few exceptions (Dolgin & Adelson, 1990) the literature suggests that the major-happy minor-sad relationship is only beginning to be made at 4 years of age, even though it has become firmly established by the age of 7 or 8 (Trunk, 1981; Kratus, 1993; Gerardi & Gerken, 1995; Dalla Bella et al., 2001).

Research on nursery songs confirms the weak link between emotional message and musical mode. The vast majority of nursery songs in Western literature are in a major key, even those with negative or sad stories such as Who killed cock robin and Humpty Dumpty (Gregory et al., 1996). And of those common nursery songs in a minor key, several have a happy message, such as Old King Cole was a merry old soul. This suggests that very young children will not be able to use mode to decipher sad/happy emotions because the generational/evolutionary process has not put pressure on streamlining nursery songs into happy-major and sad-minor categories. In other words, children's insensitivity to mode means that there is little pressure to produce songs with the major-happy, minor-sad rela- tionship. The lack of a clear relationship between mode and meaning in nursery songs also suggests a possible delay in the learning of an association between emotion and mode (Gregory et al., 1996), such that over the next 5 years, the child learns to associate major and minor key with happiness and sadness, respectively. It is important to keep in mind that this refers to the child's limited use of musical features to decode culturally encoded emotional meaning from music (that is, with respect to adult responses), and does not mean that the child's emotional response is trivial, because although they may not be as sophisticated as adults in analysing harmony, they may well have the same emotional reactions. This is why Kastner and Crowder (1990) speculate that the effect of age may result from children's 'enhanced ability to perceive emotional connotations of the major and minor modes' or 'from effects of learning superimposed on whatever tendency was present at 3 years of age'

(p. 197). Yet another possibility is that older children are more capable of understanding the types of tasks being used in studies and of therefore focusing their attention on it (Kastner & Crowder, 1990).

Even though the above evidence does not 'resolve the learned-versus-intrinsic controversy' (Kastner & Crowder, 1990, p. 200), evidence from more-recent studies (e.g., Gregory et al., 1996; Dalla Bella et al., 2001) seems to point toward a dominant contribution of a veridical mechanism in the mode-emotion connection such that repeated exposure to positive-major negative-minor exemplars help develop increasingly stronger associations over the period from 3 to 7 years of age.

Several other factors also emerge between the ages of 3 and 7. Children commence the period being better at recognizing emotion in the human voice, but by the end of the period can achieve consistent interpretation of emotion in melodies presented on musical instruments (Dolgin & Adelson, 1990). While they can judge emotions of happiness and sadness in music before the age of 3, some research demonstrates that fear and anger are more easily confused. Music expressing anger can be interpreted as being angry or fearful throughout this age bracket and beyond, in the same way that adults have difficulty deciphering these two emotions (Trunk, 1981; Terwogt & van Grinsven, 1991; Robazza et al., 1994).

The infant–child literature helps to crystallize, and to some extent substantiate Meyer's view about the cultural context required for learning major-*happy* minor-*sad* relationships. This evidence suggests that during infancy absolutist (schematic) processes are at work in determining the emotional content of musical and auditory signals. We therefore speculate that loudness, tempo, and pitch may be connected with emotion in a schematic, possibly hard-wired (innate) way. By the same token, the infant is slowly developing new ways of connecting emotional information through exposure to and participation in cultural norms, such that by the age of 7 years we see the major-*happy* minor-*sad* connotations of Western culture becoming firmly established. This age corresponds to a shift to the Piagetian concrete operational stage, where cognitive processing starts to resemble that of adults. The end of this stage is signified by several music cognition landmarks as well, such as the ability to sing with a sense of tonal stability, and reduced reliance on contour mapping for the storage of melodic information (Hargreaves & Zimmerman, 1992). In Gardner's (1973) view, 7-year-old children display all the characteristics necessary to actively participate in the artistic process and are therefore ready to perceive emotion in music in a manner not unlike adults, because the essential cultural connections between emotions and music can and have been made and are layered on top of those established from birth (see also Hargreaves, 1996).

Eight to 12 years

Emotional perception of happy from major mode and sadness from minor mode is firmly established by the age of 8. In fact, just as with their vocabulary and emotional empathy (discussed at the beginning of this chapter, under 'Perception of emotion in general'), the child has acquired a significant collection of musical experiences and connections that are so thoroughly absorbed that the emotional identification of music becomes apparently natural, automated, and increasingly consistent with adult responses.

Our view is that schematic processing also comes from the openness children show to different styles between the ages of 6 and 9 (Hargreaves & North, 1999), and at the same time, their ability to detect correctly different musical and other artistic styles (Walk *et al.*, 1971; Silverman *et al.*, 1975; Hasenfus *et al.*, 1983). At these ages, many children have built up a sizeable repertoire of musical examples and styles, without showing a strong bias towards, or rejection of, any particular style. This suggests an absolutist value in music because referentialism (veridical connection) is closely connected with specific exemplars of emotion-music connections. In contrast, this phase of openness suggests that many different styles of music can be valued intrinsically. The veridical connections built up between 3 and 7 years become highly internalized and generalized to many kinds of music. And these connections may well be fully integrated with the schematic connections made during infancy.

All of the above helps us bring into focus a picture of the development of emotional perception of music from birth to the end of childhood. At birth the principal mechanism of emotion in music is schematic. As shown in Figure 10.2, this then spirals into a layer where veridical association is the dominant mechanism, and the spiral comes full circle back to schematic association up until the age of about 12. The spiral nature of the proposed

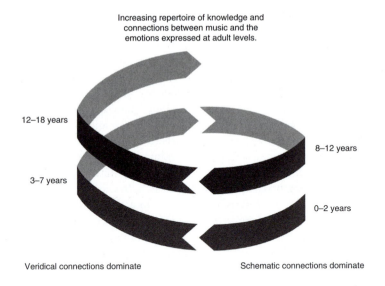

Figure 10.2 Spiral model of development of emotion perception in music. The model shows the dominating process of acquiring the ability to perceive emotion in music from birth to the end of adolescence. From birth the dominant method is through schematic connections (on the right-hand side of the diagram), but from the age of 3 veridical connections are favoured between emotions and music (that is, through the absorption of cultural norms as shown on the left-hand side of the diagram). The dominant mechanism swings back around toward schematic processes, but builds on what has been previously learnt (hence the spiral) from age 7 until the beginning of adolescence, and so forth. The model does not claim one process is in force at the exclusion of the other, only which one appears to be dominant at different ages, as assessed from the current literature.

model accounts for the accumulation of musical-emotional information at each of these three stages, and reminds us that emotional connections to music occur over a long period, are cumulative, and build on elements that are both schematic and veridical, without any necessary exclusion of one form of meaning acquisition from the other. With the above in mind, we now examine the literature for evidence of any further transitions from late childhood to adolescence.

Adolescence (12–18 years)

There exist numerous theories of why music is important during adolescence (see Chapter 7), and while the predominant explanations stem from social psychological research, the connection between emotion and music is an inextricable element in the relationship between teenage development and music. North et al. (2000) identify the reasons for the importance of music to adolescents as being to 'portray an "image" to the outside world and ...satisfy their emotional needs' (p. 255). Even when emotion is not specified as an explicit reason, the connections between emotion and enjoyment (Schubert, 1996), and emotions associated with social settings such as positive emotions experienced as part of a feeling of belonging, and negative from rejection, are undeniable and essential. In fact, Behne (1997) even argues that the focus on cognitive rather than emotional aspects of music in school curricula may be a reason for the lack of success music has in some school programmes.

In examining how adolescents process emotion in music, we acknowledge that the literature is seriously restricted in the kinds of investigations available. Nevertheless, some conclusions can be proposed by examining the available evidence. As shall become evident, there has also been a significant shift in research interest from what the child can *perceive* in music, to what the adolescent *experiences* from music. This latter dimension is best understood in the context of the critical and complex pubescent developmental processes.

Larson (1995) used a psychoanalytic framework to examine the development of self-concept. He suggests that typical adolescents lack a coherent and integrated imagery of themselves, at 'a time when responsibility for emotion self-regulation is being transferred, albeit sometimes precariously, from parent to child' (p. 2). According to Larson, fifth graders report being happy much more of the time than ninth graders (see further, Larson & Richards, 1989). This earlier age is a period of 'naïve, stable happiness' where the child still has 'a secure and unquestioning acceptance of who they are, as well as the role parents play in protecting them from emotional threats and chronic worries' (Larson, 1995, p. 2).

During adolescence popular music listening increases substantially, while TV watching decreases (Larson, 1995). The reason for this is connected with the need for developing autonomy, identity, love, and sexuality (see Marcia et al., 1993). Music listening provides adolescents with the opportunity to discover things about themselves without the guidance and interaction of parents in the family lounge-room, and as a tool for managing their emotions (Christenson & Roberts, 1998). In contrast, TV watching time is correlated with time spent with parents (regardless of whether the TV is on or off), although TV watching does allow adolescents to be in the presence of parents without having to make conversation

(Larson, 1995). But most importantly, music serves as a marker for personal space, such that the adolescent clearly shifts toward matters critically connected with their emotional and personal development.

In analysing his psychologically disturbed patients, Wooten (1992) found a link between drug use and heavy metal preference, with a referentialist explanation: The 'connection between drug use and heavy metal music may substantiate the concerns that teenagers are over-identifying with this music and its musicians' (p. 96). From this perspective the emotional connections made with the musicians are significant, and the music may act simply as a veridical reference to the image of the performer. In Western culture the idea of 'over-identifying' is characterized by the increasing tendency to idolize an individual, such as a sporting champion, movie celebrity or rock star. This behaviour peaks in early adolescence (from 10 to 11 years of age) and is decreasing by the ages of 16–17 years (Raviv et al., 1996). Idolization reflects a strong emotional connection made by the adolescent with the individual being idolized. While the music of the idolized rock star is a prime candidate for a veridical connection between the emotions associated with that individual, any piece of music can be connected with any idol. Further, having such strong connections with a piece of music can support an individual in being able to identify with peers of a subculture (Willis, 1978).

One of the few studies to specifically examine emotional responses to music from a music-perception perspective was Watson (1942). He tested emotional responses of children from the sixth grade level (age of 11 or 12) through to adulthood (in 2-year intervals) and music experts, using an adjective checklist response format (instead of basic emotions used in most childhood studies) in which subjects were asked to rate music they heard. Watson reports a consistent growth in ability to discriminate between musical meanings from sixth grade through to college levels. If adolescents are responding to emotion in music at adult levels, there should be no change in emotion from the age of 12 through to adulthood. The Watson study therefore suggests that there still are some changes, and this supports the view that emotional connections with music are still being fine-tuned, despite the implication of more recent research that suggests that by this age, emotion in music is perceived essentially at the same level as adults.

The evidence from literature on adolescents points to a dominance of veridical association between emotion and music. In a study of associations with rap music made by African-American children, Hall (1998) demonstrated a shift from general understanding of rap music toward a better understanding of the specific message of particular songs. Thus, by the age of 12, the ability to extract general information about music is superimposed with a new dimension and ability (and perhaps even a need) to form specific, veridical links with music and its meaning. In doing so, adolescents use music for the purpose of identifying with others, in developing their own sense of identity and in managing their emotions. Connections are being formed between pieces of music and the new, complex emotional changes that the adolescent experiences. So just before the teenage years, individuals start to move once again around the spiral from schematic to an additional level of veridical connectivity between music and emotion, completing the pattern of the way in which veridical and schematic processes fluctuate in dominance from birth to the end of adolescence (Figure 10.2).

Methodological issues

The spiral model shown in Figure 10.2 provides a framework to help explain data on the development of emotional perception in music. However, readers need to be cognisant of the methodological problems and limitations, which, if mitigated, may result in revisions to this model.

A general issue is the lack of specificity regarding the location (in the listener versus in the music) and structure of emotion. In this chapter we have attempted to limit our attention to the ability of the listener to observe (or perceive) emotion in music, as distinct from experiencing the emotion. However, this restriction was nearly impossible to maintain because (1) some studies are not explicit about whether they refer to the perception or experiencing of emotion, and (2) studies of adolescents are predominantly interested in the experiential aspect of emotion. This is an important limitation given the complex relationship that exists between the perception versus the experience of emotion in music (Gabrielsson, 2001; Schubert, in press).

Regarding the issue of structure, many studies make an implicit assumption that emotions are categorical, simply because of the focus on forced choice responses from a subset of basic emotions (such as happy and sad). Quite often, a dimensional perspective of emotion can identify some of the problems of categorical responses that may otherwise be overlooked. The dimensional model of emotion refers to a collection of more-or-less independent continua, such as positive to negative valence, excited to sleepy, dominant to submissive (Plutchik, 1962). For example, in the infant research 'looking-time' paradigm, a 'happy' and 'sad' video is used to determine the infant's association with a piece of music. If infants look at the allegedly 'happy' video, then we might conclude that they are associating the music with happiness (Nawrot, 2003). However, the happy video may contain a higher degree of activity than the sad video, and indeed it might be that the infant is responding to this activity dimension rather than (or in addition to) the valence dimension. The fact that in the Nawrot (2003) study most of the infant's time was spent looking at the happy video (regardless of the musical stimulus) suggests that the happiness and/or the *activity* in the video was more interesting to them than the sad/low-activity video. Despite some problems with the dimensional approach in its simplest forms (Schimmack 2002; Schimmack et al., 2002), it nevertheless provides a useful perspective in dealing with the structure of emotion. In the present case, the dimensional paradigm of emotion provides researchers with a tool for matching the amount of activity in the two videos to try to eliminate the possibility of this dimension skewing or confabulating the results.

In the child research literature, the frequent absence of the dimensional paradigm of emotional structure also appears to be responsible for some methodological problems. In studies with children researchers are able to use language to measure response. However, as linguistic skills are developing over this time, and particularly in early childhood, the limitations of language need to be overcome. The use of facial expressions is an important way of dealing with the problem of limited language. The use of faces simplifies the task for the child, who is instructed to point at the face that corresponds to the emotion the music is conveying (and in some studies to also verbalize his or her answer). However, these studies have not always been able to demonstrate an isomorphic relationship between a facial expression and its corresponding verbal labels. For example, Kastner and Crowder (1990) used four schematic faces for testing 3–12 year olds. Of the four facial expressions with intended emotions—happiness, contented, sadness, and anger—the contented face was described as 'plain' by many participants. In one of the largest ($n = 658$) studies of children's emotional responses to music, Kratus (1993) used schematic drawings of facial expressions. Kratus is one of the few researchers (Giomo, 1993 is another) who has applied information about the dimensional structure of emotion, thus ensuring that the facial expressions chosen optimize the range of emotions along the valence (positive-negative) and arousal (active-sleepy) dimensions. However, the face Kratus used for excited seems to have a strong negative valence component (fear) due to the eye-brow position. This may have skewed poles to negative—calm, rather than the intended excited—calm. It has also been demonstrated that 'excited' actually contains some positive valence (Russell, 1980), contrary to the Kratus sketch. An additional, though related problem is that, if all emotions are developed by childhood, including sophisticated strategies for interpreting social situations by children as young as 8, then we need to be moving beyond the identification of two or four emotions during this time. Finally, no research has measured children's emotional responses to music continuously. While continuous response measurement, where children move a dial or mouse connected to a computer, is in its infancy (Schubert, 2001), important questions about differences in adult versus child response patterns remain to be addressed. These issues present a new set of challenges for future researchers.

In adolescent research the focus is usually on social and psychological development, meaning that we have very little data on their perception of emotion in music. An exception is the Watson (1942) study, discussed above, which suggests that development of emotional perception is not as complete and adult-like as the late childhood literature might suggest. So it is hard to tell whether there really is a veridical mechanism dominating during adolescence, or that researchers (apart from Watson) have simply not investigated schematic connections, which may be equally present. That is, conscious attributions of why young people identify with music is not necessarily causal. For example, we know very little about whether a preference response to a piece of popular music is due to identification with the performer in the video clip, or due to the structure and qualities of the song, because the conscious attribution reported by the participant is probably filtered by the need to vindicate a badge or group membership (Zillman & Gan, 1997). An important research question therefore, is to determine the way in which adolescents perceive emotion in music because evidence is still required to confirm or detract from a weakly supported veridical explanation.

Summary and conclusions

Our view of the development of the perception of emotion in music from infancy to adolescence commences with infants who have a developed auditory perception mechanism that is highly attuned to detecting emotion information from lullabies, nursery songs, and prosodic information from their mother. They are able to detect basic emotions such as happiness in music, although the cues they use for doing so, and the level of precision are not yet the same as for adults. As this auditory system is probably present at birth, the dominant process for connecting emotional meaning to music or musical information is schematic (that is, more or less, innate). Veridical (one-to-one) connections between emotion and music become dominant from the age of about 3 years and continue to dominate until the age of about 7. Over this time, cultural associations such as the Western major-*happy* and minor-*sad* are developed and fully internalized.

From the age of 8 culturally determined musical styles and rules are so firmly established that connections between emotion perception and music are once again dominated by a schematic process. Children are able to identify numerous styles of music, but are also open to them, suggesting that they can find meaning within the various styles and structures. This period lasts until about the age of 11 or 12, at which time a new layer of veridical connections are made.

As the child moves to adolescence, music can become the most profoundly important non-human stimulation they can receive, providing meaning that appears not so much to be tied to the intrinsic value of the music, but to the way they use the music to develop their sense of identity and social bonding. The value of music for these individuals is strongly connected with factors outside the music itself. While the veridical process may not be exclusive in this period, it does appear to be dominant. We speculate that as the individual moves out of adolescence, both veridical and schematic processes have an equal footing. The young adult has developed such a long and rich set of experiences that they will be primed to extract intrinsic musical meaning, but at the same time continue to form strong associative connections between music and other stimuli, situations, and emotions (Davies, 1978). The model shown in Figure 10.2 therefore depicts a development that involves layers of associative (veridical) and intrinsic ('schematic') connections.

One of the implications of the theoretical framework is that we should not be concerned about valuing one process over another. Schematic and veridical processes are important and different ways of building up knowledge about music and emotion in a given culture. Apart from innate connections between auditory and emotional information, all truly new musical experiences are necessarily veridically connected, and with time these connections will merge into schematic representations, as the associations become thoroughly absorbed and assimilated. Our model also suggests that from early childhood both veridical and schematic mechanisms are in place, and so while there may be some value in exposing the child to music which is familiar and comfortable, they should also be challenged and exposed to new musical styles and stimuli to ensure that they can maximize their next period of openness and renewed schematic meaning. This is of critical importance because this window of openness may close in the adolescent stage where individuals tend to become restricted in the way they regulate their musical exposure. For some adolescents this may be a period of restriction that opens up again during early adulthood. Our conclusion for understanding musical development is, therefore, that early childhood up to adolescence can be regarded as a critical time during which individuals should have many, varied and positive musical experiences.

Despite all of the above, we have not been able to conclude whether changes are dependent on age or stage. That is, there is no clear evidence that the developmental landmark of being able to recognize sadness in music, for example, is a process of maturation that occurs at a certain age, or whether the recognition can be delayed or fast tracked. Some research suggests that the latter, more fluid, developmental stages are more likely to be the case (Gembris & Davidson, 2002). If this is true, then there is a degree of fluidity in that it may be possible for our spiral to be compressed or expanded. Future research should therefore seek to clarify whether the order of schematic and veridical dominance alterations occurs in a rigid order.

Acknowledgements

The authors are grateful for comments made about a draft of this chapter by Glenn Schellenberg and Alf Gabrielsson. This chapter was written with support from an Australian Research Council Discovery Project (DP-0452290) held by the first author.

References

Adachi, M. & Trehub, S. E. (1998). Children's expression of emotion in song. *Psychology of Music*, **26**(2), 133–153.

Bee, H. L. (1997). *The developing child* (8th edn). New York : Longman.

Behne, K. E. (1997) The development of 'Musikerleben' in adolescence: How and why young people listen to music. In I. Deliège and J. Sloboda (eds), *Perception and cognition of music* (pp. 143–159). East Sussex, UK: Psychology Press.

Bharucha, J. J. (1987). Music cognition and perceptual facilitation: A connectionist framework. *Music Perception*, **5**, 1–30.

Bharucha, J. J. (1994). Tonality and expectation. In R. Aiello & J. Sloboda (eds), *Musical perceptions* (pp. 213–239). Oxford: Oxford University Press.

Boone, R. T. & Cunningham, J. G. (1998). Children's decoding of emotion in expressive body movement: The development of cue attunement. *Developmental Psychology*, **34**(5), 1007–1016

Boone, R. & Cunningham, J. G. (2001). Children's expression of emotional meaning in music through expressive body movement. *Journal of Nonverbal Behavior*, **25**, 21–41.

Bower, G. (1981). Mood and memory. *American Psychologist*, **36**, 129–148.

Camras, L. A. (1992). Expressive development and basic emotions. *Cognition and Emotion*, **6**, 269–283.

Christenson, P. G. & Roberts, D. F. (1998). *It's not only rock & roll: Popular music in the lives of adolescents.* Cresskill, NJ: Hampton.

Cooper, R. P., Abraham, J., Berman, S., & Staska, M. (1997). The development of infants' preference for motherese. *Infant Behavior and Development*, **20**(4), 477–488.

Crowder, R., Reznick, J. S., & Rosenkrantz, S. (1991). Perception of the major/minor distinction: V. Preferences among infants. *Bulletin of the Psychonomic Society*, **29**, 187–188.

Cunningham, J. G. & Sterling, R. S. (1988). Developmental change in the understanding of affective meaning in music. *Motivation & Emotion*, **12**(4), 399–413.

Dalla Bella, S., Peretz, I., Rousseau, L., & Gosselin, N. (2001). A developmental study of the affective value of tempo and mode in music. *Cognition*, **80**(3), B1–B10.

Davies, J. B. (1978). *The psychology of music.* Stanford, CA: Stanford University Press.

Dissanayake, E. (2000). Antecedents of the temporal arts in early mother-infant interaction. In N. L. Wallin, B. Merker, & S. Brown (eds), *The origins of music* (pp. 389–410). Cambridge, MA: MIT Press.

Dolgin, K. G. & Adelson, E. H. (1990). Age changes in the ability to interpret affect in sung and instrumentally-presented melodies. *Psychology of Music*, **18**, 87–98.

Feinman, S. (1982). Social referencing in infancy. *Merrill-Palmer Quarterly*, **28**(4), 445–470.

Fernald, A. (1992). Human maternal vocalizations to infants as biologically relevant signals: An evolutionary perspective. In J. H. Barkow, L. Cosmides, & J. Tooby (eds), *The adapted mind: Evolutionary psychology and the generation of culture* (pp. 391–428). New York: Oxford University Press.

Fernald, A. (1993). Approval and disapproval—Infant responsiveness to vocal affect in familiar and unfamiliar languages. *Child Development*, **64**(3), 657–674.

Gabrielsson, A. (2001). Emotion perceived and emotion felt: Same or different? *Musicae Scientiae, Special Issue*, 123–147.

Gardner, H. (1973). *The arts and human development*. New York: John Wiley.

Gardner, H. & Perkins, D. N. (eds) (1989). *Art, mind, and education: Research from project zero*. Urbana, IL: University of Illinois Press.

Gardner, H., Phelps, E., & Wolf, D. P. (1990). The roots of adult creativity in children's symbolic products. In C. N. Alexander & E. J. Langer (eds), *Higher stages of human development: Perspectives on adult growth* (pp. 79–96). New York: Oxford University Press.

Gaston, E. T. (1951). Dynamic factors in mood change. *Music Educators Journal*, **37**, 42–44.

Gembris, H. & Davidson, J. (2002). Environmental influences. In R. Parncutt & G. McPherson (eds), *The science and psychology of music performance* (pp. 17–30). Oxford: Oxford University Press.

Gentile, D. (1998). *An ecological approach to the development of perception of emotion in music*, Unpublished doctoral dissertation, University of Minnesota.

Gerardi, G. M. & Gerken, L. (1995). The development of affective responses to modality and melodic contour. *Music Perception*, **12**, 279–290.

Giomo, C. J. (1993). An experimental study of children's sensitivity to mood in music. *Psychology of Music*, **21**(2), 141–162.

Gregory, A. H., Worrall, L., & Sarge, A. (1996). The development of emotional responses to music in young children. *Motivation & Emotion*, **20**(4), 341–348.

Gurucharri, C. & Selman, R. L. (1982). The development of interpersonal understanding during childhood, preadolescence, and adolescence: A longitudinal follow-up study. *Child Development*, **53**(4), 924–927.

Hall, P. D. (1998). The relationship between types of rap music and memory in African American children. *Journal of Black Studies*, **28**(6), 802–814.

Hargreaves, D. J. (1986). *The developmental psychology of music*. Cambridge: Cambridge University Press.

Hargreaves, D. J. (1996). The development of artistic and musical competence. In I. Deliege & J. Sloboda (eds), *Musical beginnings: Origins and development of musical competence* (pp. 145–170). Oxford: Oxford University Press.

Hargreaves, D. J. & North, A. C. (1999). Developing concepts of musical style. *Musicae Scientiae*, **3**, 193–216.

Hargreaves, D. J. & Zimmerman, M. P. (1992). Developmental theories of music learning. In R. Colwell (ed.), *Handbook of research on music teaching and learning* (pp. 377–391). New York: Schirmer.

Hasenfus, N., Martindale, C., & Birnbaum, D. (1983). Psychological reality of cross-media artistic styles. *Journal of Experimental Psychology: Human Perception & Performance*, **9**(6), 841–863.

Izard, C. E., Ackerman, B. P., Schoff, K. M., & Fine, S. E. (2000). Self-organization of discrete emotions, emotion patterns, and emotion-cognition relations. In M. D. Lewis & I. Granic (eds), *Emotion, development, and self-organization: Dynamic systems approaches to emotional development* (pp. 15–36). New York: Cambridge University Press.

Izard, C. E., Fantauzzo, C. A., Castle, J. M., Haynes, O., Rayias, M., & Putnam, P. (1995). The ontogeny and significance of infants' facial expressions in the first 9 months of life. *Developmental Psychology*, **31**(6), 997–1013.

Izard, C. E., Kagan, J., & Zajonc, R. B. (1984). Introduction. In C. E. Izard, J. Kagan & R. B. Zajonc (eds), *Emotions, cognition, and behavior* (pp. 1–14). Cambridge: Cambridge University Press.

Kastner, M. P. & Crowder, R. G. (1990). Perception of the major/minor distinction: IV. Emotional connotations in young children. *Music Perception*, **8**(2), 189–201.

Kratus, J. (1993). A developmental study of children's interpretation of emotion in music. *Psychology of Music*, **21**, 3–19.

Kitamura, C. & Burnham, D. (1998). The infant's response to vocal affect in maternal speech. In C. Rovee-Collier & L. Lipsitt (eds), *Advances in infancy research* (pp. 221–236). Norwood, NJ: Ablex.

Lagattuta, K. H., Wellman, H. M., & Flavell, J. H. (1997). Preschoolers' understanding of the link between thinking and feeling: Cognitive cuing and emotional change. *Child Development*, **68**(6), 1081–1104.

Lang, P. J. (1979). A bio-informational theory of emotional imagery. *Psychophysiology*, **16**, 496–512.

Larson, R. (1995). Secrets in the bedroom: adolescents' private use of media. *Journal of Youth and Adolescence*, **24**(5), 535–550.

Larson, R. W. & Richards, M. H. (eds) (1989). The changing life space of early adolescence [Special Issue]. *Journal of Youth and Adolescence*, **18**(6).

Levi, D. S. (1978). Expressive qualities in music perception and music education. *Journal of Research in Music Education*, **26**(3), 425–435.

Levine, L. J. (1995). Young children's understanding of the causes of anger and sadness. *Child Development*, **66**(3), 697–709.

Lewis, M. (2000). The emergence of human emotions. In M. Lewis & J. M. Haviland-Jones (eds), *Handbook of emotions* (pp. 265–280). New York: The Guilford Press.

Malatesta, C. Z., Culver, C., Tesman, J. R., & Shepard, B. (1989). The development of emotion expression during the first two years of life. *Monographs of the Society for Research in Child Development*, **54**(1–2), 1–104.

Malloch, S. (1999/2000). Mothers and infants and communicative musicality. *Musicæ Scientiæ* (Special issue on rhythm, musical narrative, and origins of human communication), 29–57.

Mandler, G. (1984). *Mind and body*. New York: Norton.

Mandler, G. (1990). A constructivist theory of emotion. In Stein, N. S., Leventhal, B. L., & Trabasso, T. (eds) *Psychological and biological approaches to emotion* (pp. 21–34). Hillsdale, NJ: Lawrence Erlbaum Associates.

Marcia, J. E., Waterman, A. S., Matteson, D. R., Archer, S. L., & Orlofsky, J. L. (eds), (1993). *Ego identity: A handbook for psychosocial research*. New York: Springer-Verlag.

Masterson, E. A. & Crawford, M. (1982). The defense motivation system: A theory of avoidance behavior. *The Behavioral and Brain Sciences*, **5**, 661–696.

Meyer, L. B. (1956). *Emotion and meaning in music*. Chicago, IL: University of Chicago Press.

Morton, J. & Trehub, S. E. (2001). Children's understanding of emotion in speech. *Child Development*, **72**(3), 834–843.

Nadel, L. & Butterworth, G. (eds) (1999). Immediate imitation rehabilitated at last. In *Imitation in infancy* (pp. 1–5). New York: Cambridge University Press.

Nawrot, E. S. (2003). The perception of emotional expression in music: Evidence from infants, children and adults. *Psychology of Music*, 31, 75–92.

North, A. C., Hargreaves, D. J., & O'Neill, S. A. (2000). The importance of music to adolescents. *British Journal of Educational Psychology*, 70(2), 255–272.

Oatley, K. & Jenkins, J. M. (1996). *Understanding emotions*. Oxford: Blackwell.

Plutchik, R. (1962). *The emotions: Facts, theories and a new model*. New York: Random House.

Raviv, A., Bar-Tal, D., Raviv, A. & Ben-Horin, A. (1996). Adolescent idolization of pop singers: Causes, expressions, and reliance. *Journal of Youth and Adolescence*, 25(5), 631–560.

Robazza C., Macaluso C., & Durso V. (1994). Emotional-reactions to music by gender, age, and expertise. *Perceptual and Motor Skills*, 79(2), 939–944.

Rolls, E. T. (2002). A theory of emotion, its functions and its adaptive value. In R. Trappl, P. Petta, S. Payr (eds), *Emotions in humans and artifacts* (pp. 11–34). Cambridge, MA: MIT Press.

Russell, J. A. (1980). A circumplex model of affect. *Journal of Social Psychology*, 39, 1161–1178.

Russell, J. A. (1997). How shall an emotion be called? In R. Plutchik & H. R. Conte (eds), *Circumplex models of personality and emotions* (pp. 205–220). Washington, DC: American Psychological Association.

Schimmack, U. (2002). Experiencing activation: Energetic arousal and tense arousal are not mixtures of valence and activation. *Emotion*, 2(4), 412–417.

Schimmack, U., Oishi, S. & Diener, E. (2002). Cultural influences on the relation between pleasant emotions and unpleasant emotions: Asian dialectic philosophies or individualism-collectivism? *Cognition & Emotion*, 16(6), 705–719

Schubert, E. (1996). Enjoyment of negative emotions in music: An associative network explanation. *Psychology of Music*, 24, 18–28.

Schubert, E. (2001). Continuous measurement of self-report emotional response to music. In P. N. Juslin & J. A. Sloboda (eds), *Music and emotion: Theory and research*. Series in Affective Science (pp. 393–414). Oxford: Oxford University Press.

Schubert, E. (in press). Locus of Emotion: The effect of task order and age on emotion perceived and emotion felt in response to music. *Journal of Music Therapy*.

Selman, R. L. (1977). A structural-developmental model of social cognition: Implications for intervention research. *Counseling Psychologist*, 6(4), 3–6.

Shaffer, D. R. (1999). *Developmental psychology: Childhood and adolescence* (5th edn). Pacific Grove, CA: Brooks/Cole.

Silverman, J., Winner, E., Rosentiel, A. K., & Gardner, H. (1975). On training sensitivity to painting styles. *Perception*, 4(4), 373–384.

Slaney, M. & McRoberts, G. (2003). Baby ears: A recognition system for affective vocalizations. *Speech Communication* 39, 367–384.

Solomon, R. C. (1993). The philosophy of emotions. In M. E. Lewis & J. M. E. Haviland (eds), *Handbook of emotions* (pp. 3–15). New York: The Guilford Press.

Striano, T. & Rochat, P. (2000). Emergence of selective social referencing in infancy. *Infancy*, 1(2), 253–264.

Terwogt, M. M. & van Grinsven, F. (1991). Musical expression of moodstates. *Psychology of Music*, 19(2), 99–109.

Trainor, L. J. & Trehub, S. E. (1992a). A comparison of infants' and adults' sensitivity to Western musical structure. *Journal of Experimental Psychology: Human Perception & Performance*, 18(2), 394–402.

Trainor, L. J. & Trehub, S. E. (1992b). The development of referential meaning in music. *Music Perception*, 9(4), 455–470.

Trehub, S. E. (2001). Musical predispositions in infancy. *Annals of the New York Academy Sciences*, **930**, 1–16.

Trehub, S. E. & Nakata, T. (2001). Emotion and music in infancy. *Musicae Scientiae*, 37–61 (Special Issue).

Trehub, S. E. & Schellenberg, E. (1995). Music: Its relevance to infants. *Annals of child development*, **11**, 1–24.

Trehub, S. E. & Trainor, L. (1998). Singing to infants: Lullabies and play songs. In C. Rovee-Collier & L. Lipsitt (eds), *Advances in infancy research* (pp. 43–77). Norwood, NJ: Ablex.

Trehub, S. E., Cohen, A. J., Thorpe, L. A., & Morrongiello, B. A. (1986). Development of the perception of musical relations: Semitone and diatonic structure. *Journal of Experimental Psychology: Human Perception & Performance*, **12**(3), 295–301.

Trehub, S. E., Unyk, A. M., & Trainor, L. J. (1993). Adults identify infant-directed music across cultures. *Infant Behavior & Development*, **16**(2), 193–211.

Trunk, B. (1982). *Children's perception of the emotional content of music.* Unpublished doctoral dissertation, The Ohio State University, Columbus.

Walk, R. D., Karasaitis, K., Lebowitz, C., & Falbo, T. (1971). Artistic style as concept formation for children and adults. *Merrill-Palmer Quarterly*, **17**(4), 347–356.

Walker-Andrews, A. S., & Dickson, L. R. (1997). Infants' understanding of affect. In S. Hala (ed.), *The development of social cognition. Studies in developmental psychology* (pp. 161–186). Hove, UK: Psychology Press.

Watson, K. B. (1942). The nature and measurement of musical meanings. *Psychological Monographs*, **54**.

Werker, I. E. & McLeod, P. J. (1989). Infant preference for both male and female infant-directed talk: A developmental study of attentional and affective responsiveness. *Canadian Journal of Psychology*, **43**, 230–246.

Willis, P. (1978). *Profane culture.* London: Routledge & Kegan Paul.

Wooten, M. A. (1992). The effects of heavy metal music on affects shifts of adolescents in an inpatient psychiatric setting. *Music Therapy Perspectives*, **10**(2), 93–98.

Zajonc, R. (1984). On the primacy of affect. *American Psychologist*, **39**(2), 117–123.

Zajonc, R. B. (2000), Feeling and thinking: Closing the debate over the independence of affect. In J. P. Forgas (ed.), *Feeling and thinking: The role of affect in social cognition* (pp. 31–58). Cambridge: Cambridge University Press.

Zillman, D. & Gan, S. (1997). Musical taste in adolescence. In D. J. Hargreaves & A. C. North (eds), *The Social Psychology of Music* (pp. 161–187). Oxford: Oxford University Press.

CHAPTER 11

DEVELOPING MOTIVATION

JAMES AUSTIN, JAMES RENWICK, AND GARY E. MCPHERSON

Framing motivation theories

Motivation is a theoretical construct used to explain the initiation, direction, intensity, and persistence of behaviour, especially goal-directed behaviour (Brophy, 1998). Motivation theorists working within education contexts seek to understand why some students become successful learners while others, of seemingly equal ability, do not. Since the 1970s, there has been a paradigmatic shift from motivation theories that emphasize biology (instincts, needs, drives) or behaviour (extrinsic rewards/punishments used to condition responses) to theories that recognize the role of personal cognition and social context (Pintrich & Schunk, 2002). Socio-cognitive theorists consider motivation to be largely a mentalistic or purposive process, rather than a mechanistic or reactive process. Behavioural indications of motivation include whether or not children choose to become music participants, the amount of effort they expend in their musical pursuits, and the degree to which they persevere across time.

On the broadest level, motivation may be viewed as a dynamic process involving the *self-system* (perceptions, thoughts, beliefs, emotions), the *social system* (e.g., teachers, peers, parents and siblings), *actions* (motivated behaviours including learning investment and regulation), and *outcomes* (learning, achievement). A process model, adapted from Connell (1990), is presented in Figure 11.1.

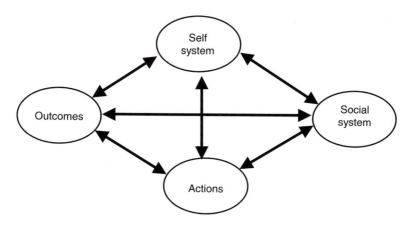

Figure 11.1 A process model of motivation depicting relations among self/social systems, actions, and outcomes.

This model implies that motivation develops in a continuous, non-linear fashion. As children encounter and engage in learning opportunities, the self system and social system constantly interact to influence actions and outcomes. In turn, actions and outcomes modify the ongoing influence of self and social systems. This reciprocal process is often context-specific (i.e., interactions in academic subjects such as mathematics may be quite distinct from those in music) but also may generalize across contexts (i.e., school-related systems influencing actions or outcomes outside of school).

In the remainder of this chapter, we explain children's motivational development by reviewing major theoretical traditions and related bodies of research in general education as well as music education. The content is organized into five sections: achievement goals, conceptions of ability, ability self-perceptions, interests and values, and attributional beliefs.

Children's achievement goals

According to Ames (1992), goals define how one approaches, engages in, and responds to achievement-type activities. Goal theory has dominated much motivation research in recent times, and the work of several theorists (e.g., Nicholls, 1984; Dweck, 1986; Ames, 1992) has coalesced around comparing types of goals that students are likely to use in guiding their academic behaviour. On the one hand, goals may be related to aspects of *learning, task-orientation,* or *mastery.* Children adopting these types of goal orientations primarily focus on learning for its own sake, how much has been learned, and the quality of their learning experiences. On the other hand, goals that focus on *performance* or that are related to *ego* characterize students who are primarily motivated to outperform others (a *performance-approach* goal) or avoid failing in comparison with others (a *performance-avoidance* goal) (Elliot & Harackiewicz, 1996). Early work has shown that learning goals are associated with the use of deeper cognitive strategies, higher levels of achievement, and the recognition of the importance of effort, whereas performance goals are more likely to be associated with an absence of these adaptive patterns of learning (Midgley *et al.*, 2001).

There has been little research regarding how children's achievement goal orientations develop (Eccles *et al.*, 1998). Whereas younger children often engage spontaneously in mastering their learning tasks, there is a tendency for older children to endorse performance goals more than learning goals. This means that while young children will use information from their peers' endeavours as a way of increasing their skill (in accord with a learning goal orientation), early adolescents tend to use social comparisons to gauge their ability as part of a performance goal orientation (Butler, 1989).

A major difficulty in assessing any developmental shifts in the achievement goals of children is the fact that educational environments typically change from primary to intermediate grades, and from intermediate grades to middle school. Thus, the shift from learning goals to performance goals may be due to changes in the school environment, children's maturation, or a combination of the two. Smiley and Dweck (1994) suggest that distinct goal orientations generally are not evident in children under 10 years of age, but that children will adopt different types of goals when classroom-level goals, learning outcomes and/or related feedback are made salient. In their study of 4 and 5 year olds in which goal conditions and performance outcomes were manipulated, for example, they found that children who adopted a learning goal orientation chose challenging tasks they viewed as interesting and sought opportunities for skill development, while children with performance goals avoided challenging tasks—opting for easier tasks that assured successful outcomes and promoted an image of competence. When experiencing failure, children in the performance goal group (particularly those with lower confidence in their abilities) expressed greater performance worries or more negative emotions, focused less on learning strategies, and were more apt to disengage altogether from the task. Conversely, learning-oriented children remained positive and engaged after failing.

More recently, researchers (Harackiewicz *et al.*, 2002) have started to move away from the binary opposition of learning and performance goals, instead proposing the existence of multiple goal patterns. As learning goals and performance goals are only weakly correlated, researchers have investigated the learning behaviour of students who strongly endorse both types of goals. The differences between performance-approach goals (reflecting a need to achieve and demonstrate competence) and performance-avoidance goals (reflecting a need to avoid failure or inferences of incompetence) have also been further distinguished.

There is some evidence that a multiple goal orientation not only enhances attitude (attributed primarily to learning goals) but also yields better grades and improved achievement on other measures of academic performance (attributed mainly to performance-approach goals). Bouffard *et al.* (1998) investigated the multiple goals of students aged 11, 13, and 15, and found that younger students were more likely to implement effective learning strategies and sustain motivation when oriented toward learning goals. Older students, by comparison, were able to adopt performance-approach goals to compensate for tasks that do not naturally elicit strong learning goals (i.e., not challenging or interesting), without adversely affecting motivation or achievement. Evidence that performance-approach goals can have some adaptive outcomes for some students is strongest with college-age students (Harackiewicz *et al.*, 2002). Austin (1988, 1991), however, has shown that elementary band students assigned to a competitive condition (emphasizing performance-approach goals) exhibit levels of motivation and performance achievement comparable with those of students assigned to a non-competitive condition (reflecting learning goals). Overall, it appears that younger children with limited ability or low self-concept are better served by adopting learning goals, whereas older children with developed knowledge/skills and high self-concept may function equally well in learning goal and performance-approach goal contexts.

Another important advance in goal theory has been the investigation of social goals (Wentzel & Wigfield, 1998). The many hours of solitary practice necessary for mastering an instrument or learning to compose, for example, are in stark contrast to the social rewards readily available when performing in a school ensemble that emphasizes popular music or in a garage band. In formal school settings, children can find support, encouragement, and understanding from their peers, especially if they possess similar interests (see Chapter 24 for further reading). It is crucial, therefore, that music students develop methods for coping when social goals are paramount but social support is lacking (Burland & Davidson, 2002).

In an application of goal theory to middle-school music students, Sandene (1998) invest-igated the associations between individuals' goal orientation and their perceptions of the achievement goals promoted within the classroom. Sandene found that students who per-ceived their classrooms as promoting performance goals were more likely to adopt personal performance goals themselves. Conversely, perceived classroom learning goals predicted personal learning goals as well as higher self-concept (i.e., estimates of one's own musical ability, see below). In turn, personal task goals and self-concept were positively associated with the strength of the students' motivation in music (see Figure 11.2). Observations of individual classrooms revealed that overt teacher behaviours, such as the ratio of negative to positive feedback, were strongly associated with students' perception of the motivational climate of the classroom and personal goal orientation.

Beyond the types of achievement goals that children adopt, goal *difficulty* also has import-ant implications for motivation and learning. Goal difficulty determines the amount of challenge that a child will encounter given a certain level of ability or skill. Music is inher-ently engaging for many young children (Custodero, 2002). This attraction involves music's physicality and its potential for the child to manipulate skill and challenge, resulting in the concentrated feeling of total immersion in an activity defined as *flow* (Csikszentmihalyi, 1990). Flow is thought to occur when there is a good match between skill and challenge.

According to Flow Theory, children who are assigned or who adopt achievement goals that are very challenging, such that the amount of challenge far exceeds their skills, will experience anxiety and diminished motivation for learning. Alternatively, children who are given or who choose very easy goals, such that their skill far exceeds the amount of challenge presented, will experience boredom and diminished motivation for learning.

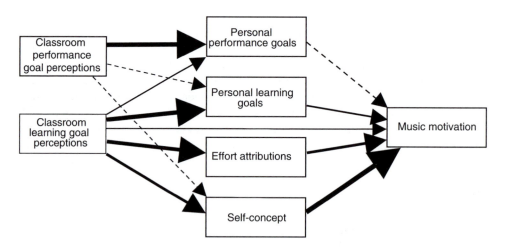

Figure 11.2 Simplification of Sandene's (1998) model of the effect of student's perceptions of classroom goals on their personal goals, attributions, self-concept and motivation in instrumental music. Factors with no significant effect on music motivation have been removed from this model for clarity. Wider arrows represent stronger effects; dotted lines indicate negative relationships.

Optimum motivation arises when skills and goal difficulty (challenge) are closely aligned, thus resulting in a mutually reinforcing and self-perpetuating cycle of musical development.

Studies involving talented adolescents (Csikszentmihalyi *et al.*, 1993) have shown that students experience a state of 'flow' most often when participating in elective school activities such as music, as opposed to academic-oriented school work (where challenge often exceeds skill and interest may be lacking) or when socializing with peers (where challenge often is lacking and goals are undefined, despite high levels of interest). Custodero (1999) videotaped 4- and 5-year-old participants in an intact music classroom over an 8-week period. Observable events (curricular activities such as singing a song or playing a keyboard piece) were analysed and coded in terms of perceived challenge. Among several factors, flow experience was associated with high self-concept or skill, perceived challenge, and active engagement. O'Neill (1999a) found interesting differences in flow experience among teenage musicians of different abilities. Those attending a non-specialist state school and high achievers at a specialist music school reported feeling in flow more often when engaged in musical activities (playing and listening to music) than moderate achievers at the specialist school. This finding shows how children with varying levels of ability or accomplishment may develop distinct perceptions of challenge when placed in a demanding instructional/evaluative context. Furthermore, it appears that excessive challenge may have detrimental effects on motivation to persist, even for young musicians who have made a commitment to pursuing specialized music training.

The theories and research reviewed in this section illustrate how achievement goals impact on children's motivation for learning and academic performance. The nature, range, complexity, and difficulty of goals adopted by children or assigned to them by teachers will determine, in part, how success and failure are defined in music learning. Young children who adopt learning goals—developing their knowledge and skills, focusing on the learning process, and defining success in relation to personal standards—are more likely to demonstrate a wide range of motivation-related behaviours and emotions that are associated with achievement. Older children who are confident in their abilities and who have a history of high achievement may be able to adopt performance-approach goals—emphasizing demonstrations of competence, focusing on performance outcomes, defining success in relation to social comparisons—in conjunction with learning goals, without experiencing a deficit in motivation or achievement. Children who adopt performance-avoidance goals often fear failure, lack motivation for learning, seek to maintain an illusory image of self-worth, and grossly underachieve in the classroom. Irrespective of a child's goal orientation, it is important that goals embody reasonable challenge and risk, so as create a sense of flow while learning, and provide for a meaningful sense of accomplishment when successes do arise.

Children's conceptions of ability

From an early age, children naturally reflect on their learning experiences and start to develop beliefs about their ability. These conceptions of ability, which continue to develop throughout the elementary years, guide students interpretations of ability-related information and their predictions of future outcomes in learning contexts.

Researchers have used many different methods to explore children's conceptions of ability or intelligence. Children, for example, have been asked to define terms such as 'smart' or to explain self-ratings of ability (Kinlaw & Kurtz-Costes, 2003). Very young children (preschool and kindergarten) often struggle to provide definitions of and criteria for ability. With age and experience, however, children define ability in a more precise, elaborate, and domain-specific fashion (Yussen & Kane, 1985; Cain & Dweck, 1995). Younger children (grades 1–4) typically define ability/intelligence globally in terms of the amount of knowledge one possesses as well as a broad range of social or behavioural traits, while older (grades 5–8) children's definitions emphasize academic skill (ability to apply knowledge) and outcomes (school grades) in addition to amount of knowledge. As children's conceptions of ability become increasingly sophisticated, they tend to interpret perceived ability differences more on the basis of specific examples of academic performance (e.g., doing well on a difficult task) and less on the basis of work habits or social interactions (e.g., trying hard, cooperating) (Stipek & Tannatt, 1984; Bempechat & London, 1991).

Children's conceptions of ability also involve beliefs about its stability, that is, whether ability is a fixed trait (i.e., *ability as capacity*) or malleable (i.e., *ability as current skill level*). To assess beliefs about stability, researchers typically ask elementary age children to rate their ability at two points in time (e.g., current and 1 year in the future) or in contrasting situations (e.g., different classrooms or schools). The responses of older children (fourth grade and above) imply that they view ability largely as a stable or fixed trait (change is possible but not probable), whereas younger children tend to believe that their ability will improve over time or vary across contexts (Stipek & Daniels, 1988; Droege & Stipek, 1993; Pomerantz & Ruble, 1997; Pomerantz & Saxon, 2001). The shift in beliefs about temporal and situational stability that arises at about ages 7–9 is often associated with the Piagetian transition from pre-operational to operational thinking (when classification skills and use of social comparisons emerge), though other theorists view the shift as having more to do with cumulative experience in processing information about achievement outcomes or the environmental influences within schools that reflect larger societal values, beliefs, and practices (Räty *et al.*, 2002; Kinlaw & Kurtz-Costes, 2003).

Despite some evidence of developmental changes in conceptions of ability, individual children clearly vary in the degree to which they see ability as fixed or malleable. Dweck and her colleagues (Dweck & Bempechat, 1983; Dweck, 1986, 2000; Dweck & Leggett, 1988; Cain & Dweck, 1989) propose that conceptions of ability influence a person's choice of achievement goals. Children who view ability as fixed and uncontrollable, for example, will focus on perceptions of their ability in relation to peers and seek out opportunities to prove they are smart. Conversely, children who view ability as malleable and controllable will strive to improve their skills through effort and experience.

Ability conceptions are also thought to influence children's learning-related behaviours and achievement outcomes, either directly or as mediated by achievement goals. Collectively, evidence suggests that children who view ability as malleable tend to adopt learning goals, implement effective learning strategies, and demonstrate adaptive responses to failure, by striving for improvement in the future. Children who view ability as fixed are inclined to

Table 11.1 Achievement goals, actions, and outcomes associated with fixed and malleable ability conceptions

	Fixed ability conception	Malleable ability conception
Self-System *Actions*	Goal is to outperform others	Goal is to learn
	Challenge avoidance	Challenge seeking
	Superficial learning strategies	Deep/active learning strategies
	Compares own performance with others'	Seeks objective feedback/help
	Maladaptive responses to failure	Adaptive responses to failure
Outcomes	Lower achievement	Higher achievement

adopt performance goals and exhibit a sense of helplessness in response to failure (particularly when they lack confidence in their abilities). The two major conceptions of ability—as a fixed or malleable construct—and the dynamics of how these conceptions relate to children's achievement goals, learning behaviours, and achievement outcomes are summarized in Table 11.1.

The applicability of ability conception theories to music was first tested in a dissertation by Ritcher (1990). Drawing on Nicholls' (1978) early work on reasoning about intellectual ability (i.e., children recognizing cause and effect relationships among ability, effort, and outcomes), students in grades 4–6 were interviewed to determine their level of reasoning about musical ability. Level of reasoning about musical ability increased across grade levels. Ritcher found that students with immature or transitional levels of reasoning held more positive attitudes toward general music, but their self-perceptions of ability were less accurate, teachers rated them as giving less effort, and their music achievement scores were lower. These findings are considered consistent with the notion that ability perceptions (self-concept) become increasingly relevant to motivation and achievement as students become mature in their thinking about the nature of ability.

Music ability conceptions were also of interest to O'Neill (1996). She studied the motivational beliefs of children aged 6–10 shortly before they commenced formal instrumental lessons, and compared these results with their performance achievement as assessed 10 months later. The children were classified as demonstrating adaptive versus helpless responses to failure (reflecting conceptions of ability as malleable versus fixed). These patterns predicted their musical achievement, whereas other important factors such as intelligence, parental involvement, and aural skills failed to discriminate between high achievers and lower achievers after a year of lessons. O'Neill suggests that a motivational orientation that allows a child to recover from the types of setbacks often encountered in the early stages of learning an instrument are an important ingredient for achieving long-term musical success.

Investigations of music ability conceptions should provide new insights about motivation because there are many subtle, but important, differences between music and the academic subjects on which most motivational research is based. Heyman and Gelman (2000) found that young children (like older children and adults) hold strong beliefs about the important role of nature in the origins of physical traits. When considering psychological traits such as intelligence, however, children increasingly endorse nurture as an explanation as they progress through school (though older children seem to recognize there are limits to the extent to which effort and experience can enhance ability). If musical activity and learning draws on both physical and psychological traits, the question remains: are conceptions of music ability based more on a nature or a nurture perspective?

Some research points to children internalizing the Western notion that musical ability is more innate and immutable than other abilities (Freedman-Doan *et al.*, 2000). Our own view, based on studies with the general public and also professional musicians, suggests that musical ability is often mistakenly seen as more innate than environmentally determined. That is, when asked to express their opinion about whether musicians are born or made (i.e., born with natural innate talent to become musicians versus acquiring skills through teaching and practice), many will place greater emphasis on an innate view of musical talent. This is in contrast to how the general public views other human endeavours, where typically environmental aspects are often given greater emphasis. A good example is a survey by Davis (1994), who asked educational psychologists, secondary teachers, primary teachers, and members of the general public to identify activities that they believed required a 'natural talent' or 'gift'. Davis reports that most of the respondents viewed musical skills as essentially innate. In fact, 75% of the educational professionals reported that playing instruments, singing, and composing were the result of a special innate gift or natural talent. The respondents gave various reasons for their belief that musical ability was innate, including the very young age when the 'talent' emerges and can be demonstrated (i.e., the unexplainable talent of child prodigies) and the fact that many youngsters try hard but often fail to develop their ability in the subject (see also, Gagné, 1999; Gagné *et al.*, 2001).

Somewhat different results emerged in a recent study by Hallam and Prince (2003) (see also Chapter 5). Professional musicians, music educators, other adults, and students were asked to complete the statement 'Musical ability is:'. A large proportion of musicians' and educators' responses reflected a belief that musical ability is something learned or developed. Adults and students (including students involved in music activities), however, made statements that reflected 'music as innate talent' beliefs to a much greater extent. This suggests that music ability conceptions may depend, in part, on whether individuals have gained enough expertise or developmental perspective, such that they are capable of recognizing the role of personal investment, experience, and learning environments in maximizing musical ability.

Children's ability self-perceptions

Children's perceptions of their own abilities have a major impact on their motivation to learn. Children who perceive themselves as highly competent are more likely to engage in learning tasks, utilize the skills and strategies they possess, persist when they confront difficulties, and achieve success. Theorists have explored a variety of constructs representing ability self-perceptions (e.g., self-esteem, self-concept, self-efficacy, perceived competence, performance expectancies). During the past 20 years, self-concept has, arguably, been measured and researched to a greater extent with children than any of the other constructs (Wylie, 1989; Byrne, 1996a).

Most self-perception research conducted prior to the 1980s was based on unitary theories—the notion being that children perceive themselves in very global terms. In the past two decades, however, self-concept theory has shifted to acknowledge the multidimensional ways in which children come to view themselves (Shavelson & Bolus, 1982; Harter, 1983; Marsh, 1990). In addition, researchers have documented developmental changes in the nature of self-concept. Younger children's self-concepts are less differentiated than those of their older peers. Children in grades K–2, for example, often rate their abilities similarly across achievement settings (i.e., ratings in various domains are highly correlated), whereas older children become more discriminating (i.e., smaller correlations exist among ratings in various domains). Put another way, a 6-year-old might claim 'I'm good at school,' while a 10-year-old states 'I'm a strong speller, and I'm a pretty fast runner, but I'm terrible at math.' When do children's self-concepts begin to take on a domain-specific character? Eccles *et al.* (1993) have reported that first-graders possess distinct beliefs about ability in various learning/activity domains. Similarly, Marsh and colleagues (1991) found evidence of domain differentiation when analysing the self-concepts of children aged 4–7.

Very young children often have inflated self-concepts that do not correlate well with objective indices of ability (Marsh, 1989; Stipek & Mac Iver, 1989; Eccles *et al.*, 1993). As children advance through the elementary years, however, they report diminished academic self-concepts that are more accurate (Chapman & Turner, 1995; Wigfield *et al.*, 1997; Marsh *et al.*, 1998). As self-concept diminishes, children may sustain motivation for learning by adopting more realistic goals and redefining what they believe they can accomplish in the near term (Anderman *et al.*, 1999) and/or by using more effective learning and regulatory strategies to improve their actual performance (and, in turn, their self-concepts). Alternatively, children can choose any number of defensive strategies designed to restore inflated self-concepts or sustain positive feelings of self-worth (Covington, 1984). Among these are choosing easy tasks, withholding effort, denying responsibility for failures, discontinuing participation, and questioning the importance of subjects in which they feel incompetent. Students opting for such self-handicapping strategies inevitably end up achieving less than otherwise might have been possible, and are academically at risk if these strategies generalize across several school subjects.

The linkage between self-concept and achievement is well documented (Marsh *et al.*, 1988). One line of research argues that children with positive self-concepts are more motivated to work hard and more capable of coping with difficult learning, and therefore achieve at a high level (Song & Hattie, 1984). According to this *self-enhancement* theory, the way to generate academic success is through interventions that directly improve children's self-concepts. However, other researchers contend that academic self-concept is heavily influenced by current and/or prior achievement (Byrne, 1996b). These *skill development* theorists recommend enhancing children's learning strategies as a precursor to improved performance, greater achievement, and more positive self-concepts. Marsh (1984) has proposed that relations between academic self-concept and achievement are reciprocal, and suggests that these two constructs may be part of a dynamic system in which a change in one produces a change in the other until equilibrium is restored (see also, Guay *et al.*, 2003). This relationship is shown in Figure 11.3.

Given the tendency for children to develop fixed conceptions of musical ability, ability self-perceptions have important consequences for learning motivation in music. Children who believe that music ability is stable or uncontrollable, and who also believe they lack ability in music, will not be very motivated to engage in music studies. Judgements of ability are very salient in music. Many school ensembles, for example, are organized to reflect a hierarchy of music ability (i.e., part assignments, leaders, or soloists within sections). In elementary music, 'learning by doing' is the modus operandi, which results in children demonstrating their abilities in front of one another. Outside of school, children often perform in very public venues (recitals, concerts, contests, festivals) where ability differences among peers may become readily apparent. All of these experiences provide information that children use to formulate their self-concept and identity as musicians.

Research focusing specifically on the *music* self-perceptions of children can be traced to an early study by Greenberg (1970), who found very low music self-concepts among grade 4–6 students who are unable to sing in tune. Since this time, a number of researchers have developed domain-specific measures of music ability self-perceptions for use with elementary students (see, for example, Svengalis, 1978; Schmitt, 1979) and adolescents (Vispoel, 1993). There is some evidence linking music self-concept to motivation/interest and participation in school and out-of-school music activities (Austin, 1990, 1991; Klinedinst, 1991). The relationship between music self-concept and achievement, however, is less clear. Some researchers have reported significant correlations between music self-concept and achievement outcomes such as notational understanding, aural skills, or adjudicated performance (Hedden, 1982; Austin, 1988), while others have found no relationship between self-concept and achievement in music (Austin, 1991; Klinedinst, 1991). In Austin's (1988) study, post-test music self-concept scores were more strongly correlated with performance achievement than pre-test scores, which provides some support for the skill development model. Collectively, studies of music self-concept provide tentative evidence that children who believe they are competent as musicians may be more inclined to participate in musical activities and demonstrate higher levels of musical achievement.

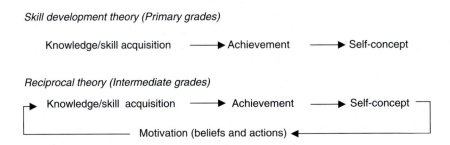

Figure 11.3 Depiction of relations between self-concept and achievement according to skill development and reciprocal theories.

How do children's music ability self-perceptions develop? Eccles, Wigfield, and their colleagues (1993; Wigfield *et al.*, 1997) have compared competence beliefs of children in different grade levels. Longitudinal data revealed sharp declines in music competence beliefs between grades 1 and 4. Importantly, children's music competence beliefs were significantly lower than competence beliefs in the other subject areas. The researchers hypothesized that instrumental music may be an activity in which 'many elementary-aged children decide not to engage or engage in for a short time and then stop' (Wigfield *et al.*, 1997, p. 463). They attributed the negative results for music competence beliefs to the fact that many children in the United States are not exposed to instrumental music until late elementary school, and so competence beliefs may be in a state of decline before children even begin receiving instruction in band or orchestra. Additionally, children's beliefs about the importance of music study may have played a part.

Austin and Vispoel (2000) sought to learn more about primary grade children's ability self-perceptions in music. Children in grades K–2 who attended urban elementary schools were asked to indicate how good they are (in general, in relation to other children, and in relation to other school subjects) at reading, mathematics, and music. Responses provided some evidence of self-concept differentiation at this early age. Children reported more positive self-perceptions in music than in reading or mathematics. Moreover, music ability self-perceptions were stable across the three grade levels. Austin and Vispoel speculated that their findings may have contrasted with those of Eccles, Wigfield, and colleagues because of developmental differences (primary grades versus middle and upper elementary) or context differences (urban versus suburban schools; daily instruction in classroom music for all students versus little or no experience in instrumental music).

Social context is also an important consideration when interpreting declines in music ability self-perceptions or unusually negative perceptions of music competence across a large population of children. Mota (1999) collected data from children attending three very different elementary schools in Portugal (different socio-economic profiles, two state schools and one music specialist school) over a 3-year period. While there were declines in students' perceptions of their music ability in all three schools, the decline was most dramatic in the music specialist school where the instructors focused on mastery of traditional music notation using didactic teaching methods. Renwick and McPherson (in preparation), who also have uncovered declines in music competence beliefs among Australian children, observe that negative self-perceptions of music ability are quite common in Western societies, where musical competence is typically perceived as a specialist, elite skill. That is in contrast to some non-Western cultures, such as the Anang Ibibo, where all community members participate actively in music-making (Sloboda *et al.*, 1994). The challenge for music educators in Western cultures then is to find optimal ways to motivate children toward high achievement and high self-concept, without diminishing their interest and involvement in music.

A self-perception construct closely related to self-concept is *self-efficacy*, defined as one's 'beliefs in one's capabilities to organize and execute the courses of action required to produce given attainments' (Bandura, 1997, p. 3). General competence beliefs of the type mentioned above relate to a child's global feelings of ability in a subject area, such as music, whereas self-efficacy relates to the person's level of confidence in their ability to perform very specific tasks, such as a difficult section in a piece they are learning. Self-efficacy has been found to be a strong predictor of achievement, independent of the effect of actual cognitive competence (Bouffard-Bouchard *et al.*, 1991). These results have been replicated in two large studies with young musicians (McCormick & McPherson, 2003; McPherson & McCormick, in press). Their analyses demonstrated the clear superiority of self-efficacy over other factors as a predictor of achievement on music performance examinations.

In the next section we turn our discussion to matters of children's interests and values.

Children's interests and values

In 1999, Brophy encouraged researchers to shift their focus from ability and expectancy beliefs toward value aspects of motivation in education. He surmised that by studying learning situations individuals find interesting and in which they sustain engagement, researchers might better understand how to promote intrinsic motivation across various learning contexts.

Research has demonstrated that children's interest is key to early stages of learning (Renninger *et al.*, 1992; Ainley *et al.*, 2002). Interest may be viewed as *individual* or *situational*. Individual interest reflects a child's more enduring personal disposition for learning in certain domains or about certain topics, whereas situational interest is generated by specific aspects of the learning environment (e.g., novelty, vividness, relevance, intensity, or choice associated with teacher presentations, class work, and assignments) and represents more immediate affective reactions that may or may not last. Within schools, students develop not just one individual interest, but a network of interests—some that might be closely related to achievement goals and others that might be antithetical to learning.

Situational interest is considered increasingly important when children do not exhibit individual interest for learning in a particular domain or might otherwise be classified as academically unmotivated. Educators might structure learning environments so as to elicit or enhance interest, just as students can work actively to maintain interest in important or required tasks that may be somewhat tedious or even boring. When situational interest is sustained and transformed into individual interest, children exhibit more enjoyment of learning, work harder, persist for longer periods of time, and attain higher levels of cognitive functioning and academic performance (O'Sullivan, 1997).

In a recent case study (Renwick & McPherson, 2002), individual and situational interest worked in combination to enhance motivation in a music learning context. A 12-year-old was observed practising a piece she had chosen herself with a highly elevated level of attention, persistence, and strategy use in comparison with repertoire assigned by her teacher. Her choice appeared to have been motivated by the situational interest in the particular piece, as well as an emerging individual interest in jazz.

The concept of interest raises a closely related body of research in motivation, namely self-determination theory (Ryan & Deci, 2000). This perspective emerges from the classic distinction between intrinsic motivation, where an activity is pursued for its own inherent satisfactions, and extrinsic motivation, where a person pursues an activity in order to obtain a separate outcome, such as praise, a reward, or the avoidance of punishment.

Self-determination theory proposes that extrinsically motivated behaviours lie along a continuum according to the level of autonomy a person feels. *External regulation* is behaviour controlled solely by the avoidance of punishment or the desire for a reward. *Introjected regulation* involves the developmental internalization of such external motivators, such that a person might start to control his or her own behaviour from within, in an attempt to gain social approval or to avoid feelings of guilt. The internalization of extrinsically motivated behaviour is increased in *identified regulation*, where behaviour is guided by a conscious valuing of the activity, such as when a committed young musician practises technical exercises that are far from being inherently pleasurable, but valued for their beneficial effect on technique.

Although this theoretical approach to the internalization of self-control is inherently developmental, there has been little empirical research on its validity. Nevertheless, there have been a number of studies of young musicians' motivation from the self-determination perspective. It appears that there is a strong association between perceived autonomy and the learning environment. Band students who more frequently engage in competitive performances (Rohrer, 1993) and who attend private schools (Miyamoto, 1997), for example, exhibit more extrinsic motivation and less autonomous behaviour. Internalized motivation has been found to be a good predictor of students' use of self-regulated practising strategies, such as monitoring their accuracy, managing their effort, and using corrective techniques (Renwick & McPherson, 2003). In addition, boys have been found to be more extrinsically motivated than girls, with girls more intrinsically motivated than boys (Rohrer, 1993; Miyamoto, 1997; Renwick & McPherson, 2006).

Recent research involving adolescent instrumentalists has found that those students that stay involved in music making seem to perceive their motivation as decreasingly extrinsic as they grow older (Renwick & McPherson, 2006). Motivation to practise 'because that's what I'm supposed to do' and to gain social approval decline markedly by the age of about 12. While internal motivation also declines at this age, it is restored among those that continue music participation in the later teenage years (cf. Sloboda & Davidson, 1996).

Another perspective on values and interest can be gained from expectancy–value theory (Wigfield & Eccles, 2000), which emphasizes the dual importance of people's beliefs about their own competence (ability, task difficulty, and expectations of success) and their valuing of the achievement tasks in which they are engaged. Children's values concerning an activity are a strong predictor of their decisions to continue engagement (Wigfield & Karpathian, 1991; Wigfield & Eccles, 1992). The other main element of the theory, children's beliefs about their own competence on various activities, has been found to be the strongest predictor of students' actual achievement (Eccles, 1983). Consequently, children who feel they are competent musicians are likely to achieve at a higher level than children who have more negative views about their musical ability, and children who believe music learning is important or who find music interesting are more likely to continue participating in music than children who attach little or no value to music.

Eccles (1983) first theorized that people's estimations of the value of an achievement activity are comprised of four main components: *attainment value* (the perceived importance of success in the activity); *utility value* (its usefulness in everyday life); *intrinsic interest* (the pleasure to be gained from engagement in the activity for itself); and *perceived cost* (the sacrifice of other activities and emotional resources that engagement entails). An additional premise (Wigfield and Eccles, 1992) was that conceptions of task value would change as children mature. Developmental research (e.g., Marsh *et al.*, 1999; Wigfield & Eccles, 2002b) depicts an age-related trend similar to that reported earlier for ability conceptions; a multifaceted conception of task value emerges from a more holistic one throughout the school years. Young children typically do not draw fine distinctions between aspects of task value. They primarily value activities for their inherent interest and enjoyment. As children progress through the elementary grades and experience a wider variety of domains and activities within domains, they begin to distinguish between the utility, importance, and enjoyment of a given pursuit. In high school, as students approach career decisions, their choices often are determined by their perception of the usefulness and costs of the activity, in conjunction with their expectation of being successful (Wigfield & Eccles, 1992). This change appears to be particularly relevant in its effect on the choices that adolescents make about continuing or discontinuing their involvement in music.

As was true for perceptions of ability/competence, children's valuing of academic domains such as reading and mathematics declined from grades 1 to 6 (Eccles *et al.*, 1993; Wigfield *et al.*, 1997; Austin & Vispoel, 2000). The decline in children's valuing of music, however, was much more pronounced than for reading and mathematics, and this trend was evident regardless of whether students have received any instruction in music (Wigfield *et al.*, 1997). With respect to values within the music domain, children's reported interest in music declined with age, but beliefs about music's usefulness and importance declined more sharply.

It is unclear whether music-related values continue to decline after elementary school when, in most instances, students have either elected to continue or discontinue studying music. Wigfield *et al.* (1999) found that adolescents who play an instrument report favouring this activity over almost all the others they were asked to rate. McPherson (2000/2001) assessed the level of commitment felt by younger children about to start learning an instrument. Commitment was measured in terms of the length of time the child anticipated continuing to play their new instrument. Together with the amount of time spent practising, this initial commitment for continuing participation accounted for a large amount of the variation in students' performance after a year of lessons. Hallam (1998) found similar associations between students' intentions to practise and whether they dropped out of a school instrumental programme. Collectively, these findings suggest that, for the minority of children who elect and continue to engage in music-making, values such as interest, usefulness, and importance may be especially influential on their learning outcomes, which would in turn foster further levels of commitment. Perhaps once a commitment is made to studying music, associated values also may remain quite strong (at least until that point in time at which an equally valued activity competes for time and resources).

Developmental trends related to children's achievement values are critically important, as research in academic learning (Pintrich & De Groot, 1990; Pokay & Blumenfeld, 1990) has found that the value placed on domains (or tasks within domains) is not only a strong predictor of activity choice, but also students' use of learning strategies and effort management, which themselves are associated with performance outcomes such as grades. Children's perceptions of music as interesting and important do appear to predict the time they will devote to practising and their choice of whether or not to participate in music over rival activities such as sport (Yoon, 1997). Further support for the importance of task value for young musicians comes from a study by O'Neill (1999b), who asked students at an average school and at a specialist music school about their competence beliefs and about the subjective importance of their music-making. While competence beliefs did not distinguish the highest-achieving and lowest-achieving groups, task value accounted for approximately 10% of the difference in reported time spent practising. McPherson and McCormick (1999), in a study of students' preparation for music performance examinations, found that task value predicted engagement across different facets of musical practice. In a follow-up study (McPherson & McCormick, 2000), the researchers investigated the predictive effects of this task value measure and several other variables on the students' examination results. Beyond self-efficacy (as reported earlier), task value contributed additional predictive power in the regression analyses. Factors traditionally assumed to play a major role, such as anxiety and weekly practice time, did not predict the music exam result when controlling for the expectancy and value measures.

To summarize, children's interest in and beliefs about the relative value or importance of learning opportunities are major determinants of task engagement (initiation and continuation of music learning) and achievement striving (time spent practising and types of practice behaviour). Value-related beliefs become more differentiated and domain-specific with age. Children often express a moderate degree of interest in music learning, but value music learning less than learning in academic domains such as reading or mathematics. As they progress through elementary school, most students find music learning (as associated with school-based learning environments) to be increasingly less important and less useful. Children who choose to pursue instrumental study within schools, however, often exhibit a strong commitment to music learning (reflecting individual interest as well as more stable beliefs about the importance and value of music learning), and adopt clear achievement goals.

In the next section, we turn our attention to children's interpretations of achievement outcomes, be they successes or failures.

Children's attributional beliefs

Children naturally seek to understand why learning outcomes occur, particularly when the outcome is important, disappointing, or unanticipated. According to attribution theory (Weiner, 1979, 1985), the factors to which individuals attribute their successes and failures affect future self-perceptions, achievement behaviours, academic performance, and affective responses. Causal attributions traditionally have been categorized as lying along two conceptual continua (internal versus external locus, stable versus unstable) as shown in Figure 11.4. Within this conceptual framework, *effort* is considered an internal attribution that is unstable because a child can choose to exert more or less effort when practising a new piece of music. This contrasts with *ability*, where children's perceptions of their own ability as a good or bad musician will tend to be relatively stable over time. *Task difficulty,* where a child may come to regard a piece as too difficult to learn or the task of writing a

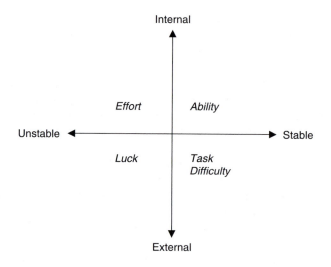

Figure 11.4 Basic types of attributions to explain success or failure.

composition as far too complex to complete, also is considered a stable, external attribution. An example of an unstable and external attribution is *luck*. Some children might believe, for example, that they achieved an excellent result in music because of having a 'lucky day.'

Internal attributions (ability, effort) are associated with more intense emotional reactions than external attributions (task difficulty, luck). Attributing a learning outcome to an internal factor yields greater pride following success, and more humiliation or shame following failure. Stable attributions (ability, task difficulty) elicit stronger expectancy beliefs than unstable attributions (effort, luck). If a student fails a music performance exam, for example, and attributes this failure to low ability, he or she might expect continued failure when subsequently engaged in the same task or similar tasks. Attributional beliefs often merge with children's conceptions of ability (Austin & Vispoel, 1998). If children believe ability is fixed, and then attribute poor performance to lack of ability, they will expect continued failure and, in some cases, ensure continued failure by adopting defensive strategies designed to avoid inferences of low ability and protect images of self-worth (Stipek, 1993).

Children often are encouraged to attribute their achievement successes and failures to amount of effort. Because one can choose to try harder, effort is viewed as being less stable and more controllable than ability (Clifford, 1984). Yet, effort attributions can be problematic. If children are struggling with a difficult musical task while expending maximum effort, attributing failure to lack of effort does not make sense, just as teacher or parent exhortations to 'try harder' will not likely alter a child's behaviour if she is already working at capacity. In situations where success is elusive, the modification of practice *strategies* may be a more productive means for encouraging children to persist. Attributional beliefs function in a similar manner. When a musical success is attributed to the use of effective practice strategies, children will experience positive affect without risking their self-concept. When a musical failure is attributed to the ineffective practice strategies, children avoid the negative consequences associated with attributing failures to low ability (humiliation) or lack of effort (guilt). They are also able to sustain motivation by approaching future learning activities as problem-solving opportunities such as by searching for alternative or more effective strategies.

As with other motivational beliefs, children's attributions become more differentiated with increasing age. Skinner (1990) reports that two factors (known versus unknown) explain the attributions of 7- and 8-year-old children, that three factors (internal, external, unknown) are typical of children aged 9–10, and that beliefs of children ages 11–12 can be represented by four factors (effort, ability, external, unknown).

Studies in which the attributional beliefs of low- and high-achieving students are compared reveal distinct orientations to interpreting success and failure (Marsh *et al.*, 1984). High achieving children commonly attribute success to high ability or effort (which leads to high self-concept, expectations for future success, and positive affect) and failure to lack of effort or use of inappropriate strategies (which implies some degree of control over future achievement outcomes). Low achieving students, on the other hand, tend to attribute success to external causes such as task ease, teacher assistance, or good luck, and attribute failure to lack of ability. In other words, low achievers do not derive motivational benefits from their successes and interpret failure as uncontrollable or inevitable.

Research on children's attributional beliefs about learning outcomes in music largely mirror those reported in the general education literature. Asmus (1985) identified the factors sixth-graders use to explain their achievement outcomes. Ability and effort attributions were the most common, with task difficulty attributions being reported much less often and luck attributions seldom mentioned (cf. Austin, 1988). Arnold (1997) asked students in grades 6, 8, and 10 to rank the importance of the same four factors in determining why some students do well or do not do well in music (i.e., separate attributional responses were obtained for music success and failure). Effort was consistently ranked first as a causal explanation and luck was consistently ranked last across grade levels and outcomes (success or failure). With age, however, students tended to de-emphasize the relative importance of effort attributions and ascribed greater import to ability and task difficulty.

In a test of Weiner's attribution model in music contexts, Asmus (1986) analysed high school music students' responses and identified five factors that best represented student beliefs about success and failure in music: ability and effort (as found in the traditional Weiner model), as well as music background (e.g., having musical parents), classroom environment (e.g., relationship with teachers and peers), and music affect (e.g., interest/enjoyment associated with making or listening to music). Using these five categories, Asmus (1986) compared attribution responses of students in grades 4–12 and found that older students are more inclined to attribute achievement outcomes to ability and less inclined to endorse effort attributions than younger students. Extending these analyses, Austin (1991) showed that effort, ability, classroom, and music affect were salient success attributions for upper elementary students, while music background was not. In addition, effort attributions for success were positively correlated with music self-concept; students with a low music self-concept did not tend to endorse effort as a reason for success, while students with moderate or high music self-concept did.

Austin and Vispoel (1992) studied the attributional beliefs of children in grades 5–8 by asking them to interpret the achievement experience of a hypothetical music student. Children predicted that the hypothetical student would demonstrate greater motivation and performance when given feedback that highlighted effort and strategy attributions as opposed to feedback that highlighted ability attributions. In a follow-up study (Austin & Vispoel, 1998) seventh-graders' attributional beliefs regarding *personal* success and failure experiences in music were directly assessed. A major finding was that beliefs about success and failure are conceptually distinct—a child who attributes success to high ability or high effort will not necessarily attribute failure to low ability or low effort. Attributions that addressed the influence of significant others (teachers, family, peers) were more strongly endorsed than generally has been reported in other research. Attributing failure to lack of ability or negative family influence (little or no history of musical ability in family) was associated with low self-concept and low achievement (standardized music test scores).

Differences in study participants' ages and in techniques used to measure attributional beliefs make it difficult to synthesize research in this area. Overall, it appears that children's explanations for why they succeed or fail centre around ability and effort. In some contexts, such as music, interest/affect as well as the influence of others (teachers, parents, classmates) also may be used to explain achievement outcomes. As children grow older, their attributional beliefs become more differentiated—they are able to associate outcomes with a wider range of specific factors. In most studies reported here, children place greater emphasis on ability attributions and less emphasis on effort attributions with age. Ability attributions for failure, in particular, are problematic when ability is conceptualized as an internal and stable factor. Children who attribute failure or other disappointing performances in music to lack of ability experience negative emotions (humiliation or shame), anticipate continued failure on similar tasks, and sense they lack control of the learning process. Ability attributions for failure are most evident among children who also report low self-concepts, limited use of learning strategies, and poor achievement.

Conclusions

Most of the literature on motivation concerns young people's motivation to learn the so-called 'academic' school subjects such as mathematics, reading, and science. However, music provides children with a wide range of opportunities for engagement, including formal settings within schools as well as more informal social and recreational contexts outside of schools (Lamont *et al.*, 2003). In contrast to disciplines that are primarily knowledge-based or cognition-intense, music also places demands on students to develop skills and express emotions. Thus, motivational processes at work in music contexts are often complex, and continuing research is needed to clarify their role in the life of young people.

We use the word 'developing' in our chapter title because of a desire to explain how children's motivation changes as a result of their engagement in music. Well-documented research in general education (Wigfield & Eccles, 2002a) shows that children's motivation develops from early childhood to late adolescence in several ways. Our interpretation of these types of development for music suggest the following key developmental processes:

First, young children tend to equate ability with effort or pro-social behaviour, and view ability as malleable—something that can be steadily improved over time. As children get older and struggle or fail despite putting forth great effort, they begin to conceive of ability as co-varying with effort (trying harder than another child to complete the same task implies less ability), base judgements of their own and others' ability on overt academic skills or specific performance outcomes, and view ability as something that is fixed or uncontrollable. Music ability, in particular, is considered by many to be an inherited trait. Thus, it is not surprising that children, at an early age, come to view music ability as something they either have in abundance or lack entirely. Children who conceive of music ability as fixed and who believe they lack ability in music, may see no point in participating in musical activity, let alone investing a great of time and effort toward developing musical expertise. Children who maintain an incremental and multifaceted view of music ability, however, will typically initiate and sustain motivation for music learning, because the challenge and positive benefits derived from improving one's own ability more than offset any negative inferences that arise from trying hard in comparison with others.

Second, young children often are overly optimistic about their ability and positively motivated toward school learning. As they develop and process social comparison information, their self-concept becomes more realistic and in line with actual achievement. The decline in self-concept is problematic only to the extent that children experience diminished motivation, adopt self-handicapping strategies, or withdraw from school achievement situations altogether. By working assiduously to improve skills and identifying realistic achievement goals, children can experience meaningful success and restore their sense of competence. In music, the very public nature of learning and evaluative processes may make it more challenging for students to sustain positive self-concepts. Young children who fall behind in their musical learning and who develop negative beliefs about their ability may reassess their musical aspirations. When these feelings of concern or doubt become entrenched, children may choose to avoid learning situations, such as private lessons or ensemble rehearsals, that provide important avenues for musical growth but that also may expose learning difficulties to others.

Third, children's beliefs, values, and behaviours become increasingly differentiated, complex, and context-specific as they progress through the elementary years. Many young children, for example, begin school with a global sense of their competence and a general interest in learning about many different things. They adopt a general orientation toward learning in school, utilize very basic cognitive strategies and organizational schemes promoted by the teacher, and interpret achievement outcomes as being due to internal or external factors. As children enter the intermediate grades and middle school, they begin to value and expect success in some activities more than others. They establish different types of goals (learning versus performance, distal versus proximal, easy versus difficult) in different learning domains. They employ more complex learning and regulatory strategies independent of the teacher, and they cite any number of causal factors when interpreting achievement outcomes. Music typically becomes an elective school subject at the very point in development when student interest, importance/usefulness beliefs, and attributional beliefs influence task engagement and course selection, and when goals and self-regulation impact classroom performance. Therefore efforts to generate situational interest, promote music as a valuable and important discipline, establish a learning goal orientation, guide students in managing their learning behaviours, and assist students in interpreting performance outcomes are vital to establishing school and community cultures in which older children and young adolescents view continued music participation and learning as the norm rather than the exception.

Fourth, there are dynamic relations between expectancies, values, goals, attributional beliefs, and academic achievement. Among young children, skill development generally is viewed as a determinant of success and motivation. The implication is that when learning to play a musical instrument, young children must invest reasonable effort and develop a modicum of proficiency before they will derive motivational benefits from the process. With age, the relationship between the various facets of motivation and achievement becomes more reciprocal in nature. Once children progress to an intermediate level of musicianship they should be able to draw on prior accomplishments to initiate motivation, and rely on motivation, in turn, to further enhance skills and ensure continued success. As children grow older, their beliefs, values, goals, and strategies also become stronger predictors of participation and performance. For music, this means that children will be inclined to continue learning only if they feel competent and believe that their learning is useful or important to what they plan to do in the future.

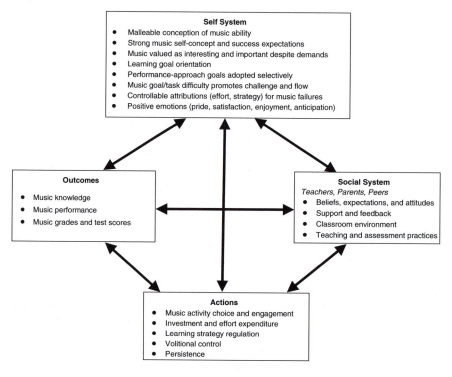

Figure 11.5 Systems profile for optimally motivated music student.

Finally, the development of motivation beliefs and behaviours reflects not only changes within the child, but also the ongoing influence of social contexts in which children learn and grow. As children grow older, they become more capable of attending to, processing, understanding, and implementing information (implicit or explicit) they receive from teachers, parents, siblings, peers, and other members of the social system.

The aim of theorists, researchers, and educators is to better understand how motivation develops so that children may become more productive and committed music learners. The process model presented at the beginning of this chapter can be expanded (see Figure 11.5) to illustrate how optimal motivation for learning might arise in various musical contexts.

References

Ainley, M., Hidi, S., & Berndorff, D. (2002). Interest, learning, and the psychological processes that mediate their relationship. *Journal of Educational Psychology*, 94, 545–561.

Ames, C. (1992). Classrooms: Goals, structures, and student motivation. *Journal of Educational Psychology*, 84, 261–271.

Anderman, E. M., Anderman, L. H., & Griesinger, T. (1999). The relation of present and possible academic selves during early adolescence to grade point average and achievement goals. *Elementary School Journal*, 100, 3–17.

Arnold, J. A. (1997). A comparison of attributions for success and failure in instrumental music among sixth-, eighth-, and tenth-grade students. *Update: Applications of Research in Music Education*, 15(2), 19–23.

Asmus, E. P. (1985). Sixth graders' achievement motivation: Their views of success and failure in music. *Bulletin of the Council for Research in Music Education*, 85, 1–13.

Asmus, E. P. (1986). Student beliefs about the causes of success and failure in music: A study of achievement motivation. *Journal of Research in Music Education*, 34, 262–278.

Austin, J. R. (1988). The effect of music contest format on self-concept, motivation, achievement, and attitude of elementary band students. *Journal of Research in Music Education*, 36, 95–107.

Austin, J. R. (1990). The relationship of music self-esteem to degree of participation in school and out-of-school music activities among upper elementary students. *Contributions to Music Education*, 17, 20–31.

Austin, J. R. (1991). Competitive and non-competitive goal structures: An analysis of motivation and achievement among elementary band students. *Psychology of Music*, 19, 142–158.

Austin, J. R. & Vispoel, W. P. (1992). Motivation after failure in school music performance classes: The facilitative effects of strategy attributions. *Bulletin of the Council for Research in Music Education*, 111, 1–23.

Austin, J. R. & Vispoel, W. P. (1998). How American adolescents interpret success and failure in classroom music: Relationships among attributional beliefs, self-concept and achievement. *Psychology of Music*, 26, 26–45.

Austin, J. R. & Vispoel, W. P. (2000). Children's ability self-perceptions and interests: Grade level, gender, and race differences for music, reading, and math. In R. G. Craven & H. W. Marsh (eds), *Self-concept theory, research, and practice: Advances for the new millennium. Proceedings of the Inaugural International Conference.* Sydney, Australia: University of Western Sydney.

Bandura, A. (1997). *Self-efficacy: The exercise of control.* New York: Freeman.

Bempechat, J. & London, P. (1991). Children's conceptions of ability in major domains: An interview and experimental study. *Child Study Journal*, 21, 11–36.

Bouffard, T., Vezeau, C., & Bordeleau, L. (1998). A developmental study of the relation between combined learning and performance goals and students' self-regulated learning. *British Journal of Educational Psychology*, **68**, 309–319.

Bouffard-Bouchard, T., Parent, S., & Larivée, S. (1991). Influences of self-efficacy on self-regulation and performance among junior and senior high-school age students. *International Journal of Behavioural Development*, **14**, 153–164.

Brophy, J. (1998). *Motivating students to learn*. Boston, MA: McGraw-Hill.

Brophy, J. (1999). Toward a model of the value aspects of motivation in education: Developing appreciation for particular learning domains and activities. *Educational Psychologist*, **34**, 75–86.

Burland, K. & Davidson, J. W. (2002). Training the talented. *Music Education Research*, **4**, 121–140.

Butler, R. (1989). Mastery versus ability appraisal: A developmental study of children's observations of peers' work. *Child Development*, **60**, 1350–1361.

Byrne, B. (1996a). *Measuring self-concept across the life span: Issues and instrumentation*. Washington, DC: American Psychological Association.

Byrne, B. (1996b). Academic self-concept: Its structure, measurement, and relation to academic achievement. In B. A. Bracken (ed.) *Handbook of self-concept: Developmental, social, and clinical considerations* (pp. 287–316). New York: Oxford University Press.

Cain, K. M. & Dweck, C. S. (1989). The development of children's conceptions of intelligence: A theoretical framework. In R. J. Sternberg (ed.), *Advances in the psychology of human intelligence* (pp. 47–82). Hillsdale, NJ: Lawrence Erlbaum Associates.

Cain, K. M. & Dweck, C. S. (1995). The relation between motivational patterns and achievement cognitions through the elementary school years . *Merrill-Palmer Quarterly*, **41**, 25–52.

Chapman, J. W. & Turner, W. E. (1995). Development of young children's reading self-concepts: An examination of emerging subcomponents and their relationship with reading achievement. *Journal of Educational Psychology*, **87**, 154–167.

Clifford, M. (1984). Thoughts on a theory of constructive failure. *Educational Psychologist*, **19**, 108–120.

Connell, J. P. (1990). Context, self, and action: A motivational analysis of self-system processes across the life-span. In D. Cicchetti (ed.), *The self in transition: Infancy to childhood*. Chicago, IL: University of Chicago Press.

Covington, M. V. (1984). The self-worth theory of achievement motivation: Findings and implications. *The Elementary School Journal*, **85**, 5–20.

Csikszentmihalyi, M. (1990). *Flow: The psychology of optimal experience*. New York: Harper and Row.

Csikszentmihalyi, M., Rathunde, K., & Whalen, S. (1993). *Talented teenagers: The roots of success and failure*. Cambridge: Cambridge University Press.

Custodero, L. A. (1999). Constructing musical understandings: The cognition-flow interface. *Bulletin of the Council for Research in Music Education*, **142**, 79.

Custodero, L. A. (2002). Seeking challenge, finding skill: Flow experience and music education. *Arts Education Policy Review*, **103**(3), 3–9.

Davis, M. (1994). Folk music psychology [Letter to the editor]. *The Psychologist*, **7**, 537.

Droege, K. L. & Stipek, D. J. (1993). Children's use of dispositions to predict classmates' behaviour. *Developmental Psychology*, **29**, 646–654.

Dweck, C. S. (1986). Motivational processes affecting learning. *American Psychologist*, **41**, 1040–1048.

Dweck, C. S. (2000). *Self-theories: Their role in motivation, personality, and development*. Philadelphia, PA: Psychology Press.

Dweck, C. S. & Bempechat, J. (1983). Children's theories of intelligence. In S. Paris, G. Olsen, & H. Stevenson (eds), *Learning and motivation in the classroom* (pp. 239–256). Hillsdale, NJ: Lawrence Erlbaum Associates.

Dweck, C. S. & Leggett, E. L. (1988). A social-cognitive approach to motivation and personality. *Psychological Review*, 95, 256–273.

Eccles, J. (with Adler, T. F., Futterman, R., Goff, S. B., Kaczala, C. M., Meece, J. L., & Midgley, C.) (1983). Expectancy, values, and academic behaviours. In J. T. Spence (ed.), *Achievement and achievement motives: Psychological and sociological approaches* (pp. 75–146). San Francisco, CA: Freeman.

Eccles, J., Wigfield, A., Harold, R. D., & Blumenfeld, P. (1993). Age and gender differences in children's self- and task perceptions during elementary school. *Child Development*, 64, 830–847.

Eccles, J. S., Wigfield, A., & Schiefele, U. (1998). Motivation to succeed. In W. Damon (series ed.) & N. Eisenberg (ed.), *Handbook of child psychology*: Vol. 4. *Social, emotional, and personality development* (5th edn) (pp. 1017–1095). New York: Wiley.

Elliot, A. J. & Harackiewicz, J. M. (1996). Approach and avoidance achievement goals and intrinsic motivation: A mediational analysis. *Journal of Personality & Social Psychology*, 70, 461–475.

Freedman-Doan, C., Wigfield, A., Eccles, J. S., Blumenfeld, P., Arbreton, A., & Harold, R. D. (2000). What am I best at? Grade and gender differences in children's beliefs about ability improvement. *Journal of Applied Developmental Psychology*, 21, 379–402.

Gagné, F. (1999). Nature or nurture? A re-examination of Sloboda and Howe's (1991) interview study on talent development in music. *Psychology of Music*, 27, 38–51.

Gagné, F., Blanchard, D., & Bégin, J. (2001). Beliefs about the heritability of abilities in education, music, and sports. In N. Colangelo & S. G. Assouline (eds), *Talent development IV: Proceedings from the 1998 Henry B. and Jocelyn Wallace National Research Symposium on Talent Development* (pp. 155–178). Scottsdale, AZ: Great Potential Press.

Greenberg, M. (1970). Musical achievement and self-concept. *Journal of Research in Music Education*, 18, 57–64.

Guay, F., Marsh, H. H., & Boivin, M. (2003). Academic self-concept and academic achievement: Developmental perspectives on their causal ordering. *Journal of Educational Psychology*, 95, 124–136.

Hallam, S. (1998). The predictors of achievement and dropout in instrumental tuition. *Psychology of Music*, 26, 116–132.

Hallam, S. & Prince, V. (2003). Conceptions of music ability. *Research Studies in Music Education*, 20, 2–22.

Harackiewicz, J. M., Barron, K. E., Pintrich, P. R., Elliot, A. J., & Thrash, T. M. (2002). Revision of achievement goal theory: Necessary and illuminating. *Journal of Educational Psychology*, 94, 638–645.

Harter, S. (1983). Developmental perspectives on the self-system. In P. H. Mussen (series ed.) & E. M. Hetherington (vol. ed.), *Handbook of child psychology*: Vol. 4. *Socialization, personality, and social development* (4th edn) (pp. 275–385). New York: Wiley.

Hedden, S. K. (1982). Prediction of music achievement in the elementary school. *Journal of Research in Music Education*, 30, 61–68.

Heyman, G. D. & Gelman, S. A. (2000). Beliefs about the origins of human psychological traits. *Developmental Psychology*, 36, 663–678.

Kinlaw, C. R. & Kurtz-Costes, B. (2003). The development of children's beliefs about intelligence. *Developmental Review*, 23, 125–161.

Klinedinst, R. E. (1991). Predicting performance achievement and retention of fifth-grade instrumental students. *Journal of Research in Music Education*, 39, 225–238.

Lamont, A., Hargreaves, D. J., Marshall, N. A., & Tarrant, M. (2003). Young people's music in and out of school. *British Journal of Music Education*, 20, 229–241.

Marsh, H. W. (1984). Relationships among dimensions of self-attribution, dimensions of self-concept, and academic achievement. *Journal of Educational Psychology*, 76, 1291–1308.

Marsh, H. W. (1989). Age and sex effects in multiple dimensions of self-concept: Preadolescence to early adulthood. *Journal of Educational Psychology*, 81, 417–430.

Marsh, H. W. (1990). A multidimensional, hierarchical model of self-concept: Theoretical and empirical justification. *Educational Psychology Review*, 2, 77–172.

Marsh, H. W., Byrne, B. M., & Shavelson, R. (1988). A multifaceted academic self-concept: Its hierarchical structure and its relation to academic achievement. *Journal of Educational Psychology*, 80, 366–380.

Marsh, H. W., Cairns, L., Relich, J., Barnes, J., & Debus, R. (1984). The relationship between dimensions of self-attribution and dimensions of self-concept. *Journal of Educational Psychology*, 76, 3–32.

Marsh, H. W., Craven, R. G., & Debus, R. (1991). Self-concepts of young children 5 to 8 years of age: Measurement and multidimensional structure. *Journal of Educational Psychology*, 83, 377–392.

Marsh, H. W., Craven, R. G., & Debus, R. (1998). Structure, stability, and development of young children's self-concepts: A multi-cohort-multi-occasion study. *Child Development*, 69, 1030–1053.

Marsh, H. W., Craven, R. G., & Debus, R. (1999). Separation of competency and affect components of multiple dimensions of academic self-concept: A developmental perspective. *Merrill-Palmer Quarterly*, 45, 567–601.

McCormick, J. & McPherson, G. E. (2003). The role of self-efficacy in a musical performance examination: An exploratory structural equation analysis. *Psychology of Music*, 31, 37–51.

McPherson, G. E. (2000/2001). Commitment and practice: Key ingredients for achievement during the early stages of learning a musical instrument. *Bulletin of the Council for Research in Music Education*, 147, 122–127.

McPherson, G. E. & McCormick, J. (1999). Motivational and self-regulated learning components of musical practice. *Bulletin of the Council for Research in Music Education*, 141, 98–102.

McPherson, G. E. & McCormick, J. (2000). The contribution of motivational factors to instrumental performance in a music examination. *Research Studies in Music Education*, 15, 31–39.

McPherson, G. E. & McCormick, J. (in press). Self-efficacy and performing music. *Psychology of Music*.

Midgley, C., Kaplan, A., & Middleton, M. (2001). Performance-approach goals: Good for what, for whom, under what circumstances, and at what cost? *Journal of Educational Psychology*, 93, 77–86.

Miyamoto, K. (1997). Japanese high school students' motivation in band as it relates to the gender of the band director and the student. *Dissertation Abstracts International*, 58, 2127A. (UMI No. 9738933)

Mota, G. (1999). Young children's motivation in the context of classroom music: An exploratory study about the role of music content and teaching style. *Bulletin of the Council for Research in Music Education*, 141, 119–123.

Nicholls, J. G. (1978). The development of the concepts of effort and ability, perception of academic attainment, and the understanding that difficult tasks require more ability. *Child Development*, 49, 800–814.

Nicholls, J. G. (1984). Achievement motivation: Conceptions of ability, subjective experience, task choice, and performance. *Psychological Review*, 91, 328–346.

O'Neill, S. A. (1996). *Factors influencing children's motivation and achievement during the first year of instrumental music tuition.* Unpublished doctoral thesis, University of Keele, England.

O'Neill, S. A. (1999a). Flow theory and the development of musical performance skills. *Bulletin of the Council for Research in Music Education*, 141, 129–134.

O'Neill, S. A. (1999b). The role of motivation in the practice and achievement of young musicians. In S. W. Yi (ed.), *Music, mind and science* (pp. 420–433). Seoul: Seoul National University Press.

O'Sullivan, J. T. (1997). Effort, interest, and recall: Beliefs and behaviours of preschoolers. *Journal of Experimental Child Psychology*, 65, 43–67.

Pintrich, P. R. & De Groot, E. V. (1990). Motivational and self-regulated learning components of classroom academic performance. *Journal of Educational Psychology*, 82, 33–40.

Pintrich, P. R. & Schunk, D. H. (2002). *Motivation in education: Theory, research, and applications* (2nd edn). Upper Saddle River, NJ: Merrill.

Pokay, P. & Blumenfeld, P. C. (1990). Predicting achievement early and late in the semester: The role of motivation and use of learning strategies. *Journal of Educational Psychology*, 82, 41–50.

Pomerantz, E. M. & Ruble, D. N. (1997). Distinguishing multiple dimensions of conceptions of ability: Implication for self-evaluation. *Child Development*, 68, 1165–1180.

Pomerantz, E. M. & Saxon, J. L. (2001). Conceptions of ability as stable and self-evaluative processes: A longitudinal examination. *Child Development*, 72, 152–173.

Räty, H., Kasanen, K., & Snellman, L. (2002). What makes one able? The formation of pupils' conceptions of academic ability. *International Journal of Early Years Education*, 10, 121–135.

Renninger, K. A., Hidi, S., & Krapp, A. (eds). (1992). *The role of interest in learning and development.* Hillsdale, NJ: Lawrence Erlbaum Associates.

Renwick, J. M. & McPherson, G. E. (2002). Interest and choice: Student-selected repertoire and its effect on practising behaviour. *British Journal of Music Education*, 19, 173–188.

Renwick, J. M. & McPherson, G. E. (2003, September). *Case studies of the practising behaviour of music students with differing reasons for striving.* Paper presented at the fifth triennial conference of the European Society for the Cognitive Science of Music, Hanover, Germany.

Renwick, J. M. & McPherson, G. E. (2006). *Age-related changes in the young musicians' beliefs about their autonomy, competence and values.* Manuscript in preparation.

Ritcher, G. K. (1990). The relationship between children's understanding of musical ability and their motivation, perceived ability, and achievement in general music class. *Dissertation Abstracts International*, 50, 2419A. (UMI No. 8924928)

Rohrer, T. P. (1993). A study of students from competitive and noncompetitive Florida high school bands using an adaptation of the Academic Motivation Scale and the Sport Competition Anxiety Test. *Dissertation Abstracts International*, 54, 857A. (UMI No. 9320341)

Ryan, R. M. & Deci, E. L. (2000). Self-determination theory and the facilitation of intrinsic motivation, social development, and well-being. *American Psychologist*, 55, 68–78.

Sandene, B. A. (1998). An investigation of variables related to student motivation in instrumental music. *Dissertation Abstracts International*, 58, 3870A. (UMI No. 9811178)

Schmitt, M. (1979). Development and validation of a measure of self-esteem of music ability. *Dissertation Abstracts International*, 40, 5357A–5358A. (UMI No. 8009164)

Shavelson, R. J. & Bolus, R. (1982). Self concept: The interplay of theory and methods. *Journal of Educational Psychology*, 74, 3–17.

Skinner, E. (1990). Age differences in the dimensions of perceived control during middle childhood: Implications for developmental conceptualizations and research. *Child Development*, 61, 1882–1890.

Sloboda, J. A., & Davidson, J. W. (1996). The young performing musician. In I. Deliège & J. A. Sloboda (eds), *Musical beginnings: Origins and development of musical competence* (pp. 171–190). Oxford: Oxford University Press.

Sloboda, J. A., Davidson, J. W., & Howe, M. J. A. (1994). Is everyone musical? *The Psychologist*, 7, 349–354.

Smiley, P. A. & Dweck, C. S. (1994). Individual differences in achievement goals among young children. *Child Development*, 65, 1723–1743.

Song, I. & Hattie, J. (1984). Home environment, self-concept, and academic achievement: A causal modeling approach. *Journal of Educational Psychology*, 76, 1269–1281.

Stipek, D. J. (1993). *Motivation to learn: From theory to practice*. Needham Heights, MA: Allyn and Bacon.

Stipek, D. J. & Daniels, D. H. (1988). Declining perceptions of competence: A consequence of changes in the child or in the educational environment. *Journal of Educational Psychology*, 80, 352–356.

Stipek, D. L. & Mac Iver, D. (1989). Developmental change in children's assessment of intellectual competence. *Child Development*, 60, 521–538.

Stipek, D. J. & Tannatt, L. M. (1984). Children's judgments of their own and their peers' academic competence. *Journal of Educational Psychology*, 76, 75–84.

Svengalis, J. (1978). Music attitude and the preadolescent male. *Dissertation Abstracts International*, 39, 4800A. (UMI No. 7902953)

Vispoel, W. P. (1993). The development and validation of the Arts Self-Perception Inventory for Adolescents. *Educational and Psychological Measurement*, 53, 1023–1033.

Weiner, B. (1979). A theory of motivation for some classroom experiences. *Journal of Educational Psychology*, 71, 3–25.

Weiner, B. (1985). An attributional theory perspective of achievement motivation and emotion. *Psychological Review*, 92, 548–573.

Wentzel, K. R. & Wigfield, A. (1998). Academic and social motivational influences on students' academic performance. *Educational Psychology Review*, 10, 155–175.

Wigfield, A. & Eccles, J. S. (1992). The development of achievement task values: A theoretical analysis. *Developmental Review*, 12, 265–310.

Wigfield, A. & Eccles, J. S. (2000). Expectancy–value theory of achievement motivation. *Contemporary Educational Psychology*, 25, 68–81.

Wigfield, A. & Eccles, J. S. (eds). (2002a). *Development of achievement motivation*. San Diego, CA: Academic Press.

Wigfield, A. & Eccles, J. S. (2002b). The development of competence beliefs, expectancies for success, and achievement values from childhood through adolescence. In A. Wigfield & J. S. Eccles (eds), *Development of achievement motivation* (pp. 91–120). San Diego, CA: Academic Press.

Wigfield, A. & Karpathian, M. (1991). Who am I and what can I do? Children's self-concepts and motivation in achievement situations. *Educational Psychologist*, 26, 233–261.

Wigfield, A., Eccles, J. S., Yoon, K. S., Harold, R. D., Arbreton, A. J. A., Freedman-Doan, C., & Blumenfeld, P. C. (1997). Changes in children's competence beliefs and subjective task values across the elementary school years: A 3-year study. *Journal of Educational Psychology*, 89, 451–469.

Wigfield, A., O'Neill, S. A., & Eccles, J. S. (1999, April). *Children's achievement values in different domains: Developmental and cultural differences*. Paper presented at the biennial meeting of the Society for Research in Child Development, Albuquerque, NM.

Wylie, R. C. (1989). *Measures of self-concept*. Lincoln, NE: University of Nebraska Press.

Yoon, K. S. (1997, April). *Exploring children's motivation for instrumental music*. Paper presented at the biennial meeting of the Society for Research in Child Development, Washington, DC.

Yussen, S. R. & Kane, P. T. (1985). Children's concept of intelligence. In S. R. Yussen (ed.), *The growth of reflection in children* (pp. 207–241). New York: Academic Press.

CHAPTER 12

GIFTEDNESS AND TALENT

GARY E. MCPHERSON AND AARON WILLIAMON

One of the most contentious debates in psychology, education, biology, and other related disciplines centres on the source of exceptional ability. To what extent can the remarkable achievements of eminent musicians, intellectuals, visual artists, writers, and so on be explained through 'nature' (innate aptitudes) or 'nurture' (the environment)? How can these achievements, regardless of their source, be identified and fostered? Certainly, the multitude of complex issues surrounding this debate have kept scholars busy for decades, and it is probably true that, in many ways, researchers are no closer to agreement than they were 20 or 30 years ago. The only possible exception to this is the general recognition that traditional views of intelligence, especially those based exclusively on a single measure such as an IQ score, are no longer seen as valid nor reliable forms of explaining the multifarious abilities evident throughout childhood and beyond (Hettinger & Carr, 2003).

In this chapter, we address fundamental issues surrounding the nature/nurture debate in music and, in doing so, scrutinize much of the folklore that typically accompanies remarkable musical abilities. Specifically, we outline a broad framework that distinguishes between 'giftedness' and 'talent' and discuss, in turn, six core components of this framework:

- giftedness
- the developmental process
- intrapersonal factors
- environmental catalysts
- chance
- talent.

We then explore the scope and potential for identifying musically gifted children. Throughout, we draw on the early experiences of Wolfgang Amadeus Mozart, commonly evoked as the paradigmatic example of childhood accomplishment, to elucidate these components.

Defining giftedness and talent

The most immediate problem one encounters when sifting through the literature on giftedness and talent is the range of competing definitions used in various sectors; moreover, as these definitions are often theoretical in nature, they can be troublesome to implement in practice (Gallagher, 1993; Gross, 1994). Frequently, terms used in one field are employed differently in another, with the added complication that some researchers use two or three terms interchangeably. This lack of standardization and agreement can consequently make it even more difficult to compare findings from one discipline with those of another (see also Gagné, 2004a).

An additional problem to the lack of standardization of terms is that conceptions of giftedness and talent are inevitably culture-specific. Shin'ichi Suzuki's (1898–1998) Talent Education method for training young violinists and pianists, for instance, is based on the principle that all children can develop requisite musical skills provided they are exposed to the 'right' education (Suzuki, 1983; see also Howe, 1999). However, this view is very much based on Japanese societal values, in which hard work is often respected above achievement.

For the purposes of this chapter, we define these terms according to their use in the field of education, as adopted by many educational systems around the world.[1] The most prevalent view is based on the work of Françoys Gagné (1985, 1993, 2000, 2003, 2004b), who distinguishes between the separate dimensions of *giftedness* and *talent*. This view takes a decidedly 'bottom up' approach to conceptualizing exceptional skills, in that it seeks to explain and identify potential and ability and then to offer direct implications for the education and training of young people. An alternative—yet equally fruitful—approach has emerged within the context of psychological research into expert performance and behaviour (for reviews, see Ericsson & Lehmann, 1996; Ericsson, 1996; Howe *et al.*, 1998; Williamon & Valentine, 2000, 2002). Here, a more 'top down' approach has been adopted, in that much effort has been directed towards studying the performance of established experts, the rationale being that such investigations can shed light on fundamental psychological mechanisms underpinning high-level performance and can eventually be used to inform the training of novices. The former, bottom up conception fits more organically with the main purpose of this chapter, which is to explain how a child, born with a range of innate gifts for music, may then develop into a talented musician. Nevertheless, we assert that only through a combination of these approaches can the most comprehensive explanation of exceptional abilities be achieved.

At the heart of Gagné's (2003) model (see Figure 12.1) is the distinction between domains of ability (gifts) and fields of performance (talent). Gagné uses the term 'giftedness' to describe individuals who are endowed with natural *potential to achieve* that is distinctly above average for their age group in one or more aptitude domains. In this conception, aptitudes are natural abilities that have a genetic origin and that appear and develop more-or-less spontaneously in every individual. The mix of these aptitudes explains the major proportion of differences between individuals when the surrounding environment and practice are roughly comparable. However, aptitudes do not develop purely by maturation alone; environmental stimulation through practice and learning is also essential.

---

[1] While the view we outline is consistent with many educational systems, we recognize also that it is decidedly different from definitions adopted by the Office of Standards in Education in the United Kingdom where 'gifted' refers to 'those with high ability or potential in the academic subjects' and 'talented' to 'those with high ability or potential in the expressive or creative arts or sports' (*Providing for gifted and talented pupils: An evaluation of excellence in cities and other grant-funded programs*, 2001, p. 2). In our view, these definitions do not adequately explain the difference between human potential and achievement.

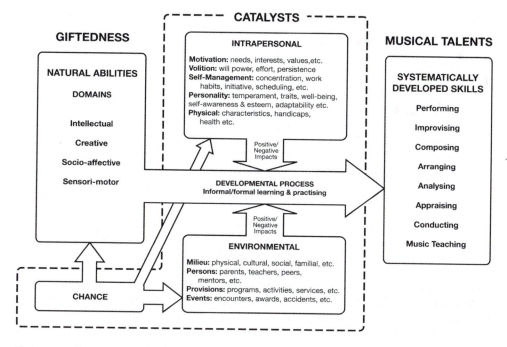

Figure 12.1 Differentiated Model of Giftedness and Talent in Music. Adapted from Gagné, F. (2003). Transforming gifts into talents: The DMGT as a developmental theory. In N. Colangelo & G. A. Davis (eds), *Handbook of gifted education* (pp. 60–74) (3rd edn). Boston, MA: Allyn and Bacon.

'Talented' can be used to describe someone who demonstrates *superior performance* (or *superior skills*) as a result of some type of systematic training in a specific field. In terms of music, it can refer to a range of competencies that encompass the defined talents shown in Figure 12.1 (i.e., performing, improvising, composing, arranging, analysis, appraising, conducting, and teaching). For example, a child's physical and mental dexterity, musicality, motor memory, and auditory memory are all evident from the first few weeks of formal training but need to be further refined and extended to a high level in order for the child to be considered a talented performer.

The most extreme cases of exceptionally talented childhood musicians—*prodigies*—develop their skills to an extraordinary high level very early, and usually before adolescence (Morelock & Feldman, 2000). Probably the most famous childhood musical prodigy is Wolfgang Amadeus Mozart, who performed at a very young age throughout Europe. Similarly, the composers J. S. Bach, Mendelssohn, and Beethoven, along with Mozart, all took great delight during their childhood in developing their capacity to improvise on the keyboard. Most importantly, superior talents in particular fields, such as performing or creating music, emerge when a child's natural abilities are mediated, not only through the support of intrapersonal and environmental catalysts, but also through systematic learning and extensive practice (Gagné, 1993, 2000).

Giftedness

Gagné (1993, 2003) identifies four basic domains of natural gifts (or high aptitudes), each involving their own distinctly different types of innate abilities:

- *Intellectual:* potentials required for learning to read, speak, and understand concepts; dimensions include the potential for fluid reasoning, being able to think abstractly, memory, a sense of observation, and metacognition.

- *Creative:* potentials related to being able to think divergently when solving problems and to produce work that is representative of such thinking; dimensions include aspects such as inventiveness, imagination, originality, and retrieval fluency.

- *Socio-affective:* social and affective abilities used when communicating with others; dimensions include perceptiveness, tact, leadership, and persuasion.

- *Sensori-motor:* potentials that influence sensory (visual, auditory, sense of smell and touch) and motor (strength, endurance, reflexes, co-ordination) development that may then give children an advantage with their learning.

From the above, we can note that the individual blending of these four basic 'natural' abilities are expected to influence the types of musical talents that will eventually evolve. In the absence of published data to elucidate this point, we tentatively draw on two relatively straightforward examples. First, creativity may not be the *key* component of some particular talents in music—such as performance within the Western art music tradition—yet it is an essential ingredient of some of the more *overtly* creative sides of the discipline, including improvising and composing (Winner & Martino, 1993, 2000). Likewise, motor aptitudes—such as physical abilities that allow for speed, endurance, strength, flexibility, and dexterity—are of vital importance in many forms of musical performance, but will be far less important for those who compose or are engaged in the analysis or appraisal of music. One of the great challenges in the discipline is for researchers to sort through this maze and to clarify the particular blend of aptitudes required for each form of music-related activity (this is discussed further in 'Identifying the musically gifted' below).

There seems to be a growing consensus of some underlying 'trait' of musical potential, perhaps related to Gagné's 'sensory' aptitude, which forms an integral component of success in all eight musical talents shown in Figure 12.1. However, researchers use different frameworks to define this potential. Gardner (1983) refers to a sensitivity to the physical and emotional aspects of sound, while Gordon (1989) talks of the ability to audiate (i.e., comprehend sound inwardly), and Mainwaring (1941, 1947, 1951a,b) places an emphasis on the ability to 'think in sound'. These earlier conceptions have been extended more recently by Brodsky (2004), who draws on findings by Papoušek (1996) to speculate about the extent to which the processing of complex musical structures might be an innate predisposition in infants that tends to 'fade away' in situations when the developing child is 'not sufficiently engaged in auditory and musical interchanges' (Brodsky, 2004, p. 87).

Although music teachers will be able to gauge a child's motor abilities and physical co-ordination within the first weeks of learning an instrument, evidence from the gifted and talented literature (Winner & Martino, 2000) suggests that a possible core ability of highly musically gifted children is their 'sensitivity to the structure of music—tonality, key, harmony, and rhythm, and the ability to hear the expressive properties of music' (p. 102). This sensitivity to structure allows gifted children to remember, play back, transpose, improvise, and create music—ways of enjoying and studying music that were evident during childhood for many of the great composers and performers throughout history. Another aspect is that musical giftedness can reveal itself as early as 1 or 2 years of age, which is earlier than practically any other domain of skill (Winner & Martino, 2000). Mozart, for example, had such delicate ears that he would become physically ill when exposed to loud sounds. In similar extreme cases of extraordinarily gifted prodigies, this intense interest in musical and environmental sounds is also accompanied by an even more sophisticated sense of the 'goodness' of tone and timbre, as evident in examples of famous musicians such as Rubinstein and Menuhin who as young children broke their toy violins because the tone was so poor (Winner & Martino, 2000).

A more universal gift that typifies highly gifted musical children, however, is their ability to sing back heard songs earlier than ordinary children, which can occur even before they learn to talk (Winner & Martino, 2000). While ordinary children start imitating songs at about 2 years (or a little after), singing whole songs by age 4 and reproducing songs accurately by 5, the most musically gifted are able to match pitches accurately by their second year and do this often after just one listening. Associated with this sensitivity to sound is the capacity for musically gifted children to represent musical relations in multiple ways (see also Chapter 4) and to respond positively to the emotional aspects of music (Persson, 1996; Persson et al., 1996). Although a young musician may not have sufficient training to follow every detail of musical structure, he or she 'can hear and respond to the emotional message of the music' (Winner & Martino, 2000, p. 105). In these ways, traditional measures of assessing musical aptitude that involve examples of telling whether two successive tonal or rhythm patterns are the same or different may be missing the point; a sharp ear for distinguishing differences in pitch and rhythm 'may be no more predictive of musicality than possessing a good eyesight is predictive of good reading ability' (Winner & Martino, 2000, p. 105; see also Davies, 1978). The two most important core ingredients of musical giftedness, therefore, seem to involve sensitivity to structural and expressive (in contrast to technical) properties of music.

Csikszentmihalyi (1998) extends this conception by asserting that 'children whose neurological makeup makes them particularly sensitive to sounds will be motivated to pay attention to aural stimulation, be self-confident in listening and singing, and likely to seek out training in music' (p. 411), while Brodsky (2003) proposes that innate potential for processing music develops as children become more aware of sound and start to identify and associate with music according to their own 'auditory style'. For Brodsky, this predisposition involves a fusion between a *responsiveness* and *preference* for music that link with the child's *awareness* of music. In our conception, these concepts of *responsiveness* and *preference* would be associated with motivation and interest, and therefore fall among intrapersonal catalysts.

As a side issue, it is important to note that the jury is still out on whether perfect (or absolute) pitch might be related to the innate capacities as described in Gagné's model. On the one hand, Trehub and Hodges (see Chapters 2 and 3) cite newly emerging evidence that this highly specialized skill of identifying and naming individual pitches involves a genetic component that only becomes evident as a result of early training between the critical ages of 4 and 6. On the other hand, absolute pitch would not seem to enhance children's sensitivity to the structural and expressive dimensions of sound as described above. In any case, the number of exceptionally talented musicians who do not possess absolute pitch suggests that this ability is not a prerequisite for achieving musical excellence, or a necessary trait that can be used to identify musically gifted children.

Developmental processes

As can be inferred from the direction of arrows in Figure 12.1, natural abilities act as the 'raw material' for the emergence of talents (Gagné, 2003), so no amount of natural aptitude will guarantee success without opportunities for intense, systematic learning and practice. In music, this is convincingly shown by a great deal of evidence for the close connection between accumulated practice and overall achievement for young and older musicians (Ericsson *et al.*, 1993; Sloboda & Davidson, 1996; Sloboda *et al.*, 1996; O'Neill, 1997). At its heart, this line of research suggests 'practice is a direct cause of achievement level rather than merely a correlate of it' (Howe *et al.*, 1998, p. 405).

Indeed, there is growing empirical support for the so-called '10-year rule', which states that a *minimum* of 10 years of dedicated practice are required to become an expert in any field—from music, drama and dance, to sport and athletics, to business and other cognitive domains (Ericsson *et al.*, 1993; Winner, 1996a,b). In the case of music, the path to eminence can actually be much longer, with requisite skills requiring constant development and maintenance (Krampe & Ericsson, 1996; Krampe, 1997). Chaffin and Lemieux (2004) expound on this point further:

> While the idea that practice is integral to success is not likely to surprise anyone, the amount of training involved is striking. It is estimated that more than 10 000 hours of practice is required before a performer is ready to begin a professional career . . . The young pianists in a study by Sosniak (1985) started their careers as concert soloists after an average of 17 years of training. For composers, the period of preparation is even longer: 20 years from first exposure to music to first notable composition for the 76 major composers whose careers were reviewed by Hayes (1981). After a lifetime of practice, the experienced pianists in Krampe's (1997) study had put in 60 000 hours of practice. (pp. 20–21)

High achievement, however, is not determined by quantity of practice alone, just as it is clear that two individuals who practice for the same amount of time will not produce exactly the same performances. Rather, the acquisition of expert-level skill is cultivated through engagement in the highest *quality* of practice (Ericsson *et al.*, 1993; Williamon & Valentine, 2000; Williamon *et al.*, 2003). Recent reviews by Chaffin and Lemieux (2004), Jørgensen (2004), and Davidson and King (2004) offer a number of suggestions for the content and form that such practice may take.

The development of *prodigious* talent in music, therefore, involves a great deal of focused, concentrated and well-directed effort from a very young age. Famous childhood performers and composers are not simply born to be musicians but work hard over many years to develop their skills to a high level. In the conception provided here, development in music consists of 'transforming specific natural abilities into the skills that define competence or expertise' in the range of musical talents shown in Figure 12.1 (Gagné, 2000).

As an example, there are many historical indications that Mozart's musical practice from a very early age was goal-oriented, structured, and effortful as described in the literature on *deliberate practice* (e.g., Ericsson, 1996). By the age of 6, Mozart was devoting large chunks of his day to practising pieces and receiving a considerable amount of daily input from his father, who was himself an eminent musician and teacher. Not only did the young Mozart practise repertoire but he also improvised for hours on end and put these thoughts on paper in the form of compositions. His remarkable learning curve meant that he was able to master all the musical clefs very early in his training, as well as sight-read any type of score on the keyboard. His learning was therefore not focused merely on performing other composers' music, but continually varying and building on what had been previously achieved. Very early in his music education, he was gaining practice in transferring what he had learned in one context to another (see Deutsch, 1966). These descriptions show that Mozart was motivated to a level akin to passion and that his extraordinary level of motivation was integrally related to his astonishing achievement.

A major implication of the discussion thus far is that a child may be gifted without displaying any specific 'talent' (but not the reverse). This is because the child may possess the potential for success but may not be able to act on it due to a number of factors such as a lack of interest.

Intrapersonal catalysts

Intrapersonal catalysts comprise at least five types of psychological and physical factors, each partially influenced by genetic endowment (Gagné, 2000). First, *motivation* is an integral part of the learning process that assists children to acquire the range of skills needed to have any chance of reaching their full potential as a musician (O'Neill & McPherson, 2002; see also Chapter 11, this volume). One line of research—achievement motivation—demonstrates how talented children seek moderate challenges and risks, in that they are attracted to tasks that are neither too hard nor too easy. These types of children are 'strivers' in that they constantly seek to improve themselves and become better in those tasks that they choose to study (Sternberg, 2000). Another kind of research has to do with children's beliefs in their own personal competence about whether or not they can do a task in a particular situation. Researchers call this 'self-efficacy' (Bandura, 1997, see also McCormick & McPherson, 2003; McPherson & McCormick, 2006). A key point, however, is that motivation affects both children's level of performance while they are undertaking a task and also the amount of time they will spend on that task (Lens & Rand, 2000). This means that the level of a child's motivation affects both the quantity and quality of their engagement with music.

Other psychological constructs, among many that could be cited, include *volition*, *self-management*, and *personality*. *Volition* comprises aspects related to a child's willingness to engage in an activity and the will-power and types of control processes that enable them to concentrate, persist, and direct their efforts in the face of personal and environmental distractions, obstacles, boredom, and failure (Corno, 1993; Gagné, 2000).

Many gifted children are highly capable in a number of areas and commit themselves to a range of activities, each of which requires vast amounts of time and energy for continuing success. This sometimes produces high levels of stress and emotional instability (Coleman & Cross, 2000). However, multitalented adolescents tend also to be good at *self-managing* their learning by focusing their efforts on a specific task for hours or even days on end, monitoring and controlling their own learning, sustaining their effort (even when tired), and efficiently planning what they need to do in order to master a new skill (Gagné *et al.*, 1996; Gagné, 1999, 2000).

Some exceptionally gifted children also display *personalities* that are different from other children, such as over-excitabilities in psychomotor, intellectual, sensual, imaginational, and emotional areas of their development. These over-excitabilities, which researchers (Coleman & Cross, 2000) define as 'expanded awareness, intensified emotions, and increased levels of intellectual and/or physical activity' (p. 204), manifest themselves in many different ways. In music, they explain why some children develop an almost fanatical love of a particular genre or composer, an intense emotional commitment to one or more forms of music, or a deep love for the sound of a particular instrument. Among many examples of the phenomena is the celebrated cellist Jacqueline du Pré, who started her musical education at the age of 4 after hearing the cello performed on the radio and then demanding that her mother arrange lessons (Wilson, 1998). Unfortunately, however, these children's highly developed capacities in music may not always match other aspects of their development, with the complication that they may experience difficulties physically, socially, or emotionally. In addition, the particular blending of the above psychological dimensions results in some gifted children placing unreasonably high expectations on themselves, which if not tempered can result in stress, burn-out, and an unhealthy self-criticism (Coleman & Cross, 2000).

Each of the above characteristics was evident in Mozart, who was so passionate about his learning that it was 'of little moment to him what he was given to learn; he simply wanted to learn' (cited in Solomon, 1995, p. 39). He was also single-minded, eager, and capable of intense concentration. 'Whatever he was given to learn occupied him so completely that he put all else, even music, on one side; e.g., when he was doing sums, the tables, chairs, walls, even the floor was covered with chalked figures' (Solomon, 1995, p. 39). By the age of 3 when his 7-year-old sister began receiving keyboard lessons from their father, Mozart was drawn to music, 'perhaps by a desire to emulate his sister and win his share of their father's attention', and spent 'endless hours at the keyboard, particularly delighting in "picking out thirds and sounding them"' (Solomon, 1995, p. 35). Mozart's efforts were so focused and concentrated that soon after he began learning he could master simple musical repertoire in a surprisingly short amount of time (Solomon, 1995). These extraordinary behaviours are not seen to the same degree in the vast majority of musically gifted children, and we need to be careful, therefore, that any conception of giftedness and talent values the uniqueness of each individual learner.

Finally, *physical* characteristics, such as body build and hand span, will affect not only the type of instrument that children may be given to learn but also the repertoire they are exposed to early in their development.

Environmental catalysts

It is impossible to survey the full range of environmental forces that come into play in the development of a gifted child musician. However, it is possible to survey some of the most important environmental catalysts, given available research that asserts the importance of parents and siblings, the influence of teachers, and the types of events in children's lives that can have a profound impact on their subsequent development.

Perhaps the most important environmental influence on children is the family, and particularly their parents. In general, researchers have found that parents of persistent learners tend to provide support and encouragement for their child during the early stages of musical development and that this tapers off as the child becomes more self-regulated with his or her practice (Sloboda & Howe, 1991). In contrast, children who give up playing their instrument tend to come from homes where there is little parental involvement during the early stages of learning and where there are greater amounts of parental pressure to practice during the teenage years, when it is obvious that motivation is waning and that the parent should make a 'last effort' to keep the child learning music.

These findings are consistent with Sosniak's (1985) work with highly talented pianists, in that exceptionally talented children typically have at least one parent or relative who cared deeply about their musical development, as confirmed by violinist Isaac Stern:

> There *has* to be someone pushing, a parent or a teacher. Every one of the kids I've guided has someone like that in their lives, pushing them, sometimes gently, sometimes horribly, sometimes, unfortunately, to the point of driving the child away from music. It's the quality of parental pushing that helps determine the eventual outcome of the prodigy.
>
> Winn (1979, p. 40)

Extending the above conception is work by Yun Dai and Schader (2001), which stresses the importance of cultural values and beliefs about learning. They report on a study of children who were taking lessons at eminent conservatory music programmes as an extension of their normal schooling. Their findings show that parents of these high-level learners tended to emphasize intrinsic rather than extrinsic rewards for their children's learning, by stressing the appreciation and aesthetic qualities, and enrichment of life as the major reasons for wanting their child to learn music. This result was consistent for both children who were beginning their training and also for those who had been studying for more than 10 years. The explanation they provide is that the parents who expressed an intrinsic orientation for their children's learning tended to nurture and foster internal motivations for them, in contrast to parents who expressed a strong extrinsic orientation and who pushed their children to a loss of effort and possible conflict. The authors of this study suggest that a social environment that reduces anxiety, external pressure, and encourages personal growth and task commitment is essential for sustained, long-term involvement (see also Sloboda, 1993; Gottfried *et al.*, 1994; Kemp, 1996; Chapter 17, this volume). Interestingly, many of the parents of the successful learners did not say they wanted their children to learn merely for musical reasons. Non-musical benefits relating to the child's holistic development (e.g., self-discipline, diligence, academic achievement) were of utmost concern. In sum, a family's life-style is important to a child's development, but there is nonetheless no ideal family, in that gifted children can spring from many and varied backgrounds (Freeman, 2000).

Research also shows that musicians who continue playing are able to differentiate between the 'personal' and 'professional' qualities of their teachers and that personal warmth is a vital characteristic of a teacher during the initial stages of development. Better students remember their first teacher 'not so much for their technical adeptness as for the fact that they made lessons fun. They communicated both their love for music and their liking for their pupil' (Sloboda & Howe, 1991, p. 110). Leopold Mozart is perhaps one of the best examples of a teacher who could inspire and nurture talent. He 'was a supreme teacher who understood how to inspire gifted children to great effort and achievement, instilling a drive for excellence and awaking in them a sense of unlimited devotion to his person and a desire to obtain his approval above all else' (Solomon, 1995, pp. 39–40). At the time, Leopold was one of the finest performers and composers in Europe and, by the time Wolfgang was born, had already published a method for teaching the violin (*Versuch einer grundlichen Violinschule*), which had brought him much acclaim (Turner, 1965). Lehmann *et al.* (2002), in a biographical study of Wolfgang and 21 lesser-known composers at the time, effectively demonstrate that it was predominantly the quality of young Wolfgang's educational opportunities that distinguished him from the others and that, among the others, it was the quality of their early music instruction that correlated with their status as a musician.

Leopold Mozart was also aware of the need to showcase his son's remarkable achievements as an added incentive to fostering his development, and by the age of 7½, Wolfgang had travelled thousands of miles across Europe to perform in almost 90 cities (Solomon, 1995). Such extensive travelling and exposure to influential patrons and contemporary trends in music making enriched Wolfgang's musical development in profoundly important ways, also leaving indelible impressions on those who were witness to his abilities. At a brief stay at a Franciscan church in Ybbs, the 6-year-old Mozart played the organ 'so well that the Franciscans . . . were almost struck dead with amazement' (Anderson, 1985, p. 6). Certainly, one can begin to imagine how the inevitable praise to follow such a performance must have left its mark on the young musician.

The above are brief examples of how parents and teachers impact on a gifted child's musical development. In contemporary society, enrichment programmes such as music camps, community ensembles, or selective schools help to accelerate the development of a talent or talents. These significant events in a child's life leave a lasting impression on subsequent vocational decisions to engage in a particular activity and are, therefore, crucial for sustaining involvement.

Chance

Chance can act positively on intrapersonal and environmental catalysts in as much as it may bring good fortune, particularly if a child is constantly engaged in exploring the environment or is simply in the 'right place at the right time'. The influence of this factor should not be underestimated, and we might wonder whether any of the great composers or performers throughout history would have made it to the top of their fields without at least some breaks during their early, developmental years.

The great jazz trumpeter Louis Armstrong, for example, worked from about 6 years of age for two emigrant brothers collecting cast-offs for their junk wagon. Normally, they would ring a bell or shout to attract customers, but one day, the brothers asked Louis to blow a simple tin-horn that was used at the time during celebrations. It worked wonders, and in the space of a short period of time, it became a tremendous asset to the business, helping to draw attention to the junk wagon with Louis playing a number of popular tunes on what was essentially a crude instrument. In his own words, Armstrong explains:

> When I would be on the junk wagon . . . I would blow this long tin-horn without the top on it. Just hold my fingers close together and blow. It was a call for old rags, bones, bottles, or anything that the people and kids had to sell. The kids loved the sound of my tin-horn. . . . One day I took the wooden top off the horn, and surprisingly I held up my two fingers close together where the wooden mouthpieces used to be and I could play a tune of some kind. Oh, the kids really enjoyed that. Better than the first time. They used to bring their bottles, Alex would give them a few pennies, and they would stand around the wagon while I would entertain them.

> cited in Bergreen (1997, pp. 55–56)

According to Bergreen (1997), the chance event of being given a tin-horn to attract attention was 'a startling discovery' that made Armstrong realize 'that he was capable of pleasing others, white and black, young and old' (p. 56). This event subsequently sowed the seeds 'to his revolutionizing jazz, and by extension, American music' (p. 56). Had he been born a decade earlier or later (and had not been exposed to all of the elements of jazz brewing in New Orleans at the time), the entire evolution of jazz may have been different, and we may not have even heard of this remarkable musician.

It would be easy to cite numerous other examples of how chance, such as the luck of being born into a particular family, helps to provide the catalyst for subsequent development. Moreover, it is important to note that Mozart's exemplary talent as a composer was at least partly influenced by his birth into the cultural milieu of eighteenth century Europe, at a time when his father could take opportunities to travel and showcase his son's remarkable achievements. The type of training, experience and exposure Leopold gave his son would simply not have been possible had Wolfgang been born decades earlier. The same could be said of many other eminent musicians.

Musical talents

Our adaptation of Gagné's model proposes that there are at least eight distinct types of musical talent: performing, improvising, composing, arranging, analysing, appraising, conducting, and teaching. All are related to professional occupations and areas of the discipline in which musicians can earn a living. Examples would include professional orchestral musicians, jazz improvisers, composers of original music or arrangers who rework existing works for a particular context, professors who teach musical analysis or music critics who write reviews of performances for newspapers, conductors of ensembles, and music teachers.

Part of the reason we define eight distinct talents is our belief that many programmes that cater for musically talented children place too much emphasis on performance. A young violinist who can perform a violin concerto is obviously talented and we must recognize and foster this type of ability. But there are many other forms of talent that go largely unrecognized, such as the child who can sit at the piano and play 'by ear' a variety of popular melodies in any key, or the teenager who can compose a catchy song directly on to a music sequencer without the need to write out the melody using traditional notation. It is here that we are reminded that 'the technical skill of Bob Dylan or John Lennon were rudimentary by classical standards, yet few would deny that these two musicians produced work which has had a profound impact on a whole generation, and whose influence is still being felt' (Hargreaves, 1994, p. 358). The point we wish to stress is that all too often children's ability to perform pieces from notation is taken as the defining skill, while the range of abilities needed to develop musically in a broader sense are often neglected (McPherson, 2005).

To add to this, it could be mentioned that while performance skills often develop early, talents in other areas—particularly composition—are rarely seen before late childhood (Winner & Martino, 1993). Simonton (1988, 1991) shows that the average famous composer begins composing during the late teens and produces unqualified masterpieces before age 30, although Mozart is an obvious exception.

Identifying giftedness and talent

The identification of musical giftedness is essentially a task of trying to predict a child's potential to succeed musically, prior to any formal musical training. However, trying to assess potential prior to formal musical training is no easy matter. Indeed, there are at least three major methodological obstacles that must be overcome in doing so.

First, the measurement of intellectual, creative, socio-affective and sensorimotor gifts is an issue of tremendous debate in and of itself. There are any number of psychometric tests, qualitative methodologies, and experimental procedures that purport to offer insight into these core features of psychological functioning; however, none are completely free of criticism concerning their basic reliability and validity or the operational definitions on which they are based (e.g., see Sternberg & Lubart, 1999, for a critique of psychometric testing in relation to creativity).

Second, beyond perhaps the most obvious examples described above, it is difficult to predict which gifts (or combinations thereof) will lead to which talents. For instance, exactly how creative must one be to excel in composition? To what extent does that level of creativity depend on or interact with other intellectual, socio-affective or sensorimotor aptitudes? Can an abundance of one gift compensate for a slight deficiency of another? Research has begun to explore the relationships between aptitudes of various types (most notably between creativity and intelligence; see Sternberg & O'Hara, 1999, for a review), but much further grassroots research is needed to determine precisely how these interrelate before one can then move on to studying how their subsequent interactions predict specific musical talents.

Third, it is typically the case that, by the time an individual is seen to be talented in a given area, the pervasive influences of the developmental process, intrapersonal and environmental catalysts and chance (as detailed above) may already have begun to mask initial, subtle differences in natural abilities. No doubt, this may be one explanation for why there has, to date, been little success in matching outstanding musical achievement with a clear-cut set of traits (Winner, 1996a; Simonton, 1999, 2001). From this viewpoint, it is not surprising that much research on expert performance (with its focus on the skills of acknowledged experts, who are usually adults) has offered so little support for the widely held belief that talent has a biological basis. An intriguing paradox here is that, *if* there is a strong genetic component to musical giftedness, then those who achieve the highest of standards will be those with the most suitable genetic make-up; therefore, for those most talented at the top of the profession, the variance in genetic material will be substantially decreased such that the remaining individual differences in heredity would be no longer easy to observe (Gagné, 2003).

These three obstacles are not necessarily insurmountable, and we believe that progress in this area is inevitable, but most likely through programmes of longitudinal research that employ a range of quantitative and qualitative methodologies and that concurrently examine giftedness in children *and* expert performance.

As explained earlier, some researchers have argued for a general trait of musical giftedness involving sensitivity to the structural and expressive dimensions of sound, rather than the physical parameters of sound as suggested by the music psychologists Seashore, Bentley, and Gordon (see also, Chapter 5, this volume). Research reviewed by Boyle (1992), however, shows that non-musical factors such as academic achievement, academic intelligence, and socio-economic background will increase the accuracy of prediction (see Rainbow, 1965; Hedden, 1982). Based on Gagné's model, it seems likely that sensorimotor abilities may emerge as the best predictor of musical potential (Gagné, 2003), and according to the model, high aptitudes in this area, though observable in older children and adults, are more easily and directly observable in young children, as environmental influences and systematic learning have exerted their moderating influence only to a limited extent. Nevertheless, a salient and robust battery of tests as such has thus far eluded researchers.

There are probably a multitude of indicators, given the nature and scope of the aptitude domains described here, in addition to the fact that some students (including those from minority or disadvantaged groups) often display their potential in ways that are unique or individual (Richardson, 1990) and that success in music may not be totally dependent on only those aptitudes identified by Gordon (1987, 1989). Moreover, Gordon (1987) himself states that 'There is no one infallible score on any music aptitude test which indicates superior potential for learning music' (p. 56) because it is up to the teacher to make a subjective evaluation of the results from each of the components of the measure. This is yet another reason why 'giftedness' should be viewed more broadly in terms of a profile of aptitudes, which, as a result of intrapersonal and environmental catalysts in addition to learning and training, may lead to the development of specific fields of talent.

Many authorities in the gifted and talented education literature suggest, for school system classifications purposes, that children in the top 10–15% of a given population can be labelled as 'gifted'. Gross (2000) for example, advocates a system whereby the top 15% of any population would fit this category while Gagné (2003) takes a more conservative view by defining the top 10%. In Gagné's conception children can be described as mildly (1:10), moderately (1:100), highly (1:1000), exceptionally (1:10 000), or extremely (1:100 000) gifted. Obviously, examples such as Mozart would occur on the extreme far end of this scale, which reinforces the importance of acknowledging and even celebrating the fact that less distinct and remarkable forms of giftedness are much more common within any given age group.

In contrast to difficulties in assessing giftedness, talent measurement is relatively straight-forward (Gagné, 2003) because soon after beginning music a child can be compared with peers of similar age and approximate training who are engaged in the same activity (Sisk, 1990; Gagné, 1993). Normative assessment in the form of teacher ratings, achievement tests, competitions, and scholarships (though occasionally criticized as subjective) are ways in which talented young musicians have traditionally been identified. According to Gagné (2003), however, the use of the term *talented* should be reserved for the top 10% of children with the emerging talent being the major criterion for further selection into advanced programmes.

Conclusions

In this chapter, we have distinguished between gifts and talents. Giftedness corresponds to potential that is distinctly above average in at least one aptitude domain, while talent refers to superior performance in a specific field of human activity (Gagné, 1985, 2000).

While the conceptual framework presented here recognizes that birth and family background, the 'two crucial rolls of the dice over which no individual exerts any personal control', impact on a child's musical development (Atkinson, 1978, p. 221), informal and formal learning and practice are also crucial for success. Clearly, there are still many issues to resolve through research. For us, however, one of the more productive means of weighing up the relative contribution of nature versus nurture would be to focus on the interactions that occur between the two, and how this might influence subsequent development (Monks & Mason, 1993). By embracing and encouraging a synthesis of competing viewpoints and methodological approaches, this is precisely what this chapter has attempted to accomplish.

References

Atkinson, J. W. (1978). Motivational determinants of intellective performance and cumulative achievement. In J. W. Atkinson & J. O. Raynor (eds), *Personality, motivation, and achievement* (pp. 221–242). New York: John Wiley.

Anderson, E. (1985). *The letters of Mozart and his family.* New York: Macmillan.

Bandura, A. (1997). *Self-efficacy: The exercise of control.* New York: Freeman.

Bergreen, L. (1997). *Louis Armstrong: An extravagant life.* New York: Broadway Books.

Boyle, J. D. (1992). Evaluation of musical ability. In R. Colwell (ed.), *Handbook of research on music teaching and learning* (pp. 247–265). New York: Schirmer.

Brodsky, W. (2004). Developing the Keele Assessment of Auditory Style (KAAS): A factor-analytic study of cognitive trait predisposition for audition. *Musicæ Scientiæ, VIII,* 83–108.

Chaffin, R. & Lemieux, A. (2004). General perspectives on achieving musical excellence. In A. Williamon (ed.), *Musical excellence: Strategies and techniques to enhance performance* (pp. 19–39). Oxford: Oxford University Press.

Coleman, L. J. & Cross, R. L. (2000). Social-emotional development and the personal experience of giftedness. In K. A. Heller, F. J. Mönks, R. J. Sternberg, & R. F. Subotnik (eds), *International handbook of giftedness and talent* (pp. 203–212) (2nd edn). New York: Elsevier.

Corno, L. (1993). The best-laid plans: Modern conceptions of volition and educational research. *Educational Researcher*, 22(2), 14–22.

Csikszentmihalyi, M. (1998). Fruitless polarities. *Behavioral and Brain Sciences*, 21, 411.

Davidson, J. W. & King, E. C. (2004). Strategies for ensemble practice. In A. Williamon (ed.), *Musical excellence: Strategies and techniques to enhance performance* (pp. 105–122). Oxford: Oxford University Press.

Davies, J. (1978). *The psychology of music*. London: Hutchinson.

Deutsch, O. E. (1966). *Mozart: A documentary biography*. London: Adam & Charles Black.

Ericsson, K. A. (ed.) (1996). *The road to excellence: The acquisition of expert performance in the arts and sciences, sports, and games*. Mahwah, NJ: Lawrence Erlbaum Associates.

Ericsson, K. A. & Lehmann, A. C. (1996). Expert and exceptional performance: Evidence of maximal adaptation to task constraints. *Annual Review of Psychology*, 47, 273–305.

Ericsson, K. A., Krampe, R. T., & Tesch-Römer, C. (1993). The role of deliberate practice in the acquisition of expert performance. *Psychological Review*, 100, 363–406.

Freeman, J. (2000). Families: The essential context for gifts and talents. In K. A. Heller, F. J. Mönks, R. J. Sternberg & R. F. Subotnik (eds), *International handbook of giftedness and talent* (pp. 573–585) (2nd edn). New York: Elsevier.

Gagné, F. (1985). Giftedness and talent: Reexamining a reexamination of the definitions. *Gifted Child Quarterly*, 29, 103–112.

Gagné, F. (1993). Constructs and models pertaining to exceptional human abilities. In K. A. Heller, F. J. Monks, & A. H. Passow (eds), *International handbook of research and development of giftedness and talent* (pp. 69–87). New York: Pergamon.

Gagné, F. (1999). The multigifts of multitalented individuals. In S. Cline & K. T. Hegeman (eds), *Gifted education in the twenty-first century: Issues and concerns* (pp. 17–45). Delray Beach, FL: Winslow Press.

Gagné, F. (2000). Understanding the complex choreography of talent development through DMGT-based analysis. In K. A. Heller, F. J. Mönks, R. J. Sternberg, & R. F. Subotnik (eds), *International handbook of giftedness and talent* (pp. 67–79) (2nd edn). New York: Elsevier.

Gagné, F. (2003). Transforming gifts into talents: The DMGT as a developmental theory. In N. Colangelo & G. A. Davis (eds), *Handbook of gifted education* (pp. 60–74) (3rd edn). Boston, MA: Allyn and Bacon.

Gagné, F. (2004a). An imperative, but, alas, improbable consensus! *Roeper Review*, 27, 12–14.

Gagné, F. (2004b). Transforming gifts into talents: The DMGT as a developmental theory. *High Ability Studies*, 15(2), 119–141.

Gagné, F., Neveu, F., Simard, L., & St Père, F. (1996). How a search for multitalented individuals challenged the concept itself. *Gifted and Talented International*, 11, 4–10.

Gallagher, J. J. (1993). Current status of gifted education in the United States. In K. A. Heller, F. J. Monks, & A. H. Passow (eds), *International handbook of research and development of giftedness and talent*. (pp. 755–770). New York: Pergamon.

Gardner, H. (1983). *Frames of mind: The theory of multiple intelligences*. New York: Basic Books.

Gordon, E. E. (1987). *The nature, description, measurement and evaluation of music aptitudes.* Chicago, IL: GIA Publications.

Gordon, E. E. (1989). *Learning sequences in music.* Chicago, IL: GIA Publications.

Gross, M. (1994). Radical acceleration. *The Journal of Secondary Gifted Education,* 5(4), 27–34.

Gross, M. (2000). Issues in the cognitive development of exceptionally and profoundly gifted individuals. In K. A. Heller, F. J. Mönks, R. J. Sternberg, & R. F. Subotnik (eds), *International handbook of giftedness and talent* (pp. 179–192) (2nd edn). New York: Elsevier.

Gottfied, A. E., Fleming, J. S., & Gottfried, A. W. (1994). Role of parental motivational practices in children's academic intrinsic motivation and achievement. *Journal of Educational Psychology,* 86, 104–113.

Hargreaves, D. J. (1994). Musical education for all. Is everyone musical?—Peer commentaries. *The Psychologist,* August, 357–358.

Hayes, J. R. (1981). *The complete problem solver.* Philadelphia, PA: Franklin Institute Press.

Hedden, S. K. (1982). Prediction of music achievement in the elementary school. *Journal of Research in Music Education,* 30, 61–68.

Hettinger, H. R. & Carr, M. (2003). Cognitive development in gifted children: Toward a more precise understanding of emerging differences in intelligence. *Educational Psychology Review,* 15(3), 215–246.

Howe, M. J. A. (1999). *Genius explained.* Cambridge: Cambridge University Press.

Howe, M. J. A., Davidson, J. W., & Sloboda, J. A. (1998). Innate talents: Reality or myth? *Behavioral and Brain Sciences,* 21, 399–442.

Jørgensen, H. (2004). Strategies for individual practice. In A. Williamon (ed.), *Musical excellence: Strategies and techniques to enhance performance* (pp. 85–103). Oxford: Oxford University Press.

Krampe, R. T. (1997). Age-related changes in practice activities and their relation to musical performance skills. In H. Jørgensen & A. C. Lehmann (eds), *Does practice make perfect? Current theory and research on instrumental music practice* (pp. 165–178). Oslo: Norwegian Academy of Music.

Krampe, R. T. & Ericsson, K. A. (1996). Maintaining excellence: Deliberate practice and elite performance in young and older pianists. *Journal of Experimental Psychology: General,* 125, 331–359.

Kemp, A. E. (1996). *The musical temperament.* Oxford: Oxford University Press.

Lehmann, A. C., Ericsson, K. A., & Hetzer, J. (2002). How different was Mozart's music education and training? A historical analysis comparing the music development of Mozart to that of his contemporaries. In C. Stevens, D. Burnham, G. McPherson, E. Schubert, & J. Renwick (eds), *Proceedings of the seventh international conference on music perception and cognition* (pp. 426–429). Adelaide, Australia: Causal Productions.

Lens, W. & Rand, P. (2000). Motivation and cognition: Their role in the development of giftedness. In K. A. Heller, F. J. Mönks, R. J. Sternberg, & R. F. Subotnik (eds), *International handbook of giftedness and talent* (pp. 193–202) (2nd edn). New York: Elsevier.

Mainwaring, J. (1941). The meaning of musicianship: A problem in the teaching of music. *British Journal of Educational Psychology,* XI(3), 205–214.

Mainwaring, J. (1947). The assessment of musical ability. *British Journal of Educational Psychology,* 17, 83–96.

Mainwaring, J. (1951a). Psychological factors in the teaching of music: Part 1: Conceptual musicianship. *British Journal of Educational Psychology,* XXI, 105–121.

Mainwaring, J. (1951b). Psychological factors in the teaching of music: Part II: applied musicianship. *British Journal of Educational Psychology,* XXI(3), 199–213.

McCormick, J. & McPherson, G. E. (2003). The role of self-efficacy in a musical performance examination: An exploratory structural equation analysis. *Psychology of Music,* 31, 37–51.

McPherson, G. E. (2005). From child to musician: Skill development during the beginning stages of learning an instrument. *Psychology of Music, 33,* 5–35.

McPherson, G. E. & McCormick, J. (2006). Self-efficacy and performing music. *Psychology of Music, 34,* 325–339.

Monks, F. J. & Mason, E. J. (1993). Developmental theories of giftedness. In F. J. Monks & E. J. Mason (eds), *International handbook of research and development of giftedness and talent* (pp. 89–101). Oxford: Pergamon.

Morelock, M. J. & Feldman, D. H. (2000). Prodigies, savants and Williams syndrome: Windows into talent and cognition. In K. A. Heller, F. J. Mönks, R. J. Sternberg & R. F. Subotnik (eds), *International handbook of giftedness and talent* (pp. 227–241) (2nd edn). Oxford: Elsevier Science Ltd.

O'Neill, S. A. (1997). The role of practice in children's early musical performance achievement. In H. Jorgensen & A. C. Lehmann (eds), *Does practice make perfect? Current theory and research on instrumental practice* (pp. 53–70). Oslo: Norwegian State Academy of Music.

O'Neill, S. & McPherson, G. E. (2002). Motivation. In R. Parncutt & G. E. McPherson (eds), *The science and psychology of musical performance: Creative strategies for music teaching and learning* (pp. 31–46). Oxford: Oxford University Press.

Papoušek, H. (1996). Musicality in infancy research: biological and cultural origins of early musicality. In I. Deliège & J. A. Sloboda (eds), *Musical beginnings: Origins and development of musical competence* (pp. 37–55). Oxford: Oxford University Press.

Persson, R. S. (1996). Musical reality: Exploring the subjective world of performers. In R. Monelle & C. T. Gray (eds), *Song and signification: Studies in music semiotics* (pp. 58–63). Edinburgh: University of Edinburgh Faculty of Music.

Persson, R. S., Partt, G., & Robson, C. (1996). Motivational and influential components of musical performance: A qualitative analysis. In A. J. Cropley & D. Dehn (eds), *Fostering the growth of high ability: European perspectives* (pp. 287–302). Norwood, NJ: Ablex.

Rainbow, E. L. (1965). A pilot study to investigate the constructs of musical aptitude. *Journal of Research in Music Education, 13,* 3–14.

Richardson, C. P. (1990). Measuring musical giftedness. *Music Educators Journal, 76*(7), 40–45.

Simonton, D. K. (1988). Age and outstanding achievement: What do we know after a century of research? *Psychological Bulletin, 104,* 251–267.

Simonton, D. K. (1991). Emergence and realization of genius: The lives and works of 120 classical composers. *Journal of Personality and Social Psychology, 61,* 829–840.

Simonton, D. K. (1999). Talent and its development: An emergenic and epigenetic model. *Psychological Review, 106,* 435–457.

Simonton, D. K. (2001). Talent development as a multidimensional, multiplicative, and dynamic process. *Current Directions in Psychological Science, 10,* 39–43.

Sisk, D. A. (1990). The state of gifted education: Toward a bright future. *Music Educators Journal, 76*(7), 35–39.

Sloboda, J. A. (1993). Musical ability. In D. Goldstein & J. J. Godfrey (eds), *The origins and development of high ability* (pp. 106–118). Ciba Foundation Symposium 178. Chichester: Wiley.

Sloboda, J. A. & Davidson, J. W. (1996). The young performing musician. In I. Deliege, & J. A. Sloboda (eds), *The origins and development of musical competence* (pp. 171–190). Oxford: Oxford University Press.

Sloboda, J. A., Davidson, J. W., & Howe, M. J. A. (1994). Is everyone musical? *The Psychologist, 7*(8), 349–354.

Sloboda, J. A., Davidson, J. W., Howe, M. J. A., & Moore, D. G. (1996). The role of practice in the development of performing musicians. *British Journal of Psychology, 87,* 287–309.

Sloboda, J. A. & Howe, M. J. (1991). Biographical precursors of musical excellence: An interview study. *Psychology of Music*, 19, 3–21.

Solomon, M. (1995). *Mozart*. London: Hutchinson.

Sosniak, L. A. (1985). Learning to be a concert pianist. In B. S. Bloom (ed.), *Developing talent in young people* (pp. 19–67). New York: Ballantine.

Sternberg, R. J. (2000). Giftedness as developing expertise. In K. A. Heller, F. J. Mönks, R. J. Sternberg, & R. F. Subotnik (eds), *International handbook of giftedness and talent* (pp. 55–66) (2nd edn). New York: Elsevier.

Sternberg, R. J. & Lubart, T. I. (1999). The concept of creativity: Prospects and paradigms. In R. J. Sternberg (ed.), *Handbook of creativity* (pp. 3–15). Cambridge: Cambridge University Press.

Sternberg, R. J. & O'Hara, L. A. (1999). Creativity and intelligence. In R. J. Sternberg (ed.), *Handbook of creativity* (pp. 251–272). Cambridge: Cambridge University Press.

Suzuki, S. (1983). *Nutured by love*. New York: Smithtown.

Turner, W. J. (1965). *Mozart: The man and his works*. London: Methuen & Co Ltd.

Williamon, A., Lehmann, A. C., & McClure, K. (2003). Studying practice quantitatively. In R. Kopiez, A. C. Lehmann, I. Wolther, & C. Wolf (eds), *Proceedings of the fifth triennial ESCOM conference* (pp. 182–185). Hanover, Germany: Hanover University of Music and Drama.

Williamon, A. & Valentine, E. (2000). Quantity and quality of musical practice as predictors of performance quality. *British Journal of Psychology*, 91, 353–376.

Williamon, A. & Valentine, E. (2002). The role of retrieval structures in memorizing music. *Cognitive Psychology*, 44, 1–32.

Wilson, E. (1998). *Jacqueline du Pré*. London: Weidenfeld & Nicolson.

Winn, M. (1979, December 23). The pleasures and perils of being a child prodigy. *New York Times Magazine*, 12–19, 38–45.

Winner, E. (1996a). *Gifted children: Myths and realities*. New York: Basic Books.

Winner, E. (1996b). The rage to master: The decisive role of talent in the visual arts. In K. A. Ericsson (ed.), *The road to excellence: The acquisition of expert performance in the arts and sciences, sports, and games* (pp. 271–301). Mahwah, NJ: Lawrence Erlbaum Associates.

Winner, E. & Martino, G. (1993). Giftedness in the visual arts and music. In K. A. Heller, F. J. Monks, & A. H Passow (eds), *International handbook of research and development of giftedness and talent* (pp. 253–281). New York: Pergamon.

Winner, E. & Martino, G. (2000). Giftedness in non-academic domains: The case of the visual arts and music. In K. A. Heller, F. J. Mönks, R. J. Sternberg, & R. F. Subotnik (eds), *International handbook of giftedness and talent* (pp. 95–110) (2nd edn). New York: Elsevier.

Yun Dai, D. & Schader, R. (2001). Parent's reasons and motivations for supporting their child's music training. *Roeper Review*, 24, 23–26.

CHAPTER 13

INCLUDING EVERYONE

JUDITH A. JELLISON

Introduction

You, the reader of this chapter, are most likely a strong supporter of music. You most likely are among the many who believe that the quality of a child's life is enriched by participation in a wide range of music activities. Individuals who have experienced personal pleasure from music are often those who advocate quality music experiences for others.

Few would question the contribution of music to the quality of life, but, for many years, quality music experiences were not accessible to hundreds of thousands of children with disabilities. Visiting volunteer musicians and perfunctory recreational music activities punctuated life in residential institutions, although few institutions were fortunate to have music therapy services.

Throughout the history of institutional care for children and adults with disabilities, physicians promoted the use of music for mental and physical health (see textbooks on music therapy for detailed descriptions of the historical foundations of music therapy). Support from the medical community, observational evidence, and eventually systematic research led to the development of music therapy organizations world-wide. Although music therapy comprises a diversity of approaches, some of which have been adapted from music education (Darrow, 2004), children with disabilities, particularly those with more severe disabilities, typically have few opportunities for a genuine music education experience.

Years of advocacy, litigation, and legislation have led to dramatic reforms in policies that deeply affect the lives of children with disabilities. Although critical dimensions of life are always at the forefront of discussions among the concerned citizenry, academic achievement, job preparation, interpersonal relationships, self-determination, and leisure now appear with increasing regularity in research related to children with disabilities. In light of legislative mandates designed to improve the quality of education of children with disabilities, the important issue among advocates, parents/guardians, and educators has become access to general education programmes, including music programmes, and access to regular environments in the community. The challenge for music education is to provide appropriate educational opportunities for all children in a variety of educational and social settings, so that children will participate happily and successfully in quality music experiences throughout their lives.

To begin to understand the musical development of children with disabilities, one must recognize that much of the knowledge in this book, and from established research on teaching and learning, applies equally to children with a wide variety of disabilities that vary in kind and degree. Much that we already know about music learning is applicable to children with and without disabilities. Recognizing similarities among seemingly diverse children is an important step toward understanding how to make educationally sound decisions for each child's musical life.

It is self-evident that musical development is influenced by biology and experiences. In this chapter, I focus on experiences that can be structured and organized by the influential and caring adults in children's lives. Socio-cultural experiences influence musical development—interpersonal relations (e.g., with family members, friends, peers, paid professionals), physical environments (e.g., the child's home, music classroom in school, and neighbourhood and community events), values, attitudes, and beliefs of people and institutions (e.g., school policies, state and federal laws, culture, tradition), and economic resources (e.g., school's budget for music instruction and resources). Research is conducted with regularity on a wide array of variables in these contexts.

In recent decades, research has identified intervention strategies that have greatly reduced the limitations associated with physical, emotional, intellectual, sensory, and specific behavioural and learning disabilities. In this chapter I explain the application of these principles in ways that allow children with disabilities to participate as independently as possible in meaningful music experiences. My intent is to illustrate ways of thinking that can lead toward greater efficiency and effectiveness in music education practice and advocacy for all children.

Although the effectiveness of music in therapeutic settings is well established (American Music Therapy Association, 2000), scant research exists that documents effective practices for children with disabilities in inclusive music education settings (Jellison, 2000a; Darrow et al., 2002). In the main, research in psychology and special education provides many of the bases for the principles I present here.

I will begin with a discussion of quality of life as an overarching principle for all efforts to nurture musical development followed by a brief overview of disabilities and issues of categorical labelling. The importance of making decisions based on quality-of-life considerations and principles of human learning leads to the presentation of six guidelines for improving the musical lives of children with disabilities followed by discussions of the principles in the guidelines. The chapter closes with comments regarding the impact of influential adults on the transformation of music education for all children.

What should be expected?

Quality of life

People strive for quality of life for themselves, for their loved ones, and perhaps for others deemed in need. The concept of quality of life is common in the vernacular of cultures and is the cornerstone of thought and action for persons with disabilities, their families and advocates. Quality of life, no matter how conceptualized, is the driving force behind socio-political changes that have positively influenced the lives of hundreds of thousands of individuals with disabilities.

The core dimensions associated with quality of life (e.g., living environments, education, employment, recreation) are used to argue and resolve inequities specific to the lives of persons with disabilities. Blatt (1970) and Shapiro (1993) have chronicled the blatant inequities of physical and social segregation that have fostered negative stereotypes and discriminatory behaviours toward individuals with intellectual and developmental disabilities. Some of these inequities were and continue to be resolved through the courts.

In many countries, years of advocacy, litigation, and legislation have led to increasing reforms in policies regarding persons with disabilities. Among the earliest and most striking victories in the United States were changes in federal and state laws associated with the deinstitutionalization movement during the late 1970s and 1980s. The initial outcomes of this change in social policy, which related to residential service systems for persons with retardation, other types of developmental disabilities, or mental illness, were less than ideal, particularly for the adults who had resided in institutions for most of their lives.

Deinstitutionalization, however, was a step forward for living for children with disabilities, many of whom now reside in real homes with their families and who attend neighbourhood schools. Deinstitutionalization led to a need for education reform for the hundreds of thousands of children who were living in communities.

Education reforms have had far-reaching consequences for children with disabilities. The Individuals with Disabilities Education Act (IDEA), first signed into United States law in 1975 as The Education for All Handicapped Children Act (Public Law 94-142), requires states and local agencies to place children in the least restrictive educational environments, which in many cases are regular classrooms. States and local education agencies develop procedures to ensure that, to the maximum extent appropriate, students with disabilities, ages 3–21, including those educated in public or private schools, or other care facilities, will be educated with students who do not have disabilities, and that the removal from regular education environments may occur only when the nature or severity of students' disabilities are such that education in regular classes with the use of supplementary aids and services cannot be achieved satisfactorily. More than 95% of children with disabilities in the United States are now educated in regular school buildings (US Department of Education, 2003; see Turnbull & Turnbull, 2000, for a reader-friendly yet thorough description of the law and its history).

Progress of improved living conditions and educational opportunities is evident for children with all types and levels of disabilities, although progress is particularly dramatic for individuals with the most severe disabilities (Ryndak & Fisher, 2003). Efforts by teachers, parents, advocates, and researchers are leading to improved living conditions for adults, but further, these efforts enrich the knowledge base on how best to prepare future generations of children for lives as adults.

Four questions can be used in describing quality of life: (1) Where is the child? (residential, community, school); (2) With whom is the child interacting? (persons with or without disabilities; classmates; acquaintances; friends; paid professionals); (3) What does the child do? (music activities, school curriculum, daily living activities, employment in the case of adults); and (4) How does the child feel? (experiences of emotional well being, autonomy, self-determination).

For many years, music was not accessible to a large number of children with disabilities. Children with disabilities were not in music classrooms (where); they had few opportunities to interact with their typical peers (with whom), or to learn and increase their ability to make music and use music knowledge (what), which limited autonomy, self-efficacy and ultimately self-determination in music contexts (feelings). Some children are still isolated from the types of meaningful music experiences their typical peers enjoy.

Who are the children?

People (children) first

Procedures to identify, assess and categorize disabilities vary among countries as do methodologies for collecting and reporting national statistics, thus prohibiting a meaningful description of disabilities world-wide. As an example of statistical reporting in the United States, the number of children with disabilities are determined by counts of infants and toddlers, preschool children (ages 3–5), and children and young adults (ages 6–21) who receive services under IDEA. Based on 2001–2002 data, the number of children with disabilities ages 3 through 21 rose to more than 6 million, representing 12% of the estimated school age population in the United States (US Department of Education, 2003).

Categorical labels used to describe children with disabilities, which differ among localities and countries have changed dramatically over the past decades. 'Typical' is a term that is now widely used to describe children without disabilities, whereas children with disabilities are described using 'person-first language' (e.g., *children with* mental retardation; *children with* learning disabilities; *children with* disabilities). Person-first language focuses attention on the commonality among all children—all people—while still acknowledging their varying abilities and disabilities as appropriate.

Children with disabilities are limited in their musical development when educational decisions rely primarily on stereotypic characteristics associated with the concept of disability. There are no specific instruments, songs, or music activities that are more successful for groups of children with the same disability label (e.g., songs for children with mental retardation). With greater opportunities for children with disabilities and with changes in disability laws, attitudes are changing for the better.

. . . *with* disabilities

Research in genetics, embryology, fetal development, and the birthing process unveils what can happen before, during, and shortly after birth that will put children at risk for disabilities. Environmental factors such as poor nutrition, substance abuse, disease, infection, and physical trauma can have dire consequences for the development of the brain, microskeletal systems, organs, and sensory systems. The developing child is also at risk when social-emotional environments are unhealthy and traumatic.

Non-discriminatory and multifaceted evaluation and re-evaluation procedures may be necessary to determine the strengths and weaknesses of a child with disabilities. Although the definitions of specific disabilities may vary, most often the broad label of disability implies conditions that are permanent.

Research has identified some of the conditions that are optimum for the cognitive, physical, social, and emotional development of typical children, and many are applicable in music environments that include children with disabilities. Advances in assistive technology and advances in medical and behavioural sciences continue to increase the levels of functional independence in all of life's activities. Inspired by a vision for the future, our responsibility now is to apply what we know in meaningful ways.

... who have music capabilities

With the exception of the very few persons identified as musical savants, or those with Williams syndrome or autism spectrum disorders (ASD) who appear to have highly developed music skills, the musical development of children with disabilities has received little attention in research literature. In a review of research with children and youth with disabilities published during the years 1975–99 (Jellison, 2000a), I found that in only a few cases were music outcomes measured. With the exception of comparative studies between groups of children with and without disabilities, most often the data were reported only for therapeutic outcomes (e.g., singing songs with activities on topics of social interaction to increase social interaction; listening to music while engaged in a physical therapy task).

Comparative studies that examine the music capabilities of children with disabilities and those of their non-disabled peers illustrate similarities between groups on a variety of music tasks, e.g.: responses to teaching strategies (Cassidy, 1992); elements associated with beat and rhythm (Darrow, 1984); descriptions of music (Flowers & Wang, 2002); singing, clapping a steady beat, preferences, and experiences (Jellison & Flowers, 1991); and tonal memory (Madsen & Darrow, 1989). Many results from comparative research studies (Jellison, 2000a), case studies (e.g., Bunt & Hoskyns, 2002), and anecdotal reports challenge the notion that students with disabilities have 'special needs' in *all* dimensions of music behaviour. Although there is insufficient empirical evidence to fully inform specific instructional strategies in music education, given the wealth of knowledge on human learning and the influence of music on behaviour, much can be done.

Guidelines and principles in music programme design and instruction

Adapting curriculum and instruction for children with disabilities is an issue that receives much attention in the educational literature. When children lack the requisite skills or when cognitive, sensory, motor, or language capabilities impede successful participation, adaptations are required. The types and variety of adaptations range from those that are easily implemented by a family member, teacher, or peer (e.g., seating and positioning; simple hand gestures; changes in room lighting) to those that are more complex, requiring training (e.g., electronic augmentative communication devices; mobility devices; hearing aids). Many simple, effective ideas for instructional adaptations are routinely developed by teachers and parents; some in consultation with occupational therapists, physical therapists, special educators, and music therapists. Children, with and without disabilities, can also suggest adaptations that prove successful.

A wide array of recommendations and opinions regarding adaptations are readily available from concerned individuals and from the Internet, books, and other printed materials. Not all recommendations are appropriate or valuable. Selecting, developing, implementing, and evaluating adaptations for any music programme or instructional situation can be overwhelming in the absence of an overall concept of what is important. Sound decision-making begins with a clear understanding of a child's strengths and weaknesses in a variety of contexts, music and otherwise, and a mindset based on sound guiding principles.

From research on human learning emerge principles that govern the development of successful experiences for children, irrespective of their disabling condition and their environments. Well-established principles comprise the foundation of effective educational practices with all children and are transferable across individuals and contexts. In the preface of his book of essays on music teaching, Duke (2005) writes '... discussions about educational practice that focus primarily on how teachers teach and that fail to consider the basic principles of human learning are fundamentally misguided. There is an expansive, rich body of data that illuminates the processes of knowledge acquisition and skill development. Intelligent teaching is predicated on a deep understanding of these processes—how knowledge and skills are acquired, refined, and applied' (p. vii).

Principles in this chapter are those derived from research and values that were and remain major forces in social policy, special education policy, research, and practice. The guidelines below are based on these principles and values and suggest that the musical lives of children with disabilities can be improved when:

1. Culturally normative music experiences and participation in socially valued roles and socially valued activities with typical children are part of the routine of daily life.

2. Collaboration and co-ordinated efforts among professionals, parents/guardians, and the child, siblings, and peers (when appropriate) are critical factors for the design, implementation, and evaluation of an individualized music education programme.

3. Transition and transfer are the basis for curricular and instructional decisions.

4. Children fully participate or at least partially participate in experiences where music skills and knowledge are chronologically age appropriate and functional.

5. Social interactions in inclusive music environments with chronological age typical peers are positive and reciprocal.

6. Self-determination is a goal and children have numerous and varied opportunities to make choices and experience autonomy.

Culturally normative music experiences and valued roles

The idea of normalization, perhaps more than any other principle, constitutes the core of practices in special education. The principle was first articulated by the philosopher Wolf Wolfensberger (1972). When applied to music teaching and learning, *the principle of normalization is evident when culturally normative music experiences and activities are part of the routine in the daily lives of children with disabilities—regardless of the severity of the disability.*

Consistent with the concept of normalization, Brown *et al.* (1983) first used the term 'natural proportion' to define the students with the most severe disabilities (1%). This concept is useful to approximate the number of children with disabilities who should be in any group of children. For example, within a school age population where 10% of the children have disabilities, a rough application suggests that three children with disabilities (perhaps one with severe disabilities) are part of a classroom of 30 children.

Living in a community, receiving an education in the least restrictive school environment, and participating with typical peers in music classes are important steps toward normalization; however, normalization alone does not ensure social inclusion and positive social interactions. Wolfensberger (1983) broadened the principle of normalization and formulated a second principle which he called social valorization (valuing people with disabilities as a result of their social role). When applied to music teaching and learning, *the principle of social value is evident when children with disabilities have roles in music activities that lead to a decrease in negative stereotyping and an increase in the probability of positive perceptions, attitudes, and behaviours among persons without disabilities.*

The music activities of typical children in a variety of settings can be used as a standard by which to evaluate whether and how children with disabilities are participating in those same activities. To the maximum extent possible, children with disabilities should attend regular music classes and school music concerts or field trips; participate in a variety of activities as part of the regular music curriculum (singing, playing instruments, listening, creating, talking about music and so on); make choices and communicate music preferences, ideas, and feelings about music; and demonstrate accomplishments valued by the child and others.

As a child with disabilities participates alongside typical peers in normalizing activities that are valued by peers, the music-learning environment is enriched as a result of influential social interactions. When children with disabilities do more than is expected by typical peers or adults, whether that be keeping a beat, playing a melody at the keyboard, or identifying a music composition, negative stereotyping of disabilities begin to diminish.

Collaboration

As the number of environments increase for the child with disabilities, so do the number of people in the child's life. When applied to music teaching and learning, *the principle of collaboration is evident when professionals, parents/guardians, and the child with disabilities, siblings, and peers (when appropriate) co-ordinate efforts for the design, implementation, and evaluation of the child's individualized music education programme.*

Collaboration is a critical component of IDEA. At least annually, parents, school representatives, teachers, the student (when appropriate), and other individuals at the discretion of the parents or school are required to meet and make critical decisions regarding the student's education programme and necessary support services. These decisions become contractual agreements and are designated as the Individualized Education Program (IEP) for ages 3–21 and the Individualized Family Service Plan (IFSP) for ages birth through 2. Although policies vary among schools, music educators can be a part of this collaborative effort and can bring a level of expertise and new information that is otherwise unavailable to the other members of the team. The unique nature of music elicits behaviours from many children that are different from those observed in academic classes.

Most often, professionals and parents/guardians agree on the importance of disciplines associated with related services (e.g., speech pathology and audiology, psychological services, physical and occupational therapy, recreation, music therapy), the assignment of trained full or part-time aides to classrooms, and other supports that occur more naturally in the child's school, classroom, and community such as classmates, acquaintances, or friends. Bernstorf (2001) discusses ways for music teachers to interact with paraprofessionals that encourage them to work more creatively and productively in inclusive music settings.

Whether collaboration is informal or formal, it is often the music teacher who must take the initiative to collaborate with others. Only a small percentage of teachers, however, initiate requests for information and support for music classrooms, and even less initiate contact with parents (Jellison *et al.*, 2006). Many parents and guardians can offer substantive information regarding their own child, but may be reluctant to make contact outside of the yearly required IEP meeting.

Teachers would do well to initiate interactions at the beginning of the school year, or if possible, prior to the first day of classes. Throughout the year, many parents of children with disabilities are eager for a positive word regarding their child's accomplishments, no matter how small the accomplishments may be viewed by others. The benefits of collaboration with parents, service providers, and other natural supports will ultimately lead to a music environment where both the child and the teacher will be more productive and successful.

Transition and transfer

Transition refers to the movement of individuals across a variety of situations and environments throughout life: In special education literature, transition refers to the movement from school to adult life. Transfer involves the application of previously learned skills and knowledge to new situations. These two ideas are closely linked in educational practice. When applied to music teaching and learning, *the principle of transition and transfer is evident when educational practices prepare children to use learned music skills and knowledge in a variety of familiar and new situations throughout life.*

Transition

The important concept of transition in special education developed as a result of observations and survey data showing that adults with disabilities continue to lag far behind other adults without disabilities in areas of employment, independent living, post secondary education, and participation in community activities. The work of advocacy groups, parents, and educators, led to legislative mandates requiring the development of transition plans for students' entry into residential, employment and recreational environments of their adult life (see Kohler & Field, 2003, who provide a thorough report of transition research literature for the past 15 years and identify effective transition practices in special education).

Transition planning is a critical component in special education, although it is not an explicit practice in regular education and music education. I have proposed an application of the concept of transition to practices in music education and music therapy in several early papers, and more recently I proposed using transition as an overarching principle for the design of music programmes for all children (Jellison, 2000b). Transition planning begins when teachers, parents, and all those concerned with the child's musical development identify meaningful music skills and knowledge and when those decisions are guided by a vision of the child participating as successfully and as independently as possible in a variety of music environments—now and in the future as adults.

Transfer

There is an abundance of research literature on the topic of transfer. In education, transfer involves two basic components: (1) tasks (what the student is observed doing), and (2) contexts (people and settings). Obviously, music tasks occur in contexts, and the goal of music education (all education for that matter) is to prepare children to perform a variety of tasks in different contexts throughout life. Varying any part of the task or any part of the context, no matter how small, creates a new situation that may affect the child's performance. All aspects of music tasks and contexts must be analysed carefully and prepared in such a way that children are initially successful and that success continues as they make progress in increasingly more difficult tasks and in new settings.

When applied to music learning, the probability of transfer is increased from one situation to another: (1) when music tasks and/or contexts are similar; (2) when there are frequent opportunities to practise the same music skills and apply the same music knowledge using numerous and varied examples in multiple contexts; and (3) when students learn a small number of meaningful principles deeply and thoroughly and apply them in different situations.

Functional value, chronological age, and partial participation

Principles of normalization and transition have greatly influenced curricular planning and instruction. Most educational practices that were followed in institutions and segregated facilities of the past are ineffective for children with disabilities today. Negative consequences of practices of the past were not evident, as children lived, played, and worked as adults in the same facility with other adults with disabilities. Errors of educational practice were tragically evident in the 1970s and into the 1980s during the deinstitutionalization movement. Individuals were not prepared to live, work, or play in a diverse society. The task for educators now is to prepare children, our future adults, to participate in the daily life experiences of typical adults to the maximum extent possible.

Functional value

Until the 1970s, the developmental model dominated curricular and instructional decisions in special education services. On the basis of decades of observing adults with disabilities, the model was deemed ineffective (Brown *et al.*, 1979). Brown *et al.* (1979) and others at the time foreshadowed sweeping changes in curricula for children with disabilities. Pressed to optimize instructional time, teachers began to prioritize meaningful learning outcomes and remove unnecessary prerequisite skills, basing curricular decisions on a principle of functional value. When applied to music teaching and learning, *the principle of functional value is evident when music skills and activities are not only interesting to the child with disabilities but lead to outcomes that have meaning and relevance for the child now and in the future.*

Among the wide variety of music activities (singing, playing instruments, improvising, reading music, listening to music, and so on), what skills and knowledge will improve the quality of children's lives now and in the future? From a national survey of arts instruction, Carey *et al.* (2002) calculate that, based on a 40-week school-year, elementary music teachers may have only 46 hours of instructional time—time in which to teach meaningful skills and knowledge and to teach for transfer. Given the problem of time, the overcrowded curriculum, and the data suggesting that we have not taught what we intended to teach in music classes, I have suggested that elementary music teachers focus on active music making for all children, including those with disabilities (Jellison, 2004).

Children with disabilities, particularly those with physical or intellectual disabilities, are often relegated to passive activities such as music listening or to playing the same classroom instruments that soon lose their attractiveness (rhythm sticks, toy tambourines, a single resonator bell, and the like). Although listening to music can be a wonderful source of pleasure, singing and playing instruments that are seen in the real world of music (keyboards, guitars, orchestral instruments) can provide a range of opportunities for personal accomplishment in many contexts throughout life. For example, playing chords for familiar school and holiday songs on a keyboard or guitar is not only a socially valued skill but a skill that can lead to a sense of personal achievement and heightened self-esteem.

Parents, guardians, and teachers who know the child's strengths and weaknesses can begin to decide what is important to teach. In determining priorities for instruction, together they can consider: (1) a child's interest as well as the context for instruction (classroom music, small group or private lessons); (2) the number of skills and kind of knowledge to be learned in the time allotted; (3) whether frequent opportunities will be available for the children to practise using the skills and knowledge in meaningful ways; and (4) whether the child will be able eventually to use the skills and knowledge and participate partially, if not fully, alone and with typical peers and adults without disabilities. In other words, will the music skill and knowledge have functional value for this child now and for the future?

Chronological age

A music curriculum that is functional is also age-appropriate. When applied to music teaching and learning, the principle of chronological age is evident when children with disabilities participate to the maximum extent possible in activities that are identical to those that would (or could) be considered appropriate for their same age typical peers.

When curricular decisions are based on 'mental or emotional age,' as was the case in institutional settings and still remains the case in some segregated schools and classrooms, history shows that many children never catch up and learn important skills for adulthood. Careful evaluation of students with disabilities, particularly those with severe disabilities, shows that rarely, if ever, can students move through the number of prerequisites and learning sequences at a rate that would enable them to participate in the activities enjoyed by their chronological age peers.

The use of chronological age as a criteria for including children with disabilities in a wide array of music settings requires teachers, parents, and classmates to have higher expectations for children and, importantly, to view partial participation and participation with assistance or with adaptation as a valid educational experience.

A child with disabilities placed in a regular music classroom with same-age peers, will have the advantage of participating in chronological age-appropriate music activities (with adaptations as necessary). Although private music lessons have advantages, care must be taken against the underestimation of the child's abilities and the use of age inappropriate instruction or materials.

Partial participation

When applied to music teaching and learning, the principle of partial participation is evident when music instruction and learning environments are arranged and adapted in such a way that children with disabilities participate in music activities as independently as possible and in as many different environments as is instructionally possible. The principle of partial participation, originally proposed for children with severe disabilities (Baumgart *et al.*, 1982), has applications for any child who is unable to learn the myriad age-appropriate skills that are required of their typical chronological age peers.

Years of observation led Ferguson and Baumgart (1991) to identify several major errors that can be made by well-intended teachers who apply this principle incorrectly in their classrooms. Teachers are cautioned against having children partially participate through passive participation—simply being present in the room or during activities. Other errors can occur when partial participation: (1) is limited to one activity (plays only simple percussion instruments); (2) is limited to one small part of the activity (starts the CD player then watches others make music); (3) involves an activity that is not valued, respected, or preferred by peers; (4) occurs only in the presence of the teacher with no transfer to other music contexts with typical peers or with parents in the home; (5) does not include extra-curricular music activities (participates in class but doesn't attend field trips to concerts with classmates); and (6) requires a high degree of assistance from other adults or students or requires changes in the activity in such a way that the activity loses its musical or educational value for other students in the class.

The movements of some dances, for example, may not be easily adapted to accommodate a child in a wheelchair or a child with other physical disabilities. As an alternative to everyone dancing, add a band to movement lessons. Bands are a part of natural settings where dancers enjoy moving to music from keyboards, guitars, and percussion instruments. The band should be comprised of students with and without disabilities (normalization). Live bands often play at dances and members of a band are often admired (valued social role), thus, the child who cannot participate fully in a movement activity can have an enjoyable, meaningful role by playing a socially desirable instrument. Electronic keyboards are desirable instruments for any band and provide a wide array of opportunities for children, including those with the most severe disabilities, to make music with peers and transfer skills to natural environments outside school and throughout life (principles of functional value and transition).

Partial participation is individualized when adaptations emphasize the student's strengths and existing repertoire of behaviour, de-emphasize those skills that are not in the student's repertoire, and, ideally, allow for the student's learning of alternative, functional skills that will transfer to new situations. In inclusive settings, individual adaptations for partial participation may require changes in materials and instruments; the sequence of activities; the use of aides and classmates; general routines; and expectations and attitudes of classmates, parents or guardians, teachers and administrators.

Social inclusion and interactions

When applied to music teaching and learning, *the principle of social inclusion and interaction is evident when children with disabilities have frequent opportunities to participate in music experiences that occur in a wide variety of regular social, school, and classroom settings and that include positive and cooperative interactions with same-age typical peers.*

Noted theorists have identified social ecology as a powerful influence on learning outcomes. There is an abundance of evidence to support the ideas of the social learning theorist Bandura (1977), who proposed that learning is closely tied to the environment created by others in the group, and developmental theorist Vygotsky (1935/1978), who suggested that social interactions were necessary for overall cognitive development and emphasized cooperation among peers as a way to build new skills and acquire new knowledge.

In a meta-analysis of peer-assisted learning interventions in elementary classrooms, Rohrbeck *et al.* (2003) found that achievement outcomes were related to peer interaction variables, particularly for 'vulnerable students, including students in the lower elementary grades, minority students, students attending school in urban settings, and possible low-income students' (p. 19). Children with disabilities were participants in several of the studies included in this analysis.

The literature is rich with effective strategies to facilitate effective social inclusion for children with disabilities, including children with severe disabilities, but only a few early studies exist in the music research literature. In a 6-month study of four inclusive music classes, positive attitudes of typical elementary-age children toward their peers with disabilities and positive behavioural interactions increased as a result of structuring small group interactions (Jellison *et al.*, 1984). In another study, positive social interactions among pre-schoolers with and without disabilities who were brought together for 15 music sessions were found to increase as a result of music activities designed to promote interactions (Humple, 1991).

Music instruction in inclusive classrooms provides a multitude of opportunities to put into practice the results of research describing the advantages of positive social interactions in learning environments for all children. For example, students who cannot play with melodic or rhythmic precision as a result of a disability can, with typical peers, participate in creating soundscapes or sound effects. Children with disabilities can choose their own instrument, and in collaboration with typical peers in small groups, help create an overall plan for the soundscape (who plays what, when, and for how long). The overall objective for each small group is to develop a piece in which everyone contributes in a meaningful way and the outcome is musically satisfying to everyone in the group. In another example, the most natural supports for a student with disabilities in a choral ensemble are those peers who sit in the same section. Teachers can provide opportunities for students to interact in small groups or with individuals from other sections to discuss group issues of concern such as choir trips, performances, recruiting, etc. In a group that has developed mutual respect and understanding for each other through positive group interactions, problems and problem solving regarding participation of the student with disabilities in any given activity will occur naturally from the student or classmates.

Self-determination and autonomy

Among the valued quality of life principles is one we often take for granted: self-determination. Although several definitions of self-determination are available, for purposes here, self-determination is considered the ability for children with disabilities to consider options and independently make choices. When applied to music teaching and learning, *the principle of self-determination is evident when children have frequent opportunities to experience autonomy in music activities, to express preferences and make decisions about music, music making, and other activities in their musical lives.*

Self-determination has become a prominent theme in research and special education practice in the United States as a result of a decade of challenges by advocacy groups to change the structure of disability services and enable more choice, freedom, authority, and responsibility for persons with disabilities ('*My Life*', 2005). Theorists Ryan and Deci (2000) have proposed that motivation to achieve in the classroom is a result of competence and autonomy and that competence and autonomy can be fostered in instructional environments. Increasingly, autonomy and self-determination are appearing as research variables for study among children with disabilities in classrooms (e.g., Wehmeyer *et al.*, 2003; Clark *et al.*, 2004), beginning with the earliest possible school setting—the preschool (Jolivette *et al.*, 2002) and early elementary classrooms (Palmer & Wehmeyer, 2003).

From research findings, choice-making has been identified as a factor that provides students with a level of control that results in a substantial effect on their motivation to participate in an activity or complete a task. In music settings, actions associated with self-determination can include teachers' providing choice, encouraging self-initiation, minimizing the use of controls, acknowledging the other's perspective and feelings, and fostering the relevance of the learning process to students' personal interests, goals, and values. There is a high probability that a child with disabilities will be more on-task to music instruction and more motivated to participate in music activities when given choices that are perceived by the child as meaningful, interesting, and within the child's capabilities.

Following the principle of normalization, the kinds of choices should be as similar as possible to those presented to same-age typical children. Choices may vary in complexity and response mode (motor or verbal) and involve music activities (e.g., choose music to sing or play; create accompaniments and improvise melodies; analyse and describe music; evaluate music) or classroom routines. As with music achievement, children should be given increasingly more difficult problems to solve and increasingly more responsibility and autonomy in music settings.

The type and severity of the disability will dictate the type of choices and the type of assistance that is necessary for children. Although appropriate assistance is to be valued, years of negative stereotyping of what people with disabilities can and cannot do, combined with a lack of knowledge by the well-intentioned but misguided actions of individuals without disabilities, has led to inappropriate helping in schools and the community.

Adults and peers who are unaware of the importance of self-determination, autonomy, and choice in children's lives can diminish important music learning opportunities with inappropriate assistance and prompting. Close proximity of adults (Giangreco *et al.*, 1997) and close proximity of *some* classmates (Jellison, 2002) can be counter-productive to students' learning. In an observation study of proximity of peers in a single inclusive music classroom, I observed well-intended typical peers unnecessarily assisting, prompting, and hovering over two children with disabilities in a music classroom. What seemed important, however, were the individual differences observed among typical children—a few children refrained from unnecessary helping and remained on-task to music instruction even when seated close to their peers with disabilities. 'In many situations, good will and positive social outcomes occur in inclusive classroom settings, but it is critical that no child's academic development be hindered as a result of inclusion. Every child must be taught to remain on-task to academic instruction and must be taught when, how, and under what conditions their social interactions and good intentions to help [their classmates with disabilities] will be both appropriate and beneficial' (Jellison, 2002, p. 352).

Closing

For years, social and educational policies impeded rather than nurtured the development of children with disabilities. Progress has been slow, but across the past several decades, changes are clearly evident in research, educational practices, and values in special education. Research that consistently identifies factors influencing learning has led to principles that have widespread applications for children with varying abilities in a variety of music teaching and learning settings. As a result of a substantive research base describing the influence of socio-cultural factors on children's development, principles of human learning, and literature and research on quality of life dimensions, much of what we need to do to improve the musical lives of children with disabilities is known.

Although there is scant research on the topic of music learning and children with disabilities, principles on how people learn and how children develop provide a wealth of knowledge that is applicable to music settings and children with varying degrees of abilities and disabilities. Many variables can be adapted by teachers, parents, and other responsible adults who share common concerns for the musical development of children. Irrespective of available knowledge, action is required to change music education practices. Individuals of good will, knowledge, and skill can contribute substantially to improving the quality of lives of future generations of people with disabilities by ensuring that music is a prominent component in the lives of *all* children.

References

American Music Therapy Association (2000). *Effectiveness of music therapy procedures: Documentation of research and clinical practice* (3rd edn). Silver Spring. MD: American Music Therapy Association.

Bandura, A. (1977). *Social learning theory.* Englewood Cliffs, NJ: Prentice Hall.

Baumgart, D., Brown, L., Pumpian, I., Nisbet, J., Ford, A., Sweet, M., Messina, R., & Schroeder, J. (1982). Principle of partial participation and individualized adaptations in educational programs for severely handicapped students. *The Journal of The Association for Persons with Severe Handicaps,* 7, 17–27.

Bernstorf, E. (2001, January). Paraprofessionals in music settings. *Music Educators Journal,* 36–40.

Blatt, B. (1970). *Exodus from pandemonium: Human abuse and a reformation of public policy*. Boston, MA: Allyn & Bacon.

Bunt, L. & Hoskyns, S. (eds) (2002). *The handbook of music therapy*. East Sussex, BN: Brunner-Routledge.

Brown, L., McLean, B. B., Hamre-Nietupski, S., Pumpian, I, Certo, N., & Gruenewald, L. (1979). *Journal of Special Education*, 13, 81–90.

Brown, L., Ford, A., Nisbet, J., Sweet, M., Donnelan, A., & Gruenewald, L. (1983). Opportunities available when severely handicapped students attend chronological age appropriate regular schools. *The Journal of the Association for the Severely Handicapped*, 8, 16–24.

Carey, N., Kleiner, B. Porch, R., & Farris, E. (2002). *Arts education in public elementary and secondary schools, 1999–2000*. Washington, DC: National Center for Education Statistics.

Cassidy, J. W. (1992). Communication disorders: Effect on children's ability to label music characteristics. *Journal of Music Therapy*, 15, 100–105.

Clark, E., Olympia, D. E., Jensen, J, Heathfield, L. T., & Jenson, W. R. (2004). Striving for autonomy in a contingency-governed world: Another challenge for individuals with developmental disabilities, *Psychology in the Schools*, 41, 143–153.

Darrow, A. A. (1984). A comparison of rhythmic responsiveness in normal and hearing impaired children and an investigation of the relationship of rhythmic responsiveness to the suprasegmental aspects of speech perception. *Journal of Music Therapy*, 22, 48–66.

Darrow, A. A. (2004). *Introduction to Approaches in Music Therapy*. Silver Springs. MD: The American Music Therapy Association.

Darrow, A. A., Colwell, C. M., & Kim, J. (2002). Research on mainstreaming: Implications for music therapists. In B. L. Wilson (ed.), *Models of music therapy interventions in school settings* (pp. 41–67) (2nd edn). Silver Spring: MD, The American Music Therapy Association.

Duke, R. A. (2005). *Intelligent music teaching: Essays on the core principles of effective instruction*. Austin, TX: Learning and Behavior Resources.

Ferguson, D. L. & Baumgart, D. (1991). Partial participation revisited. *Journal of the Association for Persons with Severe Handicaps*, 16, 218–227.

Flowers, P. J. & Wang, C. (2002). Matching verbal description to music excerpt: The use of language by blind and sighted children. *Journal of Research in Music Education*, 50(3), 202–214.

Giangreco, M., Edelman, S., Luiselli, T. E., & MacFarland, S. Z. C. (1997). Helping or hovering? Effects of instructional assistant proximity on students with disabilities. *Exceptional Children*, 64, 7–18.

Humple, M. (1991). The effects of an integrated early childhood music program on social interaction among children with handicaps and their typical peers. *Journal of Music Therapy*, 28, 161–177.

Jellison, J. A. (2000a). A content analysis of music research with disabled children and youth (1975–1999). In *Effectiveness of music therapy procedures: Documentation of research and clinical practice* (pp. 199–264). Silver Spring, MD: The American Music Therapy Association.

Jellison, J. A. (2000b). How can all people continue to be involved in meaningful music participation. In C. K. Madsen (ed.), *Vision 2020, The Housewright symposium on the future of music education* (pp. 111–137). Reston, VA: Music Educators National Conference.

Jellison, J. A. (2002). On-task participation of typical students close to and away from classmates with disabilities in an elementary music classroom. *Journal of Research in Music Education*, 50(4), 343–355.

Jellison, J. A. (2004). It's about time. MENC: Senior researcher address. *Journal of Research in Music Education*, 52(3), 191–205.

Jellison, J. A., Scott, L. P., Chappell, E. W., & Standridge, A. A. (2006, April). Talking with teachers about inclusion: Preferences, opinions, experiences. Poster session presented at the biennial meeting of MENC—The National Association for Music Education.

Jellison, J. A., Brooks, B., & Huck, A. M. (1984). Structuring small groups and music reinforcement to facilitate positive interactions and acceptance of severely handicapped students in the regular music classroom. *Journal of Research in Music Education*, **32**, 243–264.

Jolivette, K., Sticher, J. P., Sibilsky, S., Scott, T. M., & Ridgley, R. (2002). Naturally occurring opportunities for preschool children with or without disabilities to make choices. *Education and Treatment of Children*, **25**, 396–414.

My Life Going F.A.R. Freedom, authority, responsibility. (2005, March/April). [Special issue] *TASH Connections*, **31**.

Kohler, P. & Field, S. (2003). Transition-focused education: Foundation for the future. *Journal of Special Education*, **17**, 174–184.

Madsen, C. K. & Darrow, A. A. (1989). The relationship between music aptitude and sound conceptualization of the visually impaired. *Journal of Music Therapy*, **26**, 71–78.

Palmer, S. B. & Wehmeyer, M. L. (2003). Promoting self-determination in early elementary school. *Remedial and Special Education*, **24**, 115–126.

Rohrbeck, C. A., Ginsburg-Block, M D., & Fantuzzo, J. W. (2003). Peer-assisted learning interventions with elementary school students: A meta-analytic review. *Journal of Educational Psychology*, **95**, 240–257.

Ryan, R. M. & Deci, E. L. (2000). Self-determination theory and the facilitation of intrinsic motivation, social development, and well-being. *American Psychologist*, **55**, 68–78.

Ryndak, D. L. & Fisher, D. (eds), (2003). *The foundations of inclusive education: A compendium of articles on effective strategies to achieve inclusion* (2nd edn). Baltimore, MD: TASH.

Shapiro, J. P. (1993). *No pity: People with disabilities forging a new civil rights movement*. New York: Times Books.

Turnbull, H. R. & Turnbull, A. P. (2000). *Free appropriate public education: The law and children with disabilities* (6th edn). Denver, CO: Love Publishing Company.

US Department of Education (2003). *25th annual report on the implementation of the individuals with disabilities education act*. Washington, DC: US Department of Education.

Vygotsky, L. (1935/1978). *Mind in society: The development of higher psychological processes*. Cambridge, MA: Harvard University Press.

Wehmeyer, M. L., Abrey, B., Mithaug, D. E., & Stancliffe, R. (2003). *Self-determination: Theoretical foundations for education*. Springfield, IL: Charles C. Thomas.

Wolfensberger, W. (1972). *The principle of normalization in human services*. Toronto, Ontario, Canada: National Institute on Mental Retardation.

Wolfensberger, W. (1983). Social role valorization: A proposed new term for the principle of normalization. *Mental Retardation*, **21**, 234–239.

CHAPTER 14

MUSIC THERAPY FOR CHILDREN

LESLIE BUNT

Introduction

Music therapy is increasingly recognized as an appropriate and effective intervention for children with wide-ranging physical, mental, social, and emotional needs. Indications of this are, first, the acceptance of music therapy by various governments and secondly the profession's growth world-wide, witnessed by the numbers of therapists attending international music therapy conferences. A third factor is the opportunity on every continent for musicians to train in music therapy at undergraduate or postgraduate level (for further information on world-wide developments see http://www.musictherapyworld.net and the on-line journal: http://www.voices.no).

In the first part of this chapter selected case vignettes are used to indicate how children of different ages and needs benefit from music therapy. A recent survey of the range of work carried out by therapists working for one music therapy provider based in the United Kingdom will frame these vignettes. The description of part of a session with a child on the autistic spectrum (the most referred group of children to the therapists in the survey) will provide a flavour of the kinds of sounds and interactions that can emerge within a music therapy context. Additional references to selected research will be incorporated to demonstrate some effective outcomes of music therapy.

The second part of the chapter reviews current ways in which therapists provide theoretical underpinnings to their practice. One tradition within music therapy locates therapeutic changes within the music and developing musical relationships (Nordoff & Robbins, 1977; Ansdell, 1995; Lee, 1995; Aigen, 1996). This tradition can be linked to the patterns observed by developmental psychologists when young children play and interact with sound and music, biological and social roots to the understanding of the practice. Another tradition explores hypothetical connections between the music being played out externally in the space and aspects of a child's internal worlds of perception, emotion and ways of relating to self, objects and others. Within this more interpretive tradition in music therapy a focus on the music is not considered to be self-sufficient, the work being viewed through other 'lenses', for example from physiological or psychoanalytical perspectives (Pavlicevic, 1997).

The case vignettes are snapshots from ongoing therapeutic processes with their in-built history of shared repertoires of musical, personal, and relational events. A therapist adapts the music and style of approach to serve a specific child's needs. Alongside such unique needs each child will bring to the music therapy space his or her own musical preferences and history. This combination of the musical and personal is an enormous challenge to a music therapist who obviously also brings to the encounter his or her own personal musical history, abilities, and experience. Additionally, there is the therapist's theoretical knowledge and therapeutic orientation, personal value system and philosophy (Ruud, 1998). Any subsequent musical and personal meeting in the therapy room is a subtle interaction of all of these different aspects (see Bunt & Hoskyns, 2002 for an elaboration of the various elements and 'players' within a music therapy space). Cultural influences on the music therapy context cannot be overlooked and for this reason references to these broader issues will be included toward the end of the chapter (Stige, 2002).

The following definition of music therapy bridges this introduction to the main parts of the chapter.

> Music therapy is the use of sounds and music within an evolving relationship between client/patient and therapist to support and develop physical, mental, social, emotional and spiritual well-being.

Adapted from Bunt (1994, p. 8).

Examples from practice

The range of children referred to music therapy

Music therapists work with children of all ages either individually or in small groups. The wide range of settings includes: pre-school specialist nurseries, units for children with

Table 14.1 MusicSpace survey percentages by age and problem area.

	Ages			Total %
	0–5	6–10	11–18	
Autistic spectrum disorder	4.5	12.7	8.4	25.6
Profound and multiple learning difficulties	2.9	8.4	6.1	17.4
Emotional and behavioural difficulties	1.8	9.3	6.1	17.2
Mild learning difficulties (including language delay)	1.5	3.5	3.3	8.3
Other physical/neurological problems or chromosomal disorders (e.g., Down syndrome, Rett's syndrome)	3.2	1.7	0.4	5.3
Physical disabilities (e.g., cerebral palsy)	1.1	1.9	1.6	4.6
Visual impairment	1.4	1.9	1.1	4.4
Hearing impairment	2.6	0.6	1	4.2
Attention deficit hyperactivity disorder (ADHD)	0.8	1.6	1.1	3.5
Crisis intervention (mainstream schools)	0	2.1	0.5	2.6
Mental health issues	0	0	2.3	2.3
Attachment disorder	0.1	0.4	1.1	1.6
Bereavement work	0.4	0.6	0.3	1.3
Cancer and life-threatening illness	0	0.4	0.7	1.1
Abuse—history of sexual abuse	0.1	0.3	0.2	0.6
Total %	20.4	45.4	34.2	100%

language problems, special schools and units for children with learning or behavioural difficulties, mainstream schools, centres for children with visual or hearing impairments, and hospital-based units and hospices. A survey in March 2005 of the 556 members of the UK's Association of Professional Music Therapists indicated that 32% were employed by charities; 27% by the National Health Service; 20% by Local Education Authorities; 19% working privately and 2% employed by the Social Services. MusicSpace is one of the larger charities and its first community-based music therapy centre opened in Bristol in 1991. A survey of 40 mostly part-time music therapists working for the six branches throughout the UK indicated that 724 children were being seen each week during May 2004. The children were divided in three age ranges: 0–5 (21%), 6–10 (45%), and 11–18 (34%), and into 15 different areas. While acknowledging the negative aspects of labelling and of attempting to subsume a child's unique combination of difficulties into one area it is informative to discover the wide range and extent of problems that music therapy can address (see Table 14.1).

Children on the autistic spectrum

Given the difficulties these children face in a primarily verbal environment it was not surprising to discover from the survey that this was the most commonly referred group (comprising about 25% of the total cases).

Neil (not his real name) was referred by his consultant paediatrician to music therapy when he was 3 years 9 months. He was diagnosed as autistic demonstrating the 'triad of impairments' in communication, symbolic and imaginative play and social interaction exemplified by: difficulty in developing relationships; speech and language problems (he did not speak); some stereotyped movements and a need to maintain sameness (Wing, 1993). His mother brought him for weekly music therapy sessions to a dedicated music therapy centre for a period of nearly two years until Neil moved to full-time schooling. This description is taken from a video recording of the 36th session that occurred almost at the halfway stage in the therapy. From the outset it was decided to include Neil's mother in the sessions so that the therapist could facilitate further communication between mother and child via the music. Here the emphasis moved away from developing a relationship primarily with the therapist to furthering links with the primary caregiver (see Warwick, 1995; Oldfield *et al.*, 2003; Woodward, 2004). A music therapy student was involved in the session as part of a placement. It could be argued that there were too many adults in this session but, as can be noted, Neil used these different objects of reference in the music space quite effectively.

During the early part of the session Neil's music was quite fragmented. He played some of the instruments for short bursts, particularly the shiny suspended gong and metallic wind chimes. At moments he became fixated on spinning the cymbal. He vocalised using a characteristic minor third ('ah' and 'oo' sounds). There was some semblance of an emerging dialogue between his music and the therapist's singing and piano playing. Most attention was towards the instruments, with little looking towards the adults in the room. The student matched the pitch, duration, timbre and loudness of Neil's sounds on her viola, glissandi being particularly resonant with Neil's sound world.

After an extensive exploration of the viola, placing his hand on the bow and indicating the strength of movement across the string, Neil moves away. The central part of the session occurs at the piano when Neil sits at the treble end on his mother's lap. He plays fast two-handed clusters. The viola music and the therapist's piano music become faster and stronger with much syncopation and use of energetic fifths and fourths. The energy level increases as Neil's mother jiggles him up and down in the music's tempo. Neil appears to tolerate this high level of energy and activity while on his mother's lap. He looks towards the therapist. Glissandi and Neil's preferred sounds are incorporated into this stronger music. Possibly the music becomes too arousing and complex here: he breaks off any engagement and looks inside the piano, stroking the strings and moving the hammers. The viola stops and the piano music slows as he explores the inside of the piano. Long notes are sounded on the viola and the therapist sings sustained lines accompanied by repeating and rocking ostinati chords. Neil joins in the singing. The music becomes more extended—voice, viola and piano merging with Neil's vocal sounds and piano explorations. The therapist comments on Neil's actions, singing for example 'Neil is playing', or 'Neil is singing.' Neil returns to the piano clusters and plays many in quick succession, first playing with movements from his wrists and then with big gestures from his elbows. He looks to his mother and moves as if to hug her. The viola and piano harmonies provide a soft and containing support to what feels like an intimate moment between Neil and his mother. He stretches out his arms and vocalises. She replies non-verbally and holds him across her body. The music becomes quieter, slower and more reflective with falling phrases and richer harmonic textures, particularly at the end of the phrases. The music seems to articulate the tenderness of this moment between mother and child. There follows an oscillation between the faster tempo, at Neil's initiation, and the more intimate music when he looks again to his mother or the therapist. This whole piano-based section is a sustained episode and there seems to be a great deal of communication taking place between Neil and his mother.

After the focused musical and emotional intensity of this central episode his mother offers him some drumsticks. Neil resists and moves away to the corner of the room. He stays there by himself while the viola plays quiet and long low sounds. The session ends quietly.

This session had the overall shape of a gradual move to the longest and most connected contact between Neil and his mother at the piano after which he moved away. This shape was paralleled in the earlier parts of the session, such approach-avoidance behaviour being quite common with children on the autistic spectrum. Indirect, albeit at times quite fleeting, communication via the instruments did lead to more extended periods of direct communication. His mother commented that she had never seen him smile so much during a session.

There is a growing literature on the substantive role of music therapy in the assessment and ongoing work with children on the autistic spectrum (Alvin & Warwick, 1992; Howat, 1995; Robarts, 1996; Wigram, 2000). Edgerton (1994) investigated the effects of improvisational music therapy when working with 11 autistic children (aged 6–9). Her research demonstrated clear increases in communicative behaviour (responses and actions) over time. When she compared scores from the first and last of the 10 individual sessions she found significant differences between the children's scores. This controlled study, although using a small number of children and sessions, indicated that music therapy did have positive effects on the communicative behaviour of these autistic children and that the effects were beginning to be generalized.

Children with learning difficulties

The MusicSpace survey indicated a large proportion of referrals of children with learning difficulties (from mild to severe—rows 2 and 4 of Table 14.1). Music has a potential strength as an alternative non-verbal means of communication for children with such difficulties, bypassing any emphasis on verbal communication. Shared meanings and understanding can be developed and a child can learn to communicate, if appropriate, at a pre-verbal level. The flexibility and range within the different forms of music enable the therapist to adapt both the music and the approach in relation to the particular context and needs of each child.

> Louise, a 10-year old with profound learning difficulties and physical disabilities, was referred to music therapy by her class teacher to discover whether music could provide an alternative means of communication. Louise sat in a specially designed chair. A great deal of time and space was needed to listen and attend to Louise in order to begin to make any kind of connection with her. The therapist's sounds were few, short and slow, connected to the slow pace of her breathing and small bursts of attention. Louise had a preference for single long sounds, such as a pair of highly resonant Indian bells, sounds that momentarily captured her attention. She would move her head spontaneously towards the source of such sounds, sometimes with an accompanying smile and vocal sound. The therapist would match the pitch of any of Louise's sounds with his own sounds and at times a short episode of sustained engagement could be achieved. Such engagement depended on accurate matching of the duration, pitch and intensity of her sounds. A musical relationship gradually became established when Louise began to communicate her intentions. Such developments began to be transferred to the classroom and her teachers started to incorporate more vocal sounds in their communications with Louise. More of Louise's needs and feelings were being understood by both her teachers and music therapist.
>
> Adapted from Bunt & Hoskyns (2002, p. 208)

At the age of 14 Christopher still has no speech. He is currently seen regularly at his Special School for children with learning difficulties by a member of the team of music therapists at West Midlands MusicSpace. His mother, a former nurse and health service administrator, writes:

> Music therapy has been the key to unlocking many doors for my son, Christopher. . . . I am amazed by all the progress made, particularly Christopher's ability to express a range of emotions and his growing confidence and co-operation. He is learning to turn take and his co-ordination and concentration have improved. The sessions provided by MusicSpace form a valuable part of his education. It means a lot to us as a family that Christopher has found a therapy which brings him such happiness and helps him to lead a fulfilled life.

(See http://www.musicspace.org for video examples of Christopher's music-making and comments from his mother.)

There is growing evidence of the effectiveness of music therapy for children with learning difficulties. The author used video filmed at different stages in a series of interlinked projects to compare periods of individual music therapy with similar ones without music therapy. He also used individual play with well-known adults as an additional control. Music therapy was significantly effective with children with learning difficulties in such specific areas as:

- increasing the frequency, length, range, and appropriate use of vocal sounds
- increasing the amount of looking to the adult and to the musical instruments
- increasing the amount of turn taking
- developing a child's imitative skills and ability to initiate an activity
- reducing the amount of non-attentive behaviour (see Bunt, 1994, for a summary of results).

This study itemized those aspects, particularly the development of vocal sounds and turn-taking, that resulted in highly significant changes in the behaviour of the children. It also pointed to those behaviours, such as the amount of time engaged with playing the instruments, which were shared with other forms of individual intervention with children.

Aldridge and his team used both the Nordoff–Robbins scales of music therapy assessment (Nordoff & Robbins, 1977) and some standardized developmental subscales to explore differences between groups of children with developmental delay moving through periods of music therapy and no music therapy. The researchers observed 'a continuing significant difference on the hearing and speech subscale and a significantly changing ability to listen and communicate.' Aldridge noted that 'Music therapy seems to have an effect on personal relationship, emphasizing the positive benefits of active listening and performing, and this in turn sets the context for developmental change' (Aldridge, 1996, p. 262).

Further examples of work with children with learning difficulties can be found in the many published case studies (Bruscia, 1991; Tyler, 1997; Pavlicevic, 1999; Wigram & De Backer, 1999; Wigram *et al.*, 2002; Darnley-Smith & Patey, 2003).

Other groups within the MusicSpace survey

Another important subgroup was children with physical, neurological, or sensory problems. Therapists can build on the highly motivating and physical aspects of making music to help a child to become more organized in time and space, making use of the full vibrational and elemental capacities of music to compensate for any specific difficulties or impairments (Bean, 1995; Bang, 1998).

> Natalie, a bright 7-year old, was about to move upstairs into the junior part of her school. Her physical disability, a mild cerebral palsy, affected both gross and fine movements with an associated lack of confidence. Natalie walked with an irregular pattern. At the start of a short period of joint physiotherapy and music therapy sessions we discovered that her preferred spontaneous tempi were quite slow and we found the point where her pulse became steadier and her music more organised. This pulse became the basis of a walking song practised regularly with other members of her family at home, walking in the street and at school when she felt anxious as when facing large gym apparatus. During subsequent appointments it was clear that she was using the internalised tempo and pattern of the song to organise and regulate her walking. This developing self-organization transferred to her finer motor control on a horizontal level. The development of physical control was mirrored

in her increase in confidence with a far more upright girl leaving after each session (she would enjoy seeing this physically measured out). Reports from her school a few years later noted that she would still use her music as a self-help tool when feeling anxious or concerned about her level of control.

Adapted from Bunt (1994, p. 59)

A growing area indicated in the survey was children with attention deficit hyperactivity disorder (ADHD). These children often respond with highly sustained attention and concentration in individual and small group music therapy. They can find accessing the educational curriculum difficult, whereas music provides an environment where they can often succeed and build self-esteem and confidence (Jackson, 2003; Rickson & Watkins, 2003).

> The author recalls a period of music therapy with eight-year old Mark, a boy whose problems associated with living with ADHD resulted in periods out of school with home tuition. His fascination with music enabled him to attend music therapy sessions of up to forty-five minutes making careful choices from a range of instruments to create long and complex pieces of improvised music, composing his own songs and making many musical demands on his therapist. For example, he would ask for sections of a work such as Saint-Saëns' *Carnival of the Animals* to be played, demonstrating extreme sensitivity and awareness of any melodic or harmonic imperfections.

Music therapists are being asked to intervene when older children face crises, with the expectation that music will provide an emotional release and a focus for renewed access to learning (Tingle, 2002). Montello and Coons compared the behavioural effects of active rhythm-based group music therapy with listening group therapy on young people aged between 11 and 14 and exhibiting emotional and behavioural problems. Teachers used standardized procedures to rate changes in attention, motivation, and hostility. There were positively significant results for both kinds of music therapy intervention with most changes on the aggression/hostility scale. The authors concluded that the intervention was positive in the facilitation of self-expression, providing 'a channel for transforming frustration, anger and aggression into the experience of creativity and self-mastery' (Montello & Coons, 1996, p. 49).

The survey also indicated how children with mental health problems, life-threatening illnesses such as cancer and those with a history of abuse are being increasingly referred to music therapy. Such major life issues can be addressed and explored within the safety of a musical environment and therapeutic relationship (Ibberson, 1996; O'Neill & Pavlicevic, 2003; Robarts, 2003; Rogers, 2003).

Before moving to the second part of the chapter a note of caution needs to be struck regarding the complexities of overlapping problems presented by children. This is clearly demonstrated in Etkin's (1999) moving case study of a child with complex needs. This child presented with severe visual impairment related to a rare brain disorder and resulting in profound learning difficulties. However, it quickly became clear that the main therapeutic needs related more to the child's depression and acute withdrawal. Etkin related this dynamic to the work of Sinason (1992) who differentiates between the primary handicap, in this child's case her visual impairment and brain disorder, and what she refers to as a 'secondary handicap.' Sinason points out that 'the defensive use or abuse the individual makes of the primary damage can sometimes be more powerful than the original handicap itself' (p. 112).

Some theoretical underpinning and 'lenses'

Music therapy and links to early childhood development

> It is a paradox, perhaps best captured in music (or tones of voice), that it is sounds and silence that link us to our earliest states of being. Our parents would have spoken words to us as babies, but they were not words to us.
>
> Phillips (1998, p. 49)

Observers of children in music therapy often comment on the motivating quality of the music, the children seemingly demonstrating an innate curiosity in music. Some of the children described in the vignettes above found it difficult to function within a strictly verbal environment but appeared reasonably at ease within a music space. It is as if, as mentioned above, with the pressure taken away from the more customary mode of verbal communication they could begin to communicate. Often such children respond better if words and sentences are sung to them, as noted in the examples of Neil and Louise.

Children's emergent musical behaviour and music therapy

A music therapist has many opportunities to observe a child's emergent musical behaviour. Neil appeared to be at an early sensory stage of manipulating the instruments, for example his very tactile interest in the vibrations produced by the viola. Some of this activity could be viewed as reflexive yet there were times, as in his interest in playing inside the piano, when his emergent musical behaviour appeared to demonstrate intention. He was aware that sounds arose from and returned to silence, that they had a beginning and an end. His vocal sounds also appeared related to the musical context and often indicated a potential for communication. They also would often be framed by silence. Through all of his musical play and improvisations he demonstrated quite clearly his musical preferences: the sustained sounds of piano and voice, the viola and the wind chimes. Young infants show attention to preferred sounds by turning to their source, as was the case with certain musical cues presented to Louise. As with adults, young children show a marked discrimination of melodic contour before achieving precise pitch discrimination, for example Neil's vocal use of the minor third motif.

A child's explorations of the sound and musical elements of timbre, pulse, duration, loudness, silence, pitch, melody, and rhythm can provide a rich source of spontaneous material for the music psychologist. In many ways these elements can also be regarded as the tools of the music therapist's trade (Nordoff & Robbins, 1971, 1977; Alvin, 1975; Bunt, 1994, 2001; Robbins & Robbins, 1998; Darnley-Smith and Patey, 2003). In order to gain further understanding of how children connect to sound music therapists can turn to the growing evidence of the way young infants structure these basic elements of music (overviews include Hargreaves, 1986; Deliège & Sloboda, 1996).

Musical play in the context of a relationship

In music therapy a child's musical play and explorations occur within the context of a range of different relationships. These are created and built up over time between the child and the instruments in the room and indirectly through them with any adult playing other instruments. Vocal responses are similarly part of an emerging reciprocal process. In Neil's case the music was also used to facilitate as much intimate and emotional communication between himself and his mother. In a chapter entitled *Intuitive Parenting*, Papoušek (1996) notes how parents and infants share a prelinguistic code: 'musical elements, such as pitch and melody, temporal patterns and rhythm, loudness and accent, and timbre and harmony, are the most salient features of both partners' vocal utterances, and soon become the earliest means of reciprocal communication, preverbal vocal imitation, and playful vocal interchanges' (p. 90). The musical elements within sessions help to foster as much of this kind of reciprocal communication as possible. As children become more fluent in their use of the music it is hoped that more of this kind of prelinguistic code can spill over into the developing relationship between the children and other significant adults.

These natural connections between patterns in infant–parent interaction and the building blocks of music provide vital points of reference for music therapists working with children. The children described above were sufficiently motivated to play with the elements of sound and music and could discover or rediscover within a music therapy setting the very ingredients of these early stages of human communication. In spite of often quite severe difficulties in verbal communication, within music therapy healthy parts of children can be observed, parts indicating potential for communication. A music therapist can locate a musical means to reinforce what the child can do. The positive contributions that music can make to a child's potential, particularly in the early years, have been highlighted in a variety of UK governmental reports (see http://www. teachernet.gov.uk and http://www.espp.org.uk).

Early musical patterning

Researchers are finding these connections exist from the very first days of life. The early chapters in this volume discuss the evidence that very young babies not only demonstrate self-synchrony within their own patterned sound-based behaviours but that they also make instantaneous connections (interactional synchrony) with the patterned and pulse-based nature of their primary carers' vocal sounds, body movements and facial expressions. It is a highly reciprocal process with a kind of interactive dance becoming quickly established where both partners negotiate highly communicative and emotionally expressive narrative structures. These ongoing intersubjective narratives share all the jointly created sound and musical parameters discussed above and as could be observed in the case vignettes. It is a subtle process with both participants and players in the dance mutually influencing the other in order to sustain interaction and modulate emotional expression (Papoušek, 1996; Trehub *et al.*, 1997; Trevarthen & Malloch, 2000; Trevarthen, 2002; Chapter 2, this volume). Consequently, musical patterning, part of what Malloch (1999) has called 'communicative musicality,' can be regarded as being at the hub of a child's emotional development and cognition. Trevarthen (2002) has developed a theory of an 'intrinsic motive pulse' (p. 25) within the brain that enables this early engagement with music to emerge. Benzon takes up this notion and proposes that music is far more than a communicative sharing of meanings and can be regarded as 'a medium through which individual brains are coupled together in shared activity' (Benzon, 2001, p. 23), links being made here between the social, biological, and neurological.

Relational play in music therapy and links to difficulties in communication

The individual, relational, and musical exist in an interactive web within a music therapy session. Pavlicevic (1997) has drawn the personal and musical together in her exploration of the nature of 'dynamic form' in music therapy. She relates this term to Stern's notion of 'affect attunement' and his elaboration of the vitality and dynamic affects that shape, in a matrix-like fashion, the interactive play between mother and child (Stern, 1985). Pavlicevic describes Stern's vitality affects, for example, as 'the qualities of shape or contour, intensity, motion, rhythm—'amodal' properties that exist in our minds as dynamic and abstract, not bound to any particular feeling or event, and enabling us to 'make sense of the world' (Bunt & Pavlicevic, 2001, p. 194). These are 'dynamic kinesic forms of feeling ('surging,' 'fading away,' 'fleeting,' 'explosive,' 'crescendo,' 'decrescendo,' 'bursting,' 'drawn out,' etc.) that cannot be separated from the vital processes of life—breathing, getting hungry, falling asleep, etc.' (Hadley, 2003, p. 10). These forms of feeling enable connections to be made, for example, between the speed and contour of a child's hand movement and an adult's response in another modality, for example a vocal sound. Stern uses musical terminology to describe these communicative potentials and, in turn, music therapists can explore these links between the personal and musical as a further frame of reference when improvising with children (Pavlicevic, 1995, 1997; Robarts, 1996; Hadley, 2003). If we can regard musical elements to be at the root of our expressive, emotional and communicative life, then '. . . we see that disorders in any of these realms will have musical correspondences. Disturbances in communication may be seen—and experienced directly—through disturbances in the timing, sequencing, amplitude, energy and fluidity of acts and gestures, as well as in disruptions of inter-coordinating acts with another person' (Pavlicevic, 1997, p. 114).

The work described in the first part of this chapter shows that some of these disruptions and disturbances within both the musical and interactive flow as described by Pavlicevic. It took a long time for the therapist to understand the unique way that Louise timed her musical gestures before any inter-coordinated activity could develop. Neil's contact with the instruments moved from the fragmented to the more sustained. He would often break off contact at the height of maximum contact, needing to withdraw from potentially too high a level of arousal. We could observe how and when there was synchrony and co-ordination between his musical/communicative gestures and those of the other people in the room and when there were problems in sustaining such connections. Natalie's problems in organizing her responses and sequencing events were observable within both the musical and personal domains. Such observations provide the basis for furthering understanding of children's needs for ongoing therapy.

Readings of music therapy from different perspectives

Music therapy is a complex and multifaceted profession drawing from many disciplines to establish its sense of meaning. Primarily there is the music. In the previous sections the emergent patterns in music and their links to early developmental processes, in particular the socio-biological bonds established with the primary caregivers, were discussed in relation to music therapy. In this section some other frames of reference and ways of reading the work will be briefly described.

Readings through a physiological and external lens

Much can be learnt about a child's level of general development through observing behaviour in music therapy. It was clear to any observer of the children described in the first part of the chapter that music influenced a range of physical parameters. Some of the early studies indicating the effective use of music therapy show music's influence on such physiological indices as: changes in heart rate and respiration rate; electrical resistance of the skin; levels of general activity; muscle tone; pupillary reflex, and postural response (Ruud, 1980; Bunt, 1994, 1997; Aldridge, 1996). Ruud (1980) is not alone in criticizing this research for focusing on one-off experiments and short-lived effects. It is also notoriously difficult to separate out the physiological from the emotional in terms of a sensory response to music. More recently, computer-based technology and developments in, for example, vibro-acoustics have made it possible to develop extensive ongoing physiological studies linked to effective therapeutic interventions in such areas as cerebral palsy and respiratory conditions (Skille & Wigram, 1995; Wigram & Dileo, 1997).

Some links to a psychoanalytic and more internal perspective

A growing number of music therapists read their work through a psychoanalytical lens, which Heal Hughes (1995) describes as psychoanalytically informed music therapy. Children transfer positive and negative feelings on to the music, the instruments, and to any adults in the room (Bruscia, 1998). Conversely, therapists monitor their own feelings in countering such transference and in responding authentically to the children (the construct of counter-transference). Streeter (1999) has focused on the relationship within music therapy in developing the notion of the 'musical transference relationship' (p. 88).

The instruments used in music therapy and the music itself can be viewed within the constructs of transitional objects and phenomena as proposed by Winnicott (1974): 'We experience life in the area of transitional phenomena, in the exciting interweave of subjectivity and objective observation, and in an area that is intermediate between the inner reality of the individual and the shared reality of the world that is external to individuality.' (p. 64).

We can view the musical play of the children described in this chapter as exploring such transitional and transformational areas. The music was part of each child, yet also not so. The music was co-created in a space that involved another person hence the concept of intersubjectivity and the constructs of me/not me; self/other (for more exploration of such themes in relation to music therapy see, for example, Alvin, 1977; Levinge, 1993; Tyler, 1998; Brown, 2002). Viewing the work through a psychoanalytical lens therapists talk of being there for the children in a 'good enough' way as paralleled by Winnicott's notion of 'good enough mothering' (Winnicott, 1965, p. 145). There is also the notion of how the therapist and the music can contain the feelings of the child, including all the difficult ones. This is drawn from Bion (1962) and his notion of the 'container-contained'.

Shifting patterns and further areas of development

In recent years music therapists have drawn from widening areas of musical and psychological writing to underpin their clinical work. Ansdell (1997) is one of a group of therapist researchers who have made connections between music therapy and so-called 'new musicology' and in particular Small's (1998) concept of 'musicking'. Small not only sees relationships existing between the sounds themselves but also metaphorically between the various personal relationships and connections with the outside world. Ansdell also relates his own work to the context of music's expression of individual and cultural identities. This emphasis on identity has permeated the writings of music therapist Ruud (1998) and is correspondingly a growing focus within social psychology (De Nora, 2001; Davidson, 2004). Ruud has greatly influenced Stige in his search for 'a better understanding of how the participants create meaning in the communicative processes in the different contexts of music therapy' (Stige, 2002, p. 26). Stige's writings have drawn our attention to the wider cultural issues inherent in situating any therapeutic intervention within a particular context. His work is linked to the recent re-emergence of interest in Community Music Therapy, which challenges the more traditional clinical model of individual and small group music therapy practice (Pavlicevic & Ansdell, 1994).

Such challenges from recent research become clearer in the light of new developments of practice. In addition to the areas described in the MusicSpace survey music therapists are now moving into different contexts and settings, including challenging work with, among others:

- premature babies (Nöcker-Ribaupierre, 1999);
- older children with eating disorders (Robarts & Sloboda, 1994);
- children with traumatic experiences linked to early abandonment, violence, and war (Sutton, 2002);
- children in hospitals undergoing painful procedures, for example resulting from severe burns (Edwards, 1998);
- refugee children and those living in multicultural contexts in inner cities (Clough, 2004).

Final comments

It is easy to imagine that the children with profound difficulties in communication described in the vignettes in this chapter will continue to be priorities for music therapy intervention. Alongside this one striking feature of the survey was the amount of the work with older children with emotional and behavioural problems and those facing crises. More research will enable the contributions of music therapy to all the areas itemized in the survey (and to any emerging others) to be more carefully defined. There is a need for much detailed work indicating how music therapy can help children with wide-ranging ages and problems. How can music therapy make a contribution to a child's life both inside and outside of the music therapy room? There is also a need for more understanding about the musical processes that contribute towards specific therapeutic outcomes.

Reference to some of the current work in musicology contributes to potential under-standing of these processes. However, as implied in the introduction, if we only look to the music we will understand just a part of the whole picture. This chapter has attempted to indicate how a music therapist can draw on knowledge within such areas as developmental psychology, psychodynamic theory, cultural studies, as well as music. Such an integrative approach will help to deepen our understanding of how music therapy can help children with wide-ranging needs to emerge and reach their full potential.

Acknowledgement

To music therapy colleague, Sarah Hoskyns, for helpful suggestions on an earlier draft of this chapter.

References

Aigen, K. (1996). *Being in music: Foundations of Nordoff-Robbins music therapy*. The Nordoff-Robbins Music Therapy Monograph Series 1. St Louis, MO: MMB Music.

Aldridge, D. (1996). *Music therapy research and practice in medicine: From out of the Silence*. London: Jessica Kingsley.

Alvin, J. (1975). *Music therapy*. London: Hutchinson.

Alvin, J. (1977). The musical instrument as an intermediary object. *British Journal of Music Therapy*, **8**(2), 7–13.

Alvin, J. & Warwick, A. (1992). *Music therapy for the autistic child* (2nd edn). Oxford: Oxford University Press.

Ansdell, G. (1995). *Music for life: Aspects of creative music therapy with adult clients*. London: Jessica Kingsley.

Ansdell, G. (1997). Musical elaboration: What has the new musicology to say to music therapy? *British Journal of Music Therapy*, **11**(2), 36–44.

Bang, C. (1998). A world of sound and music. *Nordic Journal of Music Therapy*, **7**(2), 154–163.

Bean, J. (1995). Music therapy and the child with cerebral palsy: Directive and non-directive intervention. In T. Wigram, B. Saperston & R. West (eds), *The art and science of music therapy: A handbook* (pp. 194–208). London: Harwood Academic Press.

Benzon, W. L. (2001). *Beethoven's anvil: Music in mind and culture*. Oxford: Oxford University Press.

Bion, W. (1962). *Learning from experience*. London: Heinemann.

Brown, S. (2002). 'Hullo object! I destroyed you!' In L. Bunt & S. Hoskyns (eds), *The handbook of music therapy* (pp. 84–96). London: Routledge.

Bruscia, K. (ed.) (1991). *Case studies in music therapy*. Phoenixville, PA: Barcelona.

Bruscia, K. (ed.) (1998). *The dynamics of music psychotherapy*. Gilsum, NH: Barcelona.

Bunt, L. (1994). *Music therapy: An art beyond words*. London: Routledge.

Bunt, L. (1997). Clinical and therapeutic uses of music. In D. Hargreaves & A. North (eds), *The social psychology of music* (pp. 249–267). Oxford: Oxford University Press.

Bunt, L. (2001). Music therapy. In S. Sadie (ed.), *The new Grove dictionary of music and musicians* (pp. 534–540) **17**, London: Macmillan.

Bunt, L. & Hoskyns, S. (2002). *The handbook of music therapy*. London: Routledge.

Bunt, L. & Pavlicevic, M. (2001). Music and emotion: Perspectives from music therapy. In P. Juslin & J. Sloboda (eds), *Music and emotion*. Oxford: Oxford University Press.

Clough, L. (2004). *Finding a voice: Case study of music therapy with a young selective communicator/mute from an asylum seeker background*. Unpublished presentation to 6th European Music Therapy Congress, University of Jyväskylä, Finland (June 16–20, 2004).

Darnley-Smith, R. & Patey, H. M. (2003). *Music therapy*. London: Sage.

Davidson, J. (2004). What can the social psychology of music offer community music therapy? In M. Pavlicevic & G. Ansdell (eds), *Community music therapy*. London: Jessica Kingsley.

Deliège, I. & Sloboda, J. (ed.) (1996). *Musical beginnings: Origins and development of musical competence*. Oxford: Oxford University Press.

De Nora, T. (2001). *Music in everyday life*. Cambridge: Cambridge University Press.

Edgerton, C. L. (1994). The effect of improvisational music therapy of the communicative behaviours of autistic children. *Journal of Music Therapy*, **31**, 31–62.

Edwards, J. (1998). Music therapy for children with severe burn injury. *Music Therapy Perspectives*, **16**(2), 20–5.

Etkin, P. (1999). The use of creative improvisation and psychodynamic insights in music therapy with an abused child. In T. Wigram & J. De Backer (eds), *Clinical applications of music therapy in developmental disability, paediatrics and neurology* (pp. 155–165). London: Jessica Kingsley.

Hadley, S. (ed.) (2003). *Psychodynamic music therapy: Case studies*. Gilsum, NH: Barcelona.

Hargreaves, D. (1986). *The developmental psychology of music*. Cambridge: Cambridge University Press.

Heal Hughes, M. (1995). A comparison of mother-infant interactions and the client-therapist relationship in music therapy sessions. In T. Wigram, B. Sapertson, & R. West (eds), *The art and science of music therapy: A handbook* (pp. 296–306). London: Harwood Academic Press.

Howat, R. (1995). Elizabeth: A case study of an autistic child in individual music therapy. In T. Wigram, B. Sapertson, & R. West (eds), *The art and science of music therapy: A handbook* (pp. 239–257). London: Harwood Academic Press.

Ibberson, C. (1996). A natural end: One story about Catherine. *British Journal of Music Therapy*, **10**, 24–32.

Jackson, N. A. (2003). A survey of music therapy methods and their role in the treatment of early elementary school children with ADHD. *Journal of Music Therapy*, **40**(4), 302–23.

Lee, C. A. (1995). The analysis of therapeutic improvisory music. In A. Gilroy & C. Lee (eds), *Art and music: Therapy and research* (pp. 35–50). London: Routledge.

Levinge, A. (1993). Permission to play. The search for self through music therapy: Research with children presenting with communication difficulties. In H. Payne (ed.), *Handbook of inquiry in the arts therapies: One river many currents* (pp. 218–228). London: Jessica Kingsley.

Malloch, S. (1999). Mothers and infants and communicative musicality. *Musicae Scientae, Special Issue* (1999–2000), 29–57.

Montello, L. & Coons, E. E. (1996). Effects of active versus passive musictherapy on preadolescents with emotional, learning and behavioural disorders. *Journal of Music Therapy*, **34**, 49–67.

Nöcker-Ribaupierre, M. (1999). Premature birth and music therapy. In T. Wigram & J. De Backer (eds), *Clinical applications of music therapy in developmental disability, paediatrics and neurology* (pp. 47–65). London: Jessica Kingsley.

Nordoff, P. & Robbins, C. (1971). *Therapy in music for handicapped children*. London: Gollancz.

Nordoff, P. & Robbins, C. (1977). *Creative music therapy*. New York: John Day.

Oldfield, A., Adams, M., & Bunce, L. (2003). An investigation into short-term music therapy with mothers and young children. *British Journal of Music Therapy*, **17**, 26–46.

O'Neill, N. & Pavlicevic, M. (2003). Exploring a role for music therapy with children undergoing bone marrow transplantation at Great Ormond Hospital, London. *British Journal of Music Therapy*, 17, 8–17.

Papoušek, M. (1996). Intuitive parenting: A hidden source of musical stimulation in infancy. In I. Deliège & J. Sloboda (eds), *Musical beginnings: Origins and development of musical competence* (pp. 88–112). Oxford: Oxford University Press.

Pavlicevic, M. (1995). Music and emotion: aspects of music therapy research. In A. Gilroy & C. Lee (eds), *Art and music: Therapy and research* (pp. 51–65). London: Routledge.

Pavlicevic, M. (1997). *Music therapy in context: music, meaning, and relationship*, London: Jessica Kingsley.

Pavlicevic, M. (1999). *Music therapy: Intimate notes*. London: Jessica Kingsley.

Pavlicevic, M. & Ansdell, G. (1994). *Community music therapy*. London: Jessica Kingsley.

Phillips, A. (1998). *The beast in the nursery*. London: Faber and Faber.

Rickson, D. J. & Watkins, W. G. (2003). Music therapy to promote prosocial behaviours in aggressive adolescent boys—a pilot study. *Journal of Music Therapy*, 40(4), 283–301.

Robarts, J. (1996). Music therapy for autistic children. In C. Trevarthen, K. Aitken, D. Papoudi, & J. Robarts (eds), *Children with autism: Diagnosis and interventions to meet their needs* (pp. 134–160). London: Jessica Kingsley.

Robarts, J. (2003). The healing function of improvised songs in music therapy with a child survivor of early trauma and sexual abuse. In S. Hadley (ed.), *Psychodynamic music therapy: Case studies* (pp. 141–182). Gilsum, NH: Barcelona.

Robarts, J. & Sloboda, J. A. (1994). Perspectives on music therapy with people suffering from anorexia nervosa. *Journal of British Music Therapy*, 8, 7–15.

Robbins, C. & Robbins, C. (ed.) (1998). *Healing heritage: Paul Nordoff exploring the tonal language of music*. Gilsum, NH: Barcelona.

Rogers, P. (2003). Working with Jenny: Stories of gender, power and abuse. In S. Hadley (ed.), *Psychodynamic music therapy: Case studies*. Gilsum, NH: Barcelona.

Ruud, E. (1980). *Music therapy and its relationship to current treatment theories*. St Louis, Missouri: Magnamusic-Baton/London: Schott & Co.

Ruud, E. (1998). *Music therapy: Improvisation, communication and culture*. Gilsum, NH: Barcelona.

Sinason, V. (1992). *Mental handicap and the human condition*. London: Free Association Books.

Skille, O. & Wigram, T. (1995). The effects of music, vocalisation and vibration on brain and muscle tissue: Studies in vibroacoustic therapy. In T. Wigram, B. Saperston & R. West (eds), *The art and science of music therapy: A handbook* (pp. 23–57). London: Harwood Academic Press.

Small, C. (1998). *Musicking*. Hanover, NH: Wesleyan University Press.

Stern, D. (1985). *The interpersonal world of the infant: A view from psychoanalysis and developmental psychology*. London: Academic Press.

Stige, B. (2002). *Culture-centred music therapy*. Gilsum, NH: Barcelona.

Sutton, J. (2002). *Music, music therapy and trauma*. London: Jessica Kingsley.

Streeter, E. (1999). Definition and use of the musical transference relationship. In T. Wigram & J. De Backer (eds), *Clinical applications of music therapy in psychiatry* (pp. 84–101). London: Jessica Kingsley.

Tingle, E. (2002). Creating a paradigm: developing a new music therapy service in education. Paper presented to the *Oxford World Congress of Music Therapy* available from the website: http://www.musictherapy.org

Trehub, S., Schellenberg, G., & Hill, D. (1997). The origins of music perception and cognition: a developmental perspective. In C. Deliège & J. Sloboda (eds), *Perceptionand cognition of music* (pp. 103–128). Hove: Psychology Press.

Trevarthen, C. (2002). Origins of musical identity: evidence from infancy for musical social awareness. In R. MacDonald, D. Hargreaves, & D. Miell (eds), *Musical identities* (pp. 21–38). Oxford University Press.

Trevarthen, C. & Malloch, S. N. (2000). The dance of wellbeing: Defining the musical therapeutic effect. *Nordic Journal of Music Therapy*, 9(2), 3–17.

Tyler, H. (1997). Music therapy for children with learning difficulties. In M. Fawcus (ed.), *Children with learning difficulties: A collaborative approach to their education and management* (pp. 210–232). London: Whurr Publishers.

Tyler, H. M. (1998). Behind the mask: and exploration of the true and false self as revealed in music therapy. *British Journal of Music Therapy*, 12(2), 60–66.

Warwick, A. (1995). Music therapy in the education service: research with autistic children and their mothers. In T. Wigram, B. Saperston, & R. West (eds), *The art and science of music therapy: A handbook* (pp. 209–225). London: Harwood Academic Press.

Wigram, T. (2000). A method of music therapy assessment for the diagnosis of autism and communication disorders in children. *Music Therapy Perspectives*, 18, 13–22.

Wigram, T. & Dileo, C. (1997). *Music vibration.* Cherry Hill, NJ: Jeffrey Books.

Wigram, T. & De Backer, J. (1999). *Clinical applications of music therapy in developmental disability, paediatrics and neurology.* London: Jessica Kingsley.

Wigram, T., Pedersen, I. N., & Bonde, L. O. (2002). *A comprehensive guide to music therapy: Theory, clinical practice, research and training.* London: Jessica Kingsley.

Wing, L. (1993). *Autistic continuum disorders: An aid to diagnosis.* London: National Autistic Society.

Winnicott, D. W. (1965). *The family and individual development.* London: Tavistock.

Winnicott, D. W. (1974). *Playing and reality.* London: Penguin Books.

Woodward, A. (2004). Music therapy for autistic children and their families: a creative spectrum. *British Journal of Music Therapy*, 18, 8–15.

CHAPTER 15

MUSICAL PLAY

KATHRYN MARSH AND SUSAN YOUNG

Introduction

What do we mean by musical play and in what contexts does it take place? Educational practice and theory, rooted as it is in psychology, reflects a long-held belief that play is a form of growth that is associated positively with learning and development. Most of what we will write about in this chapter emerges from our own backgrounds and interests—and those of our fellow researchers—as music educators in countries belonging to the developed world where the simple divisions between work and play result in a view of play as a trivial, lightweight, random, and somewhat useless activity. One of our aims in this chapter is to show how the complexity and sophistication of children's play goes well beyond many adult preconceptions. To children play is neither trivial nor useless.

Assumptions about the nature of play have translated into theories that have tended to see play as merely steps on the way to more 'serious' or logical forms of thinking. Consequently, accounts of play, particularly those leaning on psychological theory, have tended to assign children's play to broad types and categories, such as 'exploratory', 'symbolic', 'functional', 'constructive', 'dramatic', and so on (Isenberg & Jalongo, 1993). Such wide-scope categories fail to capture the structural complexity of play and the social dimension of play as it is enacted by children in real-life situations. Brian Sutton-Smith (1997), a psychologist specializing in play, has explored the many theories of play and the definitions of play that they generate. From these different descriptions and versions of play he has arrived at the conclusion that the essential characteristic of play is its variability. Play varies according to the players, their situations, their motivations, and, importantly, according to the interpretive lens of those observing, describing, and theorizing play, thus eluding simplified definitional frameworks. In our own work and much of the work on play we will recount in this chapter, this variability is documented by describing and analysing the specific detail of children's play in context.

So we define children's musical play as the activities that children initiate of their own accord and in which they may choose to participate with others voluntarily. Like other modes of play, these activities are enjoyable, intrinsically motivated, and controlled by the players. They are free of externally imposed rules but may involve rules developed by the children who are playing (Rogers & Sawyers, 1988; Isenberg & Jalongo, 1993). They are 'everyday' forms of musical activity, happening in the places children inhabit when not engaged in organized educational, recreational, or economic activity. These include the home, daycare, preschool, or nursery, then as children move on to school, the playground, lunchroom, after school care settings, recreational settings, in the car or on school buses. In these places certain forms of musical play are possible, even encouraged by adults, and in others play may be severely constrained. The constraints imposed by space, the levels of acceptable noise, what might be used to produce a sound, and availability of others with whom to make music, all influence the ways in which children will play musically. Musical play is thus embedded in and blends across many features of its context.

Musical play: forms and contexts

As play is assumed in educational theory and research to be a valuable learning experience for young children, in early childhood preschool or nursery settings it is usual practice for free play to be provided for and encouraged. Spontaneous musical play, such as singing, moving rhythmically, and playing with sound making objects, is viewed positively and in some ways supported, for example, by setting out educational percussion instruments. When children reach the age at which formal school begins, usually about the age of 5 or 6 years, the play-based educational provision gradually changes in favour of a more product-oriented, skills-based approach to education. Children's play in the school context thus moves into the spaces and times between formal classroom learning activities. Forms of musical play in these settings include more stylized genres of play that constitute part of an oral tradition, such as singing games. These are the sung and chanted games that are owned, spontaneously performed, and orally transmitted by children, and incorporate the elements of text, music, and movement. They include games associated with hand clapping, mimetic movement, skipping (or jump rope), counting out or elimination, and ball bouncing, and usually occur in pair, ring or line formations. Other forms of play include singing and dance routines associated with popular music and sports chants, in addition to more improvised chants, taunts, and rhythmic movements in response to occurrences in the immediate environment (Campbell, 1998; Harwood, 1998a).

There are, however, certain characteristics of musical play that persist across all ages. A key characteristic is multimodality: children blend movement with singing and, if available, with making sounds with objects or instruments. They are therefore as visually and kinaesthetically active as they are aurally. Another defining characteristic is its unpremeditated, improvisational character. Among the youngest children, forms of musical play are often spontaneous, made up on the spot. For older children, musical play may be based on more stylized genres that form part of an oral tradition but nevertheless performances are not pre-planned. However, analyses of children's musical play show that there are creative processes of transformation that may be quite consciously enacted. Even apparently fixed forms are subject to a continual process of creative change (Marsh, 1997).

An additional characteristic of musical play is its importance as a form of social interaction. Music is a means for playing *with* others. For babies and their caregiving adults, music-like playful interactions are an essential form of communication. Young children share music play ideas, synchronize their rhythmic movements with others and imitate simple melodic ideas (Moorhead & Pond, 1941/1978; Young, 2004). In mid-childhood children suggest new text, music, or movement to their friends, actively teach them new games learnt in other contexts and jointly create variations for amusement of their playmates. Such activities promote collaboration and cohesiveness within friendship groups (Marsh, 1997). Social rules of turn-taking and hierarchical structures of social importance among friends are literally played out in the playground, reflecting and endorsing enculturated behaviours and social patterns from the wider socio-cultural environment (Blacking, 1967/1995; Brady, 1975; Eckhardt, 1975).

There is a perception that collaborative musical play becomes predominantly the province of girls once children enter formal schooling (Knapp & Knapp, 1976; Factor, 1988). What is apparent from observation of musical play in a number of international locations is that many boys continue to participate in musical playground games well into the school years, particularly in genres of musical play that incorporate counting out or elimination through chance or skill and in contexts where limited space precludes more boisterous play (Marsh, 1997, 2002–2004). Boys participate in hand clapping games though they do so less frequently, in smaller numbers and more privately than girls. Where other musical playground games such as jump rope have been endorsed through educational programmes by classroom teachers, boys may continue to play them in the playground, though once again in lesser numbers than girls (Marsh, 1997). Contexts of musical play are therefore extremely important in determining its forms and ways in which it is enacted.

The many activities that come under the term 'children's musical play' are also culturally variable. There are communities in which some adult musical activities are thought of as forms of play (Mans, 2002) or in which children's playful activities are seen as 'serious' and equitable to adult music genres. Like many aspects of music, what is understood by children's musical play becomes blurred with increased awareness of worldwide musical practices in diverse communities. However, most research into children's musical play has been carried out in the developed world. This chapter therefore focuses on play from this perspective.

Investigating musical play

In comparison with other fields of children's musical development, there is relatively little research into children's musical play. Music education researchers tend not to study musical play, focusing their attention on adult-initiated activity in formal educational settings rather than child-initiated activity. Likewise, researchers with an interest in play and early childhood education tend to neglect musical play, considering music to be a specialized area of interest (Littleton, 2002). Add to this the strong cognitive-skills orientation of education and it is of little surprise that musical play has been less central in research on children's musical development than the acquisition of 'serious' formal skills such as learning to sing, to play an instrument or to develop aural skills. One influential researcher in the field of children's folklore has deplored the 'pragmatic and utilitarian ideology that emphasizes the 'product' and evaluates the worth of a human action or idea by the profitability of its outcome' (Factor, 1988, p. 31). Play for which there is no obvious 'product' in the form of measurable learning is thus seen as trivial and unworthy of serious study. This inability to view children's play as an important object of study has been termed the 'triviality barrier' by Sutton-Smith (1970). Yet an understanding of how children choose to make music when left to their own devices, to play musically, reveals important information about children's musical development, their capabilities and what is significant and meaningful to them.

The background of research on musical play divides into two distinct areas, matching the educational contexts for children in early and mid childhood. The studies on musical play in early childhood are based on observations of children's spontaneous musical behaviours, largely in care and educational settings that have been designed by adults to promote free play. This work took its impetus from the ecological, observational studies in experimental nurseries of post-Freudian early childhood researchers such as Susan Isaacs in England in the 1930s (Isaacs, 1929). Young children were thought to possess drives and impulses that could give rise to distinct characteristic behaviours if they were allowed to play freely and follow their own inclinations.

In middle childhood, children's musical play activities are squeezed out of educational settings and so children have been mostly observed playing together in outdoor play areas. This research originally constituted a field within folklore studies and ethnomusicology, where researchers were interested in plotting the oral traditions of childhood such as singing games and in collating a corpus of traditional repertoire (Jones & Hawes, 1972/1987; Sutton-Smith, 1972; Knapp & Knapp, 1976; Opie & Opie, 1977, 1979, 1988; Segler, 1992).

Recent interest in children's musical play has shifted its priorities to explore the musical processes that underlie children's activity (for example, Marsh, 1995, 1997; Harwood, 1998a; Young, 2003a, 2005). An understanding of the intuitive ways in which children make music when left to their own resources has provided vital information for the design of educational activities that can be made more appropriate to children's self-motivated learning styles. These studies have relied on analysis of quite large data sets collected by video recording in naturalistic circumstances. This has enabled detailed analyses of movement and interaction between participants as well as the purely sonic information.

Contemporary work in the field of children's musical play has made another important shift, as exemplified in the work of Campbell (1998). Adopting an ethnomusicological stance and methods she went in search of children's spontaneous musical activity in a wide range of settings, both within school and outside. Campbell observed and interviewed children between the ages of 4 and early teens and discovered that they initiated musical activity for themselves throughout their varied experiences during the day, both alone and in the company of others. She found that children used music in many ways to help maintain emotional and social equilibriums, to entertain themselves, to relieve the boredom of their surroundings, to create and enjoy its sonic forms and to assist in the formation of identity.

Until recently most studies of childhood music have been restricted to children from developed world societies. The work of Blacking (1967/1995) on Venda children's songs is a notable exception and did much to establish the importance of understanding children's music within the framework of the culture from which it emanates, rather than as a 'universal' phenomenon. As discussed later in the chapter, Blacking's study has contributed to ideas about children's musical creativity and to an understanding of the ways in which children's music is transmitted within a culture.

Characteristics of musical play

In the next sections, musical play is discussed in four broad age phases: newborn to 3, 3–6 years, over 6 years, and on into adolescence. These age phases are not intended to be taken as specific developmental stages. They reflect the physical maturation of children and changing contexts of care and education in the home or day-care, in play-based care and education settings, and on to formal schooling. In particular, there is no attempt to differentiate between the characteristics of children's play within the age band of 6–12 years. Children appear to begin learning and performing singing games from the time they enter school and become adept within varying periods of time. Some 6-year-olds can perform quite complex games while some 9-year-olds still experience difficulty with co-ordination of text, music, and movement patterns. Children's preference for singing games seems to diminish in favour of singing and dance routines around the age of 10 years but children beyond this age still perform clapping games, though less publicly and frequently.

The majority of musical play described in the following sections is vocal. In early childhood settings and in some educational settings, depending on the nature of the curriculum, provision will be made for children to explore instruments and initiate play with them or to 'play' with recorded music by responding to it with movement or vocalizing. However, musical play for children more usually occurs in the absence of equipment. Again, this can be explained as a situational constraint. Clapping games, when played in the school context, for example, tend to be played during recess and lunch times, while waiting for a teacher, or during bus excursions. Played by pairs or small groups of children they easily fit into small spaces and limited time periods and are therefore eminently transportable both in time and place.

Birth to 3

In recent years there has been an upsurge of interest in the competencies of babies. Painstaking analysis of infant–caregiver interaction has revealed that successful communication between adult and baby depends on music-like qualities of rhythm, variations in pitch inflexion and dynamics (Trevarthen, 2000, 2002a). The adult intuitively adopts infant-directed speech characterized by short rhythmic phrases and expressively contoured variations in pitch and the baby responds with movements and vocal responses that are co-ordinated with the adult. These are spontaneous, intuitive and playful exchanges between adults and babies which, when well matched, strengthen the bond between them and enable adults to support the emotional and physical regulation of the babies they are caring for. Importantly they provide a raft of playful exchanges that enable the babies to access important aspects about the social and physical world around them.

With older babies and toddlers, parents and carers supplement these playful, music-like exchanges with a repertoire of lullabies, playsongs, rhymes, and improvised 'ditties' (Trehub et al., 1993; Trehub & Trainor, 1998; Trevarthen, 2002b; Street, 2004). They make use of all available sources for musical material and may well sing a snatch from a contemporary popular song alongside a traditional children's song. These early music play experiences are highly meaningful to very young children as they are integral to their close relationships with caregiving adults. Early music play provides a rich resource for the development of many skills and understandings, particularly the acquisition of language (M. Papoušek, 1992).

Increasing knowledge about the musical play experiences of babies and toddlers in the home is difficult for reasons of access, although some family members have kept diaries of young children's musical play in the home, noting for example vocal play (H. Papoušek & M. Papoušek, 1981; M. Papoušek, 1996), general responses to recorded music (Littleton, 2002) and body movement responses to music (Chen-Hafteck, 2004). It is easier to gain access to observe young children in daycare, although here the availability of equipment to play with; more space, freedom to move and make noise; and the higher adult-child ratio will influence the way children play in comparison with the home (Suthers, 2000; Young, 2002). However, what is striking in all contexts, is how children actively create their own opportunities for playful musical activity from what is available and show a need to repeat favourite experiences in order to deepen and develop them. For example, a toddler observed in a daycare setting requested a replay of the same recorded popular song many times and bounced rhythmically on cushions during each repetition of the chorus. Thus young children drive their own learning by selecting what they currently need, and what might appear to be arbitrary or repetitious behaviours can hold a key to children's current competencies.

The preschool years

Musical play in the preschool years (the ages of 3–6 years approximately) has been the focus of a number of studies dating from 1937 to the present. The underlying premise of the famous Pillsbury study in the USA was that young children possess an innate musicality and that if allowed freedom to play in a potentially rich environment, they would display this musicality in a coherent form embedded in their general playful behaviours (Moorhead & Pond, 1941/1978; Moorhead et al., 1951/1978; Pond, 1980). A special nursery was set up, well equipped with musical instruments, and the staff recorded their observations of children's musical activity over a number of years. The Pillsbury study inspired a number of subsequent observational studies in North America in the early 1980s (Shelley & Foley, 1979; Cohen, 1980; Shelley, 1981; Miller, 1984). What all these researchers found was that all young children are prodigious producers of a rich variety of spontaneous musical play and that there are some broad common features of this play. Overwhelmingly the majority of spontaneous musical behaviours found by all these researchers were vocal. Littleton (1991) subsequently grouped types of pre-schoolers' musical play into three categories: singing; play with instruments and sound-makers; and spontaneous movement to music. It is around these three types of play that discussion continues.

Vocal play

Although studies of young children's spontaneous vocalizations during free play are widely separated both chronologically and in geographic location, collectively they reveal a surprising similarity of findings (Bjørkvold, 1989/1992; Moorhead & Pond, 1941/1978; Sundin, 1960/1998). In summary, a general consensus emerges that identifies two broad types of singing among young children: a communicative, chant-like, repetitive singing of short verbal and musical ideas and a more introverted, solitary, free-flowing, diffuse kind of singing, often on open syllable sounds. Snatches of known songs resurface in children's spontaneous singing of either kind, often with altered words or melodic and rhythmic transformations.

A further theory was proposed by Sundin (1960/1998) as a result of his observations of 3–6-year-olds during the 'free play' hour in Swedish kindergartens. He suggested that the two types of singing were distinguished by social context; the free-flowing 'plainsong' being primarily solo and introverted, and the 'chant' (using reiterated short phrases) most often produced in group activity. Interesting comparative studies carried out among children attending pre-schools in Oslo, Russia, and the USA (Bjørkvold, 1989/1992) revealed that the repetitive 'chant' (also called 'formula song') is the dominant form of song among children in groups. It is possible that there is continuity between the preschool chant and the sociable playground games of mid and later childhood. There is less evidence for the extension of individual introverted free-flow singing into the later years of childhood, although it may be found when children improvise songs individually (Davies, 1986).

Young children's spontaneous singing is integrated not only with the social environment but also with their play in all media (Pond, 1981), exemplifying the characteristic of multimodality mentioned earlier. Children typically synchronize singing with movement, either their own physical movement or that of toys; they dramatize their toys with improvised vocalizations and act out role plays that have singing incorporated (Young, 2002).

Spontaneous play with instruments

Where instruments or other sound-makers are available, children will enjoy playing with them to explore sounds and create sequences and patterns of sounds. The idea that children are merely exploring the instruments randomly and that sounds that ensue are not 'music' but simply noise is still prevalent (Young, 1999), supported by echoes of Piagetian theory that characterize young children's activity as exploratory but without structure. However, by analysing play with instruments, two researchers (Cohen, 1980; Young, 2003a,b) demonstrated that what might appear, initially, to be random and sporadic play is generated and structured by patterns of bodily movement that are gestural or stimulated by the structure of the instruments. For example, children commonly strike or tap instruments in an ordered way, making regular rhythmic groupings and extending them into sequences.

The complexity and creativity of children's spontaneous play with instruments can often eclipse that found in more teacher-directed activities. In an interesting piece of action research, Smithrim (1997) provided a setting for eight 3- and 4-year-olds to play freely with percussion instruments, a guitar, and a piano. She found that the range, variety, and complexity of children's musical activity when left to free play far exceeded anything they would have been able to achieve in a teacher-led class. However, not surprisingly, noise was a consideration and she acknowledges that the changes in practice it implies would be difficult in many settings.

Movement play

Movement is one of the child's earliest self-initiated responses to music and a small group of studies have looked at their responses to recorded music (Gorali-Turel, 1999; Chen-Hafteck,

2004) and to songs (Hicks, 1993). Many have noticed that when recorded music is played, young children typically respond with movement. Gorali-Turel was interested to observe these movements and record them systematically in order to identify any common characteristics that emerged. She found that the youngest children of about 3 years often performed simple twirling or bouncing movements and were highly repetitive in their movements but, also, that they were responsive to the tempi, the intensity and other generalized characteristics of the music. In the Israeli daycare centre where she carried out this research, she also observed the interactions of the adults and found that if adults modelled movements, the children often attempted to imitate but only if the modelled movements took account of children's natural tempo and movement style. The way that the adult responds and partners the playing child has a crucial impact on how children play.

The adult role

When experimental situations were set up to evaluate the differences between a range of teacher interaction styles on children's musical play (Tarnowski & Leclerc, 1994) the children played in the most creative and interesting ways when 'observed' by adults and failed to extend or develop play when 'entertained' or 'directed'. Overintrusive and directive interventions tend to close down children's play, whereas interactions that the children perceive to be responsive and supportive will foster and creatively extend it (Young, 2003c). Such findings demonstrate the motivation that will sustain children's musical play when it is supported by adults who show interest and provide appropriate assistance. For this reason, some have worked carefully in early childhood settings alongside staff to help them recognize the musical learning taking place when children are playing musically so that they have a rationale for play-based approaches and pedagogical knowledge of how to support it (Suthers, 2000; Young, 2003a).

Mid-childhood

Characteristics of musical play in the playground

The differences between children's spontaneous play and that found in teacher-directed educational settings continue into the middle childhood years. It has long been assumed that children's musical play in the playground is quite rhythmically, melodically and formally simple. Such assumptions were supported by the work of ethnomusicologist Brailoiu (1954), whose analysis of children's songs and rhymes from Europe, West Africa, Russia, Canada, Japan, and Formosa (currently Taiwan) resulted in his postulation of a universal 'childish rhythm' (p. 21): a binary rhythm equal to the value of eight quavers as shown in Figure 15.1. This 'universal' rhythmic structure was subsequently endorsed by studies of Australian Aboriginal children's play (Kartomi, 1980) and Javanese children's play (Romet, 1980).

Figure 15.1 Universal childish rhythm proposed by Brailoiu.

However, these findings have related to the rhythm of game texts only and have failed to take into account the integral element of movement that accompanies the texts. While it is true that many game texts are in duple metre, the movement patterns often are metrically contrasting. Perhaps the most pervasive set of movements reported in clapping games since the late 1970s is that of a three-beat clapping pattern (Merrill-Mirsky, 1988; Riddell, 1990; Campbell, 1991; Marsh, 1997). This is seen by children in Australia, the USA, England, and Norway as a clapping pattern which is applicable to most texts, despite the fact that it creates a polymetric relationship with the text (Marsh, 2005a). This can be seen in Figure 15.2.

While children are rarely conscious of this polymetric aspect of their performance (to some extent maintaining the textual and movement rhythms independently), it nevertheless exists in sonic form, often highlighted by the regular accents provided by specific handclapping movements (clapping own hands together, for example, having a louder sound than clapping partners' hands). It is evident that the three-beat pattern is generally acquired and ably demonstrated (in conjunction with duple texts) by children at least from the age of 6 years. Children of 8 and 9 years of age have been observed performing, with remarkable fluency, a textless game, which has a seven-beat clapping pattern and additive metres as its structural core (Riddell, 1990; Marsh, 1997). The rhythm of the first three sections of this game is illustrated in Figure 15.3.

A 13-beat clapping pattern identified in the USA by Riddell (1990) and Harwood (1992) has also been performed in Sydney by children as young as 7 years (Marsh, 1997). Similar

Figure 15.2 Polymetric relationship between clapping pattern and text of a Sydney playground game.

Figure 15.3 Clapping rhythm of *Slide*.

polymetric relationships between duple text and quintuple movement rhythms of clapping games have been reported in Portugal by Prim (1989).

Environmental influences are clearly reflected in the rhythmic characteristics of playground singing games. Both the African-American game tradition and the influence of popular music, which has global dimensions, have resulted in increased syncopation in text rhythms of games over the last decades of the twentieth century (Merrill-Mirsky, 1988; Campbell, 1991; Marsh, 1997) as demonstrated in Figure 15.4.

Studies of musical play in Ghana (Addo, 1995) and South Africa (Blacking, 1967/1995) have also revealed that the polyrhythmic characteristics of adult music in these locations are maintained in children's games and songs. Complex combinations of duple and triple rhythms are identified in Balkan children's musical play by Yugoslavian ethnomusicologist Basic (1986), who has decried the 'systematic impoverishment of the children's musical creative imagination' (p. 131) by music educators who simplify children's games for classroom use.

There are also melodic differences between children's singing games and songs employed in the classroom. Melodies in children's games frequently have a melodic range of no more than a fifth and rarely exceed an octave (Campbell, 1991; Marsh, 1997), although Segler's (1992) trans-European collection and analysis of children's games includes melodies with a range of a ninth, particularly found in games from northern Europe. The minor third, which is popularly believed to be a 'universal' characteristic of children's musical play, is not any more dominant in game melodies than both major and minor seconds. In Ghanaian children's games, the melodic patterns have been linked to the speech tones of Ghanaian languages (Addo, 1995).

Of potential interest is the finding of Marsh (1997) that children's songs in an Australian playground have a unique tonality, whereby the first note of the song functions as its tonal centre. Standard tonal melodies which are part of a wider musical environment are adapted by children for performance in a playground context. When held within the repertoire of a group of children for a protracted period of time, however, what may have originated as a tonal melody is frequently transformed into a variant in which the melodic contours

Figure 15.4 Syncopation in text rhythms in a Sydney playgound game of African-American origin.

have been 'flattened'. This can be seen in the contrast between the Australian playground version of *See see my playmate* (Figure 15.2) and the original melody found in a Los Angeles rendition of the song (Figure 15.5) collected by Riddell (1990).

The tessitura of children's games appears to be much lower than that commonly found in published classroom material. A probable explanation for the low tessitura of the games is the common practice of moving from pitched song to unpitched speech. As the tonal centre of children's speech appears to be fairly low, the melodies with which the speech is interwoven are also low in pitch. In some cases melodic renditions can arise directly from exaggerated speech inflexions (Marsh, 1997).

Formally, children's singing games are frequently repetitive and cyclical. Ostinati are found in many movement patterns but these are often interrupted by mimetic movements or changes to the rhythm pattern of movements at points of textual rest or emphasis.

Say,   say,   my   play   mate,

come   out   and   play   with   me,

* Differs from original song

Figure 15.5 Los Angeles version of *See see my playmate.*

Once again the structure of games reflects environmental influences. For example, call and response forms may be found in Ghanaian or African-American games but not in the musical play of Australian children, unless they have been derived from other sources, such as the classroom or media (Riddell, 1990; Addo, 1995; Marsh, 1997).

Early adolescence

Children in their early teens often continue to play clapping games or chants with younger siblings but do this less publicly at home, rather than in the playground where cheers or dance routines may be more prominent (Harwood, 1998b). During early adolescence the boundaries between adult and child activity begin to diminish. What constitutes adolescent play is therefore less easy to define. However, a number of musical activities that are self-initiated, spontaneous, self-regulated, and enjoyable might be characterized as forms of adolescent musical play. Such activities include downloading music files from the internet and singing along with them or dancing in spontaneous response to a CD. More creative and organized endeavours such as hip hop freestyling or participation in garage bands might also be characterized as types of musical play. By this age many children have often developed competence on a musical instrument and may also be observed in solitary 'playful' improvisation.

Teaching and learning in the context of play

From early years through to early adolescence children collaborate and learn in musical play not only from adults but also from one another. Competence as musical players is increased by observation of and participation in modelled play behaviours, facilitated by physical proximity to and, physical contact with other players as evident in Figure 15.6 (Harwood, 1992, 1998a; Marsh, 2002; Moorhead & Pond, 1941/1978; Young, 2004).

Figure 15.6 Participation, modelling and observation in a playground clapping game (UK).

In the playground, among older children, games are usually transmitted between age peers and from older to young children (Harwood, 1992, 1998a; Marsh, 1999a). Children may move into a pair formation, sometimes away from the larger group, in order to practise new games or performance skills. Game transmission and skill development are always achieved by observation and attempted performance of the whole game, though hand positions are sometimes manoeuvred or demonstrated separately prior to the commencement of a game performance. Song acquisition in this context is therefore achieved by aggregative 'catching' of musical, textual and movement phrases within a musical whole. Skills are also gained within a holistic framework and never fragmented or taught in isolation from the game as a whole (Harwood, 1992, 1998a; Marsh, 2002).

Thus it can be seen that the social milieu of the setting, whether with adults or peers, allows for multiple levels of competence to coexist and be incorporated into play activities and for children to learn at their own pace. Children can choose their own level of participation, from observation, to trialling some limited form of participation, such as movements, through to full participation, perhaps joining in with singing play or playing alongside others with instruments.

Older children may develop collaborative skills to the level at which they can provide careful tuition of novice players, as observed by Marsh (1999a). Children in the school playground were aware of developmental differences in playing abilities, particularly relating to the performance of movement patterns, and accommodated these differences through a process akin to the notion of 'scaffolding' (Wood *et al.*, 1976) whereby learners' progress is supported by modelling of behaviours slightly beyond their present level of competence. Older or more adept children switched automatically to easier clapping patterns when playing with younger or less adept players. They then carefully modelled clapping patterns of greater difficulty, physically manipulating the hands of the less able player until some level of competence was reached (Marsh, 1997, 1999a).

Children do not seem to require that one skill or game genre be perfected before moving on to a new one. Rather, they create challenges for themselves by devising and adopting from external sources new variants of movement, music, or text. These variants might then be disseminated through performance with other players or by observation of the performance by child onlookers (Marsh, 1997). In his study of Venda children's play songs in South Africa, Blacking (1967/1995) states that 'children's songs are not always easier than adult songs and children do not necessarily learn the simple songs first' (p. 29). For example, more difficult songs may be learnt first by Venda children simply because they have been heard more frequently. A similar phenomenon is demonstrated by children's learning of quite complex popular songs from repeated renditions in the media (Harwood, 1987; Young, 2003a).

Creativity in children's musical play

There has been a long-standing assumption derived from developmental models of learning, both generally and in music, that young children's play is aimlessly exploratory. However, careful analysis of young children's play activity reveals creative processes of transformation. Typically, short motifs or ideas are revisited, repeated and gradually transformed, within themselves, by extending or by combining with other ideas. These processes can be identified in the musical play of even quite young children (Young, 2003a) and continue in more sophisticated and complex ways in the play of older children. This can be seen in the following vignette observed by Young in a daycare setting.

> Ahmed points to a picture of a football and declaims, Pop-ball! He repeats the word with a strong accent on the first syllable. He then turns away from the picture book, stomping across the room singing Pop-ball four times in a falling interval of a fourth expanding in the last two versions to a wider interval. His rhythmic singing is in time with his stomps. He then starts to repeat the 'pop' first to 'pop, pop-ball' and then 'pop, pop, POP—ball!'—thereby changing the rhythm and using the word not for its specific meaning but as a rhythmic idea.

Older children's quest for novelty in their games results in the generation of many variants, which are created through a process of combining short textual, melodic, and rhythmic phrases or formulae. This process of formulaic construction, which is characteristic of orally transmitted performance genres, occurs quite spontaneously during the performance of singing games and is termed 'composition in performance' (Lord, 1995). In children's generative practices there is no dichotomy between process and product, so that the repertoire is constantly evolving. Within the social safety of their friendship groups, children engage collaboratively in the generation of variants (Marsh, 1995). This is described by Blacking (1985) as a collective effort that results both in 'new cultural forms and a richer experience for the participants' (pp. 46–47).

In selecting formulae for use in games, children draw upon raw material from their auditory environment. Musical, textual, and movement formulae are therefore derived from the media, the classroom and songs or games performed by other children or adults (Marsh, 1999b). As they combine formulae in their play, children consciously consider formal, rhythmic, and melodic appropriateness and demonstrate a sophisticated array of innovative processes. These include: reorganization of formulae; elaboration through addition of new material or expansion of known material; condensation through omission or contraction of formulae; and recasting of material, for example, through substitution of new words or movements. It should be noted that these processes occur across the age range and so do not appear to develop in complexity with age, although children become more aware of their own processes of innovation from the age of approximately 8 or 9 (Marsh, 1995).

Cultural adaptation and appropriation

Globalization, a burgeoning mass media industry and large-scale patterns of migration have brought major changes to children's auditory environments since the middle of the twentieth century. Popular music, disseminated through television, radio, the internet, video, DVD, audio cassette and CD, forms a background to many activities and is heard in the home, in shops and in recreational centres (Campbell, 1998). The performance of popular music for many years has also included both aural and visual elements that are avidly absorbed and emulated by children in their play.

Electronic recordings of songs provide templates that children can use for repetitive listening and viewing. As with the learning of playground singing games, songs and dance routines are learnt holistically. Even very young children are able to reproduce portions of popular songs, often key phrases and movements (Young, 2002, 2003a) and children in the first years of schooling can reproduce songs in full (Harwood, 1987). Song and dance routines are performed individually by children in front of the television or among groups of friends well into preteen years (Harwood, 1987).

Once these adult-generated sources of entertainment are transported into the playground, however, they are immediately reappropriated and subjected to the creative endeavours of the children. As seen in Figure 15.7, children may invent new dance routines to popular songs or to cheerleaders' chants, drawing on the repertoire of movements learnt from the media or older performers. While children as young as 6 years have been observed performing popular dance routines and sports chants (Marsh, 2005), Harwood states that these genres, designated cheers, drill teams, and routines by the performers, are more regularly the province of older children in the preteen and early teen years (1998b).

Younger school-age children are more likely to invent clapping patterns with which to accompany popular songs and sports chants. These may be relatively transient, as in the renditions of the Spice Girls' *Wannabe* reported in an English playground in 1997 by Grugeon (2001) or may become part of a longer tradition, such as that of *See see my playmate*, derived from the popular song *Playmates* composed in the 1940s (Opie & Opie, 1988) which has become a clapping game still played in the UK, USA, Australia, and many

Figure 15.7 Improvisation of a dance routine for a popular song (UK).

European countries (Opie & Opie, 1988; Riddell, 1990; Segler, 1992; Marsh, 1997, 1999b) (see Figures 15.2 and 15.5).

Popular culture and its icons are also subverted in the playground. Thus *Down down baby*, a game linked with a popular song from the 1960s, *Shimmy Shimmy Ko-Ko-Bop* (Riddell, 1990), becomes a vehicle for the ridiculing of pop star Britney Spears:

> The train goes
> Down down baby down by the riverside
> Sweet sweet baby never let it go again
> Shimmy shimmy coconut shimmy shimmy ah
> Shimmy shimmy coconut shimmy shimmy ah
> I hate coffee, I hate tea
> I hate Britney, she's never with me
> Down by the fire peeling potatoes
> Britney Spears is so crap.
>
> > Recorded Keighley, England, 2002
> > (Marsh, 2005a)

Parody songs perhaps represent this subversion of adult culture at its zenith. In the middle years of school, children may adapt texts of well-known songs, advertisements or TV jingles (Harwood, 1994), creating parallel texts which mock adult concerns and reduce 'adult order to humorous disorder' (Factor, 1988, p. 153) as an 'antithetical reaction to the institutional and everyday hegemonies of the life about them' (Sutton-Smith, 1995, p. 6). Such disorder is aptly illustrated by the following example, which is sung to the melody of the Christmas carol, *Joy to the World*:

> Joy to the world, the school burnt down
> And all the teachers too.
> The principal is dead; we shot her in the head;
> The secretary too, we flushed her down the loo
> And all, and all the teachers too.

Recorded Sydney, Australia, 1994
(Marsh, 1997)

Many other songs learnt either through the media or from other adult sources, such as the classroom, become raw materials for formulaic construction in the playground. In utilizing this material for creative purposes, children exert ownership and control over it and are thus never passive recipients of adult culture. At the same time, their play is inexorably changed by its influences, as exemplified by the syncopation that has permeated the rhythms of playground games.

Within the playground, children may also be influenced by the play of children from other ethnic backgrounds. The level of cross-cultural transmission seems to vary according to circumstance. For example, where there is a wide diversity of ethnic groups within a playground, children appear to engage actively in exchanging games between groups as can be seen in Figure 15.8. This can partly be explained by an acceptance of difference but also by children's interest in novelty and the 'nonsense' characteristics of many game texts, which can be transferred readily between games in different languages (Marsh, 2001b). In a monocultural environment there may be less opportunity for or disposition towards cross-cultural transmission. In Marsh's (2005b) field observation of school children in Busan, southern Korea, the only playground game that directly appeared to transcend cultural boundaries was a textless clapping game that strongly resembled the game *Slide* found in the USA and Australia (see Figure 15.3). In this instance the absence of text probably contributed to the ease of its transmission.

Other games, such as the Punjabi *Zig Zag Zoo* may be learnt in children's (or their parents') countries of origin and then are transplanted to countries of residence and played actively at home and with friends within the ethnic group (Curtis, 2000). Studies of games in the USA seem to indicate that games are played more within ethnic groups than exchanged between them (Merrill-Mirsky, 1988). However, Merrill-Mirsky also maintains that there has been a strong transcultural influence of African-American musical styles, promulgated both by African-American games and by popular music. Programmes such as *Sesame Street* have also broadcast African-American games to an international viewing audience, thus contributing to their wider dissemination (Marsh, 2001).

Conclusions

In this chapter we have explored the variety and range of children's musical play from birth through to early adolescence. We have shown how children within their play are able to integrate, transform and generate new ideas that capitalize on the material and human

Figure 15.8 Cultural maintenance and exchange in musical play (Norway).

resources that are available to them in different settings. At any given age children may be engaged in the simultaneous development of a wide range of skills associated with different types of play and different game genres. Progress may be very irregular across different skills and even within skills and unlikely to accrue in simple linear developmental pathways. Such abilities might be harnessed in educational approaches that create ample opportunities for children to play with music. The significance of play as an essential vehicle for children's musical expression should be acknowledged and encouraged within and beyond educational settings.

References

Addo, A. O. (1995). Ghanaian children's music cultures: A video ethnography of selected singing games (Doctoral dissertation, University of British Columbia, Canada, 1995). *Dissertation Abstracts International*, 57/03, AAC NN05909.

Basic, E. (1986). Differences in the authenticity of children's expression and the viewing angle of the adults (II). In I. Ivic & A. Marjanovic (eds), *Traditional games and children of today: Belgrade: OMEP Traditional Games Project* (pp. 129–134). Belgrade: OMEP.

Bjørkvold, J. (1989). *The muse within: Creativity and communication, song and play from childhood through maturity*, (W.H. Halverson, Trans. 1992). New York: Harper Collins.

Blacking, J. (1985). Versus gradus novos ad parnassum musicum: exemplum Africanum. In *Becoming human through music: The Wesleyan Symposium on the Perspectives of Social Anthropology in the Teaching and Learning of Music* (pp. 43–52). Reston, VA: Music Educators National Conference.

Blacking, J. (1995). *Venda children's songs: A study in ethnomusicological analysis.* Chicago: University of Chicago Press. (Original work published 1967.)

Brady, M. (1975). This little lady's gonna boogaloo: Elements of socialization in the play of black girls. In R. Bauman (ed.), *Black girls at play: Perspectives on child development* (pp. 1–51). Austin, TX: Southwest Educational Development Laboratory.

Brailoiu, C. (1954). The children's rhythm-liminal notions (Trans. unknown). *In Les Colloques de Wegmont* (pp. 1–21). Brussels: International d'Etude Ethnomusicolique.

Campbell, P. S. (1991). The child-song genre: A comparison of songs by and for children. *International Journal of Music Education*, 17, 14–23.

Campbell, P. S. (1998). *Songs in their heads: Music and its meaning in children's lives.* New York: Oxford University Press.

Chen-Hafteck, L. (2004) Music and movement from zero to three: A window to children's musicality, In L. Custodero (ed.), *Proceedings of the ISME Early Childhood Conference 'Els Móns Musical Dels Infants' (The Musical Worlds of Children)*, Barcelona, Spain, July 5–10, 2004

Cohen, V. (1980) *The emergence of musical gestures in kindergarten children.* (Doctoral dissertation, University of Illinois, Champaign Urbana, 1980). *Dissertation Abstracts International*, AAT 8108471.

Curtis, M. (2000). Zig Zag Zoo and other games: The oral tradition of children of Asian origin in Keighley, West Yorkshire. *Folklife, the Journal of Folk Life Studies*, 38, 71–82.

Davies, C. (1986). Say it till a song comes (reflections on songs invented by children 3–13). *British Journal of Music Education*, 3(3), 279–293.

Eckhardt, R. (1975). From handclap to line play. In R. Bauman (ed.), *Black girls at play: Perspectives on child development* (pp. 57–99). Austin, Texas: Southwest Educational Development Laboratory.

Factor, J. (1988). *Captain Cook chased a chook: Children's folklore in Australia.* Ringwood, Victoria: Penguin Books.

Gorali-Turel, T. (1999). Spontaneous movement response of young children to musical stimulation as indicator of the hidden cognitive process. Unpublished paper. *Cognitive Processes of Children Engaged in Musical Activity*, Urbana-Champaign, IL: School of Music, University of Illinois.

Grugeon, E. (2001). 'We like singing the Spice Girl songs and we like Tig and Stuck in the Mud': Girls' traditional games on two playgrounds. In J. C Bishop & M. Curtis (eds), *The state of play: Perspectives on children's oral traditions in the school playground* (pp. 98–114). Milton Keynes, UK: Open University Press.

Harwood, E. (1987). *The memorized song repertoire of children in Grades 4 and 5 in Champaign, Illinois.* (Doctoral dissertation, University of Illinois Champaign Urbana, 1987). *Dissertation Abstracts International*, AAT 8721651.

Harwood, E. (1992). Girls' handclapping games: A study in oral transmission. *Bulletin of the International Kodály Society*, 17, 19–25.

Harwood, E. (1994). Miss Lucy meets Dr Pepper: Mass media and children's traditional playground song and chant. In H. Lees (ed.), *Musical connections: Tradition and change.* Proceedings of the 21st World Conference of the International Society for Music Education, Tampa, Florida, USA, pp. 187–194.

Harwood, E. (1998a). Music learning in context: A playground tale. *Research Studies in Music Education*, 11, 52–60.

Harwood, E. (1998b). Go on girl! Improvisation in African-American girls' singing games. In B. Nettl & M. Russell (eds), *In the course of performance: Studies in the world of musical improvisation* (pp. 113–125). Chicago: University of Chicago Press.

Hicks, W. K. (1993) An investigation of the initial stages of preparation audiation (Doctoral Dissertation, Temple University, USA) *Dissertation Abstracts International*, 54(4A), 1277.

Isaacs, S. (1929) *The nursery years: The mind of the child from birth to six years.* London: Routledge.

Isenberg, J. P. & Jalongo, M. R. (1993). *Creative expression and play in the early childhood curriculum.* New York: Macmillan.

Jones, B. & Hawes, B. L. (1987). *Step it down. Games, plays, songs & stories from the Afro-American heritage.* Athens, GA: Brown Thrasher Books, The University of Georgia Press. (Original work published 1972).

Kartomi, M. (1980). Childlikeness in play songs—A case study among the Pitjantjara at Yalata, South Australia. *Miscellanea Musicologica,* **11,** 172–214.

Knapp, M. & Knapp, H. (1976). *One potato, two potato...: The folklore of American children.* New York: W.W. Norton.

Littleton, D. (1991) *Influence of play settings on preschool children's music and play behaviours.* Doctoral dissertation, The University of Texas at Austin, USA. *Dissertation Abstracts International,* **52**(4), **1198.** (University Microfilms Order No. 91-28294).

Littleton, D. (2002). Music in the time of toddlers. *Zero to Three.* **23,** 35–38.

Lord, A. B. (1995). *The singer resumes the tale.* Ithaca, NY: Cornell University Press.

Mans, M. (2002). Playing the music—comparing performance of children's song and dance in traditional and contemporary Namibian education. In L. Bresler and C. M. Thompson (eds), *The arts in children's lives: Context, culture and curriculum* (pp. 71–86). Dordrecht: Kluwer Academic Publishers.

Marsh, K. (1995). Children's singing games: Composition in the playground? *Research Studies in Music Education,* **4,** 2–11.

Marsh, K. (1997). *Variation and transmission processes in children's singing games in an Australian playground.* Unpublished PhD thesis, University of Sydney.

Marsh, K. (1999a). Young children's negotiation of difference in playground singing games. *Australian Research in Early Childhood Education,* **6**(2), 217–227.

Marsh, K. (1999b). Mediated orality: The role of popular music in the changing tradition of children's musical play. *Research Studies in Music Education,* **13,** 2–12.

Marsh, K. (2001). The influence of the media, the classroom and immigrant groups on contemporary children's playground singing games in Australia. In J. C Bishop & M. Curtis (eds), *The state of play: Perspectives on children's oral traditions in the school playground* (pp. 80–97). Milton Keynes, UK: Open University Press.

Marsh, K. (2002). Children's song acquisition: An ethnomusicological perspective. In C. Stephens, D. Burnham, G. McPherson, E. Schubert, & J. Renwick (eds), *Proceedings of the 7th International Conference on Music Perception and Cognition* (pp. 265–268). Adelaide: Causal Productions. (CD ROM)

Marsh, K. (2002–2004). Unpublished field notes, Stavanger (Norway), Keighley (UK), Los Angeles (USA) and Busan (South Korea).

Marsh, K. (2005a). A cross-cultural study of the musical play practices of children in school playgrounds. In V. Rogers, & D. Simonds (eds), *The legacy of John Blacking: Essays on music, culture and society.* (pp. 152–166). Crawley, WA: University of Western Australia Press.

Marsh, K. (2005b). Worlds of play: The effects of context and culture on the musical play of young children.*Early Childhood Connections,* **11,** 32–36.

Merrill-Mirsky, C. (1988). *Eeny meeny pepsadeeny: Ethnicity and gender in children's musical play.* (Doctoral dissertation, University of California, Los Angeles, 1988). *Dissertation Abstracts International,* AAT 8826013.

Miller, L.W. (1984). Music in early childhood: Naturalistic observation of young children's musical behaviours. (Doctoral dissertation, University of Kansas) *Dissertation Abstracts International*, **44**(11), 3316. (University Microfilms No. 84-03616)

Moorhead, G. E. & Pond, D. (1941, reprinted 1978) Music of young children: 11. General observations. *Music of Young Children: Pillsbury Foundation Studies*. Santa Barbara: Pillsbury Foundation for Advancement of Music Education.

Moorhead, G. E., Sandvik, F., & Wight, D. (1951, reprinted 1978). Music of young children: IV. Free use of instruments for musical growth. *Music of Young Children: Pillsbury Foundation Studies*. Santa Barbara: Pillsbury Foundation for Advancement of Music Education.

Opie, I. & Opie, P. (1977). *The lore and language of schoolchildren*. Oxford: Oxford University Press. (Original work published 1959.)

Opie, I. & Opie, P. (1979). *Children's games in street and playground*. Oxford: Oxford University Press.

Opie, I. & Opie, P. (1988). *The singing game*. Oxford: Oxford University Press. (Original work published 1985.)

Papoušek, M. (1992). Early ontogeny of vocal communication in parent-infant interactions. In H. Papoušek, U. Jürgens, & M. Papoušek (eds), *Nonverbal vocal communication: Comparative and developmental approaches* (pp. 230–261). Cambridge: Cambridge University Press.

Papoušek, M. (1996). Intuitive parenting: A hidden source of musical stimulation in infancy. In I. Deliège & J. Sloboda (eds), *Musical beginnings: Origins and development of musical competence* (pp. 88–112). Oxford: Oxford University Press.

Papoušek, M. & Papoušek, H. (1981). Musical elements in the infants vocalisation: Their significance for communication, cognition and creativity. In L. P. Lipsitt (ed.), *Advances in Infancy Research*, Vol. 1 (pp. 163–224). Norwood, NJ: Ablex.

Pond, D. (1980). The young child's playful world of sound. *Music Educators Journal*, **76**(7), 38–41.

Pond, D. (1981). A composer's study of young children's innate musicality. *Bulletin of the Council for Research in Music Education*, **68**, 1–12.

Prim, F. M. 1989). The importance of girl's singing games in music and motor education. *Canadian Journal of Research in Music Education*, **32**, 115–123.

Riddell, C. (1990). *Traditional singing games of elementary school children in Los Angeles*. (Doctor of Philosophy, University of California, Los Angeles). (University Microfilms No. 9023293).

Rogers, C. S. & Sawyers, J. K. (1988). *Play in the lives of children*. Washington: National Association for the Education of Young Children.

Romet, C. (1980). The play rhymes of children—a cross-cultural source of natural learning materials for music education. *Australian Journal of Music Education*, **27**, (October), 27–31.

Segler, H. (1992). *Tänze der Kinder in Europa*. Hannover: Moeck Verlag.

Shelley, S. (1981). Investigating the musical capabilities of young children, *Bulletin of Research in Music Education*, **68**, 26–34.

Shelley, S. & Foley, J. R. (1979). Observing the nature of young children's musicality, *Current Issues in Music Education: Music of Young Children*, **12**, 44–54.

Smithrim, K. (1997). Free musical play in early childhood. *Canadian Music Educator*, **38**(4), 17–24.

Street, A. (2004). Singing to infants: How maternal attitudes to singing influence infants' musical worlds. In L. Custodero (ed.), *Proceedings of the ISME Early Childhood Conference 'Els Móns Musical Dels Infants' (The Musical Worlds of Children)*, Barcelona, Spain, July 5–10, 2004.

Sundin, B. (1960, translated into English 1998). Musical creativity in the first six years. In B. Sundin, G. E. McPherson & G. Folkestad (eds), *Children composing: Research in music education 1998* (pp. 35–56). Lund, Sweden: Malmo Academy of Music, Lund University.

Suthers, L. (2000). Music experiences for toddlers: Responses of daycare staff members. *Music Within Every Child. Proceedings of the International Society of Music Education, Early Childhood Seminar.* Kingston, Ontario, Canada: Queen's University.

Sutton-Smith, B. (1970). Psychology of childlore: The triviality barrier. *Western Folklore, 29,* 1–8.

Sutton-Smith, B. (ed.) (1972). *The folkgames of children.* Austin, TX: University of Texas Press.

Sutton-Smith, B. (1995). Introduction: What is children's folklore? In B. Sutton-Smith, J. Mechling, T. W. Johnson, & F. McMahon (eds), *Children's folklore: A source book* (pp. 3–9). New York: Garland.

Sutton-Smith, B. (1997). *The ambiguity of play.* Cambridge, MA: Harvard University Press.

Tarnowski, S. & Lerclerc, J. (1994). Musical play of pre-schoolers and teacher-child interaction. *Update: Applications of Research in Music Education, 13,* 9–16.

Trehub S. E. & Trainor, L. J. (1998). Singing to infants: lullabies and play songs. *Advances in Infancy Research, 12,* 43–77.

Trehub, S.E., Unyk, A.M., & Trainor, L. J. (1993). Maternal singing in cross-cultural perspective. *Infant Behavioral Development, 16,* 285–95.

Trevarthen, C. (2000). Musicality and the intrinsic motive pulse: Evidence from human psychobiology and infant communication. *Musicae Scientiae: Journal of the European Society for the Cognitive Sciences of Music: Special Issue* 1999–2000, 155–215.

Trevarthen, C. (2002a). Musicality and music before three: Human vitality and invention shared with pride. *Zero to Three, 23,* 10–18.

Trevarthen, C. (2002b). Origins of musical identity: Evidence from infancy for musical social awareness. In R. MacDonald, D. J. Hargreaves & D. Miell (eds), *Musical identities* (pp. 21–38). Oxford: Oxford University Press.

Wood, D., Bruner, J. C., & Ross, G. (1976). The role of tutoring in problem solving. *Journal of Child Psychology and Psychiatry, 17,* 89–100.

Young, S. (1999). Just making a noise? Reconceptualising the music-making of early childhood. *Early Childhood Connections, (USA,)* 5, 14–22.

Young, S. (2002). Young children's spontaneous vocalisations in free-play: Observations of two- to three-year-olds in a day-care setting, *Bulletin of the Council for Research in Music Education, 152,* 43–53.

Young, S. (2003a). *Music with the under-fours.* London: Routledge Falmer.

Young, S. (2003b). Time-space structuring in spontaneous play on educational percussion instruments among three- and four-year-olds. *British Journal of Music Education, 20,* 45–59

Young, S. (2003c). The interpersonal dimension: A potential source of musical creativity for young children? *Musicae Scientiae Special 10th Anniversary Conference Issue, ESCOM: European Society for the Cognitive Sciences of Music,* pp. 175–179.

Young, S. (2004). Musical collaboration between three- and four-year-olds in self-initiated play with instruments. In S. D. Lipscomb, R. Ashley, R. O. Gjerdingen, & P. Webster (eds), *Proceedings of the 8th International Conference on Music Perception and Cognition (ICMPC8).* Evanston, IL: Northwestern University School of Music. CD–ROM.

Young, S. (2005). Adults and young children communicating musically. In D. J. Hargreaves, D. Miell, & D. MacDonald (eds), *Musical communication.* (pp. 281–299) Oxford: Oxford University Press.

CHAPTER 16

SINGING AND VOCAL DEVELOPMENT

GRAHAM F. WELCH

Introduction

Despite the warmth in the room as they shook the snow off their winter coats and gathered around the kitchen table, there was a collective sense of nervousness and, in some cases, unease that was barely touched by the hostess' cheerful manner and greeting. Outside, the dark of a Newfoundland evening had already descended and the hostess wondered if some of the wind's icy chill was reflected in the body language. This gathering was to be the first of several sessions for the group when things usually unspoken, sometimes hidden for many decades, would be allowed to surface.

> You went to school, the first thing that happened, everybody had to be singing in little concerts and things. You go to class; the nuns would say, 'anybody can sing.' You'd go and you were embarrassed to tears because you knew you couldn't sing and there was no help. . . I was told. . . you really can't sing, you can go back to your classroom.
>
> Knight, S. interview with C., aged 50 (private communication)

> I remember playing skipping and singing on the street. I can't remember the tunes now. My sister—I remember singing a little bit to her, but I don't think I ever really thought I couldn't sing until Grade Seven [age 12] and the teacher and all my friends and I was in glee club and that was a major time. She stopped and said, 'Somebody is tone-deaf here.' She said, 'It's you, V, you're tone-deaf.' She said, ' You don't have any notes. You just can't sing along with the music at all.' I said, 'I really want to stay in glee club because my friends are there.' She said, 'You can stay in glee club but you're not allowed to sing. You just got to mouth the words. You can't sing.' From then on, I assumed that I was tone deaf. I never sang in any other choirs at all after that. I go to church most of the time and I mouth the words. If we are out with a bunch of friends at a party, I try to mouth the words. Maybe, if I had a drink or two, I might sing. And even when I heard myself, I felt that I couldn't sing. My voice is deep anyway. . . I know a lot of people have deep voices and are beautiful singers, but I just assumed that because my voice is deep that I couldn't sing. . . that's 35 years ago. . . I was sitting second row back and there were kids behind me. You can imagine how embarrassed I felt.
>
> Knight, S. interview with V., aged 47 (private communication)

> We always sang. We'd sit on the fence in the evening, friends and stuff like this, and we'd sing different songs that would be on the go and, of course, you would be playing and there would be songs with that. But it was always something that we did. Then in Grade Six

[age eleven], we had a two-room school and we had Grade 1 to 3 in one room and Grade 4 to 6 in the other room, and the same teacher, of course, taught the three Grades. Her daughter was in school with us and there was some kind of play or something for Christmas, and so singing—these songs were sung. I practised at home for ages and I stood up to sing it and she [the teacher] told me to sit down, that I couldn't sing. Well, I was devastated. And I thought I had done such a good job with it . . . I'm sure I wanted to cry. Of course, you came home; it was no good of telling your parents at the time that something like this had happened to you.

Knight, S. interview with L., aged 42 (private communication)

Over the next few weeks and months, these adults shared many similar detailed memories. Despite the passing of time, these episodes of childhood were vividly recalled. A sense of embarrassment, shame, deep emotional upset, and humiliation, usually accompanied by reports of a lifelong sense of musical inadequacy were commonly expressed elements. For these particular Canadians, as for many other adults around the world in different cultural contexts, the associations between singing and childhood were not positive. Within the local Newfoundland culture, singing competency either as an individual or within a group has always had high status. Consequently, any perceived singing 'failure' in childhood has often led to continued self-identify as a 'non-singer' (Knight, 1999) and has reinforced a cultural stereotype of a community that is divided in two: those who 'can sing' and those who 'cannot'.

Similar findings have been reported from other studies of adults in North America, the UK, and Scandinavia. Yet, despite such experiences, there are some adults who never give up hope of improvement and there have been several successful examples of specialist choirs being started for adult 'non-singers' (Mack, 1979; Richards & Durrant, 2003). These include a new community choir in St. John's, Newfoundland, four 'beginners' choirs in one London college that have a 20-year history, various 'Singing from Scratch' choirs in the Midlands and south-east of England and similar initiatives in Sweden, the USA, Canada, Australia, and New Zealand.

The existence of such choirs for adult 'non-singers' is one of a number of significant challenges to a bipolar 'can/cannot' categorization of singing behaviours. They are part of the evidence base for singing to be considered as a normal developmental behaviour that can be enhanced or hindered, particularly by the events and experiences of childhood. The prime source of such singing 'failure' for an individual is a particular moment in childhood and/or adolescence when there is a mismatch between developing singing competences and a set singing task (Welch, 1979, 1985, 2000a,b, 2005; Cooksey & Welch, 1998). Erroneous adult expectation often creates the problem. This mismatch may then become further 'objectified' by continuing inappropriate comment from adults or peers, which suggests that the singing problem is evidence of an underlying disability in music. Arguably, the number of singing 'failures' that are socially generated in our communities would be reduced radically if there was a greater awareness of: (1) how singing mastery develops; (2) how children of the same age can be in different phases of development (as is considered normal with other forms of culturally-biased behaviour, such as reading); and (3) how best to provide suitable 'developmentally sensitive' singing activities. The narrative that follows reviews the nature of singing development from early childhood through to (and including) adolescence.

Particular features are highlighted of how normal development may be fostered, shaped, and sometimes hindered.

Singing as a developmental behaviour

Pre-birth and infancy

The foundations of singing development originate in the auditory and affective experiences of the developing fetus during the final months of gestation, particularly in relation to the earliest perception of melodic variations in the mother's voice. The amniotic fluid that surrounds the fetus is an effective transducer of the pitch contours of maternal voicing. As the mother speaks or sings, the prosodic features of her voice (melody and rhythm) are conveyed to the developing fetus by the sound waves that transfer through her body tissue and that also are reflected from surfaces in her immediate environment. At the same time, the mother's affective state as she speaks or sings is encoded hormonally in her bloodstream through neuroendocrine activity. This emotional state is believed to be experienced by the fetus relatively concomitantly with the sound of the mother's voice because of an interfacing of the fetal and maternal bloodstreams (see Welch, 2005, for a more detailed review). The outcome is an interweaving of acoustic (prosodic/melodic) and emotional experiences pre-birth that are likely to underpin the developing infant's subsequent interactions post-birth with the sounds of the maternal culture. For example, our ability to determine particularly strong emotions in vocal behaviours in speech and singing (Johnstone & Scherer, 2000; Sundberg, 2000; Nawrot, 2003) is likely to originate in these earliest dual-channel (acoustic-affect) experiences and, arguably, to create a certain bias towards the association of particular vocal timbres with positive and negative feelings (termed 'emotional capital'—Welch, 2005). Six-month-olds, for example, exhibit endocrine (cortisol) changes after listening to their mothers singing (Trehub, 2001), becoming calmed when upset and more alert when sleepy.

The first year of life is characterized by a shaping of the infant's vocal production through an interaction with the acoustic characteristics of the maternal culture. Parents, for example, typically incorporate rich musical properties when interacting with infants: they speak and sing at higher pitch levels, use a wider pitch range, longer pauses, often at a slower rate, and use smooth, simple, but highly modulated intonation contours (for reviews, see Thurman & Welch, 2000; Welch, 2006; Chapter 2, this volume). At birth, neonates continue to be particularly sensitive to the sound of the human voice, while demonstrating a certain initial perceptual plasticity towards any language (Eimas, 1985). Two-day-old neonates, for example, listen longer to women singing in a maternal style (Masataka, 1999). Adult singing (both male and female) appears to be especially significant, as demonstrated in its beneficial effects on premature infants' physiological functioning through changes in heart rate and oxygen saturation, alongside a reduction in stressful behaviours (Coleman et al., 1997).

The earliest vocal behaviour is crying. It contains all of the ingredients of subsequent vocalization, including singing, with variations in intensity and pitch, as well as rhythmic patterning and phrasing (Vihman, 1996). At the age of 2 months, cooing and vowel-like sounds are already evidenced and being shaped by the maternal culture (Ruzza et al., 2003). Aspects of 'musical babbling' that contain definite musical features, such as pitch and rhythmic patterns, are also evidenced from 2 months onwards (Tafuri & Villa, 2002). Their incidence and quality appear to be related positively to the amount of time devoted to daily singing behaviours by the mother; the greater the amount of maternal singing, the increased likelihood of earlier musical babbling. By the age of 3–4 months, the infant is able to imitate their mother's exaggerated prosodic contours that characterize infant-mother interaction (Masataka, 1992). Vocal play emerges around the ages of 4–6 months (Papoušek, 1996). By the age of 1 year, infants are sufficiently cued into the language of the maternal culture for elements to be reflected in their own vocalizations. As examples, French infants babble using French speech units, Russian infants babble using Russian and Japanese infants using Japanese (Meltzoff, 2002).

In general, the first year of life is characterized by increasingly diverse vocal activity. The first vocalizations of infancy, with their communication of affective state (discomfort and distress, then also comfort and eustress), are expanded to include quasi-melodic features (2–4 months), developing vocal control (4–7 months), and vocal pitch behaviours that are directly linked to the prosodic features of the mother tongue.

Early childhood and pre-school

Singing development pre-school is characterized by an increasing interaction with the sounds of the experienced maternal culture. This interaction is reflected in a mosaic of different singing behaviours that are evidenced between the ages of 1 and 5 years. They relate to the young child's acquisitive, playful, creative and spontaneous nature as they engage with and make sense of their 'local' musical world. The variety of vocalization includes: 2 year olds' repetition of brief phrases with identifiable rhythmic and melodic contour patterns (Dowling, 1999), 3 year olds' vocal interplay between spontaneous improvisation and selected elements from the dominant song culture, termed 'pot-pourri' songs (Moog, 1976), and 'outline songs' (Hargreaves, 1996) in which the nature of the figurative shape of the sung melodic contour (its 'schematic' contour) is thought to reflect the current level of the young child's understanding of tonal relationships (Davidson, 1994).

There is evidence of increasing sophistication and complexity in relation to the learning of songs from the dominant culture by young children (and see later for developmental models by Rutkowski, 1997; Welch, 2002). However, the path of development is not necessarily linear for any particular individual. In a US study of the spontaneous singing of 2 year olds' first songs, for example, there is evidence that 'phrases are the initial musical units' (Davidson, 1994, p. 117). Such phrases are characterized by limited pitch range, a certain disjunction of key/tonality and a descending contour. In contrast, recent Italian data of 2–3-year-old children indicate that some young children appear to be much better at imitating a complete melody modelled by their mother (and also by a specialist course tutor) than in matching individual phrases of the same song (Tafuri & Welch, unpublished data, see Figure 16.1). These Italian children had been exposed to regular sessions of their mothers' singing since the final trimester of pregnancy, both at home and in a special infant-parent singing course organized in the local conservatoire. Yet for other children in the same Italian group, with apparently the same levels of exposure to maternal singing, the opposite is the case. Their

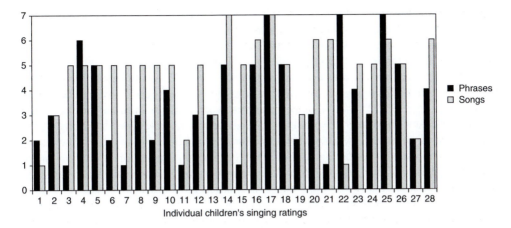

Figure 16.1 Accuracy ratings of Italian children ($n = 28$) aged 2.6–3.3 years in imitating song phrases and complete songs modelled by their mothers (Tafuri & Welch, unpublished data). Ratings are based on a seven-point scale of perceived accuracy.

sung phrase accuracy is rated as better than their whole song accuracy (Figure 16.1), in line with data from the earlier US (Davidson, 1994) study.

For the youngest children, the boundaries between singing and speaking may be blurred, or at least ambiguous to the adult listener, and are related to the dominance of a particular contour schema (Davidson, 1994) as well as to the influence of the mother tongue. For example, a longitudinal study in Canada of young girls aged 18–38 months from monolingual and bilingual backgrounds reported that 'intermediate vocalizations' (a type of vocal behaviour at the boundary between speech and song) were more prevalent in Mandarin and Cantonese-speaking children than in English-speaking children (Mang, 2000/2001). A follow-up study in Hong Kong with mono- and bilingual 3- and 4-year-olds confirmed these findings and revealed that, regardless of age, the manipulation of vocal pitch was used to distinguish between singing and speaking (Mang, 2002). The mean fundamental frequencies (F_0) for songs were reported to be consistently higher than speech, but 'own choice' songs were performed at a slightly lower pitch than a criterion song. In addition, the older English monolingual children demonstrated a wider mean F_0 differentiation between their singing and speaking behaviours compared with their Cantonese mono- and bilingual peers. Taken together, such examples from these diverse cultural settings remind us that singing behaviour is subject to developmental processes, while also being sensitive to sociocultural context (including task). In the above examples, context also includes the presence or absence of a pitch-based language as the mother tongue in which meaning is explicitly conveyed by the shaping of melodic contour.

As might be expected from the interaction of enculturation with generative skill development in music (cf. British Educational Research Association Music Education Review Group, 2001; Welch, 2006), longitudinal data on singing development in early childhood confirm the importance of the prosodic features of the mother tongue. Spontaneous singing is characterized principally by the control of melodic-rhythmic contour patterns

(Sundin, 1997; Dowling, 1999). Between the ages of 1 and 2 years, for example, a typically spontaneous infant song consists of repetitions of one brief melodic phrase at different pitch centres. By the age of 3 years, three different phrases are characteristically evidenced and one phrase singing is rare (Dowling, 1988, 1999). Furthermore, recent case study research with 2–3-year-olds in a free-play day-care setting (Young, 2002) celebrates a wide diversity in young children's spontaneous singing that is linked to context and activity, while being mediated by age. This diversity includes 'free-flow vocalizing' (a wordless vocal creation often associated with solitary play with no defined overall musical shape), 'chanting' (often short, repeated phrases), 'reworking of known songs' (the utilization of enculturated song fragments), 'movement vocalizing' (either of self or objects), singing for 'animation' (associated with dramatic play), and the imitation of actual sounds (defined as 'comic-strip type noises', usually associated with object play). As children grow older (3–4 years) and more sociable, more speaking than singing may be evidenced.

Age is also a factor in young children's perception and expression of emotion in singing. Four- and 5-year-olds are able to express happiness and sadness in their invented songs. In one Canadian study, children used conventional musical devices, such as a major modality and dotted or syncopated rhythms for 'happy' songs, contrasted by a reduced pitch range and suppression of melodic contours in 'sad' songs (Adachi & Trehub, 2000). Their song texts were also contraposed emotionally; with 'happy' songs focused on 'friends', 'family', and 'sweets', but 'sad' songs focused more on a negative version of these (e.g., 'no family'). In contrast, older children's 'sad' songs were dominated by themes related to death (Adachi & Trehub, 1999). Data from Sweden (Gabrielsson & Örnkloo, 2002) confirm the growth of children's expertise with age in the recognition and expression of intended sung emotion, particularly between the ages of 4 and 7 years.

The first years of schooling

It is common for a diverse range of singing abilities to be exhibited by children on entry to compulsory schooling. Within this diversity, it is necessary to distinguish between (1) children's (developing) skill in the performance of a taught song (Rutkowski, 1990, 1997; Welch, 1986, 1998, 2000b, 2002; Welch *et al.*, 1996, 1997, 1998), and (2) children's ability to invent songs (Davies, 1986, 1992, 1994). As with pre-school singing behaviours, context and culture are also factors (Rutkowski & Chen-Haftek, 2000; Mang, 2003).

With regard to the first of these categories concerning the skilled performance of a taught song, two major US and UK studies have drawn on developmental theories to propose phased models of singing development (Rutkowski, 1997; Welch, 1998—see footnote[1]).

---

[1] Rutkowski (1997) *Singing Voice Development Measure (SVDM)*

1   'Pre-singer' does not sing but chants the song text.

1.5   'Inconsistent Speaking Range Singer' sometimes chants, sometimes sustains tones and exhibits some sensitivity to pitch, but remains in the speaking voice range (usually A_3 to A_4 [note: the pitch labels have been altered to bring them in line with modern conventions in which middle C = C_4, 256 Hz]).

2   'Speaking Range Singer' sustains tones and exhibits some sensitivity to pitch but remains in the speaking voice range (usually A_3 to A_4).

2.5   'Inconsistent Limited Range singer' waivers between speaking and singing voices and uses a limited range when in singing voice (usually up to F_4).

The US data (Rutkowski, *op. cit.*) was generated through systematic evaluation of children's singing behaviours across a period of over 15 years. The emergent nine-phase model (which went through several versions[2]) suggests that children progress from speech-like chanting of the song text, to singing within a limited range ('speaking range singer') to the demonstration of an expanded vocal pitch range that is allied to skilled competency in vocal pitch matching. This model has an affinity with that of another US-based longitudinal study (Davidson, 1994) that suggests that children's singing development is linked to a schematic processing of melodic contour. Data from Harvard University's 6-year *Project Zero* study of children aged between the ages of 1 and 6 years indicated five specific levels of pitch development in young children's singing, expanding from an initial melodic contour scheme with a pitch interval of a third to one that embraced a complete octave.

Within the research literature, children are sometimes reported as being more skilled when copying a sung model if they used a neutral syllable rather than attempting the song with its text (e.g., Levinowitz, 1989). This finding has resonances with data from a 3-year longitudinal study of 184 children in their first 3 years of formal education in 10 UK Primary schools (Welch *et al.*, 1996, 1997, 1998). The research provided detailed evidence of how singing behaviours are age-, sex-, and task-sensitive. Over the 3 years, the participants as a collective appeared to demonstrate little overall improvement when required to match the sung pitches of the criterion songs (two songs were specially taught and assessed each year) (see Figure 16.2). However, this singing behaviour was in marked contrast to their ability to learn the words of the songs, which was extremely good, even in their first term

3	'Limited Range Singer' exhibits consistent use of initial singing range (usually D_4 to A_4).
3.5	'Inconsistent Initial Range Singer' sometimes only exhibits use of limited singing range, but other times exhibits use of initial singing range (usually D_4 to A_4).
4	'Initial Range Singer' exhibits consistent use of initial singing range (usually D_4 to A_4).
4.5	'Inconsistent Singer' sometimes only exhibits use of initial singing range, but other times exhibits use of extended singing range (sings beyond the register lift: B_4^b and above).
5	'Singer' exhibits use of extended singing range (sings beyond the register lift: B_4^b and above).

Welch (1998) *A revised model of vocal pitch-matching development (VPMD)*

Phase 1	The words of the song appear to be the initial centre of interest rather than the melody, singing is often described as 'chant-like', employing a restricted pitch range and melodic phrases. In infant vocal pitch exploration, descending patterns predominate.
Phase 2	There is a growing awareness that vocal pitch can be a conscious process and that changes in vocal pitch are controllable. Sung melodic outline begins to follow the general (macro) contours of the target melody or key constituent phrases. Tonality is essentially phrase based. Self-invented and 'schematic' songs 'borrow' elements from the child's musical culture. Vocal pitch range used in 'song' singing expands.
Phase 3	Melodic shape and intervals are mostly accurate, but some changes in tonality may occur, perhaps linked to inappropriate register usage. Overall, however, the number of different reference pitches is much reduced.
Phase 4	No significant melodic or pitch errors in relation to relatively simple songs from the singer's musical culture.

[2] The conceptualization of development as occurring in 'phases' is a common outcome of research that is undertaken over a long period with time for researcher reflection and the evaluation of new data. For example, the current author has developed and reviewed a particular model of vocal pitch matching over the past two decades (1986, 2002), which reconceptualizes the evidence and reduces the number of developmental 'phases' (rather than the originally labelled 'stages') from five to four.

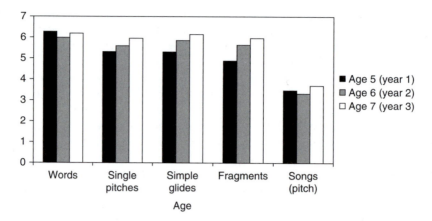

Figure 16.2 Longitudinal data on 5–7-year-old children's ($n = 184$) rated singing abilities (maximum accuracy rating = 7) for (a) words of target songs (two songs were assessed each year); (b) sung pitches of same complete songs; (c) deconstructed pitch elements of the same songs (single pitches, simple melodic contours (glides) and simple melodic fragments) (Welch *et al.*, 1996, 1997, 1998).

of compulsory schooling at age 5 (Figure 16.2: Year 1 data). Furthermore, when the pitch elements of the target songs were deconstructed into simpler musical tasks in which the children were required to match individual pitches, echo melodic contours, or copy small melodic fragments, the children were significantly more pitch accurate, as demonstrated by year-on-year improvements. There were no sex differences in their singing of these three types of deconstructed tasks. Boys and girls were equally successful and demonstrated similar improvements over time. In contrast, when the *same* boys were faced with the challenge of singing a complete song, their vocal pitch became less accurate and, as a group, they demonstrated little or no improvement in song singing across the 3 years. Overall, singing competency appeared to be closely related to the nature of the task, with many boys negatively affected in the task of singing a 'school' song. In line with these longitudinal findings, two recent studies suggest that gender stereotyping may be a factor in the lack of singing development in some young boys (Hall, 2005; Joyce, 2005). Australian research into 5-year-old boys' singing (Hall, 2005) indicates that singing may be perceived as a 'female' activity. UK research of 9- and 10 year olds (Joyce, 2005) across three primary schools found that only one-third of boys enjoyed singing (compared with two-thirds of girls) and that boys believed that girls were better singers.

In addition to age, sex/gender, and task, there are also contextual factors that can affect children's singing behaviours. For example, the UK longitudinal study data demonstrated a clear 'school effect' (Welch, 2000a). When comparing individual school data, *all* the children in one inner-city school improved their singing skills over the 3 years, notwithstanding their poor socio-economic environment and generally low academic attainment in other areas of the curriculum, whereas relatively few children made progress in another school, despite them having much higher socio-economic status and attainment levels. A major factor in these differences appears to have been teacher expectation. Progress was most marked where the class teacher expected and worked consistently for singing improvement with all their pupils over a sustained period. Similar findings concerning school effects on singing motivation, perceived self-identity as a singer and overall enjoyment of singing as a school activity are also reported by Joyce (2005).

Socio-cultural differences have been exampled also in the more advanced singing skills demonstrated by a large class of first-grade Chinese (Hong Kong) children compared with their US peers (Rutkowski & Chen-Haftek, 2000). Similarly, an assessment of the singing behaviours of 120 Hong Kong children aged 7–9 years from various language groups (Mang, 2003), using both the Rutkowski and Welch developmental profiles, reported statistically significant effects for sex (favouring girls) as well as mother-tongue. Chinese monolingual children performed consistently better than English bilingual children, even though the criterion song was in English. This was seen as a further indication (following Rutkowski & Chen-Haftek, 2000; Mang, 2000/2001) that Cantonese-speaking children achieve singing mastery earlier than their English counterparts, perhaps because the pitch centres for speech and singing of the former are more closely aligned.

Both the US- and UK-based developmental models agree that different 'phases' of singing competency are likely to be exampled within any group of children entering their first school class. Some children already will be extremely competent performers of complete songs from the experienced maternal culture (both words and music), while others will be less advanced and will be in one of the 'earlier phases' of singing development. This does not mean that the latter group of 'developing' singers will not gain singing mastery, particularly if they are provided with an appropriately nurturing environment in which singing tasks are designed to match, then to extend, current vocal behaviours. For such children, it is likely that their pre-school interactions have provided fewer opportunities to fulfil their singing potential (as outlined in the *Early childhood and pre-school* section earlier).

The effects of singing alone or with a group are equivocal in the research literature. Some research evidence suggests that children may become more accurate in reproducing the musical features of a criterion song when singing in a group compared with singing alone (e.g., Buckton, 1982; Greene, 1993). Other research (e.g., Goetze, 1985; Smale, 1988) reports the opposite in favour of increased reproductive accuracy if the young child is assessed when singing alone. It may be possible to reconcile these two positions by assuming that individual singing behaviour is likely to be framed by an interaction between current singing competency, the nature of the singing task, the competency of other singers in the group and an individual's current ability to make sense of the available feedback. There is an internal psychological feedback monitoring system that is essentially outside conscious awareness, which is used for a moment-by-moment self-monitoring of the singing behaviour. This system draws on information from internal sense receptors, as well as internal and external auditory information concerning the relative matching of vocal behaviour with an external model (see Welch, 1985, 2005). Where the individual is able to make sense of and use these different feedback channels in combination, then singing as a member of a skilled group may promote more competent behaviour. Where the individual is less able to make sense of and use this feedback, such as when surrounded by a less skilled group of singers and/or when it is difficult to 'hear' their own voice, then performing in a group context may be more disadvantageous. Data from studies of choral acoustics, for example, indicates that auditory feedback for one's own vocal output is reduced when (1) other singers are in close proximity (self-to-other ratio), and (2) when nearby singers are singing, or attempting to sing, the same pitches (Ternström, 1994; Daugherty, 2000).

Nevertheless, it is likely that singing competency will be nurtured through exposure to frequent opportunities for vocal play within an environment that encourages vocal exploration and accurate imitation (Young, 2002; Mang, 2003; Welch, 2005).

The data from various studies on early singing development were collated into a theoretical protocol 'baseline assessment of singing' for use with children on entry to school (Welch & Elsley, 1999). This was evaluated subsequently with a small class of children ($n = 19$) aged from 3 years 8 months to 5 years 10 months (King, 2000). In general, the data supported key features of the model, namely that singing competence is likely to vary at an individual level with musical task, such as in the sung reproduction of melodic contour, pitch intervals, and song text. Any assessment of singing abilities in young children, therefore, should provide a mixture of tasks (such as pitch glides and pitch patterns as well as song melodies) as a basis for diagnosis and curriculum planning. Furthermore, recent neuropsychobiological data on pitch processing modules in the brain (Peretz & Coltheart, 2003) supports a hierarchical model in which melodic contour (*pace* Davidson, 1994; Rutkowski, 1997; Welch, 1998) is analysed before the processing of intervals and tonality (see Welch, 2005 for a review).

With regard to children's ability to invent songs, a series of studies (Davies, 1986, 1992, 1994) indicate that 5–7 year olds have a range of song-making strategies. These include narrative songs (chant-like in nature, often with repeated figures), as well as songs that have more conventional features, such as an opening idea and a clear sense of closure, four-phrase structures, repetition, phrases that both 'borrow' from the immediate musical culture, and also may be transformed (sequenced, inverted, augmented) in some way. Overall, children in the first years of schooling demonstrate a clear sense of musical form and of emotional expression in their invented songs.

Older childhood

The latter years of childhood are characterized by a general singing competency for the majority. Relatively few children are reported as singing 'out-of-tune' at the age of 11 years (Welch, 1979, 2000b; Howard *et al.*, 1994). For example, evidence from a wide range of studies indicates that approximately 30% of pupils aged 7 years are reported as being relatively 'inaccurate' when vocally matching a melody within a Western cultural tradition. However, this proportion drops to about 4% of the same pupil population by the age of 11. Within each of these and the intervening age groups, 'out-of-tune' boys outnumber girls by a ratio of 2 or 3:1 (Welch, 1979). Culture, however, continues to be significant. Anthropological and ethnomusicological studies, for example, have suggested that young children from the Anang in Nigeria can sing 'hundreds of songs, both individually and in choral groups' by the age of 5 (Messinger, 1958, p. 20), Venda children in South Africa were reported as both learning special children's songs and composing new songs for themselves (Blacking, 1967), whereas Herati children in Afghanistan tended to focus on the imitation of adult models, with the children (particularly boys) of professional musicians' families (*sazendeh*) being immersed in the local music culture and often expected to perform professionally by the age of 12 (Doubleday & Baily, 1995).

The use of 'imitation' as part of an enculturated induction into the skilled practices of expert singers is evidenced in many different musical cultures, as exampled in the cathedrals where European sacred music is practised, as well as in the choral communities of sub-Saharan Africa and Scandinavia. Cathedrals in the UK, for example, typically induct their choristers at the age of 8 so that by the age of 13 they will have had 5 years immersion into a weekly (usually daily) ritual of rehearsals, performances, choral singing, and solos, embracing a wide range of compositional styles and musical genres that span over 500 years of Western classical music. Within the cathedral choir, performance skill level is signalled by singer nomenclature (such as 'head chorister', 'senior corner boy', 'probationer') and variations in the dress code, as well as by the degree of performance involvement in particular repertoire. Novices are deliberately placed in between more skilled, older choristers and normally are required to sing only certain items during the cathedral services while they deepen and develop their performance skills through listening and observing their more accomplished peers.

Although the tradition of highly skilled boy singers in the UK may be traced back to the first foundations of English cathedrals in Canterbury (AD 597), Rochester (AD 604), and St Paul's, London (AD 604), the 'all-male' hegemony of cathedral music experienced a major challenge in 1991 with the admittance of girls to Salisbury Cathedral in the west of England. Since then, by 2004, the potential for equally skilled performance by girl choristers has been recognized through the creation of separate girls' choirs in 22 cathedrals and minsters (Welch, 2004)[3]. Girl choristers are usually admitted using the same audition criteria as their male counterparts and are expected to perform the same repertoire to the same professional standard.

Evidence of the power of the musical culture in cathedrals in fostering specialist singing skills may be found both in the quality of choral outputs (such as national and international broadcasts by the BBC, commercial recordings, international tours and concerts) and also in the regular media-fuelled controversies over whether it is possible or not to perceive differences between the singing of older female and male children (Welch & Howard, 2002; Sergeant et al., 2005). With regard to perceived singer gender, a summary of recent research data (Figure 16.3) indicates that, while it is possible for an untrained solo singer's sex to be identified relatively accurately from about the age of 8 onwards, it is also equally possible for trained female choristers from the age of 8 to be systematically mistaken as male, depending on the particular piece of music being performed. However, once the female chorister moves into her mid-teens, the voice quality becomes more characteristically identifiable as 'female' ('womanly')[4]. In general, children's voices tend to be higher in pitch and have a less complex acoustic make-up than those of adults. Nevertheless, children are able to achieve similar loudness levels as adults by using relatively more breath until the age of 12, when adult-like breathing patterns are observed (Stathopoulos, 2000).

---

[3] The data for 2004 on the numbers of cathedrals with female choristers in UK cathedrals has been collated by Claire Stewart as part of her ongoing doctoral studies at the Institute of Education into their impact on the all-male choral tradition.

[4] For a detailed review of the literature on gender and chorister voice, including similarities and differences in the underlying anatomy and physiology for singing, see Welch & Howard (2002). For data on the perceived gender of untrained children's voices, see Sergeant et al. (2005).

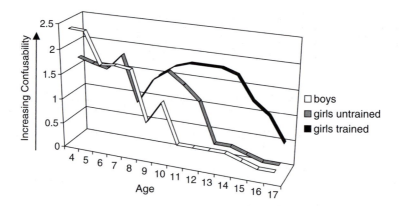

Figure 16.3 Confusability by age and gender of children and adolescents aged 4–16 years. The figure is extrapolated from measured data of perceived confusability for untrained singers (Sergeant *et al.*, 2005) and measure data of perceived confusability for trained singers (Welch & Howard, 2002). Initially, untrained young boys are confused as girls. Then, the sexes become more readily distinguishable from the age 8/9 years. However, singing training can enable girls from 8/9 years to 14 years to sound 'boy-like' in certain pieces from the repertoire. From 14 years onwards, singer sex becomes more readily identifiable.

Puberty and adolescence

The onset of puberty heralds fundamental changes to the nature and quality of the singing voice for both females and males. Whereas the actual dimensions and growth of the vocal instrument are similar across sexes during childhood (Titze, 1994), during puberty the male vocal tract becomes significantly longer and develops a greater circumference. In contrast, the growth of the female vocal tract is less marked, being about 15–20% shorter than in the male and with a different internal ratio of resonating spaces, mainly because the neck (pharynx) is relatively shorter compared with that of the male (Story *et al.*, 1997). Growth typically lasts from 10 to 18 years in females (and can begin at age 7—Herman-Giddens *et al.*, 1997), compared with 12–20 years in males (Thurman & Klitzke, 2000). The highpoint of pubertal voice change tends to be about 12–14 years of age in both females and males (Gackle, 2000; Cooksey, 2000).

There are relatively few major studies of singing voice transformation during adolescence reported in the literature, particularly with regard to the female changing voice. Those that are available draw primarily on data from populations in the USA (Williams *et al.*, 1996; Cooksey, 2000; Gackle, 2000), the UK (Geddye, personal communication; Harries *et al.*, 1996; Cooksey & Welch, 1998), Japan (Norioka, 1994), and Germany (Heidelbach, 1996). The data are consistent about the presence and characteristics of adolescent voice change.

Gackle (2000) reports the outcome of her doctoral studies in Florida (during 1987), allied to fifteen years' professional observation, to suggest that there are four distinct "stages" in female adolescent voice change (see ♀ in Figure 16.4a). In the first stage (termed 'pre-pubertal') the voice has a 'light, flute-like quality' with no apparent register changes. The comfortable singing range is between D_4 and D_5, within a wider singing range of Bb_3 to

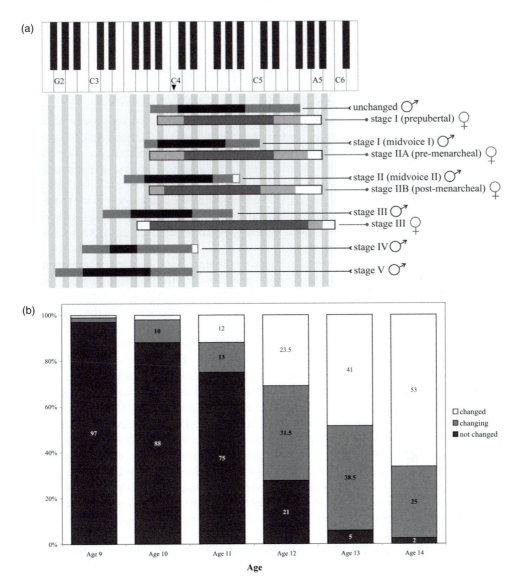

Figure 16.4 (a) Stages of singing voice change for females (based on Gackle, 2000) and males (based on Cooksey, 2000). (b) Extrapolated model of adolescent male voice change by age, based on UK (Geddye, personal communication) and Japanese data (Norioka, 1994), total $n = 3,188$.

F_5 (and up to A_5). The next stage ('pre-menarchial'—Stage IIA) is characteristic of the beginnings of female voice mutation around the ages of 11–12. The comfortable range is approximately the same as previously (D_4 to D_5), within a slightly expanded overall range (A_3 to G_5). However, there is often breathiness in the tone due to inadequate closure of the vocal folds as a result of growth occurring in the laryngeal area. A singing register transition typically appears between G_4 and B_4 and some girls may have difficulties in singing lower pitches. Singing often becomes uncomfortable and effortful and a breathy voice quality is characteristic across the range. The next stage is the peak of female voice mutation ('post-menarchial'—Stage IIb). Singing is characterized by a limited comfortable range (B_3 to C_5), discomfort (particularly at upper pitches), distinct voice qualities for each sung register and with the lower part of the voice often taking on a more 'alto' and often husky quality. The final stage ('young adult female'—Stage III) has a much-expanded comfortable singing range (A_3 to G_5), less breathiness, greater consistency in tone quality and greater singing agility. Vibrato often appears at this stage and the voice has a more adult, womanly quality. Ongoing research (Welch & Howard, 2002; Welch, 2004) indicates that adolescent voice change is the same for relatively untrained female singers as for those who have been involved in sustained vocal performance, such as through membership of a female cathedral choir. However, as with adult female singers (Lã & Davidson, 2005), there is always some individual variation in the impact of puberty on the singer's voice related to slight differences in the underlying endocrinological metabolism and physiological functioning.

Male adolescent voice change has a more extensive literature, both in Europe and the USA. One major longitudinal study was conducted by Cooksey (2000), initially based on fieldwork in California in the late 1970s, then drawing on further studies in the USA during the following decade, as well as a London-based cross-cultural study in the 1990s (Cooksey & Welch, 1998). Overall, he reports six 'stages' of adolescent male singing voice change (see ♂ in Figure 16.4a) that are characterized by an overall lowering of the sung pitch range. While the rate of voice change is unpredictable for any given individual, it is reliably sequential for all.

In the first male adolescent stage ('unchanged'), the mean sung vocal pitch range is A_3 to F_5, with the tessitura pitch boundaries $C\#_4$ to $A\#_4$. The voice quality is perceived as 'clear', with relatively little evidence of breathiness in the tone. The beginnings of voice change (termed by Cooksey as Stage I, 'Midvoice I') are marked by a reduced vocal range (Ab_3 to C_5) and instability of sung pitch, particularly for the upper frequencies, which tend to be produced with increased effort, as well as tone quality that is perceived as more effortful, strained and breathy. The sung range then descends approximately in thirds across the next three stages (see Figure 16.4a), with each stage being characterized by a reduced mean range and relative continuing instability in the production of upper pitches, but contrasted by relative stability for the lower pitches. The pitch ranges are: Stage II ('Midvoice II'), F_3 to A_4; Stage III ('Midvoice IIa'), D_3 to $F\#_4$; followed by Stage IV ('New Baritone', also termed 'New Voice'), B_2 to $D\#_4$. Within these, Stage II may be regarded as the mid-point of voice change and this is when a falsetto register (C_5 to B_5) first appears and (for some) a whistle register (C_6 to C_7). Stage III ('Midvoice IIa') is characterized by the greatest vocal instability and the least clear vocal quality. It is only in the final stage of voice change (Stage V, 'Settling Baritone', also termed 'Emerging Adult Voice' G_2 to D_4) that the mean sung pitch range opens out again and the voice timbre begins to adopt a clearer, less breathy quality. However, the number and intensity of harmonics do not yet approximate normal adult characteristics. Nevertheless, for each stage of voice change the adolescent male has a (limited) number of pitches that can be produced comfortably and musically (see the darker shaded elements in the ranges for male voices in Figure 16.4a) and it has been possible in recent years to find a greater awareness by publishers to produce repertoire that is specially written as being suitable for these changing voices.

In general, age is a poor predictor for establishing voice change stages, with any given age group likely to encompass several stages. It is possible for an individual to pass through all stages of adolescent voice change in 12 months, but is it also possible for this process to be much slower and to last several years. Nevertheless, a summation of selected UK and Japanese data for over 3000 males, aged 9–14 years, provides some indication of the possible proportions of different categories of voice change by age group (Figure 16.4b). As can be seen, the ages of 12–14 have significant proportions of males whose voices are perceived to have already 'changed', or in the process of 'changing', while embracing a reducing number that are still 'unchanged'. Ideally, choral groups of adolescent male singers in this age range are best suited, therefore, to music that has been arranged specifically for them in three parts, using the Cooksey classification guidelines (Unchanged and Stage I on a top line, Stages II and III on a middle line, and Stages IV and V on the bottom line), rather than to attempt traditional four-part music in which the tessiturae often are likely to be mismatched with current singing abilities.

Factors influencing singing development and the realization of potential

As can be seen from the previous text, singing in one form or another is an essential feature of our musical development and behaviour. In each age phase (infancy, early childhood, older childhood, adolescence), the human voice has a distinctive underlying anatomy and physiology that is capable of producing a diversity of 'singing' behaviours. These increasingly explore and approximate to the particular sonic features of models that are available in the soundworlds of the experienced maternal and global cultures. In the first months of life, these 'sung' products are driven by basic human needs, before becoming more exploratory and melodic in nature as vocal skills develop in the acquisition and mastery of musical elements. Throughout childhood and adolescence, singing development is a product of neuropsychobiological activity, potential, and change, interfaced with, and shaped by, particular socio-cultural environments in which certain patterns of sound characterize the dominant musical genres. At any age, development can be supported or hindered by a number of factors, such as the appropriateness of a given singing task set by an adult in relation to current singing capabilities, the expectations of peers and/or the value placed on singing (and certain types of singing behaviour) within the immediate culture. Opportunities to engage in vocal play and exploration, to share in singing games with peers and 'experts', as well as to improvise and compose their own songs are essential features of musical cultures that foster singing development. Children who exceed the 'norms' reported in the research literature are likely to have been provided with a nurturing environment that is designed to match, celebrate, enable, and extend individual singing expertise. Others, whose singing is perceived to be 'lacking' in some way, will not have had such appropriate opportunities. For some, entry to adolescence can confirm their identity as a 'non-singer', as someone for whom music is seen as an area of 'failure'. Yet, everyone has the potential to learn to sing. We need, therefore, to continue to seek optimal ways to allow children and adolescents to explore and extend their singing (and musical) birthright. In this, we will reduce the need for 'remedial' action in adulthood, such as the establishment of adult choirs for 'non-singers'. The stories of a lifelong sense of singing 'disability' should be confined to history.

References

Adachi, M. & Trehub, S. E. (1999). Children's communication of emotion in song. In S. W. Yi (ed.), *Music, mind and science* (pp. 454–465). Seoul: Seoul National University Press.

Adachi, M. & Trehub, S. E. (2000, April). *Preschoolers' expression of emotion through invented songs.* Paper presented at the meeting of the Society for Research in the Psychology of Music and Music Education, University of Leicester, England.

Blacking, J. (1967). *Venda children's songs.* Johannesburg: University of Witwatersrand Press.

British Educational Research Association Music Education Review Group (2001). *Mapping music education research in the UK.* Southwell, UK: British Educational Research Association.

Buckton, R. (1982). *Sing a song of six year olds.* Wellington, New Zealand: Council for Educational Research.

Coleman, J. M., Pratt, R. R., Stoddard, R. A., Gerstmann, D. R., & Abel, H.-H. (1997). The effects of the male and female singing behaviours and speaking voices on selected physiological and behavioural measures of premature infants in the intensive care unit. *International Journal of Arts Medicine*, 5(2), 4–11.

Cooksey, J. (2000). Voice transformation in male adolescents. In L. Thurman & G. F. Welch (eds), *Bodymind and voice: Foundations of voice education.* Revised Edition (pp. 718–738). Iowa: National Center for Voice and Speech.

Cooksey, J. & Welch, G. F. (1998). Adolescence, singing development and National Curricula design. *British Journal of Music Education*, 15, 99–119.

Daugherty, J. F. (2000). Choir spacing and choral sound: Physical, pedagogical, and philosophical dimensions. In B.A. Roberts & A. Rose (eds), *Conference Proceedings of the International Symposium, Sharing the Voices: The phenomenon of singing II* (pp. 77–88). St. Johns, Newfoundland, Canada: Memorial University of Newfoundland Press.

Davidson, L. (1994). Songsinging by young and old: a developmental approach to music. In R. Aiello with J. Sloboda (eds), *Musical perceptions* (pp. 99–130). New York: Oxford University Press.

Davies, C. (1986). Say it till a song comes: reflections on songs invented by children 3–13. *British Journal of Music Education*, 3(3), 279–293.

Davies, C. (1992). Listen to my song: a study of songs invented by children aged 5 to 7 years. *British Journal of Music Education*, 9(1), 19–48.

Davies, C. (1994). The listening teacher: An approach to the collection and study of invented songs of children aged 5 to 7. In H. Lees (ed.), *Musical connections: Tradition and change* (pp. 120–127). Auckland, NZ: International Society for Music Education.

Doubleday, V. & Baily, J. (1995). Patterns of musical development among children in Afghanistan. In E. J. Fernea (ed.), *Children in the Muslim Middle East* (pp. 431–444). Austin: University of Texas Press.

Dowling, W. J. (1988). Tonal structure and children's early learning of music. In J. Sloboda (ed.), *Generative processes in music* (pp. 113–128). Oxford: Oxford University Press.

Dowling, W. J. (1999). The development of music perception and cognition. In D. Deutsch (ed.), *The psychology of music* (2nd edn) (pp. 603–625). London: Academic Press.

Eimas, P. D. (1985). The perception of speech in early infancy. *Scientific American*, 252, 34–40.

Gabrielsson, A. & Örnkloo, H. (2002, August). *Children's perception and performance of emotion in singing and speech.* Paper presented at the ISME Early Childhood Conference, Copenhagen, Denmark.

Gackle, L. (2000). Understanding voice transformation in female adolescents. In L. Thurman & G. F. Welch (eds), *Bodymind and voice: Foundations of voice education.* Revised Edition (pp. 739–744). Iowa: National Center for Voice and Speech.

Goetze, M. (1985). *Factors affecting accuracy in children's singing.* Unpublished doctoral thesis, University of Colorado.

Greene, G. A. (1993). *The effects of unison singing versus individual singing on the vocal pitch accuracy of elementary school children.* Paper presented at the Southern Division of the Music Educators National Conference.

Hall, C. (2005). Gender and boys' singing in early childhood. *British Journal of Music Education,* 22, 5–20.

Hargreaves, D. J. (1996). The development of artistic and musical competence. In I. Deliege & J. Sloboda (eds), *Musical Beginnings* (pp. 145–170). Oxford: Oxford University Press.

Harries, M. L. L., Griffin, M., Walker, J. & Hawkins, S. (1996). Changes in the male voice during puberty: Speaking and singing voice parameters. *Logopedics Phoniatrics Vocology,* 21(2), 95–100.

Heidelbach, U. (1996). *Die entwicklung der knabenstimme zur mannerstimme bei chorsangern dargestellt am singstimmfeld.* Unpublished MD thesis, Technischen Universität Dresden.

Herman-Giddens, M. E., Slora, E. J. Wasserman, R. C., Bourdony, C. J., Bhapkar, M. V., Kock, G. G., & Hasemeier, C. M. (1997). Secondary sexual characteristics and menses in young girls seen in office practice: A study from the Pediatric Research in Office Settings Network. *Pediatrics,* 99(4), 505–512.

Howard, D. M., Angus, J. A., & Welch, G. F. (1994). Singing pitching accuracy from years 3 to 6 in a primary school. *Proceedings of the Institute of Acoustics,* 16(5), 223– 230.

Johnstone, T. & Scherer, K. R. (2000). Vocal communication of emotion. In M. Lewis & J.M. Haviland-Jones (eds), *Handbook of emotions* (pp. 220–235). New York: Guildford Press.

Joyce, H. (2005). *The effects of sex, age and environment on attitudes to singing in Key Stage 2.* Unpublished master's dissertation, Institute of Education, University of London.

King, R. (2000). *An investigation into the effectiveness of a baseline assessment in singing and some influential home-environmental factors.* Unpublished master's dissertation, Roehampton Institute London, London.

Knight, S. (1999). Exploring a cultural myth: what adult non-singers may reveal about the nature of singing. In B. A. Roberts & A. Rose (eds), *The Phenomenon of Singing II* (pp. 144–154). St John's, NF: Memorial University Press.

Lã, F. & Davidson, J. (2005). Investigating the relationship between sexual hormones and female Western classical singing. *Research Studies in Music Education,* 25, 75–87.

Levinowitz, L. (1989). An investigation of preschool children's comparative capability to sing songs with and without words. *Bulletin of the Council for Research in Music Education,* 100, 14–19.

Mack, L. (1979). *A descriptive study of a community chorus made up of 'non-singers.'* Unpublished EdD dissertation, University of Illinois at Urbana-Champaign.

Mang, E. (2000/2001). Intermediate vocalisations: an investigation of the boundary between speech and songs in young children's vocalisations. *Bulletin of the Council for Research in Music Education,* 147, 116–121.

Mang, E. (2002). An investigation of vocal pitch behaviours of Hong Kong children. *Bulletin of the Council for Research in Music Education,* 153/4, 128–134.

Mang, E. (2003). Singing competency of monolingual and bilingual children in Hong Kong. In L. C. R. Yip, C. C. Leung, & W. T. Lau (eds), *Curriculum Innovation in Music* (pp. 237–242). Hong Kong: Hong Kong Institute of Education.

Masataka, N. (1992). Pitch characteristics of Japanese maternal speech to infants. *Journal of Child Language,* 19, 213–223.

Masataka, N. (1999). Preference for infant-directed singing in 2-day old hearing infants of deaf parents. *Developmental Psychology*, 35, 1001–1005.

Meltzoff, A. N. (2002). Elements of a developmental theory of imitation. In A. N. Meltzoff & W. Prinz (eds), *The imitative mind* (pp. 19–41). Cambridge: Cambridge University Press.

Messinger, J. (1958). Overseas report. *Basic College Quarterly*, Fall, 20–24.

Moog, H. (1976). *The musical experience of the pre-school child.* (trans. C. Clarke). London: Schott.

Nawrot, E. S. (2003). The perception of emotional expression in music: evidence from infants, children and adults. *Psychology of Music*, 31, 75–92.

Norioka, Y. (1994). A survey of Japanese school aged poor pitch singers. In G. F. Welch, & T. Murao (eds), *Onchi and singing development* (pp. 49–62). London: David Fulton Publishers.

Papoušek, M. (1996). Intuitive parenting: a hidden source of musical stimulation in infancy. In I. Deliege & J. Sloboda (eds), *Musical Beginnings* (pp. 88–112). Oxford: Oxford University Press.

Peretz, I. & Coltheart, M. (2003). Modularity and music processing. *Nature Neuroscience*, 6(7), 688–691.

Richards, H. & Durrant, C. (2003). To sing or not to sing: A study on the development of 'non-singers' in choral activity. *Research Studies in Music Education*, 20, 78–89.

Rutkowski, J. (1990). The measurement and evaluation of children's singing voice development. *The Quarterly*, 1(1–2), 81–95.

Rutkowski, J. (1997). The nature of children's singing voices: Characteristics and assessment. In B. A. Roberts (ed.), *The Phenomenon of Singing* (pp. 201–209). St John's, NF: Memorial University Press.

Rutkowski, J. & Chen-Haftek, L. (2000, July). *The singing voice within every child: A cross-cultural comparison of first graders' use of singing voice.* Paper presented to the ISME Early Childhood Conference, Kingston, Canada.

Ruzza, B., Rocca, F., Boero, D. L., & Lenti, C. (2003). Investigating the musical qualities of early infant sounds. In G. Avanzini, C. Faienza, D. Minciacchi, L. Lopez, & M. Majno (eds), *The neurosciences and music* (Vol. 999, pp. 527–529). New York: Annals of the New York Academy of Sciences.

Sergeant, D. C., Sjölander, P., & Welch, G. F. (2005). Listeners' identification of gender differences in children's singing. *Research Studies in Music Education*, 25, 28–39.

Smale, M. J. (1988). An investigation of pitch accuracy of four- and five-year-old singers. *Dissertation Abstracts International*, AAT—8723851.

Stathopoulos, E. T. (2000). A review of the development of the child voice: an anatomical and functional perspective. In P. J. White (ed.), *Child Voice* (pp. 1–12). Stockholm: Royal Institute of Technology, Voice Research Centre.

Story, B. H., Titze, I. R., & Hoffman, E. A. (1997). Volumetric image-based comparison of male and female vocal tract shapes. *National Center for Voice and Speech Status and Progress Report*, 11, 153–161.

Sundberg, J. (2000). Emotive transforms. *Phonetica*, 57, 95–112.

Sundin, B. (1997). Musical creativity in childhood: A research project in retrospect. *Research Studies in Music Education*, 9, 48–57.

Tafuri, J. & Villa, D. (2002). Musical elements in the vocalisations of infants aged 2 to 8 months. *British Journal of Music Education*, 19, 73–88.

Ternström, S. (1994). Hearing myself with others: Sound levels in choral performance measured with separation of one's own voice from the rest of the choir. *Journal of Voice*, 8(4), 293–302.

Titze, I. (1994). *Principles of voice production.* Englewood Cliffs, NJ: Prentice-Hall.

Thurman, L. & Klitzke, C. (2000). Highlights of physical growth and function of voices from prebirth to age 21. In L. Thurman & G. F. Welch (eds), *Bodymind and voice: Foundations of voice education.* Revised edn (pp. 696–703). Iowa City, Iowa: National Center for Voice and Speech.

Thurman, L. & Welch, G. F. (eds) (2000). *Bodymind and voice: Foundations of voice education*. Revised edn. Iowa City, Iowa: National Center for Voice and Speech.

Trehub, S. E. (2001). Musical predispositions in infancy. In R. J. Zatorre & I. Peretz (eds), *The biological foundations of music* (Vol. 930, pp.1–16). New York: Annals of the New York Academy of Sciences.

Vihman, M. M. (1996). *Phonological development*. Oxford: Blackwell.

Welch, G. F. (1979). Poor pitch singing: A review of the literature. *Psychology of Music*, 7, 50–58.

Welch, G. F. (1985). A schema theory of how children learn to sing in tune. *Psychology of Music*, 13, 3–18.

Welch, G. F. (1986). A developmental view of children's singing. *British Journal of Music Education*, 3(3), 295–303.

Welch, G. F. (1998). Early childhood musical development. *Research Studies in Music Education*, 11, 27–41

Welch, G. F. (2000a). Singing development in early childhood: the effects of culture and education on the realisation of potential. In P. J. White (ed.), *Child voice* (pp. 27–44). Stockholm: Royal Institute of Technology.

Welch, G. F. (2000b). The developing voice. In L. Thurman & G. F. Welch (eds), *Bodymind and voice: Foundations of voice education* (pp. 704–717). IA: National Center for Voice and Speech.

Welch, G. F. (2002). Early childhood musical development. In L. Bresler & C. Thompson (eds), *The arts in children's lives: Context, culture and curriculum* (pp. 113–128). Dordrecht: Kluwer.

Welch, G. F. (2004). Developing young professional singers in UK cathedrals. *Proceedings, 2nd International Physiology and Acoustics of Singing Conference, Denver, USA*. Retrieved 3 June, 2005 from http://www.ncvs.org/pas/2004/pres/welch/welch.htm

Welch, G. F. (2005). Singing as communication. In D. Miell, R. MacDonald & D. J. Hargreaves (eds), *Musical communication*. (pp.239–259). New York: Oxford University Press.

Welch, G. F. (2006). The musical development and education of young children. In B. Spodek & O. Saracho (eds), *Handbook of research on the education of young children* (pp. 251–267). Mahwah, NJ: Lawrence Erlbaum Associates Inc.

Welch, G. F. & Elsley, J. (1999). Baseline assessment in singing. *Australian Voice*, 5, 60–66.

Welch, G. F. & Howard, D. (2002). Gendered voice in the cathedral choir. *Psychology of Music*, 30, 102–120.

Welch, G. F., Sergeant, D. C., & White, P. (1996). The singing competences of five-year-old developing singers. *Bulletin of the Council for Research in Music Education*, 127, 155–162.

Welch, G. F., Sergeant, D. C., & White, P. (1997). Age, sex and vocal task as factors in singing 'in-tune' during the first years of schooling. *Bulletin of the Council for Research in Music Education*, 133, 153–160.

Welch, G. F., Sergeant, D. C., & White, P. (1998). The role of linguistic dominance in the acquisition of song. *Research Studies in Music Education*, 10, 67–74.

Williams, B., Larson, G., & Price, D. (1996). An investigation of selected female singing- and speaking-voice characteristics through comparison of a group of pre-menarchial girls to a group of post-menarchial girls. *Journal of Singing*, 52(3), 33–40.

Young, S. (2002). Young children's spontaneous vocalizations in free play: Observations of two- to three year olds in a day care setting. *Bulletin of the Council for Research in Music Education*, 152, 43–53.

CHAPTER 17

PLAYING AN INSTRUMENT

GARY E. MCPHERSON AND JANE W. DAVIDSON

One of the most common and popular ways a child can be involved in music is to play an instrument, so it is important to include a chapter on this aspect of musical development in this volume. Traditionally, much of the literature on this topic has focused on performance skills and the acquisition of technique on particular instruments. More recently, however, this literature has been broadened through research dealing with a range of environmental and personal influences that impact on children's learning of a musical instrument. In this chapter we focus on this latter body of evidence in order to explain some of the underlying principles that govern how children develop their capacity to mature into performing musicians.

The chapter begins with a description of the various catalysts that shape children's initial motives to commence learning and their choice of an instrument when they begin formal training. We then explore what children expect and value from their learning and how this aspect of motivation influences their subsequent musical development. This leads to a discussion of the types of strategies children need to acquire in order to become successful performers, and the playing habits and practice techniques that either enhance or impede their progress. A final section deals with the help and encouragement children need to receive from their parents if they are to develop into successful, self-regulated learners. The chapter reviews instrumental learning within the Western musical tradition, based on the available literature and popularity of these instruments worldwide. It is our hope, however, that some of the basic principles we propose can be extrapolated and applied to the learning of different types of instruments within other musical styles and genres.

Starting age

Within reason, the adage 'the earlier the better' is probably appropriate as a general guide to when children should start learning an instrument. In practice, however, there are many differences between instruments, with physical maturation and mental attention span often being used by teachers and parents to guide decisions on whether a child is ready to begin formal lessons (Kohut, 1985; Hallam, 1998).

Children learning the keyboard can start as early as 2 or 3 years of age, preferably with informal play activities. For strings, some Suzuki teachers recommend no earlier than the age of 3, when smaller-sized instruments ensure that the physique to play these instruments does not cause problems for children with particularly small fingers. However, for brass and woodwind instruments, which require more physical strength, it is unlikely that children will have much success until at least 6 or 7 years of age when they have acquired the physical ability (and the teeth) to maintain a correct embouchure and move the air through the instrument in order to produce a characteristic tone.

Initial experiences

Technological advances during the past two decades have seen a rapid expansion of new instruments being manufactured that complement existing acoustic and electric instruments, and have also changed how music is performed and produced. This rapidly changing environment has already been experienced at a number of levels, with the palette of sound effects and recording techniques made possible by the electric keyboard being one of the most popular choices. The adoption of the electronic keyboard is in part a consequence of the broadening of the music curriculum in schools to include creative tasks such as composing and possibly also a reaction against the *squawks* produced by cheap plastic school recorders, which children regard as the least popular of all instruments (O'Neill, 2001).

Children who play either the keyboard or recorder do not necessarily take lessons, often because they are simply expected to use it in school, or if they possess one at home, it is used for 'fun' rather than for 'serious' study. However, these instruments can provide initial and unthreatening points of departure, and so their merits should not be underestimated. Indeed, Davidson *et al.* (1998) found that all of their 258 young music learners had played one of these instruments as a way of 'having fun' and 'messing around' before specializing on their chosen instrument. *Post-hoc*, some of the older students looked back on these earliest experiences as a basis for them to experiment with, get to know, understand and enjoy music. In the case of Carl (discussed in Chapter 24), the recorder was adopted as the main instrument, and the player progressed rapidly because he became obsessed by achieving more and more, through a fascination of the way in which he could manipulate the pitch and timbre of the instrument's sound.

Of course, children who begin learning traditional instruments, such as ensemble instruments or the piano, are generally much more likely to take lessons and participate in a structured learning environment right from the start. They can develop a liking for an initially disliked instrument, or a hatred for one they previously liked. In the work of Sloboda *et al.* (1996) it was discovered that some of the most successful young learners were those who had been through a range of musical instruments, often settling for their 'first study' for pragmatic reasons. For instance, Lisa (discussed in Chapter 24) changed from violin to viola at the age of 12 years, realizing that she was far more likely to have an orchestral career playing the less commonly learned viola. In this case, her participation in music was more important than the instrument itself. But, this is not necessarily the case for all individuals.

The decision to begin

In formal music programmes offered at schools, the teacher's decision about which instrument might be learned is often dictated by what instruments are available for study, plus also what instruments need to be assigned to maintain a balanced instrumentation in the school's ensembles. Typically, however, a parent's view will often evolve from an entirely different perspective. Many will be concerned about the speed at which their child will be able to learn the instrument. Very often they will also consider more pragmatic issues, such as whether the child will be able to continue learning the same instrument and perform with good ensembles after entering high school. In many cases, parents will also be concerned about the cost involved in learning, both in terms of the expense of ongoing lessons and maintenance of an instrument, as well as the eventual cost of purchasing a quality instrument if the child continues playing.

Market research by Cooke and Morris (1996) helps identify some of the important motivational concerns, from the child's perspective, that impact on long-term success in learning an instrument. They found that English children aged 5 and 6 were the most enthusiastic for expressing a desire to learn. Almost half of their sample of 5 and 6 year olds (48%) said that they were likely to start learning in the near future. However, this enthusiasm is short-lived because by the age of 7 less than half the children surveyed expressed a desire to learn an instrument, and this remained stable at about a quarter of non-playing children until 11 years. By the age of 14 only 4% of the children said that they were likely to start learning an instrument. These results need to be placed in perspective, however, because they depend on the type of instrument and music to be learned. Many rock guitarists for example, typically do not begin playing until they reach their early teenage years, but then, if they are highly motivated, make progress very quickly as a result of engaging in many hours of practice alone, with friends and in bands (Gullberg & Brändström, 2004).

Choosing an instrument

Various intrinsic and extrinsic factors impact on why a child will choose one instrument over others. Some are intrinsically attracted to a particular instrument because of a liking for its sounds, or how it looks and feels (e.g., Delzell & Leppla, 1992; Boyle et al., 1993; O'Neill & Boulton, 1996). When difficulties such as trying to get a sound out of the instrument, or carrying it around in a large and heavy case become apparent, this genuine intrinsic appeal of the way the instrument sounds, looks, or feels can help to sustain engagement with it.

In other cases, children may begin learning because of extrinsic reasons such as wanting to emulate a model they admire, such as a famous musician. A more common reason is to join with friends who are learning at the same time. Indeed, children will very often become interested in joining a school or community musical ensemble because they wish to keep up with their friends who are also beginning (MacKenzie, 1991; McPherson, 2001). Other important extrinsic motivational influences include significant others, particularly encouragement from a family member or teacher (Sloboda et al., 1994). For example, Sosniak's (1985) study of concert pianists shows that some of the highest achievers were reluctantly persuaded by a parent to start learning and it was years before they became passionately committed and intrinsically motivated to continue their own development and decide to become professional pianists.

Many children have been grateful in later life for having parents who insisted that they learn a particular instrument. In general terms, where motivation of this type is externally directed, rather than internally driven, sustaining an interest is more difficult (Alderman, 1999). If learning is merely to please a parent or teacher, a child is unlikely to make much progress or to show much enthusiasm beyond the initial stages of development (Pintrich & Schunk, 2002). This is even more apparent in situations where they encounter difficulties mastering the complex physical and mental skills involved in learning.

In terms of the advice given by teachers to their students, physical factors also appear to have some role in instrumental selection (Kohut, 1985). A very large underbite or protruding or irregularly shaped teeth may cause endless frustration to a wind instrument player, in which case teachers may advise the child to choose an instrument that does not require the use of the embouchure. But advice must be given with caution, for a casual glance at almost any professional ensemble will show that many players do not have what could be called a 'perfect body' for playing their instrument. The wonderful jazz trumpeter Chet Baker managed to play despite having lost many of his teeth, for instance.

From the examples above, it is clear that no single factor will fully explain why a child will decide to learn an instrument. This is why our longitudinal research (McPherson, 2001; McPherson & Davidson, 2002) with beginning instrumentalists across the first 3 years of their learning has tried to clarify the blend of factors that motivate each individual child to commence learning. Many of our 7- and 8-year-old beginners said they began because they felt learning an instrument might be fun, exciting or enjoyable. Their observations were often based on evidence of having seen and heard musical ensembles at their school and in the community, or knowing friends and siblings who were also involved as musicians. When asked to explain why they selected their particular instrument, almost a third of the children said that they liked the sound of the instrument, thus confirming the important intrinsic reason cited above. Children also indicated, however, that the choice of instrument was influenced by what they perceived to be 'easy' instruments to play, whether they liked the look of the instrument, whether they felt it was an appropriate size for them, or whether their friends were also playing the same instrument (see also, Boyle *et al.*, 1993; O'Neill & Boulton, 1996).

As with other studies, our research revealed gender associations with boys tending to choose so-called 'masculine' instruments such as trumpets and trombones and girls selecting more 'feminine' instruments like flutes and clarinets (Abeles & Porter, 1978; Delzell & Leppla, 1992; Bruce & Kemp, 1993; O'Neill & Boulton, 1996; Conway, 2000; Harrison & O'Neill, 2003), even though these types of associations are being increasingly challenged. One of the best examples is the images children see of Lisa Simpson playing the saxophone in *The Simpsons* TV series. However, in our study we could find no evidence that these types of images had any pronounced effect on our children's instrumental preferences.

In summary, the general evidence of our study and other related literature suggests that children not only have a projected belief about which instruments are more or less easy to learn, but also a specific view of themselves in relation to their capacity to successfully master each particular instrument, with these impressions often being influenced by gender stereotypes.

Personal expectations and values

It might be inferred from the above that children will either possess the right motivation or not to engage with music learning. To some degree this may be true, with some individuals genuinely being more intrinsically driven on specific tasks than others. In our view, a more appropriate way of thinking about this is to understand the personal beliefs that children hold and that are shaped by their experiences of the world around them. These include the expectations and values children bring to their first instrumental lessons that subsequently shape and influence their future development. For example, in our study we asked the children to explain to us before they began their instrument, how long they expected to play (McPherson, 2001). Results show that they were able to differentiate between their interest in learning a musical instrument, the importance to them of being good at music, whether they thought their learning would be useful to their short- and long-term goals, and the amount of effort they felt would be needed to continue improving. Their responses were no different to what we would have expected if they were taking up any other activity. Many seemed intrinsically interested but did not feel that they would want to play the instrument all of their lives. Others seemed more extrinsically motivated, recognizing the value of learning for their overall education. For most of the children, learning an instrument was something useful to do while they were at school but something that would be of far less value in later life. Only a small number suggested that they wanted to become professional musicians (McPherson 2001; McPherson & Zimmerman, 2002).

Our results are consistent with research in academic subjects that seek to understand what children expect and value in their learning (Wigfield & Eccles, 2000, 2001). This work demonstrated that children are goal-oriented individuals; meaning that they choose and gravitate toward activities in which they believe they can achieve and be successful. Their behaviour is directly connected to the personal beliefs they hold about the activity, such that the expectations they hold for becoming competent impact on the level of performance they achieve; while the value they place on their learning influences whether they will choose to continue participating (Wigfield & Eccles, 2000, 2001; Printich & Schunk, 2002).

The comments above show that there are many facets underpinning children's personal beliefs about learning an instrument. In terms of expectancy-value motivational theory (Eccles *et al.*, 1998; Wigfield & Eccles, 2000), six seem particularly relevant for learning to play an instrument:

- *interest:* the personal satisfaction gained when playing and practising alone and with others, plus the love for the repertoire learned;
- *importance:* the degree to which learning the instrument fits with personal goals about what the child hopes to be good at;
- *usefulness:* whether learning the instruments is constructive and functional for what the child wishes to do, both now and in the future;
- *difficulty:* whether the learning process creates obstacles or is perceived as being more difficult than other activities with which the child is engaged;

plus also whether the child believes that learning and participation will lead to a sense of:

- *competence:* for which playing and performing become activities in which the child would like to succeed, and

- *confidence:* the empowerment felt for developing the skills necessary to master challenges associated with learning and performing on the instrument, such as whether the learning process is fraught with pressures and anxieties which diminish confidence and a sense of self-worth.

Sustaining involvement

As shown above and in Chapter 11, personal beliefs associated with a desire to achieve, not only influence children's motivation to continue playing but also shape their identities as individuals and their orientations as learners. Two of the more important of these learning orientations explain why some individuals strive to achieve while others are prone to give up and deliberately avoid activities with which they believe they cannot become competent. The first of these, *adaptive mastery-oriented* students, have a tendency to continue working hard when faced with failure and enjoy putting effort into achieving their goals. These types of learners remain focused on trying to achieve, despite difficulties that might come their way. In contrast, *maladaptive helpless-oriented* students often fail to establish reasonable goals for themselves, or goals that are within their reach. When they feel that the situation is out of their control and that nothing can be done to alleviate the situation, they tend to avoid further challenges, lower their expectations, experience negative emotions, give up or perform more poorly in the future (Dweck, 1986, 2000; O'Neill & McPherson, 2002).

Convincing evidence of these types of orientations as they might apply in music comes from O'Neill (1997), who studied 6–10-year-old children during their first year of learning an instrument. Before beginning instruction, these children were given a problem-solving task and procedure used to assess their motivational patterns (O'Neill & Sloboda, 1997). Some of the children were classified as *maladaptive helpless-oriented* because they avoided challenges, showed low persistence, and performed poorly when faced with failure. Before they commenced learning, this group was compared with another group of children who were defined as *adaptive mastery-oriented*, in that they were more inclined to persist with their efforts following failure or experiencing difficulties.

O'Neill (1997) believes that studying these two motivational patterns is important, because bright and skilled children can display either orientation. Importantly, her results demonstrate how children who displayed mastery-oriented motivational patterns prior to commencing their instrument progressed to a higher level of achievement at the end of their first year of learning than children who display maladaptive helpless motivational patterns. Interpreting these findings, O'Neill suggests that the less successful students learned to feel 'helpless' because of a tendency to focus their attention on their existing level of performance with the result that they could not see that the difficulties they were having now could be overcome in the future. Because of this, they tended to feel that any further effort would be futile. In contrast, the children with mastery orientations were more focused on how to increase their competence so they could perform better in the future. Consequently, they viewed failure as a normal part of their learning instead of something that should be avoided.

Thus, we can see how children's self-beliefs shape how they cope with the challenges of learning music. This is particularly important in an area as difficult and taxing for young children as learning an instrument, where the physical, mental, and emotional effort needed to sustain long-term engagement requires a great deal of resilience and persistence (McPherson & Zimmerman, 2002). The personal beliefs that children hold for their own competence and capacity to master tasks therefore have a major effect on their subsequent ability to persist in the face of difficulties, stressful situations, and competing interests (Bandura, 1997; McPherson & McCormick, 2006). This was evident in the results of our study as well. The children's beliefs about how long they might play their instrument before starting instruction interacted with their actual practice during the first year of learning. Children who displayed short-term commitment (such as predicting that they would learn for just a few years) made the least amount of progress, irrespective of the amount of practice they undertook during their first year. The highest achieving students were those who displayed long-term commitment to playing (such as saying they intended to play all their lives) coupled with high levels of practice (McPherson, 2001).

In addition to the above results, we also compared the comments of the children who continued learning with those who ceased playing across the first 3 years of learning (McPherson & Davidson, 2002). Children who ceased typically had unrealistically high expectations about how much practice they would undertake before commencing lessons. After they started, and the reality of learning set in, they then consistently undertook far less practice than their peers who chose to continue.

The results outlined above demonstrate that children bring many preconceptions to their first lessons, and that their progress is shaped by their expectations for being able to cope and succeed with their learning, combined with the value they place on the activity as something they will enjoy doing. This does not mean, however, that children's initial motivations are fixed and that positive attitudes cannot emerge and evolve over time. As we have seen in the Sosniak (1985) study mentioned earlier, it is only after extensive experience with music that many young learners will develop a lasting desire and commitment for performing and/or becoming a professional musician.

Mental strategies

A hallmark of successful learners is the quality of the mental strategies they apply to monitor and control their learning (Harris & Pressley, 1991; Moely et al., 1992; Siegler, 1996). Being able to choose and apply appropriate strategies helps these individuals to learn faster because they are able to integrate new knowledge and skills more quickly (Bjorklund, 2000).

Identifying the range of musically appropriate mental strategies beginners and intermediate level students adopt when learning to play an instrument has been a key concern of the first author in his work with beginning through to advanced level instrumentalists (McPherson, 1993, 1995, 1997, 2005). At the heart of his research is the search to understand what children are thinking as they solve various kinds of musical problems and how the sophistication of these mental strategies impacts on their overall skill development. In these studies children are typically asked to explain what they are doing in their minds in order to prepare for or complete a variety of tasks, such as performing music that they have rehearsed at home, sight-reading, playing from memory, playing by ear, and improvising.

Importantly, this line of research suggests that many strategies concerned with learning to play an instrument are domain specific and therefore quite different to the strategies children would use to solve problems in other areas of their learning. This explains why some children experience problems very early in their development, as they try to adopt a strategy from another area of their learning or an entirely inappropriate strategy to perform on an instrument (McPherson, 1997, 2005). As an example, in one part of the study, the beginners were given a short piece of music to memorize, to assess their ability to process musical notation and perform this from memory once the notation had been removed. A variety of strategies were reported by the children, including many 'unmusical' strategies such as staring at the notation to memorize the contour of the melody or inwardly saying the names of the notes of the phrase over and over to themselves. As an example, one beginner commented: 'I picture the notes in my mind. I take a photograph and keep it in my mind. That's what my mum told me to do with phone numbers.'

On the other hand, the more successful learners employed musically appropriate strategies for each of the styles of performance very early in their development and as a result went on to achieve at a much higher level than their peers (McPherson, 2005). The best strategies children used for playing from memory and by ear, for example, linked the sound of the music directly with instrumental fingerings. This was achieved through a type of mental practice where the instrumentalist worked holistically to sing and silently finger the piece through while they were studying the score (for the memorization tasks) or listening to the recording (for the ear playing tasks).

In a similar way, the highest achieving sight-readers were those children who took the most strategic approach, by making themselves aware of the finer details of the piece in the moments before they commenced playing. In a self-regulatory fashion, they typically studied the first measure to get a feel for how the piece started and what tempo might be appropriate, identified the key- and time-signatures, scanned the music to identify possible obstacles, directed and maintained their attention throughout the performance in order to anticipate problems and to observe musical indications such as expression markings and articulation, and monitored and self-evaluated their performance in order to correct errors (McPherson, 1994, 2005).

More broadly based strategies were also identified for children's rehearsal of repertoire they learn during their home practice (McPherson, 2005). In the study with our beginners, for example, the most successful learners were children who actively kept track of what they were learning by using a practice diary to take notes about what they needed to practise and how this might be accomplished. They also organized their practice sessions by focusing on the repertoire they needed to practise first in order to improve their playing before moving on to pieces they could already play and/or enjoyed playing (in contrast to children who organized their practice by playing for enjoyment first and improvement later).

Additional strategies included a more strategic approach to problems they encountered with the repertoire they were learning, such that better players displayed a more concentrated ability to refine their playing (e.g., 'First I play it once and see how good I am, then I practise it again and again until it's at a standard that I can take to my tutor'), in contrast to less capable musicians who reported inefficient strategies (e.g., 'I play my pieces through just once. I want to get them over with'). Finally, more strategic and capable players were also more inclined to self-diagnose and correct their playing (e.g., 'I try to think about how my teacher played it, then go back over it slowly and then speed it up'). This is in contrast to poor learners who displayed virtually no evidence of being sufficiently motivated to try and improve their playing (e.g., 'I don't try to fix it, I go through everything once') (McPherson, 2005, pp. 18–19).

In the most recent publication relating to this longitudinal study, the first author reports evidence suggesting that the quality of children's performance is directly related to the quality of their thinking when playing their instrument (McPherson, 2005). Unfortunately, by the end of their third year, there were extremely wide differences between the children's performance abilities across the skills studied. Of particular importance is the finding that children who established *ear-to-hand* co-ordination skills very early in their development for aural forms of performance such as playing from memory and by ear, and *eye-to-ear-to-hand* co-ordination skills for visual forms of performance such as sight-reading, went on to achieve at the highest level and experienced far less problems with their learning compared with their less strategic peers (McPherson, 2005; see also McPherson, 1993, 1997).

Analysis of what the teachers were covering in their lessons and the types of books used in lessons suggests that many children were picking these strategies up implicitly, rather than through direct instruction from their teachers (McPherson, 1993, 1994, 2005). This point reinforces the importance for children to be exposed to quality early experiences in music so that they establish not only proper playing habits, but develop their capacity to think musically as they learn to co-ordinate their eyes, ears, and hands, and 'think in sound' (see also Rostvall & West, 2003). It also highlights the need for instruction that more explicitly links thinking skills and task-oriented strategies with actual physical performance, an element of learning that is often lacking in instrumental tuition.

Engagement with the instrument

Without doubt, one of the most important parts of learning an instrument is the time and effort put into practising by children to develop their skills between lessons. Dictionary definitions define 'practice' as involving repetition of exercises to improve and develop skill. But this limited use of the word practice, stressing the repetitive aspect of training, is far from suited to music (Hallam, 1997a). A better approach is to think of practice as encompassing the range of thoughts and behaviours that children engage in 'that are intended to influence their motivational or affective state, or the way in which they select, organize, integrate, and rehearse new knowledge and skills' (Jørgensen, 2004, p. 85).

The key function of practice is to develop the internal memory representations necessary first to understand and then execute a musical task. This involves, as we have discussed earlier, various elements such as sight-reading, aural and physical skill and dexterity, coupled with a sense of musical time and intonation in order to bring cohesion and accuracy, in addition to knowledge of musical style and form (Davidson & Scripp, 1992). The ability to generate and use mental representations efficiently is critical to instrumental learning, and the degree to which these representations have been acquired are clearly reflected in the learner's ability at any given point in time. Consider the following contrasting examples: a beginning piano student's mental representation of a piece of music might consist of a sequence of difficult and laborious fingering combinations, while a more advanced player might also represent the underlying chord progression along with some expressive information, some aural image of the sounds, and perhaps even a visual representation of how the score looks. Of course, the degree of knowledge and experience shapes the performer's goals and level of achievement (the child being far less fluent and expressive than an expert soloist, for example). So, one of the more important aims of practice therefore is for the child to acquire as much knowledge and experience as possible, in order to be able eventually to produce technically fluent and musically expressive performances of the literature he or she aims to play.

Generally, skilled musicians exert a great deal more effort and concentration during their practice than less skilled musicians, and are more likely to image, monitor, and control their playing by focusing their attention on what they are practising and how it can be improved (Ericsson, 1997). In other words, they use current information to develop more sophisticated mental representations about music and how to perform it. Williamon and Valentine (1998) have demonstrated that these individuals are able to enjoy the 'pleasurable' aspects of practice (e.g., experimenting with phrasing, dynamics, and expressiveness) at the same time as engaging with the taxing requirements of dexterity, co-ordination and so on. They therefore appear to be more intrinsically motivated. In other words, the challenges of acquiring technical skill are for the pleasure of the ultimate expressive ends.

Developing self-regulated practice habits

Studies with young learners show that their home practice is very different from the picture depicted above. As with any complex skill, it can take children years to develop to a level where their practice is efficient and effective. Unfortunately, many beginners have great difficulty moving beyond the overwhelming challenges of co-ordination. It is not surprising therefore, that after the initial burst of excitement has worn off, practising a musical instrument can cause a mix of emotions for children, many of which may not seem particularly pleasant. These negative connotations are the reason why some teachers do not use the term 'practice', preferring instead to talk about 'music time' or 'music play' as one way of refocusing this activity to try to make it more interesting and enjoyable for the student.

In the last decade a growing body of research has helped us to understand some of the processes that young children adopt in their musical practice. In our study with young beginners, a large proportion of practice time (in many cases over 90%) was spent simply playing through a piece from beginning to end, without the child adopting a specific strategy for performance improvement (McPherson & Renwick, 2001). Barry and Hallam (2002) suggest that this is because beginners have not developed appropriate internal representations to identify and correct their own mistakes and are therefore not always aware when they are going wrong.

Hallam (1997a,b) has undertaken studies that attempt to clarify the content of individual practice. Ranking student achievements, she has demonstrated that at the least successful level students focus their practice only on the early sections of the music, without completing the task. In the next level they play through the music without stopping to correct their performance. Following this, they stop when a mistake is made, but only to correct and repeat single notes in contrast to the next level, where short sections are repeated before they are able to practise larger sections. Finally, the most sophisticated practice occurs when students are able to play through the work to obtain a general overview before identifying difficult passages that can be isolated for more concentrated attention.

Definitions of effective practice should, according to Hallam (1997a), differ depending on the level of expertise acquired. Beginners need support in order to develop internal aural representations of music that they are learning and in their early stages of development repetition helps to develop the basic skills that lay a foundation for more advanced levels of skill development later on. Providing a variety of repertoire and pieces that the learner is already familiar with, plus repertoire that can be easily assimilated aurally can also help to motivate children to be more strategic with their practice. In this way, repetition may be an effective practice strategy for beginners who are trying to assimilate a variety of complex skills. The adoption of more expert practice habits is probably therefore unrealistic, given the underdeveloped knowledge base of most beginners (Hallam, 1997a,b).

Of critical importance in Hallam's (1997a) opinion, is the need for teachers to demonstrate and model the processes of effective practice, such as how to:

- obtain an overview of the work
- identify difficulties
- select appropriate strategies
- work on sections and integrate them into a whole
- monitor progress
- set personal goals, and
- self-evaluate progress.

According to Hallam (1997a), as students' expertise increases, they can be challenged to perform more difficult and more complex repertoire. As their overall mental representational skills develop, they will be more capable of reflecting on their own style of practice as well as how, and in what ways they can change their practice habits in order to produce better results. At this time also, they should be encouraged to develop their interpretative abilities, through listening, researching, and analysing a broad range of music. Obviously, the quality of teaching plays an important facilitative role in making each of these facets of a musician's development possible.

Thus, in order to practice and so develop skills more quickly and effectively, students need to become 'self-regulated learners' in the sense that they need to learn how to plan, monitor, and control aspects of their own practice. This is why the first author's research over recent years has concentrated on the context-specific set of processes that children draw upon as they promote their own learning (McPherson & Renwick, 2001; McPherson & Zimmerman,

2002). The normal cycle of development occurs when children move from being influenced by socializing processes that support and help instil attitudes, knowledge, and skills to more personal awareness in the form of active self-regulation. Key self-regulatory processes involved in musical practice include:

- *Motive:* Vicarious or direct reinforcement by others leads to children being able to establish their own personal goals, reinforce their own learning and develop a sense of purpose and confidence in their own ability to perform.

- *Method:* The strategies that children are taught or observe from others lead to them developing a repertoire of ways for dealing with problems in their playing and also the ability to self-initiate ways of practising that will enhance their development.

- *Time:* Children's use of time is socially planned and managed through suggestions and reminders from others (such as parents and teachers) leading to them eventually being able to take responsibility for, plan and manage the amount of time they devote to their practice.

- *Behaviour:* Performance is socially monitored and evaluated before children are able to self-monitor and evaluate their own progress.

- *Physical environment:* The physical environment in which practice occurs (e.g., lounge/bedroom, use of music stand) is often structured by parents as a foundation for the child to eventually be able to control and shape the physical conditions in which they feel most comfortable practising.

- *Social:* Support for practice is provided by significant others such as parents, teachers, and peers who provide emotional and psychological support leading to the child being able to directly seek help by themselves.

Practising to improve versus practising for fun

Another way of understanding why some children make rapid progress while others have difficulties or avoid practice is to examine the actual repertoire practised. Children can practice repertoire they need to learn for their teacher or the next performance situation as well as pieces they have already mastered and can already play. Some children even report a form of musical doodling: activities that are usually undertaken for the pleasure of the musical experience alone, rather than to refine specific skills.

Sloboda and Davidson (1996) report that high achieving learners tend to do significantly greater amounts of 'formal' practice, such as scales, pieces, and technical exercises, than their less successful peers but are also likely to report more 'informal' practice, such as playing their favourite pieces by ear, playing for fun, or improvising. As reported earlier in the section dealing with strategies for performing rehearsed repertoire, children who organize their practice by starting on the repertoire that they need to learn for their next lesson or upcoming performance before moving on to repertoire they enjoy and can already play tend to progress faster than children who organize their practice the other way around. However, children need to find a balance between these two elements—the discipline of practising to improve, versus the freedom of practising for personal enjoyment (McPherson, 2005).

Both aspects of practice are extremely important and relate back to the motivational issues covered earlier: that musical progression is most efficient when learning involves a sense of individual empowerment such that the child enjoys and values learning and expects to become a successful musician.

We know also, that an important way of fostering positive motivation is to take advantage of the students' own individual goals, interests, and self-perceptions (Eccles-Parsons, 1983). This was clearly apparent in another phase of our study where we analysed videotapes of a young child's practice to examine the efficiency of her practice when rehearsing repertoire assigned by her teacher as compared with pieces she chose to learn herself (Renwick & McPherson, 2002). The practice efficiency of repertoire she chose to learn herself was markedly superior to literature she had been assigned by her teacher with the result that she was able to connect to a more advanced stage of development, as she included more varied strategies into her practice such as silent fingerings, silent thinking and singing. These findings are consistent with other research showing that children who tend to be more cognitively engaged when practising, by thinking about what they are playing and actively trying to improve their playing, tend to be more motivated and do more practice (McPherson & McCormick, 1999). A clear finding, however, is that allowing students choice in their repertoire can lead to positive improvements in their intrinsic motivation and task involvement (see further, Stipek, 1998; Pintrich & Schunk, 2002). This highlights a major problem that occurs in much teaching: When students are always learning pieces that are selected by their teachers they may start to feel that they are learning these pieces to satisfy their teacher, rather than because they want to learn them. Obviously, in such situations, motivation and efficiency of practice will quickly diminish.

Parental support

An important thread in the educational literature studies connections between the family and the environment in which a child receives instruction. The socialization process is bidirectional because parents convey important 'messages' to their children even though the level at which these messages are accepted, received, and internalized varies between children (Grusec *et al.*, 2000). More recently this literature has focused on two dimensions of the parent–child relationship: *parental practices* and *parental styles* (Spera, 2005). Parental practices refer to specific behaviours used by parents to socialize their children, such as helping with practice or by attending concerts. Parental styles are concerned more with the emotional climate in which parents raise their children and act to moderate the relationship between parenting practices and children's achievement. For example, parents who are authoritarian (i.e., strict, expect obedience and assert their power) when monitoring homework are more likely to inhibit their child's school performance, whereas parents who foster a mature attitude through bidirectional communication involving explanations of their behaviour and encouragement of independence are more likely to facilitate their child's performance (Spera, 2005).

It is now well established that children's use of time is more often based on habits, rather than specific plans, which means that they will often need help to learn how to manage, plan and prioritize their use of time (Alderman, 1999). Consequently, an important area related to parental practices investigates how parents help their children acquire the necessary skills to complete their homework: by modelling the task as the child moves through the assignments, by direct instruction such as questioning and drill and practice activities, and by reinforcement through the use of praise and encouraging comments (Balli, 1998; see also Spera, 2005). If this line of research is compared with musical practice, it becomes clear that the only support parents can give to a child who is learning an instrument, especially if they do not play an instrument themselves, is the last of these categories.

The extent to which children rely on their parent's support and encouragement is evident in a number of studies on children's homework showing that very young children up to grade 2 or 3 tend not to view homework as their own responsibility (Warton, 1997). While young children may possess an understanding of the importance of doing homework as a means of improving their competence, they often fail to realize the importance of taking personal responsibility to initiate practice, preferring instead to rely on their parent's reminders (Warton, 1997). Many children therefore need constant support in the form of reminders and checking from both parents and teachers over a number of years before they can develop the self-regulatory competence needed to take personal responsibility to complete it by themselves (Chen & Stevenson, 1989; Warton, 1997).

We found very similar evidence in our study of young music learners (McPherson & Davidson, 2002), with one important exception. Whereas many parents will continue to remind their child to do his or her homework for however many years it takes, the support our children received from their parents, in the form of reminders and more general support for their musical practice, tended to drop off toward the end of the children's first year of learning—at the very time they needed ongoing encouragement to continue across the difficult period of adjusting to their instrument and gaining sufficient skill to continue into their second year of learning. Unfortunately, very soon after the children commenced learning, some of their mothers began to form judgements about their child's ability to cope with practice, as well as their own capacity to devote energy into regulating the child's practice through continual reminders and encouragement to practice. Many mothers tended to withdraw their reminders, often because they felt that the child was either not coping emotionally, believing that if the child was really interested he or she would do it anyway, or because they were unwilling to invest their personal time and effort into regulating their child's daily schedule. The overall impression we gained from these interviews was that some mothers had actually given up on their children as potential musicians, much sooner than the children had come to feel the same way.

Like children, parents form expectations and values about their child's learning that subsequently impact on how capable they will be of helping their child to take responsibility for his or her learning. Some of our parents reported very active participation, such as sitting with the child during practice sessions, being present to add support, or becoming involved in parent–teacher committees at the school. In the early months of learning, over 80% of the mothers reported actively reminding and encouraging their child to practice. But as for the children themselves, the beliefs the parents held about whether or not their child might be successful on the instrument were directly related to how much practice the children actually completed. Those mothers who expressed concerns that their child would need to be supervised in order to do sufficient practice, had children who went on to do significantly less practice than other children (McPherson & Davidson, 2002).

Some mothers had exigent standards and expected some sort of routine and a consistent approach to practice. Their children tended to flourish. In the homework literature (Hoover-Dempsey *et al.*, 2001), parental-role construction has been found to link with parental involvement in child's education. The research seeks to understand why parents believe that they should be involved in homework, the extent to which they believe that their involvement will make a difference, and also whether they feel invited by teachers (or their child) to become involved. In our study, most of the parents felt that they should be involved, but because many parents had no previous musical experience, they were often hesitant to say or do too much for fear of interfering with the teacher–child relationship. Indeed, some had little idea about how to support their child's practice, with the result that they had a very unclear perception of their role as a facilitator of their child's learning. Others actively sought out information that they could use to help their child, such as by attending lessons and ensemble rehearsals, or talking with the teacher to see how their child was progressing and how they could help overcome difficulties by assisting in the practice sessions.

Related to parental style were the interviews in our study that show the mothers had experienced times when they were frustrated with their child's attitude or approach to musical instrument learning. Sometimes these frustrations were on both sides, with the children expressing concerns that they were bored with their practice or did not know how to improve their playing, and the parent feeling frustrated that their child was not making sufficient efforts or they would argue with the child about practice. These displays of negative affect were especially evident in the post interview discussions we completed with parents and their children who had ceased instruction.

A key finding in the homework literature is that parents who stay positive when helping with homework are more likely to stimulate their child's motivation (Pomerantz *et al.*, 2005). While helping a child can cause all sorts of frustrations for a mother, it appears that if they are able to stay positive—even in the most frustrating and demanding situations—then their child is much more likely to persist and eventually become more motivated in school, as well as value and enjoy the learning process. This finding seems to have a special relevance for children's musical learning, because a parent's ability to put their own frustrations aside to help focus their child on what is enjoyable about their learning is probably one of the key elements in promoting motivation, persistence, and ongoing musical involvement. In the homework literature there is convincing evidence that parents' homework-involvement practices are directly related to children's learning, achievement, and the time they are willing to devote to their homework (Hoover-Dempsey *et al.*, 2001; Spera, 2005). For musical practice, the results of our studies suggest a similarly strong relationship (Sloboda & Davidson, 1996; McPherson & Davidson, 2002).

Concluding comments

It is clear from the literature reviewed in this chapter that children's learning of a musical instrument is shaped by many factors. Most important among these are the expectations children hold for becoming competent on their instrument, the enjoyment they experience

Table 17.1 Summary of age-related learning principles in formal learning settings.

Age	Choice of instrument	Learning processes	Learning activities	Role of significant others
Up to age 5	Determined by child's ability to produce a characteristic tone without too much effort. Keyboard and smaller stringed instruments, recorder, plus tuned and untuned percussion are common choices.	The emphasis should be on making music 'fun' with opportunities for children to explore their own and other instruments. Children should be encouraged to sing and play a variety of musical games as a foundation for developing a sense of pitch and rhythm. Learning about some basic terms allows the child to express how they feel about music.	Learning by rote (copying and repetition) is the most important and natural way for very young children to learn. Aural awareness can be developed by learning pieces that are already known or first learnt by heart through repeated singing or hearings, before being reproduced on an instrument. The sound (not the symbol) should be emphasized with formal instruction about traditional notation being left until a later stage of development. The repertoire should be interesting and challenging, not difficult and frustrating. The emphasis should be on providing a rich, varied background of experiences that will lay the foundation for future musical success.	Teachers must develop a strong personal nurturing relationship such that the child regards them as warm, caring, and lots of fun to be with. Parents have a particularly special role during this time. Because children will not have developed their self-regulatory abilities, it is advisable for parents to attend lessons so that they will be able to reinforce what has been taught during the rest of the week. They should also try to be actively involved in their children's musical progress, by frequently sitting with them when they play the instrument and helping to make them feel 'special' about their learning. Parents are also responsible for exposing their children to a variety of music around the home, such as by putting on a recording of music when they go to bed, by playing music during the day, and by singing and playing musical games whenever possible.
From 6 to 9	More choices become available, but choosing a suitable instrument is still dependent on the child's physical capacity, with larger winds still being beyond their control. Suitable instruments include most of the woodwind, brass, string families, plus keyboard, guitar, percussion (tuned and untuned), and many other less common instruments. Wind instruments require a full set of teeth while children who commence on string instruments will still need to play a smaller sized instrument. Posture will need to be carefully monitored, so that any child who is struggling to maintain a correct hand, lip or seated position does not fall into bad habits. In some cases, it is advisable for a child to commence on a more manageable instrument before progressing to a more	The emphasis should still be on making music 'fun', while at the same time ensuring that there is a reasonable amount of progress over time. During these years a child's interest and motivation will ebb and flow, depending on a variety of extrinsic and intrinsic forces. This is a natural part of growing and learning. It is therefore important to have regular exposure to enriching activities that help motivate the child, such as performing in concerts or for other family members, attending music camps, or even busking to make some extra pocket money.	Musical notation should not be emphasized until the child can demonstrate basic ear-to-hand co-ordination skills. Children should be able to play a repertoire of works by ear. In the initial stages of introducing musical notation, children should be encouraged to invent their own notations to describe well-known songs. Later this can be extended to include traditional forms of notation but only when the child has become capable of co-ordinating their eyes with their ears and hands.	The importance of a teacher retaining a strong personal relationship with the child is still paramount. Personal characteristics such as being a good communicator, showing interest and being easy to talk to and relate to the child are important. Professional characteristics, such as being able to demonstrate effectively and provide an appropriate model for the child become increasingly important. Parents should continue to provide ongoing support for their child, through gentle but persistent reminders to practice, and take an active interest in their child's learning. Ongoing praise and encouragement are also essential.

| From 10 upwards | Almost any instrument is now possible with opportunities to learn instruments informally with peers increasing. The guitar, drums, and computer synthesizers are common instruments, particularly with teenagers in informal learning settings. | Some may be motivated to learn by ear rather than a desire to become musically literate. In formal settings, however, children are able to pick up music reading skills more quickly than in the past. Unlike previous ages, they will be less likely to want to learn by repetition. | Children at this age are becoming more self-regulated and better able to monitor and control their own learning. Both the personal and professional characteristics of their teacher are important to them. They need to know that the teacher cares and will support them during difficult patches in their learning, but increasingly need to be stimulated by the quality of their teacher's abilities as a musician, in order to become inspired to reach higher levels of achievement. |
| | | This is a period when children become more independent, and in which they will want to perform repertoire that they find stimulating and challenging rather than repertoire that their teacher feels is appropriate for their technical development. | Children of this age are increasingly influence by peer pressure, so it is important that the learning environment allows opportunities for group interaction and social experiences that enable them to be immersed in the style and 'culture' of the type of music being learned. This can occur in both formal setting such as a school band or orchestra, and informal settings such as garage bands and group jamming sessions. |

when playing their instrument, the types of self-regulatory strategies they acquire to enhance their learning, and the support and encouragement they receive for their learning from their family, teachers, and peers (Sloboda & Davidson, 1996; McPherson & Zimmerman, 2002).

Table 17.1 shows a number of age-related principles of learning an instrument that we feel confident to propose, based on our understanding of the literature, our longitudinal studies with young musicians and our own teaching experiences. Our thoughts should not be considered as definitive, as children can vary markedly in both their interests as well as their mental, emotional, and physical readiness to commence and continue learning.

Overall, the principles outlined in Table 17.1 are based on our view that initial experiences in music should involve opportunities for children to:

1.   experiment with several instruments before selecting one;

2.   test out the instrument in a number of contexts; and

3.   consider what might be right both physically and expressively for them.

Later, in order to cope with the many obstacles involved with learning, young learners should be:

1.   encouraged and supported in their learning but not forced to learn;

2.   provided with ample opportunities to explore the value of instruments and their social contexts;

3.   inspired to set reasonable goals for themselves, which provide a balance between their own skill level and the challenge required to master new repertoire and techniques; and

4.   exposed to a range of learning strategies so that success is guaranteed early on.

Learning a musical instrument can be one of the most enjoyable and rewarding hobbies or pastimes that a child can pursue. However, it can also be one of the most frustrating. Because of this, teachers and parents need to understand better the many forces that impact on how children develop a deep desire for playing an instrument and eventually come to view themselves as a musician. By surveying some of the literature related to these issues, we hope that this chapter has provided a basic framework for understanding some of the more important elements in this process.

References

Abeles, H. F. & Porter, S. Y. (1978). Sex stereotyping of musical instruments. *Journal of Research in Music Education*, 26, 65–75.

Alderman, M. K. (1999). *Motivation to learn.* Mahwah, NJ: Lawrence Erlbaum Associates.

Balli, S. J. (1998). When mom and dad help: Student reflections on parent involvement with homework. *Journal of Research and Development in Education*, 31(3), 142–146.

Bandura, A. (1997). *Self-efficacy: The exercise of control.* New York: Freeman.

Barry, N. & Hallam, S. (2002). Practice. In R. Parncutt & G. E. McPherson (eds), *The science and psychology of music performance: Creative strategies for teaching and learning* (pp. 151–165). New York: Oxford University Press.

Bjorklund, D. F. (2000). *Children's thinking: Developmental function and individual differences* (3rd edn). Belmont, CA: Wadsworth/Thomson Learning.

Boyle, J. D., DeCarbo, N. J., & Fortney, P. M. (1993). A study of middle school band students' instrument choices. *Journal of Research in Music Education*, **41**, 28–39.

Bruce, R. & Kemp, A. (1993). Sex-stereotyping in children's preferences for musical instruments. *British Journal of Music Education*, **10**, 213–217.

Chen, C. & Stevenson, H. W. (1989). Homework: A cross-cultural examination. *Child Development*, **60**, 551–561.

Conway, C. (2000). Gender and musical instrument choice: a phenomenological investigation. *Bulletin of the Council for Research in Music Education*, **146**, 1–17.

Cooke, M. & Morris, R. (1996). Making music in Great Britain. *Journal of the Market Research Society*, **28**(2), 123–134.

Davidson, L. & Scripp, L. (1992). Surveying the coordinates of cognitive skills in music. In R. Colwell (ed.), *Handbook of research on music teaching and learning* (pp. 392–431). New York: Schirmer Books.

Davidson, J. W., Moore, J. W., Sloboda, J. A., & Howe, M. J. A. (1998). Characteristics of music teachers and the progress of young instrumentalists. *Journal of Research in Music Education*, **46**, 141–160.

Delzell, J. K. & Leppla, D. A. (1992). Gender association of musical instruments and preferences of fourth-grade students for selected instruments. *Journal of Research in Music Education*, **40**(2), 93–103.

Dweck, C. S. (1986). Motivational processes affecting learning. *American Psychologist*, **41**, 1040–1048.

Dweck, C. S. (2000). *Self-theories: Their role in motivation, personality and development*. Philadelphia, PA: Psychology Press.

Eccles-Parsons, J. (1983). Children's motivation to study music. In *Motivation and creativity: National symposium on the applications of psychology to the teaching and learning of music* (pp. 31–40). Washington, DC: Music Educators National Conference.

Eccles, J. S., Wigfield, A., & Schiefele, U. (1998). Motivation to succeed. In W. Damon (series ed.) & N. Eisenberg (vol. ed.), *Handbook of child psychology:* Vol. 3. *Social, emotional and personality development* (5th edn), (pp. 1017–1095). New York: Wiley.

Ericsson, K. A. (1997). Deliberate practice and the acquisition of expert performance: An overview. In H. Jørgensen & A. C. Lehmann (eds), *Does practice make perfect? Current theory and research on instrumental music practice* (pp. 9–51). Oslo, Norway: Norges musikkhøgskole.

Grusec, J. E., Goodnow, J. J., & Kucznksi, L. (2000). New directions in analyses of parenting contributions to children's acquisition of values. *Child Development*, **71**, 205–211.

Gullberg, A.-K. & Brändström, S. (2004). Formal and non-formal music learning amongst rock musicians. In J. W. Davidson (ed.), *The music practitioner. Research for the music performer, teacher and listener* (pp. 161–174). Aldershot: Ashgate.

Hallam, S. (1997a). What do we know about practicing? Toward a model synthesising the research literature. In H. Jørgensen & A. C. Lehmann (eds), *Does practice make perfect? Current theory and research on instrumental music practice* (pp. 179–231). Oslo, Norway: Norges musikkhøgskole.

Hallam, S. (1997b). Approaches to instrumental music practice of experts and novices: Implications for education. In H. Jørgensen & A. C. Lehmann (eds), *Does practice make perfect? Current theory and research on instrumental music practice* (pp. 89–108). Oslo, Norway: Norges musikkhogskole.

Hallam, S. (1998). The predictors of achievement and dropout in instrumental tuition. *Psychology of Music*, **26**(2), 116–132.

Harris, K. R. & Pressley, M. (1991). The nature of cognitive strategy instruction: Interactive strategy construction. *Exceptional Children*, **57**, 392–404.

Harrison, A. C. & O'Neill, S. A. (2003). Preferences and children's use of gender-stereotyped knowledge about musical instruments: making judgements about other children's preferences. *Sex Roles*, 49(7–8), 389–400.

Hoover-Dempsey, K. V., Battiato, A. C., Walker, J. M. T., Reed, R. P, DeJong, J. M., & Jones, K. P. (2001). Parental involvement in homework. *Educational Psychologist*, 36(3), 195–209.

Jørgensen, H. (2004). Strategies for individual practice. In A. Williamon (ed.), *Musical excellence: Strategies and techniques to enhance performance* (pp. 85–103). Oxford: Oxford University Press.

Kohut, D. L. (1985). *Musical Performance: Learning Theory and Pedagogy*. Englewood Cliffs, NJ: Prentice-Hall.

MacKenzie, C. G. (1991). Starting to learn to play a musical instrument: a study of boys' and girls' motivational criteria. *British Journal of Music Education*, 8, 15–20.

McPherson, G. E. (1993). *Factors and abilities influencing the development of visual, aural and creative performance skills in music and their educational implications*. Doctor of Philosophy, University of Sydney, Australia. *Dissertation Abstracts International*, 54/04-A, 1277. (University Microfilms No. 9317278).

McPherson, G. E. (1994). Factors and abilities influencing sight-reading skill in music. *Journal of Research in Music Education*, 42(3), 217–231.

McPherson, G. E. (1995). The assessment of musical performance: Development and validation of five new measures. *Psychology of Music*, 23(2), 142–161.

McPherson, G. E. (1997). Cognitive strategies and skills acquisition in musical performance. *Bulletin of the Council for Research in Music Education*, 133, 64–71.

McPherson, G. E. (2001). Commitment and practice: Key ingredients for achievement during the early stages of learning a musical instrument. *Council for Research in Music Education*, 147, 122–127.

McPherson, G. E. (2005). From child to musician: Skill development during the beginning stages of learning an instrument. *Psychology of Music*, 33, 5–35.

McPherson, G. E. & Davidson, J. W. (2002). Musical practice: Mother and child interactions during the first year of learning an instrument. *Music Education Research*, 4, 143–158.

McPherson, G. E. & McCormick, J. (1999). Motivational and self-regulated learning components of musical practice. *Bulletin of the Council for Research in Music Education*, 141, 98–102.

McPherson, G. E. & McCormick, J. (2006). Self-efficacy and performing music. *Psychology of Music*, 34, 325–339.

McPherson, G. E. & Renwick, J. M. (2001). A longitudinal study of self-regulation in children's musical practice. *Music Education Research*, 3(2), 169–186.

McPherson, G. E. & Gabrielsson, A. (2002). From sound to sign. In R. Parncutt & G. E. McPherson (eds), *The science and psychology of musical performance: Creative strategies for music teaching and learning* (pp. 99–115). Oxford: Oxford University Press.

McPherson, G. E. & Zimmerman, B. J. (2002). Self-regulation of musical learning: A social cognitive perspective. In R. Colwell & C. Richardson (eds), *The New handbook of research on music teaching and learning* (pp. 327–347). New York: Oxford University Press.

Moely, B. E., Hart, S. S., Leal, L., Santulli, K. A., Rao, N., Johnson, T., & Hamilton, L. B. (1992). The teacher's role in facilitating memory and study strategy development in the elementary school classroom. *Child Development*, 63, 653–672.

O'Neill, S. A. (1997). The role of practice in children's early performance achievement. In H. Jørgensen & A. C. Lehmann (eds), *Does practice make perfect? Current theory and research on instrumental music practice* (pp. 53–70, 179–231). Oslo, Norway: Norges musikkhøgskole.

O'Neill, S. A. (2001). *Young people and music participation project: Practitioner report and summary of findings*. Unit for the Study of Musical Skill and Development, Keele University, UK—see http://www.keele.ac.uk/depts/ps/ESRC/Practitionerimp.doc [accessed July 28, 2005]

O'Neill, S. A. & Boulton, M. J. (1996). Boys' and girls' preferences for musical instruments: A function of gender? *Psychology of Music*, 24, 171–183.

O'Neill, S. & McPherson, G. E. (2002). Motivation. In R. Parncutt & G. E. McPherson (eds), *The science and psychology of musical performance: Creative strategies for music teaching and learning* (pp. 31–46). Oxford: Oxford University Press.

O'Neill, S. A. & Sloboda, J. A. (1997). The effects of failure on children's ability to perform a musical test. *Psychology of Music*, 25, 18–34.

Pintrich, P. R. & Schunk, D. H. (2002). *Motivation in education: Theory, research and applications* (2nd edn), Englewood Cliffs, NJ: Prentice–Hall.

Pomerantz, E. M., Wang, Q., & Ng, F. F. (2005). Mothers' affect in the homework context: The importance of staying positive. *Developmental Psychology*, 41(2), 414–427.

Renwick, J. & McPherson, G. E. (2002). Interest and choice: Student-selected repertoire and its effect on practising behaviour. *British Journal of Music Education*, 19(2), 173–188.

Rostvall, A. & West, R. (2003). Analysis of interaction and learning in instrumental teaching. *Music Education Research*, 5, 213–226.

Siegler, R. S. (1996). *Emerging minds: The process of change in children's thinking*. New York: Oxford University Press.

Sloboda, J. & Davidson, J. (1996). The young performing musician. In I. Deliege & J. Sloboda (eds), *Musical beginnings: Origins and development of musical competence* (pp. 171–190). New York: Oxford University Press.

Sloboda, J. A. & Howe, M. J. A. (1991). Biographical precursors of musical excellence: An interview study. *Psychology of Music*, 19, 3–21.

Sloboda, J. A., Davidson, J. W., & Howe, M. (1994). Is everyone musical? *The Psychologist*, 7, 349–354.

Sloboda, J. A., Davidson, J. W., Howe, M. J. A., & Moore, D. G. (1996). The role of practice in the development of performing musicians. *British Journal of Psychology*, 87, 287–309.

Sosniak, L. A. (1985). Learning to be a concert pianist. In B. S. Bloom (ed.), *Developing talent in young people* (pp. 19–67). New York: Ballantine.

Spera, C. (2005). A review of the relationship among parenting practices, parenting styles, and adolescent school achievement. *Educational Psychology Review*, 17(2), 125–146.

Stipek, D. (1998). *Motivation to learn* (3rd edn), Needham Heights, MA: Allyn & Bacon.

Warton, P. M. (1997). Learning about responsibility: Lessons from homework. *British Journal of Educational Psychology*, 67, 213–221.

Wigfield, A. & Eccles, J. (2000). Expectancy-value theory of motivation. *Contemporary Educational Psychology*, 25, 68–81.

Wigfield, A. & Eccles, J. (2001). The development of competence beliefs, expectancies for success, and achievement values from childhood through adolescence. In A. Wigfield & J. Eccles (eds), *Development of achievement motivation* (pp. 91–120). San Diego, CA: Academic Press.

Williamon, A. & Valentine, E. (1998). 'Practice makes perfect': The effects of piece and ability level on performance preparation. In Suk Won Yi (ed.), *Proceedings of the 5th International Conference on Music Perception and Cognition* (pp. 323–328). August 26–30, 1998, Seoul National University, Korea.

CHAPTER 18

THE INDIVIDUAL AND SOCIAL WORLDS OF CHILDREN'S MUSICAL CREATIVITY

PAMELA BURNARD

Introducing creativity as a cultural construct

There are many ways in which creativity in music may be understood and its meaning constructed. The concept does not possess the same meaning from one cultural context to another. It is not surprising that children manifest and liberate themselves in the use and function of creativity in music in ways that defy traditional psychological definitions (Amabile, 1996). Taking time to reflect on how children, from early childhood through to adolescence, constitute their own forms of musical creativity (and musical culture making) is as necessary as for adults to reflect on their constructions of what musical creativity is, where it happens, with whom, and how. The vignettes that follow bring focus to how a child's personal and social worlds interface within cultural contexts to shape creativity.

> Lia's first memory of music is of singing along with and playing around on a xylophone with lots of colourful keys. From age 4, she would sing and play her own made-up songs. Her mother's recollections are of her singing and humming, bobbing and bouncing in play immersion. There were numerous recollections of middle class family gatherings with profound stories about familial and peer support, and long term participation enmeshed in a musically valued and supported world. At Primary School, Lia sang in all the choirs, played in several instrumental groups, performed solos in concerts and was recognised as 'being gifted'. Now, at 16, singing and making up her own music is the principal driving force in her life. Her ambition is 'to become a songwriter . . . a musical trendsetter'. She does not consider herself to be a high-achieving performer but in explaining significant events and crystallising experiences in music, it is clear she has had many. At age 16, she uses her voice and writes songs in distinct ways. She explores, practises and proclaims the expressive virtues of various different cultures all of which are deeply rooted in the vernacular of her many favourite singers and groups. Her song writing, as she explains, is 'very personal . . . it's totally who I am and want to be'.

> Adrian's significant musical memories recalled at 16 involve his most recent involvement with like-minded peers as members of sub-cultures which offer him opportunities for and agency in techno, hiphop, rap and hard rock. Adrian is one of several underachieving disruptive learners at school who often seems to be at the centre of some issue with the teachers. He is not into school music. His home environment is equally unpredictable. It's

an irrelevance. He redefines himself with a high profile within his peer group. Like his friends, Adrian is heavily into music. He purchases, listens to and supports playing in several different social and cultural units out-of-school. His bedroom plugs into multiple media sources which emulate a recording studio. There is nothing ambivalent about his relationship to music. His musical savvy extends across several musical contexts including his understanding of youth rock and rap cultures in which he creates, re-creates and copies songs from multi-media sources. He exchanges MP3 files and newly-created ring tones among friends. He is saving for a new mixing desk. For Adrian, music is newly made and newly created in valuable, complex, social spaces where he is seen as a leader in an expanding musical frontier of culture-makers. Adrian is not simply a consumer, he is an impassioned producer, innovator and creator of new kinds of musics.

For Lia and Adrian, who share attendance at the same schools, their personal, social, and cultural biography is central to how their development in creativity proceeds. Development does not exist in the child. Their creative development occurs from membership within various social and cultural units such as the influence of parents and carers within the nuclear culture of the family, or at the interface of social contexts with friends and peers in and out-of-school communities and as members of multiple cultures. It is these social and cultural realities that largely determine the possibility or lack of possibilities for developing creativity (Feldman, 1999). Development in musical creativity occurs as children live and interact with the inevitable influences which these units have upon their musical ideas, values, and behaviours (Campbell, 2002). It is the child's individual and social worlds which interact to create the cultural dynamic of developmental change.

Let me give another example. As soon as a child is born, adults and other knowledgeable individuals begin to contribute to the child's socialization by arranging the environment and the musical stimulus encountered within it. The developing child is located within the orbit of the work of particular parents, carers, friends, peers, teachers, artists, and pedagogical, community and cultural practices. These serve to guide children's attention to and participation in the community (or communities) of which they are a part. Children may participate and become members of a number of musical communities to creatively use music as a soundtrack to their everyday lives. These variously situated practices integrate within and draw upon the child's individual and social interests. As shown in Figure 18.1, with socialization, schooling, and enculturation, the child's world continues to expand out into ever widening networks. Thus, the development of children's musical creativity occurs through their active participation in a network of cultural systems. They can be members of the 'superculture', such as 'children', several 'subcultures', such as familiar members or Caribbean or Asian children, boys or girls, and 'intercultures' such as players, collectors or listeners of particular types of music, classrooms, groups, or clubs in or out-of-school (Campbell, 2002). They may come from Muslim families who disapprove of girls and boys making music together in the same room or even making music in single-sex groups (Halstead, 1994). It is the established norms and practices in our society and culture that identify and distinguish between ways of understanding creativity, in terms of societal judgements and values.

Csikszentmihalyi's (1999) advancement of a *systems view of creativity* offers support for the above observations (see Figure 18.1). Here creativity is conceptualized as something

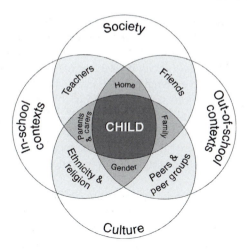

Figure 18.1 A network of cultural systems for understanding children's creativity.

that is not simply contained within the mind of person but as a cultural construct, which is given meaning by what others have to say about it. Creativity involves interaction among a *domain* discipline (for example, music, mathematics, chess playing), a *person* (individual creator), and a *field* (including specialists and appropriate observers who are familiar with the domain who make judgements about what constitutes quality in the domain).

What is important about this systems perspective of creativity is that creative endeavour and achievement in a domain ultimately arises from and becomes accepted in a particular cultural setting *as a product of societal judgements*. Thus it is the affordances and constraints constructed by and contained within specific learning communities that stimulate and fertilize creativity (Feldman, 1993, 1999). Importantly, if the individual creator is to make a significant contribution to a domain (or practice) his or her endeavours must be judged by members of the cultural community (or field).

Csikszentmihalyi's (1999) work has helped us to understand that definitions of creativity must take into account the fact that creativity is a cultural construct. It is a concept dependent upon the judgement of observers. It is a concept dependent on cultures to enhance and constrain what is possible, what is supported, what is accessible, what is valued, and what is not.

For Lia and Adrian, we know they are embedded in a complex web of social groups in contexts, which are dynamic and fluid, and are enmeshed in an ever-widening cultural network. They both reflect particular cultures within which they are raised. Their musical interests and involvements inside and outside the school are distinctive. At the same time, what is consistent is that they are musically knowledgeable, they make connections in search of meaning from within their musical lives, their individual creative endeavours are recognized and valued, and what they do musically is construed—in some ways—as expanding frontiers (that is, where the new and familiar coexist) as members of multiple musical cultures each with their own musical affiliations.

In contrast to research concerned with the development of *extreme talent* in individual creativity (Gardner, 1993; Feldman, 1999), my definition treats the ever-widening child's world of musical creativity as irrefutably a *cultural construct* related to how *individuals* construe themselves within a multiplicity of *cultural networks* (an idea conceptualized as 'cultural organism' in relation to extreme talent associated by Feldman in 1993). As I see it, a child's musical creativity develops not as something solitary (that is, in relation only to themselves) but rather in solidarity with others. According to this view, and as illustrated in the earlier observations (Burnard, 1999a,b, 2000a,b, 2004), it is the dialectic in which their *individual and social worlds* interact that provides the tacit messages, culturally embedded in and supported, as members of multiple cultures each with its own musical affiliations (Campbell, 2002).

So, how can creativity be understood in relation to children's musical development? What specific lines of development interact to create the dynamics of change in children's musical creativity?

How should we understand creativity in relation to music?

Webster (2002) characterizes the conceptual base for creativity in music as a set of *enabling conditions* (these include motivation, divergent-convergent thinking, environment, and personality) and *enabling skills* (these include musical aptitudes, conceptual understanding, craftsmanship, aesthetic sensitivity) all of which interact with the 'product intention' and the making of the 'creative product'. At the centre of his conceptual model of creative thinking, Webster places two types of thinking, which leads to many solutions: divergent (leading to many solutions) and convergent (leading to a single solution). From this starting point, Webster develops his model of creative thinking in music as a way of looking for differentiated factors that seem to shape creative thinking in music as a distinct process of thought. The larger the storehouse of enabling conditions and skills that children possess, the better equipped they will be for creative thinking in music.

Importantly, this line of argument recognizes how person-based individual differences occur in the development in creative thinking in music but doesn't articulate a position that includes roles for (and connects agents of) the cultural networks in creative development. In contrast, the systems view of creativity, as advanced by Csikszentmihalyi (1999), represents a fundamental shift from either defining creativity developmentally or as a fixed entity to one which is dependent upon people's judgements. This is important because music educators (and researchers) are often in the role of assessing and judging the creativity of children's musical endeavours. Judgements about the nature and achievement of musical creativity will depend upon the relationships that hold between the *domain* discipline (musical opportunities and constraints), the *person* (the child creator or children), and the *field* (usually teachers or researchers who make judgements about what constitutes quality in the domain). Similarly, judgements about what constitutes development in musical creativity will depend upon the relationships that hold between domain, person, and a field.

For Elliott (1995), in music education, the role of societal judgements is explained as 'tangible products or achievements that people deem valuable, useful, or exceptional in some regard' (p. 216), the function of which is a process of induction into particular musical practice. The assumption made by Elliott, among others, is that a creative achievement in music 'has its roots in specific communities of practitioners who share and advance a specific tradition of musical thinking' (p. 67). This emphasizes that there are children's discourses of creative music making, particularly when framed within the context of children's musical worlds, as occurs, for example, in analyses of the studies of children's musical play (Pond, 1981; Marsh, 1995, 1997; Addo, 1997; Sundin, 1998) and music making with computer-based digital tools (Folkestad, 1996; Nilsson & Folkestad, 2005), which provide us with evidence of children being able to position themselves as experts (as illustrated earlier with Lia and Adrian). The musical playground provides us with a powerful example of when children position themselves as creative decision-makers who make judgements from within the field and are the experts in that domain.

Importantly, this line of argument recognizes that what may be a creative endeavour and achievement in a child's musical world may not necessarily be viewed, judged, or defined as 'creative' within the adult musical world in which the child finds herself. What constitutes a creative achievement where the creative activity involves the musical practices of hiphopping or rapping, may prove highly problematic within the school setting, but not beyond it.

This raises an important issue about creative exclusion (and lack of opportunities for creative choice) where a systems view of creativity excludes creative endeavour, which is *not* created with an understanding of the field. How do we make sense of and actively contribute to educational programmes aimed at raising the overall creative endeavours and achievements of the least educationally advantaged populations of children in our formal educational systems? Forms of engagement in and judgements about musical creativity are inevitably based on and reflect the rules, traditions and practices as identified and practised within the dominant culture. Crucially, how do teachers work creatively with children of migrants and travellers in areas where there is risk of social exclusion? What about the creative endeavours that are not valued as creative by observers? This is of great concern among music educators. Often the solutions focus on the learners themselves with new innovative teaching and learning approaches, which are aimed at engaging pupils in developing capabilities of creative knowledge work rather than passively receiving information or engaging pupils in the decision-making regarding, and assessment of, their musical learning (Arnot *et al.*, 2004). From this perspective, should what constitutes musical creativity be understood in terms of its relation to both cultural and social aspects before we may enter into different contexts?

Indeed, if we argue that *musical creativity takes place as contextualized activity* and needs to be understood in different contexts, then we need to locate it both within the *individual world* of the child and where cultural dynamics interact within the *social worlds* of the child in which musical creativity grows. To illustrate, from infancy through to adolescence, children construct and enact any number of possibilities as vehicles for musical creativity. These can range from child's play explorations, to creative exchanges between adults and babies (Trevarthen, 1993), to how music happens and is played out in nurseries, playgrounds, schools, and garages (see Chapter 15), to young people as hip-hoppers and rappers who busily (re)construct repertoires from the interactive possibilities and (re) experiences of mixing and downloading internet files as representations and expressions of innovative musical style practices. Children engage creatively in music from within a wide range of communities of practice. These communities may include those within a school classroom, to a community band, to their 'peer worlds' of leisure time, to forms of creative activity, which happen in the home between the child and parents, to playgrounds and recreational settings, to any number of other musical communities in which the child interacts. For children (as with adults), whether in relation to performance, improvisation, perception, listening, arranging, or compositional practices, the kind of creative music making that we come to hold in high regard is contextual and situational (Sawyer, 1997).

Therefore, if we agree that musical creativity takes place as an interweaving of individual and social factors within specific cultural conventions then are there identifiable milestones in the development of the creative child across cultural contexts?

Problems with labelling developmental milestones: What changes?

A good deal of research has described *how* an *individual* child might show general creative developmental differences. Various descriptive models of age-related developments across the different art forms have been offered. All of these models focus on creativity as the product of single individuals and focus on development as a process within the individual.

As shown in Table 18.1, the milestones have been identified across artistic developments (Gardner, 1982), aesthetic developments (Ross, 1984), musical development (Swanwick & Tillman, 1986), and listening and generative skills in different art forms (Hargreaves & Galton, 1992).

As shown in the first column, Gardner (1982) identifies a structural progression in which children realize the universal properties of symbolization from the presymbolic period (first year of life) and the period of symbol use (between ages 2 and 7) followed by further skill developments (from the age of 8 onwards). Gardner's account of artistic development stresses the differences among children, for 'whereas all children come to explore the variety of symbolic forms made possible by a range of media, they do so in ways that are peculiarly their own' (Gardner, 1982, p. 122).

Ross (1984) suggests an outline for the process of development in the arts, in a sequence that relates stages to chronological ages. He identifies four periods of development in music, which parallel similar development in art and drama. These four 'levels of operation' refer to sets of behavioural characteristics showing how the significance of an individual's relationship with an artistic medium develops and interacts with the social and cultural.

A stage-based and age-dependent sequence of musical development is described by Swanwick and Tillman (1986). The source of data is music compositional products by school-aged children of various ages. Interestingly, these researchers identify the musical aspects of materials, expression and form to elements of developmental change. At specifiable points in development, musical schemes become organized in fundamentally new ways which profoundly alter the way in which the child understands music. More domain-specific studies in music, in addition to the UK's Swanwick and Tillman (1986), are those of Kratus (1989) in the United States and Barrett (1996) in Australia, each of who attempt to trace the different stages through which musical developmental sequences occurs by comparing compositional products of school-aged children of various ages. There is, however,

Table 18.1 Developmental milestones in children's creativity.

Gardner (1982)	Ross (1984)	Swanwick & Tillman (1986)	Hargreaves & Galton (1992)
0–1 sensorimotor presymbolic	0–2 sensuous engagement with sound materials	0–4 Materials (Mastery) Sensory and manipulative modes	0–2 sensorimotor phase characterized by physical actions and sensory involvement
2–7 symbol use; attributes of creative person; 'codes' of the culture learned	3–7 musical doodling, conventional assimilation	4–9 Expression (Imitation) Personal and vernacular modes; emphasis on expressive character. Less exploratory	2–5 Figural phase in which global or outline representations feature
Age 8 significant increase in skill development and symbol use	8–13 concern with conventions of musical production	10–15 Form (Imaginative play) Speculative and Idiomatic modes; sudden changes/surprises	5–8 Schematic phase dominated by cultural rules and standards
	14+ personal style; personal taste, embodied meaning	15+ Value (Metacognition) Symbolic and Systematic modes; wider range of styles; personal style	8–15 Rule systems phase shows the increasing mastery of the cultural codes
			16+ Professional phase mature understanding of artistic conventions; divergence and originality valued

little or no agreement regarding the ascending relationship between age and phases, and theoretical underpinnings vary considerably.

A similar developmental model, based on listening and generative skills (Hargreaves & Galton, 1992) shows five different stages of understanding: prefigural or sensorimotor, figural, schematic, rule systems, and metacognitive/professional. Importantly, this model describes rather than explains the progression.

All of these models are based to some extent on Piaget's learning theory. All are closely tied to ages and all consider that the symbolic aspect of music depends on maturation and a well developed stage of formal operational thought. In this view, creative development is normative, stage-based and age-dependent. Interestingly, none of these models relate to the development of extreme talent in individual prodigies (Feldman, 1993).

The criteria for labelling age-related changes, as sets of sequential shifts, are similar in their attempt to describe rather than explain differences between, and increases in, expertise from simple to mastery development in the domain. While there appears to be general (but disputed) agreement in terms of creativity as a universal (rather than unique) set of schematized levels across arts domains, conceptions of *how development proceeds* is not clear (Feldman, 1993, 1999).

However, what these models effectively highlight is the importance of:

1. the developmental interdependence of sensorimotor roots and action schemes;

2. the role of symbolic play in early childhood;

3. the individual cognitive and socio-culturally shared influences in the acquisition and development of creativity; and

4. children's awareness and increasing mastery of the codes of the culture as symbolic and schematic representations of their worlds.

Another important feature of Table 18.1 is that creative development is characterized first and foremost by the fact that it transpires in cultural contexts under certain conditions of dynamic change. Largely unexplored in the existing literature is whether this change arises as person-based individual differences or, as argued here, is *situated* within a *network of cultural systems*. It was Feldman (1993), in studies of extreme cases of talent development (particularly prodigies), who coined the phrase 'cultural organisms'. Similarly, Feldman argues that cultural organisms are 'specialised social structures', which act as 'humanly constructed systems for detecting, developing, protecting, promoting and rejoicing in potential within certain selected domains' (p. 246) whose purpose is 'nurture and direct the expression of extreme talent' (p. 232). Significantly, from within the network of cultural systems in which children mature, how these contexts or specific environments affect development remains little understood.

(Re-)Interpreting the literature: (Re-)Defining children's musical creativity

The literature is peppered with culturally based definitions and approaches to the study of creativity in general and musical creativity in particular, with different methodologies, developmental descriptions and research instruments. The field of developmental psychology provides us with some of the earliest literature reviews (Richardson, 1983; Hargreaves, 1986; Hargreaves & Zimmerman, 1992). One of the first reviews on the literature on musical creativity was carried out by Webster (1992) who made comparisons between the research approaches of theoretical, practical and empirical work with particular emphasis on the content analysis of creative production.

While the dominant model for research on musical creativity, and one that has interested researchers, emphasizes children's creative production, only a few studies provide descriptions of sequences of development or seek to establish *what* develops or *how* the development takes place (Swanwick & Tillman, 1986; Kratus, 1989; Davies, 1992, 1994; Barrett, 1996; Glover, 2000). Despite the conflict and disagreement about the existence or relevance of age-related changes, taken together, existing evidence suggests that what is developmentally in place by age 7 or 8, whether through ability, skill acquisition, or enculturation, will depend upon the musical opportunities, values, and choices most in currency around them (Gardner, 1973; Webster, 1992).

My own interpretation of the literature suggests that children's musical creativity does not develop in discrete phases nor is it age-dependent but rather is reliant upon contextual and environmental contextual influences. Children gain a sense of their own creative potential, strengths and developing creative self, as it were, as music makers, culture makers, and prosumers. This is argued by Leong (2003) as 'a new breed of consumers who produce what they consume [and] who proactively draw together available information, technologies and services' (p. 153). The extent to which it is possible, however, to outline developmental milestones in creativity, which applies different criteria for labelling something as a developmental change in artistic, aesthetic, and musical modalities, remains in question. Indeed, the extent to which we can generalize about the relationship between the successive levels, and rigid age timetable, and the separation of stages and sequence of general regulatory mechanisms, as explained here, remains limited. What we can say though, is that central to the importance of cultural contexts for development is that cultural effects on creativity are both enhancing and constraining. By constraints, I mean what is possible, accessible, valued, supported and what is not.

The difference in views about *what* constitutes musical creativity and *how* this knowledge is constructed, enhanced, or constrained depends upon the particular assumptions, beliefs, and understandings held about musical creativity. Researchers who have studied children as spontaneous song-makers or tune-makers (Davies, 1986, 1992; Campbell, 2002; Young, 2003) and as meaning makers (Barrett, 2001; Burnard, 2002a,b) offer surprising accounts of young children's musical creativity involving immersion in experience and tools of exploration that go with play contexts and in other out-of-classroom environments. Much of children's creative activity in play contexts focuses on the social dimension, involving interactions between individuals in pairings and groups, the principal media through which funds of knowledge and creative practices are distributed and appropriated among each other. Children's musical creativity, as with adult extreme forms of creativity, is therefore embedded within the whole spectrum of the complex worlds in which they grow (Feldman, 1993).

Thus one of the few points of widespread agreement among researchers and teachers is that across cultural domains, musical creativity underscores all forms of musical engagement. Not only is musical creativity embodied in contextual activity of (and other-than) composing, improvising and arranging but is implicated in constructing the broader realities in which the acts of performing and listening occur. The main point here is that *what* constitutes musical creativity is as much cultural constructions as *how* creativity develops throughout childhood.

Cultural contexts that shape how a child's musical creativity develops

While there appears to be no suggestion absolutely that there are universal schematized levels, themselves developmentally achieved, particular changes in children's creative engagement with music are discernible within and across cultural contexts.

Contextual influences during early childhood

As with the earliest vocal and gestural musical responses, as displayed in a baby's selective orientation to musical sound, we see from infancy, an innate psychological foundation for both creative behaviour and creativity. These innate and culturally significant creative

behaviours begin, according to Trevarthen (1993) as 'a music-like composition, an improvised song or dance of companionship with someone we trust, whom we admire, and who
admires us' (p. 35) in the production of songs and action games as an infant–parents 'playful
sharing'.

In early childhood, children's musical creativity is characterized within a wide variety
of contexts, which may involve spontaneous song-making, singing, dancing, and playing together, and improvising with instruments (Campbell, 2002; Woodward, 2005). It is
through the process of enculturation that young children learn the musical culture of their
environment (Small, 1977). Studies of musical play have also shown that the emergence of
young children's spontaneous music making is embedded within solitary and social play
settings and demonstrate how musical creation from early infancy onwards is not fortuitous but rather sophisticated and constantly evolving (Littleton, 1998; Custodero, 2002).
A pre-schooler (4 or 5 years old), for example, might sustain long periods of purposeful
inventiveness and exploration in sound making, involving spontaneous vocal and instrumental and movement play, with structures arising from a very rich variety of patterning,
sequences, repetition, and transformations of patterns (see Chapter 15).

At the same time, how children shape their own development is evidenced particularly
at infancy with much evidence to support the saliency of the social dimension of creativity,
shaped largely by those people who surround them, like their parents, carers, family, and
friends. What comes across most strongly from studies of young children is the sense of
primacy of relationships and interactions between child and adult, social contexts, which
are shaped largely by family circumstances (Young, 2003). As an example, for most preschoolers, music is created in 'music specific' (domain-specific) and 'non-music' (domain-
general) play settings in which musical play behaviours, such as voice play and instrumental
'sounding' and 'sound making' (in which objects or instruments are used musically) arise
equally from long episodes of solitary play and socially within group play, often started by
the child and taken up by the parent, carer, or by other children. More often, as Addo (1997)
suggests with specific reference to West African singing games, young children's creative
undertakings are as much connected to the socio-cultural context as learning environment
in which the child is immersed.

In a seminal study of children's spontaneous musical creativity, set in a nursery school,
Moorhead and Pond (1941/1978) observed creativity as a process characterized by originality, adaptiveness, and realization in a child's private and social worlds of sound. The
following observations by Moorhead and Pond (1941/1978) testify to how far this claim
can be justified.

> One variety of instrumental music was flexible and asymmetrically measured rhythmically;
> it endeavoured to explore wide intervals in pitch and contrasting tone colours. Another was
> rigidly and symmetrically 'rhythmical'; it seemed indifferent almost to melody or to colour
> variation; it was insistent and savage. One was most frequently quiet and produced in
> solitude, the other raucous, and associated very often with physical activity and belonging to
> the group. So also with vocal music. One variety was unfettered and free rhythmically like
> plainsong; the voice wandered over a large compass, the singer sang to himself alone, quietly,
> of everyday things, as though the melody not the words were more important. Another
> variety was rhythmic, like a ritual chant; the voice clung to one note around which it wove a

melodic pattern limited in scope and insistent in form; it was sung most often in the group, usually loudly, repeated over and over again, rising often to a high emotional pitch. (p. 8)

Clearly, very young children enter into the creative musician's experience of making music, exploring sounds, acquiring expressive vocabulary, and developing manipulative skills in response to specific cultural environments.

So, children begin to make sense of and construct with their culture's musical sounds in early childhood. Creative musical experiences occur in a variety of forms, variously defined as creativity, with a variety of fields of judges.

Contextual influences at middle to late childhood

Between 5 and 7 years of age, children's circle of creativity widens further with more and more contact in social contexts including teacher-led and peer-led experiences. In the context of playgrounds, Marsh (1995, 1997) provides us with another valuable perspective from which children's musical creative development may be viewed with the illustration of children's improvisations and variations on playground chants. In a study of children's complex playground music making, Marsh (1995, 1997) identifies how children draw socially and culturally on many musical worlds as they give voice to their own ways of transmitting cultures and operating creatively in music. They effortlessly discover, explore and negotiate polyrhythms and syncopations in highly sophisticated social music-making, driven by and creativity influenced by their cultural musical biography.

With preadolescents, creative music making in musical partnerships and small groups feature more prominently. Children aged 8–12 musically and creatively come into contact and comparison with peers of similar ages and abilities, whereupon they come to recognize and develop more situated perspectives that focus on interactive systems (that is, collaborative musical creativity) that include individuals as participants, interacting with each other as well as materials and representational systems (Burnard, 2002a,b). All of this implies that older children draw upon an increasingly sophisticated range of sources and resources, including the dual informal practices of peer learning and peer critique as they manipulate and create ideas (Savage, 2003; Jaffurs, 2004).

Peer relations and its influence on musical creativity can be identified in the following extract of children's talk about interactive rules for beginning a group improvisation. This discussion illustrates creative options that are socially constructed (Burnard, 2002a).

> *Kaytia*: I think we should start this performance with a count in and then we do our own thing
> *Dion*: Mmmm ... or what about if I give us a signal on a drum?
> *Lia*: We could come in one after another around the room
> *Ashton*: I think we should only play when we want to and end where we like.
> *Kaytia*: We don't need someone to tell us when to play
> *Chloe*: We can just join in as we go
> *Lia*: Yeah. Let's just get in when we are ready to play something.
> *Kaytia*: How about if one person starts then we all come in? Then one person could stop and then all of us would stop, one after another, until there is silence again.

> *Lia*: Yeah ... or the person who starts can then be the first to stop and then the first person starts, plays and stops and then another person plays and stops, plays and stops, until we have all had a go.
>
> *Wasim*: I think it might be easier if we organise ourselves into smaller groups and someone starts like we did before. Then we can hear what we are all doing and maybe change around more while we're playing all together.
>
> *Diane*: The thing is you can't go into your own world when you're playing together. We have to meet in the music.
>
> *Ashton*: Yeah. You have to be there together so there are no serious collisions.

At the same time, however, children experience an *awareness of audience* that can function similarly to a particular *field of judges* as foregrounded in the following vignettes (Burnard, 1999b). At the same lunchtime club for music creators, Ashton, Adrian, and Dion perform successive performances of a pop song 'I believe I can fly'. Each version is reworked giving more prominence to the new combinations of voices.

> The first presentation is introduced by Adrian who says 'We know the song and we've put it together in a new way. We've changed some bits'. In the next session, the song is rearranged to incorporate congas. In addition, Dion provides a dance routine based on a video clip of the original pop singer. The next version of the piece involves a presentation of a new arrangement of the same piece but this time its introduced as 'a piece without actions'.
>
> Burnard (1999a, p. 178)

Each one of these versions shows some deliberate manipulation and arrangement of musical elements of a known song that they all identify and can sing confidently. The performances make a favourable impression on the audience. This is evident by the frequent occurrences of each version. That arrangement and interpretation appear to be indistinguishable and yet relate to composition is evident by these three deliberately reworked and reassembled versions of a shared song. Each minded act seems to convey a new and deliberate re-presentation of a song that became the object of shared value by the members of this community.

Here, what is judged as prized by each other presupposes a shared way of thinking and acting as building blocks for that particular cultural context. Similarly, musical creativity occurs in a variety of forms, variously defined, with a variety of fields of judges.

A good deal of the research suggests that developmental differences in children's musical creativity have their origins, more often linked to and differentiated by the kinds of musical background and contexts in which music making and creating takes place (Stauffer, 2002; Younker, 2003). For example, the opportunity to learn to play an instrument can result in children composing for their own instruments. The child's instrumental proficiency and fluency may well determine their composing pathways using compositional thought processes that are rooted in the performance technique of the particular instrument at hand (Burnard & Younker, 2002, 2004). Children with prior experience of formal instrumental music tuition and who are advanced on their instruments when offered open opportunities to compose their own music, may approach composing as composers from the outset (Glover, 2000).

In Western countries, for children without formal musical training or who are just beginning to acquire some technical playing skills, the media world at home and school (that is, the arrival of networked ICT, computers, and digital arts technologies) opens new possibilities to mediate the creative process and create new meaning in their creative music making (Seddon & O'Neill, 2001, 2003; Wiggins, 2002; Nilsson & Folkestad, 2005). The research is extensive in its use of MIDI data, generated automatically by the computer and saved as a progressive series of files, as research data.

Key studies of children aged 8–12 (late childhood) similarly track progression toward the technical mastery of musical composition. Each apply fundamentally different developmental frameworks, with particular foci on the development of different skills. Similarly, each apply variously defined criteria for labelling something as a developmental change (Swanwick & Tillman, 1986; Kratus, 1989; Barrett, 1996; Glover, 2000). A common finding, however, is how children become increasingly enculturated into various musical discourses as they absorb the musical vocabulary that they experience in and out of school. The process of musical creativity becomes increasingly social as they come to know how to participate in the discourse and practices of their particular musical and learning community or communities. At this age, musically creative opportunities can range from individual to collaborative projects involving paired, small group or whole class settings, composing individually at home, with friends, in school, as homework, linked to cross-curriculum topics, based on self-devised, commissioned, or teacher-prescribed tasks, on keyboards, at a computer station using various computer software programs, using pitched percussion instruments or with a whole range of different instruments. In a study of sixth grade composers, Stauffer (2002) emphasizes the relationship between children's own musical and life experiences and composing development for this age group. Similarly, Swanwick and Tillman (1986) found that about the age of 10 or 11 children move into a 'speculative' stage whereupon they begin to introduce features that deviate from the more accepted conventions and norms.

What emerges is an awareness of personal and public expressiveness where both the individual and social worlds of preadolescent children emerge concurrently with the development of their wider awareness of their own musical creativity displaying considerable differences in the ways they experience, explain, and immerse themselves in creative activity (Hickey, 2003).

Contextual influences at adolescence

At adolescence, the development of musical creativity occurs in the context of differences in opportunities and participation in music (Cope & Smith, 1997). What also characterizes this phase is that complex social interactions take place within creative participation, which results in even greater prominence given to identity development (Fautley, 2004).

Research findings continually indicate that young people lay claim to different identities associated with musical creativity, marking out relationships and establishing and maintaining social standing from within the peer group (MacDonald & Meill, 2000a,b). While some young people prefer to work alone to author creative products (drawing upon the image of the individual inscribed as a 'lone artist'), others prefer to engage collaboratively whereupon their identity is more bound up with being a group member responsible for joint creative work (Meill & Littleton, 2004). The differences are made visible as creative activity is considered the locus of culturally significant acts, events, and meanings as observed in the ways young people engage differently in and acquire situated and contextual understandings of musical creativity (Lamont *et al.*, 2003).

What then does musical creativity look like at adolescence? Several studies have also documented the impact these new technologies have had on young people's engagement with and achievements in musical creativity (Folkestad, 1998; Savage & Challis, 2001; Jennings, 2003; Dillon, 2004). For example, Seddon (2004, in press) reports ICT has been effective in supporting creative learning in schools. It was found that music *e*-learning environments grant new opportunities for and direct access to ideas enabling collaborative composition between young people within and between schools across a global community. This allows and motivates young people to produce creative and professional products, especially those who would not otherwise be engaged. The common impression of music technologies as one of individual work at a computer has equally been debunked through the interactive musical systems developed by Dillon and Brown (forthcoming) where networked computers are used as a vehicle for real-time improvisation using digital instruments connected via electronic networks drawn from a selection of school and community-based learning spaces. Typically, in these projects, a key feature of the creative work is the *immediacy* given to the trial and error, without the fear of losing or spoiling work; the *interaction* between 'the maker' and 'the made' in which musical ideas develop through feedback and reflection; and the nature of the *collaboration* between the pairs or groups of students in designing, creating, and discussing the ways in which they could use the features of the software package to develop and present their ideas and the quality of their creative ideas.

Young people's 'informal' cultural competencies (as consumers and users of digital multimedia technology in the context of leisure) and the ever-widening range of music technologies increasingly enable them to draw on their own musical experience and access any number of highly desirable sound worlds that support their composing skills (Fung, 1997). Other features of adolescent musical creativity include the facilitative effects of friendship (MacDonald *et al.*, 2002) where socializing and learning are as closely connected as young people cultivate and co-ordinate their actions with those of others (Seddon & O'Neill, 2001, 2003; Hoyles & Noss, 2004).

A great many research questions remain to be explored, but new information and communications technology, particularly in the context of the internet, electronic mail, and multi-user domains hold the promise of giving access to new and multiple ways in which children are creative in music.

What provokes developmental change in musical creativity?

There appears to be no suggestion absolutely that there are universal schematized levels, themselves developmentally achieved, or associated with musical creativity particular to childhood, adolescence, and, eventually, adulthood. Children mature from one age to another with particular changes discernible across distinguishable contexts. This may well be a function of social beliefs and long-term participation in particular musical practices—as with everyday experience of music—all of which are known to affect the ways in which young people engage creatively in music. The extent to which individual skill and tool development underlies creative achievement also depends upon how societal judgements are communicated both explicitly and implicitly.

What is clear is that within the developing child's musical worlds, the contextual influences of their individual and social worlds change. Individual differences in beliefs about effort and ability may well influence the process of creativity, however, we know that creative practices become increasingly social, with the circle of learning ever widening as they come to know and participate in the practices of particular cultures. As contextual influences widen, so does the interdependence of individual and social dimensions. Differences in socio-cultural and politico-economic contexts thus profoundly influence the development of musical creativity and, indeed, the ways in which it is viewed. In other words, children learn and experience musical creativity differently in social practices through familial expectations, siblings, peers, teachers, and the media. At adolescence these normative frameworks and assumptions act as a constraining influence on young people's participation in various forms of and contexts for creative engagement. I would argue that it is the interrelatedness of a multitude of personal and social factors which mediate expectations and beliefs about what is possible or appropriate. For young people, their biographies are intimately linked to cultural actions that determine what is meant by and valued about musical creativity.

Widening the lens on the social bases of musical creativity

Pathways to the development of musical creativity are many and varied. Development may be facilitated by means of engagement with traditional and/or innovative cultural practices, or through manipulation of the building blocks of music as a socially mediated and culturally specific process (Espeland, 2003) enhanced through the use of technology. It may occur through experience with improvisation, seen as both an expressive and exploratory tool. In any case, children start out their lives within the context of their family, and then widen the lens to encompass multiple cultures and spheres of influence. So ever-widening are children's musical cultures that the commonly accepted concept of children's musical creativity is too small and exclusive to contain it. As with their musical knowledge, children's culture spins out in ever-widening concentric circles from family to peer, to school and beyond representing the individual and social worlds of a superculture of children's musical creativity (as shown in Figure 18.2). While songs are first sung on their mother's knee, the community widens to the playground, the nursery, and then school. With each change comes a shift to the next age-based musical creative cultures in which new contextual realms and inherent musical practices arise from within cultures made from children's memberships in particular subsets of society and socio-cultural groups.

If, as argued earlier (see Figures 18.1 and 18.2) widening the lens on the social bases and cultural action of musical creativity holds more keys for understanding how the child's

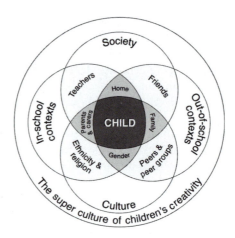

Figure 18.2 The super-culture of children's musical creativity.

musical creativity is culturally mediated, then the crucial question remains as to what might constitute a framework for examining these networks of cultural systems?

If it is accepted that what shapes and influences the development of children's musical creativity concerns the reciprocity of individual and social dimensions, then what might shed light on intersections of the 'superculture' (as in big cultures such as children's culture), 'subcultures' (as with ethnicity, age, and gender), 'microcultures' (of the classroom, the community choir or the garage band), and 'intercultures' (that constitute, for example, listeners of mass-mediated popular music), is to specify the vantage points of 'how', 'what', 'who', and 'why' specific environments work.

The significance of these vantage points for our understanding of the individual and social dimensions of children's musical creativity as a superculture is momentous in that they suggest musical creativity is as much about individual endeavour as being embedded in, constituted by, and inseparable from socially situated practices and judgements (from the domain and field). The fundamental principle underlying all of this is that music and creativity are not seen as separable parts, but as inseparable facets of a unified whole, in which no music can take place without individual and social dimensions of creativity and vice versa. The point of this is that musical creativity emerges from, is present to, and *situated* in, the multiple contexts that constitute the individual and social worlds that constitute musical creativity.

The framework, as shown in Figure 18.3, attempts to capture ways of thinking about the dimensions of musical creativity as individually and socially situated. At the same time it recognizes that there are multiple perspectives and multiple vantage points from which to view and share conceptions of musical creativity.

The significance of viewing the child's developing musical creativity, as inherently a cultural construct mediated in and across a range of settings, is that it provides a framework for a theory of musical creativity that recognizes how we come to acquire culturally constructed psychological concepts, such as creativity. The idea is predicated on cultural action which

Figure 18.3 Vantage points on individual-social dimensions of children's musical creativity.

is situated in particular cultural, historical, and institutional settings (that is, in places of formal schooling and outside the classroom as in playgrounds, garages, and community or concert halls). In other words, if there are as many cultural sites and types of creativity as there are ways of doing and making music then there are as many different views of musical creativity as there are things about which creative decisions can be made. Therefore, we need to create new understandings for re-shaping and redefining musical creativity in ways that both children and adults can construct, reconstruct, and share as they each strive to fulfil their creative potential within the social context in which they musically live.

Thus, I propose we shift our focus away from an age- or phase-related perspective on the development of musical creativity to concentrating on the practice (or 'how', 'what', 'where', and with 'whom') of musical creativity as situated cultural activity arises. From this, all ranges of cultural practices, and qualities of interactions, and relations between individuals in their social settings, can be understood. The focus here is therefore to understand the ways in which children's musical creativity can be conceptualized, gained, shared, and evaluated, all issues of which are massively influenced by cultural and contextual factors.

From here we can begin to contemporize the issues and ask questions about how children in the twenty-first century understand creativity, what constitutes and changes children's beliefs about what it takes to be and succeed creatively in music. This means observing and talking with children (and their teachers) to understand how creative practices are differently constructed and situated in cultural, historical, and institutional settings. These are questions we need also to continually ask ourselves.

Conclusions

What this chapter has argued is a socially and culturally mediated view of musical creativity. What it has tried to show is that the locus of development, for many children in the twenty-first century gives prominence to the influence of peers and other social–cultural influences in children's lives. Similarly, hearing something differently, feeling differently about something, or having new ideas, thoughts, and feelings, can be considered as constituting the development of musical creativity, whereby children construct (and reconstruct) meaning through a variety of musical experiences situated in social contexts. That is to say, it is the interrelatedness of development and learning within various contexts that shapes children's musical creativity. Thus, in the various areas in which children's musical creativity develops there is a need to be alert to the significance of culture and context and advances in our knowledge of what and how children learn musically, think musically, and think together.

By conceptualizing children both as *individual* actors and as *social* beings we may come to focus on musical creativity as cultural action, which is present and ongoing in the daily interactions of any community as something socially constructed and socially mediated. By broadening the discourse on the role and scope of musical creativity—by looking closely at what children already know, socially construct, and can represent experientially—we may learn even more about how musical creativity develops.

Acknowledgements

I wish to thank this chapter's reviewers for their inspirational feedback and Professor David Henry Feldman of Tufts University, USA for sharing his notion of 'cultural organisms' in discussion of extreme talent in creativity during the revision of this paper.

References

Addo, A. O. (1997). Children's idiomatic expressions of cultural knowledge. *International Journal of Music Education*, 30, 15–25.

Amabile, T. M. (1996). *Creativity in context: Update to the social psychology of creativity.* Boulder, CO:Westview.

Arnot, M., McIntyre, D., Pedder, D., & Reay, D. (2004). *Consultation in the classroom: Developing dialogue about teaching and learning.* Cambridge: Pearson Publishing.

Barrett, M. (1996). Children's aesthetic decision-making: an analysis of children's musical discourse as composer. *International Journal of Music Education*, 28, 37–62.

Barrett, M. (2001). Constructing a view of children's meaning-making as notators: A case-study of a five-year-old's descriptions and explanations of invented notations. *Research Studies in Music Education*, 16, 33–45.

Burnard, P. (1999a). *Into different worlds: Children's experience of musical improvisation and composition.* Unpublished PhD thesis, University of Reading, England.

Burnard, P. (1999b). Bodily intention in children's improvisation and composition. *Psychology of Music*, 27(2), 159–174.

Burnard, P. (2000a). Examining experiential differences between improvisation and composition in children's music making. *British Journal of Music Education,* 17(3), 227–245.

Burnard, P. (2000b). How children ascribe meaning to improvisation and composition: rethinking pedagogy in music education. *Music Education Research,* 2, 17–23.

Burnard, P. (2002a). Investigating the emergence of musical interaction in group improvisation. *British Journal of Music Education,* 19(2), 157–172.

Burnard, P. (2002b). Into different worlds: what improvising and composing can mean to children. *Music and Movement Education Quarterly,* 34(4), 22–28.

Burnard, P. (2004) 'A damaged dream?' adolescent realities and changing perspectives on school music. In P. Shand (ed.), *Music education entering the 21st century* (pp. 25–34). The University of Western Australia: Uniprint..

Burnard, P. & Younker, B. A. (2002). Mapping pathways: Fostering creativity in composition. *Music Education Research,* 4(2), 245–261.

Burnard, P. & Younker, B. A. (2004). Problem-solving and creativity: insights from student's individual composing pathways. *International Journal of Music Education,* 22, 59–76.

Campbell, P. S. (2002). The musical cultures of children. In L. Bresler & C. Thompson (eds), *The arts in children's lives: Context, culture and curriculum* (pp. 57–69). Netherlands: Kluwer.

Cope, P. & Smith, H. (1997). Cultural context in musical instrumental learning. *British Journal of Music Education,* 14, 283–290.

Csikszentmihalyi, M. (1999). Implications of a systems perspective for the study of creativity, In R. Sternberg, R. (ed.), *Handbook of creativity* (pp. 313–338). Cambridge: Cambridge University Press.

Custodero, L. A. (2002). Seeking challenge, finding skill: Flow experience in music education. *Arts Education and Policy Review,* 103(3), 3–9.

Davies, C. (1986). Say it till a song comes: reflections on songs invented by children 3–13. *British Journal of Music Education,* 3(3), 279–94.

Davies, C. (1992). Listen to my song: A study of songs invented by children aged 5–7 years. *British Journal of Music Education,* 9, 19–48.

Davies, C. (1994). The listening teacher: an approach to the collection and study of invented songs of children aged 5–7. In H. Lees (ed.), *Musical connections: Tradition and change* (pp. 120–128). Proceedings of the 21st World Conference of the International Society of Music Education, Tampa, Florida. New Zealand: Uniprint, University of Auckland. Auckland.

Dillon, S. & Brown, A. (forthcoming). Networked improvisation: learning through online collaborative music making. In J. Finney & P. Burnard (eds), *ICT and music in the secondary school.* Milton Keynes: Open University Press.

Dillon, T. (2004). It's in the mix baby: exploring how meaning is created within music technology collaborations. In D. Miell & K. Littleton (eds.), *Collaborative creativity, contemporary perspectives* (pp. 144–157). London: Free Association Books.

Elliott, D. (1995). *Music matters: A new philosophy of music education.* Oxford: Oxford University Press.

Espeland, M. (2003). The African drum: The compositional process as discourse and interaction in a school context. In M. Hickey (ed.), *Why and how to teach music composition* (pp. 167–192). MENC: The National Association for Music Education.

Fautley, M. (2004). Teacher intervention strategies in composing processes. *International Journal of Music Education: Practice,* 22(3), 201–218.

Feldman, D. H. (1993). Cultural organisms in the development of great potential. In R. H. Wozniak & K. W. Fisher (eds), *Development in context: Acting and thinking in specific environments* (pp. 225–251). Mahwah, NJ: Lawrence Erlbaum.

Feldman, D. H. (1999). The development of creativity. In R. J. Sternberg (ed.), *Handbook of creativity* (pp. 169–188). Cambridge: Cambridge University Press.

Folkestad, G. (1996). Computer based creative music making *Young people's music in the digital age.* Unpublished doctoral dissertation, Goteborg, Acta Universitatis Gothoburgensis.

Folkestad, G. (1998).Music learning as cultural practice: as exemplified in computer-based creative music making. In B. Sundin, G. E. McPherson, & G. Folkestad (eds), *Children composing* (pp. 97–134). Lund, Sweden: Malmö Academy of Music, Lund University.

Fung, C. V. (1997). Effect of a sound exploration programme on children's creative thinking in music. *Research Studies in Music Education,* 9, 13–18.

Gardner, H. (1973). *The arts and human development.* New York: Basic Books.

Gardner, H. (1982). *Art, mind, and brain.* New York: Basic Books.

Gardner, H. (1993). *Creating minds.* New York: Basic Books.

Glover, J. (2000). *Children composing* (pp. 4–14). London: Routledge Falmer.

Halstead, J. M. (1994). Muslim attitudes to music in schools. *British Journal of Music Education,* 11(2), 162–178.

Hargreaves, D. J. & Galton, M. (1992). Aesthetic learning: Psychological theory and educational practice. In B. Reimer & R. A. Smith (eds), *The arts, education, and aesthetic knowing* (pp. 124–150). Chicago, IL: The National Society for the Study of Education, University of Chicago Press.

Hargreaves, D. J. (1986). *The developmental psychology of music.* Cambridge, UK: Cambridge University Press.

Hargreaves, D. J. & Zimmerman, M. P. (1992). Development theories of music learning. In R. Colwell (ed.), *Handbook Of research on music teaching and learning* (pp. 377–391). New York: Schirmer.

Hickey, M. (ed.) (2003). *Music composition in the schools: A new horizon for music education* (pp. 31–54). Reston, VA: MENC.

Hoyles, C. & Noss, R. (2004). Making rules in collaborative game design. In J. Siraj-Blatchford (ed.), *Developing new technologies for young children* (pp. 55–73). Stoke on Trent, UK: Trentham Books.

Jaffurs, S. (2004). The impact of informal music learning practices in the classroom or how I learned how to teach from a garage band. *International Journal of Music Education: Practice,* 22(3), 189–200.

Jennings, K. (2003). 'Toy Symphony': An international music technology project for children. *Music Education International,* 2, 3–21.

Kratus, J. (1989). A time analysis of the compositional processes used by children ages 7–11. *Journal of Research in Music Education,* 37, 5–20.

Lamont, A., Hargreaves, D., Marshall, N., & Tarrant, M. (2003). Young people's music in and out of school. *British Journal of Music Education,* 20(3), 229–242.

Leong, S. (ed.) (2003). Musicianship in the age of the Prosumer. In S. Leong (ed.), *Musicianship in the 21st century* (pp. 151–169). Sydney: Australian Music Centre.

Littleton, D. (1998). Music learning and child's play. *General Music Today,* 12, 8–15.

MacDonald, R. & Miell, D. (2000a). Creativity and music education: The impact of social variables. *International Journal of Music Education,* 36, 58–68.

MacDonald, R. & Miell, D. (2000b). Musical conversations: Collaborating with a friend on creative tasks. In R. Joiner, K. Littleton, D. Faulkner & D. Miell (eds), *Rethinking collaborative learning* (pp. 65–78). London: Free Association Books.

MacDonald, R., Meill, D., & Mitchell, L. (2002). An investigation of children's musical collaborations: the effect of friendship and age. *Psychology of Music*, 3(2), 148–163.

Marsh, K. (1995). Children's singing games: Composition in the playground? *Research Studies in Music Education*, 4, 2–11.

Marsh, K. (1997). *Variation and transmission processes in children's singing games in an Australian playground.* Unpublished PhD thesis, University of Sydney.

Miell, D. & Littleton, K. (eds.) (2004). *Collaborative creativity, contemporary perspectives.* London: Free Association Books.

Moorhead, G. E. & Pond, D. (1941, reprinted 1978). Music of Young Children: 11. General Observations. *Music of young children: Pillsbury foundation studies.* Santa Barbara: Pillsbury Foundation for Advancement of Music Education.

Nilsson, B. & Folkestad, G. (2005). Children's practice of computer-based composition *Music Education Research*, 7, 21–38.

Pond, D. (1981). A composer's study of young children's innate musicality. *Bulletin of the Council for Research in Music Education*, 68, 1–12.

Richardson, C. P. (1983). Creativity research in music education: A review. *Research in Music Education*, Bulletin 74, Spring.

Ross, M. (1984). *The Aesthetic Impulse.* Oxford: Pergamon.

Savage, J. & Challis, M. (2001). Dunwich revisited: collaborative composition and performance with new technologies. *British Journal of Music Education*, 18(2), 139–150.

Savage, J. (2003). Informal approaches to the development of young people's compositional skills. *Music Education Research*, 5, 81–86.

Sawyer, K. (ed.) (1997). *Creativity in performance.* London: Ablex.

Seddon, F. (2004). Cross-cultural collaborative computer-mediated composition in cyberspace. Paper presented at a conference *Musical Collaboration* of the Society for Education, Music and Psychology Research (SEMPRE), Open University, Milton Keynes, United Kingdom, April, 2004.

Seddon, F. A. (in press). Cross-cultural collaborative computer-mediated composition in cyberspace. *British Journal of Music Education.*

Seddon, F. A. & O'Neill, S. A. (2001). An evaluation study of computer-based compositions by children with and without prior experience of formal instrumental music tuition. *Psychology of Music*, 29, 4–19.

Seddon, F. A. & O'Neill, S. A. (2003). Creative thinking processes in adolescent computer-based composition: An analysis of strategies adopted and the influence of instrumental music training. *Music Education Research*, 5(2), 125–137.

Small, C. (1977). *Music, society, education.* New York: Schirmer Books.

Stauffer, S. L. (2002). Connections between the musical and life experiences of young composers and their compositions. *Journal of Research in Music Education*, 50(4), 301–322.

Sundin, B. (1998). Musical creativity in the first six years: a research project in retrospect. In B. Sundin, G. E. McPherson, & G. Folkestad (eds), *Children composing* (pp. 35–56). Malmö, Malmö Academy of Music.

Swanwick, K. & Tillman, J. (1986). The sequence of musical development: A study of children's composition. *British Journal of Music Education*, 3(3), 305–339.

Trevarthen, C. (1993). The self born in intersubjectivity: the psychology of an infant communicating. In U. Neisser (ed.), *The perceived self: Ecological and interpersonal sources of self-knowledge* (pp. 121–73). New York: Cambridge University Press.

Webster, P. (1992). Research on creative thinking music: The assessment literature. In R. Colwell (ed.), *Handbook of research on music teaching and learning* (pp. 266–78). Reston, VA: MENC.

Webster, P. (2002). Creative thinking in music: advancing a model. In T. Sullivan & L. Willingham (eds), *Creativity and music education* (pp. 16–34). Canada: Britannia Printers and Canadian Music Educators' Association.

Wiggins, J. (2002). Creative process as meaningful musical thinking. In T. Sullivan & L. Willingham (eds), *Creativity and music education.* Canadian Music Educators' Association as the first in the Biennial Series, *Research to Practice,* Lee R. Bartel, series editor, (pp. 78–88). University of Alberta.

Woodward, S. (2005). Critical matters in early childhood music education. In D. Elliott (ed.), *Praxial music education: Reflections and dialogues* (pp. 249–266). London: Oxford University Press.

Young, S. (2003). Time-space structuring in spontaneous play on educational percussion instruments among three- and four-year-olds. *British Journal of Music Education,* 20, 45–60.

Younker, B. A. (2003). Fifth grade students' involvement in composition: A teacher's intentionality. *Music Education International,* 2, 22–35.

CHAPTER 19

COMPUTERS AND TECHNOLOGY

PETER R. WEBSTER AND MAUD HICKEY

There has been a steady interest in children's musical growth and development from within music education and music psychology circles for many years. Paralleling this has been the substantial development of software and hardware, which have helped in the study of musical development. What has rarely been considered is how advances in music technology might help us practically support the actual developmental understanding of music in children. Our purpose is to review important aspects of musical development in terms of music perception, performance, preference, and creation, and link these to music technology. After a summary of music technology history in the last 30 years, we will draw connections between the literature on musical development and music technology—particularly music software. We also offer a brief review of studies that have used technology to more clearly understand aspects of music learning. Our chapter concludes with thoughts about future directions in considering music technology and the understanding of musical development.

Research findings from the literature on musical development

In addition to the authors in this book, many scholars have contributed to the literature on musical development (e.g., Sloboda, 1985; Hargreaves, 1986; Bamberger, 1991; Deliege & Sloboda, 1996; Hargreaves & North 2001). The intent of the section that follows is to highlight some of the findings from this literature that might relate to the music technology development and its use in teaching and learning. We organize the literature around the topics of music perception, performance, preference of music and the role of social learning, and generative behaviours such as composition and improvisation. We also include a section on infant and pre-school development as that period is critical to further development and has some implications for early use of music technology. Music development in adulthood is also included as new interest in music learning for adults is emerging and relates well to technology and its application.

We should state at the outset that the line between musical development that occurs naturally and that development that is encouraged or facilitated by the environment is always a difficult one to draw. The use of music technology as a way to encourage music understanding is an environmental experience that ideally ought to coincide with both the natural growth patterns of children and the culture's traditions and expectations. For these reasons, solid matches between current technology and musical development are the focus of this chapter.

Pre-school development

Music awareness begins a few months before birth as the auditory system becomes formed (see Chapters 1 and 2). Infants become accustomed to structures in music and prefer patterns that conform to known structures by at least the end of the first year of life (Trehub *et al.*, 1997).

The time between 1 month and 5 years of age is marked by incredibly rapid growth in all areas of musical development. The ages from 1 to 3 years point to a time of major experimentation and play with sounds in the environment. This development can be enhanced by exposure to rich musical environments for experimentation and growth. Babbling in the early months progresses to formed songs during this period (Moog, 1976; Moorhead & Pond, 1978; McDonald & Simons, 1989; Deliege & Sloboda, 1996; Hargreaves, 1996). Studies indicate that children around age 5 understand diatonic scale structure and even begin to be sensitive to harmonic properties (Dowling, 1988; Lamont & Cross, 1994). The ability to distinguish between fast and slow tempi seems to also emerge between the third and fourth year, although comparative judgements (slow and slower) are more difficult and the language used to express this distinction may be not developed.

A more contemporary perspective of pre-school development relates to cross-modal perception. Meltzoff *et al.* (1991) have speculated that important to the development of musical perception are the connections between auditory stimuli, visual stimuli, and touch.

> The infant perceives the acoustical characteristics of the maternal voice (melody, contour, tempo, rhythmical structure, timbre) as synchronous with and analogous to his or her own sensory perception, to visual experiences, and to the movements of the mother. The development of such cross-modal perceptual schemata is likely to play an important role for the perception of musical expression.
>
> Gembris (2002, p. 491)

There is credible evidence that children by the age of 3 or 4 can identify fundamental expressivity in music and can match certain pictures correctly to music (Kastner & Crowder, 1990).

Perception

The advances in our understanding of music perception have leaped in recent years because of techniques in neurobiology, and specifically, brain research (see Chapter 3). The use of technology that allows brain imaging techniques such as PET, EEG, ERP, and MRI provide new and exciting tools for researchers to examine brain activity during musical activities such as listening. Though this research is relatively young, it is clear that different learning contexts for listening (e.g., formal versus informal musical exposure; long-term versus short-term activity; tonal versus atonal music) affect different brain areas and activities and in different ways (Gruhn & Rauscher, 2002). What is not yet clear is a developmental pattern in changes.

Outside of the technological advances, there are generalizations that can be made about the development of listening and discrimination skills. Response to and discrimination of dynamics and timbre develop first in infants, while pitch, rhythm, texture, and harmony develop later in the growth process. By the age of 6, nearly all students have developed the ability to perceive and discriminate differences in all of these areas (McDonald & Simons, 1989; Trainor & Trehub, 1992).

Dowling (1999) has shown that melodic perception in its early stages is linked to contour only and then to more specific intervallic details as age increases. This is particularly true if children are involved in formal and active music instruction, such as playing a musical instrument. Hair (1977) and Webster & Schlentich (1983) have shown that pitch perception in younger students cannot be judged by words or gestures alone and that their real perception of subtle pitch change may be more accurate at a young age than might be otherwise imagined.

Piagetian notions of 'conservation' (co-ordinating several different aspects of perception with children aged 7 or older) has inspired work in musical development. For example, Pflederer & Sechrest (1968), in an older but classic work, showed that 8-year-old children can identify different melodies as variations of the same melody when rhythmic, melodic, or tonal changes were made.

An interesting line of investigation in music perception is graphic representation of music. As a way to uncover the mental representation of sound, researchers have asked children to notate the music they hear with invented notation (Bamberger, 1991; Smith et al., 1994; Gromko, 1994). In terms of rhythm, before the age of 6, children tend to notate a sequentially ordered series of symbols in a more figural (or what Bamberger called 'intuitive') way. Older children, especially those with more musical experience, tend to order notation in a more formal or 'metric' way. Hargreaves (1986) has commented that this movement from more figural (6–7 year olds) to more metric listening (11–12 year olds) may be related to other kinds of musical development by saying that it: '. . . is very clearly paralleled in the progression from 'outline' to 'first draft' songs . . . as well as in that from pitch contours to tonal scale intervals in melodic processing . . . ' (p. 99).

Children above the age of 6 seem to prefer harmonization that is more consonant (Zenatti, 1993). Enculturation into Western tonal system seems important here and it raises an interesting question if familiarity on a regular basis with more dissonant and perhaps atonal materials in younger years might create different results.

Schellberg (1998) has determined that, by age 6, most children can perceive different instruments by their sound. Again, it is reasonable to assume that continued exposure to formal study of timbre in the early grades in general music settings and experience with music performance ensembles would further the discrimination of timbre.

Performance

As shown in Chapter 16, singing skills develop rapidly between birth and 6 years. In their second year, children can sing short phrases and spontaneous improvisations—moving toward more accurate intervals consistent with the diatonic system (Moog, 1976). By the age of 6 years, most children's sense of key is stabilized and they can sing most songs (in the appropriate range) fairly accurately (McDonald & Simons, 1989). Learning to sing as a soloist or in a choir presents a complex array of factors for success or failure. Because the body *is* the instrument, singers cannot necessarily see the physical issues to readily fix problems that arise, and the self-identity and emotion and feeling states of the person are essentially wrapped together with the singing voice. Auditory feedback is therefore essential in shaping better singing habits (Welch *et al.*, 2005).

Children who learn to play musical instruments often either start very young (such as in the Suzuki talent education programme) and learn to play by ear, or begin about the age 12–13 when they have opportunities to join a school band or chorus. While Suzuki learning emphasizes playing by ear, children who learn instruments in the more traditional way are confronted with the confounding factor of having to read notation. Studies indicate that the most efficient way to teach notation when learning an instrument is to teach 'sound before symbol'; that is when children begin to learn an instrument they should learn to play by ear first and later be introduced to the notation system (McPherson, 1993; McPherson & Gabrielsson, 2002; Haston, 2004). McPherson *et al.* (1997) found that providing students with 'enriching' activities such as composition and improvisation had a positive impact on students' ability to play by ear and improvise, while their ability to play by ear had a strong effect on their ability to sight-read.

More is known today about music practice. Barry & Hallam (2002) summarized research on practice and noted the important need for models of good practice at various stages of development and the wisdom of creating practice strategies.

Music preference and social psychology

Children's musical preferences are already formed by the ages of 4–6 years and are clearly influenced by their home and listening environment (McDonald & Simons, 1989). What happens beyond that age is obviously very complex. Hargreaves & North (1999) indicate that there may be different periods of 'openness' to musical styles, particularly in early childhood to about age 8 and in adulthood. At the beginning of adolescence, there is clear evidence that this openness decreases and the importance of peer influence in music preference emerges (LeBlanc, 1991).

The key to the study of musical preference and listening skill is understanding the role of culture and context (see Chapter 7). Musical learning through listening can happen informally as well as formally (Palmer & Krumhansl, 1987; Upitis, 1987; Serafine, 1988; Smith & Cuddy, 1989). More whole, contextualized listening experiences (as opposed to isolated or de-contextualized fragments) will provide children with richer, and more authentic learning experiences.

What is more interesting for teachers, perhaps is the growing body of research related to clear adolescent preference and identity with popular music and its associated culture. Adolescents' self-esteem and self-confidence are clearly linked to their musical tastes—their 'badges' of identity (North & Hargreaves, 1999; Tarrant *et al.*, 2002). Music serves as an important social function for teenage youth and benefits to self-identity and self-esteem often occur only through peer interaction in the type of unsupervised musical activities that typically take place outside of school (Green, 2001; Tarrant *et al.*, 2002). Adolescent youths' perception of others is also linked to musical tastes.

Of critical importance to contemporary youth and young adults is the role of music and mass media (Gembris, 2002). The availability of music by way of television, personal music players, the internet, and laser disc technology has provided delivery systems that have influenced dramatically listening preferences. This also raises interesting issues for the functionality of music. In younger children, the functionality of music is often defined by the parent and other authority figures, but in adolescents and beyond, the pervasiveness of music as distributed by media seems to be the more powerful force.

Creating music through improvisation and composition

Studies of very young children by Moorhead & Pond (1978), and Flohr (1984) show that children beginning about age 3 enthusiastically explore sounds on musical instruments, mostly using motor energy, and also show a fascination for timbre. Flohr found that children as young as 3 were able to repeat musical patterns in their improvisations showing early understanding and ability to develop basic forms.

Kratus (1996) proposed a seven-level approach to improvisation development, beginning with exploration-based behaviour with novices and ending with the highest level of personal improvisation that is transformational for the genre. Intermediate stages include: (1) improvisation that is product-based in which the individual becomes aware of the audience and traditions within a genre; (2) fluid improvisation where a student has mastered certain technical aspects of the genre; and (3) structural improvisation in which more expressive and more technically advanced improvisations are noted.

Pressing (1988) defined improvisation and surveyed teaching techniques, offering a model that utilizes intuition, memory, and decision-making skills combined with motor processes. Berliner's definitive ethnographic work (1994) on jazz improvisation offers still further insight into the development of improvisation from the jazz perspective, including the critical role of music listening and developing a vocabulary of patterns.

In addition to the growing interest in improvisation and its role in musical development, compositional thinking as a strategy for teaching music has become a major force in countries such as Australia, the United Kingdom, and the United States (McPherson & Dunbar-Hall, 2001; Wiggins, 2002). Hickey (2002) has suggested a developmental sequence for teaching composition that involves exploration of sound followed by the study of form. The cycle might move to concentration on musical elements and then the larger issues of tension, unity, and balance.

A four-stage model of composition development has been suggested by Swanwick & Tillman (1986) based on a sequence that involves the mastery of basic music materials followed by stages based on imitation, more formal property development, and metacognitve decision-making common with more adult behaviours. Each stage begins with activities that are egocentric in nature and concludes with a sense of social sharing. Similar models have been proposed by Hargreaves & Galton (1992) and Lamont (1998) and have related general musical understanding as well as creation. Interestingly, movement through these stages is highly dependent on enculturation and formal training, especially latter stages that involve movement from more figural and imitative to more formal understanding (Swanwick et al., 2004).

Webster (2002) has proposed a model of creative thinking in music that speculates on the role of enabling skills and conditions and a process of thinking that moves through cycles of divergent and convergent thinking. Based on the growing empirical, philosophical, and practical literature on creative thinking and children, the model offers a perspective on developmental issues and is intended as a springboard for such research.

Music technology

> The rise of new media technology (e.g., computers and the internet) and the emergence of new musical styles contribute to an increasing variety of musical development in the fields of composition, performance, listening, and preferences. Therefore, parents and teachers should be aware that the children's and student's musical development may differ considerably from their own.
>
> Gembris (2002, pp. 489–490)

We turn our attention now to music technology, its history and its relationship to the literature on musical development. Our intent is to suggest matches between current technology and those aspects of musical development noted earlier. The quotation from Gembris, however, reminds us of the fact that not only is it wise to consider how current technology might support what we know about development, but also how technology itself has a role in framing and perhaps even effecting this development.

History

It is fair to say that, until most recently, the history of music technology has not been driven by any interest in musical development and learning with its attendant literature. Instead, music technology's growth has been guided by: (1) practical needs in music production (music notation, sound recording and reproduction); (2) certain technical achievements in hardware (faster, smaller, and cheaper processors, laser disc technology); and (3) the Internet as a medium of communication. That said, computer-assisted instruction has always been a part of the history of music technology and certain achievements in the development of software particularly hold promise for linkages to the development literature. This is especially true now that more musicians and educators are knowledgeable about research and are engaged in formal and informal software development.

Hardware

The period from the mid 1970s to the present day can be considered the age of the integrated circuit.[1] The growth of small and powerful, personal computer systems mark this important time. Because of the effectiveness of the integrated circuit and the computer chip, number machines and electronic instruments have become smaller while increasing their ability to process digital information. The popular Apple IIe personal computer was developed in the late 1970s and add-on, digital-to-analog circuit cards gave the computer four-voice polyphony. The IBM Corporation soon followed with its own personal computer, which was emulated by many computer manufacturers in the coming years. In the mid-1980s, the Macintosh platform emerged with built-in sound to replace the Apple IIe and new IBM-type machines (commonly referred to as 'PCs') followed. New versions of both Macintosh and PC machines exist today as the dominant computers for music performance and education. Advances in hard disk and removable storage made it possible for more and more educators to experiment with their own computer programs. The development in the late 1980s of

---

[1] For a more complete review of the stages in hardware and software development, see Williams & Webster (2006, pp. 4–11).

laser-driven, CD-ROM drives that could play music audio CDs was a major event in the ability of these personal computers to actually be used for music learning.

As this computer technology developed in this modern era, so have electronic music instruments. The MIDI (Music Instrument Digital Interface) protocol was developed in the mid-1980s and allowed music devices to transmit codes that described sound. The sound resources inside these devices have improved dramatically in recent years as sound samples captured in chips has allowed the internal sounds of MIDI hardware to rival some of the best acoustic instruments. Since the beginning of the 1990s, music educators have used these MIDI-based devices to assist in music composition, performance, and listening. Today, MIDI hardware devices have become less prevalent as the sounds they produce are now easily contained in software. MIDI technology is used more often now as triggering music events either internally within the computer or from MIDI controller keyboard.

Software

The hardware advances in personal computing, MIDI, and laser technology have completely changed the nature of music instruction; however, the last 20-year period is equally impressive for its major advances in music software and it is here that some of the most important connections can be made with the musical development literature. It is during this time that music production software for music printing, sequencing, and digital audio emerged. In terms of software for computer-assisted instruction, more behaviouristic, drill-and-practice titles have been joined by more personalized, simulation and creative exploration software. Internet-based delivery of instruction marks some of the most recent trends.

From 1984 to 1994, the software aspect of music technology exploded in ways unparalleled in history. *Band-in-a-Box*[2] became the first commercial software to provide automated accompaniments for improvisation. *Practica Musica* was published as one of the first music theory/aural skills programme to incorporate options for students and teachers—creating a kind of 'flexible-practice' software that could be adapted to individual learning needs. Each of these programs use the MIDI protocol to help the computer use external hardware as interactive partners in the learning process.

In addition to these computer-assisted instruction titles, the first programs for music notation were published, including the popular *Finale* software. Software for music sequencing such as *Cubase* and *Performer* were developing at the same time, allowing arrangers and composers to develop scores more effectively for commercial music, television, and film. Such software was used by music educators as well as commercial musicians to help students experiment with music production.

It was also during this 10-year period that the audio CD greatly influenced the development of multimedia software production. In 1989, the term 'hypermedia' was coined by Ted Nelson, building on a much earlier idea of inter-related text sources. Nelson's idea was to create a learning environment that allowed software to connect graphics, sound, and text into an integrated whole. In this same year, Robert Winter designed the first commercial product

---

[2] Titles of music technology software presented in this chapter that are currently in print are documented more completely at http://www.emtbook.net/ under the link: 'Working Software List for Music Education.' Company and cost information is included there, including links to vendor sites that often offer demonstration copies.

in music to use this idea—an interactive program on Beethoven's *Symphony No. 9*, using a CD recording controlled by a software program. The software program was Apple's *Hyper-Card*, a toolkit for the development of hypermedia programs. HyperCard was a conceptual breakthrough for music software production because it allowed music educators without significant computer programming experience to create high-quality interactive software that used audio recordings on CD. This, together with Apple Computer's development of QuickTime technology, which allowed the capture and playback of digital video as part of computer software, inspired a number of professionally created interactive CD-ROMs devoted to music subjects.

The period from 1995 to the present has seen continued development of hyperme-dia titles, referred more often today as 'multimedia' experiences. In addition, software for music pedagogy has included new titles that encourage simulation and guided instruc-tion.[3] *Making Music* and *Making More Music*, both authored by famed electronic music composer, Morton Subotnik, are significant music titles for music composition. These pro-grams assume no knowledge of music notation and allow the student to discover musical structures using a drawing metaphor. The role of a composer is simulated in ways that help teach the processes of composition. *Music Ace I* and *II* use guided instruction to help students understand music theory and aural skills in an interactive environment using animation. Children are guided in their discovery of important music facts and opportunities are provided to test mastery with games and a composing space.

Music technology support for music performance has significantly increased in the last 5 years. Software such as *SmartMusic* have been successful in providing accompaniment support for instrumentalists and vocalists and has helped in the teaching of music intona-tion. Digital audio recording capabilities on modern personal computers have increased in quality in the last 5 years to a point where educators can take advantage of software that records performances directly to disc. Software such as *Audacity* and *Sound Forge* can be used to record and process sound with an impressive array of special effects. Music can now be easily recorded, processed, and 'burned' to audio CD in the basement of one's home using software such as *ProTools* and *Audition*.

Perhaps the most important trend for software recently has been the rise of Internet-based materials for music teaching and learning. As more music teachers gain skills in the development of websites and as more schools gain access to the network, music teaching materials provided on-line at any time of day or night have begun to transform both content and delivery strategies. Individuals and companies now routinely distribute recorded music on the Internet in the form of compressed audio files. The *iTunes* software and its support for the popular player, iPod, is an excellent example.

Connection to musical development

This rather condensed review of music technology in the last 30 years reveals a movement to a more constructionist posture for developers and educators. For example, software based on structured ways of rote learning, memorization, and patterns of convergent

---

[3] A complete review of many of the most influential software titles available today is contained in Williams & Webster (2006).

thinking that were commonly found in the early days of personal computers are now more likely to be augmented or even replaced with methods of discovery learning, problem-solving, and divergent thinking with more powerful hardware resources. Higher levels of synthetic thinking are seen as a more effective way to teach our children how to cope with complexity. Cooperative learning, peer teaching, and project-centred learning with the teacher in an overseeing role is much more valued than teacher-dominated interaction.

In the last 10 years, music educators have begun to use technology in a more construc-tionist context. Video, animation, text, and sound can unite to support a symbolically constructed world that represents reality in interesting and meaningful ways for children. With today's affordable personal computers, even the youngest of children can 'play along' with the computer, make increasingly more complex decisions about the composition of the music, or be asked to listen in new and exciting ways.

We believe that this use of music technology can be a powerful aid for music teachers to reinforce, extend, and refine the expected development of music perception, performance, preference, and creating that were noted in the first half of this chapter. Table 19.1 provides a suggested organization of current popular software by appropriate age level and by music content area. We also make a distinction between those software titles that are designed as computer-assisted instruction and those that are music production programs designed for personal productivity. Each of the titles can be used to match the emerging developmental aspects that were noted earlier in this chapter. In the sections that follow, we describe a few of these titles within each content area in music learning and why we feel the technology can be used as a match.

Pre-school development

Each title in the Pre-School column in Table 19.1 is designed to engage children in music experiences without the use of extensive written words. The accent is on experimenta-tion with sound using colourful graphics and recorded voice. Volume 2 of the *Thinkin' Things* series contains two sets of music activities, 'Oranga' and 'Tooney' that encourages the child to sequence sounds to create new music. Pattern formations are encouraged and pattern perception is reinforced. The *MiDisaurus* series encourages exploration of many musical elements including rhythm structures and melodies. Both programs use cross-modal exploration with graphics, sound, and movement—something that computers and software can do very well.

Perception

The *Music Ace* series and *Hearing Music* software titles are excellent for students' early development of melodic and harmonic perception. *Music Ace* provides a series of interactive, guided lessons that are consistent with what we know about music perception in the 6–10 age grouping. *Hearing Music* offers a series of game-like exercises that reinforce hearing melodic and rhythmic patterns. The *Sibelius Instruments* program offers excellent support for the development of music timbre. It supports not only timbres for individual instruments but also for ensembles.

Table 19.1 Current music software classified by music content, software type, and age

Software type	Music content	Age level for musical development			
		Pre-school	6–9	10–15	16–Adult
Computer-assisted instruction	Perception	Thinkin' Things 2 (m/pc) MiDisaurus, Vols 1–8 (m/pc) Cloud 9 (pc) New York Philharmonic(I)	Musicus (m/pc) Hearing Music (pc) Music Ace 1, 2 (m/pc) Sibelius Instruments (m/pc)	MusicTheory.net (I) MiBAC Music Lessons I, II (m/pc) Auralia (m/pc) Alfred Music Theory (m/pc)	Practica Musica (m/pc)
	Performance		Early Keyboard Skills (m/pc) Singing Coach (pc)	eMedia Guitar (m/pc) SmartMusic (m/pc)	
	Preference		Beethoven Lives Upstairs (pc)	Pianist Series (m/pc) Oscar Peterson (pc)	Carnegie Hall Listening Adventures (I) Time Sketch Editor (m/pc)
	Creating		Making Music (m/pc) Doddle Pad (m/pc) Rock Rap'N Roll (m/pc)	Berklee Shares (I) Making More Music (m/pc) Band-in-a-Box (m/pc)	Sheddin' the Basics (m/pc)
	Perception			Audacity (m/pc) Sound Forge (pc) Audition (pc) Toast (m)	Reason (m/pc) Reaktor (m/pc)
Music production	Performance				Live! (m/pc) Max MSP (m/pc)
	Preference			iTunes (m/pc) RealAudio (m/pc) QuickTime Media Player (m/pc)	
	Creating		Super Duper Music Looper (pc)	Vermont MIDI Project (I) GarageBand (m) ACID Studio (pc)	Finale (m/pc) Sibelius (m/pc) Logic (m) Sonar (pc)

Notes: a. (m/pc) = Mac and PC, (m) = Mac only, (pc) = PC only, (I) = Internet-based. b. Documentation for each product can be found in Webster Williams (2006), or online at http://www.emtbook.net

Aural skills continue to be reinforced with software such as *MiBAC Music Lessons*, *Auralia*, and *Practica Musica*. Each of these programs stresses more complicated melodic and rhythmic patterns, harmonic content, and music concepts such as cadences. Programs of this sort are appropriate for ages 10 through adult.

Development of music perception, of course, is also supported in music production software that focuses on digital audio. Sound editing programs such as *Audacity* and *Sound Forge* encourage deeper skills of sound manipulation. *Reason* and *Reaktor* are sound sculpting programs that help develop very fine levels of music perception and are appropriate for older students. It is interesting that many of these same titles, including *Audition*, which is an excellent multi-track, digital audio program, might also be considered under the 'Creating' music content area. This suggests a strong link in practice to how advanced perception work is the foundation for creative experiences in musical development.

Performance

Singing Coach is a software program useful for music singing skills. A computer and microphone are used to audit singing in real time, while offering visual feedback about accuracy. The software comes with song literature and additional music can be downloaded from the company's website. A more advanced edition of the software can support newly composed music and standard MIDI files. Such a resource can be a strong support for children learning to sing at both young ages and more advanced stages.

In a similar way, *SmartMusic* provides intelligent accompaniment for instrumental performance. The software can 'follow' the tempo of the performer and can even offer graphic representation of errors. Standard literature is provided with the software or can be created in a custom way. *SmartMusic* can be useful in reinforcing developing music performance skills and can play a dramatic role in the motivation for practice.

Technology can support live performance as well. Programs such as *Live!* and *MaxMSP* offer ways to use the computer and its sound sources as support for live performance. Such technology can assist in developing more sophisticated performance skills in older students and adults.

Music preference and social psychology

In developing preferences for music of various kinds, programs such as *Beethoven Lives Upstairs*, *Oscar Peterson*, and other multimedia programs can be most helpful. Repeated hearing of the music and learning about the social context of the music are aggressively supported in such software. Tools such as the *Time Sketch Editor* can be used by teachers and students alike to create graphic representations of the form of selected music. Various websites from music ensembles and from places such as Carnegie Hall can add greatly to the developmental growth of children of all ages. It is here that Internet-based resources can play a major part in the music preferences of children.

Of course, recent developments in music distribution have created great potential for students to learn about music of all kinds. Internet-based music stores like the Apple Music Store that supports the *iTunes* software and the iPod personal music player are good examples of this. Internet-based playback of music through *RealAudio* and *QuickTime* should also be noted. Such resources can be used wisely by teachers and parents to help broaden and focus music listening and patterns of music preference.

Creating music through improvisation and composition

This is perhaps the most powerfully supported of all music content areas. *Making Music* allows young students to draw music shapes that are then turned into music. The shapes can be manipulated much like an adult composer might do by using repetition, augmentation, inversion, and many other ways to alter a gesture. Timbre and dynamics can be changed as well. Shapes can be drawn on top of one another to create simple or very complex textures. In a more advanced version of the software, *Making More Music*, the gestures can be turned into traditional notation. Such software can be used not only to support the imaginative development of children but also for enhancing music perception development.

Traditional music notation and sequencing programs play a part in musical development for the older student. Programs such as *Sibelius* and *Sonar* are excellent for these purposes as students strive for the creation of more sophisticated music.

Other music composition programs built on the current interest in loop-based music offer exciting possibilities for musical development. Such programs as *Super Duper Music Looper, ACID,* and *GarageBand* provide excellent support for students to explore the combination of loops of various timbres and from various genres to create their own compositions. This 'instant' music making needs to be tempered with expert teaching to help challenge students to develop more sensitive and complex ways to think musically. Little is known about how this can be done well or in a way consistent with current theories such as those of Swanwick & Tillman (1986), Hargreaves & Galton (1992), Lamont (1998), or Hickey (2002).

On the improvisation side of music making, the *Band-in-a-Box* software can be used effectively to develop skills in improvisation consistent with models such as that of Kratus (1996). The software provides an intelligent backup ensemble for improvisations over chord changes that the user provides. Different styles of music are represented and the user has control over tempo. Improvisations can be recorded and changed into notation for study.

Effectiveness of music technology

Just how effective is all of this software on musical development? The evidence to date can best be described as positive but meagre in quantity and quality, especially for young children and adolescents. Higgins (1992) summarized well the classic problems with research on music technology, including poor design, Hawthorne effects, inadequate treatment, and the confounds that the changing nature of technology bring. Berz & Bowman (1994), in their review of experimental work, point to either a neutral or slightly positive overall effect of music technology in increasing learning in music. They do stress the generally positive attitudes of students toward the use of technology in learning. Webster's comprehensive review of the literature (2001) from 1990 to 2000 revealed similar results and stressed the importance of context in understanding research results. He pointed to strong gains in the use of technology for enhancing music performance and noted the need to increase our level of sophistication in evaluating the effectiveness of more exploratory and creative-based software.

Music listening and perception

In terms of music listening and perception, McCord (1993) reported on the effects of computer-assisted instruction on development of music fundamentals understanding in middle school instrumental students. Using an interactive, multimedia program with MIDI support, she found gains in low, middle and high-level music performance groups in the understanding of music fundamentals such as note name identification, key and time signature understanding, and knowledge of symbols and scales.

Goodson (1992) documented the development and trial of an interactive hypermedia program for basic music listening. Her study involved 128 sixth-grade students. Using a four-group comparison model that included groups with no contact, traditional instruction, computer instruction in small groups, and computer instruction with one large group, she found interactive hypermedia instruction required less instructional time in order to achieve equal or higher scores on a 22-item music listening test.

Bush (2000) investigated 84 sixth- and seventh-grade students after individually completing either a 40-minute session with two specially designed multimedia programs or a group expository lesson on the same subject. He was interested in the effect of multimedia software use on cognitive style (field dependence/independence) and on gender in terms of performance on retention of factual information. The subject matter was a lesson on the steel bands of Trinidad. Hypermedia content included text, audio, digital photographs, and movies. The dependent variable was a 20-question, multiple-choice test that was evaluated for validity and reliability. This post-test was given once at the end of the experiment and again after a 6-week time period. Results indicated statistically significant differences with both post-tests for treatment in favour of the control group (expository lecture) and for field independent students. There were no differences for gender. The results for cognitive style, which showed field independent students doing well in both conditions but field dependent doing less well in computer-based group, reinforced past research. The gender result demonstrated that, despite evidence that male/female attitudes may differ for technology, real achievement as measured by the test does not. The result for the main effect of treatment was a surprise in light of other studies on multimedia in music instruction. Bush speculated that the nature of the multiple-choice test might not be a good predictor of what was learned in multimedia work. He also wondered if the expository lecture was better at preparing the students for multiple-choice assessment. Another possibility might be the short time for software use in an unstructured environment has no real effect on factual recall.

In a more qualitative study, Greher (2003) provided evidence that multimedia music used in an inner city, at-risk middle-school population encouraged thoughtful discussion about music outside of the student's experience and highly motivated student discussion and attention. Multiple tracks of audio, video images, and digital movies were combined and students were encouraged to watch and listen, then answer questions before moving on to other music. Opinions were solicited and recorded in a database. There were also possibilities for students to compose their own music to match film clips. Field notes, teacher interview data, and student surveys showed very positive reactions to the music and to the use of the technology.

Taken as a group these studies are representative of what we seem to know from current research about technology and music listening and perception. Certain factual knowledge about music can be effectively taught by computer-based resources, freeing teachers to focus on more complex and meaningful aspects of the art form. Multimedia use can be very effective, especially if designed to encourage personal involvement and higher-level thinking skills. Our ability as researchers to measure the effects of technology's use in music listening and perception remains a problem.

Music performance

The evidence of the role of technology in helping music performance skills develop is growing in both quantity and quality. Orman (1998) reported results of a project to evaluate the effect of a multimedia program on beginning saxophonists' achievement and attitude. Experimental and control groups were formed from sixth-grade students ($n = 44$) in four middle schools. Content was based on a number of topics in beginning saxophone books and verified by experts. She designed her work to support short periods of instruction by having students in the experimental group complete sections of 8–15 minutes with the computer in a nearby room, then return to regular band class. Results on post-tests of both written knowledge and video recorded ability to apply understanding favoured the experimental group significantly. Data also demonstrated strong, positive attitudes for the computer-assisted instruction.

Simpson (1996) investigated pitch accuracy among high school choral students and its possible improvement with technology-assisted visual and aural feedback. The subjects were 69 students in an urban, multi-ethnic high school, divided evenly into three groups. The first group received teacher-guided instruction in a small group in addition to the regular choral rehearsal. The second group received visual/aural feedback on pitch as part of the choral rehearsal. The third group received both the small group instruction and the technology help. Comparison between post-tests demonstrated no significant difference, but the second group, which received just the technology treatment, did improve from post-test scores.

Work with intelligent accompaniment programs continues to be done. Tseng (1996) described its use with flute students using a cross-participant, case study approach. Her results supported the notion that the software helps music learning, intonation, and performance preparation. Ouren (1998) also used this software, but with middle school wind performers. Using pre- and post-interviews and independent assessments of performance achievement, he studied eight students' progress over a 6-week period. No control group was employed. Performance evaluations showed improvement for seven of the eight students, especially in rhythm and interpretation/musicianship. Interview data indicated positive reactions to the technology.

Creating music through improvisation and composition

Some of the most extensive and rich work done on computer-based, compositional thinking was reported by Folkstead and his associates (Folkestad *et al.*, 1998). The purpose was to document the process of creation for 129 pieces by 14, 15, and 16 year olds over a 3-year period in Sweden. MIDI files were collected during the process of composition and interviews and observations of participants were recorded. Students with no previous compositional experience worked after school, once a week. Interviews with the students were conducted after the completion of a composition in order to understand how each student worked and what the thought processes were. The interviews were undertaken at the computer workstation (computer with standard sequencing software and keyboard synthesizer) and access to previous versions of the compositions was possible. From the data, a typology for compositional strategies emerged. Two principal types were labelled 'horizontal' and 'vertical.' Horizontal composers worked at the start with a conception of the piece from beginning to end. Further divisions of this approach included how the composer used the keyboard or the computer. Horizontal composers tended to complete one line at a time. Some composers worked exclusively on the computer and others would opt to use an acoustic instrument, such as a guitar, to work out ideas first before entering them into the computer. Vertical composers worked on bits of the whole at a time with one part completed before moving on to the next vertical space. Some vertical composers had an idea of the whole 'orchestra' ahead of time and defined each line of the vertical space from the start. Others worked this out as they composed bits of the work. This research is useful because it resulted in a model that other researchers can use to investigate different aged children, differences caused by past experience, or with different media.

Stauffer (2001) reported work with one child on a limited number of projects and used the *Making Music* software. After describing her role as a consultant in the development of the software, Stauffer described the composition processes of one 8-year-old child, Meg, as she manipulated the software to compose. The description tells a rich story of how Meg developed a musical style by exploring and developing fluency with sound over time. Different types of exploring and developing are described. In telling the story, Stauffer integrates previous research in composition and creative thinking as examples of Meg's behaviour. A more recent study by Stauffer (2002) also includes case-study data on sixth-grade composers and connections between life experiences and their music. In this study, several computer-based composition programs were used and rich information about cultural context and music was revealed.

Younker (1997) used technology in an imaginative way to offer a platform for composition that allowed for the analysis of thought processes and strategies of different aged children. Nine students, ranging in age from 8 to 14, were asked to compose using a standard software sequencer with a computer and MIDI keyboard much like the one used by Folkestad. Students were asked to think aloud while composing at the computer and respond to questions in an unstructured fashion. Data revealed differences in thought processes and strategies that could serve as the basis for a developmental model.

Lendáyi (1995) used a qualitative case study approach to examine the compositional thought processes of four high school students from a suburban high school. A computer and MIDI keyboard was used, together with a music notation program. Evaluation of both open and close-ended tasks revealed very different compositional styles. One of her major findings was that there may well be four classifications of novice composers at this level: (1) archetypal (possessing the 'gift' of imaginative ideas, but without much experience and knowledge); (2) style emulator (strongly influenced by popular genres with few original ideas of their own); (3) technician (students who seem to concentrate on surface details without connecting to deeper musical meaning); and (4) super composer (students with the 'gift' and with past training and experience to achieve a high level of attainment).

Hickey has completed studies evaluating creative thinking ability. Process and product data were compared from a creative thinking perspective with 21 fourth and fifth grade subjects (Hickey, 1995). MIDI data were unobtrusively captured from a custom program stack that controlled a keyboard synthesizer and was designed to encourage compositional thinking. The program guided the subjects through a variety of possibilities organized around five musical elements: melody, rhythm, texture, timbre, and dynamics. The MIDI data created by the custom program was cleverly collected for both the process and product data analysis. Final compositions were evaluated by a panel of judges using consensual assessment techniques. Compositions rated in the high third and low third were then evaluated descriptively and quantitatively. Hickey used this same custom program to explore two subjects in detail (Hickey, 1997). In this work, she was interested in the subjects' moments of most creative output in relation to a theory of interaction between reward and task conditions. Because the technology records experimentation with musical materials unobtrusively, she was able to capture and compare compositional thinking products when the subjects were exploring and developing ideas (presumably not under pressure for a final, evaluated product) and under more demanding conditions for a final product. She provided background information on both students, placing the resulting data in context. The comparison of musical content under both conditions revealed qualitatively different descriptions, with the less pressured situation resulting in far more creative content based on the established notions of divergence and convergence. The relationships between these conditions of task structure and creative music making await much more systematic work, but the use of technology to reveal these subtleties is worth note.

Daignault (1996) examined children's computer-mediated strategies in relation to craftsmanship and creative thinking. Twenty-five subjects, ranging in age from 10 to 11 were asked to: (1) record three to eight improvisations into a typical sequencer program; (2) select the one they preferred; and (3) develop the selection further using graphic, 'piano-roll' notation. The main data came by observing carefully the development process using a video camera trained on the computer screen. Interestingly this use of a video camera for data collection was greatly improved by Seddon & O'Neill (2000) who reported use of a special video card in a computer that recorded student behaviour directly to video-tape. Using techniques similar to Hickey, Daignault asked judges to assess consensually the final developed compositions for craftsmanship and creativity and the top and bottom rated compositions served as an indicator of which process data to evaluate carefully. Analyses of process data for high and low craftsmanship and creativity lead to conclusions about compositional thinking.

The future

Advances in the science of how people learn have influenced teaching and are worth mentioning here because of the potential intersection with the advancements in music technology. A 2-year study by 16 individuals on the 'Committee on Developments in the Science of Learning' resulted in a text[4] that compiles the latest research about how people learn and the best way to teach and create learning environments based on these findings (Brandsford *et al.*, 1999). They conclude that most effective learning takes place in constructive, learning-centred environments where children learn by doing and by replicating, as well as possible, 'real-world' learning problems: 'Because many new technologies are interactive, it is now easier to create environments in which students can learn by doing, receive feedback, and continually refine their understanding and build new knowledge. . . . The new technologies can also help people visualize difficult-to-understand concepts.' (pp. 206–207).

While the thrust of these findings relate to learning in science and math, many of the conclusions are as appropriate and important for learning in music. Technology provides for constructive learning instances: students find problems to solve and can work these out in creative ways through new technologies such as music notation, sequencing, and CAI programs. Technology brings 'real-world' experience into the classroom. Students hear sounds that are real, can manipulate sound and obtain immediate feedback. Technology is also creating a new literacy that children may grasp quicker than (and in spite of) their music teachers (Hickey, 2004).

Perhaps the most exciting potential for technology relates to the topic of this chapter: the intersection of music technology tools, games, and software with musical development. The newest software presents new windows into the musical actions of children because it offers constructive, learning-centred environments where children *are* learning by doing. What if researchers *observed* or experimented with children using the software, for instance, listed in Table 19.1, to learn more about the developmental aspects of preference, performance, perception, and creating. How a 6-year-old child interacts and learns with Subotnik's colourful CAI program *Hearing Music,* may inform us more about musical development than we've ever known. The choices adolescents make to create music in *GarageBand* may provide researchers with answers concerning the musical preferences, learning style, and developmental peaks that have not yet been revealed in research to date. It is also conceivable that not only will new technology and software enhance our understanding of children's musical development, but it may also *advance* the development process of musical learning and understanding in those that use it.

Folkestad *et al.* (1998), Savage (2005), and many others whose work is summarized in the previous section are examples of researchers who have used technology to gather powerful information about the musical understandings (and hence, potential developmental information) of adolescent musicians. However, the connection between music technology and our understanding of musical development in children has yet to be fully bridged. More research must be done in this area: observing and experimenting with children as they work in the music technology environments such as those provided in the most popular and recent software (see Table 19.1). The potential for major advances in our knowledge of musical development is very great indeed.

---

[4] The full text is also available as a website at: http://books.nap.edu/html/howpeople1

References

Bamberger, J. (1991). *The mind behind the musical ear: How children develop musical intelligence.* Cambridge, MA: Harvard University Press.

Barry, N. & Hallam, S. (2002). Practice. In R. Parncutt & G. E. McPherson (eds), *The science and psychology of music performance: Creative strategies for teaching and learning* (pp. 151–166). New York: Oxford University Press.

Berliner, P. (1994). *Thinking in jazz.* Chicago, IL: University of Chicago Press.

Berz, W. L. & Bowman, J. (1994). *Applications of research in music technology.* Reston, VA: Music Educators National Conference.

Brandsford, J., Brown, A. L., & Cocking, R. R. (eds) (1999). *How people learn: Brain, mind, experience, and school.* Washington, DC: National Academies Press.

Bush, J. E. (2000). The effects of a hypermedia program, cognitive style, and gender on middle school students' music achievement. *Contributions to Music Education, 27,* 9–26.

Daignault, L. (1996). *Children's creative musical thinking within the context of a computer-supported improvisational approach to composition.* (Doctor of Philosophy, Northwestern University). *Dissertation Abstracts International.* 57/11-A, 4681. (University Microfilms No. 9714572).

Deliege, I. & Sloboda, J. (eds) (1996). *Musical beginnings: Origins and development of musical competence.* New York: Oxford University Press.

Dowling, J. (1988). Tonal structure and children's early learning of music. In J. Sloboda (ed.), *Generative processes in music: The psychology of performance, improvisation, and composition* (pp. 113–128). New York: Oxford University Press.

Dowling, J. (1999). The development of music perception and cognition. In D. Deutsch (ed.), *The psychology of music* (pp. 603–625). San Diego, CA: Academic Press.

Folkestad, G., Hargreaves, D. J., & Lindström, B. (1998). Compositional strategies in computer-based music-making. *British Journal of Music Education, 15,* 83–97.

Flohr, J. (1984). *Young children's improvisations: A longitudinal study.* Paper presented at the Music Educators National In-Service Conference (49th, Chicago, IL, March 23, 1984)

Gembris, H. (2002). The development of musical abilities. In R. Colwell & C. Richardson (eds), *The new handbook of research on music teaching and learning* (pp. 487–508). New York: Oxford.

Goodson, C. A. (1992). *Intelligent music listening: An interactive hypermedia program for basic music listening skills.* Doctor of Philosophy, The University of Utah.) *Dissertations Abstracts International,* 53/11-A, 3837. (University Microfilms No. 9307303).

Greher, G. R. (2003). Multimedia in the classroom: Tapping into an adolescent's cultural literacy. *Journal of Technology in Music Learning, 2*(2), 21–43.

Green, L. (2001). *How popular musicians learn: A way ahead for music education.* Burlington, VA: Ashgate Publishing.

Gromko, J. E. (1994). Children's invented notations as measures of musical understanding. *Psychology of Music, 22*(2), 136–147.

Gruhn, W. & Rauscher, F. (2002). The neurobiology of music cognition and learning. In R. Colwell & C. Richardson (eds), *The new handbook of research on music teaching and learning* (pp. 445–460). New York: Oxford University Press.

Hair, H. I. (1977). Discrimination of tonal direction on verbal and nonverbal tasks by first-grade children. *Journal of Research in Music Education, 25*(3), 197–210.

Hargreaves, D. J. (1986). *The developmental psychology of music.* New York: Cambridge University Press.

Hargreaves, D. J. (1996). The development of artistic and musical development. In I. Deliege & J. A. Sloboda (eds), *Musical beginnings: Origins and development of musical competence* (pp. 145–170). Oxford: Oxford University Press.

Hargreaves, D. J. & Galton, M. J. (1992). Aesthetic learning: psychological theory and educational practice. In B. Reimer & R. A. Smith (eds), *The arts, education, and aesthetic knowing* (pp. 124–150). Chicago: National Society for the Study of Education; distributed by University of Chicago Press.

Hargreaves, D. J. & North, A. C. (1999). Developing concepts of musical style. *Musicae scientiae: Journal of the European Society for the Cognitive Sciences of Music*, **3**(2), 193–216.

Hargreaves, D. J. & North, A. C. (2001). Complexity, prototypicality, familiarity, and the perception of musical quality. *Psychomusicology*, **17**(1–2), 77–80.

Haston, W. (2004). *Comparison of a visual and an aural approach to beginning wind instrument instruction.* (Doctor of Philosophy, Northwestern University). *Dissertation Abstracts International*, 65/05-A, 1711. (University Microfilms No. 3132535).

Hickey, M. (1995). *Qualitative and quantitative relationships between children's creative musical thinking processes and products.* (Doctor of Philosophy, Northwestern University). Dissertations Abstracts International. 57/01-A, 145. (University Microfilms No. 9614754).

Hickey, M. (1997). The computer as a tool in creative music making. *Research Studies in Music Education*, **8**(July), 56–70.

Hickey, M. (2002). Creative thinking in the context of music composition. In M. Hickey (ed.), *Why and how to teach music composition: A new horizon for music education* (pp. 31–54). Reston, VA: MENC.

Hickey, M. (2004). Music technology in schools—the 'Garage bands' of the future? *Triad*, **71**(4), 27–19.

Higgins, W. (1992). Technology. In R. Colwell (ed.), *Handbook of research on music teaching and learning* (pp. 480–497). New York: Schirmer Books.

Kastner, M. P. & Crowder, R. G. (1990). Perception of the major/minor distinction. IV: Emotional connotation in young children. *Music perception: An interdisciplinary journal*, **8**(2), 189–201

Kratus, J. (1996). A developmental approach to teaching music improvisation. *International Journal of Music Education*, **26**, 27–37.

Lamont, A. (1998). Music, education, and the development of pitch perception: The role of context, age and musical experience. *Psychology of Music*, **26**, 7–25.

Lamont, A. & Cross, I. (1994). Children's cognitive representations of musical pitch. *Music Perception*, **12**, 27–55.

LeBlanc, A. (1991). Some unanswered questions in music preference research. *Contributions to Music Education*, **18**, 66–73.

Lendáyi, K. (1995). *Processes of musical composition facilitated by digital music equipment.* (Doctor of Philosophy, University of Illiois at Urbana-Champaign.) *Dissertation Abstracts International*. 56/09-A, 3494. (University Microfilms No. 9543638).

McCord, K. (1993). Teaching music fundamentals through technology in middle school music classes. In K. Walls (ed.), *Third international conference on technological directions in music education* (pp. 68–71). San Antonio, TX: IMR Press.

McDonald, D. T. & Simons, G. M. (1989). *Musical growth and development: Birth through six.* New York: Schirmer Books.

McPherson, G. E. (1993). Factors and abilities influencing the development of visual, aural and creative performance skills in music and their educational implications (Doctor of Philosophy, University of Sydney–(Australia)). *Dissertation Abstracts International*, 54/04-A, 1277. (University Microfilms No. 9317278).

McPherson, G. E. & Dunbar-Hall (2001). Australia. In D. J. Hargreaves & A. C. North (eds), *Musical development and learning: The international perspective* (pp. 14–26). New York: Continuum.

McPherson, G. E. & Gabrielsson, A. (2002). From sound to sign. In R. Parncutt & G. E. McPherson (eds), *The science and psychology of music performance: Creative strategies for teaching and learning* (pp. 99–116). New York: Oxford University Press.

McPherson, G. E., Bailey, M., & Sinclair, K. E. (1997). Path analysis of a theoretical model to describe the relationship among five types of musical performance. *Journal of Research in Music Education*, 45, 103–112.

Meltzoff, A. N., Kuhl, P., & Moore, M. K. (1991). Perception, represenation, and the control of action in newborn and young infants towards a new synthesis. In M. J. S. Weiss & P. R. Zelazo (eds), *Newborn attention: Biological constraints and the influence of experience* (pp. 377–411). Norwood, NJ: Ablex.

Moog, H. (1976). The development of musical abilities in the first years of life. *Psychology of Music*, 1, 14–20.

Moorhead, G. E. & Pond, D. (1978). *Music of young children*. Santa Barbara, CA: Pillsbury Foundation.

North, A. C. & Hargreaves, D. J. (1999). Music and adolescent identity. *Music Education Research*, 1, 75–92.

Orman, E. K. (1998). Effect of interactive multimedia computing on young saxophonists' achievement. *Journal of Research in Music Education*, 46, 62–74.

Ouren, R. W. (1998). *The influence of the* Vivace *accompaniment technology on selected middle school instrumental students*. (Doctor of Philosophy, University of Minnesota). *Dissertation Abstracts International*, 58/07-A, 2456. (University Microfilms No. 9738468).

Palmer, C. & Krumhansl, C. (1987). Independent temporal and pitch structures in determination of musical phrase. *Journal of Experimental Psychology: Human Perception and Performance*, 13, 116–126.

Pflederer, M. & Sechrest, L. (1968). Conversation-type responses of children to musical stimuli. *Council for Research in Music Education*, 13, 19–36.

Pressing, J. (1988). Improvisation: methods and models. In J. Sloboda (ed.), *Generative processes in music: The psychology of performance, improvisation and composition* (pp. 129–178). New York: Oxford University Press.

Savage, J. (2005). Sound2Picture: *Developing compositional pedagogies from the sound designer's world*. Proceedings of the Fourth International Research in Music Education Conference (RIME) (pp. 182–185). Exeter, UK: University of Exeter, April, 2005.

Schellberg, G. (1998). *Zur entwicklung der klangfarben-wahrnehmung von vorschulkindern*. Münster, Germany: Lit Verlag.

Seddon, F. & O'Neill, S. (2000). Influence of formal instrumental music tuition (FIMT) on adolescent self-confidence and engagement in computer-based composition. In C. Woods, G. Luck, R. Brochard, F. Seddon, & J. Sloboda (eds), *Sixth International Conference on Music Perception and Cognition* (CD-ROM). Keele, UK: Keele University.

Serafine, M. L. (1988). *Music as cognition: The development of thought in sound*. New York: Columbia University Press.

Simpson, E. H. (1996). *The effects of technology-assisted visual/aural feedbgack upon pitch accuracy of senior high school choral singing*. (Doctor of Musical Arts, University of Hartford.) *Dissertation Abstracts International*, 57/03-A, 1070. (University Microfilms No. 9622215).

Sloboda, J. (1985). *The musical mind: The cognitive psychology of music*. New York: Oxford University Press.

Smith, K. C. & Cuddy, L. L. (1989). Effects of metric and harmonic rhythm on the detection of pitch alterations in melodic sequences. *Journal of Experimental Psychology: Human Perception and Performance*, 15(3), 457–471.

Smith, K. C., Cuddy, L. L., & Upitis, R. (1994). Figural and metric understanding of rhythm. *Psychology of Music*, 22, 117–135.

Stauffer, S. L. (2001). Composing with computers: Meg makes music. *Council for Research in Music Education*, 150, 1–20.

Stauffer, S. L. (2002). Connections between the musical and life experiences of young composers and their compositions. *Journal of Research in Music Education.* 50(4), 301–322.

Swanwick, K. & Tillman, J. (1986). The sequence of musical development: A study of children's compositions. *British Journal of Music Education*, 3(3), 305–339.

Swanwick, K., Hallam, S., Lamont, A., O'Neill, S., Green, L., Cox, G., Hennessy, S., Farrell, G., & Welch, G., (2004). Mapping music education research in the UK. *Psychology of Music*, 32(3), 239–290.

Tarrant, M., North, A. C., & Hargreaves, D. J. (2002). Youth identity and music. In R. MacDonald, D. J. Hargreaves, & D. Meill (eds), *Musical identities* (pp. 134–150). New York: Oxford University Press.

Trainor, L. J. & Trehub, S. E. (1992). The development of referential meaning in music. *Music Perception*, 9(4), 455–470.

Trehub, S. E., Hill, D. S., & Kamenetsky, S. B. (1997). Parents' sung performances for infants. *Canadian Journal of Educational Psychology*, 51(4), 385–396.

Tseng, S. (1996). *Solo accompaniments in instrumental music education: The impact of the computer-controlled Vivace on flute student practice.* (Doctor of Philosophy, University of Illinois at Urbana-Champaign.) *Dissertation Abstracts International*, 57/04-A, 1536. (University Microfilms No. 9625203).

Upitis, R. (1987). Children's understanding of rhythm: the relationship between development and music training. *Psychomusicology*, 8, 141–160.

Webster, P. (2001). Computer-based technology and music teaching and learning. In R. Colwell & C. Richardson (eds), *The new handbook of research on music teaching and learning* (pp. 416–439). New York: Oxford.

Webster, P. (2002). Creative thinking in music: advancing a model. In T. Sullivan & L. Willingham (eds), *Creativity and music education* (pp. 16–33). Edmonton: Canadian Music Educator's Association.

Webster, P. & Schlentrich, K. (1983). Discrimination of pitch direction by preschool children with verbal and nonverbal tasks. *Journal of Research in Music Education*, 30, 151–161.

Wiggins, J. (2002). Creative process as meaningful musical thinking. In T. Sullivan & L. Willingham (eds), *Creativity and music education* (pp. 78–88). Edmonton AB: Canadian Music Educators' Association.

Williams, D. B. & Webster, P. R. (2006). *Experiencing music technology* (3rd edn). Belmont, CA: Thomson Higher Education.

Younker, B. (1997). *Thought processes and strategies of eight, eleven, and fourteen year old students while engaged in music composition.* (Doctor of Philosophy, Northwestern University.) *Dissertation Abstracts International*, 58/11-A, 4217. (University Microfilms No. 9814345).

Zenatti, A. (1993). Children's musical cognition and taste. In T. J. Tighe & W. J. Dowling (eds), *Psychology and music: The understanding of melody and rhythm* (pp. 177–196). Hillsdale, NJ: Erlbaum.

HISTORICAL PERSPECTIVES

GORDON COX

My purpose in this chapter is to assemble four examples taken from different historical periods of children's experience of learning music in formal educational settings in the west. They include: the English medieval song schools, instrumental instruction in eighteenth century Britain, school music teaching in late nineteenth century Europe, and recapitulation and musical childhoods in the twentieth century. The first three of these were selected in order to illustrate children's musical experiences in the formal educational settings of churches, studios, and schools, respectively, while the fourth charts the progress of an influential theory concerning the evolutionary development of music, and the evolutionary stages of childhood. I do not attempt to provide a comprehensive view, but rather by use of selected examples drawn from music education in formal educational settings, illustrate the notion that childhood is historically constructed.

Underpinning the account are fundamental questions of a general nature concerning childhood: Did children come into the world innocent, or with the stain of original sin upon them? Were children like a blank sheet at birth, or did they arrive with a number of innate characteristics already in place? Should they experience a 'short' or a 'long' childhood? These relate in turn to a repertoire of themes that have been used to construct and reconstruct images of the child and the adolescent in the west: depravity/innocence; nature/nurture; independence/dependence (Heywood, 2001).

My contention is that the changing ideas about what childhood is like and how children develop has influenced the nature of formal music education, whether in church, studio, or school.

There are two particular challenges for historians of childhood: to tease out the relationship between ideas about childhood and the experience of being a child, and how it has changed over time, and to unearth source material on past childhoods as children themselves leave few records (Cunningham, 1995). Bearing these challenges in mind, I hope we will be able to hear children's musical voices, albeit somewhat faintly at times through such diverse evidence as cathedral records, travellers' observations, official reports produced by schools inspectors, instructional manuals, literary accounts and paintings, and polemical works generated by debates concerning musical childhoods.

Song schools in Medieval England

The popular view is that children in the medieval period were regarded as small adults, and that childhood was impoverished and disregarded by modern standards.

Much of this stems from the work of Philippe Ariès (1962) who believed that medieval children lived very dissimilar lives from their early-modern successors. More recent historians, however, have rebutted Ariès's assertions, and have gathered copious evidence to demonstrate that medieval people did have concepts of what childhood was: the arrival of children in the world was a notable event, and their upbringing and education were taken seriously (see Shahar, 1990; Orme 2001).

Opinions within the medieval Christian tradition were sharply polarized on whether children were channels of diabolical or divine influence. The belief in original sin, which could only be remitted through baptism, has to be balanced with the belief, rooted in the Christian tradition, in the original innocence of children (Heywood, 2001).

The Church was an all-powerful force, and in medieval England music education derived strength and privilege from its place within the liturgy and devotions of the church, although music itself, according to Augustine, was morally ambivalent and indeed could ensnare one (Mark, 1982).

The Judaeo-Christian tradition of psalm and hymn singing provided an important medium for worship, and the founding of the Schola Cantorum in Rome in the fourth century ensured firm and lasting connections between music, the liturgy, and education. The song schools subsequently set up throughout Europe for the purpose of disseminating Roman church music were to have a permanent effect on the general development of music teaching. Until the Reformation song schools were necessities for all monasteries and cathedrals. Generally speaking, children were admitted to these schools at the age of 7, and attended them until the age of 10 or 12 (Shahar, 1990). The founding of universities throughout western Europe from the twelfth century onwards led to an increase in grammar and song schools (Plummeridge, 2001).

But what kind of musical education did pre-Reformation choristers receive in such institutions? We have been provided with a detailed picture by Flynn (1995) drawing upon the evidence of indentures of Masters of Choristers in 11 major English and Scottish choral institutions dating from the mid-fifteenth century (see also Orme, 1978, 2003). The aim of choristers' training was not primarily musical; it was focused upon the liturgy, the performance of which demonstrated practically the way to live a virtuous Christian life. In addition to acquiring musical skills, choristers learned to read and write English and Latin, and their morals were based upon Christian teaching. The training was practical rather than academic: lessons were designed to reinforce the knowledge and expertise necessary for participation in the liturgy. The boys practised their lessons as a group, usually in one room, reciting and listening to others, and being corrected by the master.

From the evidence available, Flynn (1995) has listed the musical skills acquired by pre-Reformation choristers, which suggests a progressive order of attainment:

- 'Plainsong'. All students in the song schools, not only choristers, began their education at around 7 years of age with 'song', a combination of Latin grammar and chant. They learned to read and write, and memorized the psalms with their psalm tones and other liturgical texts such as Canticles. Solmization (singing by sol-fa syllables introduced by Guido at the beginning of the eleventh century) helped them to memorize intervals that they learned to sing in tune. They did not need to learn the letter names of notes nor how to read music in the early stages. However, the more advanced choristers would find the ability to read music preferable to additional memorizing. They learned how to read music by using the 'gamut', the sequence of note names over the three octaves of the human voice, which beginners had to commit to memory (see Rainbow, 1989).

- 'Pricksong'. The boys learned the note values and ligatures characteristic of mensural music (polyphonic music with specific time values as opposed to plainchant with free rhythm). In order to reinforce such learning, some ligature shapes (in which two or more notes were combined) were painted on one of the walls of the classroom at St George's Chapel, Windsor. A well-used way of learning mensuration was to sing canons.

- 'Figuration'. This was the singing of chant, in equal notes and regular mensuration for others to improvise against (see Morley, 1597/1952, pp. 169–170 for three ways of performing it).

- 'Faburden'. Singing in faburden, a form of improvisation on a chant, involved little more than doubling the chant a fourth above in the top voice and a third below in the third voice except at cadences. The cantus firmus was in the middle voice (Caldwell, 1991).

- 'Descant' was another more varied form of improvisation less dependent on parallelism. The boys began learning note against note counterpoint, while more advanced descanters would improvise two or more notes against each note of the chant, sometimes involving imitation.

- 'Square-note', apparently improvisation on a 'square'. A square originated as the lowest part in a polyphonic composition, and was used as the basis for an improvisation or a new notated composition.

- 'Counter', that is, improvising a melody below a chant, suitable for choristers who were older, singing in the lower range.

- 'Organ'. Older choristers learned to play the organ, in the course of which they applied to the keyboard descant skills originally acquired through vocal music.

It would be misleading to imply that these various disciplines were part of some kind of fixed and universal medieval curriculum. However, it is significant that things appear to have been taught in a more or less fixed order; teaching was certainly progressive. A student began with pre-existing material, first learning largely by memory, then by reading notation; next, others improvised while the student provided the part for them to improvise against ('figuration'); then the student learned to improvise himself, beginning with the most straightforward method ('faburden'). All this was achieved through the mind and the voice. The final stage was technology—the organ.

This outline shows that in the finest song schools usually connected with the great cathedrals, boys acquired a sophisticated musical education through a way of sequencing material so that they were able to develop their musical competence as quickly as possible, even though we are unsure about the extent to which their practice exemplified their teachers' intentions. We gain a rare glimpse, however, of the day-to-day realities of life in such institutions from a sermon preached on Christmas Day 1553 by the Boy Bishop, John Stubbs, himself a chorister. He admonished his fellow choristers for their behaviour in church, 'how rashly thei cum into quire without any reverence', and reprimanded the school master: 'Yf a scoler of the song scole syng out of tune, he is well wrong by the ears, or else well beatyn' (Harris 1939, pp. 119–120).

The song schools were not only placed in the grand institutions, they were also kept in many of the parishes of the land, frequently in humble circumstances (Thompson, 1942). For example, one London parish church, St Mary at Hill, had a choir school that was conducted in a separate chamber in 1523. The school had one or two forms and a desk, and the floor was covered with rushes. Some of the children were sent at the expense of the parishioners who paid for clothing, boots, and board in addition to tuition (Littlehales, 1905; Hanawalt, 1993). Chaucer's 'little clergeon' attended a song school in the *Prioress's Tale*, learning

> Swich maner doctrine as men used there,
> This is to seyn, to singen and to rede,
> As smale children doon in hir childhede
>
> in Lawson & Silver (1973, p. 69)

Song schools thus provided opportunities for boys, often from humble backgrounds, to specialize in music. We must recollect that only a tiny minority of boys would receive such instruction, and that essentially it provided an induction into the adult musical world, in which mastery of specialist skills was paramount. Whereas the Church recruited boys to do duties such as singing the liturgy in cathedrals, colleges, monasteries, friaries, or parish churches, girls could be utilized only in nunneries of which there were never more than 146 throughout England and Wales (Orme, 2001).

In England the Dissolution of the Monasteries between 1536 and 1540 saw the demise of the majority of song schools apart from those connected with cathedrals. The teaching of music declined in schools with the result that children of the poor lost their chance to develop their musical skills (Harris, 1939).

The medieval song schools of England provided a musical education based upon the comprehensive religious organizations that were the backbone of social life. Although for only a small minority of children these educational settings provided musical instruction sometimes of the highest order to a range of pupils from diverse social backgrounds. The underlying theological emphasis was on the doctrine of original sin, while the practical function of schooling was to furnish the liturgy appropriately.

Instrumental tuition in eighteenth century Britain

There is a general agreement among historians that from the late seventeenth century a new attitude towards children (and notions of childhood) began to manifest itself (Hendrick, 1997). The key to this change, according to Cunningham (1995) lay in the long-term secularization of attitudes to childhood and children, with a decline in belief in original sin. Some people began to see childhood not as a preparation for something else, but as a stage in life to be valued for its own sake.

In 1693 John Locke had published *Some thoughts concerning education*, which included an attack on the idea of infant depravity, and portrayed a new-born child's mind as a tabula rasa, a blank sheet of paper, a clean sheet. Implicit is a doctrine of egalitarianism, so different from the medieval outlook. Locke was a follower of Francis Bacon (Bantock, 1980) who maintained that the materials of knowledge should be placed before the senses, and that further enlightenment should derive from proper methods of instruction.

As far as schools were concerned, during this period children received little opportunity for musical experience, at least in England, where the arts came to be considered as a mere diversion. In fact it was the same John Locke who famously (or infamously) in 1684 allocated music the last place in his list of educational accomplishments (Rainbow, 1989).

However, private music instruction began to flourish. In this section I shall focus upon textbooks and manuals published in Britain between 1814 and 1830 in order to demonstrate how in the early stages of learning, young upper-class children were taught the rudiments of music, and their first steps in playing a musical instrument (Kassler, 1976). We need to recollect that musical ability was thought to be manifest in infants if they had a musical ear. Interestingly, aptitude was considered *a priori* to be inborn, and part of a child's 'organization'.

Once the factors of social rank and musical ability were decided, a child's first lessons in music began about the age of 5 or 6. The acquisition of musical knowledge was *a posteriori*, the mental faculty chiefly employed was the memory. Charles Burney writing in 1779 had pointed out:

> A child is not thought capable of profiting from the instructions of a music- master till five or six years old, though many have discovered an ear capable of being pleased with musical tones, and a voice that could imitate them much sooner ...in music the undirected efforts of an infant must be ...circumscribed: for without the aid of reason and perseverance he can only depend on memory and a premature delicacy and acuteness of ear for his guides.
>
> in Kassler (1976, p. 70)

Hence music teachers were concerned primarily to communicate facts suitable for impressing 'simple ideas' on their young pupils' memories. As the mind at this early stage was thought to be passive, various educational tools were devised to assist teachers in 'imprinting' these simple musical ideas. The most numerous were music instruction books. For infants these covered such elements as the stave, lines and spaces, leger lines, names of notes in different clefs, accidentals, rests, proportions, etc.

Along with musical facts infants were to acquire physical dexterity by singing, playing an instrument, or copying music. Instruction books included material pertaining to the body and the mind: fingering, sitting, scales, and arpeggios. The musical education of infants was patterned after their education in language, the elements being taught grammatically. In music, infants learned the different kinds of single elements (etymology) their union into larger structures (syntax) and writing correctly (orthography). These books (for example Keith's *A Musical Vade Mecum* c.1820; see Kassler, 1979) may be called the 'ABCdaria' (after ABC books) for they taught the musical alphabet. Some ABCdaria were in the form of a catechism, either as dialogue or question and answer. These tutors might also contain pictures and verses. There was, however, no room for rhetorical ornament. Universal concerns in all the instructional materials focused upon musical ciphers, the reduction of the number of musical characters and substituting them for symbols of a more universal application. The reform of musical notation was undertaken so that infants could remember more easily simple musical ideas.

Musical games connected with instruction have not been located before the 1790s, when new developments in educational theory held that the child should be amused as well as interested. Play was being prioritized: the earliest instructive game appears to be musical dominoes in 1793. Anne Gunn's *Instructions for playing musical games* (1801) (see Kassler, 1979) described how following each throw of the dice, two players were to compete by arranging on their separate boards the notes, clefs, chords, and key signatures called for. The intent was to make the learning of music rudiments amusing and instructive. There were also mechanical aids to assist good bodily habits in musical performance. The Hand Director or Chiroplast (1814) as featured in Logier's *Companion to the Royal Patent Chiroplast* of 1815 (see Kassler, 1979), was based on the physiological theory that part of the body cast into a mould while soft and tender will be better formed than if left to chance.

Music instruction, therefore, was patterned after the study of language where elementary grammar consisted of two domains, knowledge and practice. Musical knowledge pertained to the mind, practice to the body. The child learned by having the elements merely impressed on the memory by having the model placed before the senses. Further explication beyond naming was not required. In the practice of music children were encouraged by the teacher to inculcate correct bodily habits. Music instruction books and mnemonic aids impressed this musical knowledge on the mind.

There are examples from English eighteenth century paintings, drawings, and prints of representations of children from the middle and upper social orders making music. They show us some of the prevailing attitudes to musical childhoods. Leppert (1988) points out that portraits of male children at music, or in the proximity of musical instruments, are extremely rare. Those that do exist are concerned to establish maleness. Images associating boys with drums were acceptable, but there are very few that include keyboard instruments on account of their association with effeminacy. In contrast visual representations of girls at music, including keyboard instruments, are most common. Indeed singing and instrumental competence came to be regarded as worthy and graceful social skills especially for young women from the middle and upper classes in the seventeenth and eighteenth centuries.

In summary, with the Age of Reason came a more egalitarian outlook and the powerful notion of the child's mind as a tabula rasa. All this raised questions concerning *nature* vs. *nurture*. Musical knowledge was impressed upon the infant's memory, instruction became highly systematized and modelled upon language teaching. The place of music in schools declined, with the view that music was a mere diversion suited more for girls than boys.

Observing the teaching of school music in Europe in the late nineteenth century

An essential factor in the universalizing of childhood was the introduction of compulsory mass schooling in Europe in the 1870s and 1880s, 'the classic period in which childhood was transformed' (Hendrick, 1997). Compulsory schooling replaced wage earning as the accepted occupation for children aged five to about twelve and thirteen. The entire ideological apparatus of education lay in the proper segregation of children from adults, a 'truly national childhood', a childhood which was now, in a large measure, institutionalized and made into an age-graded condition. According to Hendrick (ibid) the majority opinion is that schooling during the 1870–1918 period was a fairly miserable experience with children separated from the community, and governed by regimentation and drill.

In England the 1870 Education Act ushered in compulsory schooling for children, and 'singing' became a compulsory subject in 1872 governed by specific codes. It is not surprising therefore that officials were dispatched to countries on the continent to see what lessons could be learnt or avoided. An independent and influential observer of school music abroad was John Spencer Curwen (1847–1916) who was the oldest son of John Curwen, the founder of the Tonic Sol-fa movement. J.S. Curwen received his musical education at the Royal Academy of Music in London and succeeded his father as president of the Tonic Sol-fa College in 1880, and thereafter was responsible for the exponential growth of the 'movement' (Simon, 1973). He made a number of independently organized visits to observe the teaching of music in schools over a period of 19 years between 1879 and 1901, ranging through Europe, Scandinavia, and North America. His intention was 'to ascertain what was the highest level reached in the subject in Europe; to know whether our children have as good capacity for singing as the children of other countries; to find whether the difficulties that our teachers meet in teaching singing were met with abroad' (Curwen 1901, p. iii). Curwen's accounts were intended for the information of supporters of the Tonic Sol-fa movement at home. Finally, these were assembled into a book *School Music Abroad* (1901). I shall draw upon his observations in Europe in order to present a picture of nineteenth century music education focusing on what children were learning and how they were learning. Curwen was very precise about the ages of pupils, and so I will present this material in order from the youngest to the oldest.

In Paris, Curwen found that the syllabus for communal schools was minutely laid down, and based on the fixed-doh system (i.e. 'doh' is always 'C'). For 6–8 year olds notation was explained in small doses, so that by the end of the second year in school, children were singing songs in unison by ear, and singing from notation those they had already learned by ear. They would also know the common signs of the staff, being still in the key of C. The 8–9 year olds were required to sing easy solfeggios (vocal exercises using sol-fa syllables) in unison, and easy two-part and unison songs. The keys of G and F major, E and D minor were specified, with dictation exercises and the introduction of the three-pulse measure. By the end of the following year pupils were supposed to sing at sight an easy piece containing simple time divisions and two changes of key.

The weekly 1-hour lessons included 10 minutes each of instruction on theory and dictation plus 20 minutes each on blackboard exercises and solfeggios, and songs with words. For 10–11 year olds, singing in two and three parts was required, as well as knowledge of such details as compound time, less used signs, and the enharmonic scale. Every lesson at this stage it was stated should start with singing a major, a minor and a chromatic scale.

To sample what Curwen saw in practice I shall focus upon his visits to Swiss and German schools. Although he found that the public schools on the Continent did not generally include an infant department, an agreeable exception was l'Ecole Enfantine de Malagnon in Geneva. The head teacher was doing all she could to carry out Froebel's principles with her children who were aged 3–7. Curwen observed a class of 24 children of 6–7 year olds who began to sing 'with tiny soft sweet tone' (Curwen, 1901, p. 140). He remarked on the absence of a piano. The singing was all by imitation, there were no exercises, and the lesson was mixed with games and with the topics of the stories and pictures. The songs were appropriate to the season, and the teachers 'headed the children in their marches and evolutions, singing with them and inspiring their organised play'. For Curwen (1901) 'it was a pretty sight, and one which dwelt in my mind' (p. 140).

Curwen noted that the Chevé system, based on cipher notation (Rainbow, 1989) had been taught in Geneva for 40 years, and that Rousseau, a Genevan himself, was the first to produce such a notation of figures. It depended upon the representation of the degrees of the rising major scale by the figures 1–7, where the figure 1 always referred to the keynote of a major key (see Rousseau, 1742). This is shown in Figure 20.1.

Figure 20.1 Rousseau's cipher notation from his *Dictionnaire de la Musique*.

Curwen found the influence of Chevé and cipher notation in the music teaching he witnessed in a girls high school on the Quai de la Poste, Geneva, a 'Secondary and Superior School for Young Ladies' where he observed a class of 12–13 year olds. The teacher was M. Henri Kling, a distinguished horn player and teacher. The blackboard behind the teacher's desk had two octaves of crotchets on the treble stave painted on it. Below this were a number of phrases painted in the Chevé figures. The girls sang phrases from the staff in C, then from the figures. M. Kling next sang to 'la' a phrase of 18 notes in C, which the girls wrote down in the Chevé notation. The time was eventually sorted, although the dictation of time, according to Curwen was found by the girls to be more difficult than the tune. The passage was finally copied into notebooks into staff notation. This dictée took 20 minutes. The last quarter of an hour was devoted to singing two-part songs from a collection in the Chevé notation. Four songs were given, and the Loreley was sung in German, the first foreign language song the French-Swiss learn.

In Zürich, Curwen visited a girls' secondary school close to the Grossmunster, and observed a class of thirty pupils aged 13–15 in an impressive lesson. After they had sung from their books a two-part solfeggio to alphabetical names, the pupils sight-read a simple E minor melody from the blackboard, and then tried it in the major key. A two-part song was sung, and after it the girls stood up one by one and answered questions on notes, rests, and intervals. This class was followed by one of 20 girls, aged 15–17, who began with long holding tones to 'laa', ascending by semitones, then the minor scale to alphabetical names. A difficult melody was written on the blackboard, with a tricky syncopation. The teacher accompanied well on the piano, but talked little himself. Intervals were discussed, followed by three-part singing exercises to 'laa'. The girls received 2 hours per week of music.

Curwen was critical of those schools that did not focus upon the teaching of sight-singing skills. In Berlin's Victoria Schule, a high school for girls, Curwen heard 18 year olds singing in four parts: 'the voices were pure and soft, and the lowest part of all seemed to me more resonant than we find in England' (Curwen, 1901, p. 9). Great expenditure of time was spent in rehearsing the separate parts, the different parts having only their own score, which led Curwen to comment acerbically that 'Blinkers on a horse prevent his seeing too much, and these single voice parts are the expression of feeble reading power' (p. 9). The teacher agreed that the girls could hardly read music at all. Their motets were unaccompanied. But while the single parts were being rehearsed 'the rest are yawning, whispering, nudging or staring' (p. 9).

At the Training College for Men teachers in Hamburg he observed a class of 25 'lads' of 18 years old. They took up Bertalotti's Solfeggios, which had sol-fa syllables printed under the staff. F sharps were very 'sore places' even after much prompting with the violin. The tune 'God speed the right' came next, sung to a drinking song. There were two tenor parts and two bass parts. There was a lot of repetition over a short phrase: 'time after time the violin led them through this passage, and rasped out the right notes against their wrong ones a second apart. The students 'began to gape and look bored' (Curwen, 1901, p. 26). The situation reminded Curwen of Herbart's observation 'Weariness is the cardinal sin of instruction' (p. 26). There evidently was plenty of weariness in the class while this piece was being learnt. The 'lads' had soft rich voices and the feeling for singing, but their reading power was practically nil—although Curwen noted that they had entered the school when they were 7. If the 11 years produced this result, a shorter time would do still less. Curwen admitted 'sight-reading is not the whole business of the teacher of singing, but choral music will never spread widely where new music has to be taught laboriously by ear' (p. 27).

What do we conclude from all this? That for the most part children were receiving a structured programme of tuition characterized by the imperatives of regimentation and drill. We should recollect that this reflected the general trend that pedagogical methods were governed by imperatives of codes and examinations, size of classes, attitudes about the status of children, and philosophies about what education should be preparing children for in adult life.

Most systematic instruction appeared to be based upon the fixed doh, but also included influences from Chevé. In those schools, which proved musically effective in Curwen's eyes, the pupils must have felt a progression through their school musical life, so that by the time they were 18 some of them were in classes singing in four parts. Curwen was convinced that the fixed-doh system itself was unsuitable for such teaching, compared with the tonic sol-fa method based upon the movable-doh. However, he also found a tendency in some schools to aim for vocal performance without sufficient background knowledge of notation, which meant the loss of musical independence. Curwen characterised this tension as 'the old conflict between technic and sensibility, which will never be settled' (p. iv). We will find this tension at the heart of our discussion of twentieth-century notions of music and childhood.

In the nineteenth century compulsory mass schooling derived from the hegemony of the Nation-State, progress demanded the active participation of all subjects (see Ramirez & Boli, 1994). With respect to the theme of independence/dependence, children became dependent as schooling replaced working. Mass schooling by its very nature was inclusive, and it developed a standardized curriculum dominated by regimentation and drill. Singing became a part of compulsory education in most of the countries of Europe. Ideally there was an age-related plan, leading from singing by ear, to singing at sight often in several parts. Curwen was convinced of the paramount need for a systematic pedagogical method for the effective teaching of sight singing.

Rediscovery of the primitive child in the twentieth century

A number of authorities have regarded the late nineteenth and early twentieth centuries as significant in the construction of modern childhood (Heywood, 2001). I shall focus on one particularly influential model as far as music education is concerned, derived from evolutionary theory: racial recapitulation (although a more vaguely defined version of it had been propounded previously by Rousseau, Pestalozzi, Froebel, and Herbart) (Gould, 1977). It is not surprising that Darwin's theory of evolution should have profoundly influenced views of childhood. It came to be believed that in their embryonic development individuals passed through stages similar to those through which their ancestors had evolved. The idea of racial recapitulation was thus developed. It stated that the ontogenesis of the individual, or the development of the individual, is a short and quick repetition (recapitulation) of phylogenesis, or the development of the tribe to which it belongs: ontogeny recapitulates phylogeny (Gould, 1977). This led to the theory of cultural epochs: 'The somewhat poetic idea, which certainly has biological analogy, that each child …passes through the same general stages that the race has passed through in its rise from savagery to civilisation.' (Cleverley & Phillips, 1976, p. 40).

This theory soon appeared as a basis for the school curriculum. One suggestion was that curriculum materials in each grade should draw the child along the path travelled by the race. By 1900 the doctrine of recapitulation was an unchallenged truth in the influential child study movement and championed by its leader, the American psychologist, G. Stanley Hall (1844–1924) (Selig, 2004). Essentially, the idea was that 'infancy, childhood and youth are three bunches of keys to unlock the past history of the race' (Cleverley & Phillips, 1976, pp. 41–42).

Within Hall's psychological theories, sound was the most primitive of our contacts with self and environment (see Rideout, 1982). Music was regarded as a primal element in humankind's mental constitution, and the best and truest expression of the pre-intellectual phase, comprising feeling, instinct and impulse (Hall, 1911). More specifically Hall identified three stages of development (Humphreys, 1985). The first (3–8 years) corresponded to the primitive man stage in evolution. Rhythm consequently should be emphasized as the most basic element in music teaching. The second stage (8–12 years) corresponded to the time between the simian and historic periods of evolution. This was the time for the development of thought and morals and the growth of skills, including musical ones. The third stage witnessed the continued development of character and emotions and an increasing interest in a variety of subjects. Musical and other types of drill were de-emphasized, in favour of an approach refined to an appreciation of cultural history.

Indeed it was Hall who wrote the foreword to the first edition of the book by the American music educator Satis N.Coleman (1878–1960) *Creative Music for Children: A plan of training based on the natural evolution of music including the making and playing of instruments dancing–singing–poetry* (1922). Coleman was an innovative music educator who later worked at the progressive Lincoln School in New York (see also, Cremin, 1964; Boston, 1992; Volk, 1996). While not attempting to support or discuss what she called 'the once popular Recapitulation Theory', Coleman nevertheless believed that most primitive peoples were musical, and the music employed by them was a necessity of life. In our midst, she continued, it is the children who are the primitives, they are musical in the beginning, but this tendency does not always survive their training. She believed that her young pupils were little savages, and this gave Coleman her mission: 'Being little savages, they can understand savage music. I shall find the child's own savage level, and lift him gradually up to higher forms…The natural evolution of music shall be my guide in leading the child from the simple to the complex.' (Coleman, 1922, p. 29).

In her book Coleman describes how by their own creative work children shall experience the most important stages in the evolution of music. Her experiment proper began in October 1918 after a summer of preliminary experiment with two children aged 5 and a half, and 7 and a half. Others aged 3–9 joined them. There was a weekly lesson of 1 hour, but some children came four times a week, others twice. After the first year, Saturday lessons were also scheduled.

The children made percussion instruments first 'as primitive peoples do' (Coleman, 1922, p. 39), then ventured into making among others the Pipes of Pan, Shepherd's pipe, Ocarinas, Squash leaf oboes, Petunia blossom oboes, cornstalk fifes, Cocoa nut fiddles, and dulcimers.

Coleman then emphasized movement and rhythm: 'Many dances of primitive peoples are excellently suited to little children' (p. 84). The children invented new steps and pantomimes, improvised to music almost daily, made dance dramatizations of fairy tales, poems and original stories and impersonated natural phenomena.

After a clear rhythmic grounding came singing and voice control for the children. Coleman (1922) believed that although the union of song and dance was almost universal among primitive peoples, all primitive music stressed rhythm rather than melody. In its turn, singing was more elemental than playing: 'Most savage children are trained in keenness of ear perception' (p. 103). She drew on the writings of a British music historian, J.F. Rowbotham, whose key work was *A history of music to the time of the Troubadors* (1885). Rowbotham believed that the story of vocal music commenced with a one-note stage, and he cited the inhabitants of Tierra del Fuego as living examples of primitive peoples emerging from that period: he claimed this was followed historically by a two-note period, later the third note was added and so on. As an 'evolutionist' he followed the fashionable anthropological method of treating contemporary 'primitive' music as a survival from the past, 'a kind of living fossil' (Blacking, 1987, p. 8; for a discussion of Rowbotham's ideas see Zon, 2000, pp. 193–120).

These ideas permeated Coleman's thinking and practice. For instance, after improvising chants, her pupils 'naturally' began to sing Mother Goose rhymes to melodies of three notes, then progressed to the pentatonic scale (see Figure 20.2).

Figure 20.2 Dorianne's *Goosey Gander* from Coleman, 1922.

Coleman employed numerical names: "'Do-re-mi" is a foreign language to the young child, and complicates his singing progress' (Coleman 1922, p. 107). Indeed she believed that notation should be postponed until after the child has had wide experience in making music. As the child plays by imitation and by ear, no symbols whatever are needed in the beginning. The first thought of written signs usually comes when a child had made up a little song 'which he plays and would like to remember, and thinks he might forget' (p. 118). Composing was a definitely prescribed activity in each phase of the work. Song improvisations really began in mere singing conversations, making up songs on the spot.

Coleman (1922) is worth quoting in this summary of her philosophy:

> Those early years of the child's development correspond to the stage of primitive music and the simplest of instruments. The music of the childhood of the race belongs to him while he is yet a little child ...Heretofore in most of our instrumental training for children we have forced the child to skip a very important and a very broad stage in his indigenous evolution. We have urged him while still in swaddling clothes to take on adult culture, as one who would try to teach a savage to drive an automobile before he has had any simpler experiences with machinery. (p. 154).

The theory of racial recapitulation has had a lasting effect upon education (see Malvern, 1994, for an account of its impact upon art education), although in the USA the child study movement was superseded by the powerful progressive education movement (Cremin, 1964; Humphreys, 1985). In music education, however, its influence was still apparent in the 1960s in England as we can trace in the educational writings of Wilfrid Mellers (b.1914). It was Mellers, a distinguished academic and composer, who founded the Department of Music at the University of York in 1964, which subsequently gained an international reputation for its adventurous curriculum and for its espousal of the importance of music education, specifically in the work of John Paynter (1970) who is known for his work in encouraging creative music making in schools.

Mellers wrote three articles for the *Musical Times* in 1964 under the heading 'Music for 20th century Children' in which he expounded his beliefs in the nature of childhood and musical experience. Underpinning these articles is a sociological and psychological view of the law of Recapitulation, with progress through childhood to adulthood recapping the primitive, the medieval, and the positivistic stages of development (Boas, 1966). In a related publication, *The Resources of Music* (Mellers, 1969), which in essence is a musical working out of these ideas, it is significant that Mellers referenced the work of the music historian Curt Sachs whose thinking bears similarities with earlier musical 'evolutionists' (Blacking, 1987).

In the first of his *Musical Times* series of articles, Mellers (1964a) addressed 'magic and ritual in the junior school'. His main point was: 'as children, we start as little savages, and must do if we are to grow to consciousness. If we miss out the savage phase in childhood, it will find an outlet later on, at the wrong time, in the wrong place.' (Mellers 1964a, p. 342).

He pointed out that a return to primitive intuition had been one of the mainsprings of music since Wagner's Tristan. Stravinsky and Bartók used rhythm in a directly corporeal manner. The New World avant-garde from Varèse to Partch, Cage and Feldman manifest 'aboriginal childishness still more unequivocally' (Mellers, 1964a, p. 343). Children recognized in Cage's prepared piano music an experience parallel to their own, and indeed his later music was of a type that the child, given appropriate facilities, would create from his or her own subconscious.

Carl Orff, according to Mellers, explored the rebirth of melody and achieved a liberation of corporeal rhythm. *Schulwerk* is music as inseparable from action: 'The mythology of the child's world, of the rune and nursery rhyme, is the only wonder-creating magic that is still available to us in our urban society...Orff's children's music is thus a necessary and blessedly innocent renewal of pagan delight, whereby the senses are enriched and the limbs rejoiced.' (p. 344).

After the first and 'pagan' phase of children's musical awareness, Mellers (1964b) considered the dramatic conflict characteristic of Christianity. Orff's undulating organum-like triads are harmony before puberty, while the homophonic part songs of Peter Maxwell-Davies are an embryonic consciousness in which the parts move in restricted compass and in very close harmony (note the evolutionary correspondences), as though the music were half eager to escape from the innocence of the monodic state, 'and this must be why children, growing through puberty, could recognise it as particularly their music' (p. 422).

In his final article for the series, 'The Teenager's World', Mellers (1964c) asked, what happens as we cross the borderline from childhood to adolescence, and then to an adult state? He concluded that neither Orff, Kodály, nor Britten really addressed the teenager's world. Orff's music for adolescents seemed inadequate, Kodály's music was inseparable from his own creativity and the culture in which he lived and worked, while the popularity of Britten's beautiful and moving music for children was largely a middle class phenomenon. Instead, Mellers concluded, we should look to jazz and blues as urban folk arts whose creative essence lay in their honesty.

We see in all this discussion a linking of the child with the primitive. It develops the idea that teaching should follow the child's innate and natural development, but this view of the child was also central to the modernist view of 'primitivism'. Musically, this accords with Mellers' view of musical childhood which he connects with the music of those 'American aboriginals' (his words) of the twentieth century, John Cage and Harry Partch.

Mellers' writings on education appear to have had an impact upon the thinking that lay behind the so-called creative music movement in UK schools and then elsewhere in the 1960s and 1970s. For example, the influential writer on music education, Christopher Small (1968) aligned himself with reformers such as Mellers and Paynter, stating that they were bearing out the biologist's truism that 'ontogeny recapitulates phylogeny'. The individual showed the various phases of the evolution of the species. As music teachers we must co-operate with the recapitulative process: 'We are trying to do nothing less than re-establish the lifeline to the subconscious and harness its energies' (p. 304).

It is somewhat surprising that the racial theory of recapitulation, which no longer has any currency (Malvern, 1994), should have had such long lasting influence in music teaching. Musically we now comprehend that music does not simply progress from the simple to the complex (Blacking, 1987), and that there is a danger in equating the natural with the socially limited: the potentialities of human nature become ignored.

Rideout (in Boston, 1992) makes the same point, 'the evolutionary theory as Hall defined it did not allow for active self-interest or will' (p. 95). Nevertheless in spite of its flaws, recapitulation 'became the strongest argument for child-centered education' (Gould, 1977, p. 155), which reached its climax in the 1960s and 1970s.

This offshoot of the romantic conception of childhood attempted to establish a connection between the primitive and the child. This resulted in a movement that tried to encourage a flowering of creativity and expressive freedom for children, and also a relationship with contemporary musical developments. However, we need to bear in mind that, although as a racial theory, recapitulation is no longer respected, the innate/learned question remains central to considering the nature of creativity and its place in musical experience.

Conclusions

What I have attempted to demonstrate in these examples from the historical record is that the character of institutionalized music education is always related to ideas about what childhood is like and how the child develops. Cultural ideas about childhood will have a structuring effect on educational practices: different cultural ideas about childhood will produce significantly different educational ideas and practices. However, we also need to bear in mind that institutional arrangements construct as much as reflect childhood and perspectives on it, so the ideas and the institutions are always in some kind of tension. An exploration of ways in which changes in music education both mirror and shape the shifts in the historical constructions of musical childhoods should help music educators to become more aware of the cultural influences that impinge on the construction of childhood, and more specifically to understand better how children can be encouraged to fulfil their musical potential.

Acknowledgements

My thanks to Hugh Benham and Marie McCarthy for pointing me towards key references, and to Nicholas Bannan, Hugh Benham, Kevin Brehony, Vic Gammon, Stephanie Pitts, and the anonymous reviewers for helpful comments on previous drafts.

References

Ariès, P. (1962). *Centuries of childhood*. London: Jonathan Cape (Trans. R. Baldick).

Bantock, G. H. (1980). *Studies in the history of educational thought 1: Artifice and nature 1350–1765*. London: George Allen & Unwin.

Blacking, J. (1987). '*A commonsense view of all music*': *Reflections on Percy Grainger's contribution to ethnomusicology and music education*. Cambridge: Cambridge University Press.

Boas, G. (1966). *The cult of childhood*. London: The Warburg Institute, University of London.

Boston, S. (1992). *Satis N.Coleman (1878–1961): Her career in music education*. Doctoral dissertation. University of Maryland College Park.

Caldwell, J. (1991). *The Oxford history of English music*. Vol. 1: *From the beginnings to c.1715*. Oxford: Clarendon Press.

Cleverley, J. & Phillips, D. C. (1976). *From Locke to Spock: Influential models of the child in modern western thought*. Melbourne: Melbourne University Press.

Coleman, S. N. (1922). *Creative music for children: A plan of training based on the natural evolution of music including the making and playing of instruments dancing-singing-poetry*. New York: G. P. Putnam's Sons.

Cremin, L. A. (1964). *The Transformation of the school: Progressivism in American education 1876–1957*. New York: Alfred A. Knopf.

Cunningham, H. (1995). *Children and childhood in Western society since 1500*. London: Longman.

Curwen, J. S. (1901). *School music abroad: A series of reports on visits to schools in Prussia, Saxony, Bavaria, Austria, Switzerland, France, Belgium, Holland, Sweden, Norway, Denmark, Italy and American during the years 1882 to 1901*. London: J. Curwen.

Flynn, J. (1995). The education of choristers in England during the sixteenth century. In J. Morehen (ed.), *English choral practice 1400–1650* (pp. 180–199). Cambridge: Cambridge University Press.

Gould, S. J. (1977). *Ontogeny and phylogeny*. Cambridge MA: The Belknap Press of Harvard University Press.

Hall, G. S. (1911). *Educational problems*. 2 volumes. New York: D. Appleton.

Hanawalt, B. (1993). *Growing up in medieval London: The experience of childhood in history*. New York: Oxford University Press.

Harris, D. G. T. (1939). Musical education in Tudor times. *Proceedings of the Royal Musical Association*, **65**, 109–139.

Hendrick, H. (1997). *Children, childhood and English society, 1880–1990*. Cambridge: Cambridge University Press.

Heywood, C. (2001). *A history of childhood: Children and childhood in the west from medieval to modern times*. Cambridge: Polity.

Humphreys, J. (1985). The child-study movement and public school music education. *Journal of Research in Music Education*, **33**(2), 79–86.

Kassler, J. C. (1976). Music made easy to infant capacity. *Studies in Music*, **10**, 67–78.

Kassler, J. C. (1979). *The science of music in Britain, 1714–1830: A catalogue of writings, lectures and inventions*. 2 volumes. New York: Garland.

Lawson, J. & Silver, H. (1973). *A social history of education in England*. London: Methuen.

Leppert, R. (1988). *Music and image: Domesticity, ideology and socio-cultural formation in eighteenth century England*. Cambridge: Cambridge University Press.

Littlehales, H. (ed.), (1905). *The medieval records of a London city church (St. Mary at Hill) A.D. 1420–1559*. London: published for the Early English Text Society by Kegan Paul, Trench, Trübner & Co.

Malvern, S. (1994). Recapping on recapitulation: Or how to primitivize the child, *Third Text. Third World Perspectives on Contemporary Art and Culture*, **27**, 21–30.

Mark, M. L. (1982). *Source readings in music education history*. New York: Schirmer.

Mellers, W. (1964a). Music for 20th-century children: 1: Magic and ritual in the junior school. *Musical Times*, May, 342–345.

Mellers, W. (1964b). Music for 20th-century children: 2: From magic to drama. *Musical Times*, June, 421–427.

Mellers, W. (1964c). Music for 20th-century children: 3: The teenager's world. *Musical Times*, July, 500–505.

Mellers, W. (1969). *The resources of music: Vocal score and commentary*. Cambridge: Cambridge University Press.

Morley, T. (1597/1952). *A plain and easy introduction to practical music* (R. Alec Harman). London: J. M. Dent.

Orme, N. (1978). The early musicians of Exeter cathedral. *Music and Letters, LIX,* 395–410.

Orme, N. (2001). *Medieval children.* New Haven: Yale University Press.

Paynter, J. (1970). *Sound and silence: Classroom projects in creative music.* Cambridge: Cambridge University Press.

Plummeridge, C. (2001). Music in schools (2nd edn). In S. Sadie & J. Tyrrell (eds), *The new Grove dictionary of music and musicians* (pp. 614–629). London: MacMillan.

Rainbow, B. (1989). *Music in educational thought and practice: A survey from 800 BC.* Aberystwyth: Boethius.

Ramirez, F. O. & Boli, J. (1994). The political institutionalisation of compulsory education: The rise of compulsory schooling in the western cultural context. In J. A. Mangan (ed.), *A significant social revolution: Cross-cultural aspects of the evolution of compulsory education* (pp. 1–20). London: The Woburn Press.

Rideout, R. R. (1982). On early applications of psychology in music education. *Journal of Research in Music Education* 30(3), 141–150.

Rousseau, J.-J. (1742/1982). *Project concerning new symbols for music.* Translated and introduced by Bernarr Rainbow. Kilkenny: Boethius.

Rowbotham, J. F. (1885). *A history of music.* London: Trübner & Co. 3 vols.

Selig, D. (2004). Granville Stanley Hall. In P. Fass (ed.), *Encyclopedia of children and childhood in history and society* (pp. 413). New York: MacMillan Reference.

Shahar, S. (1990). *Childhood in the middle ages.* London: Routledge.

Simon, H. (1973). *Songs and words: A history of the Curwen press.* London: George Allen & Unwin.

Small, C. (1968). Music in a liberal education forum—3. *Music in Education,* **31,** *November/December,* 302–304.

Thompson, A. H. (1942). *Song schools in the middle ages.* London: SPCK & Humphrey Milford. Church-Music Occasional Papers No. 14.

Volk, T. (1996). Satis Coleman's 'creative music'. *Music Educators Journal,* **May,** 31–33, 47.

Zon, B. (2000). *Music and metaphor in nineteenth-century British musicology.* Aldershot: Ashgate.

CHAPTER 21

GLOBAL PRACTICES

PATRICIA SHEHAN CAMPBELL

Children are learning the music of their heritage, and of children's culture, from their earliest childhood experiences. Across the globe, they know similarities in their early developing musical expressions and interests, and in the manner through which they acquire music. Yet even as they grow musically in ways that are common across cultures, they are also musically enculturated so as to reflect the local facets of their homes, families, and neighbourhood communities. They are trained and entrained, educated and schooled, according to national policies and cultural preferences.

This chapter examines the acquisition by children of musical knowledge in selected environments, with attention to the role of music within their society, and the means of transmission that are traditionally practised by adults in the process of passing on musical repertoire and techniques, behaviours, and values. In exploring global practices of children's learning of music, and through music their learning of social mores, reference will be made to the cultural underpinnings of children's own playful repertoire, as well as to their musical heritage of adult-influenced culture in which they are enculturated and schooled. Attention will be drawn to cases of music learning engagements among children and youth in Ireland, Japan, the Philippines, Thailand, within North American First Nations circumstances, and in a selection of societies spread across eastern and western Africa. While the promise of a full global scope on the subject is tantalizing, it was necessary to select out and only briefly sample musical cultures, with the aim of highlighting events and behaviours in the process of transmitting and acquiring music. The writer's own North American perspective may surface here in references to geographic places and peoples 'off the beaten track' in the Americas, yet the fieldwork of notable scholars (often American ethnomusicologists) of various music cultures across the world is consulted and cited for issues and insights. Similarities and distinctions will be evident, and prominent techniques will be traced to their use in formal settings such as school and the one-on-one private lesson where musical training is known for its successful process of teacher–student interactions.

Music learning by degrees of formality

There are constructs to consider in a discussion of children's global practices in music learning, each of them definitive yet also somewhat overlapping and adding meaning to the other. A spectrum of learning may be found, extending from the most formal means to the non-formal processes found beyond institutionalized settings, all the way to completely informal, indirect, and unintentional forms of learning. Learning may be defined through a differentiation of it as: (1) formal, occurring through a teacher's intervention in highly structured settings such as school; (2) non-formal and only partly guided, occurring outside institutionalized settings through the prompting of non-consecutive directives, frequently by expert musicians to novices; and (3) enculturative, occurring naturally, non-consciously, and without direct instructional activity of any sort (Campbell, 2001).

The first realm of learning is thoroughly linked to teachers' selection, presentation, and rehearsal of students in schools in explicit knowledge and skills to be learned, while the second, non-formal, process may be a father's occasional coaching at home of his daughter in the bar chords on a guitar, or a neighbour's infrequent modelling for a youngster of repertoire and techniques at the piano. In the last realm, enculturative learning, the psychic structure of a societal group is passed from one generation to the next through a cultural immersion process, so that a child develops an implicit understanding of the knowledge and values of a repertoire by nature of his membership and participation in that society. Language and communications, including self-identity, gender role, kinaesthetics (body language), and daily rhythms are learned but not taught; they are acquired in ways that are automatic and outside children's own conscious awareness. These cultural patterns appear always to have been there as part of the ambience of a people's lifestyle, permeating the manner and style of their thought, expression, and behaviour (Hall 1992).

Further differentiations and descriptions of learning have been offered: apprenticeships and live-in private study with a teacher (as in the case of Thai *piphat* houses or Indian *gharanas*) outside of institutionalized settings, growth-oriented experiences that are arranged within a community (such as Suzuki instruction), and socialization, the process by which a group shares its beliefs and values in a learner- (rather than teacher-) constructed learning experience (Jorgensen, 1997). There may be further gradations than these, yet it is useful to consider them as degrees of formality in the means by which music is transmitted and acquired. These spectral points of music learning, along with particular techniques of pedagogy and reception by children and other learners, will find their illustration in the selected cultures described below.

Multiple bases for the study of children

Through a diversity of disciplines, music learning as global practice can be explored, and a conceptualization of its features can be understood. Scholars of anthropology, ethnomusicology, sociology, and (music) education are only beginning to awaken to the study of children from their own perspective, and as such are discovering their perceived beliefs, interests, and needs. Even while Rousseau's *Emile* drew attention two centuries ago to the unique conditions of children and childhood, as a group they have always existed on the sidelines and in the margins of disciplines. A movement is afoot to know children as they naturally are within their local social and cultural environments, with intent to piece their culture-specific cases together in order to develop a broader and more global understanding of them. The recent emphases given by these various disciplinary fields to the study of children are worthy of consideration prior to a review of culture cases that probe music learning practices, if only to explain the scant attention that children have received in the past concerning their own cultural, artistic, and specifically musical expressions. In many instances, they have been swept together with adult novices and beginning students in a discussion of the transmission of a musical tradition, even when there may be reason to believe that children learn in ways that are unique to them.

Tracing the evolution of children's music and its relationship (or not) to adult culture is a task ahead that may require the expertise of scholars from multiple disciplines. How does the music of a Malay child differ from that of children in Labrador, or Yoruba culture? Will these children sound alike as members of child culture, or will they vary by way of their socio-cultural influences? In fact, will Malay children differ also in the music that they express, based upon the region in which they live, and the economic and social condition of their families? What features of the mature 'adult' music of a culture are found in children's music? How is children's music more alike than different, cross-culturally? When does children's music end and youth music begin? How do the unique facets of contemporary children's music and culture hang on and shape adult music? Such questions are likely directives for scholarly study of children and their expressive selves.

Children, their developmental processes and practices, and their means of growing into the knowledge systems of their culture and society, were never central to the scholarly concerns of anthropologists. They were marginalized in anthropological descriptions of social organization and kinship, individual personality and collective culture, and have even been dismissed altogether by adult 'outsiders' to their culture (Schwartzman, 2001). Where children did surface in the literature, it was often as a means of gauging their imitation of adults or tracing the origin and development of adult behaviours. Typically, anthropologists were concerned with what adults do to children, and what adults give to children or make for children. An 'anthropology of children' is a fairly recent phenomenon within the field, in which children are increasingly examined for who they are within culture, and even as their own culture (Hardman, 1973; Stephens, 1995; Goldman, 1998). Where anthropologists once used children as specimens for examining, collecting, and measuring culture, frequent and more rigorous 'child-focused studies' (Benthall, 1992) in anthropology are beginning to be aimed at understanding children themselves. In the last decade, studies of children for their family and peer relationships, household activity, school achievement, spiritual development and religious beliefs reflect and foreshadow a deeper commitment to the study of children by anthropologists.

Likewise, an 'ethnomusicology of children' is only just beginning to emerge (Campbell, 1998; Minks, 2002). Early studies of musical culture assumed that children passively received the artistic and linguistic expressions from adults, participating in the song and dance that came 'from above to below'. Children were left out of descriptions of a musical culture, as they were viewed by ethnomusicologists as incomplete in their representation of adult expressive practices. Diffusionist scholars, mostly active as folklorists (if not anthropologists at the edge of ethnomusicology), collected children's songs to examine as the source of understanding not just the concept of 'child as primitive' but also the 'primitive as child'. A study of their songs was considered a way of knowing children as early 'stages' of human development, thus a means of examining theories of socio-cultural evolution. Cross-cultural comparisons of children's musical expressions surfaced occasionally in ethnomusicology, if only to seek a more homogeneous child culture that transcends specific music cultures

(Herzog, 1950; Brailiou, 1984). Socialization of music-cultural norms has been of interest to scholars who contribute to an enculturative paradigm, where adult-to-child socio-cultural education is examined for its influences in raising (musical) citizens within communities (Waterman, 1956; Blacking, 1967). In the last decade, however, border crossings by music educators employing an ethnomusicological method have brought attention to children's musical expressions as a means of studying their patterns of thought and social behaviour (Campbell, 2003).

As in anthropology and ethnomusicology, children were less ignored by sociologists than minimalized and moved to the rim of more central concerns. They were considered more for what can be known about adult society rather than for who they are in their current lives, needs, and desires (Corsaro, 1997). Rather than viewing children in the process of constructing their own social worlds, sociologists typically examined their socialization, the processes by which they are shaped by family and passively developed into adult members of their society. Early work of a behaviouristic mode gave way to a study of their cognitive development (best represented in the work of Jean Piaget), after which a socio-cultural view was formulated of their internalization of culture (as in Vygotsky's approach). (While the two theorists were contemporaries, it was not until Vygotsky's work was translated into English that his perspective on broader cultural contexts of children became influential beyond a Russian-speaking readership.) Piagetian thought emphasized developmental outcomes, however, with little attention to the complexity of children's own social structures, their collective activities, and their membership as active participants in both children's and adult cultures.

An understanding of children as children, as having their own identities, growing in the midst of their own peer culture, in the locus of their roles within the family, and under the influence or through interaction with mediated forces, is yet within the realm of sociological method to discover. Some sociologists are providing frameworks for studying the status of children and childhood, constructing relevant metatheories and suitable methodologies (James et al., 1998; Mayall, 2002). Such perspectives would be well-suited to music-education research, in which the study of children at musical play and in non-formal learning circumstances might lend insight to their academic and social–emotional behaviours at school. A sociological approach would be likely to shed light on children's musical experiences within families and peer groups, and a pastiche of local cases might provide a global understanding of their sociomusical nature.

Research by music teacher-scholars

Music education scholarship has been concerned with the musical achievement of children and adolescents, and the instructional procedures and curricular values of teachers within elementary and secondary school music courses and in tertiary programmes of music and music teacher education. Topics for study in the field have included children's development of music perception abilities, their singing skills, and their capacities as instrumentalists, composers (and improvisers), and eurhythmic 'movers' and dancers. Secondary school students have been less likely subjects than elementary students, although some attention is paid to skill development and attitudes of students in choral and instrumental ensembles.

Research has also concentrated on the pre-service training of university students as musicians and teachers, and of practising teachers' attitudes and in-service training. Clearly, music education scholarship has been centred on the outcomes of formal instruction, with attention to teachers as curriculum designers, communicators, conductors, and facilitators, and their students as beneficiaries of this instruction. Much less attention has been paid to their non-formal and informal music-learning processes and children's natural means of learning through socialization and play (Marsh, 1997; Campbell, 1998; Harwood, 1998). British scholars working within the overlaps of sociology, psychology, and education are notable for their attention to children's socialization in music and informal music learning processes, as well as to their emergent identities as performing musicians, listeners, and consumers of popular forms of mediated music (Hargreaves & North, 1997; Juslin & Sloboda, 2001; MacDonald *et al.*, 2002). The examination of children's 'musical incubation' and musical engagement at home and in school has been a developing interest among Scandinavian scholars, too, notably Bjorkvold's *The Muse Within* (1992). Yet global practices of children's music and music learning have not been addressed systematically. An understanding of children's natural inclinations and interests, and their interactions with siblings, peers, and various adults in (and beyond) musical venues may lead to understanding effective avenues for their in-school learning of musical skills, repertoire, and overall knowledge.

Questions of children's views, experiences, and behaviours are increasingly being put to children by disciplinary scholars, so as to investigate their sense of themselves, and of the society and culture in which they live. Adjustments of theoretical and methodological orientations are beginning to bring out the expressive voice of children on their thoughts and actions. Such developments are long overdue, however, such that an understanding of cross-cultural patterns of children's music learning now comes largely through the scholarship on music and its transmission among adults. This adult-oriented perspective will become clear in a recounting of culture-cases that address the manner in which music learning unfolds for young people, and by extension how it is taught and transmitted in a selection of traditions and locations in the world. Running through the descriptive text as a central strand are fieldwork observations of children at the edge of adult culture, learning by doing, living in musical worlds that are steered and directed by adults, listening intently or lapping up the soundscape into their daily lives. There is an acknowledgement of music across the world as an aural expression, too, and thus the aural–oral components will be noted as prominent in the means by which it is transmitted to and acquired by children. Despite the mostly marginal mention of children in the extant scholarship on music in and as culture, a careful telling and interpretation of it may offer provocative points in study of global practices of the child as musician.

Lilting the legacy of a cultural heritage (Ireland)

Irish tunes, from sung ballads to the jigs, hornpipes, and reels of flutes and fiddles, have long been learned by ear. The traditional transmission and learning process is a social one, where novice and accomplished musicians alike have continued a traditional give-and-take process through the sociomusical realm of the group session, and in the fashion of a personalized lesson with an expert musician. Musical elders act as role models, offering to young and less-experienced singers and players the musical repertoire and the stylistic nuances and technicalities of their performance. They pass on social behaviour and history as well, in which the 'Celtic Tiger' character of a postmodern and economically successful Ireland can be viewed as but a recent development away from the rich traditions of a long-standing rural agrarian society.

Children are naturally there in the midst of family music-making in traditional Ireland, in those families with members who have for decades and even centuries fiddled, played flute, pipes, harp, or concertina, or sung *sean-nos* style. They are there also for celebrations of weddings, christenings, holidays, and family reunions at which music and dance are prominent features. They may participate in the equally festive occasions of the wake, when the memory of the deceased is honoured in the family home and tribute is paid through song and sessions lasting long into the night and over several days. Like the air they breathe, music surrounds the children of professional and amateur musicians in Ireland, and the melodies become a part of their natural sonic fabric. In the changing scene of a contemporary Ireland, adults and children, including those with no past family history in musical practice, are finding their musical selves as an important component of their Irish identity (M. O'Suilleabhain, personal communication).

Professional performers recall house parties as one important context of their musical learning. Mary McNamara, a concertina player growing up in the west-coast county of Clare, recalled that her father would take the children to his sessions: '. . . he would go to different houses . . . maybe twice a week and we'd sit down and we'd listen to these musicians. And listen to the stories they had to tell, listen to them playing. We'd have the tea and the corncake and all the rest, and then we'd play a few tunes with them, might dance a set' (Hast & Scott, 2004, p. 44). As in the case of so many Irish musicians who grew up with the music as part of their family activity, her participation as a child at these musical house parties consisted mostly of listening. The music was just part of a scene that mixed well with visits with family and neighbours, conversation, dancing, and tea.

Just as it is natural to listen, it follows that children living within an environment where Irish traditional music is actively performed also 'pick up' instruments to play. Pennywhistles are sometimes played by children as an entry-point to instrumental music, as they are useful in unloading the tunes that settle in the ear from countless listening occasions. Some pick up the fiddle, or transfer tunes from pennywhistle to the Irish flute, and girls might be drawn to the concertina as an acceptable woman's instrument. Years of listening to the elders in their informal playing together form the basis of their repertoire and sense of style, so that performance can advance more rapidly than if they had not absorbed the music. Children may graduate into lessons with more expert players, and of course continue to learn within the sociomusical realm of the session.

With the growth of Irish national identity in the early part of the twentieth century, the markers of Irish culture—its Gaelic language and its Catholic religion—were promoted in government-sponsored schools for children and youth. This promotion of the Irish national language as part of state policy led to the support of traditional Irish song. By the early 1930s, Irish song and the liturgical repertoire of the Catholic Church were widespread in the national schools (McCarthy, 1999). Pennywhistles were an additional development in school music instruction, so that Irish song and common tunes could be performed together in class groups of students playing monophonically *en masse* under the tutelage of their teacher. Thus it was that children at large and far beyond the families of musicians came to know in a formal fashion a standard musical repertoire. Such a system of musical education is continuing in some schools, even as curricular changes have also entered the scene to include Western art music and occasionally other world traditions as well.

One of the strongest contemporary supports for the continuation of traditional music outside school, and a means of musically training children and youth of Ireland in their cultural music is the organization known as *Comhaltas Ceoltoiri Eireann* (or just 'Comhaltas'). Established in 1951, the organization seeks to promote Irish traditional music, dance, and language nationally and abroad, by motivating the young to remain actively involved in learning these traditions. The funding of more than 400 branches in Ireland and internationally is based largely on government grants, which thus finance the competitions that occur at county, regional, provincial, and all-Ireland levels. The competitions include all major traditional instruments, 'lilting' (singing vocables to the dance tunes), Irish and English singing, and are divided into age levels to suit those children under 12 years, youth from 12 to 15, from 15 to 18, and over 18. The Comhaltas branches are responsible for organizing the community schools, arranging sessions, teaching the music, and preparing the young musicians for competitions. The songs and tunes are selected by Comhaltas, and so both the musical content and its means of transmission are in the hands of the organization to preserve or modify.

Living old and new 'traditions' (Japan)

In Japan, where Westernization has been an integral part of Japanese identity since the late nineteenth century, children have within their school music repertoire a set of Western orchestral and chamber works to perform and appreciate and songs translated to Japanese from English, French, German, and other languages of the world. In after-school programmes, many opt for experiences in wind band performance, where musical standards are high and competition can be fierce. Their knowledge of their own Japanese musical traditions and song repertoire has been minimal, due to priorities set by the Ministry of Education to promote 'basic musical skill' and 'encourage children's love of music' through a Western-styled repertoire that has been a measure of excellence in musical education for nearly a century (Takizawa, 1997). Yet some path-breaking developments by Japanese educators and ethnomusicologists are beginning to redirect materials and methods of teaching to musical genres, repertoire, and processes beyond the West, including Japan's own unique instrumental, musical theatre, and *minyo* (folk song) traditions. Thus, despite the enormous success of Western art music in Japanese schooling, a curricular shift is now in progress to raise young people to understand their Japanese musical identity as well as to know a broader and more global view of musical cultures.

When Americans first arrived to Japan in 1868 and for the following several decades of frequent exchanges between Japan and the West, a grand assortment of musical instruments, styles, and explicit pieces were introduced to children in Japanese schools. Japanese educator Seiji Izawa invited American educator Luther Whiting Mason to Japan for a period in the 1880s, and a curriculum was forged for elementary school music classes that was to bring Japanese school children the songs of not only their American peers but also of European traditions. This musical transformation came rapidly, too, so that by the turn of the 20th century, young women in preparation as future teachers (and mothers) were also taught these multicultural children's songs (Howe, 1997). The Japanese Ministry of Education developed *shoka*, a specific way of school singing in which Western song melodies were imbued with Japanese moral and patriotic texts. The aim of these curricular actions was to radically alter the culture by influencing the children and the women who would work with them, in music and through music.

Yet even while shoka singing and Western songs were the musical mainstay in Japanese schools at the end of the nineteenth century, children continued a traditional repertoire of children's songs, singing games, and chants (called collectively *warabe-uta*) when off on their own and at play. By the 1920s, composers and poets were creating new songs of high artistic quality for children with texts thought to be relevant to their needs and interests (Gottschewski, 1998). These songs merged Japanese and Western musical and textual sensibilities, which became the centrepoint of a school-based repertoire for much of the twentieth century. Yet when post-war Japan was in search of its own identity, *warabe-uta* were 're-discovered' and viewed as central to not only children's culture but also the Japanese spirit (Suzuki, 1993). These traditional children's songs were even seen as having been a musical foundation or inspiration for other genres such as the *nagauta* (the 'long songs' of *kabuki* theatre) and instrumental music for koto, shamisen, and shakuhachi. Traditional children's songs continue to be sung by Japanese children today, even in the midst of Western art music, Japanese traditional music, and the ubiquitous sounds of mediated popular music.

The study of traditional Japanese instruments by beginners of all ages typically transpires through highly stylized individual lessons beyond school, where the teacher's own musical competence is useful in modelling appropriate techniques. Verbal explanations are rare, while demonstration and the physical interaction of teacher and student in clarifying finger and arm positions are commonly practiced. Pieces for koto, as well as shamisen and shakuhachi, are learned through mnemonics—semantically meaningless aural cues that use pitched or rhythmic syllables to represent the music. Japanese teachers transmit phrases of melody and rhythm orally, singing, or chanting them to the student who immediately repeats them; they may sing and chant together before or during their performance of these phrases on the instrument. Even as notation is available, learning by rote or at least in a combination of rote and note is preferable, so that notation becomes a trigger for remembering what had transpired in aural and kinaesthetic terms within the lesson. The beauty of the physical execution of the music is a key aesthetic component in Japanese traditional music, and a teacher's modelling of posture and graceful movement is yet another component of the student's efforts at observation and imitation (Campbell, 1991). Instrumental study in Japan typically commences in childhood, and while there is a steady stream of young people in piano and violin lessons, a significant number are drawn also to the traditional instruments both for their sonic appeal as for the performance rituals that are embraced by the teacher and the culture at large.

Formal schooling in the traditional music of Japan typically emphasizes listening and appreciation. As in any music curriculum, there are some pieces and genres that are 'fixed' and others that 'go missing'. The song, 'Sakura', is a constant among teaching materials in Japan, and a handful of minyo are typically spread through textbooks. Koto music, especially, 'Rokudan', a shakuhachi piece called 'Shika No Tone', a kabuki nagauta selection, and the *gagaku* court ensemble piece, 'Entenraku', are commonly featured. The musical canon in Japanese school texts does not feature, however, music of the fourteenth century *noh* theatre, Buddhist *shomyo* chant, *biwa* lute music, or *gidayu* (the duo of musicians that perform in the *bunraku* puppet theatre) (Takizawa, 1997). Where Japanese traditional music is taught in schools, the emphasis is frequently given to understanding musical structure, cultural and historical context, and aesthetic values. Still rare for children in Japanese schools is the mass-class performance-based study of traditional instruments or vocal music beyond select minyo and warabe-uta.

Of Maystros and Kulintangs (the Philippines)

While continuing a long history of European and American-styled systems of schooling in the Philippines that includes both Western content and pedagogical processes, a movement is in motion for the rediscovery in curriculum and courses of indigenous musical expressions that comprise the unique identity of the Filipino people. The urban concert scene, and the content of music within established conservatories and university departments of music, is overwhelmingly Western in flavour. Still, there are folk ensembles, vocal forms, and instrumental genres that reflect the indigenous, colonial, and immigrant groups that comprise the nation, and which are increasingly becoming a presence in formal studies of Filipino music. The local music genres are often the first sounds that children may hear, and are likely to be the sounds that remain closest to them even as they grow into adulthood; these are now finding further validation through their inclusion in educational settings.

The Western tradition of established conservatories is tied to Western standard pedagogical methods, but within communities and schools, the *maystro* works to revive folk ensembles that have known a considerable history in the Philippines, and which continues to be important in rural areas and provincial towns. From the Spanish *maestro* (master or teacher) comes the maystro system, where individual musician-educators teach, arrange, and conduct music for school-age members of *banda* (band) and *rondalla* (string) ensembles. The maystro prepares music arrangements in staff notation, many players are taught by rote. Every banda and rondalla player knows the melodic line by heart, and can sing it, and thus shares this identical aural and kinetic referent so that no one can get lost in the ensemble. Solfege is frequently utilized in learning melody and parts, so that a comprehensive musicianship develops in players that goes beyond keys and bowings (Trimillos, 1989).

The maystro system provides a template for social relationships in and through music. The maystro is coach and mentor of the students, and he typically takes on the person of a family member when he offers his home as the location of instructional sessions and rehearsals. Student players learn to help novice players, and to seek out the advice and support of players more expert than themselves. In the case of improvisation, which is standard practice within the rondalla ensemble, young students learn the idiomatic ways of their instrument and a certain technical proficiency through the experience of playing the maystro's arrangements and from listening to others. On cue from the maystro, adolescent and adult musicians are expected to take off from the arrangements, trying out new harmony parts and counter-melodies (Atabug, 1984). The maystro, as authority figure and benefactor, provides encouragement and guidance and is viewed as the source of all early knowledge of the instruments and their repertoire.

Within the Philippines is the large island of Mindanao, where the Maranao reside and retain their brilliant Muslim traditions. The Maranao have a signature vocal form, *bayok*, a love song of artistic merit sung by artists called *onor* from either gender. The onor must be prepared intellectually and artistically for the task of performing bayok, and so the cultivation begins in childhood when onors learn Arabic language, Qur'anic recitation, Maranao social ethics, the principal Maranao epic, called Darangen, performance techniques and repertoire for the *kulintang* (set of knobbed gongs). The skill of a performing onor is measured by how well the onor delivers an improvised musical discourse with high literary value, using classical Maranao language, proverbs, humour, and poetic devices. The training requires long tutorial sessions filled with rote learning, with texts to be memorized in set melodic phrases. The Maranao bayok is highly specialized, and thus requires rigorous lessons and practice sessions before a public performance is permitted (Santos, 1996).

The Yakan people, an Islamic community of Basilan island in the Sulu archipelago, perform instrumental music that is related to their agricultural cycle. Their instruments include small graduated bossed gongs that are laid in a row (*kwintangan*), hanging log beams (*kwintangan kayu*), bamboo xylophone (*gabbang*), a percussion plank with jar resonator (*tuntungan*), a bamboo clapper (*kopak-kopak*), and a digging stick topped by a clapper (*daluppak*). They are played solo and ensemble, and their music is created through improvization on one of hundreds of *lebad* (nuclear melodies) from which to select. The lebad are learned from childhood, as are the instruments, when children learn within the immediate family circle or surrounding neighbourhood; in fact, many of the Yakan instrumental ensembles are comprised of family members. Children study with known masters and artists as arranged by their parents, and the process is kinaesthetically driven where the teacher holds the hands of the student and perform the music on the instrument at the proper performance speed. This is done repeatedly until the sound and feel of the music is comprehended, at which point the teacher steps away, observes, and provides commentary.

The kulintang is by far the ultimate national musical symbol of the Philippines, and is fast becoming the instrument of choice for many young Filipinos living there and abroad. Kulintang is both the name of the ensemble as it is also a single instrument, which appears as an oblong wooden box with cords strung within it so as to support eight kettle-shaped embossed bronze gongs. Two long, light wood mallets are used to play the gongs, each with a small head of wrapped yarn and cloth. The ensemble includes this instrument along with several hanging gongs and a single-headed barrel drum, and plays a percussive melody along with punctuating rhythms that drive the sound forward and motivate listeners to want to dance. The transmission of Filipino kulintang music occurs through an oral/aural process where demonstration and imitation are prominently featured, and singing the melody line may spontaneously occur while attempting to play it. The visual-kinaesthetic channels of information are critical to learning, too, so that young players watch as much as listen to other players perform at high speed and then reproduce the gestures of the hands as they fly across the gongs. In early listening and performing attempts, student players 'catch' the motifs and partial phrases and realize the general ideas of melodic contour, but may take many trials before they can fill in the details that replicate the music as it is meant to be played (Campbell, 2001). Kulintang music is rhythmically sophisticated, and the ensemble of instruments sounds in interlocking fashion where one rhythm fits in between or surrounds another one to create a complex musical groove that is immensely appealing to Filipino youth.

Varied venues for learning music (Thailand)

Thailand is considered a gong-chime culture, but it is not only the resonant tuned gongs that provide a soundscape for children growing up Thai. There are as well wooden xylophones, stringed instruments, flutes, quadruple-reed instruments, and various drums, wood blocks, and cymbals that comprise the classical court music ensembles; these are heard in elaborate public ceremonies to honour the royal family, to commemorate important national events, to perform for tourists, to play for dance and theatre shows, and to continue the long-standing Thai musical identity. Children hear the music of the classical *pi phat* and *mahori* ensembles on TV, if not live, and grow to expect their sounds in conjunction with performances by dancers, actors, and even puppets re-enacting the *Ramakien* legend. They are immersed in the popular songs imported from Hong Kong, Japan, Taiwan, Great Britain and the USA that are played in restaurants and shops. They are also grounded in Thai folk songs and singing games, many passed by the generations before them, and they know the music of weddings, funerals, and other landmark events in their lives. Three musical streams—classical, popular, and folk—are prominent in the lives of children in modern Thailand, filling needs and functions over the course of their growing up in cities, towns, and villages (Phaosavadi & Campbell, 2003).

Alongside the more informal and non-formal learning, there appear to be three venues for children's formal learning of traditional Thai music. Piphat houses (*ban piphat*) were once the primary means of musical training for classical musicians, where as many as 50 or 60 disciples, usually boys or young men, lived with a master teacher to study traditional instruments and play daily in the house ensemble. Although the houses are nearly all gone today, the pedagogical approach of a ban piphat master parcelling out small phrases from a larger work to teach to his student by rote continues on in private lessons. Community institutes are a second venue for instrumental tuition, developed over the last several decades to serve tuition-paying students who wish to study stringed instruments, particularly *khim* (a hammered dulcimer), after school and on Saturdays. Teaching techniques include the use of written notation, including staff notation, solfege notation, numerical notation, and tablature, even while the oral/aural process is also very much in play (Miller, 1992).

In public schools, children may sing Thai folk songs, and depending upon the teacher's interest, perform the basic movements of Thai classical and folk dances, play Thai melodies together on recorder-like *khlui,* or join together in playing *angklung* ensembles of bamboo idiophones. The establishment of Thai Music Clubs give students in some schools opportunities to study traditional instruments and singing style; they follow the model of such clubs at universities where campus piphat and mahori ensembles perform competitively (Campbell, 1995).

An important element in the learning of Thai music is the custom of *wai kru,* or honouring the teacher. Children learn to show the sign of salutation (*wai*) by the time they enter school, raising both hands, joining palm to palm, and lightly touching the body somewhere between the face and chest. School-days, lessons, and even performances begin with this gesture of respect. Yet the wai kru is more than this: it is a ceremony to mark the time at which, following a trial period of study, the child or youth becomes a student of a particular teacher for life. The student brings gifts of food and money to the teacher when he (or she) has agreed to open the riches of his musical knowledge to the student. As Thai classical music was once learned only through oral means, the teacher's acceptance of the student is a significant event. For young people wishing to devote themselves to learning this revered music, the teacher's selection of a student is the gateway to labour-intensive practice that may lead to musical excellence.

Yet while few Thai children will follow a pathway to classical music studies, they all know a repertoire of singing games and rhythmic chants that are frequently the focal point of their play. Children sing songs of the elephant ('Chaang'), imitating its lumbering movement and swinging 'trunk', and of the blind fisherman with a trap ('Poong Paang') meant to catch the fish swimming near him. They chant in games that resemble 'Drop the Handkerchief' and 'London Bridges', their language sounding rich with melodic nuances due to the five-tone nature of Thai language. There are clapping games, circle games, double-line games, all in which children's live music-making is prominent (Phaosavadi & Campbell, 2003). Along with this playful song repertoire they trade among themselves, there are also the heritage songs passed to children from parents and grandparents. This is the music close to the heart of the Thai, music that cuts across age, class, and gender, the folk music of their history, customs, and beliefs that all are invited to sing.

Musical grooves from infancy onward (West Africa)

Much has been written about the musical engagement of children and youth in West Africa. Children of the Ewe of Ghana (Agawu, 1995), the Yoruba of Nigeria (Waterman, 1991), and the Kpelle of Liberia (Stone, 2004) are naturally enculturated into social worlds in which music plays a high-profile and prominent role in their daily lives. They sing, dance, and play from their earliest childhoods. In the arms of their mothers, or strapped to their mothers' backs, children learn from infancy the rhythms and tunes of their culture. In rural societies, they continue as infants and toddlers in a cultural practice of listening and feeling the rhythmic movement and sound vibrations of their mothers at work, walking, talking, chopping, stirring, stamping, singing. Their sound worlds are extended beyond infancy as they come under the watchful eye of older siblings and neighbour-children, who teach them songs, stories, and games through which they may learn useful life skills and initial understandings of their cultural roles.

West African societies perceive music, dance, and even drama as a tightly bound complex of the performing arts. The Kpelle people of Liberia describe a beautifully performed song, drum pattern, or dance with the same term, 'sang', a deliberate choice of a word that reflects the blending of the arts into one entity. In illustration of the term, a drummer comments upon a dancer's performance might be 'The dance she spoke', just as a dancer might say of a drummer, 'The music he moved' (Stone, 2004, p. 21). Children generally see the arts as blended, too, and in West African societies they are encouraged to hold this concept into adolescence and adulthood, as song, speech, movement, and instrumental music are viewed as part of an artistic continuum.

The performance practice of West African musicians typically encompasses both tradition and creative change. Among the Yoruba of Nigeria, the point is not to create a perfect imitation of music that has come before but rather to catch the 'feel' of music for specific functions and to portray it with new energy (Waterman, 1991). The performance practice influences the manner of its learning, so that a combination of informed listening with mimesis, or learning through imitation, is a powerful one. This is the way they learn stories and riddles, songs and dances, often combining the interspersing spoken and sung interludes in their stories, interjecting their spontaneous exclamations, and dancing as it suits the story and the song. Yoruba children learn singing games at play with their peers in this manner, as they also learn their church hymns, the rhythms of the *dundun* (talking drum) and drumming ensembles, and the grooves of popular music such as *juju* and *fuji*.

Even as they sing their clapping games and counting songs, young children are perfecting some of the essential characteristics of the music of their culture. Where non-overlapping call and response structure is a key musical component, children infuse it within their songs. They have heard adults performing call and response songs as they plant rice, chop wood, cut and harvest sugar cane, pound maize into powder, and weave straw into baskets. They themselves learn as children to pound cassava in a mortar, or to grind recently harvested rice in order to remove the husks, all the while incorporating interactive rhythmic exchanges between them (Agawu, 1995). The call and response melodies and rhythms of ensembles of xylophones, drums, flutes, horns, harps, and lutes have surrounded them, too, so that this organizing element comes easily to them as they sing familiar and spontaneously created songs. Children learn the timing and turn-taking of call and response, even so far as to understand the importance of an equal balance in some genres between the length of the call phrase and the response phrase (Stone, 2004).

There are important social groups in some areas of West Africa that function as secret societies, in which older children are expected to leave their homes to live for a time in Poro (for males) and Sande (for females) enclosures in the forest. There they receive instruction in the traditions and values of their culture, which is an intensive training for the adult roles they will one day play. Music and dance are featured within this training for all students, and for the talented there is even a specialized training for becoming solo singers, instrumentalists, or dancers in their communities (Stone, 2004). Everyone performs the dances they learned in Poro and Sande as a part of their graduation exercise, after they are declared ready to take on some of the challenges of the adult lives into which they will grow.

In describing their life history, Wolof griots of Senegal offer detailed accounts of their childhoods as prominent in their growth as musicians and tellers of tales (Tang, 2002). Most learn their drumming early, and the critical period of developing their drumming talent falls between the ages of 2 and 10 years. Children are exposed to drums and drummers from infancy, so that an immersion phenomenon occurs. With drums in the home and yard, babies may grab them to steady themselves when learning to walk, or might be offered a turn on the drum to appease and reward them. Young Wolofs watch and then imitate the adult drummers, sometimes playing on empty cans and plastic containers when they are just 3 and 4 years old. As they are brought to adult gatherings that feature music, children hear characteristic rhythms and complicated phrases, and may chant them and dance to them. They then apply the music to their toy drums the next morning, sometimes alone or together in small groups. If a child is observed to be particularly talented, he was taken under the wing of a male relative and trained until he was sufficiently skilled to contribute his minor part in a public festival. While Wolof griots may describe the music they know as inherited, it is often the presence of the music within their environment that allows them to know it intimately.

Ngoma to grow on (East Africa)

East African societies in Kenya, Tanzania, Uganda, and the Cape Horn countries of Ethiopia, Eritrea, Somalia, and Djibouti embrace the participation of all their members, including children, in traditional music and dance. *Ngoma* (in as many translations as there are languages) is the combined music–dance form of performance that spreads across the region, where singers dance, dancers sing, and instrumentalists may sing and move as they play. Traditional ngoma serves important rituals and routines throughout East Africa, including music for education, entertainment, and funerals, in work and as therapy, and for communication (through metalinguistic drumming from one village to another) and timekeeping (as in calling villagers to worship where no church bells chime). It also serves diadactic and educational purposes as well in village Uganda (Barz, 2004). Music is viewed as an appropriate means of handling social problems, where stories are sung as warnings to villagers of wrong-doings and encouragement to individuals to mend their ways. It is used for coping with diseases such as HIV/AIDS, so that songs, dances, and dramatic performances of people suffering and dying are presented so that they might be more thoughtful about the issues.

Some genres function in multiple ways, including as means for enhancing the quality of young workers as well as for entertaining them. *Bugobogobo* is a genre of the Sukuma of Tanzania found in the context of field labour and as a refined stage art (Gunderson, 1999). It was initially intended as music made by youth and adult labourers to facilitate their work in harvesting, hauling, and planting. The benefits of music-making for those engaged in this physical labour are multiple: to create a desire to work together, to work longer hours without being tired, to calm listeners and focus their mental energies and organizational skills, to cast off worries and create joy, and to pass on important life testimonies and teaching within the songs. The music and dance of Bugobogobo are carefully synchronized, and even as it has risen from the field to become a refined performance art, the origins of the form are seen in the young dancers who demonstrate the motions of hoeing the earth and spreading seeds. A popular genre in clubs throughout East Africa due to its pulsive, energetic, and colourful nature, Bugobogobo serves as a symbolic of Tanzanian national identity. Performers are not 'taught' how to perform it, but they have been imitating their elders—both farmers and performers—since early in their childhoods. As early as 5 and 6 years of age, children witness the workers and the performance troupes, and commence playing the intricate rhythms of Bugobogobo on discarded tin cans and wooden sticks (Barz, 2004). This active participation thus assures their place on the receiving end of the process of transmission of traditional culture, and often motivates their fuller involvement in Bugobogobo later in their lives.

At home and in the Islamic schools of Kenya, children learn to recite the Qur'an in Arabic. They can be heard performing their devotional chants in school choirs, with texts from the Qur'an, called *kaswida*, that enhance the religious sentiment. They do not perform *nyimbo* (songs), as their more melodic styles would be considered a distraction from the religious beliefs of the texts (Barz, 2004). In the same rehearsal, the girls may take to performing *chakacha*, a traditional ngoma that is sung, danced, and drummed exclusively by women. The dance features the rhythmicized rotation of the hips, which are accented by tying their *hijab* headscarves at the hips of their traditional Muslim black robes. Its virtuosically played drum rhythms and sensual movements have contributed to its popularity as the national musical symbol of Kenya across the generations (Campbell & Eastman, 1984).

In much of East Africa, as in sub-Saharan Africa at large, girls are typically discouraged from playing musical instruments. The gender roles are often clearly delineated from childhood onward, such that while everyone sings, only men play instruments and women more typically dance. In some villages, women are discouraged from touching or even passing near musical instruments; to do either is considered a transgression of a social taboo. This value system is changing in urban centres such as Nairobi, Kampala, Dar-es-Salaam, and Mogadishu, where boys and girls are taught in schools on many different musical instruments. Yet even while youth understand and appreciate the changes, the older generation still maintains these beliefs about gender (Ephrem, personal communication; see also comments by Ephrem, in Campbell *et al.*, 1994).

One way of understanding the sociomusical life of children is to learn from the reflections of a performer well-attuned to his own development as well as those of others whom he now teaches. Centurio Balikoowa, a performer of the *ntongooli* (a multistring bowl-lyre) of Uganda, recalled beginning his musical education by playing musical games as early as 3 years of age (Barz, 2004). He learned the ntongooli by observing his father, who had in turn learned by observing his grandfather. He remembered also playing *endere* (flute) by ear, having heard the melodies played by shepherds as they took care of the grazing cows in the neighbouring field. Like all children in his village, Balikoowa learned to play *embaire* (xylophone). Because there was no electricity, a communal embaire was constructed by the adults, who would take turns playing it through the evenings. As there was no television, radio, or videos, one resident after another in the village would play for a period of time, and sometimes residents in neighbouring villages would contribute their own complementary performances, too. For the master and professional musicians with whom he is associated, learning happens through a combination of listening, imitation, and repetition.

Keeping culture through traditional song (North American First Nations)

Among the people of the First Nations, or Native Americans, of North America (including Canada and the USA), music is a communal event as it is also a deeply personal phenomenon. Its transmission may be a matter of one's age, gender, and rank within a community, or it may be a result of a personal journey that leads to spiritual inspiration. Music is deeply embedded in ritual and social customs of the clan or tribe, in coming-of-age ceremonies, and in coming-to-terms with the supernatural, the ancestral spirits, and the spirits of nature and of living creatures. Some songs are group-owned and intended for all to know, while others are considered personal property, to be sung only by those whose songs they are or by permission given for their use. For many people of the First Nations, song is the equivalent of the Bible's Genesis and Leviticus in the moral lessons it holds, and those without knowledge of song are considered 'poor', uneducated, or lacking an important piece of who they are.

For children growing up in their Native American communities, music is a part of their personal and social identities. Concepts of traditional indigenous knowledge to be passed to the young allow for the music as a way of recounting history, predicting the future, passing on local wisdom, reflecting on meaningful places and contexts, and clarifying one's role within a nation and a clan. Modern indigenous music and dance has emerged even as older layers are continued, so that a group of unaccompanied singers and dancers can still hold its own even as wired rock and country music bands perform their own blend of contemporary and indigenous expressions. Inter-tribal celebrations are raising new issues of ownership, borrowing, and sharing, as songs cross groups and become fused with different cultural expressions. Meanwhile, young people are often caught in the middle of contemporary cultural revitalization that is occurring, trying to make sense of older layers of culture, including music, in their changing world.

Families are responsible for teaching songs and dances to family members in order to perpetuate its traditions. The Spokane and Coeur d'Alene tribes of the interior of the American Northwest assert the primary place of song in their development as children. They remember it as the sound they awakened to, and to which they would go to sleep, when mothers, fathers, grandparents, and other family members sang alone and together. From birth to death, songs are there for points through the day and through their lives, from the morning song, the song for the birth of a child, of becoming a man or woman, of being in love, for marriage, for sickness and death. There are welcoming songs, songs for learning dances, for being a warrior, and for battle itself (Sijohn, 1999).

The Coast Salish groups who live along the Pacific Rim of the USA and Canada continue to pass the lessons of their culture to young people through their songs. While stories are significant in that they contain metaphors, and important cultural knowledge about ancestors, family, animals, and plants, the elders believe that 'You have to sing the most important teaching of a story for children to remember it' (Miller, 1999, p. 31). Singing is often reserved for the moral of the story, the bottom-line lessons to be learned, the story's most important turn of events. One account of the song-learning among the Snohomish people underscores the means of ensuring that the substance of stories and songs is learned. 'My great-grandmother would sing the songs that went with the stories. Then somewhere during the story, my great-grandmother would stop and pretend to try to remember what came next (it was a test). One of the older children, who had heard the song many times before, would have to say 'Kaya [grandmother], this is what they did' (Miller, 1999, p.30). A singer of the Makah Nation remembered the importance of repeated listening: 'My dad . . . would make us sit down and listen to a new song 'til we were very tired of it! He'd just play the drum and sing the song, every day' (Swan, 1999, p. 86). Although the oral method continues to be practised by the Makah, children now learn songs via tape recordings given them by their elders. However, as children may no longer be 'forced' to sit and listen repeatedly to their parents and grandparents, they do not practise regularly. The same is true of the dance, where videotapes are available, but the viewing by First Nations' children is sporadic when left to chance. With no one there to help them out physically and to correct their errors, children and youth know less of the traditional repertoire than they once did.

For the Mescaleros, as well as other Apaches of the American Southwest, a coming-of-age ceremony combines ritual with song, prayer, rattles, and ritual, in order to prepare young adolescent girls for marriage and child-bearing ahead in their future. An older woman serves as sponsor of the girl, who is selected by the family because of her knowledge of Apache traditions, including the puberty rite and its songs. The ceremony brings the girl into womanhood over a period of 5 days, when powwow dancing occurs outside even as the girl is taking instruction by her sponsor within her specially constructed private tipi (thought to be the home of the goddess). The sounds of the girl's tin-cone jingles, sewn into her ceremonial dress, can be heard as she dances. Male ritual singing is punctuated by female ritual cries, and supportive singing is offered by women who know the rituals. On the fourth night, the singing and dancing extend until dawn, when the girls are painted with red and white clay. Adolescent Mescalero girls remain largely silent through the ceremony, but they hear the music and prayers that swirl around them (Shapiro & Talamantez, 1986). Some of them later become sponsors themselves, drawn to the music, beginning their learning of it at their very own puberty rite.

As in many First Nations cultures, Navajo children learn the songs of their adult culture by joining in as singing participants in the rituals and social functions in which adults play prominent roles. They may also sing the adult songs, or parts of them, away from adults, sometimes converting them into their own new expressions, adding interactive movements or combining them with games they know or invent. Among the Oglala Sioux of the Dakotas, where the word for 'compose' is *yatun,* literally 'to give birth to a song', and yet the connotation of *tun* is 'to give rise to something that has already existed in another form' (Powers, 1980, p. 33). Thus it appears that there may be an unconscious recycling of songs that occurs from person to person, with the singer uncertain of the song's evolution. Since country, rock, rap, gospel and other popular forms have become embedded in the ambience of their communities, these styles are also influential in the music children make. There are, of course, traditional children's songs, too, and singing games, lullabies, and humorous songs, which are all part of the oral tradition passed to them by adults (McAllester, 1996).

The traditional music continues, despite an attempt that was underway in the nineteenth century to 'civilize' the children of First Nations communities. Indigenous people in Canada and the USA were banned from practising their Native rituals, religious celebrations, and extended family gatherings, children and youth were sent to boarding schools where traditional practices, including heritage songs and dances, could be replaced by the curricular content of mainstream schools. By the 1890s, these schools were mandatory for all Native children, where they were subjected to studies that were far afield from their tribal life, and they were clothed in uniforms. Their hair was cut short, they were housed in barracks-styled halls, and fed a new menu of foods foreign to them. Many schools were run like military academies, and wind and brass bands similar to those found in the military were established (Swan, 1999). These actions were intended to bring assimilation to Native American children, and to focus attention away from the culture they would have known at home that would not serve to bring them into the mainstream of society. Yet in summer, when school was out and the children were back at home, the traditions, including the music, crept back into their lives. They serenaded one another, sang and danced with their families, and (depending upon the particular tribe) found drums to beat, rattles to shake, and flutes to play. People of the First Nations survived the boarding schools, and gradually the government-sponsored schools closed and children were returned to their families to be educated in their local schools, where curricular subjects today include Native American cultural studies and celebrations of music and dance with standard public-school fare.

Living and learning music

The manner by which children and youth learn music may vary from culture to culture, and yet in interesting ways this learning by individuals may also be seen as transpiring across a continuum of aural–oral techniques and formal, non-formal, and informal processes. Children's musical involvement may encompass active and engaged learning at times, and more passive, receptive, and indirect modes at other times. Further, as surely as they acquire music, children are also involved in transmitting it (often to other children), thus preserving it. In examining settings and situations of music learning by young people across cultures, comparisons may be made of the strategies employed by children in the process of knowing music well enough to be able to perform it, to create it anew, to understand its meaning. As they live, children learn, and many are keen to know the music that suits them and their view of the world—as well as to reflect the musical values of adults who are influential in shaping their cultural identities.

Across the globe, childhood is a period of life in which learning one's membership in a cultural group is a crucial accomplishment. This learning transpires within the immediate family group and in the wider community, and includes language (and dialect), social skills, religious beliefs and rituals, values, and culturally based artistic expression to adhere to and strive for as children progress into adolescence and toward adulthood. Children pledge their allegiances to family, friends, community values, and gradually they shift their focus towards achieving competence in economically useful skills they will use in their future. They acquire leisure skills, too, that include sport and the arts, some of which become life-long pursuits that fill and fulfil them. Stretching from childhood into adolescence is the period of exploration in how best one might participate in one's collective culture, as well as to learn how to shape oneself in the direction of one's individual future; here, too, music is often a choice that young people make to engage in, and to be engaged by, its performance. Children's social lives evolve as they graduate from a dependence upon adults exclusively as caregivers to one of an interdependence with family members, other children, and adults (teachers, youth leaders, relatives, and others within their community). Children come to an understanding of self in relationship to others, and they learn their roles and responsibilities, and their strengths in the contributions they will make to their culture and society. Through the stages of children's growth, their musical expressions and interests are evident and often significant means of their learning.

Music is emblematic of personal and collective identity, so that whether or not they study it and specialize in its performance, children and youth are at least subconsciously aware of its expressive power and symbolism. A few will become highly competent in music so as to choose it for their life's work, while the vast majority will find music a component of their life within family, social, and religious communities. As children, they sing because they must, they move because the music prompts them, and they dabble with instruments and sound sources out of curiosity, a need for tactile experience, and because it 'feels good' to do so. It is this dabbling that may lead to ever-deepening involvement in instrumental play, even when it begins with mere whistling, tooting, tapping, key-clicking, and other exploratory behaviours. Children learn the role of music within their society simply by living in their culture, and the musical grammar they develop is a direct result of what sounds come into their ears. As they grow, children are developing a sense of their musical heritage, for it is apt to be their own soundscape of live and mediated expressions. Their inventions of a musical nature derive from this musical sound-surround.

As music is a human phenomenon, it is also a learned behaviour. Children are to an extent similarly 'wired', regardless of where they live, so that some facets of the manner in which they perceive, receive, and grow to know music are evident across cultures. Yet if there is variance in musical expression from one culture to another, it follows also that the manner in which it is learned may be affected by the music itself, and by the ways, means, and values of the locality concerning the transfer of knowledge. The function of music, including the role it plays in the daily lives of people, may influence the circumstances of its transmission, as do also the values placed upon the music by a society as either the rare endowment of expert artists or a characteristic shared by all its citizens. Who learns the music, and how it is learned, is thus reflective of its internal content and the collective cultural thought about it. However, a central interest is the extent to which music learning is similar in process regardless of its content and the context of its learning.

Clearly, music moves from teacher to learner, from master to apprentice, from adult to child. It also moves from child to child, even from child to adult, and from mediated sources to anyone who will listen. Sensory avenues are exercised by children in 'getting the music', and learning may embrace aural, visual, and kinaesthetic/tactile capacities. Beginners may need to listen, observe, and then imitate the teacher, and so students across many traditions use their ears and eyes in learning the fiddle of Ireland, the shakuhachi of Japan, the kulintang of The Philippines, the khim of Thailand, the dundun of Nigeria, and the ntongooli of Uganda, the songs of the Coast Salish. So it is in popular music genres, too, in which the ear is challenged to learn the nuances of the style and piece, both those parts that are fixed and certain as well as those parts that are improvised. Verbal explanations are largely unnecessary, notation systems may or may not be utilized (even when such notation is available), and 'rote' imitation of those who already know the music is frequently viewed as a positive component of learning. In remarkable ways, it may be that adult student musicians may emulate children's learning strategies, finding their musical way through observation and imitation, becoming active in the kinaesthetic process of performance as a result of looking and listening (Campbell, 1991).

When learning requires the retention of skills for performance, vocalization and mnemonic devices may be critical components of the process. Orally spoken cues serve the memory well, which may be semantically meaningless and yet key to storing and later recalling passages. Japanese instruments have their own sets of syllables to designate pitches, rhythms, and the performing positions for koto, shamisen, and various drums. Drumming traditions have elaborate mnemonic system, too, to communicate durations and drumstrokes, including a wide variety of percussion instruments in sub-Saharan Africa. Prerequisite to instrumental performance in many traditions may be the vocalization by way of the chanting and singing of syllables, including solmization. In order to play the drums of the Wolof, there is an expectation that students chant first the principal rhythmic themes. Similarly, players of Irish tunes on various traditional instruments may first have learned by ear, and even through song. This practice extends to artistic and popular forms beyond those mentioned, as jazz musicians, for example, claim that singing must naturally precede instrumental performance, and that their ear-training is enhanced through vocalization (Berliner, 1994).

Approaches to the study of the child as musician must encompass cross-cultural studies of their musical engagements in order to grasp the multisplendored realities of children's interests, needs, behaviours, and values. Concurrently, considerations of music as global practice must encompass the ways in which children musically grow to express themselves, and ways in which they are enculturated, trained, and educated. Children are a product of social organization, and they do not move through increasingly advanced stages of their biological and neurological growth without being shaped by a constellation of forces within their environments, not the least of which are the musical genres which their societies value and thus preserve. Yet also, as a perspective of children as their own social system becomes more readily apparent through cross-disciplinary scholarship, they will need to be studied further as the young musicians they are rather than as unfinished products in motion towards adult culture. Of course, adults have much to offer children by way of musical knowledge and skills that have since the beginning of time been transmitted generationally, and yet children—their own development, their means of socialization with other children, of learning, exchanging (and even discarding) particular points of their knowledge and views, deserve support and the freedom to evolve beyond the direct influence of well-intentioned adults. With an open and receptive approach to the study of children within school, in public places such as parks and playgrounds, in their social clubs, and in their homes, they may be better understood for their musical interests and values, for how they perceive and grow their musical behaviours, so that adults can contribute in relevant ways to their musical lives.

References

Agawu, K. (1995). *African rhythm: A northern Ewe perspective.* Cambridge: Cambridge University Press.

Atabug. A. C. (1984). Music education in a multicultural society: The Philippine experience. *International Society of Music Education Yearbook* 11, 25–40.

Barz, G. (2004). *Music in East Africa.* New York: Oxford University Press.

Benthall, J. (1992). Child-focused research. *Anthropology Today* 8, 23–25.

Berliner, P. (1994). *Thinking in jazz.* Chicago, IL: University of Chicago Press.

Bjorkvold, J. (1992). *The muse within* (trans. W. H. Halverson). New York: Harper Collins.

Blacking, J. (1967). *Venda children's song: A study in ethnomusicological analysis.* Chicago, IL: University of Chicago.

Brailiou, C. (1984). *Problems of ethnomusiocology* (trans. A. L. Lloyd). Cambridge: Cambridge University Press. (Original work published 1954.)

Campbell, C. A. & Eastman, C. M. (1984). *Ngoma*: Swahili Adult Song Performance in Context. *Ethnomusicology* 28(3), 467–493.

Campbell, P. S. (1991). *Lessons from the world.* New York: Schirmer Books.

Campbell, P. S. (1995). The making of musicians and musical audiences in Thailand. *International Journal of Music Education* 25, 20–28.

Campbell, P. S. (1998). *Songs in their heads: Music and its meaning in children's lives.* New York: Oxford University Press.

Campbell, P. S. (2001). Unsafe suppositions? Cutting across cultures on questions of music's transmission. *Music Education Research,* 32, 215–226.

Campbell, P. S. (2003). Ethnomusicology and music education: Crossroads for knowing music, education, and culture. *Research Studies in Music Education* 21, 16–30.

Corsaro, W. A. (1997). *The sociology of childhood.* Thousand Oaks, CA: Pine Forge Press.

Ephrem, H. (1994). In P.S. Campbell, E. McCullough-Brabson, & J. Cook Tucker (eds), *Roots and branches.* (pp. 11–12). Danbury, CT: World Music Press.

Goldman, L. (1998). *Child's play: Myth, mimesis and make-believe.* Oxford: Berg.

Gottschewski, H. (1998). The development of the language of music during the introduction of European music to Japan between 1853 and 1945. *Japan Foundation Newsletter,* 25(6), 7–9.

Gunderson, F. (1999). *Music labor associations in Sukumaland, Tanzania: History and practice.* Unpublished PhD dissertation, Wesleyan University.

Hall, E. T. (1992). Improvisation as an acquired, multilevel process. *Ethnomusicology* 36, 223–245.

Harwood, E. (1998). Go on girl! Improvisation in African-American girls' singing games. In B. Nettl & M. Russell (eds), *In the course of performance* (pp. 13–25). Chicago: University of Chicago Press.

Hardman, C. (1973). Can there be an anthropology of children? *Journal of the Anthropological Society of Oxford,* 4, 85–99.

Hargreaves, D. J. & North, A. J. (eds) (1997). *The social psychology of music.* New York: Oxford University Press.

Hast, D. & Scott S. (2004). *Music in Ireland.* New York: Oxford University Press.

Herzog, G. (1950). Song. In M. Leach & J. Fried (eds), *Dictionary of folklore, mythology, and legend* (Vol. 2), (pp. 1043–1050). New York: Funk & Wagnall.

Howe, S. W. (1997). *Luther Whiting Mason: International music educator.* Warren MI: Harmonie Park Press.

James, A., Jenks, C., & Prout, A. (1998). *Theorizing childhood.* New York: Teachers College Press.

Jorgensen, E. (1997). *In search of music education.* Urbana, IL: University of Illinois Press.

Juslin, P. N. & Sloboda, J. A. (2001). *Music and emotion: Theory and research.* New York: Oxford University Press.

McAllester, D. P. (1996). *David P. McAllester on Navajo music.* In P. S. Campbell (ed.), *Music in cultural context* (pp. 5–11). Reston, VA: Music Educators National Conference.

McCarthy, M. (1999). *Passing it on: The transmission of music in Irish culture.* Cork: Cork University Press.

MacDonald, R., Hargreaves, D. J., & Miell, D. (2002). *Musical identities.* New York: Oxford University Press.

Marsh, K. (1997). Children's singing games: Composition in the playground? *Research Studies in Music Education*, **4**, 2–11.

Mayall, B. (2002). *Toward a sociology for childhood: Thinking from children's lives.* Buckingham, UK: Open University Press.

Miller, B. S. (1999). Seeds of our ancestors. In W. Smyth & E. Ryan (eds), *Spirit of the first people* (pp. 25–43). Seattle: University of Washington Press.

Miller, T. E. (1992). The theory and practice of Thai musical notations. *Ethnomusicology*, **36**(2), 197–221.

Minks, A. (2002). From children's song to expressive practices: Old and new directions in the ethnomusicological study of children. *Ethnomusicology*, **46**(3), 379–408.

Phaosavadi, P. & Campbell, P. S. (2003). *From Bangkok and beyond.* Danbury, CT: World Music Press.

Powers, W. K. (1980). Oglala song terminology. *Selected Reports in Ethnomusicology*, **7**, 23–42.

Santos, R. (1996). Beyond the song. In J. Katsumura & Y. Tokumaru (eds), *Report of world musics forum: Hamamatsu 1996* (pp. 96–106). Tokyo: Foundation for the Promotion of Music Education and Culture.

Schwartzman, H. B. (2001). Children and anthropology: A century of studies. *Children and anthropology: Perspectives for the 21st century.* Westport, CT: Bergin & Garvey.

Shapiro, A. D. & Talamantez, I. (1986). The Mescalero Apache girls' puberty ceremony: The role of music in structuring ritual time. *Yearbook of the International Council for Traditional music*, **18**, 77–90.

Sijohn, C. (1999). The circle of song. In W. Smyth & E. Ryan (eds), *Spirit of the first people* (pp. 45–49). Seattle: University of Washington Press.

Stephens, S. (ed.), (1995). *Children and the politics of culture.* Princeton, NJ: Princeton University Press.

Stone, R. (2004). *Music in west Africa.* New York: Oxford University Press.

Suzuki, A. (2003). *The change and diversity of singing games in England and Japan: A comparative approach to their roles and construction.* Unpublished Doctoral dissertation, The University of Reading.

Swan, H. (1999). Makah music. In W. Smyth & E. Ryan (eds), *Spirit of the first people* (pp. 81–93). Seattle: University of Washington Press.

Takizawa, T. (1997). A new paradigm of world musics in Japanese music education: Japan's learning from ASEAN countries' access roads to world music. In J. Katsumura & Y. Tokumaru (eds), *Report of World musics forum: Hamamatsu 1996* (pp. 33–39). Tokyo: Foundation for the Promotion of Music Education and Culture.

Tang, P. (2002). *Masters of the Sabar: Wolof Griots in contemporary Senegal.* Unpublished Ph.D. dissertation, Harvard University.

Trimillos, R. (1989). Halau, hochschule, maystro, and ryu: Cultural approaches to music learning and teaching. *International Journal of Music Education*, 14, 32–43.

Waterman, C. (1991). *Juju music: A social history*. Chicago, IL: University of Chicago Press.

Waterman, R. (1956). Music in Australian Aboriginal culture—Some sociological and psychological implications. In E. T. Gaston (ed.), *Music therapy* 1955 (pp. 40–49). Lawrence KS: The Allen Press.

CHAPTER 22

CULTURAL TRADITIONS

ROBERT WALKER

Introductory explanation

The importance of music to a sense of culture

In writing about cultural traditions in children's music-making one should attempt to highlight the special and distinct behaviours, practices, and beliefs that define a culture. One problem, of course, is that there are few cultures that have not been infiltrated to some degree by Western culture and especially its entertainment products. None the less, my purpose in writing about cultural traditions is to explain about the special ways in which music helps define a culture.

Merriam (1997) points out that although '. . . no culture escapes the dynamics of change over time . . . culture is also stable, that is, no cultures change wholesale and overnight, the threads of continuity run through every culture, and this change must always be considered against a background of stability' (p. 305). I would add that this background is of the most interest. But Merriam makes an important point about music: 'Ethnomusicologists make frequent reference to the idea that music is considered to be one of the most stable elements of culture' (p. 304). This is commensurate with my own work among the Haida, Tsimsian, and Salish peoples of the Pacific North West (Walker, 1986, 1987, 1990, 1997). It is my experience that music is one of the most important elements through which a child maintains a stable cultural identity, even when cultural traditions and associated life-styles have all but disappeared. Indeed, Frith (1996), De Nora (2000), and MacDonald *et al.* (2002) make a similar point in their accounts of how urban teenagers today use popular music to both generate and support their individual and group identities. And ethnomusicologists and anthropologists explain that the traditional music of any culture somehow encapsulates and symbolizes the nature or the essence of a culture for its people thus enabling them to identify with their culture through its music.

From a common sense viewpoint it is probably impossible to eradicate from one's psyche the imprints, the memories of both vicarious and actual events of the culture into which one is born, develops and matures (Draaisma, 2000, 2004). And while today most children's contemporary social reality is shaped by globalization and the socio-political concept of the multicultural society, it would be misleading to imagine that children regard themselves simply as multicultural beings or as total slaves to popular entertainment deep inside their persona. I refer not to some nostalgic longing of memories of a past that no longer exists but rather to the ineradicable psychological and emotional phantasms of one's birth culture and early experiences.

Most industrialized societies have changed dramatically over the last century as a result of rapidly evolving technology and improved communications, as well as social, political, and economic change. This process of change can be observed 'either as it has occurred in the past or as it is occurring in the present. The former is usually subsumed under the rubric of diffusion, defined as achieved cultural transmission, while the latter is approached under the heading of acculturation, defined in this frame of reference as cultural transmission in process' (Merriam, 1997, p. 303).

Given all this, cultural perspectives on children's musical development should, I argue, be concerned with the more stable aspects of cultural life and less with the effects of 'cultural transmission in process'. However, contemporary issues of acculturation, especially concerning the effects of the global entertainment industry as it targets the financial capacities of young people in order to persuade them to buy its products, require some mention. I have, therefore, chosen to comment on three cultures, two in some detail, which show stable cultural values, practices, and beliefs about music established over time through the processes of diffusion, and also to challenge the relevance of some contemporary Western notions of development to non-Western cultures.

I take as a starting point Clifford Geertz's notion of art as a cultural system (Geertz, 1983), and the idea that the 'human is an animal suspended in webs of significance [s/he] has spun, and the analysis of it to be therefore not an experimental science in search of [a] law but an interpretive one in search of meaning' (Geertz, 1973, p. 5). Consequently, I explain children's music making as both reflecting and reinforcing through music the culture they inhabit and the role music plays in the particular social group in which they grow and mature. The musical activities in the cultures I describe below are unconnected with those of Western popular entertainment and its music and consequently the children of these cultures are exposed only to their own birth culture.

The global music entertainment industry is not a product of culture, nor is it a culture in its own right. It does not satisfy Geertz's (nor anyone else's) criteria for defining a culture. The global entertainment industry owes its existence to one driving force: selling products. It contains no deep-rooted cultural beliefs, no passing on of cultural wisdom and knowledge from one generation to the next (indeed each successive wave of pop music idols is deliberately distinct from the previous one because of the selling power of the new), no commonly agreed moral and ethical values by which to live, no sense of one's history and connection with ancestors. Instead there is the continual rise of the new, the novel, the sensational and the attractions of instant gratification where membership of a social group involves spending money and reacting in empathy with one's chronological peer group rather than with a society as a whole involving all its members across the generations (Neufeld & Mate, 2004). As will become evident in this chapter, the distinction between what is known as 'popular culture' with its commercially manufactured products and a naturally occurring culture with its rituals, beliefs, and practices developed over time through Merriam's idea of 'diffusion' and Geertz's notion of 'webs of significance' forming a cultural system is an important one.

I chose to explain children's music-making in some detail in two societies which, by virtue of time or remote location, are either completely free from the influences of the contemporary global music entertainment industry and Western culture in general, as is certainly the case of historical Korea, or at least free from the intrusive effects of the entertainment industry of the last two or three decades, as is the case of reports from a remote area of Papua New Guinea where the *Kaulong* people live. In less detail I refer to a third from central Africa describing something of the role of music in the life-style of the Ituri Pygmies, the ancient culture mentioned by Plato. The reports on the latter two cultures were based on observations made earlier in the twentieth century depicting life-styles, which then were virtually untouched by Western culture and the global entertainment media. However, an important part of my examination is also to contrast and compare notions of psychological and physical development in these cultures with those current in contemporary Western culture.

Problems defining development and music across cultures

In attempting to describe and comment on involvement with what Western culture describes as children's music in these three different cultures there are certain definitional problems concerning what Western terms like music and child development might mean if applied to each of these traditions. The term development attracts considerable debate in Western society, especially the concept of adolescence, and in the three cultural settings I describe there appears to be no recognition of a state of adolescence. In fact, there is convincing evidence that in these cultures adulthood begins immediately at the onset of puberty, and the concept of the teenager or adolescent as neither child nor adult but something in between is unknown in these cultures. Moreover, childhood in the three cultures is regarded as a state of miniature adulthood within the mores of the culture making it difficult to identify developmental stages in terms defined by Western developmental psychology. Of course, one may argue that development as described in Western psychology probably occurs in all humans whether or not they recognize it. On the other hand, at issue is the extent to which the nature of a society encourages or even causes a particular type of growth and developmental trajectory. I present arguments supporting a close connection between the structures and practices of a culture and development, especially in music. Consequently, I describe development in these societies as defined and circumscribed by the traditions of the culture, guided and controlled by the adults of the culture who carry the cultural memes (Dawkins, 1989) in their heads and whose duty it is to pass them on to the next generation. Through this process one can identify a clear difference between the effects of contemporary popular entertainment in the West on many children and young adults who are defined as adolescents (Neufeld *et al.*, 2004) and those of the specific cultural tradition I describe.

Significantly, one major difference lies in the fact that there is little evidence in the societies I describe of children spending time listening to music from outside their traditional cultural surroundings; a marked contrast with the vast majority of young people's listening habits in contemporary Western society where 3–5 hours of listening to commercial popular music each day is reported (North *et al.*, 2000; Sloboda, 2001; Boal-Palheiros *et al.*, 2001; Lamont *et al.*, 2003). Only a minority of Western adolescents appear to be engaged with performing or listening to what might be called Western art music; i.e. the long-term, stable products of Western culture. This is markedly different in the three cultures I describe where active participation with all members and generations of the social group in the performance of music as it occurs in the regular rituals of daily life is normal as the child develops and where music of another culture is unknown, even regarded as alien. This situation has implications for musical development as the West might describe it.

The various transition stages found in Western developmental psychology do not appear to be acknowledged in the cultures I describe. One main reason for this is that there are no socio-political and economic structures and practices in these societies similar to those of Western culture. Two of the societies I describe are agrarian and hunter-gatherer (the *Kaulong* and the *Ituri*) where children do not go to school and are not separated from adults at large during their development and training. Instead they learn life skills from the whole social group as part of daily living, and music instruction is a communal preparation for the various ceremonies and daily rituals that form the essential framework of their cultural identity and their very existence. In the third, historical Korea, the monarchical structure of that society determined the nature of its social structures, how each social stratum lived and worked, and how instruction in music served the purpose of preparing young people for their roles in various court ceremonies.

First, I deal further, but briefly, with definitional issues concerning both adolescence and music. I focus some attention on the former because of the powerful influence of popular culture in Westernized societies today on young people of both pre-teen and teenage years, and the fact that puberty is now seen to occur earlier than hitherto in Western countries, especially among females, meaning that adolescence, as the West knows it, now lasts from the ages of about 8 to10 (Herman-Giddens *et al.*, 1997) to late teens or even beyond. In which case, I argue, adolescence is probably the most important and lengthy stage affecting emotional, and therefore musical, development in Western culture. In musical development, especially where listening is concerned, the emotions figure largely, as many studies of, and commentaries on, Western teenagers and their idolization of their favourite pop idol confirm (Frith, 1996; North *et al.*, 2000; Sloboda, 2001; Boal-Palheiros *et al.*, 2001; Lamont *et al.*, 2003).

Traditionally, as Plato, Confucius, and many early thinkers in many cultures claim, music affects the human emotions and behaviours generally more profoundly and immediately than any other expressive art form. The music of the global entertainment industry specifically targets young people's emotions in order to build allegiances for financial gain rather than cultural benefit with the result that young people attribute great significance to popular music and their own special pop idol wherever Western entertainment and its technology are available. It is this difference between cultural bonding through participation in traditional musical performances with the whole age group, and engagement in peer group idolization of pop stars through listening to popular music and watching pop videos that I want to highlight. I will concentrate most on the adolescent state in my analysis since music affects the emotions so immediately and profoundly, plus the fact that the Western concept of adolescence is traditionally associated with emotional turmoil.

Defining music

The term music in Western culture now refers specifically to singing and playing instruments. This has not always been the case in Western culture. The Western term music is derived from the Greek word *mousike* referring to the activities of the nine Muses, which ranged from poetry, dancing, astronomy, to flute playing, among others (Landels, 1999). During medieval times the Latin term *musica* was further defined by categories 'and one cannot always be immediately sure whether a writer . . . is talking about . . . the music of speech in verse or prose, or about acoustical theory, or the metaphorical harmony of gesture, or dance, or the movements of the spheres' (Stevens, 1986, p. 25).

The distinction between *musica mundana* (the music of the spheres: i.e. proportional mathematics and the cosmic purpose) and *musica instrumentalis* (the sounds of music in performance and therefore the lowest form of knowledge) was crucial to the Pythagoreans, for their proportional theory 'was really promulgating the inverse square law of gravitation' not just explaining musical temperament (Walker, 1978, p. 26). Actual musical sound was merely the sonic analogy of the perfect (or imperfect) harmony (what we would call gravity) which kept the planets in their celestial positions and the earth intact and functioning, and 'the difference between a musician and a singer is that between a grammarian and the man who reads the lesson' (Stevens, 1986, p. 376). Distinctions were made between instrumentalists and singers, and the more important theoreticians who were dealing with how music acted as a surrogate for the very nature of the cosmos expressed mathematically (Stevens, 1986). All this signifies the profound connections developed over time in Western culture between the musical theory of temperament and eventually the diatonic key system, expressed in the proportional mathematics used to define musical intervals (e.g. 2:1, the octave, 3:2 the fifth, and so on), the proportional theory itself, which explained cosmic matter and relationships between celestial objects, and the sounds of music, which were regarded as cosmic metaphors linked by proportional theory. To understand the meaning of the term music and its practices as they have evolved in Western culture requires some understanding of these ancient connections. In the Western traditions the term music has profound and ancient connotations that inform its current practices. The same is true of the 'music' of all cultures.

Many societies have no word for music *per se*, preferring instead to signify either specific activities or combinations of activities in the relevant social context. In some cultures music is defined by its specific context in ritual and its associated activities, whether dancing, miming, singing, or playing instruments. Among the Kaulong people of Papua New Guinea the term *lut* means the human voice, which is further defined by context. Thus we get the term *lut a yu* (singing with pigs who are then sacrificed: Goodale, 1995, p. 198), or *lutngin* (singsings with elders where children learn to sing: Goodale, 1995, p. 196). A totally different term, *dikaiyikngin*, means singing around (Goodale, 1995, p. 198) involving visitors to the village and thus distinguishing it from activities involving only village members. There are few societies in Africa where dancing is not an intrinsic part of what the West calls singing, and for many indigenous societies of North America playing the drum and singing, often together with dancing, are inseparable activities and all are defined by terms signifying their place in ritual.

Adolescence

The term adolescence became applied to teenagers during the mid-twentieth century specifically in North America, and then England. Some argue that it was an invention of commercial interests of the time because of the growing affluence of this age group (Ariès, 1962; Palladino, 1996). Of some importance to this argument is the fact that for the first time in Western history during the mid-twentieth century attendance at school was universally compulsory up to the age of about 14 or 15 years thus isolating this whole age group from adult society as a whole. After that age young people went to work and joined adulthood. Nowadays, because of governmental pressures to develop a highly educated workforce, most young people in Western countries are schooled until their late teens, further isolating the adolescent age group from adult society and encouraging the feeling of being a separate cultural entity.

Typically in Western societies during the twentieth century up to the 1950s the whole family would listen to the radio as a social group, and the content of music broadcasts would be aimed at the whole family. However, the invention of transistor radios coinciding with the emergence, during the 1950s, of *rock 'n roll* as a distinctly youth-oriented music resulted in teenagers being able to listen in isolation to their own choice of music without parental or family involvement. The emergence of a genre of popular music solely associated with teenagers and adolescence whose role was that of a spectator rather than performer marks the crucial difference between Western adolescent involvement in music and that of their chronological equivalents in the three traditional cultures I refer to.

Brief introduction to the three cultures

Whether it is the practice of *Lut u yu* (singing with pigs) in Papua New Guinea, the ancient Chinese elegant music of *Aak* in Korea, or the *elima* songs of the Ituri Pygmy in central Africa, children in these cultures were making adult music from their early childhood. Thus describing these activities as simply children making music is misleading, especially if the implication is that there might be a genre of children's music different from that of adult music in these societies.

The *Kaulong* people of Papua New Guinea, the historical kingdoms of ancient Korea, and the Ituri Pygmy society of the Ituri Forest have many words for the many different activities involving what the West sees as singing, dancing, acting, and playing instruments. Each word signifies the special socio-cultural importance of the ritualized context of the activity as well as reflecting the special and unique belief system and epistemology of the society. The *Kaulong* see pigs as central to their epistemology and their sense of being human. The Chinese practice of *Aak* in ancient Korea reflects the profound influence on that society of Confucian thought. And the *elima* puberty rites of the Ituri Pygmies reflect their deep attachment to their forest home. Children in these societies grow up with such cultural traditions and practices and learn adult ways of performing from their earliest years.

Singing with pigs and concepts of musical development among the *Kaulong* people

In *Kaulong* society, child development, if we can call it such in any Western sense, can be characterized as more teleological than psychological. Children learn early to perform adult duties involving tasks deemed essential for the survival of both the individual and the village community as a whole within their particular environment and epistemological system. In such a context, epistemological concerns arise from group beliefs about cause and effect, and often events and happenings are explicable only by attribution to magical or spiritual forces. Consequently, control of these forces is an essential part of the daily ritual of such societies where music plays a vital, even central role. Placation of higher forces and powers is achieved through singing, dancing, acting, and sacrificial offerings. It is within such a context that children acquire knowledge and life skills within which musical performance skills are essential. Psychological development as the West knows it becomes a somewhat irrelevant concept as the child learns from the very earliest how to sing, how to dance, how to hunt, and eventually to make magic spells, in the way adults do such things. Such learning is acquired by observation and participation rather than systematic instruction. Among the *Kaulong*, the child is regarded, ideologically, as a replacement adult for their parents almost immediately at birth (Goodale, 1995). There is little point to Western idealism regarding education in such societies, nor for theoretical notions of educational experience aimed at different stages of development, nor for philosophical speculation about what it might mean to be educated or to learn. Such ideals are not just unknown they are alien to the *Kaulong* knowledge system.

Pigs hold a central role in *Kaulong* life. Wild pigs can be killed at will for feasts. Domestic pigs, however, are sacred. They live with the family and are groomed and trained by the family as family members. Young pigs, for example, are put on a leash for the process of training. Pork is an important symbol of political and social power and used as a form of currency. Pigs with large tusks are considered most valuable, and often the upper teeth are removed in order that the lower canines can grow into tusks (Goodale, 1995). Ceremonies involving singing, acting, dancing, and spell making, are used to enhance the growth of tusks and train the pigs. There is an annual cycle of ceremonial pig-killing, which only happens in the morning and must be preceded by specially appropriate all-night singing—*lut u yu*. This is one of the most important ceremonies in the *Kaulong* calendar, and everyone takes part. *Lut u yu* (singsing with pigs) are also performed for all initiation rites, both male and female, and which involve the eventual ritual killing of the pig for a feast. However, no owner will eat his own pig. They will only eat someone else's because they tend to form an attachment to the animal as it enables them to affirm their 'humanness'. Here it should be mentioned that the *Kaulong* live very closely to various animals and other fauna and establishing and affirming their difference as humans is important to them. Other ceremonies all involving singing include the: *dikaiyikgin* (singing along with visitors or making crops grow or to settle disputes or to celebrate); *sasungin* (tooth blackening ceremony); *sasokngin* (funerals, *laugnin*—singing with skulls); *tubuan* (with masks); and *sia* (a masked dance) (Goodale, 1995).

If one must conceptualize the growth and development of children in the *Kaulong* society there are most probably only three such stages of child development that might be acknowledged. The first is the infant stage, where the baby relies on the mother's or another woman's milk for sustenance. Usually this lasts until the child is about 4 or 5 years old during which the infant spends its time exclusively in the care of women especially, but not exclusively, with their mother. During this time the infant will participate in singing and dancing as an appendage to the mother, and will attempt to imitate adult behaviour. The second stage is the time between having been weaned off the mother's milk and the onset of puberty. This usually lasts between the ages of about 4 or 5 and 10 or 12. This period is perhaps the most problematic to Western notions of development because these young children spend their time with adults and do not function socially as a separate age group. They are expected to start immediately learning the skills and traditions of the social group from adults by imitation. In effect they are regarded as small adults, an approach to children which was apparent in pre-industrial Western societies. As Ackland (1995) comments, in some paintings of village life prior to the seventeenth century, small children were depicted as little adults in their dress, their apparent demeanour, and their position in the group. Peter Bruegel's (1568) painting *The peasant dance*, for example, clearly depicts children as miniature adults (Abowitz & Rees, 2003).

Singing is considered equal to speaking for the *Kaulong*. Goodale (1995) reports that *Kaulong* children learn to sing at the same time as they learn to form the first phonemes of their language. Singing and speaking, while not being synonymous, are certainly contemporaneous in the learning processes. Children often sing before they can speak adequately (Simon, 1978, p. 447). Singing soon becomes for the child a main form of communication and expression. The *Kaulong* sing as they walk through the forest on the way to their gardens, on their way to the hunt, as they return in the afternoon, and in their houses at any time. Singing is extremely important to children as a means of establishing their individuality and essential humanity. Songs are learned through participation in the communal *singsings*. Children observe, and sometimes participate, or dance together arm in arm. Music is everywhere (Goodale, 1995). Men and women sing the same songs, and it is sometimes difficult to tell which gender is singing because they use the same tessitura, a practice that makes it easier for children to participate on equal terms.

Everyone in the community joins in singing and dancing on a daily basis. There are occasions, such as rituals and festivals, where only certain groups or genders were allowed to sing or dance, but these were for socially decided reasons to do with guarding magical spells, hiding ritualistic practices until people were ready, or maintaining some social hierarchy. They were not to do with any musical capability of lack of it due to musical developmental issues. Some songs proclaim social status: *pomidan* signifies an 'important big man', and *polamit* an 'important big woman'. Tooth blackening is an important ritual that is performed at the celebration of young adulthood where *sasungin* songs are sung and a pig is sacrificed (Goodale, 1995). Young men and women have an enormous amount of freedom and do a lot of visiting, and much of this visiting is to attend all-night singings with the whole group. There is no category of children's or teenager's songs. All songs are learned through a form of osmosis through imitation (Simon, 1978).

Development of musical ability

Despite the inclusive nature of children's music making in *Kaulong* society there is evidence that high ability is recognized in some children and not others. Goodale (1995) reports that 'some children are seen to be exceptional at a very early age … and that they often begin singing before they speak' (p. 120). Therefore, as in Western societies, it appears that some *Kaulong* children are regarded very early as more gifted than their peers and singled out for special treatment, and high standards in dancing and singing are expected of them. However, the Kaulong ideal of musical ability is confined strictly to their own traditions. As an illustration, there is an interesting account of the *Kaulong* people of Papua New Guinea hearing recordings of African *Yaruba* drummers for the first time, played to them by Jane Goodale in the early 1960s (Goodale, 1995). The adult *Kaulong* drummers commented somewhat contemptuously that 'these people don't know how to play the drums' (p. 196). As Goodale (1995) points out, to the Western ear the Yaruba would appear to be exceptionally fine drummers performing amazingly complex rhythms but the *Kaulong* react differently, displaying little awareness of, or even interest in, any norms other then their own relating to standards of musical complexity or excellence. Furthermore, Goodale (1995) explains that, for the *Kaulong* people, knowledge and its acquisition is considered to be an entirely individual problem rather than a collective or societal concern. Such an approach is almost the antithesis of the modern Western position towards education and development, and it produces a great deal of individualistic and idiosyncratic performance practice making stages of development difficult if not impossible to identify in terms of societal norms and standards. Nevertheless, the early emergence of giftedness appears to be recognized similarly in both Western and *Kaulong* societies. And while musical standards of excellence are clearly identifiable in the Western traditions, the highest levels of excellence in music performance in *Kaulong* society are individualistic and idiosyncratic.

Howe *et al.* (1998) argue that the evidence from a variety of research studies shows that lengthy, persistent, and focused practice provides the most reliable predictors of musical achievement. Even if there is such a thing as innate ability, they argue, no one has achieved high standards in music or any other activity without hard work and focused practice. Further, the evidence for innate ability is, they argue, unreliable and unconvincing, largely because of the retrospective and anecdotal nature of the accounts of its occurrence. However, respondents to their article argued differently. Csikszentmihaly (1998, p. 411) states that 'at this point, there is no conclusive support for either position, and it is doubtful that talent could be explained exclusively by only one of them'. Detterman *et al.* (1998), describe Howe *et al.*'s position as 'Absurd Environmentalism', and argued that studies supporting practice over talent' are incapable of showing differences because subjects are self-selecting on talent' (p. 411). Feldman and Katzir (1998, p. 411) argue for innate talent: 'Irvin Rosen, principal violinist of the Philadelphia Orchestra's second violin section, said after a performance by the then 11-year-old MiDori, if I practiced three thousand years, I couldn't play like that. None of us could' (p. 411). They go on to assert that 'in the presence of superior talent, most practitioners would acknowledge that such talent is a natural gift' (p. 411). Gagné's (1967) distinction between giftedness and talent is important here: the former being innate, the latter developed (see Chapter 12 for further reading).

It is clear from these exchanges that there is as much support for early recognition of giftedness in Western society as there is in *Kaulong* society, and the ways of recognizing it appear to be similar. The *Kaulong* describe exceptional children as

> bright eyed, fat and active, have shiny skins, bubbling over with good humour and joy at being themselves. They often begin singing before speaking. They are clowns, perceptive of

everything around them, and able to repeat imitate and mimic easily. Their language learning is accelerated and their entire childhood education and growth are intensified once they are identified, and it is carried out by all the inhabitants of the village.

Goodale (1995, p. 120)

Goodale (1995) mentions that she knew

one such charmer in Angelek. I was told that if anything happened to this four year old, his parents would hang themselves. Kawang, the young child, once performed an original dance to the acclaim of nearly two hundred people . . . His father said he had invented the steps when he was visiting in another hamlet. (p. 121)

Such descriptions are similar to those of the young Mozart who, during a family visit to Paris in 1766 was described by Friedrich Grimm as 'one of the most lovable of creatures imaginable, who puts wit and spirit into everything he says and does, with all the grace and sweetness of his age' (Landon, 1990, p. 65). And in 1770, the composer Hasse described him as 'handsome, vivacious, graceful and full of good manners; and knowing him, it is difficult to avoid loving him' (Kerst, 1965, p. 45) This gives some cause for speculating that children of high, and apparently, natural ability or giftedness display the same characteristics in any culture. One thing certainly seems universal, that the parents of such children feel an immense obligation to provide special nurturing to ensure the rapid development of such children. Many studies of Western musicians show strong parental involvement similar to that indicated above in the *Kaulong* parent of *Angelek*. Sloboda and Howe (1991) state that 'without strong parental encouragement . . .their children would never make good progress' (p. 18). Davidson *et al.* (1996) state that 'sustained parental encouragement was evident in almost all successful young musicians' (p. 402).

Making Aak in the Royal Courts of Korea

A clear distinction can be made between the education system established in ancient Korea in order to meet the musical requirements of the Royal Court and the child's induction into the music of the *Kaulong* people. The highly structured and organized courts of the kings of Korea administered the education and development of the musicians who performed at the various functions and locations required by court protocol. Court musicians were generally 'looked down upon, and excluded from certain privileges enjoyed by [court officials] . . . their status was one of the lowest within the court hierarchy' (Lee, 1980, p. 201). There were two different groups, *aksaeng* who came from aristocratic families, and *agong* from the common people. The *agong* performed the music at the Royal Ancestor's Shrine and at court banquets, and it was this group who played a 'more significant role in the history of Korean music' (Lee, 1980). The *aksaeng* performed the elegant music of *Aak*, which was Chinese ritual court music. Several hundred musicians were employed at any one time. The training was arduous. In order to reach the status of a 'qualified regular court musician in the Office of Performers, four stages of training were required' (Lee, 1980, p. 202).

Children entered training early in order to be accepted into the appropriate musical institute for their social class. The Korean Royal Courts were centres of learning, literacy, and elegance, with highly complex ceremonials accompanied by sophisticated and highly trained musical ensembles and dancers. In many ways, the musical establishments of the Korean Royal Courts appear to resemble those of monastic Europe during both the period of religious social and political hegemony up to the Reformation, and certainly parallel those of the more secular rulers during the European Enlightenment. The development and training of Korean court musicians were highly institutionalized and controlled by complex bureaucratic and administrative structures, paralleling the contemporary institutionalized monastic training schools of medieval and early Renaissance Europe. Additionally, the introduction of notation systems was an important development in Korean court music during the reign of King Sejong (1418–1450), resulting in more efficient training methods. In Europe, Guido D'Arezzo's introduction of staff notation, solfege, and the Guidonian Hand (*gamut)* in the eleventh century was a similarly important development in Western monastic musical training.

There is another parallel of sorts between the historical European traditions and those of the Royal Courts of Korea in the exclusive use of males as musicians. However, female entertainers were 'attached to the court and regional governments [and] had been chosen as young girls from the common people and sent to the court to learn court entertainment' (Lee, 1980, p. 201). Chang (1983) reports that the training of female musicians was associated with the training of doctors, which began in 1406 at the Office of Medical Affairs. Females practised diagnosis and acupuncture and were also trained in singing and dancing. Prior to being accepted for such training, young girls were first trained in Chinese classical practices in their home town and further educated at the *Chesaengwon,* the Office of Medical Affairs. These female entertainers, or *kisaeng,* were also recognized prostitutes and were 'often chosen as concubines of the king and high officials' (Lee, 1980). Lee further explains that 'despite their low social status and insignificant family background, the contribution of the *kisaeng* to Korean music and dance was considerable. It was through the *kisaeng* that the songs and dances of court music (called *yoak*: female music) were carried beyond the palace and transmitted to the general public' (p. 201).

Outside the court, traditional folk musicians and dancers, *kwangdae,* travelled the country playing to the general public. One such tradition was that of *p'ansori,* a one-person opera accompanied by a drummer. The *p'ansori* singing style, as performed by females, is unique, and requires long and arduous training in order to develop the harsh and penetrating sound required. Chang (1983) explains that, as a part of this training, young girls shouted at the hills daily for several years until their voices were hoarse.

The traditional Korean kingdoms referred to stretch back well over 2000 years. The Three Kingdoms period (57 BC to AD 668) was a time when each state in the kingdom emphasized a different instrument. The music of this period was heavily influenced by China and to a lesser extent by contact with Japan. Yet despite this, Korea developed its own distinct musical style and content. This was followed by the United Shilla period (AD 668–936), when Korea became unified. China's high Buddhist culture became a major influence (Lee, 1980), but there arose a clear distinction between traditional Korean music and that of China. The Koryo dynasty (AD 918–1392) chose Buddhism as its dynastic religion, yet much of the Shilla musical traditions continued.

Another important development was the creation of *Aak,* an elegant court ritual music associated with Confucianism (Lee, 1980). This firmly instituted the court orchestra, which in 1430 constituted an ensemble ranging up to 33 different musical instruments (Chang, 1983, p. 85). These included stone chimes (*p'yon'g yong*), bell chimes (*p'yonjong*), pounded wooden boxes (*ch'uk*), clay pots (*pu*), transverse flutes (*taegom*), double reed instruments such as the *chongmyoak*, a variety of drums such as the *chin'go* (a barrel drum), and zithers, such as the seven-stringed *Ajaeng*, or the *Kayago*, a 12-stringed zither (Lee, 1980).

Such a variety of complex instruments signals the need for long and arduous training. Although there is scant evidence indicating the age at which young Korean boys began to learn these instruments, it is clear from what we know of learning similarly complex Western instruments that it must have begun at least as early as about the age of 8–10 or even earlier. Apart from the complexities of performing on individual instruments, their use in large groups such as an orchestra would also require significant training in ensemble playing. It seems credible, then, to speculate that boys and girls who became *kisaeng* must have started their training as young children, probably in their homes. To this extent, the development and training of Korean court musicians would resemble that of their Western counterparts in Medieval, Renaissance, and Enlightenment Europe.

The Choson dynasty (AD 1392–1910) is usually divided into two main parts, the first up to 1593, and the second from AD 1593–1910. The earlier of these two saw major developments in music notation, the firm establishment of a Royal Music Department, and the emergence of tuning systems based on the cycle of fifths using the principal pitch of the *huang-chung*, the bronze bell of the Chinese Ming dynasty (Lee, 1980, p. 194). During this time, the processes and organization of music education for court musicians remained relatively unchanged in its methods except that it became more focused and organized. Learning was based on the master-disciple relationship where music was taught orally. The masters demonstrated performance practice and the pupils (disciples) imitated and repeated pieces many times until they mastered all the skills necessary (Chang, 1986). In such a system musical development was clearly circumscribed by the needs of the various court ceremonies at which musicians had to perform.

The students in the musical institutes were examined, much as they are today through performance examination boards such as the *Australian Music Examination Board, Trinity College of Music*, and the *Associated Board of the Royal Schools of Music*. Chang (1983) reports that in 1471, 'the examinees were asked to perform the following numbers: candidates for Chinese style court music were to play three court music numbers, a song, a civilian and a military ritual dance. Candidates for Chinese style folk music were to perform five examples as well as other numbers.' (p. 85).

These candidates would be aged approximately 10–13 years old and expected to go through the next stages and be examined even more rigorously at its conclusion. For example, those later 'wanting to specialise in Chinese folk music had to perform 41 numbers, while those for traditional Korean music performed 31 numbers'. (Chang, 1983, p. 85).

There is no evidence of the existence of children's music that was different to that of adults, and it appears from the historical records that in the traditions of the Korean Royal Courts young people were trained from the beginning in the same music as that performed by adults.

Social structures and children's singing and dancing

Significant differences can be observed distinguishing children's involvement in singing and dancing as a function of the social structuring of a society. In monarchies, where society is stratified and divided by social class, position, and wealth, children are musically trained systematically to serve the needs of the Royal Court protocols. Part of this training involves examinations to determine their level of competence in adult performance. Only when the rigorous training is satisfactorily completed can the child participate in performances at court. This was the developmental pathway in music for children in the ancient kingdom of Korea where boys were trained from a young age to perform at the various court ceremonies and girls were trained in dancing and singing. However, in hunter and agrarian societies such as the Kaulong of Papua New Guinea or hunter-gatherer societies such as the Ituri Pygmies of Central Africa, children participated in the ritualized daily singing and dancing from early childhood, imitating the adults and gradually becoming able to participate fully. In such societies there is no sense of needing to be trained to acquire specific levels of skills before being able to participate. It is not so much that these were acquired through a process of osmosis, but rather that a young person's performance was valued as much as the individual who provided it.

This is for two main reasons: epistemologically each individual developed their own knowledge, which was personal and private indicating that each individual also developed their own ways of singing, dancing, and participating in the group ritual. Evidence from the Kaulong suggests that some children appeared to be born with special musical skills and they made up their own dancing and singing at a very early age. In comparison, we can see how Western culture has been structured first by the church, with is own musical demands and training system, then by the aristocracy and the demands of court life, and then by political and commercial forces. Each of these requires training in musical performance relevant to the various religious, political, or commercial interests and purposes of adult society. The growth of a specific music for children different in style and content from adult music emerged in the West from the late eighteenth century onwards inspired by the writings of Rousseau and the educational practices of Pestalozzi, Montessouri, Froebel, Steiner, and many others who advocated a more child-centred approach to learning.

Considering the state of adolescence, its music, and comparisons between the modern West, the Kaulong, the Ituri Pygmies, and ancient Korea

The above description highlights what I believe are substantial differences between contemporary Western and the traditional societies. Many studies of teenagers demonstrate conclusively that popular music is one of the most important sources of emotional sustenance in a Western teenager's life (Steele & Brown, 1995; Frith, 1996; North *et al.*, 2000; MacDonald *et al.*, 2002; Neufeld *et al.*, 2004). Among the Kaulong, the Ituri, and the ancient Korean people music is quite clearly important to their lives, but there are two caveats: one is the fact that the music each refers to is the music of their culture as a whole, not some special commercial category, which is aimed solely at teenagers and excludes adults; the other is the way in which Western teenagers appear to use music compared with their counterparts in the other cultures mentioned. Concerning the latter, music is something that forms a significant part of everyday life in the culture and it serves the community as a whole, probably in much the same way it did in Western culture prior to the rise of the transistor radio, rock 'n roll, MTV, and other global popular music media outlets. In this way there is a sharing and a bonding between all members of the culture through music in ways that do not occur in contemporary Western society where popular music and many teenagers are concerned.

Puberty naturally forms a division between childhood and adulthood because of the emergence of sexual capabilities for reproduction. The troubled teenager or the alienated adolescent has become a Western stereotype over the last half of the twentieth century and commensurate with such portents of antisocial behaviour has developed successive genres of popular music signalling stressful relationships with the adult world. This music is not part of the European-based traditions of Western music. It is essentially the music of African-American societies that has been appropriated for commercial purposes, thus diminishing the uniquely expressive and powerful music of the African-American. Rock 'n Roll was first abducted into its role of signifying Western teenage angst by the entertainment industry during the 1950s. However, the original African-American Blues music, which became Rock 'n Roll, was adult music with adult themes in the lyrics and associated dances. It had nothing to do with the state of adolescence, and in some ways its blatant commercial use outside its cultural embedding degrades this unique cultural form of music (Lomax, 1993). The first major Rock 'n Roll teenage hits were little more than adult Rhythm and Blues numbers played fast and sung by young Caucasian Americans. For example, Elvis Presley's 1956 hit *Hound Dog* was originally a slow Rhythm and Blues number written by Jerry Leiber and Mike Stoll for Big Mama Thornton (1926–84) who first recorded it in 1953.

The teenage years without commercially generated angst

Nothing could be further from the reality of emergent adulthood for Kaulong teenagers in Papua New Guinea, or the *Ituri Pygmie* teenagers in central Africa, than the manufactured Western concept of teenagers as troubled beings. The *Kaulong* celebrate the transition to adulthood at puberty with a *Lut u yu*, a ceremony of 'singing with pigs' (Goodale, 1995). The *Lut u yu* is a major event where literally singing with pigs is the focus. For a major ritual and celebration, such as puberty rites, a pig is killed and a major 'singing' held, which often lasts for days. These 'singsings' include special songs for the puberty rituals celebrating the coming to womanhood or manhood. For the *Ituri Pygmie* people, the '*elima*' celebration is the puberty ritual where songs and dances welcome both boys and girls into adulthood (Turnbull, 1976). The '*elima*' songs and dances are joyful and celebratory. Young men show their courage to fight and kill an animal. Young women at first stay in the '*elima*' house at the beginning of the ceremony, but eventually emerge to chase the men of their choice, often with whips for compelling the men to go with them (Turnbull, 1976). Such gender roles are circumscribed by tribal laws and tradition. Importantly, the *Kaulong* and *Ituri* adolescent are fully active participants in the music and dancing, unlike many of their Western counterparts who spend up to 3 or 4 hours each day passively listening to someone else performing teenage popular music (North *et al.*, 2000) and whom they only experience vicariously through visual and auditory recordings.

We can observe the Western entertainment industry version of puberty and adolescence in the form of Britney Spears, currently regarded as a popular music 'diva', who sings about a supposed in-between state with the words 'I'm not a girl, not yet a woman', a major hit in 2001. In this 'pop' song it is as though puberty is some sort of limbo with the female lost in an in-between world. For the young women of the Kaulong and the Ituri people, puberty is a time for celebration: they are ritually accepted as women, able and free to marry and conceive. On the first menstruation, their transition from small form of adult to adult woman is instant and cause for jubilation through singing and dancing. The same is true of young males who, at their puberty, immediately become men, with all the responsibilities, through ritual celebration.

In contrast, in the invented world of mass entertainment, puberty from the 1950s onwards was characterized as a time of crisis, turmoil, and confusion in the music and lyrics of Rock 'n Roll through to Grunge, Rap, and all the other genres of commercial pop. This intrusion by the music entertainment media into developmental issues started in 1954 with the 19-year-old Elvis Presley singing a Rhythm and Blues number 'That's all right Mama' in Sam Parker's Memphis Studio. Parker 'realized he had found the kind of singer he'd been looking for—a white kid who sounded black' (Bronson, 1995, p. 6).

Prior to the twentieth century, the teenage years in Western culture were regarded quite differently to the way they are now depicted in mass entertainment. There is no historical or literary evidence of either a troubled adolescent state nor a specially designed music for channelling teenage emotions. That astute observer of human behaviour, William Shakespeare, provided no verbal portraits of teenage angst. If such had existed in his day as a natural and inevitable stage of human development, one can be certain that Shakespeare would have captured its essence somewhere in his works, especially in Romeo and Juliet where both main characters were teenagers. Their problem was not adolescent angst but the ancient feud that existed between their respective families. The nearest we come to any reference to the teenager years is in the play As you like it and the passage spoken by Jaques, beginning 'All the world's a stage'. The seven ages of man depicted by Shakespeare move from the schoolboy directly to the lover:

> Then the whining school-boy, with his satchel
> And shining morning face, creeping like a snail
> Unwillingly to school. And then the lover,
> Sighing like a furnace, with a woeful ballad
> Made to his mistress' eyebrow.

Act 2, Scene 7

Shakespeare's young man is not raging against the oppression of an adult world; he is merely a young man in love and relishing the power of his manhood as he woos his lady. And prior to Shakespeare another highly observant literary figure, Geoffrey Chaucer, describes some young renegades dancing, gambling, and womanizing as follows:

> In Flanders, once, there was a company
> Of young companions, given to folly,
> Riot and gambling, brothels and taverns,
> They danced and played at dice both day and night.

Chaucer's young men are not railing at the inequities of adult oppression. Instead they are tasting all the fruits life has to offer. A few lines later, their foolishness (but note, it is not emotional turmoil due to some adolescent state) becomes bravado when, in their drunken condition, they decide to avenge the deaths of some locals by taking on Death himself:

> Yea, by God's arms! Exclaimed this roisterer
> Is it such peril, then, this Death to meet?
> I'll seek him in the road and in the street.
> As I now vow to God's own noble bones!
> Hear, comrades, we're of one mind, as each owns;
> Let each of us hold up his hand to other
> And each of us become the other's brother,
> And we three will go slay this traitor Death.

> From The Pardonner's Tale,
> in *The Canterbury Tales*, by Geoffrey Chaucer

Ariès (1962) explains that in medieval Europe, 'the movement from child to adult was instantaneous ... once he had passed the age of five or seven, the child was immediately absorbed into the world of adults ... by the age of ten, girls were already little women ... and they were taught to behave very early in life like grown-ups' (p. 329). Palladino (1996, p. 52) argues that the concepts teenager and adolescence are inventions of mid-twentieth century commerce and advertising in the USA. The fact that from the 1940s teenagers in the USA were suddenly compelled to spend much of their teenage years in school because of legislation requiring them to be educated as opposed to working in the adult world for wages, meant that this age group became socially isolated from adults to form a new socio-economic group ready for commercial exploitation. Palladino (1996) argues that this is precisely what happened through popular music, movies, and associated clothing and other paraphernalia specifically targeting the teenage market. In the UK this occurred about a decade later following the 1944 Education Act which provided free and compulsory secondary education for all (Hebdidge, 1988, 1997).

The world of commercial entertainment made it their business to invent and then to accommodate the musical tastes of teenagers (Palladino, 1996). In the USA and UK, from the mid-twentieth century on, teenagers were suddenly confronted with an array of choices in music that were different from those of their parents and adult society at large. Thus, the alienation of teenagers from adult society was manufactured largely through music and entertainment (Ackland, 1995; Palladino, 1996). The very idea of giving teenagers a choice in music marks a major difference between practices in the West and in traditional societies such as the Kaulong. In the latter, the idea of choice in such things as which songs to listen to or peer group pressures supporting one song or performer over another are alien to the culture.

There are other important issues relating to puberty and the concept of development that arose in Western thinking over the last century. I briefly examine two: the Recapitulation theory, and the Freeman–Mead controversy. My reason for this concerns societal attitudes to emerging sexuality, the Western stereotypes of the 'troubled' adolescent and the adolescent *per se* as a person inevitably in a traumatic, confused, and stressed state, misunderstood and treated badly by adults. The musical corollary to this is the teenage pop-idol who first emerged during the 1950s essentially in the form of Elvis Presley. There is no evidence of either adolescent storm and stress or matching teenage music in the three cultures I have described above. Most important, however, is the academic controversy focusing on this precise issue: the Freeman–Mead controversy beginning in the1980s. Its provenance is highly relevant as well as illuminating. The recapitulation theory has had significant influence on Western music education pedagogy during the twentieth century where ironically there is reference to the use of 'primitive' music as a foundation for Western music education of young children.

The Freeman–Mead controversy

A view of adolescence, purporting to show that in some cultures there was no stress nor angst and rebellion, was that proposed by Margaret Mead during the 1920s in Samoa. Mead (1928/1973) suggested that Samoan adolescents 'experienced a transition to adulthood that was relatively stress-free in relation to Western societies' (Côté, 2000, p. 525), by which Mead meant the USA. She argued that since all adolescents undergo the same biological changes, the reason must be cultural.

Freeman (1983, 1999) led a ferocious attack on Mead in both the academic press and the media. Freeman made the accusation that 'Mead's account of Samoan culture . . . is fundamentally in error' (Côté, 2000, p, 533). Côté (2000) states that 'there is a consensus that Freeman's case . . . is flawed in several ways' (p. 536). The controversy caused problems on at least two fronts: one moral, the other political involving which type of determinism is involved, biological or cultural. Freeman appears to be a staunch advocate of biological determinism. However, Freeman's statements about Samoan society displayed an astonishing lack of knowledge and understanding of the role of sexual mores among different world cultures. The males and females of some South Pacific cultures regard sexual activity as a normal and unexceptional part of the human condition, as reported by Goodale (1995) in her account of life among the Kaulong at puberty rites. Moreover, Goodale (1995) reports that the Kaulong regard any sexual activity between men and women as 'placing both permanently in the category of married persons' (p. 23). Here it should be mentioned that some contemporary studies of Western adolescence show that there is little evidence of the expected 'storm and stress' associated with adolescence in homes where parents and children get along well, and where the young person has developed a sense of personal worth and well-being (Ben-Zur, 2003). The point being that Western pop music signifying teenage angst and rebellion is media generated, not culturally instigated.

Mead's findings of fewer signs of the inevitable storm and stress among the Samoan adolescents provided, she claimed, evidence for a culturally determined affect on behaviour, and not an automatic biologically determined one. Freeman's aim was to attack the culturally determined position through his overt attacks on Mead and what he termed her 'obeisance' to the supervisor of Mead's research project, Franz Boas, the first Professor of Anthropology at Columbia University, New York. Boas was a strong advocate of cultural determinism. He was of expatriate German Jewish origin and he specifically targeted the Nazi deterministic view of race during the 1930s.

The influence on development and music education of the recapitulation theory

A controversial Western concept of human development was formulated during the second half of the nineteenth century. Ernst Haeckel (1866), a zoologist, postulated that onto-geny recapitulates phylogeny. At the beginning of the twentieth century supporters of the recapitulation theory of human development saw it as essentially a Darwinian perspective on human development but without any empirical basis of proof it was entirely speculative. The basic premise was that as children grew up they inevitably went through the various stages of evolution through which the species had emerged, starting as fish in the womb, becoming amphibious as young children, which explains their fascination with water, and so on. The absurdity of such an idea has been fully exposed by Gould (1977) who reports that the recapitulation theory had been thoroughly discredited scientifically by the second decade of the twentieth century. Nevertheless, this doctrine affected many aspects of edu-cation, especially the concept of development and music education pedagogy from early in the twentieth century. Piaget was trained as a zoologist during what Gould (1977) describes as 'the heyday of Haeckelian recapitulation' (p. 144) and while, according to Gould, Piaget 'believes in parallels between ontogeny and phylogeny, he denies Haeckelian recapitulation as the mechanism' (p. 144). However, the Piagetian stages of development are essentially based on the recapitulation approach (Gould, 1977).

The idea of children going through developmental stages that replicate some part of the organism's history had, for some music educators, profound implication for the type of music children should be exposed to during their educational development and sub-sequently for music education practices in general. The pedagogy of Carl Orff, a most significant influence in music education for children across the world, relied on aspects of the recapitulation theory approach. Most pertinent, however, is the evidence of musical engagement by children in the many non-Western societies that have been studied by ethnomusicologists over the last century. This evidence clearly shows that in these tra-ditional societies there is no such thing as children's or teenager's music (Simon, 1978; Turnbull, 1976; Goodale, 1996). All young people listen to and perform adult music from birth. And much of this music is very complex indeed, even by Western standards of art music. Empirically, and logically, there can be no justification for applying the recapitulation theory of development to music education using the music of so-called primitive societies, especially as the theory posited that children pass through a stage of musical development equivalent to that of adults in primitive societies on their way to the more sophisticated stages of Western musical culture and its associated music (i.e., from simple to complex music). The logical problem is this. If all children pass through this primitive stage in their musical development towards sophisticated adult music, and since the Kaulong and Ituri children only experience adult music from birth, what developmental stages in music could they pass through?

Perhaps the most influential advocate of the recapitulation approach was the American G. Stanley Hall (1904), 'the father of a scientific psychology of adolescence' (Muuss, 1996, p. 1). He applied the approach to child development with conviction and enthusiasm to become very influential in American educational theory and practice. Hall's (1904) text on adolescence was the beginning in the West, especially in the USA, of a scholarly identification of adolescence as a period of stress, bad behaviour, rebellion, and emotional outbursts because of sexual awakening and associated tension. It is this that the commercial world revived to exploit during the 1940s and 1950s. Hall argued that because this supposed state was biologically based 'ontogenesis recapitulates phylogenesis as a normal part of human development (hence it applies to all people regardless of their culture)' (Côté, 2000, p. 527). Consequently, one would expect to find evidence of adolescent angst in all societies.

In music education, the *Schulwerk* method of Carl Orff (Horton, 1980), developed in Germany during the 1920s, is loosely based on this idea of recapitulation of musical practices from the primitive and simple to the complex, sophisticated, and civilized. Orff became interested in the correlation between dance and music in children's development through his contact with Mary Wigman, a pupil of both Emile-Jacques Dalcroze and Rudolf von Laban (Horton, 1980). Dalcroze developed his concept of Eurhythmics (Dalcroze, 1921/1967) as a method of teaching music very early in the twentieth century, trying it out first in primary schools. Darwinism infected most areas of intellectual endeavour at the time, and rhythm was considered the most obviously primitive component in music from which children could develop towards the more sophisticated uses of melody, harmony and musical structure. The reason for this was the clear connection between dance and song observed in the musical performances of many so-called primitive non-Western societies which, by this time, had appeared at many European exhibitions from the mid-nineteenth century onwards as well as in many reports of European explorers and early anthropologists. The inextricable connection in many traditional societies between dance and music was, therefore, well known in Europe early in the twentieth century. Similarly, instruments such as the xylophone and the metallophone became known in Europe during the nineteenth century. The Indonesian gamelan instruments became known to musicians because of their appearance at the Paris Exposition of 1889, and they represented a so-called primitive stage of musical development to some Europeans, especially those convinced of the efficacy of the recapitulation theory of development.

Orff saw the gamelan and the African xylophone, especially in their use of moveable metal or wooden bars for each individual pitch, as a natural starting point for children as they progressed through their phylogenetic development in music. In 1924 he and Dorothee Günter founded a school in Munich for the 'coordinated teaching of music, gymnastics, and dance' (Horton, 1980, p. 707). The first part of Orff's *Schulwerk* appeared in 1930. Günter and Orff believed that children should learn simple repetitive patterns first because, as primitives in their stage of development, they naturally take to primitive music because it was repetitive and simple. They then progress to more complex music as they develop physically and psychologically, especially cognitively. Such an idea invalidates the musical sophistication of societies such as the *Kaulong* and the *Ituri Pygmies*, not to mention that of the Indonesian gamelan traditions in general. It implies that such music is considered childish in the larger canvas of the development of music among humans, *per se*. Nothing could be further from the truth.

The fact that children in the cultures described in this chapter participated from early childhood in the ceremonies of their culture, and were thus inducted straight into the adult music of their society, indicates a clear difference from Western practices in attitudes to musical development. In the West, musical development is thought by many to be evident in discrete stages of cognitive and affective development matched by incremental progressions from simple to complex musical activities, eventually leading to adult music.

Acknowledgements

I wish to thank Myung-sook Auh, of the University of New England, who translated from Korean relevant sections from *Korean Music History* by Chang, Sa Hoon. This provided me with information I cite in this chapter. Dr Auh also explained many details of the references that were in Korean, including the instruments played and the notation system, which allowed me to use another important source in her possession, *Traditional Korean Music*, a text edited by the Korean National Commission for UNESCO. I am also grateful to Christine Yau for helping me find the references to Mozart's childhood.

References

Abowitz, K. K. & Rees, R. (2003). *What is a teenager?* http://www.units.muohio.eduleadership/courses

Ackland, C. R. (1995). *Youth, murder, spectacle: The cultural politics of 'Youth in Crisis'*. Boulder, CO: Westview Press.

Ariès, P. (1962). *Centuries of childhood*. London: Jonathan Cape. Trans. R. Baldick.

Ben-Zur, H. (2003). Happy adolescents: the link between subjective well-being, internal resources, and parental factors. *Journal of Youth and Adolescence*, 23(2), 67–79.

Boal-Palheiros, G. & Hargreaves, D. J. (2001). Listening to music at home and at school. *British Journal of Music Education*, 18(2), 103–118.

Bronson, F. (1995). *Hottest hits*. New York: Billboard.

Chang, S. (1983). Education in Korean Music. *Part 3: Traditional Korean Music*. Edited by the Korean National Commission for UNESCO. Seoul: Si-sa-yong-o-sa Publishers Inc. Korea.

Csikszentmihaly, M. (1998). Fruitless polarities. *Behavioural and Brain Sciences*, 21, 411.

Côté, J. E. (2000). The Mead-Freeman controversy in review. *Journal of Youth and Adolescence*, 29(5), 525–538.

Dalcroze, J. (1921/1967). *Rhythm, music, and education* (trans. H.F. Rubenstein). Geneva: The Dalcroze Society.

Davidson, J. W., Howe, M. J., Moore, D. G., & Sloboda, J. (1996). The role of parental influences in the development of musical performance. *British Journal of Developmental Psychology*, 14, 399–442.

Dawkins, R. (1989). *The selfish gene*. Oxford: Oxford University Press.

DeNora, T. (2000). *Music in everyday life*. Cambridge: Cambridge University Press.

Detterman, D. K., Gabriel, L. T., & Ruthsatz, J. M. (1998). Absurd environmentalism. *Behavioural and Brain Sciences*, 21, 411.

Draaisma, D. (2000). *Metaphors of memory: A history of ideas about the mind*. Cambridge: Cambridge University Press.

Draaisma, D. (2004). *Why life speeds up as you get older: How memory shapes our past*. Cambridge: Cambridge University Press.

Feldman, D. H. & Katzir, T. (1998). Natural talents: An argument for the extremes. *Behavioural and Brain Sciences*, 21, 414.

Freeman, D. (1983). *Margaret Mead and Samoa: The making and unmaking of an anthropological myth.* Cambridge MA: Harvard University Press.

Freeman, D. (1999). *The fateful hoaxing of Margaret Mead: An historical analysis of her Samoan research.* Boulder, CO: Westview Press.

Frith, S. (1996). *Performing rites.* Cambridge, MA: Harvard University Press.

Gagné, R. (1967). *Learning and individual differences.* Columbus, OH: C. Merrill.

Geertz, C. (1973). *The interpretation of cultures.* New York: Basic Books.

Geertz, C. (1983). *Local knowledge.* New York: Basic Books.

Goodale, J. C. (1995) *To sing with pigs is human: the concept of person in Papua New Guinea.* Seattle: University of Washington Press.

Gould, S. J. (1977) *Ontogeny and phylogeny.* Cambridge MA: Harvard University Press.

Hall, G. S. (1904). *Adolescence.* New York: Appleton.

Haeckel, E. (1866). *General morphology of organisms.* Berlin: Georg Reimer.

Hawkins, J. (1776/1969). *A general history of the science and practice of music.* New York: Dover Press.

Hebdidge, D. (1988). *Hiding in the light.* London: Routledge

Hebdidge, D. (1997). *Posing threats, striking poses: Youth surveillance and display.* In K. Gelder & S. Thornton (eds), *The subcultures reader* (pp. 393–405). New York: Routledge.

Herman-Giddens, M. E., Slora, E. J., Wasserman R. C., Bourdony, C. J., Bhapkar, M. V., Koch, G. G., & Hasemeier, C. M. (1997). Secondary sexual characteristics and menses in young girls seen in office practice: a study from the Pediatric Research in Office Settings network. *Pediatrics*, 99, 505–512.

Horton, J. (1980). Carl Orff. In S. Sadie (ed.), *The new Grove dictionary of music and musicians*, Vol. 13 (p. 707). London: MacMillan.

Howe, J. A. H., Davidson, J. W., & Sloboda, J. A. (1998). Innate talents: Reality or myth. *Behavioural and Brain Sciences*, 21, 399–442.

Kerst, F. (1965). *Mozart—The man and the artist revealed in his own words* (trans. H. E. Krehbiel). New York: Dover.

Lamont, A., Hargreaves, D.J., Marshall, N.A., & Tarrant, M. (2003). Young people's music in and out of school. *British Journal of Music Education*, 20(3), 229–241.

Landels, J. G. (1999). *Music in ancient Greece and Rome.* London: Routledge.

Landon, H. C. R. (1990). *The Mozart compendium. A guide to Mozart's life and music.* London: Thames & Hudson.

Lee, B.W. (1980). Korea. In S. Sadie (ed.), *The new Grove dictionary of music and musicians*, Vol. 10 (pp. 192–208). London: MacMillan.

Lomax, A. (1993). *The land where the blues began.* New York: Pantheon Books

McDonald, R., Hargreaves, D. J., & Miell, D. (2002). *Musical identities.* Oxford: Oxford University Press.

Mead, M. (1928/1973). *Coming of age in Samoa: A psychological study of primitive youth for western civilization.* New York: Morrow Quill Paperbacks.

Merriam, A. P. (1997). *The anthropology of music.* Chicago, IL: Northwestern University Press.

Muuss, R. (1996). *Theories of adolescence.* New York: McGraw-Hill.

Neufeld, G. & Mate, G. (2004). *Hold on you lids: Why parents matter.* Toronto: Knopf.

North, A. C., Hargreaves, D. J., & O'Neill, S. A. (2000). The importance of music to adolescents. *British Journal of Educational Psychology*, 70, 255–272.

Palladino, G. (1996). *Teenagers: an American history.* New York: Basic Books.

Simon, A. (1978). Types and functions of music in the eastern highlands of West Irian. *Ethnomusicology,* 22(3), 441–455.

Sloboda, J. (2001). Conference keynote: Emotion, functionality and the everyday experience of music: Where does music education fit? *Music Education Research,* 3(2), 243–253.

Sloboda J. A. & Howe, M. (1991). Biographical precursors of musical excellence: an interview study. *Psychology of Music,* 19, 3–21.

Steele, J. R. & Brown, J. D. (1995). Adolescent room culture: Studying media in the context of everyday life. *Journal of Youth and Adolescence,* 24(5), 551–575.

Stevens, J. (1986). *Words and music in the middle ages.* Cambridge: Cambridge University Press.

Turnbull, C. (1976). *The forest people.* London: Pan Books.

Walker, D. P. (1978). *Studies in musical science in the late renaissance.* London: The Warburg Institute.

Walker, R. (1986). Music and multi-culturalism. *International Journal of Music Education,* 8, 43–52.

Walker, R. (1987). The effects of culture, environment, age, and musical training, on choices of visual metaphors for sound. *Perception and Psychophysics,* 42(5), 491–502.

Walker, R. (1990). *Musical beliefs: Psychoacoustic, mythical, and educational perspectives.* New York: Teachers College Press, Columbia University.

Walker, R. (1997). Musically significant acoustic parameters and their notations in vocal performances across different cultures. *Journal of New Music Research,* 26(4), 315–345.

CHAPTER 23

POSITIVE YOUTH MUSICAL ENGAGEMENT

SUSAN A. O'NEILL

A new vision of youth musical involvement has emerged in recent years. This vision is predicated on the idea that every young person has the potential and capacity for positive engagement in musical activities. What makes this vision particularly exciting is that it comes at a time in the history of civilization when there is an unprecedented amount of musical diversity in our culture. Opportunities for young people's musical involvement are multifaceted, diverse, and heterogeneous; they extend to a wide range of activities, take place in a variety of social contexts, cater to varied interests, and include many different approaches, styles, and genres. Never before has there been such a strong awareness of the importance of music in the lives of females and males from diverse educational, economic, racial/ethnic and multicultural backgrounds, and from all ages across the lifespan. And all this is happening at a time when there is growing recognition of the need to provide opportunities for all young people to develop more than the musical skills and competencies associated with formal systemic and structural music and music education traditions. We must also provide opportunities for young people to develop the beliefs and values that will foster their sense of self and self-responsibility, desire, and motivation for positive musical engagement, as well as respect for the diversity of musical practices in their world.

Although music is an integral part of the lives of children and adolescents, the experiences that maximize their involvement in musical activities from the earliest years of development until they have moved beyond the reach of formal music education are deeply rooted in the concept of *generativity*. This concept can be traced back at least 2500 years to Plato's notion of immortality and the externalization of the self—a concern for establishing and guiding the next generation (see further McAdams & de St Aubin, 1998). More recently, the concept of generativity is discussed *vis-à-vis* Erik Erikson's (1968) theoretical ideas of identity formation, in terms of its ontology in the development and well-being of the next generation. It is about caring for and educating young people by assuming the role of responsible adult (e.g., parent, guardian, mentor, teacher). It is also about being a responsible citizen, a contributing member of a community, a leader, an enabler. As such, generativity provides a useful framework for thinking about musical development at many different levels.

In this chapter, I will consider the concept of *diversity* and the social groups associated with musical engagement during childhood and adolescence. In particular, I will focus on new directions that the concept of diversity provides in guiding our thinking about musical development from a number of different perspectives. I will then outline a theory of *generativity* that provides a framework for examining how generative processes influence young people's conceptions of themselves as music-learners and the implication of these processes for music educators. Before considering these issues, I will begin by summarizing a key perspective that is receiving increasing attention in child and adolescent developmental theory and research. This perspective, known as *positive youth development*, provides a vital framework for considering young people's musical development and positive engagement in musical activities.

Positive youth development and positive musical engagement

Historically, child development researchers spent a great deal of time identifying and focusing on the unusual or 'abnormal' developmental characteristics of young people and comparing them to youth considered 'normal' or healthy. Psychologists relied primarily on *deficit* models that emphasized negative outcomes or *risk factors* associated with only a minority of young people (Roth *et al.*, 1998; Lerner, 2002). A reverse but equally deficit-orientated approach has been prevalent in studies of musical development where researchers have focused on identifying 'talented' children or adolescents in terms of their musical ability, precociousness, or skill expertise and comparing them with young people considered non-musicians or musically 'untrained' (O'Neill, 2001).

This deficit approach to musical development has manifested itself in the discourses and practices that researchers, practitioners, and the general public use (albeit at times inadvertently). Parker (1990) defines discourses as 'coherent systems of meaning' and argues that some discourses are used to legitimize or reinforce existing social structures. This is evident in relation to Western classical music where there is a long tradition of emphasis placed on the acquisition of performance skills that require the accurate reproduction of printed music notation, structured teaching methods that are taught by specialists, and some form of evaluative performance achievement or competition (O'Neill, 2005). These practices have contributed to a sense of musical elitism that evokes a superiority view of formal training and leads to a sense of inadequacy on the part of those who have not received formal instrumental music training. For example, Green (2001) highlighted the neglect of informal learning practices in formal music education and the alienation and sense of inadequacy that popular musicians often feel towards formal classical instrumental training. I have argued elsewhere that this focus on expertise and differences in performance outcomes acts as a constraining influence on young people's engagement in music and understanding of what it means to be a *musician* (O'Neill, 2002). Additionally, there has been growing criticism of the narrow conceptualization that exists in relation to what it means to be *musical* (e.g., Cook, 1990; Trevathen, 1999; DeNora, 2000), although the notion that *everyone is musical* has also been met with some resistance (for a detailed discussion see Howe *et al.*, 1998 and peer commentaries).

In recent years, researchers interested in child and adolescent development have shifted their emphasis away from deficit models toward initiatives that promote, build on, and strengthen the competencies and social contexts that foster young people's resiliency or ability to thrive in the face of adversity (Lerner *et al.*, 2002b; Villarruel *et al.*, 2003). This shift in emphasis is referred to as *positive youth development* and its main premise is that *all* young people have the *potential* and *capacity* for healthy growth and development. In terms of music, this translates into the notion that every young person has the potential and capacity for positive musical development, or more specifically that engagement in musical activities should be associated with positive or healthy outcomes for all young people. No longer are musical skills and knowledge viewed as the domain of a few talented individuals, and no longer are distinctions made in terms of the relative merits of formal or informal musical activities or teaching and learning practices. Rather, the focus shifts to the development of musical strengths and competencies that are present within *all young people* in *all contexts* in which their development occurs.

Contexts of development or person–context relations (i.e., individual and contextualized interrelationships such as family, peer group, community) are the focus of bioecological systems theoretical models (e.g., Bronfenbrenner, 1979, 2001; Spencer *et al.*, 1997; Overton, 1998). These models attempt to provide an integrated approach to understanding the complexity inherent in human development (Lerner *et al.*, 2002a). The basic structure and content of all bioecological systems models are based on two main propositions. The first proposition asserts that in order to develop (e.g., intellectually, emotionally, socially, morally, musically) a person, regardless of age, requires active participation in progressively more complex, reciprocal interaction with persons, objects and symbols in the individual's immediate environment on a fairly regular basis and over extended periods of time. These are referred to as *proximal processes*. The second proposition asserts that as proximal processes cannot structure, steer or sustain themselves, their form, power, content, and direction vary systematically as a function of: (1) the reciprocal interactions that take place between the developing person and the environment (including immediate and more remote manifestations of educational institutions, public policy, government, and economic systems); (2) time through the life course and the historical period during which the person lives; and (3) the nature of the developmental outcome under consideration. As such, the *characteristics of the person* function as both an *indirect producer* (influencing the form, content, and direction of proximal processes) and as a *product of development* (the quality of the developing person that emerges at a later point in time).

For young people to become fully engaged in active learning, the activities they are involved in should occur in a context that provides opportunities for self-expression and self-direction (Kleiber, 1999). Such contexts promote the bioecological developmental space necessary for youth to function as both indirect producers (e.g., self-directed learners) and as products of their own musical engagement (e.g., the emotional and creative expressions of musical outcomes). According to Pittman (1992), a leading youth advocate, identifying (and even solving) young people's problems in terms of providing adequate opportunities does not necessarily prepare them for the future. And preparing youth in terms of acquiring specific skills and knowledge does not necessarily mean they will be fully engaged in active learning or active agents in their own development. 'Effectively preparing young people to meet challenges requires providing them with the foundation to make decisions that will promote their own positive development.' (Perkins *et al.*, 2003, p. 2). This has important implications for musical development as the vast majority of young people have a great deal of autonomy in the way they engage with musical activities both as consumers and performers. As such, they are already active agents and constructors of their own musical skills and knowledge (O'Neill, 2005). This suggests a need for collaborative engagement on the part of all individuals and institutions within a community in promoting youth involvement in musical activities. Such an approach has much to offer in terms of developing young people's sense of self, self-responsibility, interest, and motivation in relation to their own musical development (O'Neill, 1999; O'Neill & McPherson, 2002).

Positive youth development initiatives provide frameworks that focus on strengthening both the *protectors* and *supporters* in the lives of young people. *Protectors* have been identified as competencies or developmentally appropriate assets that foster resiliency and provide a protective 'buffer' or shield against adverse circumstances. *Supporters* refer to the notion that opportunities for youth to develop these competencies are embedded within multiple social contexts in which youth and others in their environment interact (i.e., families, peers, teachers, other adults in their community). Drawing on the ecological systems theory of human development proposed by Bronfenbrenner (1979), Benson (1997, 2002) refers to these protectors and supporters as *developmental assets*. Developmental assets are grouped into *internal assets* (e.g., desire, passion, striving), and *external assets* (e.g., supportive features of the ecology and environment in which one is situated). One important difference between the two is that we can do a considerable amount to influence external assets that provide support and cover a range of opportunities for experiencing approval and acceptance within multiple settings such as the family, community, and school. These experiences include relational support and a warm, caring, and safe environment. However, internal assets develop gradually over time as a result of numerous life experiences. The growth of internal assets can be a slow, complex, and idiosyncratic process of self-regulation.

Positive youth development frameworks shift the focus from the individual to the interactions that take place between individuals and multiple levels of their environment. In other words, fostering positive youth development requires 'positive supports, opportunities for skill and competence development, and partnerships with youth at multiple levels of young people's ecology and within the systems that comprise that ecology' (Perkins *et al.*, 2003, p. 6). Positive youth development frameworks offer the potential to provide meaningful accounts of the processes associated with young people's musical engagement that take into account both the generative objectives and the diversity of contexts and approaches that characterize involvement in musical activities by all young people. The next section considers the nature of diversity in relation to young people's musical development.

Diversity and social contexts

Diversity is a popular term in recent theorizing across a number of scholarly disciplines. Simply put, diversity refers to the presence in one population (however, broadly or narrowly defined) of a wide variety of social groups (e.g., based on differences in ethnicity, gender, age, physical abilities/qualities, religious status, national origin, sexual orientation, geographical location, etc.), as well as a combination of characteristics that are unique to individuals, such as styles of communication, education, work, and life experiences, and so on. As such, the negotiated positions of individuals within particular structures and practices are reflected in the concept of diversity. The notion of diversity is socially constructed by individuals and groups from a broad spectrum of demographics and ideologies through *discourse* or discursive practices. There are a number of dominant discourses that inform and shape our understanding of diversity among individuals and social groups, such as economics, cultural factors, and the balance of power. These can be identified as both contradictory and complementary parameters in the identification of diverse social groups (O'Neill & Green, 2004). For example, in relation to gender issues, more men than women are involved in professional musical activities and men reach higher levels of achievement in their musical careers (see further O'Neill, 1997; O'Neill *et al.*, 2002).

Although diversity has been used as a heuristic for the identification, classification, and differentiation of individuals and social groups, the concept also entails a number of social practices (Beckham, 2002). These social practices represent at least two universal and fundamental features of human musical development: (1) the interdependence of people, cultures, and the environment, and (2) that musical development includes ways of *being involved with music* as well as ways of *knowing about music.* By recognizing and legitimizing these social practices it becomes morally and ethically necessary to put into practice a mutual respect for musical qualities and experiences that are different from our own. For this to happen we must first recognize that personal, cultural, and institutional discrimination creates and sustains privileges for some while creating and sustaining barriers and constraints for others. The concept of diversity helps us move beyond the mere categorization of individuals and social groups in relation to musical development and becomes instead a vehicle for social action that can be used to inform, challenge, and broaden our conceptualizations and representations of the musical structuring of society.

By acknowledging diversity as a social practice rather than merely a mechanism for categorization, we begin to recognize the futility of attempts to clarify and illuminate specific features of musical development in relation to one or even several narrowly defined groups or categories. In other words, an understanding of the complex processes involved in the musical development of racially, ethnically, and culturally diverse young people requires more than an examination of the characteristics, beliefs, attitudes, and abilities of researcher-defined groupings. Musical involvement and outcomes are the result of the history of person–context relations that are 'fused' within a dynamic developmental system that individuals experience as they grow and develop (and the ways in which they interpret these experiences). Indeed, one could argue that social groupings themselves are anticategorical in the sense that the number of components that comprise diversity in any society is indeterminate and dependent on fluid and complex interrelationships. These interrelationships are embedded in particular situations and intertwined with the particular functions they serve and actions they accomplish. Each person is always involved at some level in a multitude of social groups, some of which may correspond with each other, some of which may conflict, and some of which may change over time (O'Neill & Green, 2004).

In the past, researchers have tended to focus on one or more social groups without acknowledging the possible influences of characteristics and identities from other social groups. This has tended to universalize experiences and create an acceptance of commonality among theories of musical development without fully recognizing heterogeneity.

The term *intersectionality* refers to the consequences of holding two or more social identities simultaneously and the recognition that multiple identities do not only operate in an additive or mutually exclusive function (e.g., an individual who is a popular musician, and a female, and a vocalist), but also interact (e.g., an individual who is a female pop vocalist). As a result, the experience of being a 'female vocalist' is qualitatively different for a popular musician than for a classical musician because a female vocalist is defined and constructed differently by the two musical groupings. It is often impossible for an individual to separate her experiences into those that are a result of being a popular musician and those that are result of being a female vocalist (Green, 1997).

Although the concept of intersectionality can create a formidable number of potential intersecting identities, some identities do not intersect in conflicting ways. For example, 'classical orchestral musician' and 'violinist' are two intersecting identities that are less conflicting than 'jazz musician' and 'violinist'. However, other identities may intersect depending on the situational context. Individuals who reside at the intersections of identity as members of multiple social groups are often forced to divide their loyalties and make a choice. This has important consequences for representing aspects of musical development. For example, in an interview study that focused on the social construction of meaning systems and adolescent identity, one African-American adolescent female told us she gave up the idea of a career that involved playing classical music on the piano because her parents and teachers confirmed what she had already begun to recognize for herself; black females have little chance of ever becoming professional concert pianists (O'Neill, 2003). These perceptions can lead to the devaluation of particular musical pursuits and the adoption of self-defeating behaviours that inhibit possibilities for success. A popular explanation for this type of perception is known as the 'glass ceiling effect', whereby a transparent barrier appears to prevent the advancement and achievement of women and members of minority groups. All adolescents struggle to develop their own identities and strive for acceptance and approval. However, this struggle is compounded for minority youth as they gain an understanding of the negative stereotypes, barriers, and constraints associated with being a member of one or more minority groupings. This increases the amount of negative anxiety that is experienced when trying to construct a particular notion of 'self' (for a detailed discussion of anxiety and self-identity in musical performance see Senyshyn & O'Neill, 2001). According to Spencer *et al.* (1997, 2001), youth react to negative anxiety by employing coping strategies, which in turn yield stable coping responses, or 'emergent identities'. In other words, if the black adolescent female in our study perceived one or more aspects of being a classical concert pianist as occurring in a particular context where she is devalued, she may cope reactively by defining the expectations of this context as belonging to particular identities that are oppositional to her own developing sense of self.

Emergent and oppositional identities may involve a number of intersecting identities based on gender, ethnicity, age, physical abilities/qualities, and so on. In addition, there is the potential for intersecting identities to be based on the notion of what it means to be a musician. For example, an individual may construct the notion of a *musician identity* as someone who belongs to a particular musical grouping and that the part of one's thinking, perceptions, feelings, and behaviour is related to that musical group membership (e.g., classical, jazz, popular, instrumental, solo, orchestral, etc. musician). This would be distinct from the notion of a *musical identity* as being the significance and meaning that individuals attribute to their musical behaviour within their self-concepts (e.g., talented, soulful, passionate, authentic, etc.). Intersections between these identities may be more or less salient based on available cultural discourses and personal histories.

According to Suzuki (1997), 'We derive our history, identity, purpose and ways of thinking from the social grouping in which we are born and raised and on which we depend.' (p. 165). As such, even if we go so far as to acknowledge that the isolation and categorization of social groups are artificial and arbitrary, they are none the less established practices in our society and culture. Most of us are not aware of the fact that our musical activities are totally enmeshed in a social and cultural world. Indeed, this fundamental relationship is often lost or forgotten in the daily routine that expresses our musical values, tastes, and practices. In addition, many of the established research methods are not sophisticated enough to deal with the complexity of considering overlapping and combinations of various entities within social groups. Although there are many examples of research where reductionism has been useful in terms of analysing isolated parts or simple concepts, it remains relatively ineffective in explaining complex social and developmental phenomena. Ultimately, researchers will have to find a way to examine musical development as a social phenomenon in terms of its embeddedness in a temporal and social world. In the meantime, we can use the concept of diversity as a mechanism for identifying barriers or constraints to young people's musical engagement and for promoting positive change. The mere acknowledgement of a problem that may be hidden or etched in our thinking can: (1) create possibilities for new spaces, positions, and positive identities; (2) legitimize what was previously denied or negatively valued; (3) unravel negative associations; (4) discover how 'locking' occurs within different restrictive discourses; (5) challenge the 'deficit discourse' associated with negative positioning; and (6) offer voice to young people who may have been previously unheard.

Although critics of the concept of diversity may argue that the term tends to force people to tolerate musical practices that they would otherwise condemn, I believe that this only highlights the need for more debate about what constitutes an inclusive, respectful, and equitable approach to the musical development of all young people. It does this by providing a structure for scrutinizing the myriad of beliefs that currently exist about the nature and function of youth musical engagement and the presuppositions or taken-for-granted assumptions that certain beliefs are based on. It also enables us to challenge the value and validity of certain beliefs in terms of the various practices and outcomes that result from them. For example, when examining the outcomes of research that investigates specific social groups in isolation or that relies on reductionism as a framework for defining specific social groups, the concept of diversity may provide a framework for new interpretations of the results or for new questions to emerge that may have been previously overlooked. The concept of diversity can also provide a framework for considering the integration of past and present positioning in our understanding of contemporary musical structures. This process of integration can encourage demystification of previously unchallenged common sense beliefs or myths about the nature of musical engagement (e.g., the notion of innate musical ability being a necessary precursor for fulfilling one's musical potential).

Finally, diversity provides a direction for working toward creating alternative methods and practices based on a critical awareness of how certain beliefs influence not only our understanding of young people's musical involvement but also the meanings we share about musical engagement in our culture. It is extremely important to support and protect diversity because by valuing individuals and groups, and by fostering a climate where equity and mutual respect are inherent, music educators will help to create a success-oriented, cooperative, and caring community of music learners that produce creative musical outcomes. In this way, music educators will create a learning environment that enhances the human potential of all members of a community. These issues are discussed further in the next section, which considers the concept of *generativity* in relation to positive musical development.

Generativity and positive musical development

Philosophers, since at least the time of Plato, have been engrossed in the question of immortality, not only in terms of having an eternal life or existence, but also in terms of leaving behind a legacy after death—something that will be remembered and passed on to future generations. The term that is used to describe the need for human beings to establish and guide the next generation is *generativity*. In Erik Erikson's theoretical ideas of identity formation, generativity is discussed in terms of its ontology in the development and well-being of the next generation (Erikson, 1968). David Suzuki, a scientist and leading environmental activist, discusses the notion of generativity in relation to the way that nearly half of the world's children today grow up in an urban environment that lacks the diversity of other species so that the important emotional bonding that needs to take place between children and nature is lost. This means that as adults we have little protection against developing ecologically destructive attitudes and behaviours (Suzuki, 1997). In addition, social psychologists have discussed generativity as both a concept and as a developmental phenomenon (McAdams & de St Aubin, 1998; McAdams *et al.*, 1998) that is heavily influenced by the work of Giddens (1991) on self-identity.

Although the concept of generativity has taken many forms, I believe it can also provide a rich framework for thinking about musical development. The proportion of originality in my conceptualization probably lies as much in my attempt to integrate previous work in philosophy, ecology, and social psychology than in new thinking *per se*. However, I believe it is useful if we can borrow profitably from the ideas found in different ways of thinking and knowing. This is particularly important for musical development researchers and educators who strive to understand the epistemology and the growth points in their discipline that enable them to focus on music praxis in a way that will help to maximize the musical development of self and others.

Simply put, the concept of generativity is about caring and educating young people by assuming the role of responsible adult (e.g., parent, guardian, mentor, teacher). It is also about being a responsible citizen, a contributing member of a community, a leader, an enabler. As such, generativity provides a framework for building musical competencies and promoting positive life-long musical development, opportunities, and experiences (e.g., a generative music educator), as well as providing a framework for understanding musical development and young people's positive engagement in musical activities. It is a process for both the definition and fulfilment of the self in relation to musical structures and practices. The components of musical generativity are part of a complex, interrelated system that operates at a number of different levels simultaneously. These components are part of the systemic (bidirectional, fused) relations between individuals and contexts and the temporal embeddedness of a developmental process. Thus, when considering the main components it is necessary to keep in mind that they are not separate, but rather interrelated processes.

The components of generative musical development include a combination of motivational sources, personal beliefs and values, and musical behaviours known to enhance the development of musical skills, knowledge, and understanding, as well as the definition and fulfilment of self or a sense of identity in terms of music. Motivational sources involve both internal and external developmental assets, including parent and teacher attitudes, encouragement, involvement, and modelling. The quality of both formal and informal musical activities matters, as well as peer groups and communities that pay attention to, and show an interest in, musical activities. The components of beliefs, values, and musical behaviours, referred to as the six Cs—confidence, character, commitment, connection, competence, and contribution—are an integral part of positive youth development frameworks (Villarruel *et al.*, 2003). The beliefs and values components include *confidence, character, commitment,* and *connection.* Confidence is often mistakenly equated with self-esteem (i.e., a relatively stable sense of self-worth), or with the idea that it is developed through the experience of frequent success and praise (Dweck, 2000). However, confidence is a complex, changeable belief in one's ability that is inextricably linked to particular situations and contexts (O'Neill & Sloboda, 1997). Confidence is also heavily influenced by contingent feedback (i.e., feedback that provides an accurate evaluation of one's ability) and on young people's views of themselves in relation to who one is becoming (self-identity), self-esteem, sense of purpose, and power or control over one's actions.

Character refers to qualities within individuals that guide their decisions and choices. As such, the notion of character and musical development is deeply rooted in the values that young people develop in relation to music and musical activities. However, character is not about 'blind adherence to rigid principles and values [nor does it] happen through a simple process of telling young people how to be and how to behave' (Pace, 2003, p. 261). Rather, character development is a complex life-long process that results from maturation, socialization, and education. Although adults are powerful guides in the process of character development, young people can also guide the development of adults' musical values through a 'mutually respectful atmosphere of trust, care, and support' (Pace, 2003, p. 262). The character component is closely tied to commitment, which involves taking responsibility for one's actions and meeting obligations that contribute to the greater good of others in the community.

Connection or a sense a belonging is an important component within both positive youth development and generative musical development frameworks. Musical development, like all human development, proceeds through social experience. As such, character development is intertwined with connections that young people have with significant people in their lives. Children's natural inclinations towards music are strengthened and enhanced through positive relationships and interactions within a musical grouping. It is not enough, however, to simply create opportunities to connect young people with peers and adults.

Rather, connections with peers and adults that foster generative musical development must also include opportunities for equitable and respectful engagement in musical activities.

The components of musical behaviour in generative musical development framework include *competence* and *contribution*. Competence involves more than observable skills and achievements. It also involves the ability to think and reason about musical ideas, to understand others' musical choices and to make decisions based on abstract principles. Contribution is about finding the purpose and meaning of music-making in relation to oneself and others. It is about making a respectful and meaningful contribution to valued cultural art forms involving diverse groups of people to benefit the common good in communities.

The combination of motivational sources, personal beliefs and values, and musical behaviours contribute to the gradual construction and reconstruction of a positive identity in relation to music. A positive musical identity means having a sense of being or becoming a musical person. A musical identity integrates past, present, and anticipated future musical involvement and at the same time specifies ways in which the individual fits into and distinguishes herself or himself in the social world. This is a challenging notion in contemporary society where young people are exposed to media-drenched music idols that are admired as much, if not more, for their appearance and sexual image than for their musicality or musicianship. The ways in which young people come to view themselves in relation to musical activities are based, in part, on their understanding of the musical structuring of society. They learn this by observing the different roles and positions that musicians occupy in the adult world. The presence or absence of musicians viewed by young people as similar to themselves implicitly conveys information about the possibilities for their own futures. As such, these representations of opportunity have enormous implications for students' educational aspirations and achievement. Young people only pursue educational goals they can imagine are possible. It is therefore important that we understand those aspects of the social and cultural context that frame students' sense of musical opportunities in relation to their sense of self-identity.

The processes involved in what might be described as generative musical development include *introspection, service,* and *action*. Introspection or reflection involves recognizing enablers, barriers and constraints, setting goals, refining principles, and preparing for the future. For example, we need to recognize some of the problems that young people face today and their impact on musical opportunities and participation, such as high rates of family mobility, greater anonymity in neighbourhoods and schools, extensive media exposure to negative or problem behaviours, deterioration of music resources, and programmes aimed at youth in diverse contexts, increasingly complex, technological, and multicultural experiences, extended length of adolescence (i.e., pathways to adulthood are less clear and more numerous). The process of introspection requires us to ask the question: how do young people's negotiated understandings of their world sustain or exclude certain actions in relation to musical opportunities or barriers, enablements or constraints?

Service refers to the ways in which we aid others in the community. In terms of musical development, service refers to a focus on youth-centred learning contexts, the ability to respond to diverse talents, skills, and interests by providing a rich array of musical activities that provide opportunities for young people to participate at all levels of expertise.

The process of service within a generative musical development framework also involves: (1) identifying and building on the strengths of each participating youth by providing opportunities for individuals to do what they can do best as well as to learn new skills; (2) using developmentally and culturally appropriate materials that allow youth to grow in skills and leadership roles within specific musical activities; (3) providing extensive personal attention from adults; (4) fostering a recognition of musician role models based on relevance and attainability; and (5) actively recruiting youth using a variety of locally appropriate methods.

The final process of generative musical development, action, involves doing, creating, and experiencing music in a way that benefits one's self and others; a way of bringing about positive change in one's self, in others, or in one's environment through active engagement in the process of transformation. The action demonstrated by generative music educators reveals a strong commitment to planning, implementing, evaluating, and facilitating youth empowerment. For example, a music teacher who loves teaching music and spends her life doing it is helping others generatively. All three elements (introspection, service, action) are positively engaged in this generative process. Conversely, a music teacher who hates teaching music and spends her life doing it is at best making a great personal sacrifice— giving up her happiness to help others, and at worst, she may be instilling in her students an irrevocable negative attitude towards musical involvement. Although this scenario may accomplish something in terms of producing successful results among students (e.g., having students who win competitions or who achieve high marks on graded music examinations), the main element involved is service and this element alone does not constitute a generative process or transmit to others an authentic sense of musical meaning in one's life. A negative learning experience increases the likelihood that young people will become adults with a weak sense of musical generativity.

The individuals who play a critical role in nurturing the positive musical development of young people often find themselves lacking the necessary knowledge, support, and resources for fostering generative musical development. For example, generative music educators need access to a range of training, education, and research options that provide an understanding of relevant theory (i.e., educational, developmental, musical) and current cultural trends affecting young people. They need to be part of an ongoing system of professional development that recognizes the legitimacy and value of their work. In addition, they need to work in supportive environments and contexts that provide safe learning opportunities for youth to experience meaningful roles and responsibilities that will foster their own sense of development, growth, transformation, and excellence. Finally, generative music educators need to understand the ways in which they are publicly accountable. They need to use a common language with a shared optimistic vision of all youth as having the potential and capacity for positive musical growth and to be part of a system for advocating and influencing others to see the positive benefits of young people's engagement in musical activities. Music education practices are tied to prevailing ideologies that contain many tensions and contradictions that can so often be construed as negative or problematic. Although a generative approach to musical development recognizes these problems, it does so from within a framework that focuses on and builds on strengths rather than deficits.

Conclusions

Positive youth development frameworks offer the potential to provide meaningful accounts of the components and processes associated with young people's positive engagement in musical activities. Although there are multiple dimensions and complexity inherent in our representations of musical development, these frameworks provide essential ingredients for furthering our understanding of both the diversity of contexts and the generative processes and approaches that create opportunities for young people to develop the beliefs and values that will foster their sense of self and self-responsibility, desire, and motivation for positive musical engagement, as well as the development of tolerance, acceptance, and respect for the diversity of musical practices in their world. Together, these theoretical components and processes create a vital framework for building musical competencies and promoting positive musical identities among youth in diverse contexts, particularly as they navigate in multiple cultural settings, and make key transitions from childhood, through adolescence, and into adulthood.

By ensuring the primary focus of musical development is on positive musical engagement and youth-centred learning contexts, we can respond to the diverse talents, skills, and interests of young people by providing a rich array of musical activities that allow opportunities for youth to participate at all levels of expertise. In addition, we need to focus on the contexts of development that lead to the positive definition and fulfilment of self in terms of music. The contexts in which musical activities take place can either foster positive beliefs and values or create barriers that can lead to motivational and/or behavioural problems. To date, there is a tendency to categorize or specify too precisely the boundaries of acceptable contexts for musical development and attributes of those boundaries thereby limiting our understanding of the musical opportunities that will best assist young people in their understanding, interpretation, and representations of the musical structuring of the society and culture in which they live. We still know far too little about how to create and sustain musical experiences that will be valued by and acceptable to young people from diverse backgrounds in order to engage them in musical activities as part of a life-long learning process of growth and development. The difficult task now is in trying to map the multiple pathways that can lead to generative musical development within diverse contexts and cultures. By increasing our understanding in these areas, we will be in a much stronger position to assist children and adolescents in taking an active role in their own musical development. In this way, we can ensure that youth continue to make meaningful contributions to a valued cultural art form so that it will continue to flourish and nurture future generations.

References

Beckham, E. F. (2002). Diversity at the crossroads: Mapping our work in the years. Paper presented October 27, 2002 at AAC&U's Diversity and Learning: Education for a World Lived in Common conference. http://www.aacu.org/meetings/diversityandlearning/DL2002/beckham_crossroads.cfm

Benson, P. L. (1997). *All kids are our kids: What communities must do to raise caring and responsible children and adolescents.* San Francisco, CA: Jossey-Bass.

Benson, P. L. (2002). Adolescent development in social and community context: A program of research. *New Directions for Youth Development*, **95**, 123–148.

Bronfenbrenner, U. (1979). *The ecology of human development: Experiments by nature and design.* Cambridge, MA: Harvard University Press.

Bronfenbrenner, U. (2001). Bioecological theory of human development. In N. J. Smelser & P. B. Baltes (eds), *International encyclopedia of the social and behavioral sciences* (pp. 6963–6970). Oxford: Elsevier.

Cook, N. (1990). *Music, imagination, culture.* Oxford: Clarendon Press.

DeNora, T. (2000). *Music in everyday life.* Cambridge: Cambridge University Press.

Dweck, C. S. (2000). *Self-theories: Their role in motivation, personality and development.* Philadelphia, PA: Psychology Press.

Erikson, E. (1968). *Identity: youth and crisis.* New York: W. W. Norton & Company.

Giddens, A. (1991). *Modernity and self-identity: Self and society in the late modern age.* Cambridge: Polity Press.

Green, L. (1997). *Music, gender, education.* Cambridge: Cambridge University Press.

Green, L. (2001). *How popular musicians learn: A way ahead for music education.* Aldershot, Hants: Ashgate.

Howe, M. J. A., Davidson, J. W., & Sloboda J. A. (1998). Innate talents: Reality or myth? *Behavioral and Brain Sciences*, **21**(3), 99–407.

Kleiber, D. (1999). *A dialectical interpretations: Leisure experience and human development.* New York: Basic Books.

Lerner, R. M. (2002). *Concepts and theories of human development* (3rd edn). Mahwah, NJ: Lawrence Erlbaum Associates.

Lerner, R. M., Brentano, C., Dowling, E. M., & Anderson, P. M. (2002a). Positive youth development: Thriving as the basis of personhood and civil society. *New Directions for Youth Development*, **95**, 11–33.

Lerner, R. M., Taylor, C. S., & von Eye, A. (eds) (2002b). Pathways to positive development among diverse youth. *New Directions for Youth Development*, **95**, 1–164.

McAdams, D. P. & de St. Aubin, E. (eds) (1998). *Generativity and adult development: How and why we care for the next generation.* Washington, DC: American Psychological Association.

McAdams, D. P., Hart, H. M., & Maruna, S. (1998). The anatomy of generativity. In D. P. McAdams & E. de St Aubin (eds), *Generativity and adult development: How and why we care for the next generation* (pp. 7–74). Washington, DC: American Psychological Association.

O'Neill, S. A. (1997). Gender and music. In D. J. Hargreaves & A. C. North (eds), *The social psychology of music* (pp. 46–63). Oxford: Oxford University Press.

O'Neill, S. A. (1999). Flow theory and the development of musical performance skills. *Bulletin of the Council for Research in Music Education*, **141**, 129–134.

O'Neill, S. A. (2001). Psychology of music. In S. Sadie (ed.), *The new Grove dictionary of music and musicians*, Vol. 20, (2nd edn) (pp. 527–562). London: Macmillan.

O'Neill, S. A. (2002). The self-identity of young musicians. In R. A. R. MacDonald, D. J. Hargreaves, & D. Meill (eds), *Musical identities* (pp. 79–96). Oxford: Oxford University Press.

O'Neill, S. A. (2003). Meaning systems in the construction of adolescents' social identities. Paper presented at the *Society for Research on Child Development Biennial Conference*, Tampa, Florida, USA, April 2003.

O'Neill, S. A. (2005). Youth music engagement in diverse contexts. In J. L. Mahoney, R. W. Larson, & J. S. Eccles (eds), *Organized activities as contexts of development: Extracurricular activities, after-school and community programs* (pp. 255–273). Mahwah, NJ: Lawrence Erlbaum Associates.

O'Neill, S. A. & Green, L. (2004). Social groups and research in music education. Mapping music education research in the UK. *Psychology of Music*, 32(3), 252–258.

O'Neill, S. A. & McPherson, G. E. (2002). Motivation. In R. Parncutt & G. E. McPherson (eds), *The science and psychology of music performance: Creative strategies for teaching and learning* (pp. 31–46). Oxford: Oxford University Press.

O'Neill, S. A. & Sloboda, J. A. (1997). The effects of failure on children's ability to perform a musical test. *Psychology of Music*, 25, 18–34.

O'Neill, S. A., Ivaldi, A., & Fox, C. (2002). Gendered discourses in musically 'talented' adolescent females' construction of self. *Feminism & Psychology*, 12, 153–159.

Overton, W. F. (1998). Developmental psychology: Philosophy, concepts, and methodology. In R. M. Lerner (ed.), *Theoretical models of human development: Vol. 1. The handbook of child psychology* (pp. 107–189) (5th edn) (W. Damon, ed. in chief). New York: Wiley.

Pace, K. L. (2003). The character of moral communities: A community youth development approach to enhancing character development. In F. A. Villarruel, D. F. Perkins, L. M. Borden, & J. G. Keith (eds), *Community youth development: programs, policies, and practices* (pp. 248–272). London: Sage.

Parker, I. (1990). Discourse: definitions and contradictions. *Philosophical Psychology*, 3, 189–204.

Perkins, D. F., Borden, L. M., Keith, J. G., Hoppe-Rooney, T. L., & Villarruel, F. A. (2003). Community youth development: partnership creating a positive world. In F. A. Villarruel, D. F. Perkins, L. M. Borden, & J. G. Keith, (eds), *Community youth development: programs, policies, and practices* (pp. 1–24). London: Sage.

Pittman, K. J. (1992). *Defining the fourth R: Promoting youth development*. Washington, DC: Center for Youth Development and Policy Research.

Roth, J., Brooks-Gunn, J., Murray, L., & Foster, W. (1998). Promoting healthy adolescents: Synthesis of youth development program evaluations. *Journal of Research on Adolescence*, 8, 423–459.

Senyshyn, Y. & O'Neill, S. A. (2001). Subjective experience of anxiety and musical performance: a relational perspective. *Philosophy of Music Education Review*, 9 (1), 42–53.

Spencer, M. B., Dupree, D., & Hartmann, T. (1997). A phenomenological variant of ecological systems theory (PVEST): A self-organization perspective in context. *Development and Psychopathology*, 9, 817–833.

Spencer, M. B., Noll, E., Stoltzfus, J., & Harpalani, V. (2001). Identity and school adjustment: Questioning the 'Acting White' assumption. *Educational Psychologist*, 36(1), 21–30.

Suzuki, D. (1997). *The sacred balance: rediscovering our place in nature*. Vancouver, BC: Greystone Books.

Trevathen, C. (1999). Musicality and the intrinsic motive pulse: evidence from human psychobiology and infant communication. *Musicae Scientiae, Special Issue (1999–2000)*, 155–215.

Villarruel, F. A., Perkins, D. F., Borden, L. M., & Keith, J. G. (eds) (2003). *Community youth development: programs, policies, and practices*. London: Sage.

CHAPTER 24

MUSICIAN IDENTITY FORMATION

JANE W. DAVIDSON AND KAREN BURLAND

Introduction

By the time children reach adolescence they have acquired most of the cognitive and biomechanical skills necessary to become a musician (Shuter-Dyson & Gabriel, 1981; Bamberger, 1986). As the range of chapters in this book show, children often spend thousands of hours accumulating practice, learning about instrumental and musical styles and techniques, as well as playing in different ensembles. Furthermore, social influences on the developing child musician are important for motivating and regulating the initial musical participation. The personality characteristics of teachers, for example, are thought to be key in initiating and sustaining a child's interest in music, and high levels of parental support are necessary for a child to become a successful child musician. However, is the same true for the adolescent? Through adolescence a major part of the developmental process is a move away from the childhood identity and the earlier dependence on the parent, with a shift towards independence (Coleman, 1960; Larson, 1995). In Western classical music where the learner needs to have financial support for the purchase of instruments and lessons, transportation to and from musical activities, and ample time for labour-intensive practice, it could be that the profile of those individuals who go on to be highly successful adult solo musicians may in fact not comply with the adolescent social norms. This chapter, therefore, will consider how the adolescent musician develops and makes decisions about the future position of music in their lives and how, in turn, these decisions shape or are shaped by the adolescent's emerging sense of self.

A life-span theory proposed by Erikson (1959) is a useful point of departure for the current discussion as it provides an account for how individuals change throughout their lives according to the demands placed upon them. Erikson divides the life-span into eight stages, each of which has a distinct task that needs to be achieved. His fifth stage—adolescence—is labelled as the period of identity versus role confusion. Erikson describes how the main goal in adolescence is to establish a secure 'social, sexual and occupational identity'. If we accept this view, it is not surprising that other researchers suggest that the transition through adolescence is perhaps the most significant and stressful of all life-span changes (Gecas & Mortimer, 1987; Hendry & Kloep, 2002). Indeed, socializing that has previously centred around peers and parents often shifts during this period to intimate, often sexually oriented peer relationships, and the need to make decisions about a future career emerges.

In view of Erikson's claims, the ways in which adult figures such as parents and teachers interact with the adolescent are bound to have a crucial role in influencing engagement with music. Peers too are likely to play a fundamental role, perhaps one even more significant than adults. It is these elements that form the primary focus of the literature reviewed in this chapter.

The social environment

Among 257 school-aged music learners interviewed by Davidson *et al.* (1996, 1998) almost half were between the ages of 14 and 18 years. The findings indicated that prior to adolescence, children in the highest achieving group of these young musicians were given the greatest levels of support most consistently from their parents, but thereafter the parents' support diminished while the teenagers were increasingly driven by intrinsic motives to do practice. For those in groups with lower levels of achievement or the ones who gave up, parental support was initially weak and conversely, by adolescence the parents attempted to enforce a practice regime. The authors interpreted this result as the parents' last (and often unsuccessful) attempt to keep their children playing.

Teachers were also critically important social influences. How they interacted with the learners was highly significant, with the most successful learners having experienced teachers who changed from playing parent-like roles when the children were under 12 years of age, to mentors at the later adolescent stage. Thus, the most successful learners found their initial teachers to be entertaining, friendly, and proficient musicians, ascribing positive attributes to them, even when they were remembered as not being very proficient musicians. Later, during adolescence, the role model of the teacher as a professional player seemed more important than personal dimensions such as friendliness. Thus the teacher who could be perceived as 'a brilliant musician from whom there is a lot to learn', could also be regarded as a 'not very nice person'. The lowest achieving adolescent students remembered their teachers as being generally incompetent and also unfriendly. Thus, it seems that in the low achievers, an external attribution was being made in which their own failures were being linked to negative perceptions of the teacher: incompetence in playing/teaching, and so these teachers were also perceived as being unfriendly. They did not seem to be able to see the possibility that their own lack of progress or commitment may have led the teacher to behave in an unfriendly manner. The possible interpretations of these kinds of external attributions raise a central concern for the rest of this chapter: that is, how to understand research participants' thoughts about themselves and their life circumstances. It is evident that what someone reports as a belief is only one possible interpretation of an event, circumstances or feelings. In these particular data sets, Davidson *et al.* always tried to triangulate data sources to achieve as objective a view as possible, and these particular students' attributions relating to teachers were supported by parents. However, later in the chapter, we shall reveal data that were based only on the musician reporting on his or her adolescence, so external and internal attributions need to be considered.

The ideas raised so far in this chapter link to others in this volume, which consider factors such as cognitive style, self-efficacy in practice, and emotional orientation as central factors in learning classical music. We shall not deal with these factors in detail here, but offer an interim conclusion that certain strategies need to be implemented by significant others if a young learner is to be able to gain assistance in developing his or her skills. Moreover, a certain mental style (which sort of attributions, for instance) may lend itself to more or less musical progress when operating within the social dimensions of the key interactions. For the adolescent classical musician, their adult guides as mentors, and the ability to discern which technical and expressive musical elements are of crucial importance seem to play a significant role.

Of course, in areas where a stylistic canon need not be acquired or synthesized, or where virtuosity is not a prerequisite, adolescent energy and a form of rebellion against adults might be key to the process of musical success. For instance, in hip-hop or heavy metal, creativity and innovation is built upon the culture of rebellion (Larson, 1995; Csikszentmihalyi, 1999). Work by Gullberg and Brändström (2004) indicates that in popular music in general, it can be negative to conform and work under the 'older generation's supervision', whereas novelty and innovation in performance are important in classical music of many sorts (Indian, Chinese, etc.), these styles are all heavily governed by form; therefore, the handing down of traditions is essential.

In terms of peers and friendship groups, playing some musical instruments can lead to a child being bullied and socially rejected in school, which can eventually result in a decision to stop learning (Kemp, 1996). By socializing with like-minded peers, in this case other musicians, the child has access to emotional support (Freeman, 1985), and may be motivated and stimulated by his/her peers' musical achievements (Feldhusen, 1986). In the study by Davidson et al. (1996), the teenagers who were more successful in music and more motivated to participate were those who surrounded themselves with other teenagers engaging in similar musical activities.

The notion of 'an idol in touching distance' (a description made by Hall, 1969) further highlights the importance of peers: role models close in age and expertise to the student have more influence on the child than a master in the field (Sosniak, 1990). Older students in the field were used for setting goals and skills to be mastered: the younger musicians were able to identify with the older ones simply because they were aware that they were not alone in work they dedicated to the pursuit of expertise (see Sosniak, 1990 for further details).

It seems that another component in the adolescent developing as a musician is the need to feel understood and supported by all around them, and especially being valued as musicians. If an adolescent possesses a strong self-identity as a musician, they will be more resilient to social pressure, and therefore more determined to achieve their musical goals. This line of argument is based on data from Davidson et al. (1996), which showed that some adolescents had a 'stubborn' attitude towards their learning. Indeed, the more they were teased by older siblings or non-musician friends about their involvement in music, the more they were determined to show those people that being a high achiever in classical music was to be admired, not scorned. So, as the chapter unfurls we see how important it is for the adolescent to have a self-belief and a mechanism for 'coping with' how others behave towards them within the context of their music learning.

A rare life-span study of classical musicians provides further key information on adolescence and musical progress. Manturzewska (1990) worked with 165 musicians, and developed a model in which the third stage of the musician's lifespan development was 'the stage of formation and development of the artistic personality' (p. 134) between 12 and 20 years of age. Manturzewska believed this was dependent upon the 'master–student' relationship, the student modelling his/her behaviours and goals according to those of the teacher.

However, Manturzewska fails to consider a range of individual characteristics relating to self-identity and personality, and does not consider the role of peers sufficiently. While she suggests that teachers play a crucial part in shaping 'aesthetic attitudes, life philosophy, professional standards and attitudes' (Manturzewska, 1990, p. 135), there is little mention of the complex dynamics of the gamut of other social relationships. However, underlying her work and all the previously mentioned research is that the adolescent musician is indeed developing an identity as a musician.

Developing an identity

A recent contribution to our understanding of how individuals implement significant life changes (the example comes from the domain of business consultancy) is the notion of 'provisional selves' (Ibarra, 1999). The term describes the process by which individuals 'try out' different identities in order to develop strategies to help them to succeed in their chosen field. Ibarra describes two ways this happens: wholesale, where the individual adopts the characteristics of a single role model (that is, someone who is already successful in the chosen area), or selective, where the individual adopts a range of characteristics from different role models. These identities are either confirmed or rejected by other people (colleagues/family). In terms of musical development, we have already seen that becoming a musician might depend upon close contact with musical role models (see above discussion regarding 'idols in touching distance') in order to develop the necessary knowledge of the skills involved and the behaviours required to succeed, but equally, it also requires other people around us to confirm or reject our emerging musician identity (supporting and admiring family and friends).

The emergent picture, therefore, is that the transition of the adolescent musician may be dependent upon critical environmental elements: the influence of significant others is vital in guiding the developing musician in terms of practical skill, but also in helping the individual to confirm or reject emerging identity traits. But, identity may not simply emerge from others. Music as a communicative medium has a strong mood regulating and emotional expression component (Juslin & Sloboda, 2002; Bailey & Davidson 2003) and so we also can develop an internal relationship with it. Research into music listening has shown that adolescents from the West often rely on music listening activities and so 'musical taste' to present a particular self-image to others (North *et al.*, 2000). This suggests that music has a major impact on the way in which an individual chooses to perceive and so develops him/herself. It is likely that performers use music in an equivalent way to listeners; that is, as an identity construct and as an emotional outlet. Gullberg and Brändström (2004) have shown this to be the case with pop music, but there is less obvious evidence from classical music learning. If music does contribute to the identity of the individual, it would contribute further to his/her motivation to study music throughout adolescence and beyond into adulthood. As the discussion about the role of peers demonstrated, perhaps a strong musician identity helps the individual to ignore the potential criticism from peers and teachers, and motivates him/her to continue in musical participation.

Of course, it could be that social and personal factors interact, leading to the eventual development of a specific form of musician/musical identity, which may be central to becoming a professional performing musician or a keen amateur listener. In other words, negotiating the adolescent period in a specific manner may well shape adult musical engagement and success. Such identity management will certainly affect how an individual will appraise situations, and this in turn will feed into his or her belief system. Without research precedents in developing adolescent musicians, we decided to pursue these matter ourselves in a project which followed up the earlier work by Davidson *et al.* (1996, 1998). (Note that Davidson is the first author in this current chapter.)

What happens to musical performance achievements and motivations during the adolescent transition?

Using semistructured interview schedules, we (Burland & Davidson, 2002) interviewed 20 of the highly successful childhood musicians from the original study—10 in pursuit of performing careers, and 10 working in non-performance careers (primary school teachers, solicitors, sales). The interviews aimed to gain insight into the development of the individuals throughout their adolescent transition, asking them to reflect on the reasons affecting their decisions to pursue a professional musical performance career or not. Specifically, we focused on the role played by other people during their musical development, and perhaps most importantly, the nature of their changing relationships with music (emotional, self-identity related). Transcripts of the interviews were analysed using Interpretative Phenomenological Analysis (Smith *et al.*, 1997). This particular technique was used because it is a method that enables participants, through self-reflection, to tell their own story, in their own words. Then, through a technique of repeated observation, analysis, and feedback, themes from the transcripts emerge to be theorized, grounded in the participants' own experiences and perceptions. Of course, these are subjective positions, but that is the intention: to investigate how an individual attributes his or her own success, and then to investigate how viable such a theory is, based on the evidence taken from their biographies. The theoretical approach is not far removed from the traditions established by Erikson, borrowing most strongly from the social psychologist William James, who views a theory of selves being relational, and so dependent on how the individual connected with and perceived his or her relationships to be with others.

Analysis of the data revealed that there were distinct differences in biography and self-beliefs between the musicians who became professional performers and those who did not: the two groups of musicians had very different experiences with other people, their training and had specific self-beliefs associated with these, which seemed contingent on a relationship each one of them described as having with the music itself. For example, the musicians who decided not to pursue a performance career reported how, during adolescence, they felt pressured and overwhelmed by experiences of competition and felt unable to cope with criticism from teachers and peers—a negative external attribution. Those who became performers, on the other hand, regarded similar experiences as more positive learning experiences to help them improve in the future. As a result of these findings, we proposed that through the adolescent years self-belief coupled with the external attributions of the treatment by and perceptions of the behaviours and attitude of others, alongside a positive

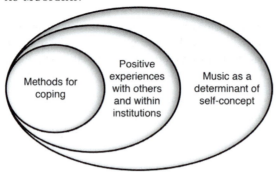

Figure 24.1 Tripartite model of professional music performer success.

internalized view of music as a key determinant of self-identity were features of success. From these findings we formulated a tripartite model of success comprising: (1) a need for strategies for coping with social pressures; this in turn interfaced with (2) positive experiences with others; and finally, and perhaps most importantly, (3) music as a determinant of self-concept. A slightly modified version of our original model can be seen in Figure 24.1. If all three elements were reported, then the transition through adolescence to being a professional musician was achieved. Where one of the elements was absent, it was unlikely that the musician would succeed in becoming a professional. The aim of the remainder of this chapter is to examine in more detail the ideas discussed so far. We do this by discussing three case study examples[1] from our study to demonstrate how adolescent musical development shaped the musicians' eventual career choices, their relationships with music, and how they perceived themselves as musicians.

The successful adult professional musician performer: Daniel

Daniel was one of the musicians to become a professional performer. At the time the interviews took place he was a fine string player, working in a prestigious chamber ensemble. His perceptions and experiences during adolescence seem to have influenced his decision to become a performer, and also had an impact on his emergent performer identity. He believed that his professional musician parents played an important role in his musical development:

> They've helped me a lot. . .without the things I learned just from them doing it at the time, and experiencing, and knowing, and contact with professional musicians from a very early age. . .was invaluable, and helped me not only in terms of being a musician, but in terms of understanding the profession and the good things about it and the bad things about it, and what to avoid and what to aim for.

Circumstantial evidence—phone calls, letters, attendance at his performances—revealed that Daniel's parents did indeed provide a positive contact with the music profession and

---

[1] Note that for reasons of confidentiality, pseudonyms are used in all cases.

he still, as a young adult (26 years old at the time of follow-up interview), turned to them for advice and support. He attributed this form of relationship as being key to his success.

The emergent picture of Daniel as a developing professional musician came from his father who was interviewed at the height of Daniel's adolescence (aged 16 years old):

> I mean Daniel is just a natural musician. He loves it, and he is so able. We wanted to give him all the opportunities we had missed in our backgrounds – we didn't have musician parents ourselves. Being able to show him the way to deal with performance, the ups and downs of the job…Well, it has been very important. He's come through his school career even more determined to be a player.

However, Daniel described how the influence of an idol slightly older than him was potentially negative: 'There was a time when I thought I just wanted to play like him and even be like him as a person as well even though I knew there were things about his personality that people didn't like'.

Despite the influence, it was this experience that was of importance to the emergence of Daniel's own performer identity: his realization that it was unhealthy for him to try to copy someone else's style and limit his goals to those of his idol enabled him to see his own strengths and ambitions. For example, when Daniel first went to music college he realized that he did not like the teaching he was receiving, nor the politics within the institution, and so he decided to change to a different college. His experiences greatly improved at the new college, although he still perceived negative elements: 'I think I came into contact with maybe more cynical people, and maybe more realities, and that was obviously a good thing in the long run, and also, it was when I started to realise that I had to, there were things about my personality and things about my playing that weren't right, and I wasn't being true to myself'.

This internal reflection, at an important time of personal and psychological development, seems to have signified a turning point: Daniel was beginning to acquire the strategies necessary for coping with life as a professional musician by realizing that there were inherent aspects of his personality that did not suit the profession, which he knew he would have to accept and attempt to deal with. There was certainly much internal reflection during this period, which seemed to offer Daniel a positive and 'realistic' way to reflect on his experiences as a musician.

> When you discover something about your playing that you don't like, that you haven't thought of before, it's initially very depressing and you think 'Oh God, how have I not noticed that before, I can't believe I ever expected to be successful if I can't do that'. At first you think it's all over, and then you realise it's a good thing you realised that and then you come through it and put it right and then once you've done that you feel great, and 'I've done it'.

Daniel showed a self-determination, and he additionally spoke about always challenging himself to achieve the highest possible standards through his music.

> I worked very, very hard [for my second college audition], in fact, I don't think I've ever worked that hard for anything, to the point that I was just going to work as hard as I could, and then I realised that was the only way to do things really, to want them and really put

everything into it, and once I got the audition and got the trial and became a member of the orchestra I was unbelievably happy for a while, and then a couple of months later I thought 'I'm very happy, but I need something else to do, I need another challenge', and so I set myself another challenge, and so it goes from there.

Throughout Daniel's interview it was evident that he felt passionately about music. Perhaps the fact that he had overcome a number of negative experiences by himself made him feel that his destiny was somehow entwined with music. He described how music was always on his mind and determined how he perceived himself:

There's nothing like it really, especially if you do a performance that you're happy with, even if you've had one good day of practice, or you've discovered one tiny thing that helps your playing, or you've made a breakthrough, or just feeling things are going well and you're playing well, it just puts me in a different frame of mind. And if I've had a bad day, or bad concert, that's even worse.

The connection that Daniel felt with his playing certainly appears to have been a motivation for him to work so hard at it. Despite the setbacks and occasional negative experiences, he explained that he loved being a professional musician and his overriding motivation to play came from the enjoyment that making music offers. Additionally, though, he stated that he would only be a musician for as long as it was enjoyable: '[Music offers me] passion I suppose, something to be passionate about, something to look for and enjoy, and something that will always be there and no-one will ever be able to take away from me'.

Of course, as we mentioned earlier, much of Daniel's thinking may be a *post-hoc* rationalization of his thoughts and actions through the adolescent period; however, his views were similar to all of those who achieved similar standards. This suggests that whether or not everything happened or shaped him as he believes may be questionable, but the way he and his like-achieving colleagues attribute their successes and failures suggests a biographical and so motivational similarity.

Perhaps one of the most striking pieces of data to emerge from the interview with Daniel was his description of how he 'needed' music and could not imagine life without it. Even when experiencing a bad day, he still turned to music for a source of comfort. 'I can always go and play my violin, or I can put a CD on, and listen to the music that will completely change my mood. It's always there basically'.

Thus, the emotional and psychological connection that Daniel felt with music may have been a key factor in motivating him to be a musician. Through his experiences at the specialist music school and the key support from his parents, he began to discover his own identity and this was focused around himself as a musician, being someone who loved music. Within this framework, he seemed to have developed strategies for coping with the negative experiences. Daniel's data show all three elements of the tripartite model of success described above.

In our study there were a number of participants who explained their success in terms of their adolescent experiences with music, although for some, the 'success' outcome was not to become a professional musician.

The musical amateur: Lisa

At the time of the interviews, Lisa was a trainee solicitor and had not played her musical instrument for several years. Lisa's story emphasizes how her beliefs and experiences with music during adolescence shaped her self-identity, which she believed equipped her with skills necessary to pursue a chosen non-music related-career.

Lisa began her musical life as a violinist, but spoke about soon realizing that she would have more opportunities as a viola player. This decision signified a turning point in her personal development:

> I gained a lot more confidence from playing it [the viola] to be honest. I think because it was the first time I was doing really well at something, and people were recognising it . . .Just swapping over instruments, just increased my confidence which was what I needed, and I think that tumbled into all other aspects of my life as well. . .including. . .making a confident decision to go to Cambridge and that kind of thing. I'm sure that had I stayed on the violin I would have just felt a little bit average, and just probably not have done as well as I have done now.

Here we see an external factor—changing to the viola—as precipitating a considerable and positively perceived internal shift, enabling Lisa to build her self-confidence. It also shows how she seems to attribute her sense of self to academic achievement (she mentions Cambridge specifically) perhaps rather more than the music itself. Her perceived emergent aim through this adolescent period was to become 'the best,' with music being not a serious or 'best' career choice.

Overall, Lisa discusses her experiences with other people during her musical development as being overwhelmingly positive. She describes how inspiring she found her viola teacher, and like Daniel, Lisa's parents were highly supportive and still share a very close bond through their music. Lisa also described herself as having a close personal relationship with music: 'I think about music a lot, and I love music, and whenever I am down about anything I would always rather listen to classical music than anything else'.

However, it is possible to see a somewhat different belief system to Daniel. In fact, Lisa was very concerned about the kind of future that music could offer: 'With music you've got no stable future, there's so many things to think about, all the things that can go wrong with tendonitis and backache and it just seemed like it was always going to be uphill, and I just didn't want that'.

From these descriptions, it seems as though she uses music as a sort of 'self-therapy', but she is able to bring many reasons to the fore to explain why it would not be a suitable career. We know that these were sentiments Lisa's parents presented when Lisa was only 14 years old, and presumably had become a shared family 'belief' that Lisa went along with, indeed, so did her sister Laura, who had also gone to Cambridge a few years before to study English. Indeed, the family values were placed upon academic achievement. The mother was a school secretary and seemed to value and prioritize academic achievement. For example, when the girls were first interviewed as teenagers for the original study, both parents were also interviewed and the father expressed their views as follows:

> We have always tried to give our girls opportunities that we never had. My wife and I have ordinary jobs and we never had the opportunity for further or higher study. We hope that

the girls will be able to go as far as they are able and do what they want to do. To get a good profession would be marvellous. Imagine, our eldest is off to Cambridge, and although she's a musician of a very high standard (she also goes to the same specialist school as Lisa), Laura is going to study English. From our perspective, that is a marvellous achievement.

To add further detail to Lisa's belief that music should be for 'comfort', it is important to note that the father had always wanted to learn music as a child and when Lisa and her older sister, Laura, began playing, he joined in lessons too. He joined in to 'feel close and together with the girls'. He helped them with their music practice, orchestras and so on. But, the music was always for 'sharing', 'love', and 'enjoyment', it was not for a profession. Broadly speaking, Lisa seemed to be re-iterating her father's sentiments. Of course, as Byng-Hall (1973, 1982, 1985, 1988, 1995, 1998) points out, many of our belief systems are developed from the playing out of 'family scripts'; that is, continuing a 'story' initiated by our forebears. The psychological power of this for Lisa seems to be that she created herself a highly meritorious 'niche' by becoming the lawyer in the family.

Placing music firmly into the niche of career options that 'can go badly wrong' suggests that Lisa did at some level have a negative self-image as a musician. This is explained a little more fully when Lisa describes her experiences at music school: 'It's just made me a more confident person doing something other than music, it's just a battlefield trying to get noticed, and it was crazy [at school], and for being so young, I think it's slightly unnatural to be like that at that age'.

So, while she loved music, she was evidently battling with her identity as a performer and the competitive elements experienced at school. Ironically, of course, academic study can be just as competitive, and indeed she attributed some of the seemingly negative aspects of her music education as being formative, and so positive for her emerging career as a lawyer.

Speaking of herself as a 25 year old, she describes her experiences as a musician as follows:

> I think it has helped a lot in so many ways that it would shock people. I think maybe people thought they had an advantage over me because I was from music. [Speaking about other Law students.] Because music builds you up to be a performer it makes you a performer and law is all about, certainly if you're going to be a barrister, it's all about performing, talking to clients, being confident, being articulate, and I think these are all skills that I did pick up at school, and also, at school you had to work really, really hard to get something right and I think. . .I'm just the kind of person that does work hard. I'm not frightened of studying or working hard to get something. . .I think as long as you have got something to aim for then you're always going to do well, and I've always got that instilled in me. I'm always aiming to achieve.

Lisa's story about her life as a musician highlights how she uses her mix of positive and negative experiences to explain her development as a solicitor.

Within this framework, it is possible to interpret Lisa's career decisions in part as being a consequence of following her family script which was to love music, but not earn a living at it. Furthermore, she did follow in her sister's footsteps at two levels: attending the specialist school and going to Cambridge University to study a subject other than music. Interestingly, at the point we interviewed her (as a 25 year old) she was also trying for the 'highest achievement' of studying for a professional qualification in law. This contrasts somewhat with Daniel's family, where music was central to everything: careers, expression and achievements (remember that both his parents were professional musicians). For Daniel music, especially musical performance, was the catch-all, the 'be all' of his life; for Lisa it was a channel to access enjoyment and to focus her towards a perceived higher career goal.

The discussion so far has shown how the experiences during adolescence shaped the career ideals and the professional identities of two individuals who had relatively positive perceptions of their musical development. But what happens when our musical training is generally negative, even when the achievements are prodigious?

The chameleon musician: Carl

Carl's early life was quite 'special'. He grew up with his mum, living in a commune. Reading original interview transcripts for Carl and his mum, it seems that they had an extremely close bond, especially as the mother had put a lot of energy into educating her son herself until he went to secondary school. When Carl began formal school, he describes having to face the humiliation associated with getting bottom marks for a music test, and so Carl, perhaps not surprisingly, had turned to his mum for help. Knowing only the recorder, his mum armed herself with a basic study manual and bought two recorders. Her evident care and support, coupled with Carl's determination to prove himself to his school music teacher, resulted in Carl investing in much practice and making rapid progress. At the time of the original study—when Carl was just about to go to music college—his mum commented: 'After six week of starting to play the recorders, I could not keep up with Carl's progress ... It was staggering. He was a 'cool kid' of thirteen, with a bee in his bonnet, practising for three hours a day. He was completely driven, but it was also apparent that he had found something he loved. He just loved it.'

Thus far, Carl's story is particular, especially given his early years, but shares much in common with the other two stories, in terms of the emotional bonding with family and the enjoyment brought through musical activities.

At the time of the follow-up study, Carl (who was 27 years old) was working in the education department of a music technology company. He played very rarely but was focused on creating dance music from which he eventually hoped to earn his living. Carl was the only participant to have moved away from classical performance to composing in a different musical idiom. Examination of his story shows that he had very negative perceptions of his training at music college, but an emotional reliance on music as a vehicle for self-expression. It was perhaps because of his internal attribution of music's value that meant that, although the idiom for expression changed, the music itself remained central to his life. He also believed that music had been important in providing a very special bond with his mum. In fact, by the time Carl was 13 years old, his mum had married and moved him and herself into a more traditional lifestyle, so when he took up the recorder, the musical activity seems to have taken him into a 'special emotional place' with his mum. This is indeed something he and his mother spoke about. To explain his decision to give up music college and so the recorder, Carl described how his instrumental teachers rarely challenged him, and felt that the course he studied was not particularly tailored to his skills and ability.

[My teacher] wanted it done one way, and it felt totally unnatural and unmusical to do it the way he wanted me to. . .I've got to be honest, there were things I could do that he couldn't, and he was well known for being one of the most technically able recorder players in the world. . .and I could play faster than him. He used to say 'I know you can play it' and he was a bit resentful of that. My other teacher actually indicated to me that he could actually be deliberately holding me back.

Whether the teachers really said this, or whether Carl chose to understand what they said in this manner is for debate, however, it is evident that dissatisfaction pervaded his music college experiences. An internal view of himself as a superior player might be one explanation for some of the dissatisfaction, for Carl presented a view of himself as a player with a great deal of confidence in his abilities: 'I've never actually ever needed to do the practice, to get results.'

He, accounts therefore, for his eventual disillusionment with the recorder because of a lack of a challenge: '. . .I think that was half the problem, keeping my hours up, I didn't practise that much, I'd do about an hour a day, and everybody else was doing five or six hours a day, and I had hours to kill and I was getting so bored'.

However, there are contradictions in his story too. For instance, he described the final motivation behind his decision as follows: 'I was getting bored with the rigidity of the routine and I didn't get on well with it. . .I started going to clubs and stuff and hearing music that I really liked and could identify with that wasn't classical based'.

So, a possible interpretation of this is that he could no longer motivate his practice, therefore, the playing was not progressing. His new musical niche could have been his attributed lack of 'identification with' classical music. But, an increasing desire to give up performance involved certain emotional difficulties due to the feelings of obligation Carl had to his mother. As described above, initially it had been Carl's mother who had taught him how to play the recorder, and had supported him throughout his musical development. He explained that he was afraid of disappointing his mum.

Music was certainly the described key to his emotional expression, and unlike other interests in his life, listening offered Carl a key outlet: 'Good music has the ability to take me to a better space, I'd say. A better space within myself. Listening to a good track I can, when I hear a really good track that I like, it's like all of the bad emotion in me just tightens up and explodes and totally just goes, and then I'm just feeling totally light, and totally ready to dance, and so it sort of shatters any stress I've got'.

If we consider Carl's experience in terms of the tripartite model of success, a lack of positive experience, and not developing the appropriate strategies for coping with the 'bad times' are possible explanations for why he chose not to become a professional performer. The fact that music is such a crucial part of his self-concept may be the reason why Carl aimed at earning his living from creating rather than performing music.

Music and identity formation

This chapter has shown that in the case of classical music exposure, experiences during mid to late adolescence seems to shape the career decisions made by Western classical musicians.

From the data discussed, it seems that the development of a close relationship with music—personal emotional expression through listening and making music—is common to all musicians, and this seems critical to making music a key part of their future lives. However, extra-musical factors such as coping strategies connected with social forces such as peer pressure, parents, and teachers, and how this connects to an individual's self-esteem seem to affect whether or not a musician feels able to pursue music performance as a professional career. So, how might we understand the career choices made by these young musicians theoretically? The data suggest that the transition from adolescent to young adult involves the individual identifying and pursuing what seems necessary to fulfil his/her idealized personal identity. It is our belief that music as a key identity construct, relating to self-expression, must be at the core of this identity. Coping strategies for difficulties faced while engaging with music (social pressures, or technical difficulties) need a form of positive attribution and so self-management through the adolescent period if the emergent identity as a classical musician is to stabilize. The perceptions of feedback provided by key and respected others (family, teachers, and peers) regulate the emergent identity by confirming or rejecting characteristics displayed. From pre-existing theoretical models, we believe that the notion of 'provisional selves' (Ibarra, 1999) might be applied here. As individuals experience career transitions, changes in identity occur due to changing roles and work demands. Ibarra describes a process of adaptation as the individual uses possible selves to negotiate a new 'work' identity. According to Ibarra, individuals use imitation strategies that are either 'wholesale' (imitation of a single role model') or 'selective' (using characteristics of a number of different role models), and these are moderated by the second part of the process, which involves being true to self (thus providing a sense of congruence between adopted characteristics and those already existing). The role of others is an important part of this process, as external evaluations from others influence the individual's attribution process and lead to either confirming or rejecting particular characteristics through the positive or negative feedback they provide.

Let us return to each of our case study participants to see how their provisional selves were constructed and then confirmed. As discussed above, Daniel was highly influenced by an older musician during his teenage years, and in this instance, Daniel's 'provisional self' was a 'wholesale imitation' of his idol (Ibarra, 1999). He was able to realize that he had his own ideas about musicianship and the kind of musician he would like to become, so the provisional self was able to shift, based more around Daniel's own characteristics, plus what was applicable to him from his idol. He was helped in this formulation and re-formulation of self by being able to reflect on his actions having considered the concerns expressed by his family. Daniel's experiences demonstrate that the route to becoming a professional musician is not necessarily a straightforward one, and had the support of his family not been in place, then it is possible that his transition may not have been so successful. However, despite the potentially negative influence of his idol, Daniel emerged as a determined and focused musician, with a secure sense of himself as a musician, and it seemed that his positive attributes for music and his own dependence upon it for emotional release and expression motivated him to persevere and become a professional violinist.

Like Daniel, Carl's experiences also highlight similar difficulties and setbacks. Having lost motivation for classical music, his new passion did not 'fit' a view of self as a potential professional classical performer, and so he had to make changes in his life in order to reach a balance between his current provisional and an emergent possible self. Listening to and writing dance music became central to Carl's daily activities, and although at the time of the follow-up interview he was working for a music technology company, he spent most of his leisure time creating music or listening to it. It is likely that Carl's passion for music, which did not change throughout his identity transition, was the primary reason for his desire to continue working with music, but in a different way. He clearly depended upon music for a sense of comfort and security, and as a vehicle for emotional expression, and these elements perhaps led him to leave college and immerse himself in a more suitable environment for pursuing his new 'possible' self.

Lisa's story highlights that music itself did not appear to be treated as a central agent in her self-identity, though arguably, motivationally, helped her to develop skills she could turn, through positive attributions, to her career advantage as a lawyer identity emerged. So, music provided Lisa with a channel for career success in another field, but she did not report an emotional connection with, or passion for, music in the same way as Daniel and Carl. It is our belief that this, in association with her goal-focus in the pursuit of a legal career and a decline in her musical participation, highlights a lack of personal identification with music. Lisa's story seems to demonstrate that developing an identity in and through music is a central and necessary component of becoming a professional musician; without it, a musician is unlikely to develop the attributes linked with the drive and coping strategies of self-management around practice and performance style needed in order to succeed. Lisa did have drive and coping strategies, but these were focused around academic achievement goals.

An individual's identity in and through music appears to comprise motivation for music and a passion to become a professional musician. Coping strategies seem to provide the relevant skills of self-management to deal with the often negative experiences associated with the classical music profession. These are linked with the use of music as a medium of close personal/emotional expression. The case studies above demonstrate that a musician's transition between adolescence and young adulthood is characterized by the him/her trying to find a balance between the current self and the future self, and it seems that this process is moderated by external influences, such as family or peers, but ultimately it is the individual's personally attributed values and passions in and for music that drive the formation of a musician identity, consequently motivating him or her to pursue a professional career as a performer.

References

Bailey, B. & Davidson, J. W. (2003). Amateur group singing as a therapeutic agent. *Nordic Journal of Music Therapy*, 12, 18–32.

Bamberger, J. (1986). Cognitive issues in the development of musically gifted children. In R. J. Sternberg and J. E. Davidson (eds), *Conceptions of giftedness* (pp. 388–413). Cambridge: Cambridge University Press.

Burland, K. & Davidson, J. W. (2002). Training the talented. *Music Education Research*, 4, 121–140.

Byng-Hall, J. (1973). Family myths used as defence in conjoint family therapy. *British Journal of Psychology*, **46**, 239–250.

Byng-Hall, J. (1979). Re-editing family mythology during family therapy. *Journal of Family Therapy*, **1**, 103–116.

Byng-Hall, J. (1982). Family legends: Their significance for the family therapist. In A. Bentovim, A. Cooklin and G. G. Barnes (eds), *Family therapy: complementary frameworks of theory and practice* (Vol. 2). London: Academic Press.

Byng-Hall, J. (1985). The family script: A useful bridge between theory and practice. *Journal of Family Therapy*, **7**, 301–305.

Byng-Hall, J. (1988). Scripts and legends in families and family therapy. *Family Process*, **27**, 167–180.

Byng-Hall, J. (1995). *Rewriting family scripts* (1st edn.), (Vol. 1). London: Guilford.

Byng-Hall, J. (1998). Evolving ideas about marriage: Re-editing the re-editing of family mythology. *Journal of Family Therapy*, **29**, 133–141.

Coleman, J. S. (1960). The adolescent Subculture and academic achievement. *The American Journal of Sociology*, **4**, 337–347.

Csikszentmihalyi, M. (1999). Implications of a systems perspective for the study of creativity. In R. J. Sternberg (ed.), *Handbook of creativity* (pp. 313–335). New York: Cambridge University Press.

Davidson, J. W., Howe, M. J. A., Moore, D. G., & Sloboda, J. A. (1996). The role of parental influences in the development of musical performance. *British Journal of Developmental Psychology*, **14**, 399–412.

Davidson, J. W., Moore, D. G., Sloboda, J. A., & Howe, M. J. A. (1998). Characteristics of music teachers and the progress of young instrumentalists. *Journal of Research in Music Education*, **46**, 141–160.

Erikson, E. (1959). *Identity and the life cycle.* New York: International University Press.

Feldhusen, J. F. (1986). A conception of giftedness. In R. J. Sternberg and J. E. Davidson (eds), *Conceptions of giftedness* (pp. 112–127). Cambridge: Cambridge University Press.

Freeman, J. (1985). Emotional aspects of giftedness. In J. Freeman (ed.), *The psychology of gifted children: Perspectives in development and education* (pp. 247–264). Chichester: John Wiley & Sons.

Gecas, V. & Mortimer, J. T. (1987). Stability and change in the self-concept from adolescence to adulthood. In T. Honess and K. Yardley (eds) *Self and identity: perspectives across the lifespan*, 265–285. London: Routledge and Kegan Paul.

Gullberg, A.-K. & Brändström, S. (2004) Formal and non-formal music learning amongst rock musicians. In J. W. Davidson (Ed.), *The music practitioner* (pp. 161–174). Aldershot: Ashgate.

Hall, R. (1969). Sleeve note to 'Masters of Irish music: Martyn Byrnes'. Leader Sound Ltd.

Hendry, L. B. & Kloep, M. (2002). *Lifespan development: Resources, challenges and risks.* Oxford: The Alden Press.

Ibarra, H. (1999). Provisional selves: Experimenting with image and identity in professional adaptation. *Administrative Science Quarterly*, **44**, 764–791.

Juslin, P. & Sloboda, J. A. (eds) (2002). *Music and emotion.* New York: Oxford University Press.

Kemp, A. E. (1996). The musical temperament: Psychology and personality of musicians. Oxford: Oxford University Press.

Larson, R. (1995). Secrets in the bedroom: Adolescents' private use of media. *Journal of Youth and Adolescence*, **24**, 535–550.

Manturzewska, M. (1990). A biographical study of the life-span development of professional musicians. *Psychology of Music*, **18**, 112–139.

North, A. C., Hargreaves, D. J., & O'Neill, S. A. (2000). The importance of music to adolescents. *British Journal of Educational Psychology*, **70**, 255–272.

Shuter-Dyson, R. & Gabriel, C. (1981). *The psychology of musical ability*. London: Methuen.

Smith, J. A., Flowers, P., & Osborn, M. (1997). Interpretative phenomenological analysis and the psychology of health and illness. In L. Yardley (ed.), *Material discourses of health and illness* (pp. 68–91). London: Routledge.

Sosniak, L. A. (1990). The tortoise, the hare, and the development of talent. In M. J. A. Howe (ed.), *Encouraging the development of exceptional skills and talents* (pp. 165–178). Leicester: The British Psychological Society.

INDEX